Ford Contour and Mercury Mystique Automotive Repair Manual

by Mark Jacobs
and John H Haynes
Member of the Guild of Motoring Writers

Models covered:

All Ford Contour and Mercury Mystique models
1995 through 2000

(3G10 - 36006)

ABCD

Haynes Publishing Group
Sparkford Nr Yeovil
Somerset BA22 7JJ England

Haynes North America, Inc
861 Lawrence Drive
Newbury Park
California 91320 USA

A book in the Haynes Automotive Repair Manual Series

Printed in the U.S.A.

ISBN 1 56392 399 8

Library of Congress Catalog Card Number 00-109294

04-344

Contents

Haynes mechanic, author and photographer with a 1995 Contour

About this manual

Its purpose

The purpose of this manual is to help you get the best value from your vehicle. It can do so in several ways. It can help you decide what work must be done, even if you choose to have it done by a dealer service department or a repair shop; it provides information and procedures for routine maintenance and servicing; and it offers diagnostic and repair procedures to follow when trouble occurs.

We hope you use the manual to tackle the work yourself. For many simpler jobs, doing it yourself may be quicker than arranging an appointment to get the vehicle into a shop and making the trips to leave it and pick it up. More importantly, a lot of money can be saved by avoiding the expense the shop must pass on to you to cover its labor and overhead costs. An added benefit is the sense of satisfaction and accomplishment that you feel after doing the job yourself.

Using the manual

The manual is divided into Chapters. Each Chapter is divided into numbered Sections, which are headed in bold type between horizontal lines. Each Section consists of consecutively numbered paragraphs.

At the beginning of each numbered Section you will be referred to any illustrations which apply to the procedures in that Section. The reference numbers used in illustration captions pinpoint the pertinent Section and the Step within that Section. That is, illustration 3.2 means the illustration refers to Section 3 and Step (or paragraph) 2 within that Section.

Procedures, once described in the text, are not normally repeated. When it's necessary to refer to another Chapter, the reference will be given as Chapter and Section number. Cross references given without use of the word "Chapter" apply to Sections and/or paragraphs in the same Chapter. For example, "see Section 8" means in the same Chapter.

References to the left or right side of the vehicle assume you are sitting in the driver's seat, facing forward.

Even though we have prepared this manual with extreme care, neither the publisher nor the author can accept responsibility for any errors in, or omissions from, the information given.

NOTE

A **Note** provides information necessary to properly complete a procedure or information which will make the procedure easier to understand.

CAUTION

A **Caution** provides a special procedure or special steps which must be taken while completing the procedure where the Caution is found. Not heeding a Caution can result in damage to the assembly being worked on.

WARNING

A **Warning** provides a special procedure or special steps which must be taken while completing the procedure where the Warning is found. Not heeding a Warning can result in personal injury.

Introduction

Introduced in 1995, the Contour/Mercury Mystique models are available in a four-door Sedan configuration. The Contour comes in GL, LX and SE trim levels. The Mystique comes in GS and LS trim levels. The Contour/Mystique features a high standard of equipment, with driver/passenger safety in accidents being a particularly high design priority; all models are fitted with features such as side impact bars in all doors, seat belt grabbers and pre-tensioners, and an airbag fitted to the steering wheel. Dual airbags are optional. Vehicle security is enhanced, with an in-built alarm system as well as double-locking doors with shielded locks, and security-coded audio equipment.

The base engine is a 2.0 liter four-cylinder model. Standard on the sporty SE and optional on all other models is a 2.5 liter V6. Both engines are controlled by a sophisticated engine management system, which combines multi-point sequential fuel injection and distributorless ignition systems with evaporative emissions control, exhaust gas recirculation and a three-way regulated catalytic converter to ensure that the vehicle complies with the most stringent of the emissions control standards currently in force, and yet provides the levels of performance and fuel economy expected.

The transversely mounted engine drives the front wheels through either a five-speed manual transaxle with a hydraulically actuated clutch, or through an electronically controlled four-speed automatic transaxle.

The fully independent suspension is by MacPherson strut on all four wheels, located by transverse lower arms at the front, and by transverse and trailing arms at the rear; stabilizer bars are fitted at front and rear.

The steering is power-assisted. The pump is belt-driven from the engine, and the rack-and-pinion steering gear is mounted behind the engine.

The power-assisted brakes are disc at the front, with drums at the rear on most models; disc rear brakes and an electronically controlled Anti-lock Braking System (ABS) are available on some models. A Traction Control System (TCS) is available as a further option where ABS is fitted.

Vehicle identification numbers

VIN engine and model year codes

Two particularly important pieces of information found in the VIN are the engine code and the model year code. Counting from the left, the engine code is the 8th digit and the model year code designation is the 10th digit.

On the models covered by this manual, the engine codes are:

3...................... 2.0 liter four-cylinder
L...................... 2.5 liter V6

On the models covered in this manual, the model year code are:

S 1995
T...................... 1996
V...................... 1997
W 1998

Vehicle Certification Label

The certification label is located on the driver's side door end post (lock panel). The label contains the name of the manufacturer, month and year of manufacture, gross vehicle weight rating (GVWR), gross axle weight rating (GAWR) and the certification statement.

The Vehicle Identification Number (VIN) is visible through the driver's side of the windshield

Engine identification number

The engine number is stamped into a flat-machined surface on the front-facing side of the cylinder block **(see illustration)**.

Transaxle identification number

The transaxle number is printed on a label affixed to the transaxle pan **(see illustration)**.

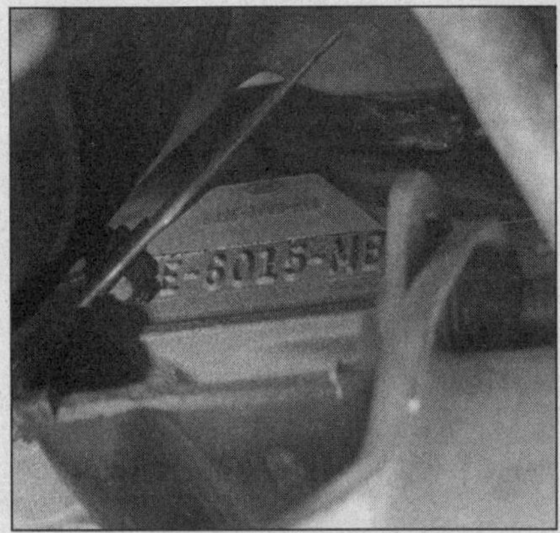

The engine identification number is stamped on the front side of the cylinder block

Vehicle Emissions Control Information (VECI) label

The emissions control information is printed on a label affixed to the bottom of the hood. This label contains information regarding the emissions control equipment installed on the vehicle, tune-up specifications and a vacuum hose routing diagram **(see illustration)**.

The transaxle identification number is printed on a label affixed to the transaxle pan

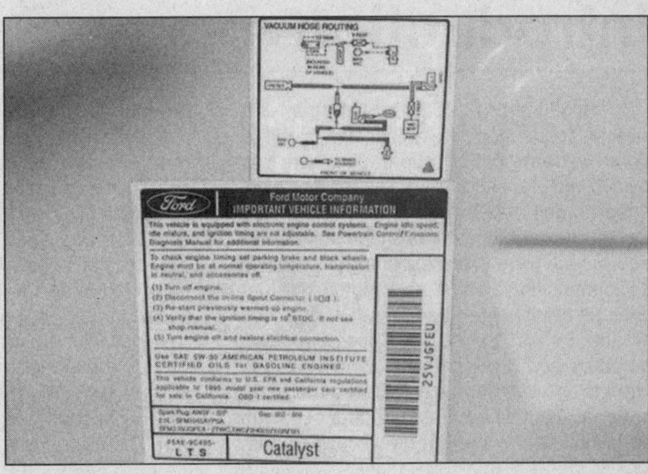

The vehicle emissions control information (VECI) label is located on the underside of the hood

Buying parts

Replacement parts are available from many sources, which generally fall into one of two categories - authorized dealer parts departments and independent retail auto parts stores. Our advice concerning these parts is as follows:

Retail auto parts stores: Good auto parts stores will stock frequently needed components which wear out relatively fast, such as clutch components, exhaust systems, brake parts, tune-up parts, etc. These stores often supply new or reconditioned parts on an exchange basis, which can save a considerable amount of money. Discount auto parts stores are often very good places to buy materials and parts needed for general vehicle maintenance such as oil, grease, filters, spark plugs, belts, touch-up paint, bulbs, etc. They also usually sell tools and general accessories, have convenient hours, charge lower prices and can often be found not far from home.

Authorized dealer parts department: This is the best source for parts which are unique to the vehicle and not generally available elsewhere (such as major engine parts, transmission parts, trim pieces, etc.).

Warranty information: If the vehicle is still covered under warranty, be sure that any replacement parts purchased - regardless of the source - do not invalidate the warranty!

To be sure of obtaining the correct parts, have engine and chassis numbers available and, if possible, take the old parts along for positive identification.

Maintenance techniques, tools and working facilities

Maintenance techniques

There are a number of techniques involved in maintenance and repair that will be referred to throughout this manual. Application of these techniques will enable the home mechanic to be more efficient, better organized and capable of performing the various tasks properly, which will ensure that the repair job is thorough and complete.

Fasteners

Fasteners are nuts, bolts, studs and screws used to hold two or more parts together. There are a few things to keep in mind when working with fasteners. Almost all of them use a locking device of some type, either a lockwasher, locknut, locking tab or thread adhesive. All threaded fasteners should be clean and straight, with undamaged threads and undamaged corners on the hex head where the wrench fits. Develop the habit of replacing all damaged nuts and bolts with new ones. Special locknuts with nylon or fiber inserts can only be used once. If they are removed, they lose their locking ability and must be replaced with new ones.

Rusted nuts and bolts should be treated with a penetrating fluid to ease removal and prevent breakage. Some mechanics use turpentine in a spout-type oil can, which works quite well. After applying the rust penetrant, let it work for a few minutes before trying to loosen the nut or bolt. Badly rusted fasteners may have to be chiseled or sawed off or removed with a special nut breaker, available at tool stores.

If a bolt or stud breaks off in an assembly, it can be drilled and removed with a special tool commonly available for this purpose. Most automotive machine shops can perform this task, as well as other repair procedures, such as the repair of threaded holes that have been stripped out.

Flat washers and lockwashers, when removed from an assembly, should always be replaced exactly as removed. Replace any damaged washers with new ones. Never use a lockwasher on any soft metal surface (such as aluminum), thin sheet metal or plastic.

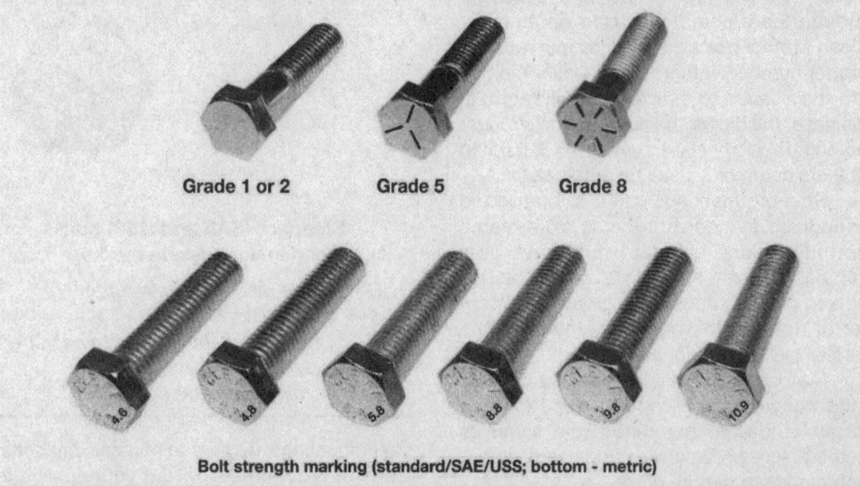

Bolt strength marking (standard/SAE/USS; bottom - metric)

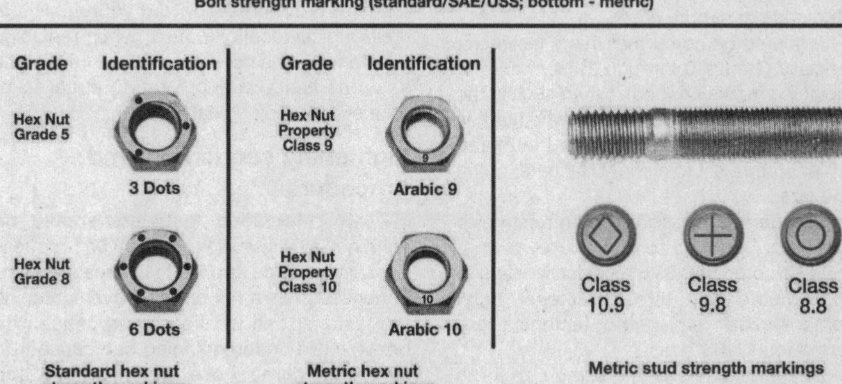

Standard hex nut strength markings

Metric hex nut strength markings

Metric stud strength markings

Fastener sizes

For a number of reasons, automobile manufacturers are making wider and wider use of metric fasteners. Therefore, it is important to be able to tell the difference between standard (sometimes called U.S. or SAE) and metric hardware, since they cannot be interchanged.

All bolts, whether standard or metric, are sized according to diameter, thread pitch and length. For example, a standard 1/2 - 13 x 1 bolt is 1/2 inch in diameter, has 13 threads per inch and is 1 inch long. An M12 - 1.75 x 25 metric bolt is 12 mm in diameter, has a thread pitch of 1.75 mm (the distance between threads) and is 25 mm long. The two bolts are nearly identical, and easily confused, but they are not interchangeable.

In addition to the differences in diameter, thread pitch and length, metric and standard bolts can also be distinguished by examining the bolt heads. To begin with, the distance across the flats on a standard bolt head is measured in inches, while the same dimension on a metric bolt is sized in millimeters (the same is true for nuts). As a result, a standard wrench should not be used on a metric bolt and a metric wrench should not be used on a standard bolt. Also, most standard bolts have slashes radiating out from the center of the head to denote the grade or strength of the bolt, which is an indication of the amount of torque that can be applied to it. The greater the number of slashes, the greater the strength of the bolt. Grades 0 through 5 are commonly used on automobiles. Metric bolts have a property class (grade) number, rather than a slash, molded into their heads to indicate bolt strength. In this case, the higher the number, the stronger the bolt. Property class numbers 8.8, 9.8 and 10.9 are commonly used on automobiles.

Strength markings can also be used to distinguish standard hex nuts from metric hex nuts. Many standard nuts have dots stamped into one side, while metric nuts are marked with a number. The greater the number of dots, or the higher the number, the greater the strength of the nut.

Metric studs are also marked on their ends according to property class (grade). Larger studs are numbered (the same as metric bolts), while smaller studs carry a geometric code to denote grade.

It should be noted that many fasteners, especially Grades 0 through 2, have no distinguishing marks on them. When such is the case, the only way to determine whether it is standard or metric is to measure the thread pitch or compare it to a known fastener of the same size.

Standard fasteners are often referred to as SAE, as opposed to metric. However, it should be noted that SAE technically refers to a non-metric fine thread fastener only. Coarse thread non-metric fasteners are referred to as USS sizes.

Since fasteners of the same size (both standard and metric) may have different strength ratings, be sure to reinstall any bolts, studs or nuts removed from your vehicle in their original locations. Also, when replacing a fastener with a new one, make sure that the new one has a strength rating equal to or greater than the original.

Metric thread sizes	Ft-lbs	Nm
M-6	6 to 9	9 to 12
M-8	14 to 21	19 to 28
M-10	28 to 40	38 to 54
M-12	50 to 71	68 to 96
M-14	80 to 140	109 to 154
Pipe thread sizes		
1/8	5 to 8	7 to 10
1/4	12 to 18	17 to 24
3/8	22 to 33	30 to 44
1/2	25 to 35	34 to 47
U.S. thread sizes		
1/4 - 20	6 to 9	9 to 12
5/16 - 18	12 to 18	17 to 24
5/16 - 24	14 to 20	19 to 27
3/8 - 16	22 to 32	30 to 43
3/8 - 24	27 to 38	37 to 51
7/16 - 14	40 to 55	55 to 74
7/16 - 20	40 to 60	55 to 81
1/2 - 13	55 to 80	75 to 108

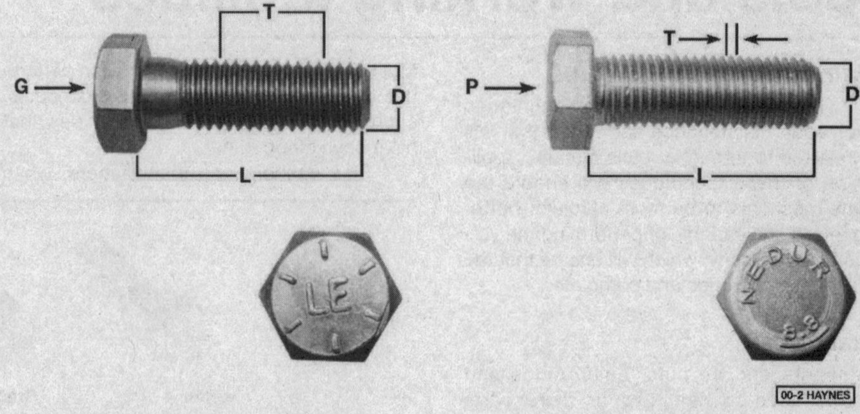

Standard (SAE and USS) bolt dimensions/grade marks

- G Grade marks (bolt strength)
- L Length (in inches)
- T Thread pitch (number of threads per inch)
- D Nominal diameter (in inches)

Metric bolt dimensions/grade marks

- P Property class (bolt strength)
- L Length (in millimeters)
- T Thread pitch (distance between threads in millimeters)
- D Diameter

Tightening sequences and procedures

Most threaded fasteners should be tightened to a specific torque value (torque is the twisting force applied to a threaded component such as a nut or bolt). Overtightening the fastener can weaken it and cause it to break, while undertightening can cause it to eventually come loose. Bolts, screws and studs, depending on the material they are made of and their thread diameters, have specific torque values, many of which are noted in the Specifications at the beginning of each Chapter. Be sure to follow the torque recommendations closely. For fasteners not assigned a specific torque, a general torque value chart is presented here as a guide. These torque values are for dry (unlubricated) fasteners threaded into steel or cast iron (not aluminum). As was previously mentioned, the size and grade of a fastener determine the amount of torque that can safely be applied to it. The figures listed here are approximate for Grade 2 and Grade 3 fasteners. Higher grades can tolerate higher torque values.

Fasteners laid out in a pattern, such as cylinder head bolts, oil pan bolts, differential cover bolts, etc., must be loosened or tight-

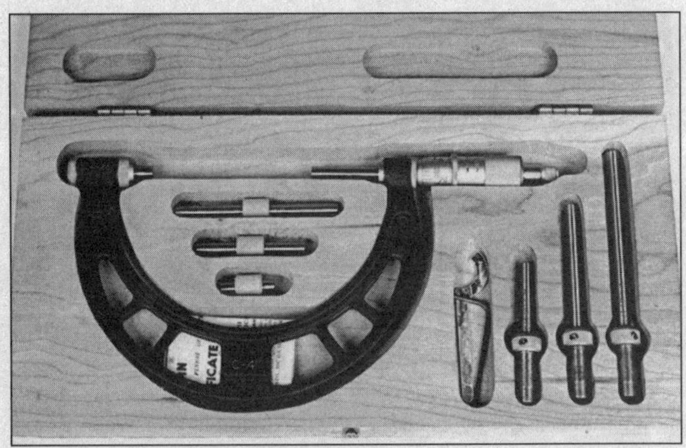

Micrometer set

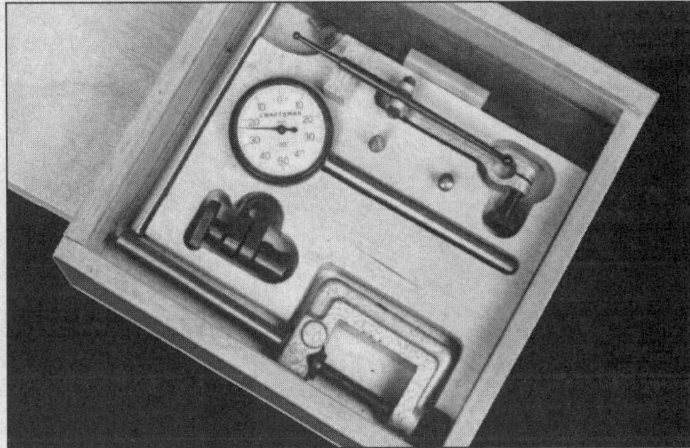

Dial indicator set

ened in sequence to avoid warping the component. This sequence will normally be shown in the appropriate Chapter. If a specific pattern is not given, the following procedures can be used to prevent warping.

Initially, the bolts or nuts should be assembled finger-tight only. Next, they should be tightened one full turn each, in a criss-cross or diagonal pattern. After each one has been tightened one full turn, return to the first one and tighten them all one-half turn, following the same pattern. Finally, tighten each of them one-quarter turn at a time until each fastener has been tightened to the proper torque. To loosen and remove the fasteners, the procedure would be reversed.

Component disassembly

Component disassembly should be done with care and purpose to help ensure that the parts go back together properly. Always keep track of the sequence in which parts are removed. Make note of special characteristics or marks on parts that can be installed more than one way, such as a grooved thrust washer on a shaft. It is a good idea to lay the disassembled parts out on a clean surface in the order that they were removed. It may also be helpful to make sketches or take instant photos of components before removal.

When removing fasteners from a component, keep track of their locations. Sometimes threading a bolt back in a part, or putting the washers and nut back on a stud, can prevent mix-ups later. If nuts and bolts cannot be returned to their original locations, they should be kept in a compartmented box or a series of small boxes. A cupcake or muffin tin is ideal for this purpose, since each cavity can hold the bolts and nuts from a particular area (i.e. oil pan bolts, valve cover bolts, engine mount bolts, etc.). A pan of this type is especially helpful when working on assemblies with very small parts, such as the carburetor, alternator, valve train or interior dash and trim pieces. The cavities can be marked with paint or tape to identify the contents.

Whenever wiring looms, harnesses or connectors are separated, it is a good idea to identify the two halves with numbered pieces of masking tape so they can be easily reconnected.

Gasket sealing surfaces

Throughout any vehicle, gaskets are used to seal the mating surfaces between two parts and keep lubricants, fluids, vacuum or pressure contained in an assembly.

Many times these gaskets are coated with a liquid or paste-type gasket sealing compound before assembly. Age, heat and pressure can sometimes cause the two parts to stick together so tightly that they are very difficult to separate. Often, the assembly can be loosened by striking it with a soft-face hammer near the mating surfaces. A regular hammer can be used if a block of wood is placed between the hammer and the part. Do not hammer on cast parts or parts that could be easily damaged. With any particularly stubborn part, always recheck to make sure that every fastener has been removed.

Avoid using a screwdriver or bar to pry apart an assembly, as they can easily mar the gasket sealing surfaces of the parts, which must remain smooth. If prying is absolutely necessary, use an old broom handle, but keep in mind that extra clean up will be necessary if the wood splinters.

After the parts are separated, the old gasket must be carefully scraped off and the gasket surfaces cleaned. Stubborn gasket material can be soaked with rust penetrant or treated with a special chemical to soften it so it can be easily scraped off. A scraper can be fashioned from a piece of copper tubing by flattening and sharpening one end. Copper is recommended because it is usually softer than the surfaces to be scraped, which reduces the chance of gouging the part. Some gaskets can be removed with a wire brush, but regardless of the method used, the mating surfaces must be left clean and smooth. If for some reason the gasket surface is gouged, then a gasket sealer thick enough to fill scratches will have to be used during reassembly of the components. For most applications, a non-drying (or semi-drying) gasket sealer should be used.

Hose removal tips

Warning: *If the vehicle is equipped with air conditioning, do not disconnect any of the A/C hoses without first having the system depressurized by a dealer service department or a service station.*

Hose removal precautions closely parallel gasket removal precautions. Avoid scratching or gouging the surface that the hose mates against or the connection may leak. This is especially true for radiator hoses. Because of various chemical reactions, the rubber in hoses can bond itself to the metal spigot that the hose fits over. To remove a hose, first loosen the hose clamps that secure it to the spigot. Then, with slip-joint pliers, grab the hose at the clamp and rotate it around the spigot. Work it back and forth until it is completely free, then pull it off. Silicone or other lubricants will ease removal if they can be applied between the hose and the outside of the spigot. Apply the same lubricant to the inside of the hose and the outside of the spigot to simplify installation.

As a last resort (and if the hose is to be replaced with a new one anyway), the rubber can be slit with a knife and the hose peeled from the spigot. If this must be done, be careful that the metal connection is not damaged.

If a hose clamp is broken or damaged, do not reuse it. Wire-type clamps usually weaken with age, so it is a good idea to replace them with screw-type clamps whenever a hose is removed.

Tools

A selection of good tools is a basic requirement for anyone who plans to maintain and repair his or her own vehicle. For the owner who has few tools, the initial investment might seem high, but when compared to the spiraling costs of professional auto maintenance and repair, it is a wise one.

To help the owner decide which tools are needed to perform the tasks detailed in this manual, the following tool lists are offered: *Maintenance and minor repair, Repair/overhaul* and *Special.*

The newcomer to practical mechanics

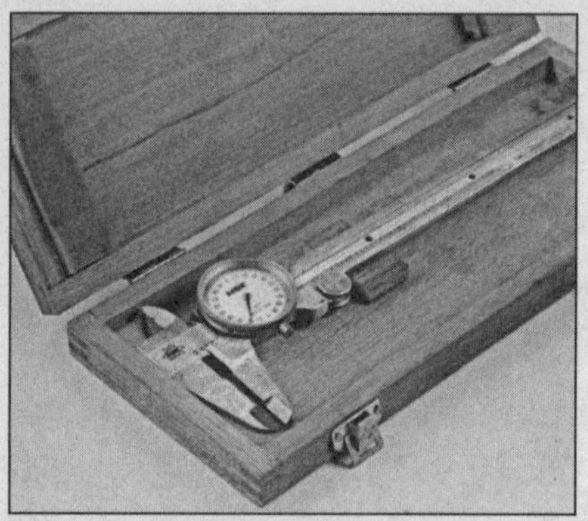
Dial caliper

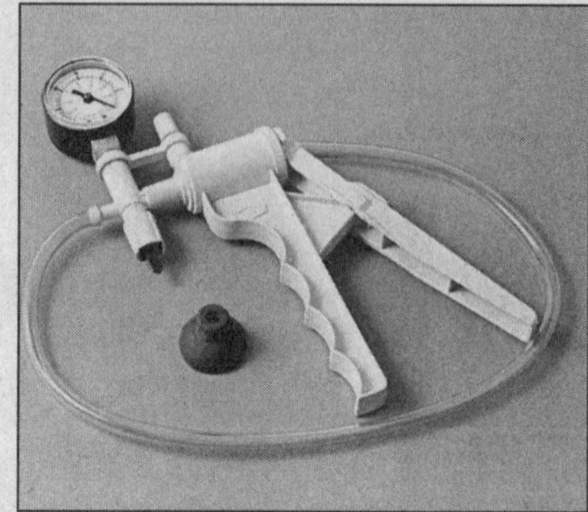
Hand-operated vacuum pump

Timing light

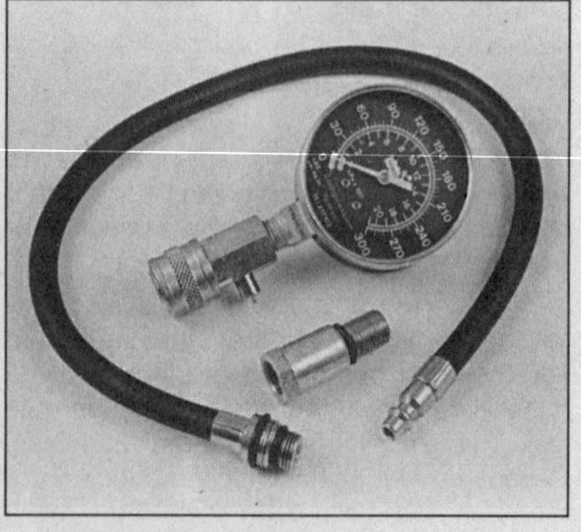
Compression gauge with spark plug hole adapter

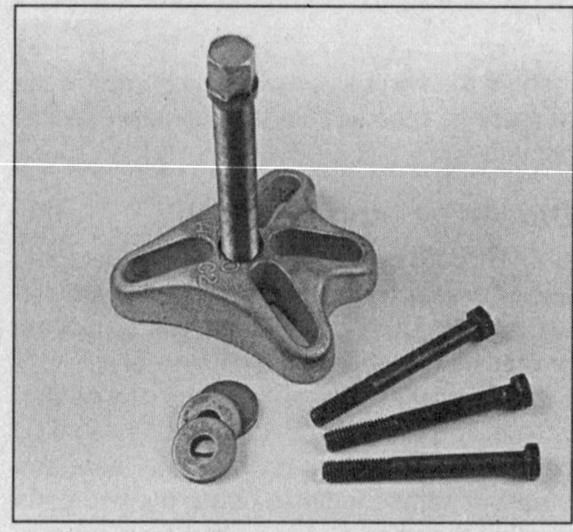
Damper/steering wheel puller

General purpose puller

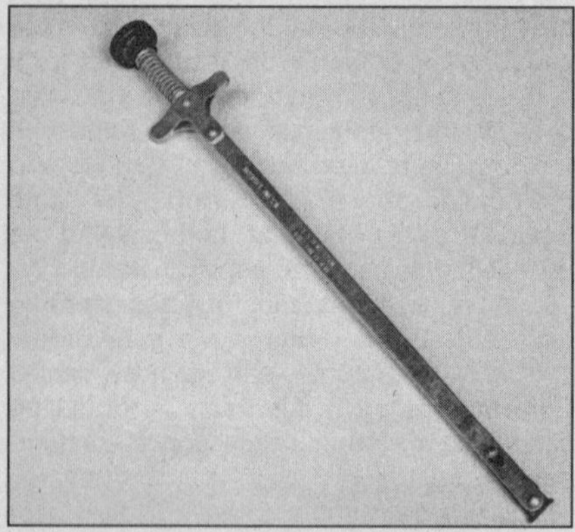
Hydraulic lifter removal tool

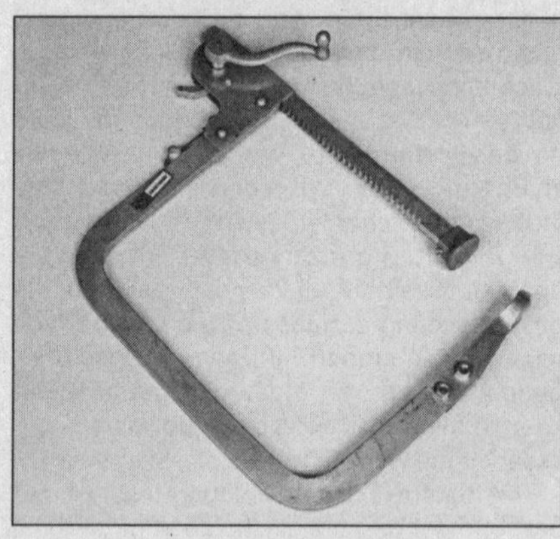
Valve spring compressor

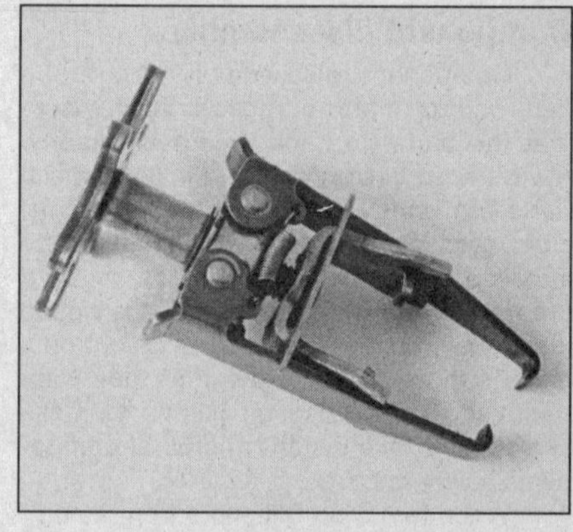
Valve spring compressor

Ridge reamer

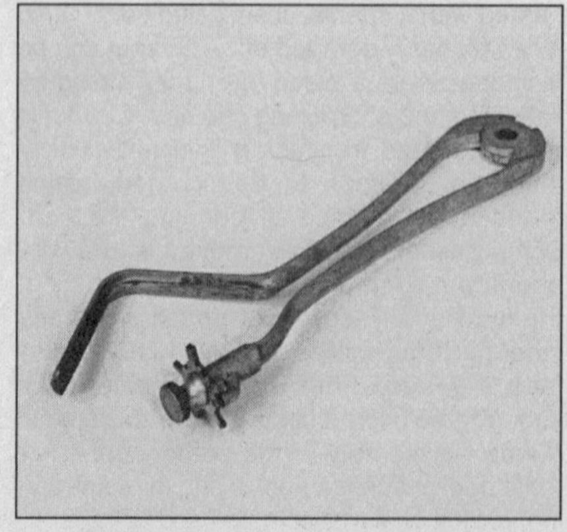
Piston ring groove cleaning tool

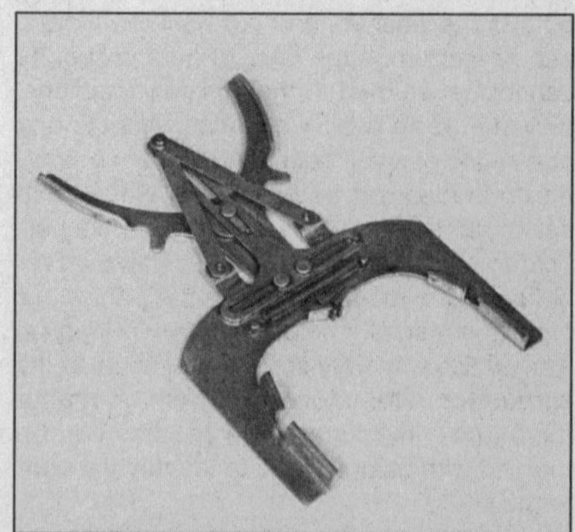
Ring removal/installation tool

Ring compressor

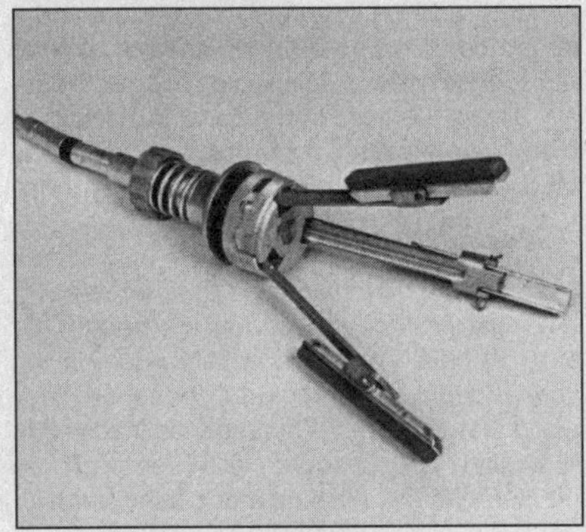
Cylinder hone

Brake hold-down spring tool

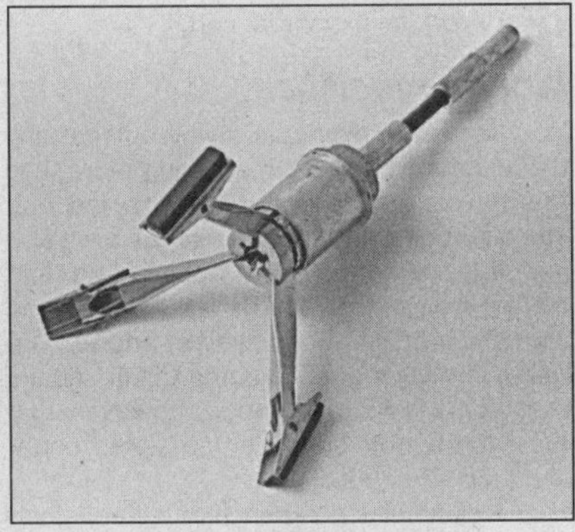
Brake cylinder hone

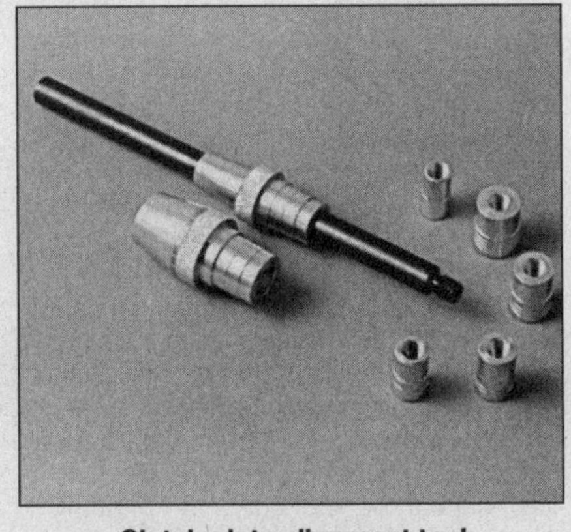
Clutch plate alignment tool

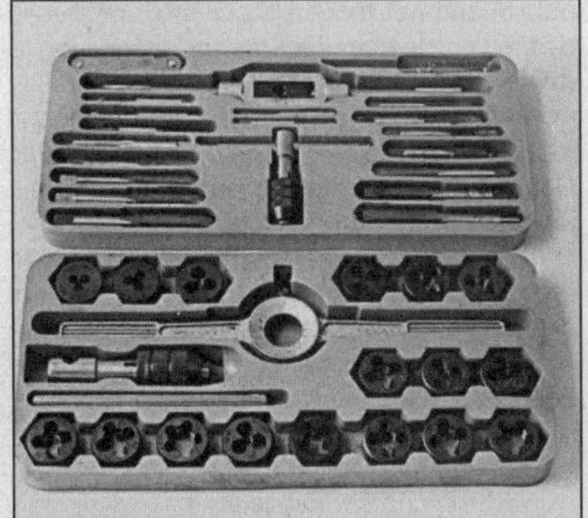
Tap and die set

should start off with the *maintenance and minor repair* tool kit, which is adequate for the simpler jobs performed on a vehicle. Then, as confidence and experience grow, the owner can tackle more difficult tasks, buying additional tools as they are needed. Eventually the basic kit will be expanded into the *repair and overhaul* tool set. Over a period of time, the experienced do-it-yourselfer will assemble a tool set complete enough for most repair and overhaul procedures and will add tools from the special category when it is felt that the expense is justified by the frequency of use.

Maintenance and minor repair tool kit

The tools in this list should be considered the minimum required for performance of routine maintenance, servicing and minor repair work. We recommend the purchase of combination wrenches (box-end and open-end combined in one wrench). While more expensive than open end wrenches, they offer the advantages of both types of wrench.

Combination wrench set (1/4-inch to 1 inch or 6 mm to 19 mm)
Adjustable wrench, 8 inch
Spark plug wrench with rubber insert
Spark plug gap adjusting tool
Feeler gauge set
Brake bleeder wrench
Standard screwdriver (5/16-inch x 6 inch)
Phillips screwdriver (No. 2 x 6 inch)
Combination pliers - 6 inch
Hacksaw and assortment of blades
Tire pressure gauge
Grease gun
Oil can
Fine emery cloth
Wire brush
Battery post and cable cleaning tool
Oil filter wrench
Funnel (medium size)
Safety goggles
Jackstands (2)
Drain pan

Note: *If basic tune-ups are going to be part of routine maintenance, it will be necessary to purchase a good quality stroboscopic timing light and combination tachometer/dwell meter. Although they are included in the list of special tools, it is mentioned here because they are absolutely necessary for tuning most vehicles properly.*

Repair and overhaul tool set

These tools are essential for anyone who plans to perform major repairs and are in addition to those in the maintenance and minor repair tool kit. Included is a comprehensive set of sockets which, though expensive, are invaluable because of their versatility, especially when various extensions and drives are available. We recommend the 1/2-inch drive over the 3/8-inch drive. Although the larger drive is bulky and more expensive, it has the capacity of accepting a very wide range of large sockets. Ideally, however, the mechanic should have a 3/8-inch drive set and a 1/2-inch drive set.

Socket set(s)
Reversible ratchet
Extension - 10 inch
Universal joint
Torque wrench (same size drive as sockets)
Ball peen hammer - 8 ounce
Soft-face hammer (plastic/rubber)
Standard screwdriver (1/4-inch x 6 inch)
Standard screwdriver (stubby - 5/16-inch)
Phillips screwdriver (No. 3 x 8 inch)
Phillips screwdriver (stubby - No. 2)
Pliers - vise grip
Pliers - lineman's
Pliers - needle nose
Pliers - snap-ring (internal and external)
Cold chisel - 1/2-inch
Scribe
Scraper (made from flattened copper tubing)
Centerpunch
Pin punches (1/16, 1/8, 3/16-inch)
Steel rule/straightedge - 12 inch
Allen wrench set (1/8 to 3/8-inch or 4 mm to 10 mm)
A selection of files
Wire brush (large)
Jackstands (second set)
Jack (scissor or hydraulic type)

Note: *Another tool which is often useful is an electric drill with a chuck capacity of 3/8-inch and a set of good quality drill bits.*

Special tools

The tools in this list include those which are not used regularly, are expensive to buy, or which need to be used in accordance with their manufacturer's instructions. Unless these tools will be used frequently, it is not very economical to purchase many of them. A consideration would be to split the cost and use between yourself and a friend or friends. In addition, most of these tools can be obtained from a tool rental shop on a temporary basis.

This list primarily contains only those tools and instruments widely available to the public, and not those special tools produced by the vehicle manufacturer for distribution to dealer service departments. Occasionally, references to the manufacturer's special tools are included in the text of this manual. Generally, an alternative method of doing the job without the special tool is offered. However, sometimes there is no alternative to their use. Where this is the case, and the tool cannot be purchased or borrowed, the work should be turned over to the dealer service department or an automotive repair shop.

Valve spring compressor
Piston ring groove cleaning tool
Piston ring compressor
Piston ring installation tool
Cylinder compression gauge
Cylinder ridge reamer
Cylinder surfacing hone
Cylinder bore gauge
Micrometers and/or dial calipers
Hydraulic lifter removal tool
Balljoint separator
Universal-type puller
Impact screwdriver
Dial indicator set
Stroboscopic timing light (inductive pick-up)
Hand operated vacuum/pressure pump
Tachometer/dwell meter
Universal electrical multimeter
Cable hoist
Brake spring removal and installation tools
Floor jack

Buying tools

For the do-it-yourselfer who is just starting to get involved in vehicle maintenance and repair, there are a number of options available when purchasing tools. If maintenance and minor repair is the extent of the work to be done, the purchase of individual tools is satisfactory. If, on the other hand, extensive work is planned, it would be a good idea to purchase a modest tool set from one of the large retail chain stores. A set can usually be bought at a substantial savings over the individual tool prices, and they often come with a tool box. As additional tools are needed, add-on sets, individual tools and a larger tool box can be purchased to expand the tool selection. Building a tool set gradually allows the cost of the tools to be spread over a longer period of time and gives the mechanic the freedom to choose only those tools that will actually be used.

Tool stores will often be the only source of some of the special tools that are needed, but regardless of where tools are bought, try to avoid cheap ones, especially when buying screwdrivers and sockets, because they won't last very long. The expense involved in replacing cheap tools will eventually be greater than the initial cost of quality tools.

Care and maintenance of tools

Good tools are expensive, so it makes sense to treat them with respect. Keep them clean and in usable condition and store them properly when not in use. Always wipe off any dirt, grease or metal chips before putting them away. Never leave tools lying around in the work area. Upon completion of a job, always check closely under the hood for tools that may have been left there so they won't get lost during a test drive.

Some tools, such as screwdrivers, pliers, wrenches and sockets, can be hung on a panel mounted on the garage or workshop wall, while others should be kept in a tool box or tray. Measuring instruments, gauges, meters, etc. must be carefully stored where they cannot be damaged by weather or impact from other tools.

When tools are used with care and stored properly, they will last a very long time. Even with the best of care, though, tools will wear out if used frequently. When a tool is damaged or worn out, replace it. Subsequent jobs will be safer and more enjoyable if you do.

How to repair damaged threads

Sometimes, the internal threads of a nut or bolt hole can become stripped, usually from overtightening. Stripping threads is an all-too-common occurrence, especially when working with aluminum parts, because aluminum is so soft that it easily strips out.

Usually, external or internal threads are only partially stripped. After they've been cleaned up with a tap or die, they'll still work. Sometimes, however, threads are badly damaged. When this happens, you've got three choices:

1) *Drill and tap the hole to the next suitable oversize and install a larger diameter bolt, screw or stud.*
2) *Drill and tap the hole to accept a threaded plug, then drill and tap the plug to the original screw size. You can also buy a plug already threaded to the original size. Then you simply drill a hole to the specified size, then run the threaded plug into the hole with a bolt and jam nut. Once the plug is fully seated, remove the jam nut and bolt.*
3) *The third method uses a patented thread repair kit like Heli-Coil or Slimsert. These easy-to-use kits are designed to repair damaged threads in straight-through holes and blind holes. Both are available as kits which can handle a variety of sizes and thread patterns. Drill the hole, then tap it with the special included tap. Install the Heli-Coil and the hole is back to its original diameter and thread pitch.*

Regardless of which method you use, be sure to proceed calmly and carefully. A little impatience or carelessness during one of these relatively simple procedures can ruin your whole day's work and cost you a bundle if you wreck an expensive part.

Working facilities

Not to be overlooked when discussing tools is the workshop. If anything more than routine maintenance is to be carried out, some sort of suitable work area is essential.

It is understood, and appreciated, that many home mechanics do not have a good workshop or garage available, and end up removing an engine or doing major repairs outside. It is recommended, however, that the overhaul or repair be completed under the cover of a roof.

A clean, flat workbench or table of comfortable working height is an absolute necessity. The workbench should be equipped with a vise that has a jaw opening of at least four inches.

As mentioned previously, some clean, dry storage space is also required for tools, as well as the lubricants, fluids, cleaning solvents, etc. which soon become necessary.

Sometimes waste oil and fluids, drained from the engine or cooling system during normal maintenance or repairs, present a disposal problem. To avoid pouring them on the ground or into a sewage system, pour the used fluids into large containers, seal them with caps and take them to an authorized disposal site or recycling center. Plastic jugs, such as old antifreeze containers, are ideal for this purpose.

Always keep a supply of old newspapers and clean rags available. Old towels are excellent for mopping up spills. Many mechanics use rolls of paper towels for most work because they are readily available and disposable. To help keep the area under the vehicle clean, a large cardboard box can be cut open and flattened to protect the garage or shop floor.

Whenever working over a painted surface, such as when leaning over a fender to service something under the hood, always cover it with an old blanket or bedspread to protect the finish. Vinyl covered pads, made especially for this purpose, are available at auto parts stores.

Booster battery (jump) starting

Booster battery (jump) starting

Observe the following precautions when using a booster battery to start a vehicle:

a) *Before connecting the booster battery, make sure the ignition switch is in the Off position.*

b) *Ensure that all electrical equipment (lights, heater, wipers etc.) are switched off.*

c) *Make sure that the booster battery is the same voltage as the discharged battery in the vehicle.*

d) *If the battery is being jump started from the battery in another vehicle, the two vehicles MUST NOT TOUCH each other.*

e) *Make sure the transaxle is in Neutral (manual transaxle) or Park (automatic transaxle).*

f) *Wear eye protection when jump starting a vehicle.*

Connect one jumper lead between the positive (+) terminals of the two batteries. Connect the other jumper lead first to the negative (-) terminal of the booster battery, then to a good engine ground on the vehicle to be started **(see illustration)**. Attach the lead at least 18 inches from the battery, if possible. Make sure that the jumper leads will not contact the fan, drivebelt of other moving parts of the engine.

Start the engine using the booster battery and allow the engine idle speed to stabilize. Disconnect the jumper leads in the reverse order of connection.

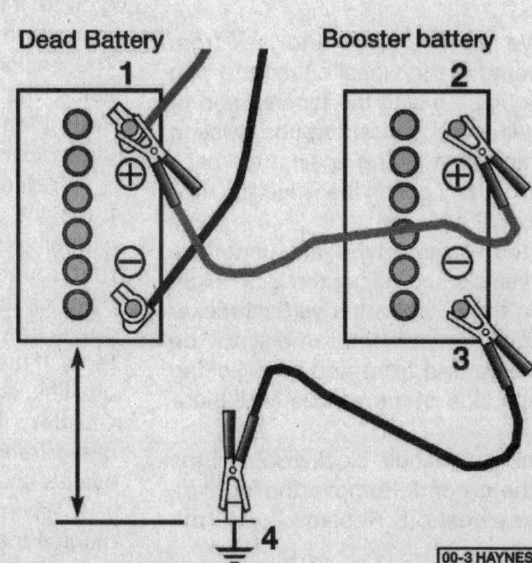

Make the booster battery cable connections in the numerical order shown (note that the negative cable of the booster battery is NOT attached to the negative terminal of the dead battery)

Jacking and towing

Jacking

Warning: *The jack supplied with the vehicle should only be used for changing a tire or placing jackstands under the frame. Never work under the vehicle or start the engine while this jack is being used as the only means of support.*

The vehicle should be on level ground. Place the shift lever in Park, if you have an automatic, or Reverse if you have a manual transaxle. Block the wheel diagonally opposite the wheel being changed. Set the parking brake.

Remove the spare tire and jack from stowage. Remove the wheel cover and trim ring (if so equipped) with the tapered end of the lug nut wrench by inserting and twisting the handle and then prying against the back of the wheel cover. Loosen the wheel lug nuts about 1/4-to-1/2 turn each.

Place the scissors-type jack under the side of the vehicle and adjust the jack height until it fits in the notch in the vertical rocker panel flange nearest the wheel to be changed. There is a front and rear jacking point on each side of the vehicle **(see illustration)**.

Turn the jack handle clockwise until the tire clears the ground. Remove the lug nuts and pull the wheel off. Replace it with the spare.

Install the lug nuts with the beveled edges facing in. Tighten them snugly. Don't attempt to tighten them completely until the vehicle is lowered or it could slip off the jack. Turn the jack handle counterclockwise to lower the vehicle. Remove the jack and tighten the lug nuts in a diagonal pattern.

Install the cover (and trim ring, if used) and be sure it's snapped into place all the way around.

Stow the tire, jack and wrench. Unblock the wheels.

Towing

As a general rule, the vehicle should be towed with the front (drive) wheels off the ground. If the vehicle must be towed from the rear, place the front wheels on a towing dolly. The ignition key must be in the ACC position, since the steering lock mechanism isn't strong enough to hold the front wheels straight while towing.

Vehicles equipped with an automatic transaxle can be towed from the front only with all four wheels on the ground, provided that speeds don't exceed 30 mph and the distance is not over 40 miles. Before towing, check the transaxle fluid level (see Chapter 1). If the level is below the HOT line on the dipstick, add fluid or use a towing dolly.

Caution: *Never tow a vehicle with an automatic transaxle from the rear with the front wheels on the ground.*

When towing a vehicle equipped with a manual transaxle with all four wheels on the ground, be sure to place the shift lever in neutral and release the parking brake.

Equipment specifically designed for towing should be used. It should be attached to the main structural members of the vehicle, not the bumpers or brackets.

Safety is a major consideration when towing and all applicable state and local laws must be obeyed. A safety chain system must be used at all times.

Place the jack on firm level ground and locate the jack head in the jacking point indentation (arrow) - there are two jacking points on each side of the vehicle, indicated by a notch in the rocker panel flange

Automotive chemicals and lubricants

A number of automotive chemicals and lubricants are available for use during vehicle maintenance and repair. They include a wide variety of products ranging from cleaning solvents and degreasers to lubricants and protective sprays for rubber, plastic and vinyl.

Cleaners

Carburetor cleaner and choke cleaner is a strong solvent for gum, varnish and carbon. Most carburetor cleaners leave a dry-type lubricant film which will not harden or gum up. Because of this film it is not recommended for use on electrical components.

Brake system cleaner is used to remove brake dust, grease and brake fluid from the brake system, where clean surfaces are absolutely necessary. It leaves no residue and often eliminates brake squeal caused by contaminants.

Electrical cleaner removes oxidation, corrosion and carbon deposits from electrical contacts, restoring full current flow. It can also be used to clean spark plugs, carburetor jets, voltage regulators and other parts where an oil-free surface is desired.

Demoisturants remove water and moisture from electrical components such as alternators, voltage regulators, electrical connectors and fuse blocks. They are non-conductive and non-corrosive.

Degreasers are heavy-duty solvents used to remove grease from the outside of the engine and from chassis components. They can be sprayed or brushed on and, depending on the type, are rinsed off either with water or solvent.

Lubricants

Motor oil is the lubricant formulated for use in engines. It normally contains a wide variety of additives to prevent corrosion and reduce foaming and wear. Motor oil comes in various weights (viscosity ratings) from 0 to 50. The recommended weight of the oil depends on the season, temperature and the demands on the engine. Light oil is used in cold climates and under light load conditions. Heavy oil is used in hot climates and where high loads are encountered. Multi-viscosity oils are designed to have characteristics of both light and heavy oils and are available in a number of weights from 5W-20 to 20W-50.

Gear oil is designed to be used in differentials, manual transmissions and other areas where high-temperature lubrication is required.

Chassis and wheel bearing grease is a heavy grease used where increased loads and friction are encountered, such as for wheel bearings, balljoints, tie-rod ends and universal joints.

High-temperature wheel bearing grease is designed to withstand the extreme temperatures encountered by wheel bearings in disc brake equipped vehicles. It usually contains molybdenum disulfide (moly), which is a dry-type lubricant.

White grease is a heavy grease for metal-to-metal applications where water is a problem. White grease stays soft under both low and high temperatures (usually from -100 to +190-degrees F), and will not wash off or dilute in the presence of water.

Assembly lube is a special extreme pressure lubricant, usually containing moly, used to lubricate high-load parts (such as main and rod bearings and cam lobes) for initial start-up of a new engine. The assembly lube lubricates the parts without being squeezed out or washed away until the engine oiling system begins to function.

Silicone lubricants are used to protect rubber, plastic, vinyl and nylon parts.

Graphite lubricants are used where oils cannot be used due to contamination problems, such as in locks. The dry graphite will lubricate metal parts while remaining uncontaminated by dirt, water, oil or acids. It is electrically conductive and will not foul electrical contacts in locks such as the ignition switch.

Moly penetrants loosen and lubricate frozen, rusted and corroded fasteners and prevent future rusting or freezing.

Heat-sink grease is a special electrically non-conductive grease that is used for mounting electronic ignition modules where it is essential that heat is transferred away from the module.

Sealants

RTV sealant is one of the most widely used gasket compounds. Made from silicone, RTV is air curing, it seals, bonds, waterproofs, fills surface irregularities, remains flexible, doesn't shrink, is relatively easy to remove, and is used as a supplementary sealer with almost all low and medium temperature gaskets.

Anaerobic sealant is much like RTV in that it can be used either to seal gaskets or to form gaskets by itself. It remains flexible, is solvent resistant and fills surface imperfections. The difference between an anaerobic sealant and an RTV-type sealant is in the curing. RTV cures when exposed to air, while an anaerobic sealant cures only in the absence of air. This means that an anaerobic sealant cures only after the assembly of parts, sealing them together.

Thread and pipe sealant is used for sealing hydraulic and pneumatic fittings and vacuum lines. It is usually made from a Teflon compound, and comes in a spray, a paint-on liquid and as a wrap-around tape.

Chemicals

Anti-seize compound prevents seizing, galling, cold welding, rust and corrosion in fasteners. High-temperature ant-seize, usually made with copper and graphite lubricants, is used for exhaust system and exhaust manifold bolts.

Anaerobic locking compounds are used to keep fasteners from vibrating or working loose and cure only after installation, in the absence of air. Medium strength locking compound is used for small nuts, bolts and screws that may be removed later. High-strength locking compound is for large nuts, bolts and studs which aren't removed on a regular basis.

Oil additives range from viscosity index improvers to chemical treatments that claim to reduce internal engine friction. It should be noted that most oil manufacturers caution against using additives with their oils.

Gas additives perform several functions, depending on their chemical makeup. They usually contain solvents that help dissolve gum and varnish that build up on carburetor, fuel injection and intake parts. They also serve to break down carbon deposits that form on the inside surfaces of the combustion chambers. Some additives contain upper cylinder lubricants for valves and piston rings, and others contain chemicals to remove condensation from the gas tank.

Miscellaneous

Brake fluid is specially formulated hydraulic fluid that can withstand the heat and pressure encountered in brake systems. Care must be taken so this fluid does not come in contact with painted surfaces or plastics. An opened container should always be resealed to prevent contamination by water or dirt.

Weatherstrip adhesive is used to bond weatherstripping around doors, windows and trunk lids. It is sometimes used to attach trim pieces.

Undercoating is a petroleum-based, tar-like substance that is designed to protect metal surfaces on the underside of the vehicle from corrosion. It also acts as a sound-deadening agent by insulating the bottom of the vehicle.

Waxes and polishes are used to help protect painted and plated surfaces from the weather. Different types of paint may require the use of different types of wax and polish. Some polishes utilize a chemical or abrasive cleaner to help remove the top layer of oxidized (dull) paint on older vehicles. In recent years many non-wax polishes that contain a wide variety of chemicals such as polymers and silicones have been introduced. These non-wax polishes are usually easier to apply and last longer than conventional waxes and polishes.

Conversion factors

Length (distance)

Unit		Factor	Equals		Factor	Equals
Inches (in)	X	25.4	= Millimeters (mm)	X	0.0394	= Inches (in)
Feet (ft)	X	0.305	= Meters (m)	X	3.281	= Feet (ft)
Miles	X	1.609	= Kilometers (km)	X	0.621	= Miles

Volume (capacity)

Unit		Factor	Equals		Factor	Equals
Cubic inches (cu in; in^3)	X	16.387	= Cubic centimeters (cc; cm^3)	X	0.061	= Cubic inches (cu in; in^3)
Imperial pints (Imp pt)	X	0.568	= Liters (l)	X	1.76	= Imperial pints (Imp pt)
Imperial quarts (Imp qt)	X	1.137	= Liters (l)	X	0.88	= Imperial quarts (Imp qt)
Imperial quarts (Imp qt)	X	1.201	= US quarts (US qt)	X	0.833	= Imperial quarts (Imp qt)
US quarts (US qt)	X	0.946	= Liters (l)	X	1.057	= US quarts (US qt)
Imperial gallons (Imp gal)	X	4.546	= Liters (l)	X	0.22	= Imperial gallons (Imp gal)
Imperial gallons (Imp gal)	X	1.201	= US gallons (US gal)	X	0.833	= Imperial gallons (Imp gal)
US gallons (US gal)	X	3.785	= Liters (l)	X	0.264	= US gallons (US gal)

Mass (weight)

Unit		Factor	Equals		Factor	Equals
Ounces (oz)	X	28.35	= Grams (g)	X	0.035	= Ounces (oz)
Pounds (lb)	X	0.454	= Kilograms (kg)	X	2.205	= Pounds (lb)

Force

Unit		Factor	Equals		Factor	Equals
Ounces-force (ozf; oz)	X	0.278	= Newtons (N)	X	3.6	= Ounces-force (ozf; oz)
Pounds-force (lbf; lb)	X	4.448	= Newtons (N)	X	0.225	= Pounds-force (lbf; lb)
Newtons (N)	X	0.1	= Kilograms-force (kgf; kg)	X	9.81	= Newtons (N)

Pressure

Unit		Factor	Equals		Factor	Equals
Pounds-force per square inch (psi; lbf/in^2; lb/in^2)	X	0.070	= Kilograms-force per square centimeter (kgf/cm^2; kg/cm^2)	X	14.223	= Pounds-force per square inch (psi; lbf/in^2; lb/in^2)
Pounds-force per square inch (psi; lbf/in^2; lb/in^2)	X	0.068	= Atmospheres (atm)	X	14.696	= Pounds-force per square inch (psi; lbf/in^2; lb/in^2)
Pounds-force per square inch (psi; lbf/in^2; lb/in^2)	X	0.069	= Bars	X	14.5	= Pounds-force per square inch (psi; lbf/in^2; lb/in^2)
Pounds-force per square inch (psi; lbf/in^2; lb/in^2)	X	6.895	= Kilopascals (kPa)	X	0.145	= Pounds-force per square inch (psi; lbf/in^2; lb/in^2)
Kilopascals (kPa)	X	0.01	= Kilograms-force per square centimeter (kgf/cm^2; kg/cm^2)	X	98.1	= Kilopascals (kPa)

Torque (moment of force)

Unit		Factor	Equals		Factor	Equals
Pounds-force inches (lbf in; lb in)	X	1.152	= Kilograms-force centimeter (kgf cm; kg cm)	X	0.868	= Pounds-force inches (lbf in; lb in)
Pounds-force inches (lbf in; lb in)	X	0.113	= Newton meters (Nm)	X	8.85	= Pounds-force inches (lbf in; lb in)
Pounds-force inches (lbf in; lb in)	X	0.083	= Pounds-force feet (lbf ft; lb ft)	X	12	= Pounds-force inches (lbf in; lb in)
Pounds-force feet (lbf ft; lb ft)	X	0.138	= Kilograms-force meters (kgf m; kg m)	X	7.233	= Pounds-force feet (lbf ft; lb ft)
Pounds-force feet (lbf ft; lb ft)	X	1.356	= Newton meters (Nm)	X	0.738	= Pounds-force feet (lbf ft; lb ft)
Newton meters (Nm)	X	0.102	= Kilograms-force meters (kgf m; kg m)	X	9.804	= Newton meters (Nm)

Vacuum

Unit		Factor	Equals		Factor	Equals
Inches mercury (in. Hg)	X	3.377	= Kilopascals (kPa)	X	0.2961	= Inches mercury
Inches mercury (in. Hg)	X	25.4	= Millimeters mercury (mm Hg)	X	0.0394	= Inches mercury

Power

Unit		Factor	Equals		Factor	Equals
Horsepower (hp)	X	745.7	= Watts (W)	X	0.0013	= Horsepower (hp)

Velocity (speed)

Unit		Factor	Equals		Factor	Equals
Miles per hour (miles/hr; mph)	X	1.609	= Kilometers per hour (km/hr; kph)	X	0.621	= Miles per hour (miles/hr; mph)

*Fuel consumption**

Unit		Factor	Equals		Factor	Equals
Miles per gallon, Imperial (mpg)	X	0.354	= Kilometers per liter (km/l)	X	2.825	= Miles per gallon, Imperial (mpg)
Miles per gallon, US (mpg)	X	0.425	= Kilometers per liter (km/l)	X	2.352	= Miles per gallon, US (mpg)

Temperature

Degrees Fahrenheit = (°C x 1.8) + 32

Degrees Celsius (Degrees Centigrade; °C) = (°F - 32) x 0.56

**It is common practice to convert from miles per gallon (mpg) to liters/100 kilometers (l/100km), where mpg (Imperial) x l/100 km = 282 and mpg (US) x l/100 km = 235*

Safety first!

Regardless of how enthusiastic you may be about getting on with the job at hand, take the time to ensure that your safety is not jeopardized. A moment's lack of attention can result in an accident, as can failure to observe certain simple safety precautions. The possibility of an accident will always exist, and the following points should not be considered a comprehensive list of all dangers. Rather, they are intended to make you aware of the risks and to encourage a safety conscious approach to all work you carry out on your vehicle.

Essential DOs and DON'Ts

DON'T rely on a jack when working under the vehicle. Always use approved jackstands to support the weight of the vehicle and place them under the recommended lift or support points.

DON'T attempt to loosen extremely tight fasteners (i.e. wheel lug nuts) while the vehicle is on a jack - it may fall.

DON'T start the engine without first making sure that the transmission is in Neutral (or Park where applicable) and the parking brake is set.

DON'T remove the radiator cap from a hot cooling system - let it cool or cover it with a cloth and release the pressure gradually.

DON'T attempt to drain the engine oil until you are sure it has cooled to the point that it will not burn you.

DON'T touch any part of the engine or exhaust system until it has cooled sufficiently to avoid burns.

DON'T siphon toxic liquids such as gasoline, antifreeze and brake fluid by mouth, or allow them to remain on your skin.

DON'T inhale brake lining dust - it is potentially hazardous (see *Asbestos* below).

DON'T allow spilled oil or grease to remain on the floor - wipe it up before someone slips on it.

DON'T use loose fitting wrenches or other tools which may slip and cause injury.

DON'T push on wrenches when loosening or tightening nuts or bolts. Always try to pull the wrench toward you. If the situation calls for pushing the wrench away, push with an open hand to avoid scraped knuckles if the wrench should slip.

DON'T attempt to lift a heavy component alone - get someone to help you.

DON'T rush or take unsafe shortcuts to finish a job.

DON'T allow children or animals in or around the vehicle while you are working on it.

DO wear eye protection when using power tools such as a drill, sander, bench grinder, etc. and when working under a vehicle.

DO keep loose clothing and long hair well out of the way of moving parts.

DO make sure that any hoist used has a safe working load rating adequate for the job.

DO get someone to check on you periodically when working alone on a vehicle.

DO carry out work in a logical sequence and make sure that everything is correctly assembled and tightened.

DO keep chemicals and fluids tightly capped and out of the reach of children and pets.

DO remember that your vehicle's safety affects that of yourself and others. If in doubt on any point, get professional advice.

Asbestos

Certain friction, insulating, sealing, and other products - such as brake linings, brake bands, clutch linings, torque converters, gaskets, etc. - may contain asbestos. Extreme care must be taken to avoid inhalation of dust from such products, since it is hazardous to health. If in doubt, assume that they do contain asbestos.

Fire

Remember at all times that gasoline is highly flammable. Never smoke or have any kind of open flame around when working on a vehicle. But the risk does not end there. A spark caused by an electrical short circuit, by two metal surfaces contacting each other, or even by static electricity built up in your body under certain conditions, can ignite gasoline vapors, which in a confined space are highly explosive. Do not, under any circumstances, use gasoline for cleaning parts. Use an approved safety solvent.

Always disconnect the battery ground (-) cable at the battery before working on any part of the fuel system or electrical system. Never risk spilling fuel on a hot engine or exhaust component. It is strongly recommended that a fire extinguisher suitable for use on fuel and electrical fires be kept handy in the garage or workshop at all times. Never try to extinguish a fuel or electrical fire with water.

Fumes

Certain fumes are highly toxic and can quickly cause unconsciousness and even death if inhaled to any extent. Gasoline vapor falls into this category, as do the vapors from some cleaning solvents. Any draining or pouring of such volatile fluids should be done in a well ventilated area.

When using cleaning fluids and solvents, read the instructions on the container carefully. Never use materials from unmarked containers.

Never run the engine in an enclosed space, such as a garage. Exhaust fumes contain carbon monoxide, which is extremely poisonous. If you need to run the engine, always do so in the open air, or at least have the rear of the vehicle outside the work area.

If you are fortunate enough to have the use of an inspection pit, never drain or pour gasoline and never run the engine while the vehicle is over the pit. The fumes, being heavier than air, will concentrate in the pit with possibly lethal results.

The battery

Never create a spark or allow a bare light bulb near a battery. They normally give off a certain amount of hydrogen gas, which is highly explosive.

Always disconnect the battery ground (-) cable at the battery before working on the fuel or electrical systems.

If possible, loosen the filler caps or cover when charging the battery from an external source (this does not apply to sealed or maintenance-free batteries). Do not charge at an excessive rate or the battery may burst.

Take care when adding water to a non maintenance-free battery and when carrying a battery. The electrolyte, even when diluted, is very corrosive and should not be allowed to contact clothing or skin.

Always wear eye protection when cleaning the battery to prevent the caustic deposits from entering your eyes.

Household current

When using an electric power tool, inspection light, etc., which operates on household current, always make sure that the tool is correctly connected to its plug and that, where necessary, it is properly grounded. Do not use such items in damp conditions and, again, do not create a spark or apply excessive heat in the vicinity of fuel or fuel vapor.

Secondary ignition system voltage

A severe electric shock can result from touching certain parts of the ignition system (such as the spark plug wires) when the engine is running or being cranked, particularly if components are damp or the insulation is defective. In the case of an electronic ignition system, the secondary system voltage is much higher and could prove fatal.

Troubleshooting

Contents

This section provides an easy reference guide to the more common problems which may occur during the operation of your vehicle. These problems and possible causes are grouped under various components or systems; i.e. Engine, Cooling System, etc., and also refer to the Chapter and/or Section which deals with the problem.

Remember that successful troubleshooting is not a mysterious black art practiced only by professional mechanics. It's simply the result of a bit of knowledge combined with an intelligent, systematic approach to the problem. Always work by a process of elimination, starting with the simplest solution and working through to the most complex - and never overlook the obvious. Anyone can forget to fill the gas tank or leave the lights on overnight, so don't assume that you are above such oversights.

Finally, always get clear in your mind why a problem has occurred and take steps to ensure that it doesn't happen again. If the electrical system fails because of a poor connection, check all other connections in the system to make sure that they don't fail as well. If a particular fuse continues to blow, find out why - don't just continue replacing fuses. Remember, failure of a small component can often be indicative of potential failure or incorrect functioning of a more important component or system.

Engine

1 Engine will not rotate when attempting to start

1 Battery terminal connections loose or corroded. Check the cable terminals at the battery. Tighten the cable or remove corrosion as necessary.
2 Battery discharged or faulty. If the cable connections are clean and tight on the battery terminals, turn the key to the On position and switch on the headlights and/or windshield wipers. If they fail to function, the battery is discharged.
3 Automatic transaxle not completely engaged in Park or Neutral or clutch pedal not completely depressed.
4 Broken, loose or disconnected wiring in the starting circuit. Inspect all wiring and connectors at the battery, starter solenoid and ignition switch.
5 Starter motor pinion jammed in flywheel ring gear. If manual transaxle, place transaxle in gear and rock the vehicle to manually turn the engine. Remove starter and inspect pinion and flywheel at earliest convenience (Chapter 5).
6 Starter solenoid faulty (Chapter 5).
7 Starter motor faulty (Chapter 5).
8 Ignition switch faulty (Chapter 12).

2 Engine rotates but will not start

1 Fuel tank empty.
2 Fault in the fuel injection system (Chapters 4 and 6).
3 Battery discharged (engine rotates slowly). Check the operation of electrical components as described in the previous Section.
4 Battery terminal connections loose or corroded (see previous Section).
5 Fuel injector or fuel pump faulty (Chapter 4).
6 Excessive moisture on, or damage to, ignition components (Chapter 5).
7 Worn, faulty or incorrectly gapped spark plugs (Chapter 1).
8 Broken, loose or disconnected wiring in the starting circuit (see previous Section).
9 Distributor loose, causing ignition timing to change. Turn the distributor as necessary to start the engine, then set the ignition timing as soon as possible (Chapter 1).
10 Broken, loose or disconnected wires at the ignition coil or faulty coil (Chapter 5).
11 Broken or stripped timing chain or belt (Chapter 2).

3 Starter motor operates without rotating engine

1 Starter drive pinion sticking. Remove the starter (Chapter 5) and inspect.
2 Starter drive pinion or flywheel teeth worn or broken. Remove the flywheel/driveplate access cover from the oil pan and inspect the ring gear teeth and starter drive pinion gear.

4 Engine hard to start when cold

1 Battery discharged or low. Check as described in Section 1.
2 Fault in the fuel injection system (Chapters 4 and 6).
3 Fuel not reaching the fuel injection system (see Section 2).

5 Engine hard to start when hot

1 Air filter clogged (Chapter 1).
2 Fault in the fuel injection system (Chapters 4 and 6).
3 Fuel not reaching the fuel injection system (see Section 2).

6 Starter motor noisy or excessively rough in engagement

1 Drive pinion or flywheel gear teeth worn or broken. Remove the cover at the rear of the engine (if so equipped) and inspect the ring gear teeth and starter pinion.
2 Starter motor mount bolts loose or missing.

7 Engine starts but stops immediately

1 Loose or faulty electrical connections at distributor, coil or alternator.
2 Fault in the fuel injection system (Chapters 4 and 6).
3 Insufficient fuel reaching the fuel injectors. Check the fuel pressure (Chapter 5) or have the fuel injection pressure checked by your dealer or a properly equipped shop.
4 Vacuum leak at the gasket surfaces of the intake manifold, fuel charging assembly or throttle body. Make sure that all mount bolts/nuts are tightened securely and that all vacuum hoses connected to the fuel injection assembly and manifold are positioned properly and in good condition.

8 Engine lopes while idling or idles erratically

1 Vacuum leakage. Check the mount bolts/nuts at the fuel injection unit and upper and lower intake manifolds for tightness. Make sure that all vacuum hoses are connected and in good condition. Use a stethoscope or a length of fuel hose held against your ear to listen for vacuum leaks while the engine is running. A hissing sound will be heard if a vacuum leak is located. A soapy water solution will also detect leaks. Check the fuel injector and intake manifold gasket surfaces.
2 Fault in the fuel injection system (Chapters 4 and 6).
3 Leaking EGR valve or plugged PCV valve (see Chapters 1 and 6).
4 Air filter clogged (Chapter 1).
5 Fuel pump not delivering sufficient fuel to the fuel injectors (see Chapter 4).
6 Leaking head gasket(s). If this is suspected, take the vehicle to a repair shop or dealer where the engine can be pressure checked.
7 Timing chain, belt or sprockets worn (Chapter 2).
8 Camshaft lobes worn (Chapter 2).

9 Engine misses at idle speed

1 Spark plugs excessively worn or not gapped properly (Chapter 1).
2 Fault in the fuel injection system (Chapters 4 and 6).
3 Faulty spark plug wires (Chapter 1).

10 Engine misses throughout driving speed range

1 Fuel filter clogged and/or impurities in the fuel system (Chapter 1).
2 Faulty or incorrectly gapped spark plugs (Chapter 1).
3 Fault in the fuel injection system (Chapters 4 and 6).
4 Incorrect ignition timing (Chapter 5).
5 Defective spark plug wires (Chapter 1).
6 Faulty emissions system components (Chapter 6).
7 Low or uneven cylinder compression pressures. Remove the spark plugs and test the compression with a gauge (Chapter 2).
8 Weak or faulty ignition system (Chapter 5).
9 Vacuum leaks at the fuel injection unit, upper and/or lower intake manifold or vacuum hoses (see Section 8).

11 Engine stalls

1 Idle speed incorrect. Refer to the VECI label and Chapter 4, then take the vehicle to a dealer (idle speed is not adjustable).
2 Fuel filter clogged and/or water and impurities in the fuel system (Chapter 1).
3 Fault in the fuel injection system (Chapters 4 and 6).
4 Faulty emissions system components (Chapter 6).
5 Faulty or incorrectly gapped spark plugs (Chapter 1). Also check the spark plug wires (Chapter 1).
6 Vacuum leakage. Check as described in Section 8.

12 Engine lacks power

1 Incorrect ignition timing (Chapter 5).
2 Fault in the fuel injection system (Chapters 4 and 6).
3 Faulty or incorrectly gapped spark plugs (Chapter 1).
4 Fuel filter clogged and/or impurities in the fuel system (Chapter 1).
5 Faulty coil (Chapter 5).
6 Brakes binding (Chapter 1).
7 Automatic transaxle fluid level incorrect (Chapter 1).
8 Clutch slipping (Chapter 8).
9 Restricted catalytic converter or exhaust system (Chapter 4).
10 Emissions control system not functioning properly (Chapter 6).
11 Use of substandard fuel. Fill the tank with the proper octane fuel.
12 Low or uneven cylinder compression pressures. Test with a compression tester, which will detect leaking valves and/or a blown head gasket (Chapter 2).

13 Engine backfires

1 Emissions system not functioning properly (Chapter 6).
2 Fault in the fuel injection system (Chapters 4 and 6).
3 Ignition timing incorrect (Chapter 5).
4 Faulty secondary ignition system (cracked spark plug insulator, faulty plug wires) (Chapters 1 and 5).
5 Vacuum leakage. Check as described in Section 8.
6 Valves sticking (Chapter 2).

14 Pinging or knocking engine sounds during acceleration or uphill

1 Incorrect grade of fuel. Fill the tank with fuel of the proper octane rating.
2 Fault in the fuel injection system (Chapters 4 and 6).
3 Ignition timing incorrect (Chapter 5).
4 Improper spark plugs. Check the plug type against the VECI label located in the engine compartment. Also check the plugs and wires for damage (Chapter 1).
5 Faulty emissions system (Chapter 6).
6 Vacuum leak. Check as described in Section 8.

15 Engine diesels (continues to run) after switching off

1 Idle speed too high. Refer to Ignition timing section in Chapter 5; take vehicle to a dealer.
2 Fault in the fuel injection system (Chapters 4 and 6).
3 Excessive engine operating temperature. Probable causes of this are a malfunctioning thermostat, clogged radiator, insufficient coolant level, faulty water pump (Chapter 3).

Engine electrical system

16 Battery will not hold a charge

1 Accessory drivebelt defective or not adjusted properly (Chapter 1).
2 Electrolyte level low or battery discharged (Chapter 1).
3 Battery terminals loose or corroded (Chapter 1).
4 Alternator not charging properly (Chapter 5).
5 Loose, broken or faulty wiring in the charging circuit (Chapter 5).
6 Short in the vehicle wiring causing a continual drain on battery (refer to Chapter 12 and the Wiring Diagrams).
7 Battery defective internally.

17 Charging system light fails to go out

1 Fault in the alternator or charging circuit (Chapter 5).
2 Accessory drivebelt defective or not properly adjusted (Chapter 1).
3 Mega fuse blown (Chapter 5).

18 Ignition light fails to come on when key is turned on

1 Instrument cluster warning light bulb defective (Chapter 12).
2 Alternator faulty (Chapter 5).
3 Fault in the instrument cluster printed circuit, dashboard wiring or bulb holder (Chapter 12).

Fuel system

19 Excessive fuel consumption

1 Dirty or clogged air filter element (Chapter 1).
2 Incorrect ignition timing (Chapter 5).
3 Emissions system not functioning properly (Chapter 6).
4 Fault in the fuel injection system (Chapters 4 and 6).
5 Low tire pressure or incorrect tire size (Chapter 1).

20 Fuel leakage and/or fuel odor

1 Leak in a fuel feed or vent line (Chapter 4).
2 Tank overfilled. Fill only to automatic shut-off.
3 Evaporative emissions system filter clogged (Chapter 6).
4 Vapor leaks from system lines (Chapter 4).
5 Fault in the fuel injection system (Chapters 4 and 6).

Cooling system

21 Overheating

1 Insufficient coolant in the system (Chapter 1).
2 Water pump drivebelt defective or not adjusted properly (Chapter 1).
3 Radiator core blocked or radiator grill dirty and restricted (Chapter 3).
4 Thermostat faulty (Chapter 3).
5 Fan blades broken or cracked (Chapter 3).
6 Radiator cap not maintaining proper pressure. Have the cap pressure tested by gas station or repair shop.
7 Ignition timing incorrect (Chapter 5).

22 Overcooling

Thermostat faulty (Chapter 3).

23 External coolant leakage

1 Deteriorated or damaged hoses or loose clamps. Replace hoses and/or tighten the clamps at the hose connections (Chapter 1).
2 Water pump seals defective. If this is the case, water will drip from the vent hole in the water pump body (Chapter 3).
3 Leakage from radiator core or tank. This will require the radiator to be professionally repaired (see Chapter 3 for removal procedures).
4 Engine drain plug leaking (Chapter 1) or water jacket core plugs leaking (see Chapter 2).

24 Internal coolant leakage

Note: *Internal coolant leaks can usually be detected by examining the oil. Check the dipstick and inside of the rocker arm cover for water deposits and an oil consistency like that of a milkshake.*
1 Leaking cylinder head gasket. Have the cooling system pressure tested.
2 Cracked cylinder bore or cylinder head. Disassemble the engine and inspect (Chapter 2).

25 Coolant loss

1 Too much coolant in the system (Chapter 1).
2 Coolant boiling away due to overheating (see Section 15).
3 External or internal leakage (see Sections 23 and 24).
4 Faulty radiator cap. Have the cap pressure tested.

26 Poor coolant circulation

1 Inoperative water pump. A quick test is to pinch the top radiator hose closed with your hand while the engine is idling, then let it loose. You should feel the surge of coolant if the pump is working properly (Chapter 1).
2 Restriction in the cooling system. Drain, flush and refill the system (Chapter 1). If necessary, remove the radiator (Chapter 3) and have it reverse flushed.
3 Water pump drivebelt defective or not adjusted properly (Chapter 1).
4 Thermostat sticking (Chapter 3).

Clutch

27 Fails to release (pedal pressed to the floor - shift lever does not move freely in and out of Reverse)

1 Defective hydraulic system, low fluid level in clutch master cylinder reservoir or air trapped in hydraulic system (Chapter 8).
2 Clutch plate warped or damaged (Chapter 8).

28 Clutch slips (engine speed increases with no increase in vehicle speed)

1 Clutch plate oil soaked or lining worn. Remove clutch (Chapter 8) and inspect.
2 Faulty pressure plate (Chapter 8).

29 Grabbing (chattering) as clutch is engaged

1 Oil on clutch plate lining. Remove clutch (Chapter 8) and inspect. Correct any leakage source.
2 Worn or loose engine or transaxle mounts. These units move slightly when the clutch is released. Inspect the mounts and bolts (Chapter 2).
3 Worn splines on clutch plate hub. Remove the clutch components (Chapter 8) and inspect.
4 Warped pressure plate or flywheel. Remove the clutch components and inspect.

30 Squeal or rumble with clutch fully disengaged (pedal depressed)

1 Worn, defective or broken release bearing (Chapter 8).
2 Worn or broken pressure plate springs (or diaphragm fingers) (Chapter 8).

31 Clutch pedal stays on floor when disengaged

Linkage or release bearing binding. Defective clutch master cylinder or slave cylinder. Air in clutch hydraulic system. Low clutch fluid level. Inspect the clutch components as necessary.

Manual transaxle

32 Noisy in Neutral with engine running

1 Input shaft bearing worn.
2 Damaged main drive gear bearing.
3 Worn countershaft bearings.
4 Worn or damaged countershaft endplay shims.

33 Noisy in all gears

1 Any of the above causes, and/or:
2 Insufficient lubricant (see the checking procedures in Chapter 1).

34 Noisy in one particular gear

1 Worn, damaged or chipped gear teeth for that particular gear.
2 Worn or damaged synchronizer for that particular gear.

35 Slips out of high gear

1 Transaxle loose on clutch housing (Chapter 7).
2 Shift rods interfering with the engine mounts or clutch lever (Chapter 7).
3 Shift rods not working freely (Chapter 7).
4 Dirt between the transaxle case and engine or misalignment of the transaxle (Chapter 7).
5 Worn or improperly adjusted linkage (Chapter 7).

36 Difficulty in engaging gears

1 Clutch not releasing completely (see clutch adjustment in Chapter 8).
2 Loose, damaged or out-of-adjustment shift linkage. Make a thorough inspection, replacing parts as necessary (Chapter 7).

37 Oil leakage

1 Excessive amount of lubricant in the transaxle (see Chapter 1 for correct checking procedures). Drain lubricant as required.
2 Driveaxle oil seal (Chapter 8) or speedometer oil seal in need of replacement (Chapter 7).

Automatic transaxle

Note: *Due to the complexity of the automatic transaxle, it's difficult for the home mechanic to properly diagnose and service this component. For problems other than the following, the vehicle should be taken to a dealer or reputable mechanic.*

38 General shift mechanism problems

1 Chapter 7 deals with checking and adjusting the shift linkage on automatic transaxles. Common problems which may be attributed to poorly adjusted linkage are:

a) Engine starting in gears other than Park or Neutral.
b) Indicator on shifter pointing to a gear other than the one actually being used.
c) Vehicle moves when in Park.

2 Refer to Chapter 7 to adjust the linkage.

39 Transaxle will not downshift with accelerator pedal pressed to the floor

Chapter 7 deals with adjusting the throttle cable to enable the transaxle to downshift properly.

40 Transaxle slips, shifts rough, is noisy or has no drive in forward or reverse gears

1 There are many probable causes for the above problems, but the home mechanic should be concerned with only one possibility - fluid level.
2 Before taking the vehicle to a repair shop, check the level and condition of the fluid as described in Chapter 1. Correct fluid level as necessary or change the fluid and filter if needed. If the problem persists, have a professional diagnose the probable cause.

41 Fluid leakage

1 Automatic transaxle fluid is a deep red color. Fluid leaks should not be confused with engine oil, which can easily be blown by air flow to the transaxle.
2 To pinpoint a leak, first remove all built-up dirt and grime from around the transaxle. Degreasing agents and/or steam cleaning will achieve this. With the underside clean, drive the vehicle at low speeds so air flow will not blow the leak far from its source. Raise the vehicle and determine where the leak is coming from. Common areas of leakage are:

a) ***Pan:*** *Tighten the mount bolts and/or replace the pan gasket as necessary (see Chapter 7).*
b) ***Filler tube:*** *Replace the rubber seal where the tube enters the transaxle case.*
c) ***Transaxle oil lines:*** *Tighten the connectors where the lines enter the transaxle case and/or replace the lines.*
d) ***Vent tube:*** *Transaxle overfilled and/or water in fluid (see checking procedures, Chapter 1).*
e) ***Speedometer connector:*** *Replace the O-ring where the speedometer cable enters the transaxle case (Chapter 7).*

Driveaxles

42 Clicking noise in turns

Worn or damaged outer CV joint. Check for cut or damaged seals. Repair as necessary (Chapter 8).

43 Knock or clunk when accelerating after coasting

Worn or damaged inner CV joint. Check for cut or damaged seals. Repair as necessary (Chapter 8)

44 Shudder or vibration during acceleration

1 Worn or damaged CV joints. Repair or replace as necessary (Chapter 8).
2 Sticking CV joint assembly. Correct or replace as necessary (Chapter 8).

Rear axle

45 Noise

1 Normal road noise. No corrective procedures necessary.
2 Tire noise. Inspect tires for abnormal wear (cupped or uneven wear). Also check tire pressures (Chapter 1).
3 Rear wheel bearings loose, worn or damaged (Chapter 10).

Brakes

Note: *Before assuming that a brake problem exists, make sure that the tires are in good condition and inflated properly (see Chapter 1), that the wheel alignment is correct and that the vehicle is not excessively loaded.*

46 Vehicle pulls to one side during braking

1 Defective, damaged or oil contaminated disc brake pads on one side. Inspect as described in Chapter 9.
2 Excessive wear of brake pad material or disc on one side. Inspect and correct as necessary (Chapters 1 and 9).
3 Loose or disconnected front suspension components. Inspect and tighten all bolts to the specified torque (Chapter 10).
4 Defective caliper assembly. Remove the caliper and inspect for a stuck piston or other damage (Chapter 9).

47 Noise (high-pitched squeal with the brakes applied)

1 Disc brake pads worn out. The noise comes from the wear sensor rubbing against the disc (does not apply to all vehicles) or the actual pad backing plate itself if the material is completely worn away (grinding noise). Replace the pads immediately (Chapter 9). If the pad material has worn completely away, the brake discs should be inspected for damage as described in Chapter
2 High-pitched squeal can be caused by excessive dust accumulation in the brake mechanism or loose brake pad mount hardware. Anything that can allow the brake pads to vibrate during brake application will cause brake squeal.

48 Excessive brake pedal travel

1 Partial brake system failure. Inspect the entire system (Chapter 9) and correct as required.
2 Insufficient fluid in the master cylinder. Check (Chapter 1), add fluid and bleed the system if necessary (Chapter 9).
3 Rear brakes not adjusting properly. Make a series of starts and stops while the vehicle is in Reverse. If this does not correct the situation, remove the drums and inspect the self-adjusters (Chapter 9).

49 Brake pedal feels spongy when depressed

1 Air in the hydraulic lines. Bleed the brake system (Chapter 9).
2 Faulty flexible hoses. Inspect all system hoses and lines. Replace parts as necessary.
3 Master cylinder mount bolts/nuts loose.
4 Master cylinder defective (Chapter 9).

50 Excessive effort required to stop vehicle

1 Power brake booster not operating properly (Chapter 9).
2 Excessively worn linings or pads. Inspect and replace if necessary (Chapter 9).
3 One or more caliper pistons or wheel cylinders seized or sticking. Inspect and rebuild as required (Chapter 9).
4 Brake linings or pads contaminated with oil or grease. Inspect and replace as required (Chapter 9).
5 New pads or shoes installed and not yet seated. It will take a while for the new material to seat against the drum (or disc).

51 Pedal travels to the floor with little resistance

Little or no fluid in the master cylinder reservoir caused by leaking wheel cylinder(s), leaking caliper piston(s), loose, damaged or disconnected brake lines. Inspect the entire system and correct as necessary.

52 Brake pedal pulsates during brake application

1 Caliper improperly installed. Remove and inspect (Chapter 9).
2 Disc defective. Remove the disc (Chapter 9) and check for excessive lateral runout and parallelism. Have the disc resurfaced or replace it with a new one.

Suspension and steering systems

53 Vehicle pulls to one side

1 Tire pressures uneven (Chapter 1).
2 Defective tire (Chapter 1).
3 Excessive wear in suspension or steering components (Chapter 10).
4 Front end in need of alignment.
5 Front brakes dragging. Inspect the brakes as described in Chapter 9.

54 Shimmy, shake or vibration

1 Tire or wheel out-of-balance or out-of-round. Have the wheel professionally balanced.
2 Loose or worn wheel bearings (Chapter 10).
3 Shock absorbers (struts) and/or suspension components worn or damaged (Chapter 10).

55 Excessive pitching and/or rolling around corners or during braking

1 Defective shock absorbers (struts). Replace as a set (Chapter 10).
2 Broken or weak springs and/or suspension components. Inspect as described in Chapter 10.

56 Excessively stiff steering

1 Lack of fluid in power steering fluid reservoir (Chapter 1).
2 Incorrect tire pressures (Chapter 1).
3 Front end out of alignment.

57 Excessive play in steering

1 Excessive wear in suspension or steering components (Chapter 10).
2 Rack and pinion steering assembly damaged (Chapter 10).

58 Lack of steering power assist

1 Steering pump drivebelt faulty or not adjusted properly (Chapter 1).
2 Fluid level low (Chapter 1).
3 Hoses or lines restricted. Inspect and replace parts as necessary.
4 Air in power steering system. Bleed the system (Chapter 10).

59 Excessive tire wear (not specific to one area)

1 Incorrect tire pressures (Chapter 1).
2 Tires out-of-balance. Have the wheels professionally balanced.
3 Wheels damaged. Inspect and replace as necessary.
4 Suspension or steering components excessively worn (Chapter 10).

60 Excessive tire wear on outside edge

1 Inflation pressure incorrect (Chapter 1).
2 Excessive speed in turns.
3 Front end alignment incorrect (excessive toe-in). Have professionally aligned.
4 Suspension component bent or twisted (Chapter 10).

61 Excessive tire wear on inside edge

1 Inflation pressure incorrect (Chapter 1).
2 Front end alignment incorrect. Have professionally aligned.
3 Loose or damaged steering components (Chapter 10).

62 Tire tread worn in one place

1 Tires out-of-balance.
2 Damaged or buckled wheel. Inspect and replace if necessary.
3 Defective tire (Chapter 1).

Notes

Chapter 1
Tune-up and routine maintenance

Contents

Specifications

Cooling system

Radiator cap opening pressure	16 psi

Fuel system

Idle speed	Not adjustable
Fuel filter	Motorcraft FG-800A

Ignition system

Firing order	
Four-cylinder engine	1-3-4-2
V6 engine	1-4-2-5-3-6
Spark plugs	
Four-cylinder engine	
Type	
1995 through 1998	Motorcraft AZFS-22PP
1999 and later	
Cylinders #1 and #2	AZFS-22F
Cylinders #3 and #4	AZFS-32FE
Gap	0.050 inch
V6 engine	
Type	Motorcraft AWSF-32F
Gap	0.054 inch
Brake system	
Disc brake pad thickness (minimum)	1/8 inch
Drum brake shoe thickness (minimum)	
Bonded	1/8 inch
Riveted	1/16 inch

1 2 3 4
FRONT
36006-1-A HAYNES

Cylinder location and coil terminal identification diagram - four-cylinder engine

1 2 3
4 5 6
FRONT
36006-1-B HAYNES

Cylinder location and coil terminal identification diagram - V6 engine

Recommended lubricants and fluids

Note: *Listed here are manufacturer recommendations at the time this manual was written. Manufacturers occasionally upgrade their fluid and lubricant specifications, so check with your local auto parts store for current recommendations.*

Engine oil	
Type	API grade SF or SE
Viscosity	SAE 5W-30 or 10W-30
Engine coolant	50/50 mixture of ethylene glycol antifreeze and water
Brake fluid	Dot 3 heavy duty brake fluid
Power steering fluid	Motorcraft Type F automatic transaxle fluid
Automatic transaxle fluid	Mercon automatic transaxle fluid
Manual transaxle fluid	Mercon automatic transaxle fluid

Capacities*

Engine oil (with filter change)	
Four-cylinder engine	4.5 quarts
V6 engine	5.8 quarts
Cooling system (including heater core)	
Automatic transaxle	
Four-cylinder models	
1995 through 1997	7.5 quarts
1998	7.0 quarts
V6 models	
1995 through 1998	9.1 quarts
1998 and later	10.2 quarts
Manual transaxle	
Four-cylinder models	
1995 through 1997	7.0 quarts
1998	7.0 quarts
V6 models	
1995 through 1998	8.9 quarts
1999 and later	10.0 quarts
Transaxle	
Automatic	
Dry fill (after an overhaul, for example)	
Four-cylinder models	
1995 through 1997	9.0 quarts
1998	7.6 quarts
V6 models	10.3 quarts
Drain and refill **	4.0 quarts (starting point, then add as necessary, in small quantities, to bring to the appropriate level)
Manual transaxle	5.5 pints

* *All capacities approximate. Add as necessary to bring up to the appropriate level.*
** *When draining and refilling the automatic transaxle, purchase four extra quarts of the specified automatic transmission fluid (this will be used for flushing).*

Torque specifications

	Ft-lbs (unless otherwise indicated)
Engine oil drain plug	15 to 21
Automatic transaxle drain plug	18 to 22
Manual transaxle fill/level plug	26
Drivebelt tensioner mounting bolt(s)	
Four-cylinder engine	35
V6 engine	15 to 22
Spark Plugs	
Four-cylinder engine	
1995 through 1997	108 to 156 in-lbs
1998 and later	132 in-lbs
V6 engine	
1995 through 1997	84 to 180 in-lbs
1998 and later	144 in-lbs
Wheel lug nuts	95

Engine compartment component locations - V6 engine

1. *Automatic transaxle fluid dipstick (Section 7) (not visible)*
2. *Ventilation system filter - under cowl grille panel (Section 33)*
3. *Brake fluid reservoir (Section 3)*
4. *Air filter housing (Section 23)*
5. *Auxiliary fuse box (Chapter 12)*
6. *Battery (Section 10)*
7. *PCV hose (one of two shown) (Section 24)*
8. *Radiator hose (Section 15)*
9. *Water pump drivebelt (under cover) (Section 21)*
10. *Engine oil filler cap (Section 3)*
11. *Engine oil dipstick (Section 3)*
12. *Windshield washer fluid reservoir (Section 3)*
13. *Drivebelt (Section 21)*
14. *Coolant expansion tank (Section 3)*
15. *Power steering fluid reservoir (Section 6)*

Engine compartment components - four-cylinder engine

1 *Spark plugs (Section 30)*
2 *Engine oil filler cap (Section 3)*
3 *Brake fluid reservoir (Section 3)*
4 *Auxiliary fuse box (Chapter 12)*
5 *Air filter housing (Section 23)*
6 *Battery (Section 10)*
7 *Coolant expansion tank (Section 3)*
8 *Ventilation system filter - under cowl grille panel (Section 33)*
9 *Air intake resonator (Chapter 4)*
10 *Radiator upper hose (Section 15)*
11 *Cooling system expansion tank filler cap (Section 3)*
12 *Air intake plenum chamber (Chapter 4)*
13 *Engine oil dipstick (Section 3)*
14 *Vehicle Identification Number (VIN) plate*
15 *Windshield washer reservoir (Section 3)*
16 *Accessory drivebelt (Section 21)*
17 *Power steering fluid reservoir (Section 6)*

Front underbody view (four-cylinder model shown, V6 similar)

1 *Radiator lower hose (Section 15)*
2 *Exhaust gas oxygen sensor (Chapter 6)*
3 *Brake system, fuel and emission control system lines*
4 *Front disc brake (Section 19)*
5 *Manual transaxle drain plug (Section 30)*
6 *Front suspension subframe (Chapter 2)*
7 *Manual transaxle filler/level plug (Section 20)*
8 *Radiator shield (Section 28)*
9 *Catalytic converter (Section 26)*
10 *Exhaust system rubber hangers (Section 26)*
11 *Engine oil drain plug (Section 8)*
12 *Engine oil filter (Section 8)*

Maintenance Schedule

The following maintenance schedule is based on the assumption that the vehicle owner will be performing the maintenance or service work, as opposed to having a dealership service department or other repair shop do the work. Although the time/mileage intervals are loosely based on factory recommendations, most have been shortened to ensure, for example, that such items as lubricates and fluids are checked/changed at intervals that promote maximum engine/drivetrain service life. If you wish to keep your vehicle in peak condition at all times, you may wish to perform some of these procedures even more often. Because frequent maintenance enhances the efficiency, performance and resale value of your vehicle, we encourage you to do so. If your usage is not normal, shorter intervals are also recommended - the most important examples of these are noted in the schedule. These shorter intervals apply particularly if you drive in dusty areas, tow a trailer, sit with the engine idling or drive at low speeds for extended periods (i.e., in heavy traffic), or drive for short distances (less than four miles) in below-freezing temperatures.

When your vehicle is new, it should be serviced at a factory-authorized dealership service department to protect the factory warranty. In many cases, the initial maintenance check is done at no cost to the owner (check with your dealer service department for more information). Note that this first free service (performed by the selling dealership 1500 miles or 3 months after delivery), although an important check for a new vehicle, is not part of the regular maintenance schedule, and is therefore not mentioned here.

Every 250 miles or weekly, whichever comes first

Check the engine oil level (Section 3)
Check the engine coolant level (Section 3)
Check the windshield washer fluid level (Section 3)
Check the brake fluid level (Section 3)
Check the tire pressures, including the spare (Section 4)
Visually check the tires for excessive tread wear, or damage (Section 4)
Check the operation of all (exterior and interior) lights, the horn, wipers and windshield washer system (Section 5)
Replace any blown bulbs (Chapter 12), and clean the lenses of all exterior lights

Every 3000 miles or 3 months, whichever comes first

All items listed above, plus:
Check the power steering fluid level (Section 6)
Check the automatic transaxle fluid level (Section 7)
Change the engine oil and filter (Section 8)
Check clutch pedal freeplay (Section 9)

Every 6000 miles or 6 months, whichever comes first

All items listed above, plus:
Check and service the battery (Section 10)
Inspect and replace, if necessary, the windshield wiper blades (Section 11)
Rotate the tires (Section 12)
Check seat belt operation (Section 13)

Every 15,000 miles or 12 months, whichever comes first

All items listed above, plus:
Inspect and replace, if necessary, all underhood hoses (Section 14)
Inspect the cooling system (Section 15)
Check the fuel system (Section 16)
Inspect the steering and suspension components (Section 17)
Inspect the driveaxle boots and CV joints (Section 18)
Inspect the brakes (Section 19)
Check the manual transaxle lubricant level (Section 20)

Every 30,000 miles or 24 months, whichever comes first

Check the engine accessory drivebelt (Section 21)
Inspect and replace, if necessary, the ignition system components (Section 22)
Replace the air filter element (Section 23)*
Check the PCV valve and replace if necessary (Section 24)
Replace the fuel filter (Section 25)
Inspect the exhaust system (Section 26)
Change the automatic transaxle fluid (Section 27)**
Service the cooling system (drain, flush and refill) (Section 28)
Replace the brake fluid (Section 29)

Every 60,000 miles or 48 months, whichever comes first

Replace the spark plugs (Section 30)
Change the manual transaxle lubricant (Section 31)
Replace the timing belt on four-cylinder models (Section 32)
Ventilation system filter replacement (Section 33)

**Replace more often if the vehicle is operated under dusty conditions.*
***If the vehicle is operated in continuous stop-and-go conditions or in mountainous areas, change at 15,000 miles.*

3.2a On four-cylinder models, the engine oil dipstick (arrow) is located at the front, near the center of the engine

3.2b On V6 models, the engine oil dipstick (arrow) is located adjacent to the oil filler cap

1 Introduction

This Chapter is designed to help the home mechanic maintain the Contour/Mystique models for peak performance, economy, safety and long life.

On the following pages are Sections dealing specifically with each item on the maintenance schedule. Visual checks, adjustments, component replacement and other helpful items are included. Refer to the accompanying illustrations of the engine compartment and the underside of the vehicle for the location of various components.

Servicing your Contour/Mystique in accordance with the mileage/time maintenance schedule and the following Sections will provide it with a planned maintenance program, which should result in a long and reliable service life. This is a comprehensive plan, so maintaining some items but not others at the specified service intervals will not produce the same results.

As you service your Contour/Mystique, you will discover that many of the procedures can - and should - be grouped together, because of the nature of the particular procedure you're performing, or because of the close proximity to one another of two otherwise-unrelated components.

For example, if the vehicle is raised for any reason, you should inspect the exhaust, suspension, steering and fuel systems while you're under the vehicle. When you're checking the tires, it is good practice to check the brakes and wheel bearings, especially if the wheels have already been removed.

Finally, let's suppose you have to borrow or rent a torque wrench. Even if you only need to tighten the spark plugs, you might as well check the torque of as many critical fasteners as time allows.

The first step of this maintenance program is to prepare yourself before the actual work begins. Read through all the Sections which are relevant to the procedures you're planning to perform, then make a list of, and gather together, all the parts and tools you will need to do the job. If it looks as if you might encounter problems during a particular segment of some procedure, seek advice from a professional mechanic or experienced do-it-yourselfer.

2 Tune-up general information

The term tune-up is used in this manual to represent a combination of individual operations rather than one specific procedure.

If, from the time the vehicle is new, the routine maintenance schedule is followed closely and frequent checks are made of fluid levels and high-wear items, the engine will be kept in relatively good running condition and the need for additional work will be minimized.

More likely than not, however, there will be times when the engine is running poorly due to lack of regular maintenance. This is even more likely if a used vehicle, which has not received the proper care, is purchased. In such cases, an engine tune-up will be needed outside of the regular maintenance interval.

The first step in any tune-up or diagnostic procedure to help correct a poor running engine is a cylinder compression test. A compression test (Chapter 2 Part B) will help determine the condition of internal engine components and should be used as a guide for tune-up and repair procedures. If, for instance, a compression check indicates serious internal engine wear, a conventional tune-up will not improve the performance of the engine and would be a waste of time and money. Because of its importance, the compression test should be done by someone with the right equipment and the knowledge to use it properly.

The following procedures are those most often needed to bring a generally poor running engine back into a proper state of tune.

Minor tune-up

Check all engine-related fluids (Section 3)
Clean, inspect and test the battery (Section 10)
Check all underhood hoses (Section 14)
Check the cooling system (Section 15)
Check the accessory drivebelts (Section 21)
Inspect the spark plug wires (Section 22)
Check the air filter (Section 23)

Major tune-up

All items listed under Minor tune-up, plus:
Check the fuel system (Section 16)
Replace the spark plug wires (Section 22)
Replace the spark plugs (Section 22)
Replace the air filter (Section 23)
Replace the PCV valve (Section 24)
Replace the fuel filter (Section 25)
Check the charging system (Chapter 5)

3 Fluid level checks (every 250 miles or weekly)

General

1 Fluids are an essential part of the lubrication, cooling, braking and other systems. Because these fluids gradually become depleted and/or contaminated during normal operation of the vehicle, they must be periodically replenished. See *Lubricants and fluids and capacities* at the beginning of this Chapter before adding fluid to any of the following components. **Note:** *The vehicle must be on level ground before fluid levels can be accurately checked.*

Engine oil

Refer to illustrations 3.2a, 3.2b and 3.4

2 Check the engine oil level with a dipstick located at the front, near the center of the engine on four-cylinder models and adjacent to the oil filler cap on V6 models **(see illustrations)**. The dipstick extends through a metal

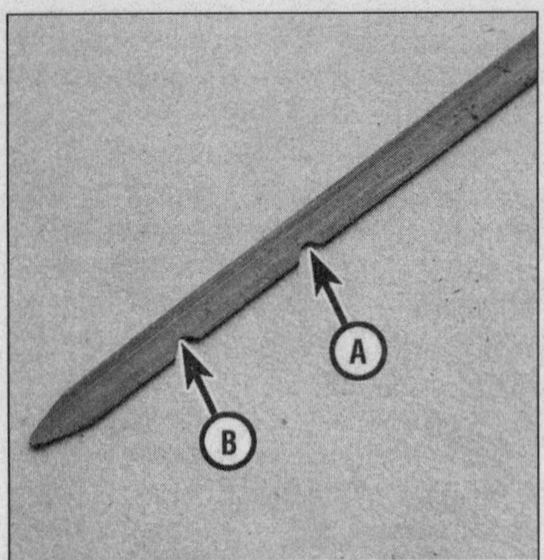

3.4 On four-cylinder models, the oil level should be at or near the maximum level notch (A) on the dipstick. On V6 models, the two notches are replaced by two small holes and the marks MIN (minimum) and MAX (maximum). If necessary, add enough oil to correct the level. It takes approximately one quart of oil to raise the level from the minimum level mark to the maximum level mark

tube, from which it protrudes down into the oil pan at the bottom of the engine.

3 The oil level should be checked before the vehicle is driven, or about five minutes after the engine has been switched off.

4 Pull the dipstick from the tube, and wipe all the oil from the end with a clean rag or paper towel; note the dipstick's maximum and minimum levels, indicated by notches or holes **(see illustration)**. Insert the clean dipstick all the way back into its metal tube, and pull it out again. Observe the oil on the end of the dipstick; its level should be between the minimum and maximum level marks, preferably near the maximum level.

5 Do not allow the level to drop below the minimum level mark, or oil starvation may cause engine damage. Conversely, overfilling the engine (adding oil above the maximum level mark) may cause oil-fouled spark plugs, oil leaks or oil seal failures.

6 The plastic oil filler cap is screwed into the left end of the valve cover on four-cylinder engines or the right end of the front valve cover on V6 engines; clean the area around the cap, then unscrew it to add oil. When adding oil, use only the correct grade and type of oil, as given in the Specifications Section of this Chapter. Use a funnel if necessary to prevent spills. It takes approximately one quart of oil to raise the level from the dipstick's minimum level mark to its maximum level mark. After adding the oil, install the filler cap hand-tight. Start the engine, and allow it to idle while the oil is redistributed around the engine - while you are waiting, look carefully for any oil leaks, particularly around the oil filter or drain plug. Stop the engine and check the oil level again, after waiting approximately five minutes for the oil to drain back into the oil pan.

3.10 The cooling system expansion tank is located on the right-hand side of the engine compartment. Maintain the coolant level between the MIN and MAX marks (arrows) with the engine cold

7 Checking the oil level is an important preventive maintenance step. A continually dropping oil level indicates oil leakage through damaged seals and from loose connections, or oil consumption past worn piston rings or valve guides. If the oil looks milky in color, or has water droplets in it, the cylinder head gasket may be blown - the engine's compression pressure should be checked immediately (see Chapter 2B). The condition of the oil should also be checked. Each time you check the oil level, slide your thumb and index finger up the dipstick before wiping off the oil. If you see small dirt or metal particles clinging to the dipstick, the oil should be changed (Section 8).

Coolant

Refer to illustration 3.10

Warning: *Do not allow antifreeze to come in contact with your skin or painted surfaces of the vehicle. Flush contaminated areas immediately with plenty of water. Don't store new coolant, or leave old coolant lying around, where it's accessible to children or pets - they're attracted by its sweet smell. Ingestion of even a small amount of coolant can be fatal! Wipe up garage-floor and drip-pan spills immediately. Keep antifreeze containers covered, and repair cooling system leaks as soon as they're noticed.*

8 All vehicles covered by this manual are equipped with a sealed, pressurized cooling system. A translucent plastic expansion tank, located on the right-hand side of the engine compartment, is connected by a hose to the radiator. As the coolant heats up during engine operation, the expanding coolant fills the reservoir. As the engine cools, the coolant is drawn back into the radiator.

9 The coolant level in the reservoir should be checked regularly. **Warning:** *Do not remove the expansion tank cap to check the coolant level when the engine is warm!* The level in the tank varies with the temperature of the engine. When the engine is cold, the coolant level should be at nor slightly above the MIN mark on the tank. If the engine is warm, the level should be at or near the MAX mark. If it isn't, add a 50/50 mixture of ethylene glycol based antifreeze and water.

10 For an accurate check of the coolant level, the engine must be cold. The level must be between the MAX and MIN level lines on the tank **(see illustration).** If it is below the MIN level line, add coolant as follows.

11 Add a sufficient quantity of coolant mixture, using clean, soft water and antifreeze of the recommended type, in the specified mixture ratio. Don't use rust inhibitors or other additives. If only a small amount of coolant is required to bring the system up to the proper level, plain water can be used. However, repeatedly adding water will dilute the antifreeze/water solution. To maintain the specified antifreeze/water ratio. It is therefore essential to top-up the coolant level with the correct mixture, as described here. Use only ethylene/glycol type antifreeze, and *do not* use supplementary inhibitors or additives. **Warning:** *Never remove the expansion tank cap when the engine is running, or has just been switched off, as the cooling system will be hot, and the consequent escaping steam and scalding coolant could cause serious injury.* If the coolant level drops consistently, there may be a leak in the system. Inspect the radiator, hoses, filler cap, drain plugs and water pump (see Section 15). If no leaks are evident, have the expansion tank cap pressure tested by a service station. If significant leakage is noted, use an antifreeze hydrometer to check the concentration of the antifreeze in the system.

12 If you must remove the expansion tank cap, wait until the engine has cooled completely, then wrap a thick cloth around the cap and slowly unscrew it, stopping if you hear a hissing noise. If coolant or steam escapes, let the engine cool longer, then continue to unscrew the cap. At all times, keep your face, hands and other exposed skin away from the filler opening.

13 Also check the condition of the coolant. It should be relatively clear. If it's brown or rust colored, the system should be drained, flushed and refilled. Even if the coolant appears to be normal, the corrosion inhibitors wear out, so it must be replaced at the specified intervals.

14 Coolant hydrometers are available at most automotive accessory shops. If the specific gravity of a sample taken from the recovery reservoir (with the engine Off and fully cooled) is less than that specified, the coolant strength has fallen below the minimum required. If this is found, either the coolant strength must be restored by adding antifreeze or by draining and flushing the system, then refilling it with a fresh coolant and water mixture.

Windshield washer fluid

Refer to illustration 3.15

15 Fluid for the windshield washer system

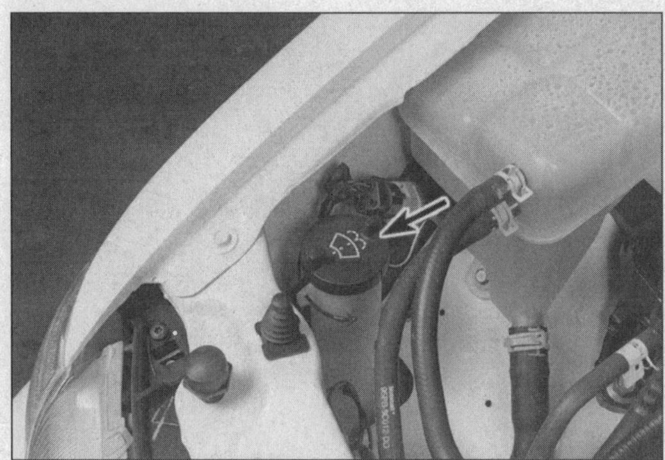

3.15 The windshield washer reservoir (arrow) is located on the right-hand side of the engine compartment, in front of the coolant expansion tank

3.16 On an unsealed battery, maintain the electrolyte level of all cells between the minimum and maximum levels (arrows). The electrolyte should be approximately 3/8-inch above the plates. Use distilled water and never overfill the cells

is stored in a plastic reservoir, which is located at the right front corner of the engine compartment **(see illustration)**. In milder climates, plain water can be used to top-up the reservoir. In colder climates, use windshield washer antifreeze, available at your dealer or any automotive parts store, to prevent freezing. Do not use regular (engine) antifreeze - it will damage the vehicle's paint.

Battery electrolyte

Refer to illustration 3.16

16 On models not equipped with a sealed battery (see Section 10), check the electrolyte level of all six battery cells. The level must be approximately 3/8-inch above the plates; this may be shown by maximum and minimum level lines marked on the battery's casing **(see illustration)**. If the level is low, remove the filler/vent caps and add distilled water. Install and securely retighten the cap. **Caution:** *Overfilling the cells may cause electrolyte to spill over during periods of heavy charging, causing corrosion or damage. Refer also to the warning at the beginning of Section 10.*

Brake fluid

Refer to illustration 3.17

17 The master cylinder fluid reservoir is located on the top of the brake master cylinder, which is attached to the front of the power booster unit **(see illustration)**.

18 The brake fluid in the translucent reservoir is readily visible. Maintain the brake fluid level between the MIN and MAX marks on the side of the reservoir (vehicle on level ground).

19 If the fluid level is low, wipe the top of the reservoir and the cap with a clean shop towel to prevent contamination of the system as the cap is removed.

20 Add only the specified brake fluid to the reservoir (refer to *Recommended lubricants and fluids* at the front of this Chapter). Mixing different types of brake fluid can damage the system. Fill the reservoir to the MAX line. **Warning:** *Brake fluid can harm your eyes and damage painted surfaces. Use extreme caution when handling or pouring brake fluid. Don't use brake fluid that has been standing open or is more than one year old. Brake fluid absorbs moisture from the air, which will contaminate the brake hydraulic system and can cause a dangerous loss of braking efficiency.*

21 While the reservoir cap is off, check the master cylinder reservoir for contamination. If rust deposits, dirt particles or water droplets are present, the system should be drained and refilled at a dealership service department or other qualified repair shop.

22 After filling the reservoir to the proper level, make sure the cap is seated to prevent fluid leakage and/or contamination.

23 The fluid level in the master cylinder will drop slightly as the brake shoes or pads wear during normal operation. If the brake fluid level drops consistently, check the entire system for leaks immediately. Examine all brake lines, hoses and connections, along with the disc brake calipers, wheel cylinders and master cylinder (see Section 19).

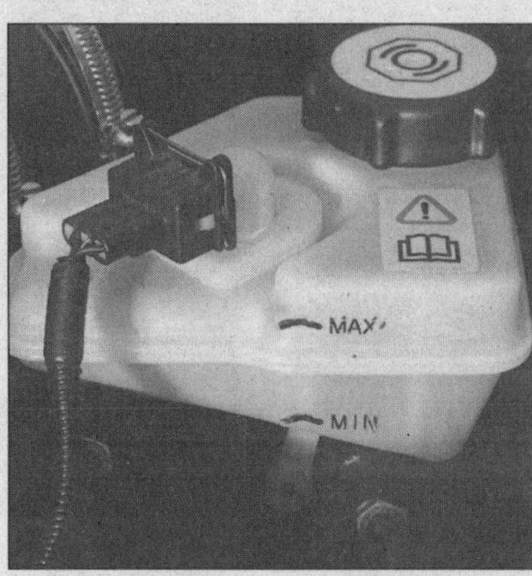

3.17 Master cylinder fluid reservoir showing the MIN and MAX marks

Clutch fluid

24 The clutch master cylinder uses brake fluid and shares the same reservoir as the brake system master cylinder.

4 Tire and tire pressure checks (every 250 miles or weekly)

Refer to illustrations 4.2, 4.3, 4.4a, 4.4b and 4.8

1 Periodic inspection of the tires may spare you the inconvenience of being stranded with a flat tire. It can also provide you with vital information regarding possible problems in the steering and suspension systems before major damage occurs.

2 The original tires on this vehicle are equipped with 1/2-inch wide bands that will appear when tread depth reaches 1/16-inch, at which point the tires can be considered worn out. Tread wear can be monitored with a simple, inexpensive device known as a tread depth indicator **(see illustration)**.

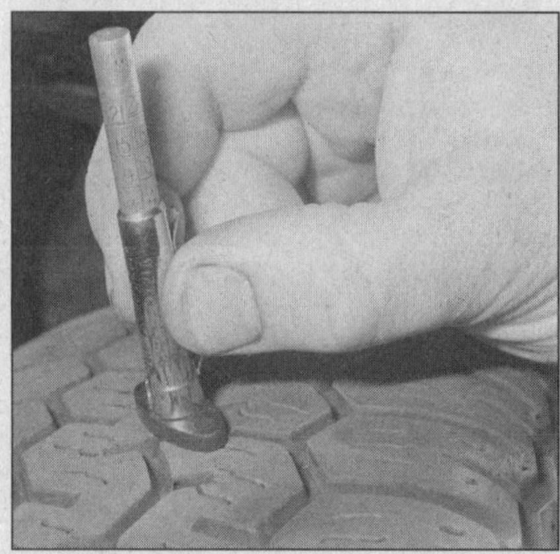

4.2 Use a tire tread depth indicator to monitor tire wear - they are available at auto parts stores and service stations and cost very little

UNDERINFLATION

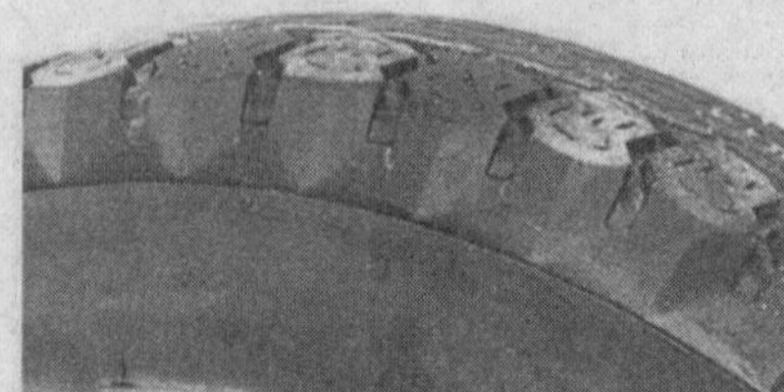

CUPPING

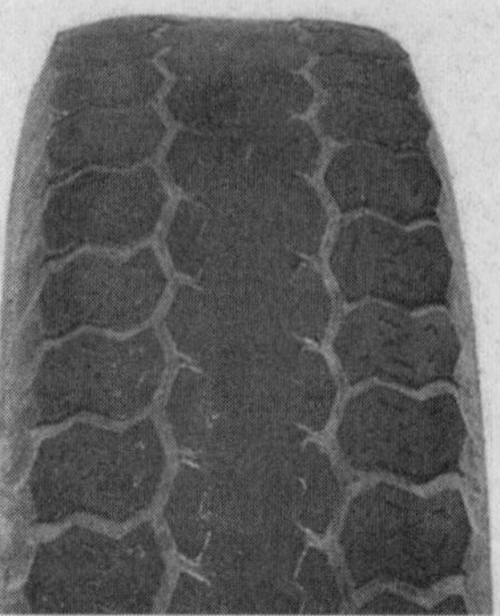

OVERINFLATION

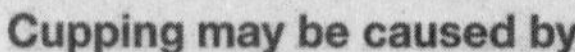

Cupping may be caused by:

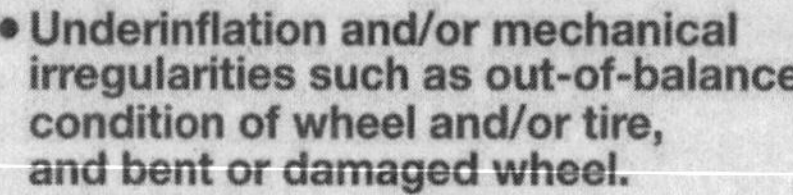

- Underinflation and/or mechanical irregularities such as out-of-balance condition of wheel and/or tire, and bent or damaged wheel.
- Loose or worn steering tie-rod or steering idler arm.
- Loose, damaged or worn front suspension parts.

INCORRECT TOE-IN OR EXTREME CAMBER

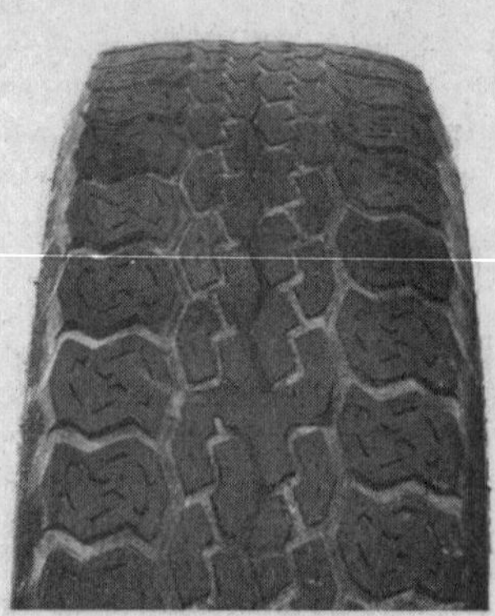

FEATHERING DUE TO MISALIGNMENT

4.3 This chart will help you determine the condition of the tires, the probable cause(s) of abnormal wear and the corrective action necessary

3 Note any abnormal tread wear **(see illustration)**. Tread pattern irregularities such as cupping, flat spots and more wear on one side than the other are indications of front end alignment and/or balance problems. If any of these conditions are noted, take the vehicle to a tire shop or service station to correct the problem.

4 Closely inspect the tires for cuts, punctures and embedded nails or tacks. Sometimes a tire will hold air pressure for a short time or leak down very slowly after a nail has embedded itself in the tread. If a slow leak persists, check the valve stem core to make sure it is tight **(see illustration)**. Examine the tread for an object that may be embedded in the tire. If a puncture is suspected, it can be easily verified by spraying a solution of soapy water onto the puncture area **(see illustration)**. The soapy solution will bubble if there is a leak. Unless the puncture is unusually large, a tire shop or service station can usually repair the tire.

5 Carefully inspect the inner surface of the tires for evidence of brake fluid leakage. If brake fluid leakage is noted, inspect the brake system immediately.

6 Correct air pressure adds miles to the lifespan of the tires, improves fuel economy and overall ride quality. Tire pressure cannot

4.4a If a tire loses air on a steady basis, check the valve stem core first to make sure it's snug (special inexpensive valve core tools are commonly available at auto parts stores)

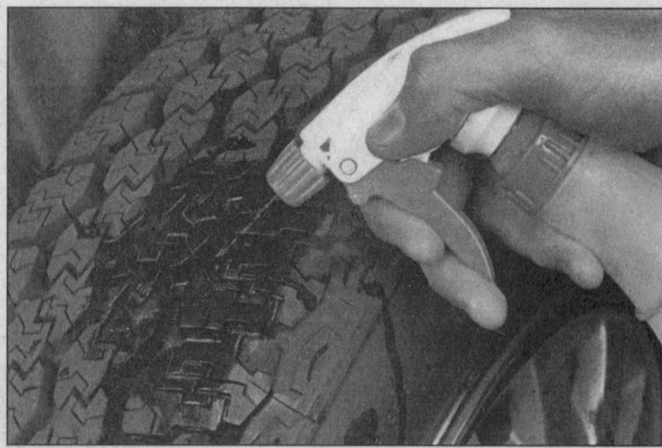

4.4b If the valve stem core is tight, raise the corner of the vehicle with the low tire and spray a soapy water solution onto the tread as the tire is turned slowly - leaks will cause small bubbles to appear

4.8 **To extend the life of the tires, check the air pressure at least once a week using an accurate gauge (don't forget the spare)**

6.4 **Power steering fluid reservoir showing the MAX and MIN marks**

be accurately estimated by looking at a tire, especially if it's a radial tire. A tire pressure gauge is essential. Keep an accurate gauge in the glove compartment. The tire pressure gauges attached to the nozzles of air hoses at gas stations are often inaccurate.

7 Always check tire pressure when the tires are cold. Cold, in this case means the vehicle has not been driven over a mile in the three hours preceding a tire pressure check. A pressure rise of four-to-eight psi is not uncommon once the tires are warm.

8 Unscrew the valve cap protruding from the wheel or hubcap and push the gauge firmly onto the valve stem **(see illustration)**. Note the reading on the gauge and compare the figure to the recommended tire pressure shown on the tire placard on the driver's side door. Be sure to reinstall the valve cap to keep dirt and moisture out of the valve stem mechanism. Check all four tires, and if necessary, add enough air to bring them up to the recommended pressure.

9 Don't forget to keep the spare tire inflated to the specified pressure (refer to your owner's manual or the sidewall of the tire). Note that the pressure recommended for the temporary (mini) spare is higher than for the tires on the vehicle.

5 Electrical system check

1 Check the operation of all external lights, including turn signals (front and rear).

2 Check for satisfactory operation of the instrument panel, its illumination and warning lights, the switches and their function lights.

3 Check the horn(s) for proper operation.

4 Check all other electrical equipment for proper operation.

5 Check all electrical wiring in the engine compartment for correct routing, evidence of damage or loose or corroded connections.

6 Power steering fluid level check (every 3000 miles or 3 months)

Refer to illustration 6.4

1 Check the power steering fluid level periodically to avoid steering system problems, such as damage to the pump. **Caution:** *Do not hold the steering wheel against either stop (extreme left or right turn) for more than five seconds. If you do, the power steering pump could be damaged.* The power steering fluid reservoir is located at the right rear corner of the engine compartment.

2 Park the vehicle on level ground and apply the parking brake.

3 Run the engine until it is at normal operating temperature. With the engine at idle, turn the steering wheel back-and-forth several times to purge any air from the steering system. With the front wheels facing straight ahead, stop the engine.

4 Check that the fluid level is up to the MAX mark on the reservoir **(see illustration)**.

5 If fluid is required, first use a clean rag to wipe clean the filler cap and the surrounding area, to prevent foreign matter from entering the system. Unscrew and remove the filler cap.

6 Add the recommended fluid as necessary to bring the level to the MAX mark. **Caution:** *Do not overfill the reservoir. If too much fluid is added, remove the excess using syringe or suction pump.*

7 Install the filler cap.

7 Automatic transaxle fluid level check (every 3000 miles or 3 months)

Refer to illustrations 7.4 and 7.6

1 The automatic transaxle fluid level should be carefully maintained. Low fluid level can lead to slipping or loss of drive, while overfilling can cause foaming, loss of fluid. Either condition can cause transaxle damage.

7.4 **Remove the automatic transaxle dipstick from its tube**

2 The transaxle fluid level should only be checked when the transaxle is warm (at normal operating temperature). If the vehicle has just been driven over 10 miles (15 miles in a cold climate), the transaxle can be considered sufficiently warm. **Caution:** *If the vehicle has just been driven for a long time at high speed or in city traffic in hot weather, or if it has been pulling a trailer, an accurate fluid level reading cannot be obtained. In these circumstances, allow the fluid to cool down for about 30 minutes.*

3 Park the vehicle on level ground, apply the parking brake, and start the engine. While the engine is idling, depress the brake pedal and move the selector lever through all the gear ranges three times, beginning and ending in Park.

4 Allow the engine to idle for one minute, then (with the engine still idling) remove the dipstick from its tube **(see illustration)**. Note the condition and color of the fluid on the dipstick.

5 Wipe the fluid from the dipstick with a clean rag, and re-insert it into the filler tube until the cap seats.

6 Pull the dipstick out again, and note the fluid level. The level should be between the MIN and MAX marks **(see illustration)**. If the level is on or below the MIN mark, stop the engine, and add the specified automatic transaxle fluid through the dipstick tube, using a clean funnel if necessary. It is important not to introduce dirt into the transaxle when adding fluid.

7 Add the fluid a little at a time, and keep checking the level as previously described until it is correct.

8 If the transaxle requires fluid on a regular basis, the transaxle has a leak which must be repaired as soon as possible.

9 The condition of the fluid should also be checked along with the level. If the fluid at the end of the dipstick is black or a dark reddish-brown color, or if it has a burned smell, the fluid should be changed. If you are in doubt about the condition of the fluid, purchase some new fluid, and compare the color and smell of the new and old fluids.

8 Engine oil and filter change (every 3000 miles or 3 months)

Refer to illustrations 8.1, 8.7, 8.9 and 8.10

Note: *Changing the oil and filter frequently is the most important preventive maintenance that can be done by the home mechanic. As engine oil ages, it becomes diluted and contaminated, which leads to premature engine wear.*

1 Make sure that you have all the necessary tools before you begin this procedure **(see illustration)**. You should also have plenty of rags or newspapers handy, for cleaning up oil spillage.

2 To avoid any possibility of burning yourself, and to protect yourself from possible skin irritation, it is advisable to wear gloves when carrying out this work.

3 Access to the oil drain plug and filter is improved if the vehicle can be lifted on a hoist, driven onto ramps, or supported by jackstands. **Warning:** *Do not work under a vehicle which is supported only by a jack of any kind or, or by bricks or, blocks of wood - always support the vehicle securely using jackstands.*

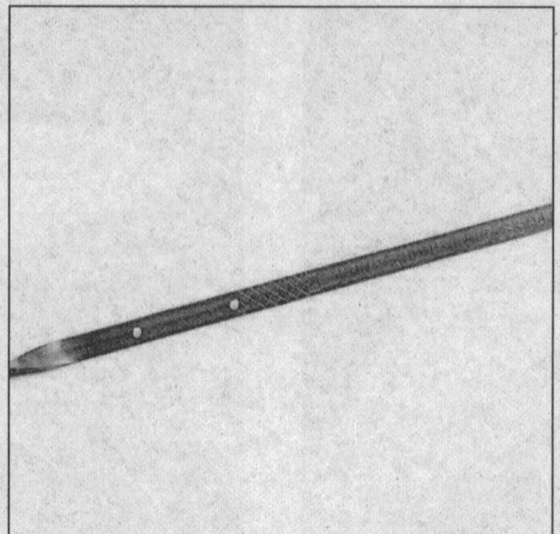

7.6 MIN and MAX marks on the dipstick

4 If this is your first oil change, get under the vehicle and familiarize yourself with the position of the engine oil drain plug, which is located at the rear of the oil pan. The engine and exhaust components will be warm during the actual work, so try to anticipate any potential problems while the engine and accessories are cool.

5 The oil should preferably be changed when the engine is warm (at normal operating temperature). The sludge and contaminants will flow from the oil pan more easily if the oil is warm. Park the vehicle on firm, level ground and apply the parking brake firmly. Open the hood and remove the engine oil filler cap from the valve cover, then remove the oil level dipstick from its tube (see Section 3).

6 If you're working on a four-cylinder model, loosen the right-front wheel lug nuts. On all models, raise the front of the vehicle and support it securely on jackstands. Block the rear wheels to prevent the vehicle from rolling. On four-cylinder models, remove the right-front wheel to provide access to the oil filter; if the additional working clearance is

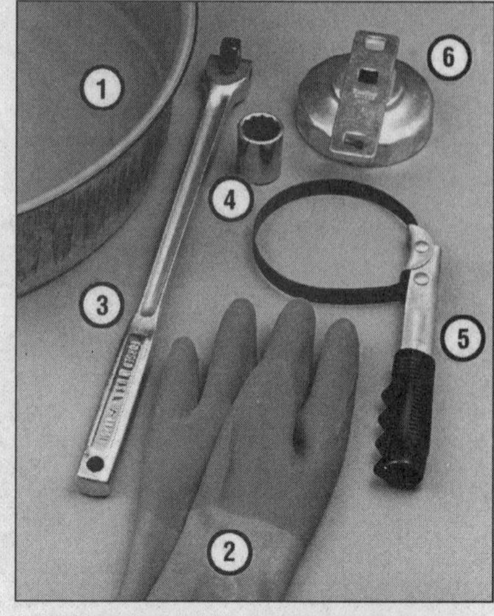

8.1 These tools are required when changing the engine oil and filter

1 **Drain pan** - *It should be fairly shallow in depth, but wide to prevent spills*
2 **Rubber gloves** - *When removing the drain plug and filter, you will get oil on your hands (the gloves will prevent burns)*
3 **Breaker bar** - *Sometimes the oil drain plug is tight, and a long breaker bar is needed to loosen it*
4 **Socket** - *To be used with the breaker bar or a ratchet (must be the correct size to fit the drain plug - six-point preferred)*
5 **Filter wrench** - *This is a metal band-type wrench, which requires clearance around the filter to be effective*
6 **Filter wrench** - *This type fits on the bottom of the filter and can be turned with a ratchet or breaker bar (different-size wrenches are available for different types of filters)*

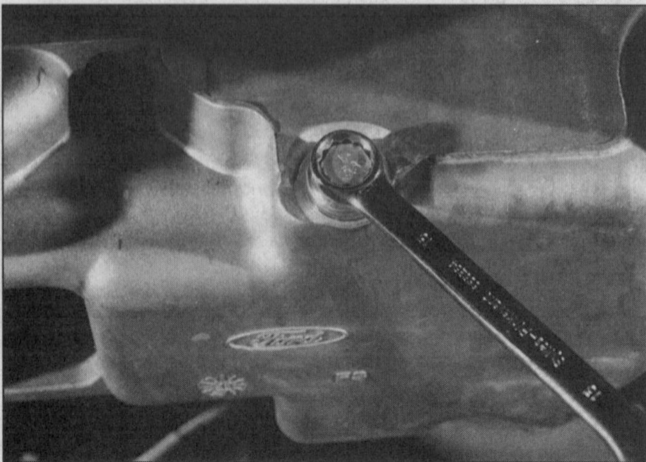

8.7 Remove the oil pan drain plug using a box-end wrench or a socket

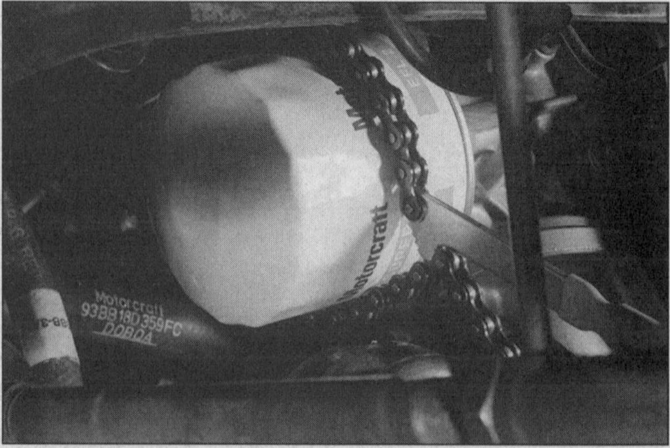

8.9 The oil filter is usually very tight and requires a special oil filter wrench to remove it - do not, however, use the filter wrench to tighten the new filter

8.10 Lubricate the oil filter gasket with clean engine oil before installing the filter

required. **Warning:** *To avoid personal injury, never work under the vehicle if it is supported by only by a jack. Always use jackstands to support the vehicle when it becomes necessary to place your body under the vehicle.*

7 Being careful not to touch the hot exhaust components, place the drain pan under the drain plug, then unscrew the plug **(see illustration)**. If possible, try to keep the plug pressed into the oil pan while unscrewing it by hand the last couple of turns. As the plug releases from the threads, move it away quickly, so the stream of oil flowing from the oil pan runs into the drain pan. Allow the oil to drain into the drain pan, and check the condition of the plug's gasket. Replace the gasket if it's worn or damaged.

8 Allow the oil to drain completely - it may be necessary to reposition the drain pan as the oil flow slows to a trickle. When the oil has completely drained, wipe clean the drain plug and its threads in the oil pan and reinstall the plug. Tighten the plug to the torque listed in this Chapter's Specifications.

9 Using a suitable filter wrench, unscrew the oil filter **(see illustration)**. On four-cylinder engines it's located on the rear of the engine block. On V6 engines it's located on the front of the engine block. Check the old filter to make sure that its rubber gasket isn't stuck to the engine. If the gasket sticks to the engine, carefully remove it. Withdraw the filter, taking care to spill as little oil as possible.

10 Using a clean, lint-free rag, wipe the filter sealing surface on the block. If there are no specific instructions supplied with it, install a new oil filter as follows. Apply a light coat of clean engine oil to the filter gasket **(see illustration)**. Screw the filter into position on the engine until the filter gasket contacts the block, then tighten it an additional three-quarters of a turn. Tighten the filter by hand only - do not use any tools.

11 Remove the drain pan and all tools from under the vehicle, reinstall the wheel, and lower the vehicle to the ground.

12 Refill the engine with oil, using the correct grade and type of oil, as listed in the Specifications Section of this Chapter. Pour in half the specified quantity of oil first, then wait a few minutes for the oil to settle into the oil pan. Continue adding oil until the level is up to the lower mark on the dipstick. Adding approximately one quart will raise the level to the dipstick's upper mark.

13 Start the engine. The oil pressure warning light will take a few seconds to go out while the new filter fills with oil. Do not race the engine while the light is on. Run the engine for a few minutes, while checking for leaks around the oil filter seal and the drain plug.

14 Shut off the engine, and wait a few minutes for the oil to settle in the oil pan once more. With the new oil circulated and the filter now completely full, recheck the level on the dipstick. Add oil as necessary to bring the level up to the Full range.

15 During the first few trips after an oil change, make it a point to check frequently for leakage and the proper oil level.

16 The old oil drained from the engine cannot be re-used in its present state and should be discarded. Check with your local refuse disposal company, disposal facility or environmental agency to see whether they will accept the oil for recycling. Don't pour used oil into drains or onto the ground. After the oil has cooled, it can be drained into a suitable container (capped plastic jugs, topped bottles, milk cartons, etc.) for transport to one of these disposal sites.

9 Clutch pedal adjustment

The clutch is actuated by hydraulic pressure and does not require adjustment. See Chapter 8 for a description of the clutch system and the bleeding procedure.

10 Battery check, maintenance and charging (every 6000 miles or 6 months)

Refer to illustrations 10.1, 10.6a, 10.6b, 10.7a, 10.7b and 10.8

Warning: *Certain precautions must be followed when checking and servicing the battery. Hydrogen gas, which is highly flammable, is always present in the battery cells, so keep lighted tobacco and all other open flames and sparks away from the battery. The electrolyte inside the battery is actually diluted sulfuric acid, which will cause injury if splashed on your skin or in your eyes. It will also ruin clothes and painted surfaces. When disconnecting the battery, always disconnect the negative lead first and reconnect it last!*

Note: *Before disconnecting the battery, refer to Section 1 of Chapter 5.*

General information

1 A routine preventive maintenance program for the battery in your vehicle is the only way to ensure quick and reliable starts. Before performing any battery maintenance, make sure that you have the proper equipment necessary to work safely around the battery **(see illustration)**.

2 There are also several precautions that should be taken whenever battery maintenance is performed. Before servicing the battery, always turn the engine and all accessories off, and disconnect the cable from the negative (-) terminal of the battery - see

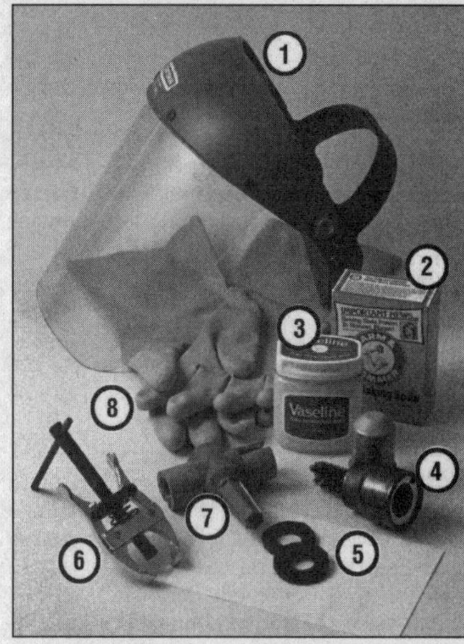

10.1 Tools and materials required for battery maintenance

1 ***Face shield/safety goggles*** *- When removing corrosion with a brush, the acidic particles can easily fly up into your eyes*
2 ***Baking soda*** *- A solution of baking soda and water can be used to neutralize corrosion*
3 ***Petroleum jelly*** *- A layer of this on the battery posts will help prevent corrosion*
4 ***Battery post/cable cleaner*** *- This wire brush cleaning tool will remove all traces of corrosion from the battery posts and cable clamps*
5 ***Treated felt washers*** *- Placing one of these on each post, directly under the cable clamps, will help prevent corrosion*
6 ***Puller*** *- Sometimes the cable clamps are very difficult to pull off the posts, even after the nut/bolt has been completely loosened. This tool pulls the clamp straight up and off the post without damage*
7 ***Battery post/cable cleaner*** *- Here is another cleaning tool which is a slightly different version of Number 4 above, but it does the same thing*
8 ***Rubber gloves*** *- Another safety item to consider when servicing the battery; remember that's acid inside the battery!*

1

10.6a Battery terminal corrosion usually appears as light, fluffy powder

10.6b Removing the battery cable from the battery post - always remove the negative (-) cable first and reconnect it last

Chapter 5, Section 1.

3 The battery produces hydrogen gas, which is both flammable and explosive. Never create a spark, smoke, or light a match around the battery. Always charge the battery in a well-ventilated area.

4 Electrolyte contains poisonous and corrosive sulfuric acid. Do not allow it to get in your eyes, on your skin or on your clothes. Never ingest it. Wear protective safety glasses when working near the battery. Keep children away from the battery.

5 Note the external condition of the battery. If the positive (+) post and cable clamp on the vehicle's battery is equipped with a plastic cover or rubber protector, make sure that it's not torn or damaged. It should completely cover the terminal. Look for any corroded or loose connections, cracks in the case or cover or loose hold-down clamps. Also check the entire length of each cable for cracks in the insulation and frayed cables.

6 If corrosion, which looks like white, fluffy deposits **(see illustration)** is evident, particularly around the terminals, remove the battery for cleaning. Loosen the cable clamp nuts using a wrench, being careful to remove the negative (-) cable first. Slide the cable clamps off the battery posts **(see illustration)**. Then unscrew the hold-down clamp nuts, remove the clamp, and lift the battery from the engine compartment.

7 Clean the cable clamps thoroughly, using a soft wire brush or a terminal cleaner, with a solution of warm water and baking soda. Wash the terminals and the top of the battery case with the same solution, but make sure that the solution doesn't get into the battery cells. When cleaning the cable clamps, battery posts and battery top, wear safety goggles and rubber gloves, to prevent any solution from coming in contact with your eyes or hands. Wear old clothes too - even when diluted, sulfuric acid splashed onto clothes will burn holes in them. If the cable clamps and battery posts are severely corroded, clean them using a terminal cleaner **(see illustrations)**. Thoroughly rinse all cleaned areas with plain water.

8 Make sure that the battery tray is in good condition and the hold-down clamp nuts are tight **(see illustration)**. If the battery is removed from the tray, make sure no parts remain in the bottom of the tray when the battery is reinstalled. When reinstalling the hold-down clamp nuts, do not overtighten them.

9 Information on removing and installing the battery can be found in Chapter 5. Information on jump starting can be found at the front of this manual. For more detailed battery checking procedures, refer to the Haynes *Automobile Electrical and Electronic Systems Manual.*

Cleaning

10 Corrosion on the hold-down components, battery case and surrounding areas can be removed with a solution of water and baking soda. Thoroughly rinse all cleaned areas with plain water.

11 Any metal parts of the vehicle damaged by corrosion should be covered with a zinc-based primer, then painted.

Charging

Warning: *When batteries are being charged, hydrogen gas, which is very explosive and flammable, is produced. Do not smoke, or allow open flames, near a charging or a recently charged battery. Wear eye protection when near the battery during charging. Also, make sure the charger is disconnected before connecting or disconnecting the battery from the charger.*

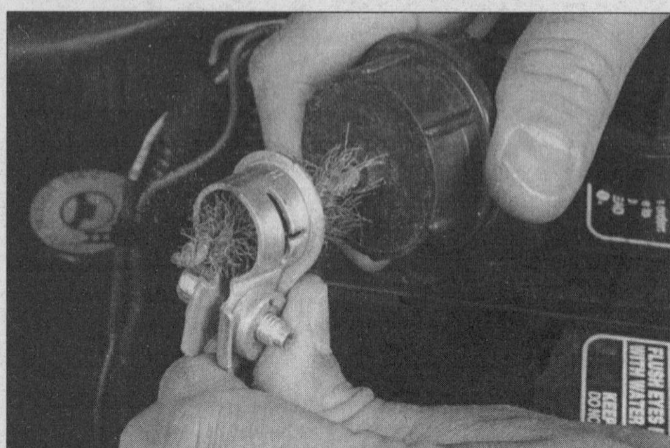

10.7a When cleaning the cable clamps, all corrosion must be removed

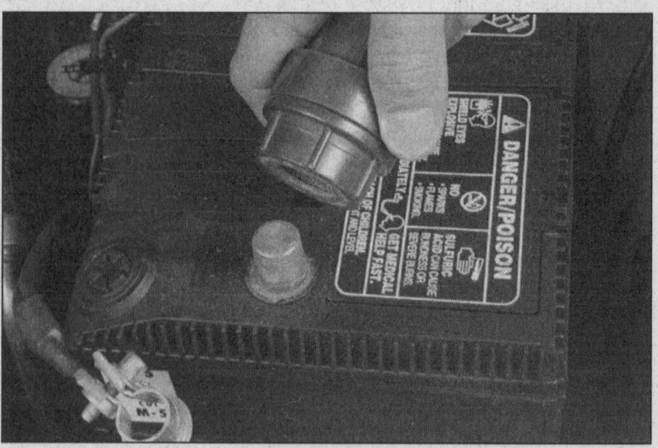

10.7b Regardless of the tool used to clean the battery posts, a clean shiny surface should be the result

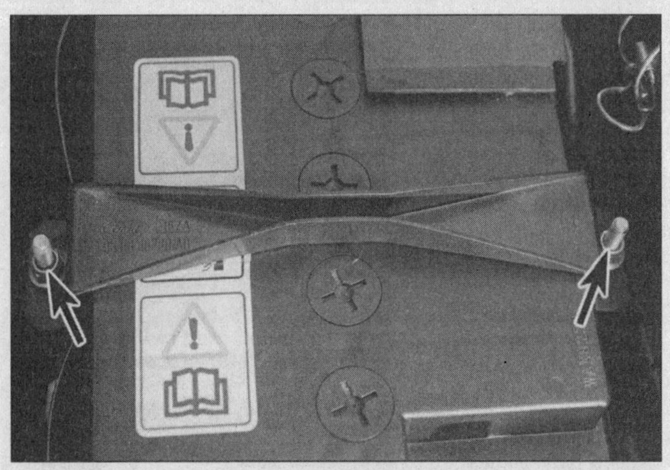

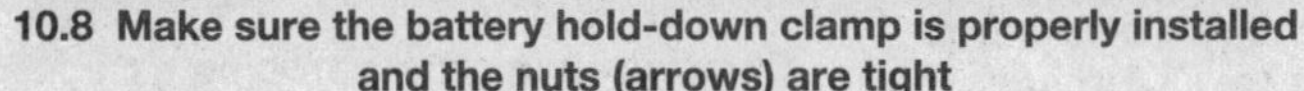

10.8 Make sure the battery hold-down clamp is properly installed and the nuts (arrows) are tight

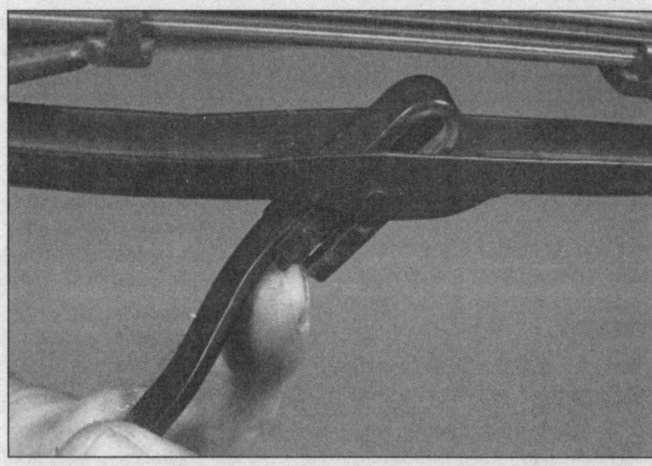

11.6 Release the catch to remove a windshield wiper blade

12 Slow-rate charging is the best way to recharge a discharged battery. It's also a good way to maintain the battery charge in a vehicle that's only driven a few miles between starts. Maintaining the battery charge is particularly important in winter, when the battery must work harder to start the engine, and electrical accessories that drain the battery are in greater use.

13 It's best to use a one- or two-amp battery charger (sometimes called a trickle charger). They are the safest and put the least strain on the battery. They are also the least expensive. For a faster charge, you can use a higher-amperage charger, but don't use one rated more than 1/10th the amp/hour rating of the battery (for example, no more than 5 amps, typically). Rapid boost charges that claim to restore the power of the battery in one to two hours are hardest on the battery, and can damage the battery if it is not in good condition. This type of charging should only be used in an emergency situation.

14 The average time necessary to charge a battery should be listed in the instructions provided with the charger. As a general rule, a trickle charger will charge a battery in 12 to 16 hours.

11 Windshield wiper blade inspection and replacement (every 6000 miles or 6 months)

Refer to illustration 11.6

1 Inspect the windshield wipers and blades at the specified intervals for damage, loose components and cracked or worn blade elements.

2 Road film can build up on the wiper blades and adversely affect their efficiency. Therefore, they should be washed regularly with a mild detergent solution.

3 The action of the wiper mechanism can loosen bolts, nuts and fasteners, so they should be checked and tightened, as necessary, at the same time the wiper blades are checked.

4 If the wiper blade elements are cracked, worn or warped, or no longer clean adequately, replace the wiper blades.

5 Lift the wiper arm and blade away from the windshield.

6 To remove the windshield wiper blade, release the catch on the arm, then turn the blade 90 degrees and withdraw the blade from the end of the arm **(see illustration)**.

7 If the frame of the wiper blade is in good condition, it may be possible to replace the rubber insert separately. The insert can be obtained from an auto parts store.

8 Reinstall the wiper blade assembly using a reversal of the removal procedure, making sure that it fully engages with the spring clip.

9 Check that the washer jets direct the windshield washer fluid onto the upper part of the windshield, and if necessary, adjust the small jet with a small screwdriver or needle-nose pliers.

12 Tire rotation (every 6000 miles or 6 months)

Refer to illustration 12.2

1 Rotate the tires at the specified intervals and if uneven wear is noted. Since the vehicle will be raised and the tires removed, check the brakes also (see Section 19).

2 Radial tires must be rotated in a specific pattern **(see illustration)**. If the vehicle has a compact spare tire, don't include it in the rotation pattern.

3 Refer to the information in *Jacking and towing* at the front of this manual for the proper procedure to follow when raising the vehicle and changing a tire. If the brakes must be checked, don't apply the parking brake as stated.

4 The vehicle must be raised on a hoist or supported on jackstands to get all four wheels off the ground. Make sure the vehicle is safely supported!

5 After rotating the tires, check and adjust the tire pressures as necessary and be sure to check the lug nut tightness.

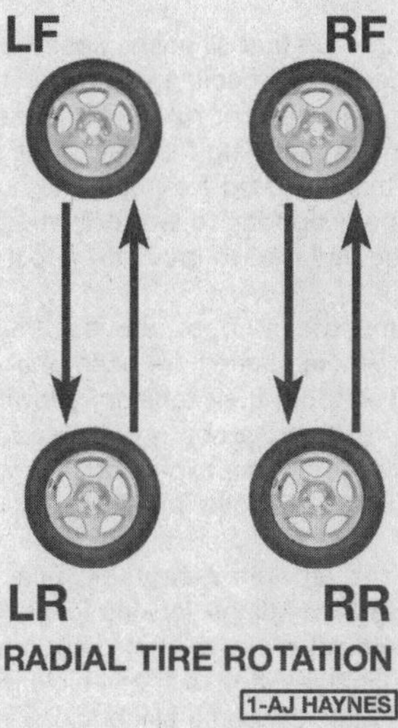

12.2 The recommended tire rotation pattern

13 Seat belt check (every 6000 miles or 6 months)

1 Check the seat belts, buckles, latch plates and guide loops for obvious damage or evidence of wear.

2 Make sure the seat belt reminder light comes on when the key is turned to the Run or Start position. A chime should also sound. On passive restraint systems, the should belt should move into position in the A-pillar.

3 The seat belts are designed to lock during a sudden stop or impact, yet allow free movement during normal driving. Make sure the retractors return the belt against your chest while driving and rewind the belt fully when the buckle is unlatched.

4 If any of the above checks reveal problems with the seat belt system, replace parts as necessary.

14 Underhood hose check and replacement (every 15,000 miles or 12 months)

Warning: *Replacement of air conditioning hoses must be left to a dealership service department or air conditioning specialist who has the equipment to evacuate the system safely. Never remove air conditioning components or hoses until the system has been evacuated.*

General

1 High temperatures in the engine compartment can cause the deterioration of the rubber and plastic hoses used for engine, accessory and emission systems operation. Periodic inspection should be made for cracks, loose clamps, material hardening and leaks.

2 Make sure that all hose connections are tight. A leak in the cooling system will usually show up as white- or rust-colored deposits on the areas adjoining the leak; if the spring clamps that are used to secure the hoses in this system appear to be loosening, they should be replaced to prevent the possibility of leaks.

3 Some other hoses are secured with clamps. Where clamps are used, make sure they haven't lost their tension, allowing the hose to leak. If clamps aren't used, make sure the hose has not expanded and/or hardened where it slips over the fitting, allowing it to leak.

4 Check all fluid reservoirs, filler caps, drain plugs and fittings, looking for engine oil, transaxle fluid, brake fluid, coolant or power steering fluid leakage. If the vehicle is regularly parked in the same place, close inspection of the ground under it will soon show any leakage; ignore the puddle of water if the air conditioning system is in use. As soon as a leak is noted, locate its source and repair it. If oil has been leaking for some time, it is usually necessary to use a steam cleaner or pressure washer to clean the accumulated dirt, so the exact source of the leak can be located.

Vacuum hoses

5 It's common for vacuum hoses, especially those in the emissions system, to be color-coded, or to be identified by colored stripes molded into them. Various systems require hoses with different wall thicknesses, collapse resistance and temperature resistance. When replacing hoses, be sure the new ones are made of the same material.

6 Often the only effective way to check a hose is to remove it completely from the vehicle. If more than one hose is removed, be sure to label the hoses and fittings to ensure correct installation.

7 When checking vacuum hoses, also inspect all plastic fittings for cracks. Make sure the hoses are a tight fit on all fittings.

8 A small piece of vacuum hose (one quarter-inch inside diameter) can be used as a stethoscope to detect vacuum leaks. Hold one end of the hose to your ear, and probe around vacuum hoses and fittings, listening for the hissing sound characteristic of a vacuum leak. **Warning:** *When probing with the vacuum hose stethoscope, be very careful not to come into contact with moving engine components.*

Fuel hoses

Warning: *Gasoline is extremely flammable, so take extra precautions when working on any part of the fuel system. Work in a well-ventilated area, and do not allow open flames (cigarettes, appliance pilot lights, etc.) or bare light bulbs near the work area. Clean up any spills immediately and do not store fuel-soaked rags where they could ignite.*

9 Check all fuel hoses for deterioration and chafing. Check especially for cracks in areas where the hose bends and also just before fittings, such as where a hose attaches to the fuel filter.

10 If replacing a fuel hose, use only hose that is specifically designed for the fuel injection system. Never, under any circumstances, use regular fuel hose, vacuum hose, clear plastic tubing or water hose for fuel lines.

11 Spring-type clamps are commonly used on fuel lines. These clamps often lose their tension over a period of time, and can be deformed during removal. Replace all spring-type clamps with screw clamps whenever a hose is replaced.

Metal lines

12 Sections of metal line are often used for fuel line between the fuel filter and the engine. Check carefully to be sure the line isn't bent, crimped or cracked.

13 If a section of metal fuel line must be replaced, use only seamless steel tubing because copper and aluminum tubing don't have the strength necessary to withstand normal engine vibration.

14 Check the metal brake lines where they enter the master cylinder, brake proportioning valve and ABS hydraulic unit (if used) for cracks in the lines or loose fittings. Any evidence of brake fluid leakage calls for an immediate and thorough inspection of the brake system.

PCV system hose

15 To reduce hydrocarbon emissions, crankcase blow-by gas is vented through the PCV valve to the intake manifold via a rubber hose. The blow-by gas mixes with incoming air in the intake manifold before being burned in the combustion chambers.

16 Check the PCV hose for cracks, leakage or other damage. Disconnect the hose and check it for restrictions. If plugged or restricted, clean or replace the hose.

Check for a chafed area that could fail prematurely.

Check for a soft area indicating the hose has deteriorated inside.

Overtightening the clamp on a hardened hose will damage the hose and cause a leak.

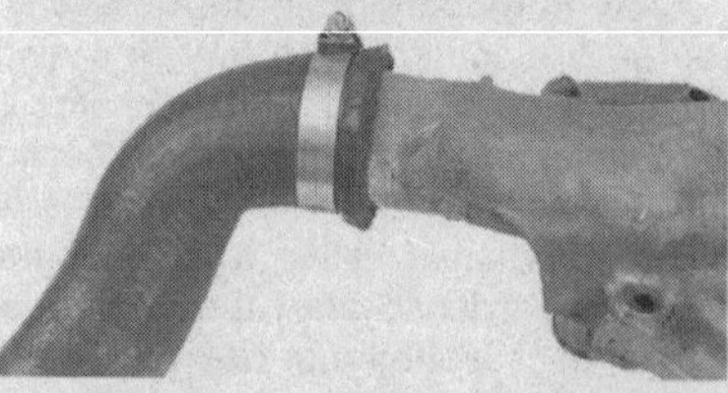

Check each hose for swelling and oil-soaked ends. Cracks and breaks can be located by squeezing the hose

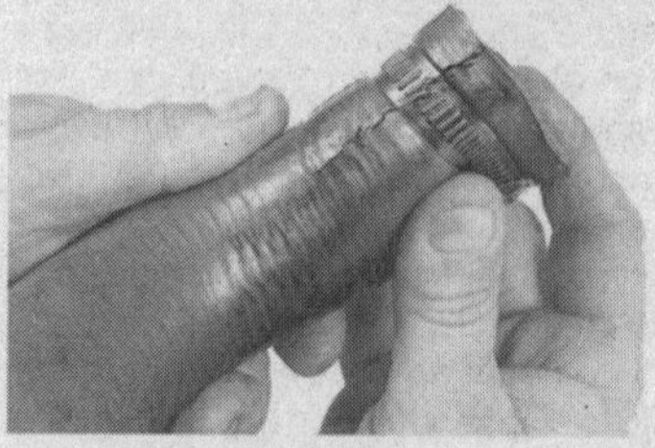

15.4 Hoses, like drivebelts, have a habit of failing at the worst possible time - to prevent the inconvenience of a blown radiator or heater hose, inspect them carefully as shown here

15 Cooling system check (every 15,000 miles or 12 months)

Refer to illustration 15.4

1 Many major engine failures can be attributed to a faulty cooling system. The cooling system also plays an important role in prolonging automatic transaxle life because it cools the fluid.

2 The engine should be cold for the cooling system check, so perform the following procedure before the vehicle is driven for the day or after it has been shut off for at least three hours.

3 Remove the filler cap from the coolant expansion tank (see Section 3). Clean the cap thoroughly, inside and out, with clean water. The presence of rust or corrosion in the tank means the coolant should be changed (see Section 28).

17.2a Check the tie-rod ends for torn rubber boots (arrow)

17.2b Check the lower balljoints for torn rubber boots (arrow)

4 Carefully check the radiator hoses and heater hoses **(see illustration)**. Inspect each coolant hose along its entire length and replace any hose that is cracked, swollen or deteriorated. Cracks will show better if the hose is squeezed. Pay close attention to hose clamps that secure the hoses to the cooling system components. Hose clamps can pinch and puncture hoses and result in a coolant leak. Some hoses are hidden from view so it is sometimes difficult to locate a coolant leak.

5 Make sure that all hose connections are tight. A leak in the cooling system will usually show up as white or rust colored deposits on the area next to the leak. If wire-type clamps are used to secure the hoses, it is good practice to replace them with screw-type clamps if removed.

6 Clean the front of the radiator and air conditioning condenser with compressed air, if available. If compressed air is not available use a soft brush. Remove all insects, leaves, or other material from the radiator/condenser fins. Be extremely careful not to damage the cooling fins.

7 If the coolant level has been consistently dropping, but no leakage can be located, have the radiator cap and cooling system pressure tested at a dealership or other qualified shop.

16 Fuel system check (every 15,000 miles or 12 months)

Warning: *Gasoline is extremely flammable, so take extra precautions when working on any part of the fuel system. Don't smoke or allow open flames or bare light bulbs near the work area, and don't work in a garage where a natural gas-type appliance (such as a water heater or clothes dryer) with a pilot light is present. Since gasoline is carcinogenic, wear latex gloves when there's a possibility of being exposed to fuel, and, if you spill any fuel on your skin, rinse it off immediately with soap and water. Clean any spills immediately and don't store fuel soaked rags where they could ignite. If performing any kind of work on the fuel system, wear safely glasses and have a Class B type fire extinguisher nearby. The fuel system is under constant pressure, so before disconnecting any fuel lines, relieve fuel system pressure (see Chapter 4).*

1 If you smell gasoline while driving or after the vehicle has been sitting in the sun, inspect the fuel system immediately.

2 Remove the fuel tank filler cap and inspect it for damage and corrosion. The gasket should have an unbroken sealing imprint. If the gasket is damaged, install a new cap.

3 Inspect the fuel feed and return lines for cracks. Make sure that the connections between the fuel lines and the fuel injection system and between lines and fuel filter are tight. **Warning:** *The vehicle is fuel injected, so relieve system pressure before servicing any fuel system components. The fuel system pressure relief procedure is described in Chapter 4.*

4 Since some of the components of the fuel system are under the vehicle (fuel tank and lines), they can be inspected more easily with the vehicle raised on a hoist. If that's not possible, raise the vehicle and support it on jackstands.

5 With the vehicle raised and safely supported, inspect the fuel tank and filler neck for punctures, cracks and other damage. The connection between the filler neck and the tank is particularly critical. Sometimes a rubber filler neck will leak because of loose clamps or deteriorated rubber. Inspect all fuel tank mount brackets and straps to be sure that the tank is securely attached to the vehicle. **Warning:** *Do not, under any circumstances, try to repair a fuel tank (except rubber components). A welding torch or any open flame can easily cause fuel vapor in the tank to explode.*

6 Carefully check all rubber hoses and metal lines leading away from the fuel tank. Check for loose connections, deteriorated hoses, crimped lines and other damage. Repair or replace damaged sections as necessary (see Chapter 4).

17 Steering, suspension and wheel check (every 15,000 miles or 12 months

Refer to illustrations 17.2a, 17.2b, 17.2c and 17.4

Note: *The steering linkage and suspension components should be inspected periodically. Worn or damaged suspension or steering components can cause excessive and abnormal tire wear, poor ride quality, poor handling and reduced fuel economy. For detailed illustrations of the steering and suspension systems, refer to Chapter 10.*

Front suspension and steering check

1 Apply the parking brake, then raise the front of the vehicle and support it on jackstands. Block the rear wheels to prevent the vehicle from rolling.

2 Inspect the balljoint boots and the steering gear boots for splits, chafing or deterioration **(see illustrations)**. Any wear of these components will cause loss of lubricant, and dirt and water contamination which will result in rapid deterioration of the balljoints or steering gear.

17.2c Check the steering gear boots for cracks and leaking fluid

17.4 Check for wear in the front suspension and wheel bearings

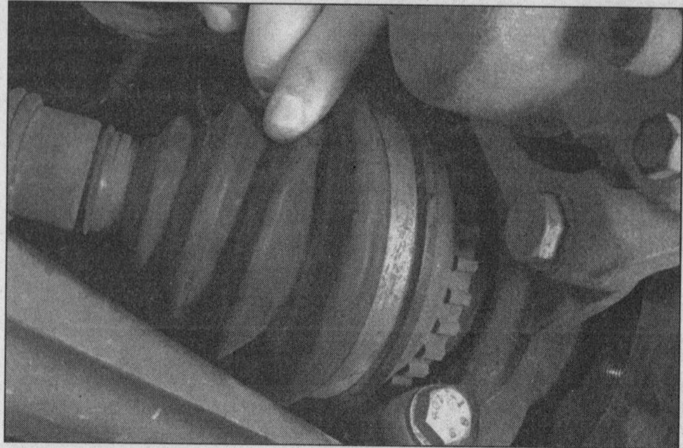
18.2 Inspect the CV joint boots for splits, cracks and/or leaking grease

3 Check the power steering hoses for chafing, deterioration and leakage. Also check for fluid leakage from the steering gear rubber boots, which would indicate failed seals inside the steering gear.

4 Grasp the wheel at the 12 o'clock and 6 o'clock positions, and try to rock it **(see illustration)**. Very slight play may be felt, but if the movement is appreciable, further inspection is necessary to determine the source. Continue rocking the wheel while an assistant depresses the brake. If the movement is now eliminated or significantly reduced, it is likely that the wheel bearings are worn. If the freeplay is still evident with the brake depressed, there is wear in the balljoints or suspension.

5 Now grasp the wheel at the 9 o'clock and 3 o'clock positions, and try to rock it as before. Any movement felt now may be caused by wear in the wheel bearings or the steering tie-rod ends. If the outer tie-rod end is worn, the visual movement will be obvious. If inner joint wear is suspected, it can be felt by placing a hand over the rack-and-pinion rubber boot, and gripping the tie-rod while the wheel is rocked as previously described.

6 Using a large screwdriver or prybar, check for wear in the suspension bushings by prying between the relevant suspension component and its attachment point. Some movement can be expected as the mounts are made of rubber. Excessive wear, however, should be obvious. Also check the condition of all rubber bushings, looking for splits, cracks or contamination of the rubber.

7 With the front wheels on the ground, have an assistant turn the steering wheel back-and-forth, about an eighth of a turn each way. There should be very little, if any, play between the steering wheel and wheels. If excessive play is evident, closely observe the joints and mounts previously described. Also check the steering column universal joints and rack-and-pinion steering gear assembly for excessive wear.

Rear suspension check

8 Securely block the front wheels, then raise the rear of the vehicle and support it on jackstands.

9 Check the rear wheel bearings for wear, using the method described for the front wheel bearings (paragraph 4).

10 Using a large screwdriver or pry bar, check for wear in the suspension bushings by prying between the relevant suspension component and its mount point. Some movement can be expected as the mounts are made of rubber. Excessive wear should be obvious, however.

Wheel check and balancing

11 Periodically remove the wheels, and clean any dirt or mud from the inside and outside surfaces. Inspect the wheel rims for rust, corrosion or other damage. Alloy wheels are easily damaged by hitting a curb while parking. Steel wheels can be easily bent in the same way. If bent or damaged, wheel replacement is often necessary. Steel wheels can sometimes be repaired, but repair of alloy wheels is difficult.

12 The balance of each wheel and tire assembly should be maintained, not only to avoid excessive tire wear, but also to prevent wear in the steering and suspension components. Wheel imbalance is normally noticed by vibration through the steering wheel or the vehicle's body. Conversely, it should be noted that wear or damage in the suspension or steering components may cause excessive vibration and tire wear. Out-of-round or out-of-true tires, damaged wheels and excessively worn wheel bearings also fall into this category. Balancing will not usually cure vibration caused by such wear.

13 Wheel balancing may be performed with the wheel either on or off the vehicle.

18 Driveaxle boot and CV joint check

Refer to illustration 18.2

1 The rubber CV joint boots are very important, because they prevent dirt, water and foreign material from entering and damaging the constant velocity (CV) joints. External contamination can cause the boot material to deteriorate prematurely, so it's a good idea to wash the boots with soap and water occasionally.

2 With the vehicle raised and securely supported on jackstands, inspect the condition of the outer constant velocity (CV) joint rubber boots. Rotate the tires to inspect the boots around their entire circumference. Check for cracking, splits or deterioration of the rubber, which would allow the grease to leak out and water and road grit to contaminate the joint **(see illustration)**. Also check the condition of the boot clamps. Repeat these checks on the inner CV joints. If any damage or deterioration is found, replace the boots as described in Chapter 8.

3 Check the general condition of the outer CV joints, by first holding the driveshaft and attempting to rotate the wheels. Repeat this check on the inner joints, by holding the inner joint yoke and attempting to rotate the driveshaft.

4 Any appreciable movement in the CV joint indicates wear in the joint, wear in the driveshaft splines, or a loose driveshaft retaining nut.

19 Brake check (every 15,000 miles or 12 months)

Warning: *The dust created by the brake system may contain asbestos, which is harmful to your health. Never blow it out with compressed air and don't inhale any of it. An approved filtering mask should be worn when working on the brakes. Don't, under any circumstances, use petroleum-based solvents to clean brake parts. Use brake system cleaner only! Try to use non-asbestos replacement pads and shoes when possible.*
Note: *For detailed photographs of the brake system, refer to Chapter 9.*

1 The work described in this Section should be performed at the specified intervals, or whenever a defect is suspected in the braking system.

19.5 You will find an inspection hole (arrow) like this in each caliper - placing a ruler across the hole should enable you to determine the thickness of the remaining pad material for both inner and outer pads

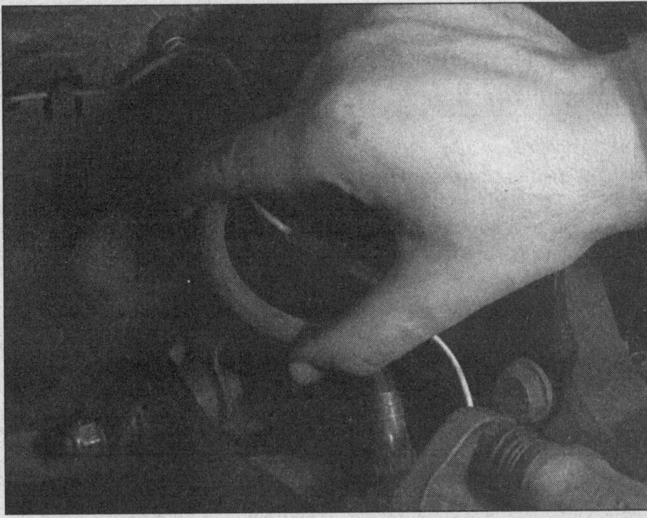

19.10 Bend the brake hose to check for cracks in the casing

2 Any of the following symptoms could indicate a potential brake system defect:

(a) *The vehicle pulls to one side when the brake pedal is depressed.*
(b) *The brakes make scraping or dragging noises when applied.*
(c) *Brake pedal travel is excessive.*
(d) *The brake fluid requires repeated topping-up.*

Disc brakes

Refer to illustrations 19.5 and 19.10

3 Loosen the front or rear wheel lug nuts. Raise the front or rear of the vehicle, as applicable, and support it on jackstands.
4 Remove the wheels.
5 Look through the inspection window in the caliper, and check that the thickness of the lining material on each of the pads is not less than the recommended minimum thickness given in the Specifications. **Note:** *The lining material is normally bonded to a metal backing plate.*
6 If it is difficult to determine the exact thickness of the pad linings, or if you are concerned about the condition of the pads, remove them from the calipers for further inspection (refer to Chapter 9).
7 Check the remaining brake caliper(s) in the same way.
8 If any one of the brake pads have worn to, or below, the specified limit, replace *all four* pads at that end of the vehicle (for example all the front pads or all the rear pads).
9 Measure the thickness of the discs with a micrometer, if available, to make sure that they still have service life remaining. If any disc is thinner than the specified minimum thickness, replace it (refer to Chapter 9). Check the general condition of the discs. Look for excessive scoring and discoloration caused by overheating. If these conditions are noted, remove the disc and replace it or have it resurfaced (refer to Chapter 9).
10 Before reinstalling the wheels, check all brake lines and hoses (refer to Chapter 9). In particular, check the flexible hoses in the vicinity of the calipers, where they are subjected to the most movement. Bend them between your fingers (but do not actually kink or crimp them, as the casing may become damaged) and check that this does not reveal previously hidden cracks, cuts or splits **(see illustration)**.

Rear drum brakes

Refer to illustration 19.13

11 Securely block the front wheels, then raise the rear of the vehicle and support it on jackstands.
12 To check the brake shoe lining thickness without removing the brake drums, pry the rubber plugs from the backing plates and use a flashlight to inspect the linings of the leading brake shoes. Make sure the thickness of the brake shoe lining is not less than the minimum thickness provided in this Chapter's Specifications.
13 If it is difficult to determine the exact thickness of the brake shoe linings, or if you are concerned about the condition of the shoes, remove the rear drums for a more comprehensive inspection (refer to Chapter 9) **(see illustration)**.
14 With the drum removed, check the shoe return and hold-down springs for correct installation, and check the wheel cylinders for fluid leakage. Check the friction surface of the brake drums for scoring and discoloration. If excessive, the drum should be resurfaced or replaced.
15 Before reinstalling the wheels, check all brake lines and hoses. On completion, apply the parking brake and make sure the rear wheels are locked. The parking brake is self-adjusting, and no manual adjustment is possible.

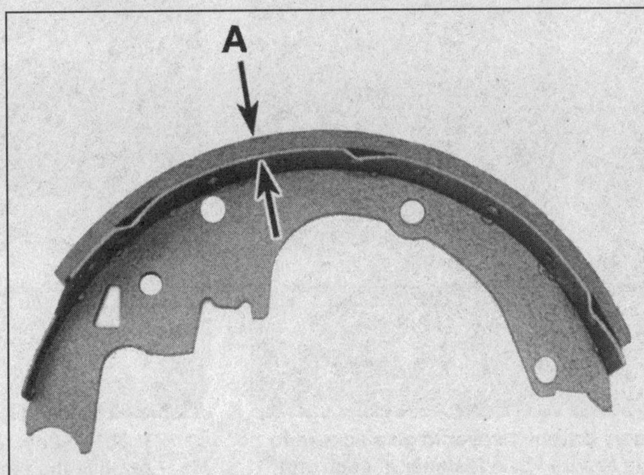

19.13 If the lining is bonded to the brake shoe, measure the lining thickness from the outer surface to the metal shoe, as shown (A). If the lining is riveted to the shoe, measure from the lining outer surface to the rivet head

20 Manual transaxle lubricant level check (every 15,000 miles or 12 months)

Refer to illustration 20.2

1 The manual transaxle does not have a dipstick. To check the lubricant level, raise the vehicle and support it securely on jackstands, making sure that the vehicle is level. The filler/level plug is located on the lower front side of the transaxle housing. Unscrew and remove the plug. If the lubricant level is correct, the oil should be even with the lower edge of the hole.

2 If the transaxle needs more lubricant (if the oil level is not even with the hole), use a syringe, or a plastic bottle and tube, to add more **(see illustration)**. Stop filling the transaxle when the lubricant begins to run out of the hole.

20.2 Adding fluid to the manual transaxle

3 Reinstall the filler/level plug, and tighten it to the torque listed in this Chapter's Specifications. Drive the vehicle a short distance, then check for leaks.

21 Drivebelt check and replacement (every 30,000 miles or 24 months)

General information

1 The drivebelt is of the flat, V-ribbed type. On four-cylinder models, the drivebelt is located on the right end of the engine and drives the alternator, water pump, power steering pump (if so equipped) and air conditioning compressor from the engine crankshaft pulley. V6 models are equipped with two drive belts - the belt located on the right end of the engine drives the alternator, power steering pump and air conditioning compressor from the engine crankshaft pulley. A separate drivebelt located on the left end of the engine drives the water pump from a pulley attached to the front intake camshaft.

2 The good condition and proper tension of the drivebelt(s) is critical to the operation of the engine. Because of their composition and the high stresses to which they are subjected, drivebelts stretch and deteriorate as they age. Therefore, they must be inspected regularly.

Drivebelt inspection

Refer to illustrations 21.3a, 21.3b, 21.3c and 21.4

3 With the engine Off, open and support the hood, then locate the drivebelt on the right-hand end of the engine, under the engine right-hand mount bracket. For improved access, raise the front right-hand side of the vehicle, support it securely on jackstands, remove the wheel, then remove the drivebelt cover (two fasteners) from inside the inner fender area. To access the water pump drivebelt on V6 models, remove the fasteners securing the water pump pulley cover and remove the cover from the engine **(see illustrations)**.

4 Inspect the entire length of the drivebelt. Rotate the engine when necessary using a wrench on the crankshaft pulley bolt. Check the drivebelt for cracks, separation of the rubber and torn or worn ribs **(see illustration)**. Also check for fraying and glazing, which gives the drivebelt a shiny appearance. Both sides of the drivebelt should be inspected, which means you will have to twist the drivebelt to check the underside. Use your fingers to feel the drivebelt where you can't see it. If you are in any doubt as to the condition of the drivebelt, replace it.

21.3a Remove the accessory drivebelt cover to gain access to the drivebelt - the cover is secured by a fastener at each end (arrows) and is located inside the right-hand inner fender area

21.3b To access the water pump drivebelt on V6 models, remove the fasteners (arrows) securing the pulley cover and remove the cover

FORD
1998 CONTOUR 2.0L

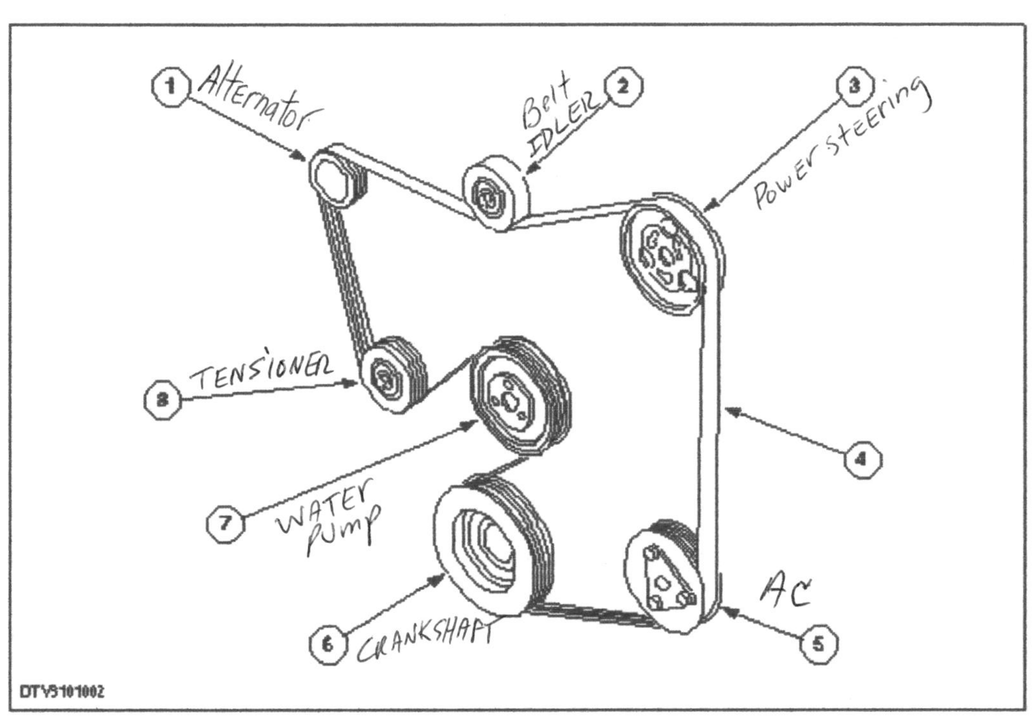

SERPENTINE
Belt DRIVE ROUTING

* you have to take Rightfront tire off to get access to.

* tensioner/and belt Pulley

use 13MM wrench on bolt

push "away" from drivebelt (to left)

FORD
1998 CONTOUR 2.0L

SERPENTINE
Belt DRIVE Routing

push "away" from
drivebelt (to left)

21.3c Water pump drivebelt on V6 models (arrow)

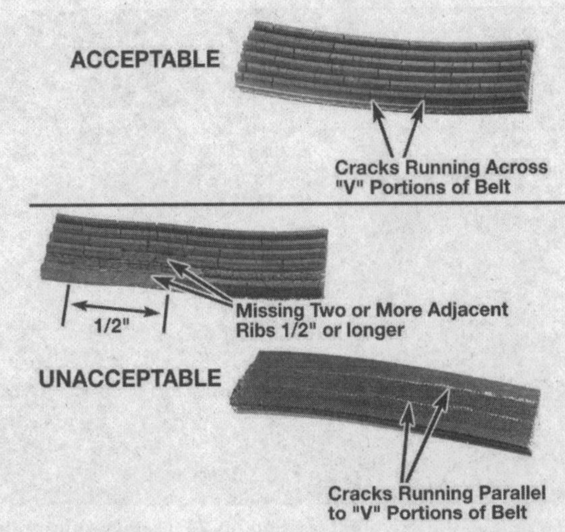

21.4 Inspect the accessory drivebelt for excessive wear. Very small cracks across the drivebelt ribs are acceptable. If the cracks are deep, or if the drivebelt appears excessively worn or damaged, replace it

21.6a On four-cylinder models, remove these two bolts (arrows) to remove the drivebelt tensioner

21.6b On V6 models, remove this bolt (arrow) to remove the drivebelt tensioner (water pump drivebelt tensioner is similar)

Drivebelt tension

Refer to illustrations 21.6a and 21.6b

5 The drivebelt is tensioned by an automatic tensioner. Regular checks or adjustment are not required.

6 If you suspect that the drivebelt is slipping and/or loose, or that the tensioner is otherwise faulty, it must be replaced. To do this, remove the drivebelt as described below, then remove the tensioner bolt(s) and remove the tensioner **(see illustrations)**. To install the new tensioner, place it on the engine and align it on its mount. Install the tensioner bolt(s) and tighten them to the torque listed in this Chapter's Specifications.

Replacement (except water pump drivebelt on V6 models)

Refer to illustrations 21.10, 21.11 and 21.13

7 Open the hood. On models equipped with a four-cylinder engine, raise the front right-hand side of the vehicle and support it securely on a jackstand and remove the wheel.

8 Remove the drivebelt cover (two fasteners) from the inner fender area (if necessary).

9 If the existing drivebelt is to be re-used, mark it, so it can be installed to run in the same direction.

10 On models equipped with a four-cylinder engine, reach up between the body and the engine (above and to the rear of the crankshaft pulley) and place a 13 mm wrench on the tensioner bolt. Rotate the tensioner pulley away from the drivebelt to release its pressure, then slip the drivebelt off the crankshaft pulley **(see illustration)**. Then release the tensioner. Note the drivebelt routing and slip it off the remaining pulleys.

11 On models equipped with a V6 engine, engage the square hole in the tensioner with a 3/8-inch breaker bar and rotate the ten-

21.10 On four-cylinder models, rotate the tensioner pulley away from the drivebelt to relieve the tension from the drivebelt, then slip the drivebelt off the crankshaft pulley

21.11 To relieve the drivebelt tension on V6 models, rotate the tensioner clockwise using a 3/8-inch breaker bar placed in the square hole in the tensioner

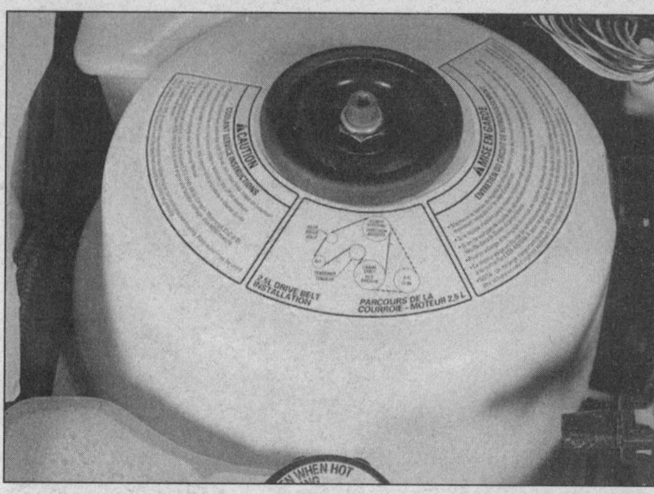

21.13 The drivebelt routing decal is usually located on the radiator shroud or strut tower as shown (this diagram is for the V6 engine)

sioner clockwise to relieve tension from the drivebelt **(see illustration)**. Slip the drivebelt off the crankshaft pulley. Note the drivebelt routing and slip it off the remaining pulleys.

12 Check all the pulleys, ensuring that their grooves are clean. Remove all traces of oil and grease from the pulley grooves. Make sure the tensioner operates properly. The tensioner should have strong spring pressure and should return smoothly when released.

13 Route the new belt over the various pulleys, again rotating the tensioner to allow the belt to be installed, then release the tensioner. Make sure the belt is correctly routed **(see illustration)** and that it fits properly into the pulley grooves - it must not overlap either edge of the pulley.

14 Rotate the crankshaft two or more full turns (in the normal direction of rotation) using a wrench on the crankshaft pulley bolt. This will seat the belt and allow you to check for correct belt installation.

15 Reinstall the drivebelt cover and wheel, then lower the vehicle to the ground.

Water pump drivebelt replacement (V6 engine)

16 Remove the water pump pulley cover as described in paragraph 3.

17 Rotate the drivebelt tensioner clockwise by hand and slip the belt off the pulleys.

18 Rotate the tensioner clockwise, install the belt, then release the tensioner.

22 Ignition system component check and replacement (every 30,000 miles or 24 months)

Spark plug check and replacement

See Section 30 for spark plug inspection and replacement procedures.

Spark plug wires

Note: *Each time a spark plug wire is disconnected from a spark plug or ignition coil, apply silicone dielectric compound (available at auto parts stores) to the inside of each wire boot before reconnection. Use a small screwdriver to coat the entire inside surface of each boot with a thin layer of the compound.*

1 The spark plug wires should be checked and, if necessary, replaced at the same time as the spark plugs. Start by making a visual check of the leads while the engine is running. In a dark garage (make sure there is adequate ventilation) start the engine and observe each plug wire. Be careful not to come into contact with any moving engine parts. If there is a break in a plug wire, a spark or arcing will be noted at the damaged area.

2 Inspect the spark plug wires one at a time, beginning with the wire for the number one cylinder, to prevent confusion. Clearly label each plug wire with a piece of tape marked with the correct cylinder number. The plug wires must be reinstalled in the correct order to ensure proper engine operation.

3 Check inside the boot for corrosion, which will look like a white crusty powder. Clean this off as much as possible. If excessive corrosion is present, replace the plug wire. The boot should fit tightly onto the end of the plug. If it doesn't, remove the lead and use pliers carefully to crimp the metal connector inside the boot until the wire fits tightly.

4 Using a clean rag, wipe the entire length of the plug wire to remove dirt and grease. Once the wire is clean, check for burns, cracks and other damage. Do not bend the lead sharply, because the conductor might break.

5 Disconnect the lead from the ignition coil pack. Check for corrosion and for a tight fit. Reinstall the wire to the coil pack, noting that each coil terminal is marked with its respective cylinder number.

6 Inspect the remaining plug wires. Make sure that all plug wires are securely attached at both ends. If any sign of arcing, corrosion, burns, cracks or other damage is noted, replace the spark plug wires as a set. If new spark plug wires are installed, remove and reinstall them one at a time, to ensure the correct firing order is maintained.

Ignition coil packs

7 Clean the coil packs with a dampened cloth and dry them thoroughly.

8 Inspect the coil pack for cracks, damage and carbon tracks. If damage is noted, refer to Chapter 5 for the replacement procedure.

23 Air filter element replacement (every 30,000 miles or 24 months)

Refer to illustrations 23.1a, 23.1b and 23.2

1 The air filter element is located in the air cleaner assembly on the left side of the engine compartment. Release the clips and lift the air cleaner cover off **(see illustrations)**.

2 Lift out the filter element, and wipe out the housing **(see illustration)**. Check that no foreign matter is present in the air intake duct or in the mass airflow sensor.

3 If performing routine service, replace the element regardless of its condition. Note that the small foam filter in the right rear corner of the air cleaner housing must be cleaned whenever the air filter element is replaced (see Section 24).

4 If you are checking the element for any other reason, inspect its lower surface. If it is oily or very dirty, replace the element. If it is only moderately dusty, it can be cleaned and re-used by blowing it clean from the upper to the lower surface using compressed air. Because it is a pleated-paper type filter, it cannot be washed or re-oiled. If it cannot be

23.1a Release the wire clips to remove the air cleaner cover . . .

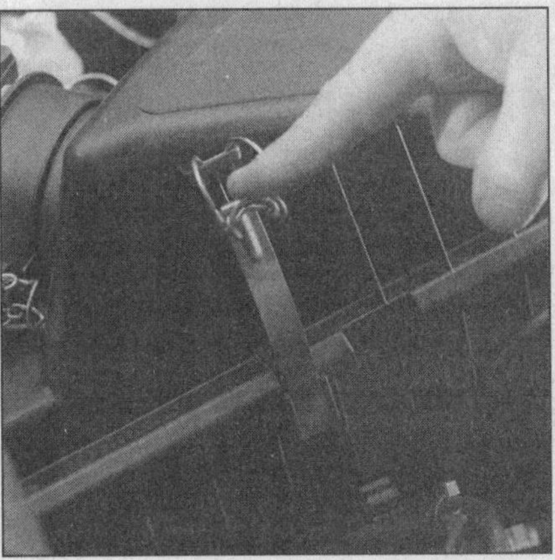

23.1b . . . noting the long clip normally hidden by the battery . . .

23.2 . . . then remove the cover and lift the filter element out of the filter housing. Wipe out the inside of the housing before installing the new filter element

cleaned satisfactorily with compressed air, replace the filter element. **Warning:** *Wear eye protection when using compressed air!* **Caution:** *Never drive the vehicle with the air filter element removed. Excessive engine wear could result, and backfiring could even cause a fire under the hood.*

5 Installation is the reverse of the removal procedure. Ensure that the element and cover are securely seated, so that unfiltered air cannot enter the engine.

24 Positive Crankcase Ventilation (PCV) system check and filter cleaning (every 30,000 miles or 24 months)

Refer to illustrations 24.1 and 24.5

Note: *To maintain efficient operation of the PCV system, clean the hoses and check the PCV valve at the intervals recommended in the maintenance schedule. For additional information on the PCV system, refer to Chapter 6.*

1 On four-cylinder models, the Positive Crankcase Ventilation (PCV) valve is located at the front of the engine, under the exhaust manifold (at the oil separator). On V6 models, the PCV valve is located in a rubber tube connected to the oil separator, which is mounted under the lower intake manifold **(see illustration)**.

2 Make sure all PCV system components are securely fastened, correctly routed (with no kinks or sharp bends to restrict flow) and in good condition. Replace any worn or damaged components.

3 If oil leakage is noted, disconnect the various hoses and tubes and check that all are clear. Remove the air cleaner cover, then check that the hose(s) from the valve cover(s) to the air cleaner housing is clear and undamaged.

4 The PCV valve is designed to allow gases to only flow out of the crankcase, so slight vacuum is created in the crankcase under most operating conditions, especially at idle. Therefore, if either the oil separator or the PCV valve are restricted, they must be replaced (see Chapter 6). The PCV valve should rattle when shaken. If it doesn't, replace the valve.

5 With the air filter element removed (see Section 23), wipe out the housing and withdraw the small foam filter from its location in the rear right-hand corner of the housing **(see illustration)**. If the filter is badly plugged with dirt or oil, it must be cleaned by soaking it in a suitable solvent. Allow the filter to dry before reinstalling it.

25 Fuel filter replacement (every 30,000 miles or 24 months)

Refer to illustrations 25.5, 25.7a and 25.7b

Warning 1: *Gasoline is extremely flammable, so take extra precautions when you work on any part of the fuel system. Don't smoke or allow open flames or bare light bulbs near the work area, and don't work in a garage where a natural gas-type appliance (such as a water heater or a clothes dryer) with a pilot light is present. Since gasoline is carcinogenic, wear latex gloves when there's a possibility of*

24.1 On V6 models, the PCV valve (arrow) is located in a hose connected to the oil separator which is mounted under the lower intake manifold

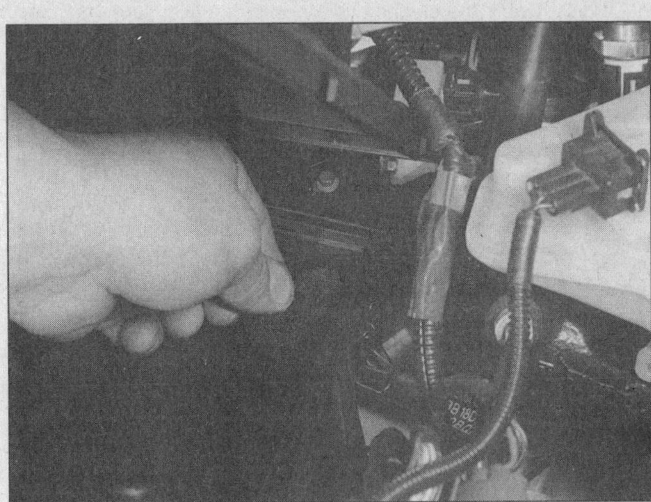

24.5 The Positive Crankcase Ventilation (PCV) system filter in the air filter housing must be cleaned whenever the air filter is removed

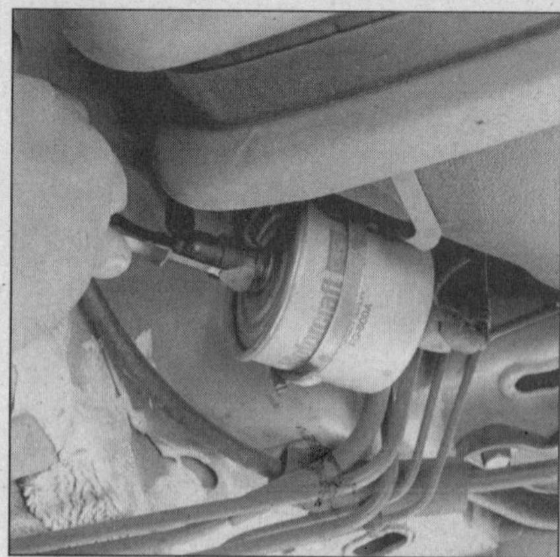

25.5 Use a small screwdriver to pry the fuel line fitting retaining clips off

25.7a When installing the fuel filter, make sure the arrow on the filter is facing toward the engine . . .

25.7b . . . then slip the fuel lines onto the filter and secure them with the retaining clips - do not overtighten the filter clamp (arrow)

being exposed to fuel, and, if you spill any fuel on your skin, rinse it off immediately with soap and water. Mop up any spills immediately and do not store fuel-soaked rags where they could ignite. The fuel system is under constant pressure, so, if any fuel lines are to be disconnected, the fuel pressure in the system must be relieved first (see Chapter 4). When you perform any kind of work on the fuel system, wear safety glasses and have a Class B type fire extinguisher on hand.

Warning 2: *After the fuel pressure has been relieved, it's a good idea to lay a shop towel over any fuel connection to be disassembled, to absorb the residual fuel that may leak out when servicing the fuel system.*

1 The fuel filter is located at the right front corner of the fuel tank, just forward of the vehicle's right-hand rear jacking point. The filter performs a vital role in keeping impurities out of the fuel system, and therefore must be replaced at regular intervals, or if there is reason to suspect that it may be restricted.

2 Relieve residual pressure in the system by removing the fuel pump fuse (No 14) and starting the engine. Allow the engine to idle until it dies. Crank the engine over once or twice using the starter, to ensure that all pressure is released, then switch off the ignition. **Warning:** *This procedure will merely relieve the pressure in the fuel system. Remember that fuel will still be present in the system components, so take precautions before disconnecting them.*

3 Noting the comments made in Section 1 of Chapter 5, disconnect the cable from the negative terminal of the battery.

4 Raise the rear of the vehicle and support it securely using a jackstand. Block the front wheels to prevent the vehicle from rolling.

5 First, spread the two clip legs apart about 1/8-inch to disengage them, then push in on them. Pry out the other end of the clips using a small screwdriver to detach them from the fittings **(see illustration)**. Then, pull the fuel lines from the fittings. Be prepared for fuel spillage as the lines are disconnected from the filter. **Caution:** *If the new filter doesn't include new fuel line retaining clips, don't use any tool that will damage the clips, which must be reused.*

6 Noting the arrow on the filter that indicates the direction of fuel flow (arrow toward engine). Loosen the filter clamp screw and remove the filter. Note that the filter still contains fuel. Use care to avoid spillage and to minimize the risk of fire.

7 To install the filter, slide the filter into its clamp so the arrow marked on it faces the correct direction (toward engine). Slide each fuel line onto the filter until they are seated fully, then install the fuel line retaining clips **(see illustrations)**. Make sure the clips are securely attached - if they come off, the fuel lines could back off the filter and a fire could result! Tighten the filter mount clamp screw, until the filter is just prevented from moving; do not overtighten the clamp screw, or the filter casing may be crushed.

8 Reinstall the fuel pump fuse and reconnect the battery cable. Turn the ignition switch on and off five times, to pressurize the system. Check for fuel leakage around the filter before lowering the vehicle to the ground and starting the engine.

26 Exhaust system check (every 30,000 miles or 24 months)

Refer to illustration 26.2

1 With the engine cold (at least three hours after the vehicle has been driven), check the complete exhaust system, from the engine to the end of the tailpipe. Ideally, this should be done on a hoist, where unrestricted access is available. If a hoist is not available, raise and support the vehicle on

26.2 Check the exhaust system hangers for cracks or damage

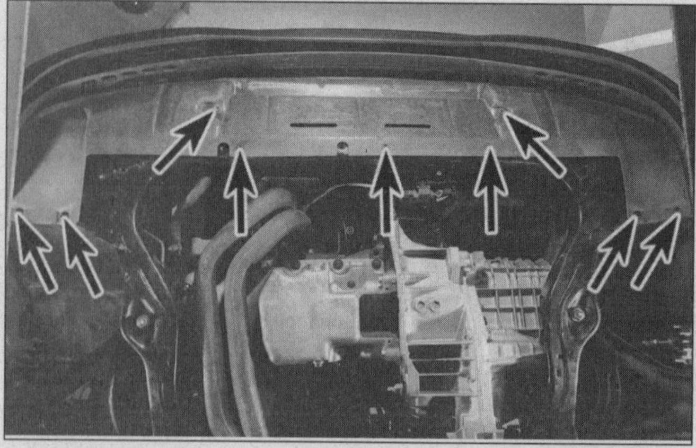

28.3a If necessary for added clearance, remove the screws (arrows) and remove the radiator lower shield

28.3b Unscrew the radiator drain plug (arrow) and drain the cooling system

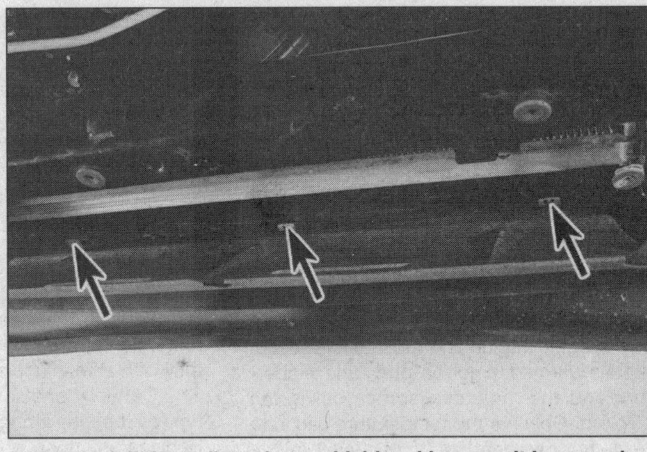

28.7 Install the radiator lower shield making sure it is properly secured in the three clips at the front edge (arrows)

jackstands.

2 Check the exhaust pipes and connections for evidence of leaks, corrosion, or damage. Make sure that all brackets and rubber hangers are in good condition, and tight. If any of the hangers must be replaced, ensure that the replacements are of the correct type **(see illustration)**. Leakage at any of the joints or in other parts of the system will usually show up as a black sooty stain in the vicinity of the leak. **Note:** *Exhaust sealant should not be used on any part of the exhaust system upstream of the catalytic converter - even if the sealant does not contain additives harmful to the converter, pieces of it may break off and contaminate the element, causing local overheating.*

3 At the same time, inspect the underside of the body for holes, corrosion or open seams, which could allow exhaust gases to enter the passenger compartment. Seal all body openings with RTV sealant or body putty.

4 Rattles and other noises can often be traced to the exhaust system, especially the rubber hangers. Try to move the system, muffler(s) and catalytic converter. If any components can touch the body or suspension parts, secure the exhaust system with new hangers.

5 Check the running condition of the engine by inspecting inside the end of the tailpipe. The exhaust deposits here are an indication of the engine's state of tune. The inside of the tailpipe should be dry and should vary in color from dark gray to light gray/brown. If it is black and sooty, or coated with white deposits, the engine is in need of a thorough fuel system inspection.

27 Automatic transaxle fluid change (every 30,000 miles or 24 months)

1 The transaxle fluid should be changed at the specified intervals or if the fluid is contaminated, discolored (brown or black) or smells burnt. Discolored fluid and a burned smell could indicate a transaxle overheating condition or clutch disc or band failure.

2 The transaxle fluid will remain hot long after driving. Therefore, change the fluid after the engine and transaxle has cooled completely.

3 Raise the front of the vehicle and support it securely using jackstands. Place a suitable drain pan under the transaxle drain plug.

4 Remove the transaxle drain plug and allow the fluid to drain, then reinstall the drain plug. Closely inspect the fluid in the drain pan. A slight amount of very fine metal particles or friction material can be considered normal. If however, excessive metal particles or friction material is noted, the transaxle likely requires further service.

5 Lower the vehicle to the ground and add four quarts of the specified transaxle fluid. Start the engine and shift through each transaxle range at idle speed. Allow the engine to run at idle speed to warm the fluid.

6 Again, raise the vehicle and drain the transaxle fluid (see Steps 3 and 4). After the fluid is completely drained, install and tighten the transaxle drain plug to the torque listed in this Chapter's Specifications.

7 Lower the vehicle and add four quarts of the specified fluid. Start the engine and allow it to run at idle speed. Shift through all gears to ensure that all internal passages are filled with fluid. Check the fluid level and add as necessary (see Section 7).

28 Coolant replacement

Warning: *Do not allow antifreeze to contact with your skin or painted surfaces of the vehicle. Flush contaminated areas immediately with plenty of water. Don't store new coolant, or leave old coolant lying around, where it's accessible to children or pets - they're attracted by its sweet smell. Ingestion of even a small amount of coolant can be fatal! Wipe up spilled antifreeze immediately. Keep antifreeze containers covered, and repair cooling system leaks as soon as they're noticed.*

Warning: *Never remove the expansion tank cap when the engine is running, or has just been switched off, as the cooling system will be hot, and the consequent escaping steam and coolant could cause serious injury.*

Coolant draining

Refer to illustrations 28.3a and 28.3b

Warning: *Wait until the engine is completely cool before starting this procedure.*

1 To drain the system, first remove the expansion tank cap (see Section 3).

2 If the additional working clearance is required, raise the front of the vehicle and support it securely on jackstands.

3 Remove the radiator lower shield, then place a large drain pan under the radiator. Unscrew the radiator drain plug and allow the coolant to drain **(see illustrations)**.

System flushing

4 Once the system is completely drained, flush the radiator with fresh water from a garden hose until clean water flows from the drain. The flushing action of the water will remove sediments from the radiator but will not remove rust and scale from the engine and cooling tube surfaces.

5 These deposits can be removed by the chemical action of a cleaner available from an auto parts store. Follow the manufacturer's instructions when using such products. If the radiator is severely corroded, damaged or leaking, remove it and have it cleaned and/or repaired at a radiator shop.

6 Remove the hoses from the expansion tank. Flush the tank with clean water, then reconnect the hoses.

Coolant filling

Refer to illustration 28.7

7 With the cooling system drained and flushed, ensure that all hoses are correctly secured and that the radiator drain plug is securely tightened. Reinstall the radiator lower shield, noting that it is located by three clips at its front edge. Tighten the retaining screws securely **(see illustration)**. Lower the vehicle to the ground.

8 Prepare a sufficient quantity of the specified coolant mixture (see Step 15).
9 Slowly fill the system through the expansion tank; since the tank is the highest point in the system. All the air in the system should be displaced into the tank by the rising liquid. Adding the coolant slowly reduces the possibility of air being trapped in the cooling system.
10 Continue filling until the coolant level reaches the MAX level line on the expansion tank, then cover the filler opening to prevent coolant from splashing out.
11 Start the engine and run it at idle speed, until it is warmed to normal operating temperature and the radiator electric cooling fan activated. Observe the temperature gauge to check for overheating. If the level in the expansion tank drops significantly, add coolant to bring the level to the MAX level line, to minimize the amount of air circulating in the system.
12 Stop the engine, allow it to cool down *completely* (overnight, if possible), then remove the filler cap and add coolant to the MAX level line. Reinstall the filler cap, tightening it securely and wash off any spilled coolant from the engine compartment and bodywork.
13 After refilling, always check all components of the system for coolant leaks. Repair any leaks found.
14 **Note:** *If, after draining and refilling the system, the engine overheats (but didn't previously), the problem is almost certainly due to trapped air at some point in the system, causing an air lock and restricting the flow of coolant. Usually, the air is trapped because the system was refilled too quickly. In some cases, air locks can be released by tapping or squeezing the various hoses. If the problem persists, stop the engine and allow it to cool completely, then remove the expansion tank cap or disconnect the radiator upper hose to purge trapped air.*

Antifreeze mixture

15 Always be replace the coolant at the suggested intervals. This is necessary not only to maintain the antifreeze properties, but also to prevent the corrosion which would otherwise occur as the corrosion inhibitors become progressively less effective. Always use ethylene glycol-based antifreeze which is compatible for use in aluminum engines.
16 To give the recommended mixture ratio for the antifreeze a 50/50 mixture of antifreeze and water should be used. It is best to mix slightly more than the system's capacity, so that a supply is available for subsequent topping-up.
17 After filling with antifreeze, attach a label to the recovery reservoir, stating the type and concentration of antifreeze used and the date installed. Any subsequent topping-up should be made with the same type and concentration of antifreeze.
18 Do not use engine antifreeze in the windshield washer system, as it will damage the vehicle's paint.

General cooling system checks

19 The engine should be cold for the cooling system checks, so perform the following procedure before driving the vehicle or after it has been shut off for at least three hours.
20 Remove the expansion tank cap and clean it thoroughly inside and out with a rag. The presence of rust or corrosion in the tank indicates that the coolant should be changed. The coolant inside the tank should be relatively clean and transparent. If it is rust-colored, drain and flush the system, and refill with a fresh coolant mixture.
21 Carefully check the radiator hoses and heater hoses along their entire length. Replace any hose which is cracked, swollen or deteriorated (see Section 15).
22 Inspect all other cooling system components for leaks. A leak in the cooling system will usually show up as white- or rust-colored deposits on the area near the leak.
23 Clean the front of the radiator using a soft brush to remove all insects, leaves or other debris. Be careful not to damage the radiator fins, or cut your fingers on them.

29 Brake fluid replacement (every 30,000 miles or 24 months)

Warning: *Brake fluid can harm your eyes and damage painted surfaces, so use extreme caution when handling or pouring it. Do not use brake fluid that has been standing open or is more than one year old. Brake fluid absorbs moisture from the air. Excess moisture can cause a dangerous loss of braking effectiveness.*
1 At the specified intervals, drain and replace the brake fluid. Since the brake fluid may drip or splash when pouring it, place plenty of rags around the master cylinder to protect the surrounding painted surfaces.
2 Before beginning work, purchase the specified brake fluid (see *Recommended lubricants and fluids* at the beginning of this Chapter).
3 Remove the cover from the master cylinder reservoir.
4 Using a hand suction pump or similar device, withdraw the fluid from the master cylinder reservoir.
5 Add new fluid to the master cylinder until it rises to the base of the filler neck.
6 Bleed the brake system as described in Chapter 9 at all four brakes until new fluid flows from each bleeder screw. Be sure to maintain the fluid level in the master cylinder as you perform the bleeding process. If the master cylinder is allowed to run dry, air will enter the system.
7 Refill the master cylinder with fluid and check the operation of the brakes. The pedal must feel solid when applied, with no softness or sponginess. **Warning:** *Do not operate the vehicle if you are in doubt about the effectiveness of the brake system.*

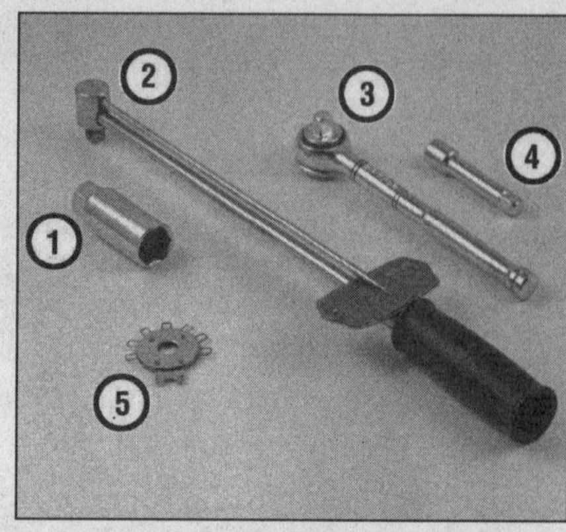

30.2 Tools required for changing spark plugs

1 **Spark plug socket** - *This will have special padding inside to protect the spark plug's porcelain insulator*
2 **Torque wrench** - *Although not mandatory, using this tool is the best way to ensure the plugs are tightened properly*
3 **Ratchet** - *Standard hand tool to fit the spark plug socket*
4 **Extension** - *Depending on model and accessories, you may need special extensions and universal joints to reach one or more of the plugs*
5 **Spark plug gap gauge** - *This gauge for checking the gap comes in a variety of styles. Make sure the gap for your engine is included*

30 Spark plug replacement (every 60,000 miles or 48 months)

Refer to illustrations 30.2, 30.12, 30.13 and 30.15

1 It is vital for proper engine operation, optimum performance and economy that the spark plugs perform with maximum efficiency. The most important factor in ensuring this is that the plugs installed are appropriate for the engine. The suitable type is given in the Specifications Section at the beginning of this Chapter, on the Vehicle Emissions Control Information (VECI) label located on the underside of the hood or in the vehicle's Owner's Manual. If these sources specify different plugs, purchase the spark plug type specified on the VECI label, as that information is provided specifically for your engine. If this type is used and the engine is in good condition, the spark plugs should not need attention between scheduled replacement intervals. Spark plug cleaning is rarely necessary, and should not be attempted unless specialized equipment is available as damage can easily be caused to the spark plug electrodes.
2 Spark plug removal and installation requires a spark plug socket with an extension which can be turned by a ratchet handle. This socket is lined with a rubber sleeve, to protect the porcelain insulator of the spark

30.12 Use a wire-type feeler gauge to check spark plug gap - if the wire doesn't slide between the electrodes with a slight drag, adjustment is necessary

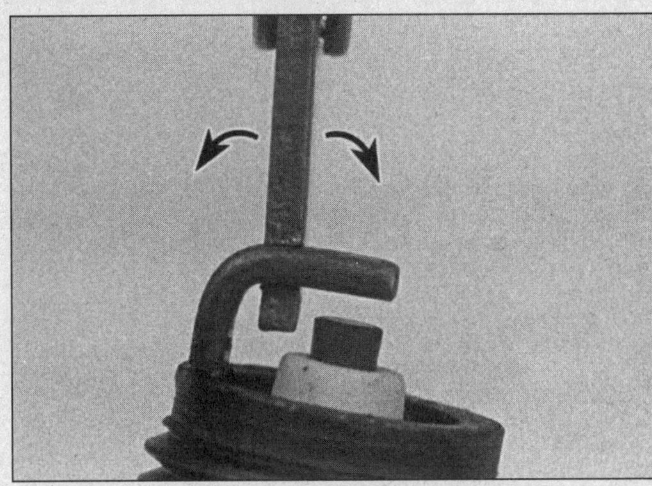

30.13 To adjust the gap, bend the side electrode only, as indicated by the arrows, and be very careful not to crack or chip the porcelain insulator surrounding the center electrode

plug and to hold the plug while you insert it into the spark plug hole. You also need a wire-type feeler gauge to check and adjust the spark plug electrode gap and a torque wrench to tighten the new plugs to the specified torque **(see illustration)**.

3 Note how the spark plug wires are routed and secured by clips at various locations on the engine. To prevent the possibility of mixing up the spark plug wires, it is a good idea to try to work on one spark plug at a time.

4 If the marks on the original-equipment spark plug wires cannot be seen, mark the wires to correspond to their respective cylinder. Pull the wires from the plugs by gripping the rubber boot and simultaneously twisting it. Do not pull on the plug wire or the wire will be damaged.

5 It is advisable to soak up any water in the spark plug recesses with a rag and to remove any dirt from them using a clean brush, vacuum cleaner or compressed air before removing the plugs, to prevent any dirt or water from dropping into the cylinders. **Warning:** *Wear eye protection if using compressed air!*

6 Unscrew the spark plugs, ensuring that the socket is kept in alignment with each plug - if the socket is forcibly moved to either side, the porcelain top of the plug may be broken off. If the spark plugs are difficult to remove, carefully check the cylinder head threads and tapered sealing surfaces for wear, excessive corrosion or damage. If any of these conditions are found, seek the advice of a dealer service department or other qualified repair shop as to the best method of repair.

7 As each plug is removed, examine it as follows - this will give a good indication of the condition of the engine. Also, compare the plugs to the spark plug condition chart on the inside back cover of this manual. If the insulator nose of the spark plug is clean and white with no deposits, this is indicative of a lean fuel/air mixture.

8 If the tip and insulator nose are covered with hard black-looking deposits, the fuel/air mixture is too rich. If the plugs are black and oily, the engine is excessively worn - the fuel/air mixture may also be too rich.

9 If the fuel/air mixture is correct and the engine is in good condition, the plug insulators will be covered with light tan to grayish-brown deposits.

10 Check the new plug for cracked insulators or damaged threads. Note also that, whenever the spark plugs are replaced during routine service, the spark plug wires should be checked as described in Section 22.

11 The spark plug electrode gap is of considerable importance. If it is too large or too small, the size of the spark and its efficiency will be seriously impaired. The gap should be set to the dimension given in the Specifications Section of this Chapter. New plugs will not necessarily be set to the correct gap, so they should always be checked before installation.

12 Special spark plug electrode gap adjusting tools are available from most auto parts stores **(see illustration)**.

13 To set the electrode gap, measure the gap with a feeler gauge, then bend open, or closed, the outer plug electrode until the correct gap is achieved **(see illustration)**. The center electrode should never be bent, as this will crack the insulation and cause plug failure. If the outer electrode is not exactly over the center electrode, bend it gently to align them.

14 Before installing the spark plugs, make sure the threaded connector sleeves at the top of the plugs are tight and that the plug exterior surfaces and threads are clean. Brown staining on the porcelain, immediately above the metal body, is normal, and doesn't necessarily indicate a leak between the body and insulator.

15 When installing the spark plugs, first make sure the cylinder head threads and sealing surface are as clean as possible. Use a clean rag wipe clean the sealing surface.

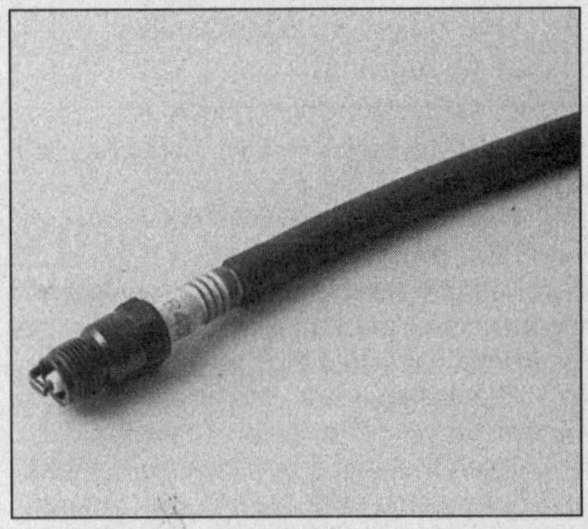

30.15 A length of rubber hose will save time and prevent damaged threads when installing the spark plugs

Apply a smear of anti-seize compound to the threads of each plug and screw them in by hand where possible. Take extra care to start the plug threads correctly, as the cylinder head is of aluminum alloy - it's often difficult to insert spark plugs into their holes without cross-threading them. It's a good idea to slip a length of rubber hose over the end of the plug to use as a tool to thread it into place **(see illustration)**. The hose will grip the plug well enough to turn it, but will start to slip if the plug begins to cross-thread in the hole.

16 When each spark plug is started correctly, screw it down until it just seats lightly, then tighten it to the torque listed in this Chapter's Specifications. If a torque wrench is not available - and this is one case where the use of a torque wrench is strongly recommended - tighten each spark plug through *no more than* 1/16 of a turn after it is seated lightly. *Do not* exceed the specified torque setting, and *NEVER* overtighten these spark plugs - their tapered seats mean they are almost impossible to remove if overtightened.

17 Reconnect the spark plug wires in their correct order, using a twisting motion on the boots until they are firmly seated on the end of the spark plug and valve cover.

33.4a Gently peel back the rubber seal...

33.4b ... and lift out the cowl panel

31 Manual transaxle lubricant change (every 60,000 miles or 48 months)

1 Raise the vehicle and support it securely on jackstands.

2 Place a drain pan and the necessary wrenches under the transaxle.

3 Remove the transaxle drain plug from the bottom of the transaxle case. Allow the lubricant to drain into the pan.

4 After the lubricant is completely drained, reinstall the plug and tighten it securely.

5 Clean the area around the fill/level plug and remove the plug. Using a hand pump, syringe or funnel, fill the transaxle with the specified lubricant until it is level with the lower edge of the fill/level plug hole.

6 Lower the vehicle. Drive the vehicle a short distance then check for leakage.

32 Timing belt replacement (four-cylinder engine) (every 60,000 miles or 48 months)

Refer to Chapter 2, Part A, for the timing belt replacement procedure.

33 Ventilation system filter replacement (every 60,000 miles or 48 months)

Refer to illustrations 33.4a, 33.4b and 33.5

1 The air entering the vehicle's ventilation system is passed through a paper air filter element, which removes particles of pollen, dust and other airborne foreign matter. To ensure its continued effectiveness, this filter's element must be replaced at the specified intervals.

2 Position the windshield wiper arms out of the way by switching off the ignition switch when the wipers are at the top of their arc.

3 Pry off the trim caps on the right side cowl grille panel, then unscrew the two screws securing the windshield edge of the cowl grille panel. Open the hood and remove the remaining three retaining screws.

4 Peel back the rubber seal and withdraw the cowl grille panel **(see illustrations).**

5 Releasing the clip at each end, lift out the filter housing and withdraw the element **(see illustration).**

6 Wipe out the ventilation system intake and the filter housing, removing any leaves, dead insects or other debris.

7 If carrying out a routine service, the element must be replaced regardless of its apparent condition. If you are checking the element for any other reason, inspect its front surface - if it is very dirty, replace the element. If it is only moderately dusty, it can be re-used by blowing it clean from the rear to the front surface using compressed air. Because it is a pleated-paper type filter, it cannot be washed or re-oiled. If it cannot be cleaned satisfactorily with compressed air, discard and replace it. **Warning:** *Wear eye protection when using compressed air!*

8 Installation is the reverse of the removal procedure. Ensure that the element and housing are securely seated so that unfiltered air cannot enter the passenger compartment.

33.5 Release the two retaining clips on each side

Chapter 2 Part A
Four-cylinder engine

Contents

Specifications

General

Engine type	Four-cylinder, in-line, double overhead camshafts
Displacement	2.0 liters (122 cubic inches)
Oil pressure (with oil hot)	
1995 through 1997	20 to 45 psi at 1500 rpm
1998	35 to 65 psi at 2000 rpm
Compression pressure	Lowest reading cylinder must be within 75-percent of highest cylinder
Firing order	1-3-4-2 (No 1 cylinder at timing belt end)
Direction of crankshaft rotation	Clockwise (seen from right-hand side of vehicle)

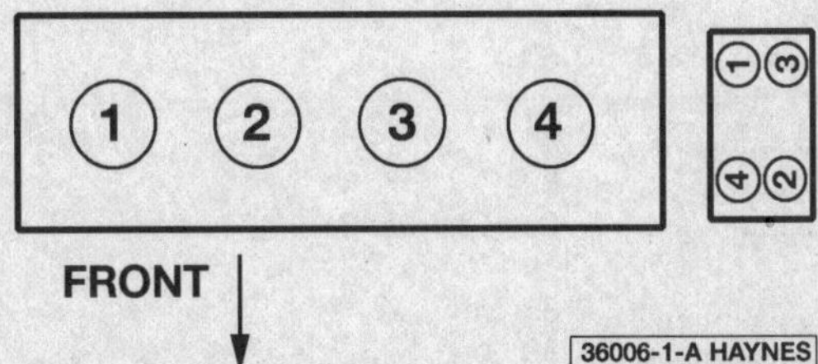

Cylinder and coil terminal locations

Camshafts and lifters

Camshaft bearing journal diameter	1.022 to 1.023 inches
Camshaft journal oil clearance	0.0008 to 0.0027 inch
Camshaft endplay	
1995 through 1998	0.003 to 0.009 inch
1999 and later	0.0007 to 0.008 inch
Lifter diameter	
1995 through 1997	1.116 to 1.117 inches
1998 and later	0.8740 to 0.8745 inch
Lifter clearance in bore	
1995 through 1997	0.0010 to 0.0027 inch
1998 and later	0.0009 to 0.0026 inch
Lobe lift at zero lash	
1995 through 1997	
Intake (primary)	0.35 inch
Intake (secondary)	0.36 inch
Exhaust	0.31 inch
1998 and later (intake and exhaust)	0.245 inch
Valve clearance at room temperature, 1998 and later	
Intake	0.004 to 0.007 inch
Exhaust	0.011 to 0.013 inch

Torque specifications

	Ft-lbs (unless otherwise indicated)
Valve cover bolts	
1995 through 1997	53 to 71 in-lbs
1998 and later	62 in-lbs
Timing belt idler pulley bolts	
1995 through 1997	47 to 53
1998 and later	38
Camshaft bearing cap bolts	
1995 through 1997	
Stage 1	90 in-lbs
Stage 2	180 in-lbs
1998 and later	132 in-lbs
Cylinder head bolts*	
1995 through 1997	
Stage 1	15 to 22
Stage 2	30 to 37
Stage 3	Tighten an additional 90 to 120-degrees
1998 and later	
Stage 1	18
Stage 2	33
Stage 3	Tighten an additional 105-degrees
Timing belt cover fasteners	
Upper cover bolts	27 to 44 in-lbs
Center (except 1998) and lower cover bolts	53 to 71 in-lbs
Center cover (1998)	36
Cover studs-to-cylinder head or block	78 to 96 in-lbs
Timing belt tensioner bolt	
1995 through 1997	26 to 30
1998 and later	18
Timing belt tensioner back plate locating peg	72 to 96 in-lbs
Timing belt tensioner spring retaining pin	71 to 97 in-lbs
Timing belt sprocket-to-camshaft bolts	
1995 through 1997	47 to 53
1998	
Intake camshaft	50
Exhaust camshaft	88
1999 and later	
Intake camshaft	50
Exhaust camshaft	
Stage 1	44
Stage 2	89
Water pump bolts	See Chapter 3
Drivebelt idler pulley	
1995 through 1998	35
1999 and later	30
Intake manifold nuts and bolts	144 to 180 in-lbs

Alternator mount bracket-to-cylinder block bolts	
1995 through 1997	35
1998 and later	48
Cylinder head support plates:	
Front plate Torx screws - to power steering pump/air conditioning compressor mount bracket and cylinder head	35
Rear plate/engine lifting eye - to alternator mount bracket and cylinder head bolts	35
Front engine lifting eye bolt	
Left-hand	120 to 156 in-lbs
Right-hand	29 to 40
Intake manifold studs-to-cylinder head	84
Exhaust manifold heat shield bolts:	
Shield-to-cylinder head	60 in-lbs
Shield/dipstick tube	84 in-lbs
Shield/coolant pipe-to-manifold	17
Exhaust manifold nuts	132 in-lbs
Crankshaft pulley bolt	81 to 89
Oil pump-to-cylinder block bolts	72 to 96 in-lbs
Oil pick-up tube-to-pump screws	71 to 97 in-lbs
Oil baffle/pump pick-up tube nuts	156 to 180 in-lbs
Oil filter adapter-to-pump	13 to 18
Oil pan bolts	
1995 through 1997	15 to 18
1998	84 in-lbs
1999 and later	18
Oil pan-to-transaxle bolts	25 to 34
Rear main oil seal retainer bolts	156 to 192 in-lbs
Coolant tube-to-oil pan bolt	84 in-lbs
Flywheel/driveplate bolts	79 to 88
Transaxle-to-engine bolts	25 to 34
Engine/transaxle front mount:	
Mount-to-subframe bolts/nuts - stage 1	84 in-lbs
Mount-to-subframe bolts/nuts - stage 2	35
Mount center bolt	89
Engine/manual transaxle rear mount:	
Mount bracket-to-transaxle 12 mm fasteners	58 to 62
Mount bracket-to-transaxle 10 mm fasteners	35
Mount-to-subframe bolts and nut - stage 1	84 in-lbs
Mount-to-subframe bolts and nut - stage 2	35
Mount center bolt	89
Engine/automatic transaxle rear mount:	
Mount bracket-to-transaxle	35 to 36
Mount-to-subframe bolts - stage 1	84 in-lbs
Mount-to-subframe bolts - stage 2	35
Mount center bolt	89
Engine/transaxle left-hand mount:	
Bracket-to-transaxle nuts	61
Mount center bolt	Not available
Mount-to-body bolts	Not available
Engine/transaxle right-hand mount:	
Bracket-to-engine and mount nuts	61 to 66
Mount-to-body bolts	82

**Cylinder head bolts must be replaced after each use.*

1 General information

This Part of Chapter 2 is devoted to in-vehicle repair procedures for the 2.0L four-cylinder engine. This engine design utilizes a cast-iron block with four cylinders. The cylinder head is aluminum and the overhead camshafts operate the valves through hydraulic lifters.

All information concerning engine removal and installation and engine block and cylinder head overhaul can be found in Part C of this Chapter. The following repair procedures are based on the assumption that the engine is installed in the vehicle. If the engine has been removed from the vehicle and mounted on a stand, many of the steps outlined in this Part of Chapter 2 will not apply.

The Specifications included in this Part of Chapter 2 apply only to the procedures contained in this Part. Part C of Chapter 2 contains the Specifications necessary for cylinder head and engine block rebuilding.

2 Repair operations possible with the engine in the vehicle

Many major repair operations can be accomplished without removing the engine from the vehicle.

Clean the engine compartment and the exterior of the engine with some type of pressure washer before any work is done. It will make the job easier and help keep dirt out of the internal areas of the engine.

It may help to remove the hood to improve access to the engine as repairs are performed (refer to Chapter 11 if necessary).

If vacuum, exhaust, oil or coolant leaks develop, indicating a need for gasket or seal replacement, the repairs can generally be made with the engine in the vehicle. The intake and exhaust manifold gaskets, oil pan gasket, crankshaft oil seals and cylinder head gaskets are all accessible with the engine in place.

Exterior engine components, such as the intake and exhaust manifolds, the oil pan (and the oil pump), the water pump, the starter motor, the alternator, and the fuel system components can be removed for repair with the engine in place.

Since the cylinder head can be removed without pulling the engine, valve component servicing can also be accomplished with the engine in the vehicle. Replacement of the timing belt and sprockets is also possible with the engine in the vehicle.

In extreme cases caused by a lack of necessary equipment, repair or replacement of piston rings, pistons, connecting rods and rod bearings is possible with the engine in the vehicle. However, this practice is not recommended because of the cleaning and preparation work that must be done to the components involved.

3 Compression test

This procedure is substantially the same as for the V6 engine. Refer to Chapter 2, Part B and follow the procedure there.

4 Top Dead Center (TDC) for number one piston - locating

Refer to illustrations 4.9a and 4.9b

This procedure is substantially the same as for the V6 engine. Refer to the accompanying illustrations, but follow the procedure in Chapter 2, Part B. Note that the number one cylinder is the one closest to the drivebelts. After placing the number one piston at TDC, rotate the crankshaft 180-degrees clockwise to bring each of the remaining cylinders to TDC (in the firing order sequence).

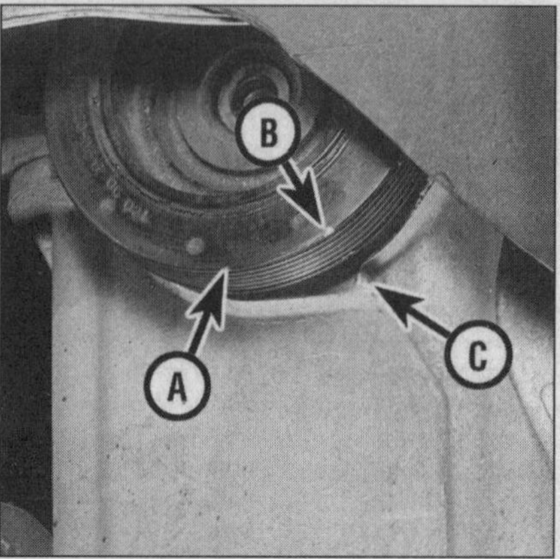

4.9a Don't use the crankshaft pulley's first pair of notches (A) - align the second pair of notches (B) with the raised rib on the oil pan (C) . . .

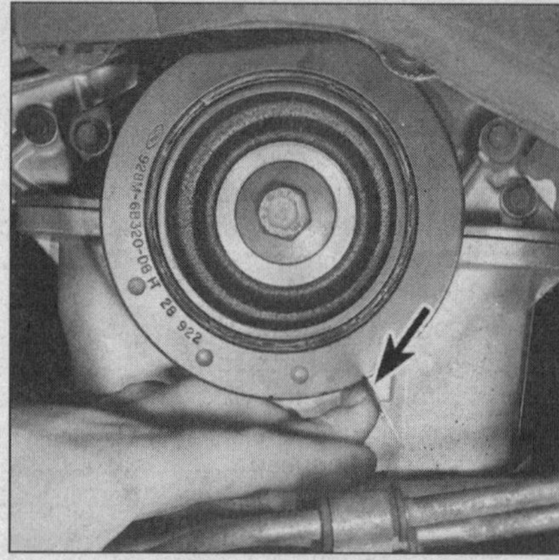

4.9b . . . using a straight edge extended out from the oil pan (arrow) if greater accuracy is required

5 Valve cover - removal and installation

Refer to illustrations 5.4, 5.6, 5.8 and 5.9

1 Remove the two electrical connectors and disconnect the vacuum hose (if equipped), then remove the air cleaner assembly cover with the mass airflow sensor, the resonator and the plenum chamber (see Chapter 4).

2 Disconnect the accelerator cable from the throttle linkage as described in Chapter 4. Where equipped, disconnect also the cruise control actuator cable (see Chapter 12).

3 Remove the timing belt upper cover (see Section 9).

4 Disconnect the crankcase breather hose from the valve cover union **(see illustration)**.

5 Remove the spark plug wires from the spark plugs and remove them, unclipping the leads from the cover.

6 Working in stages, unscrew the valve cover retaining bolts, noting the spacer sleeve and rubber seal at each, then remove the cover **(see illustration)**.

7 Discard the cover gasket; this *must* be replaced whenever it is disturbed. Check that the sealing faces are undamaged, and that the rubber seal at each retaining bolt is ser-

5.4 Disconnecting the crankcase breather hose from the valve cover

5.6 Removing the valve cover

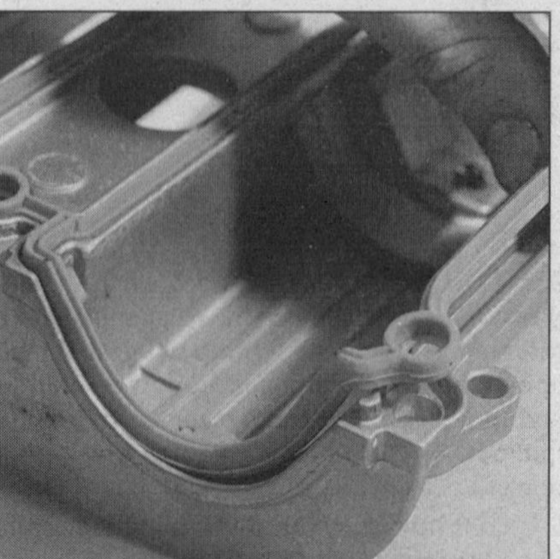

5.8 Ensure the gasket is located correctly in the cover groove

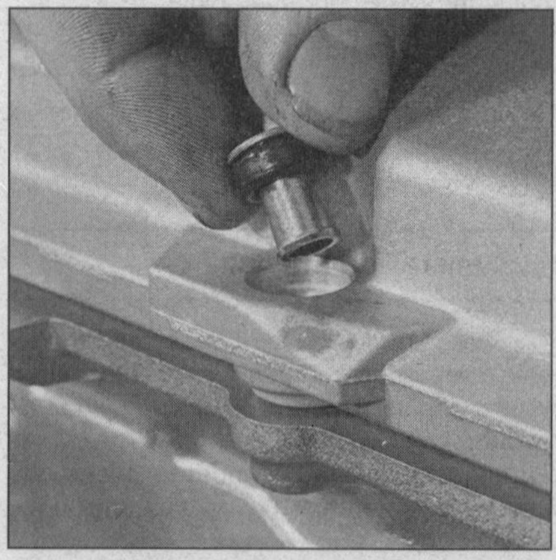

5.9 Ensure the rubber seal is installed on each valve cover bolt spacer

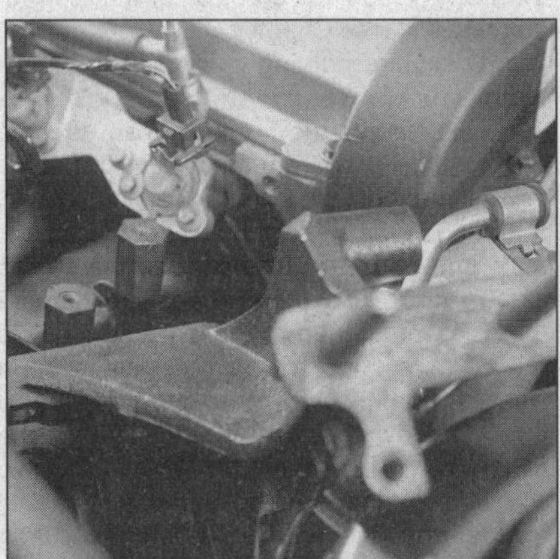
6.15 The alternator mounting bracket must be unbolted from the rear of the cylinder block to permit access to the intake manifold nut

6.16 Removing the intake manifold - take care not to damage delicate components

6.17a Always replace the intake manifold gasket - don't rely on sealants

viceable; replace any worn or damaged seals.

8 On installation, clean the cover and cylinder head gasket faces carefully, then install a new gasket to the cover, ensuring that it locates correctly in the cover grooves **(see illustration)**.

9 Install the cover to the cylinder head, then insert the rubber seal and spacer sleeve at each bolt location **(see illustration)**. Start all bolts finger-tight, ensuring that the gasket remains seated in its groove.

10 Working in a diagonal sequence from the center outwards, and in two stages tighten the cover bolts to the torque listed in this Chapter's Specifications.

11 Install the spark plug wires, clipping them into place so that they are correctly routed; each is numbered, and can also be identified by the numbering on its associated coil terminal.

12 Reconnect the crankcase breather hose, then install the timing belt upper cover. Reconnect and adjust the accelerator cable, then install the air cleaner assembly cover with the mass airflow sensor, the resonator and the plenum chamber (see Chapter 4).

6 Intake manifold - removal and installation

Warning: *Gasoline is extremely flammable, so take extra precautions when disconnecting any part of the fuel system. Don't smoke, or allow open flames or bare light bulbs in or near the work area. Don't work in a garage where a natural gas appliance (such as a clothes dryer or water heater) is installed. If you spill gasoline on your skin, rinse it off immediately. Have a fire extinguisher rated for gasoline fires handy, and know how to use it.*

Removal

Refer to illustrations 6.15 and 6.16

1 Park the vehicle on firm, level ground, apply the parking brake firmly, and loosen the nuts securing the right-hand front wheel (the wheel will be removed to ease access to the alternator mounting bolts).

2 Relieve the fuel system pressure (see Chapter 4).

3 Disconnect the battery negative cable - see Chapter 5, Section 1.

4 Disconnect the two electrical connectors and disconnect the vacuum hose (if equipped), then remove the air cleaner assembly cover with the mass airflow sensor, the resonator and the plenum chamber (see Chapter 4).

5 Disconnect the accelerator cable from the throttle linkage as described in Chapter 4 - if equipped, disconnect also the cruise control actuator cable.

6 Disconnect the crankcase breather hose from the valve cover union.

7 Unbolt the upper part of the exhaust manifold heat shield; unclip the coolant hose to allow it to be removed. Loosen the sleeve nut securing the EGR tube to the manifold, remove the two screws securing the tube to the ignition coil bracket, then unscrew the sleeve nut securing the tube to the EGR valve - see Chapter 6 for full details if required.

8 Remove the two screws securing the wiring rail to the top of the manifold - this is simply so that it can be moved as required to reach the manifold bolts. Remove the electrical connectors to disconnect the camshaft position sensor and the coolant temperature sensor, then unclip the wiring from the ignition coil bracket, and secure it to the manifold.

9 Remove the three screws securing the wiring rail to the rear of the manifold. Releasing its wire clip, remove the large electrical connector (next to the fuel pressure regulator) to disconnect the wiring of the manifold components from the engine wiring harness.

10 Marking or labeling them as they are removed, disconnect the vacuum hoses as follows:

(a) *One from the rear of the throttle housing (only the one hose - there is no need to disconnect the second hose running to the fuel pressure regulator).*
(b) *One from the union on the manifold's left-hand end.*
(c) *The braking system vacuum servo unit hose (see Chapter 9 for details).*
(d) *One from the Exhaust Gas Recirculation (EGR) valve.*

11 Equalize the pressure in the fuel tank by removing the filler cap, then undo the fuel feed and return lines connecting the engine to the chassis (see Chapter 4). Plug or cap all open attachments.

12 Unbolt the power steering high-pressure tube and the ground lead from the cylinder head rear support plate/engine lifting eye, then unscrew the bolt securing the support plate/lifting eye to the alternator mount bracket.

13 Unscrew the six nuts securing the engine/transaxle right-hand mount bracket, then remove the bracket.

14 Remove the alternator (see Chapter 5).

15 Unbolt the alternator mount bracket from the rear of the cylinder block and remove it, together with the cylinder head rear support plate/engine lifting eye **(see illustration)**.

16 Unscrew the bolts and nuts securing the manifold to the cylinder head and remove it **(see illustration)**. Take care not to damage vulnerable components such as the EGR tube and valve as the manifold assembly is maneuvered out of the engine compartment.

Installation

Refer to illustrations 6.17a and 6.17b

17 Installation is the reverse of the removal procedure, noting the following points:

(a) *When using a scraper and solvent to remove all traces of old gasket material and sealant from the manifold and cylinder head, be careful to ensure that you don't scratch or damage the material of either; the cylinder head is of aluminum alloy, while the manifold is plastic - any solvents used must be suitable for this application. If the gasket was leaking, have the mating surfaces checked for warpage at an automotive machine shop. While it may be possible to have*

6.17b Check all disturbed components - such as this brake booster hose - for leaks on reassembly

the cylinder head gasket surface resurfaced if necessary, to remove any distortion, the manifold must be replaced if it is found to be excessively warped or cracked - check with special care around the mount points for components such as the idle speed control valve and EGR tube.

(b) *Provided the relevant mating surfaces are clean and flat, a new gasket will be sufficient to ensure the joint is gas-tight.* ***Don't*** *use any kind of silicone-based sealant on any part of the fuel system or intake manifold.*

(c) *Install a new gasket, then locate the manifold on the head and install the nuts and bolts* **(see illustration)**.

(d) *Tighten the nuts/bolts in three or four equal steps to the torque listed in this Chapter's Specifications. Work from the center outwards, to avoid warping the manifold.*

(e) *Install the remaining parts in the reverse order of removal - tighten all fasteners to the torque specified.*

(f) *When reassembling the engine/transaxle right-hand mount, replace the self-locking nuts, and don't allow the mount to twist as the middle two of the bracket's six nuts are tightened.*

(g) *Before starting the engine, check the accelerator cable for correct adjustment and the throttle linkage for smooth operation.*

(h) *When the engine is fully warmed up, check for signs of fuel, intake and/or vacuum leaks* **(see illustration)**.

(i) *Road test the vehicle, and check for proper operation of all disturbed components.*

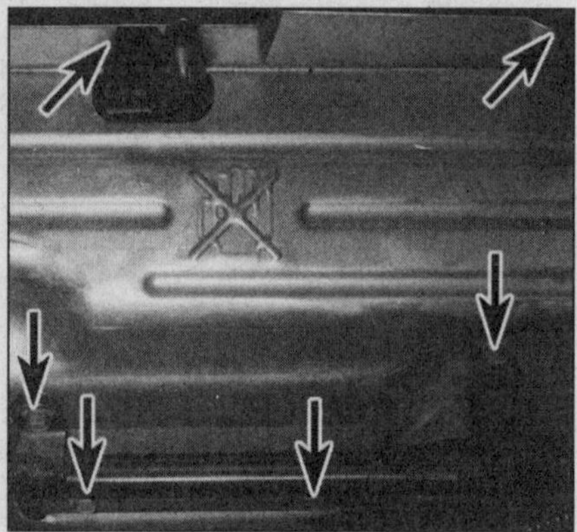

7.5 Upper exhaust manifold heat shield bolts (arrows)

7 Exhaust manifold - removal, inspection and installation

Warning: *The engine must be completely cool before beginning this procedure.*

Note: *In addition to the new gasket and any other parts, tools or facilities needed to perform this operation, a new plastic guide sleeve will be required on reassembly.*

Removal

Refer to illustrations 7.5, 7.9a and 7.9b

1 Disconnect the battery negative cable - see Chapter 5, Section 1.

2 Unbolt the resonator support bracket from the engine compartment front crossmember, loosen the two clamp screws securing the resonator to the mass airflow sensor and plenum chamber hoses, then swing the resonator up clear of the thermostat housing (see Chapter 4).

3 Drain the cooling system (see Chapter 1).

4 Disconnect the coolant hose and the coolant tube/hose from the thermostat housing; secure them clear of the working area.

5 Unbolt the exhaust manifold heat shield, and remove both parts of the shield **(see illustration)**. Apply penetrating oil to the EGR tube sleeve nut, and to the exhaust manifold mount nuts (also to the pulse-air system sleeve nuts, if they are to be unscrewed).

6 Unscrew the sleeve nut securing the EGR tube to the manifold, remove the two screws securing the tube to the ignition coil bracket, then loosen the sleeve nut securing the tube to the EGR valve - see Chapter 6 for full details if required.

7 Disconnect the oxygen sensor electrical connector to avoid straining its wiring, then

8 Unscrew the nuts to disconnect the exhaust system front pipe from the manifold (see Chapter 4).

9 Remove the nuts and detach the manifold and gasket **(see illustration)**. Take care not to damage vulnerable components such as the EGR tube as the manifold assembly is maneuvered out of the engine compartment. When removing the manifold with the engine in the vehicle, additional clearance can be obtained by unscrewing the studs from the cylinder head; a female Torx-type socket will be required **(see illustration)**.

10 Always install a new gasket on reassembly, to carefully cleaned components (see below). *Don't* attempt to re-use the original gasket.

Inspection

Refer to illustrations 7.13a, 7.13b and 7.14

11 Use a scraper to remove all traces of old gasket material and carbon deposits from the manifold and cylinder head mating surfaces. If the gasket was leaking, have the manifold checked for warpage at an automotive machine shop, and have it resurfaced if necessary. **Caution:** *When scraping, be very careful not to gouge or scratch the delicate*

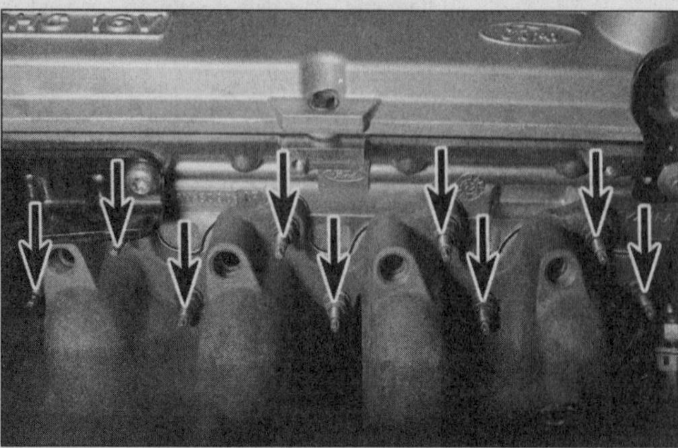

7.9a Unscrew these nuts (arrows) to remove the exhaust manifold

7.9b The exhaust manifold studs can be unscrewed, if necessary, to provide additional working space

7.13a Exhaust pipe-to-manifold bolt - note coil spring and shoulder on bolt

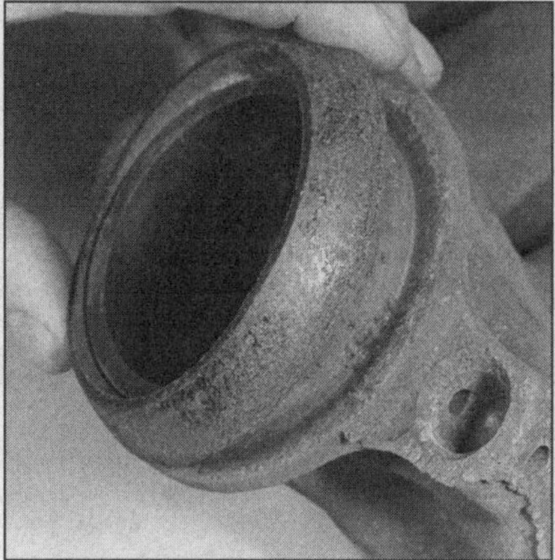
7.13b Replace the pipe-to-manifold gasket to prevent leaks

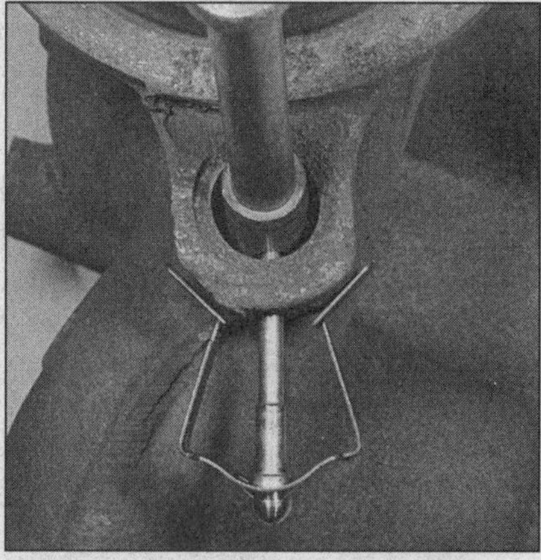
7.14 Release the spring clip to extract the bolt from the manifold

aluminum alloy cylinder head.

12 Provided both mating surfaces are clean and flat, a new gasket will be sufficient to ensure the joint is gas-tight. *Don't* use any kind of exhaust sealant upstream of the catalytic converter.

13 Note that the exhaust pipe is secured to the manifold by two bolts, with a coil spring, spring seat and self-locking nut on each. On installation, tighten the nuts until they stop on the bolt shoulders; the pressure of the springs will then suffice to make a leakproof joint **(see illustrations)**.

14 Don't overtighten the nuts to cure a leak - the bolts will shear; replace the gasket and the springs if a leak is found. The bolts themselves are secured by spring clips to the manifold, and can be replaced easily if damaged **(see illustration)**.

Installation

Refer to illustration 7.15

15 Installation is the reverse of the removal procedure, noting the following points:

(a) *Position a new gasket over the cylinder head studs, and install a new plastic guide sleeve to the stud nearest to the thermostat housing, so that the manifold will be correctly located* **(see illustration)**. ***Don't*** *install the manifold without this sleeve.*

(b) *Install the manifold, and finger-tighten the mount nuts.*

(c) *Working from the center out, and in three or four equal steps, tighten the nuts to the torque given in the Specifications Section of this Chapter.*

(d) *Install the remaining parts in the reverse order of removal. Tighten all fasteners to the specified torque .*

(e) *Refill the cooling system (see Chapter 1).*

(f) *Run the engine, and check for exhaust leaks. Check the coolant level when fully warmed-up to normal operating temperature.*

8 Crankshaft pulley - removal and installation

Refer to illustration 8.4

1 Remove the drivebelt - either remove the drivebelt completely, or just secure it clear of the crankshaft pulley, depending on the work to be performed (see Chapter 1).

2 If necessary, rotate the crankshaft until the timing marks align (see Section 4).

3 The crankshaft must now be locked to keep it from rotating while loosening the bolt. On models with manual transaxles, shift into fifth gear and have an assistant apply the brakes hard. On models with automatic transaxles, remove the starter (see Chapter 5) and wedge a large screwdriver into the flywheel ring gear teeth.

4 Unscrew the pulley bolt and remove the pulley **(see illustrations)**.

5 Installation is the reverse of the removal procedure; ensure that the pulley's keyway is aligned with the crankshaft's locating key, and tighten the pulley bolt to the specified torque.

9 Timing belt covers - removal and installation

Refer to illustrations 9.1, 9.7, 9.8, 9.11 and 9.14

Upper cover

1 Unscrew the cover's two mount bolts and remove it **(see illustration)**.

2 Installation is the reverse of the removal

7.15 Install the plastic guide sleeve (arrow) on the stud before installing the exhaust manifold

8.4 Unscrew the pulley bolt to release the crankshaft pulley

9.1 Remove the bolts (arrows) to release the timing belt upper cover

9.7 Loosen the water pump pulley bolts (arrows) and remove the pulley

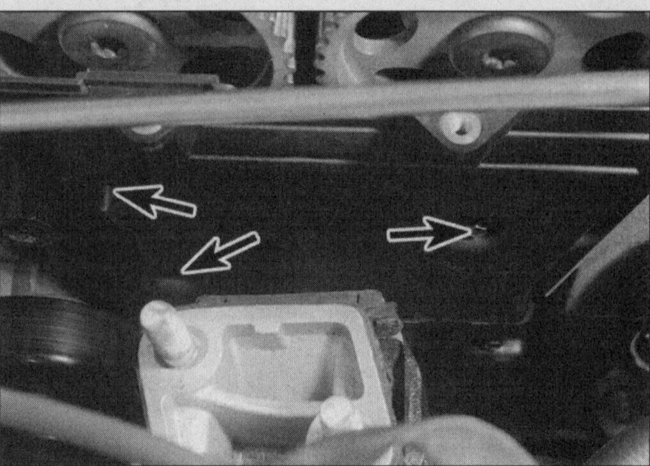

9.8 Remove the fasteners (arrows) to release the timing belt middle cover

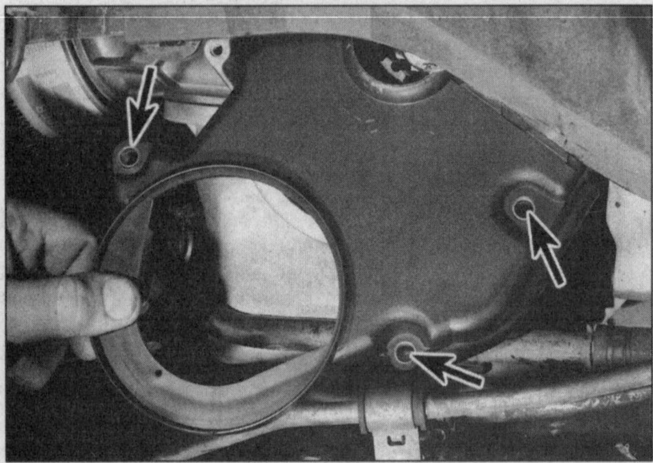

9.11 Removing the timing belt lower cover (arrows at bolt locations)

9.14 Timing belt inner shieldfasteners (arrows)

procedure; ensure the cover edges engage correctly with each other, and note the torque specified for the bolts.

Middle cover

3 Unscrew the nuts securing the engine/transaxle right-hand mount bracket, then remove the bracket.

4 Loosen the water pump pulley bolts.

5 Remove the timing belt upper cover (see Step 1 above).

6 Remove the drivebelt (see Chapter 1).

7 Unbolt and remove the water pump pulley **(see illustration)**.

8 Unscrew the middle cover fasteners (one bolt at the front, one at the lower rear, one stud at the top rear) and remove the cover **(see illustration)**.

9 Installation is the reverse of the removal procedure. Ensure the cover edges engage correctly with each other, and note the torque specified for the various fasteners. When reassembling the engine/transaxle right-hand mount, replace the self-locking nuts, and don't allow the mount to twist as the middle two of the bracket's six nuts are tightened.

Lower cover

10 Remove the crankshaft pulley (see Section 8).

11 Unscrew the cover's three securing bolts and remove it **(see illustration)**.

12 Installation is the reverse of the removal procedure; ensure the cover edges engage correctly with each other, and note the torque specified for the various fasteners.

Inner shield

13 Remove the timing belt, its tensioner components and the camshaft sprockets (see Sections 10 and 11).

14 The shield is secured to the cylinder head by two bolts at the top, and by two studs lower down; unscrew these and remove the shield **(see illustration)**.

15 Installation is the reverse of the removal procedure; note the torque specified for the various fasteners.

10 Timing belt - removal, installation and adjustment

Refer to illustrations 10.8, 10.10, 10.14, 10.15, 10.19a, 10.19b, 10.20, 10.22, 10.25 and 10.26

Note: *To perform this operation, a new timing belt (where applicable), a new valve cover gasket, and some special tools (see text) will be required. If the timing belt is being removed for the first time since the vehicle left the factory, a tensioner spring and retaining pin must be obtained for installation on reassembly.*

1 With the vehicle parked on firm level ground, open the hood and disconnect the battery negative cable - see Chapter 5, Section 1.

2 Unbolt the power steering high-pressure tube from the cylinder head rear support plate/engine lifting eye, and from the front support plate/pump bracket.

3 Unscrew the nuts securing the engine/transaxle right-hand mount bracket, then remove the bracket.

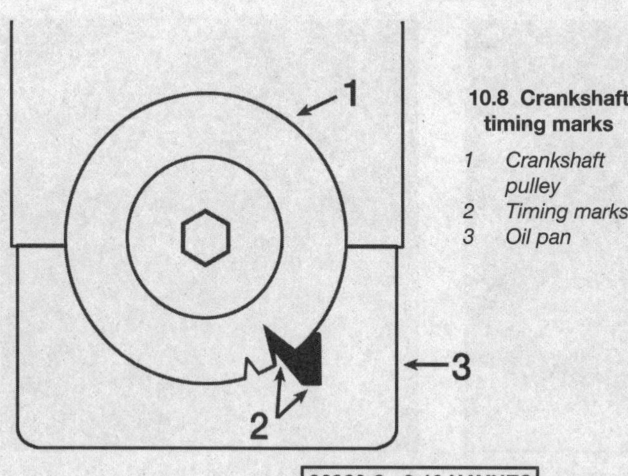

10.8 Crankshaft timing marks

1 *Crankshaft pulley*
2 *Timing marks*
3 *Oil pan*

10.10 Install the camshaft aligning tool to ensure the engine is locked with Nos 1 and 4 cylinders at TDC

4 Loosen the water pump pulley bolts.

5 Remove the valve cover (see Section 5).

6 Remove the spark plugs, covering their holes with clean rag, to prevent dirt or other foreign bodies from dropping in (see Chapter 1).

7 Remove the drivebelt (see Chapter 1).

8 Rotate the crankshaft clockwise until the second notch in the pulley rim aligns with the edge of the oil pan mark, so that cylinders 1 and 4 are at TDC **(see illustration)**.

9 Unbolt and remove the water pump pulley and the drivebelt idler pulley.

10 Fabricate a tool from a strip of metal 0.20 inch thick (while the strip's thickness *is* critical, its length and width are not, but should be approximately 7 to 9 inches by _ to 1-1/4 inches). Check that cylinders 1 and 4 are at Top Dead Center (TDC) - No 1 on the compression stroke - by resting this tool on the cylinder head mating surface, and sliding it into the slot in the left-hand end of both camshafts **(see illustration)**. The tool should slip snugly into both slots while resting on the cylinder head mating surface; if one camshaft is only slightly out of alignment, it is permissible to use an open-end wrench to rotate the camshaft gently and carefully until the tool will fit.

11 If both camshaft slots (they are machined significantly off-center) are below the level of the cylinder head mating surface, rotate the crankshaft through one full turn clockwise and install the tool again; it should now fit as described in the previous Step.

12 With the camshaft aligning tool remaining in place, remove the crankshaft pulley. *Don't* use the locked camshafts to prevent the crankshaft from rotating - use only the locking methods described in Section 8.

13 Remove the timing belt lower and middle covers (see Section 9).

14 **Note:** *1998 models are equipped with an additional timing belt idler pulley located near the crankshaft sprocket.* With the camshaft aligning tool still in place, loosen the tensioner bolt, and use an Allen key inserted into its center to rotate the tensioner clockwise as far as possible away from the belt; retighten the bolt to secure the tensioner clear of the timing belt **(see illustration)**.

15 If the timing belt is to be re-used, use white paint to mark its direction of rotation, and note from the manufacturer's markings to see which way it is installed. Remove the belt **(see illustration)**. *Don't* rotate the crankshaft until the timing belt is installed.

16 If the belt is being removed for reasons other than routine replacement, check it carefully for any signs of uneven wear, splitting, cracks (especially at the roots of the belt teeth) or contamination with oil or coolant. Replace the belt if there is the slightest doubt about its condition. As a safety measure, the belt should be replaced routinely. Also, check the tensioner spring (if equipped), replacing it if there is any doubt about its condition. Check the sprockets for wear or damage, and ensure that the tensioner and guide pulleys rotate smoothly on their bearings; replace any worn or damaged components. If signs of oil or coolant contamination are found, trace the source of the leak and rectify it, then wash down the engine timing belt area and related components, to remove all traces of oil or coolant.

17 On reassembly, temporarily install the crankshaft pulley, to check that the pulley notches and oil pan rib are aligned as described in Step 8 above, then ensure that both camshafts are aligned at TDC by the special tool (Step 10). If the engine is being reassembled after major disassembly, both camshaft sprockets should be free to rotate on their respective camshafts; if the timing belt alone is being replaced, both pulleys should still be securely fastened.

18 **Note:** *On 1998 models, the oil plug must be removed from the exhaust camshaft sprocket before its retaining bolt can be removed.* A holding tool is required to prevent the camshaft sprockets from rotating while their bolts are loosened and retightened, or fabricate a substitute as follows. Find two lengths of steel strip, one approximately 23.5 inches long and the other about 8 inches, and three bolts with nuts and washers; one nut and bolt forming the pivot of a forked tool, with the remaining nuts and bolts at the tips of the forks, to engage with the sprocket spokes as shown in the accompanying illustrations. **Note:** *Don't use the camshaft aligning tool to prevent rotation while the camshaft sprocket bolts are loosened or tightened; the risk of damage to the camshaft concerned and to the cylinder head is far too great. Use only a forked holding tool applied directly to the sprockets, as described.*

19 If it is being installed for the first time,

10.14 Loosen the tensioner bolt, and use an Allen key to rotate the tensioner away from the timing belt . . .

10.15 . . . then remove the timing belt

10.19a Installing the tensioner spring retaining pin

10.19b Hook the spring onto the tensioner and install it as shown - engage the tensioner back plate on the locating peg (arrow) . . .

10.20 . . . then use an Allen key to position the tensioner so that the timing belt can be installed

screw the timing belt tensioner spring retaining pin into the cylinder head, tightening it to the specified torque. Unbolt the tensioner, hook the spring onto the pin and the tensioner back plate, then install the tensioner, engaging its back plate on the locating peg **(see illustrations)**.

20 In all cases, loosen the tensioner bolt (if necessary), and use an Allen key inserted into its center to rotate the tensioner clockwise as far as possible against spring tension, then retighten the bolt to secure the tensioner **(see illustration)**.

21 Install the timing belt; if the original is being reinstalled, ensure that the marks and notes made on removal are followed, so that the belt is reinstalled in the same position, and to run in the same direction. Starting at the crankshaft sprocket, work counterclockwise around the camshaft sprockets and tensioner, finishing off at the rear guide pulley. The front run, between the crankshaft and the exhaust camshaft sprockets, *must* be kept taut, without altering the position either of the crankshaft or of the camshaft(s) - if necessary, the position of the camshaft sprockets can be altered by rotating each on its camshaft (which remains fixed by the aligning tool). Where the sprocket is still fastened, use the holding tool described in Step 18 above to prevent the sprocket from rotating while its retaining bolt is loosened - the sprocket can then be rotated on the camshaft until the belt will slip into place; retighten the sprocket bolt.

22 When the belt is in place, loosen the tensioner bolt gently until the spring pulls the tensioner against the belt; the tensioner should be retained correctly against the timing belt inner shield and cylinder head, but must be just free to respond to changes in belt tension **(see illustration)**.

23 Tighten both camshaft sprocket bolts (or check that they are tight, as applicable) and remove the camshaft aligning tool. Temporarily install the crankshaft pulley, and rotate the crankshaft through two full turns clockwise to settle and tension the timing belt, returning the crankshaft (pulley notches) to the position described in Step 8 above. Install the camshaft aligning tool; it should slip into place as described in Step 10. If all is well, proceed to Step 26.

24 If one camshaft is only just out of line, install the forked holding tool to its sprocket, adjust its position as required, and check that any slack created has been taken up by the tensioner; rotate the crankshaft through two further turns clockwise, and install the camshaft aligning tool to check that it now fits as it should. If all is well, proceed to Step 26.

25 If either camshaft is significantly out of line, use the holding tool described in Step 18 above to prevent its sprocket from rotating while its retaining bolt is loosened - the camshaft can then be rotated (gently and carefully, using an open-ended wrench) until the camshaft aligning tool will slip into place; take care not to disturb the relationship of the sprocket to the timing belt. Without disturbing the sprocket's new position on the camshaft, tighten the sprocket bolt to its specified torque **(see illustration)**. Remove the camshaft aligning tool, rotate the crankshaft through two further turns clockwise and install the tool to check that it now fits as it should.

26 When the timing belt has been settled at its correct tension, and the camshaft aligning tool fits correctly when the crankshaft pulley notches are exactly aligned, tighten the tensioner bolt to its specified torque **(see illus-**

10.22 Loosen the tensioner bolt to give initial belt tension

10.25 Using a forked holding tool while the camshaft sprocket bolt is tightened

10.26 When the setting is correct, tighten the tensioner bolt to the torque listed in this Chapter's Specifications

11.3 Removing the timing belt tensioner

11.8 Note the FRONT marking on the outside face of the crankshaft sprocket - note which direction the round thrustwasher is facing

11.13 Tighten the timing belt guide pulley bolts to the torque listed in this Chapter's Specifications

tration). Installing the forked holding tool to the spokes of each sprocket in turn, check that the sprocket bolts are tightened to their specified torque. Remove the camshaft aligning tool, rotate the crankshaft through two further turns clockwise, and install the tool to make a final check that it fits as it should.

27 The remainder of the reassembly procedure is the reverse of removal, noting the following points:

(a) *Tighten all fasteners to the torque specified.*

(b) *When reassembling the engine/transaxle right-hand mount, replace the self-locking nuts, and don't allow the mount to twist as the middle two of the bracket's six nuts are tightened.*

11 Timing belt tensioner, sprockets and pulleys - removal, inspection and installation

Tensioner

Refer to illustration 11.3

Note: *If the tensioner is being removed for the first time since the vehicle left the factory, a tensioner spring and retaining pin must be obtained for installation on reassembly.*

1 While it is possible to reach the tensioner once the timing belt upper and middle covers only have been removed (see Section 9), the whole procedure outlined below must be followed, to ensure that the valve timing is correctly reset once the belt's tension has been disturbed.

2 Release the tension from the timing belt as described in Section 10, Steps 1 to 14.

3 Unscrew the tensioner bolt and remove the tensioner, unhooking the spring, if so installed **(see illustration)**. Check the tensioner and spring as described in Step 16 of Section 10.

4 On reassembly, if it is being installed for the first time, screw the timing belt tensioner spring retaining pin into the cylinder head, tightening it to the specified torque. Hook the spring onto the pin and the tensioner back plate, then install the tensioner, engaging its back plate on the locating peg.

5 Use an Allen key inserted into its center to rotate the tensioner clockwise as far as possible against spring tension, then tighten the bolt to secure the tensioner.

6 Reassemble, checking the camshaft alignment (valve timing) and setting the timing belt tension, as described in Steps 22 to 27 of Section 10.

Camshaft and crankshaft sprockets

Refer to illustration 11.8

7 While it may be possible to remove the sprockets once their respective covers have been removed, the complete timing belt removal/installation procedure (see Section 10) must be followed, to ensure that the valve timing is correctly reset once the belt's tension has been disturbed.

8 With the timing belt removed, the camshaft sprockets can be detached once their retaining bolts have been unscrewed as described in Steps 18 and 21 of Section 10. The crankshaft sprocket can be pulled off the end of the crankshaft once the crankshaft (grooved) pulley and the timing belt have been removed. Note the FRONT marking identifying the pulley's outboard face, and the thrustwasher behind it; note the direction the thrustwasher is installed **(see illustration)**. Note the pulley-locating Woodruff key; if this is loose, it should be removed for safe storage with the pulley.

9 Check the pulleys as described in Step 16 of Section 10.

10 Installation is the reverse of the removal procedure.

Timing belt idler pulleys

Refer to illustration 11.13

11 Remove the timing belt covers (see Section 9).

12 Unbolt and remove the pulley(s); check their condition as described in Step 16 of Section 10.

13 Installation is the reverse of the removal procedure; tighten the pulley bolts to the specified torque **(see illustration)**.

2A

12 Camshaft oil seals - replacement

Refer to illustrations 12.5 and 12.6

Note: *While it is possible to reach either oil seal, once the respective sprocket has been removed (see Section 11) to allow the seal to be pried out, this procedure isn't recommended. Not only are the seals very soft, making this difficult to do without risk of damage to the seal housing, but it would be very difficult to ensure that the valve timing and the timing belt's tension, once disturbed, are correctly reset. Owners are advised to follow the whole procedure outlined below.*

1 Release the tension from the timing belt as described in Section 10, Steps 1 to 14. **Note**: *If the timing belt is found to be contaminated by oil, remove it completely as described, then replace the oil seal (see below). Wash down the engine timing belt area and all related components, to remove all traces of oil. Install a new belt on reassembly.*

2 If the timing belt is still clean, slip it off the sprocket, taking care not to twist it too sharply; use your fingers only to handle the belt. *Don't* rotate the crankshaft until the timing belt is reinstalled. Cover the belt, and secure it so that it is clear of the working area and cannot slip off the remaining sprocket.

3 Unfasten the sprocket bolt and remove the sprocket (see Section 11).

4 On 1995 through 1997 models, unbolt the camshaft bearing caps, and remove the defective oil seals. Clean the seal bores and polish off any burrs or sharp edges. On 1998 models, the camshaft front bearing cap is one piece for both camshafts. Remove the four bolts securing the cap and remove the seals. Clean the seal bores and polish off any burrs or sharp edges.

5 To install a new seal with the camshaft bearing cap in place, use a socket with an outside diameter slightly smaller than that of

12.5 Using a socket and a sprocket bolt to install the camshaft oil seal

12.6 Alternatively, install the seal when the camshaft bearing cap is unbolted

the seal bore and the sprocket bolt **(see illustration)**. Grease the seal lips and periphery to ease installation, and draw the seal into place until it is flush with the housing/bearing cap outer edge. Install the bearing cap, using sealant and tightening the cap bolts as described in Section 13.

6 For most owners, the simplest answer will be to grease the seal lips, and to slide it onto the camshaft (until it is flush with the housing's outer edge). Install the bearing cap, using sealant and tightening the cap bolts as described in Section 13 **(see illustration)**. Take care to ensure that the seal remains absolutely square in its housing, and isn't distorted as the cap is tightened down.

7 Install the sprocket to the camshaft, tightening the retaining bolt loosely, then slip the timing belt back onto the sprocket (refer to Steps 18 and 21 of Section 10) and tighten the bolt securely.

8 The remainder of the reassembly procedure, including checking the camshaft alignment (valve timing) and setting the timing belt tension, is as described in Steps 22 to 27 of Section 10.

13.3 Using a forked holding tool while the camshaft sprocket bolt is loosened

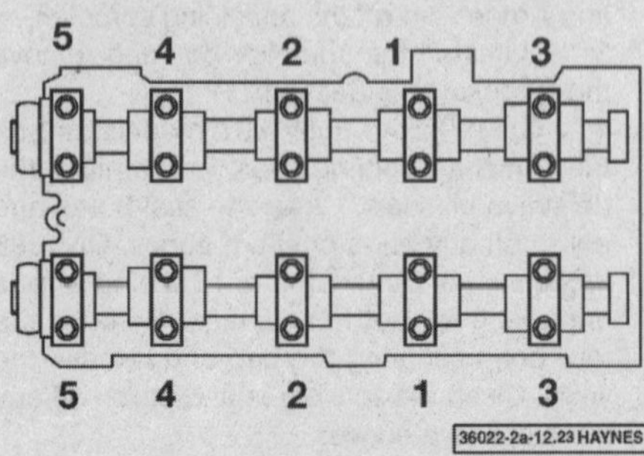

13.4 Camshaft bearing cap loosening sequence

13 Camshafts and lifters - removal, inspection and installation

Removal

Refer to illustrations 13.3, 13.4, 13.5a, 13.5b, 13.6a and 13.6b

1 Release the tension from the timing belt as described in Section 10, Steps 1 to 14.

2 Either remove the timing belt completely (Section 10, Steps 15 and 16) or slip it off the camshaft sprockets, taking care not to twist it too sharply; use the fingers only to handle the belt. Cover the belt, and secure it so that it is clear of the working area. *Don't* rotate the crankshaft until the timing belt is reinstalled.

3 Remove the sprocket bolts as described in Section 10, Steps 18 and 21, and remove the sprockets. Keep the sprockets separate; it is good working practice to mark them so that each is reinstalled only to its original location **(see illustration)**.

4 Working in the sequence shown, loosen progressively, by half a turn at a time, the camshaft bearing cap bolts **(see illustration)**. Work only as described, to release gradually and evenly the pressure of the valve springs on the caps.

5 Remove the caps, noting their markings and the presence of the locating dowels. On 1998 models, remove the two bolts (located on the sprocket end of the engine) from the oil feed flange then remove the camshafts and remove their oil seals. On 1998 models, the oil feed flange is removed along with the exhaust camshaft. The intake camshaft can be identified by the reference lobe for the camshaft position sensor; therefore, there is no need to mark the camshafts **(see illustrations)**.

6 Obtain sixteen small, clean containers, and number them 1 to 16. Using a suction cup, remove each hydraulic lifter in turn, invert it to prevent oil loss, and place it in its respective container, which should then be filled with clean engine oil **(see illustrations)**. Don't interchange the lifters, or the rate of wear will be much increased. Don't allow them to lose oil, or they will take a long time to refill on restarting the engine, resulting in incorrect valve clearances.

Inspection

Refer to illustrations 13.8, 13.10, 13.12, 13.13a and 13.13b

7 With the camshafts and lifters removed, check each for signs of obvious wear (scoring, pitting, etc.) and for out-of-round, and replace if necessary.

13.5a Note the locating dowels when removing the camshaft bearing caps

13.5b The intake camshaft has a lobe for the camshaft position sensor

13.6a Removing the lifters

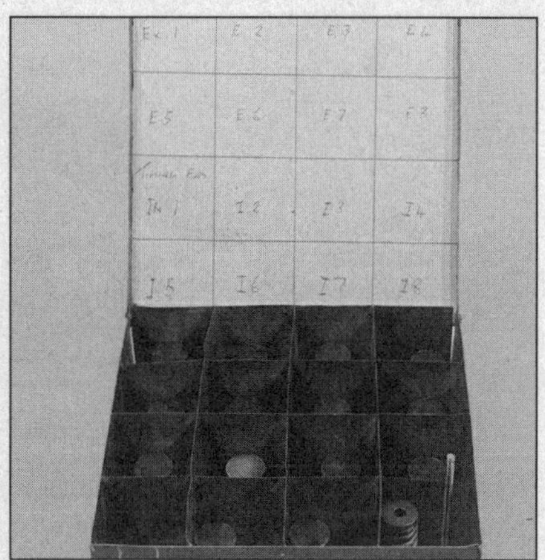
13.6b The hydraulic lifters must be stored as described in the text

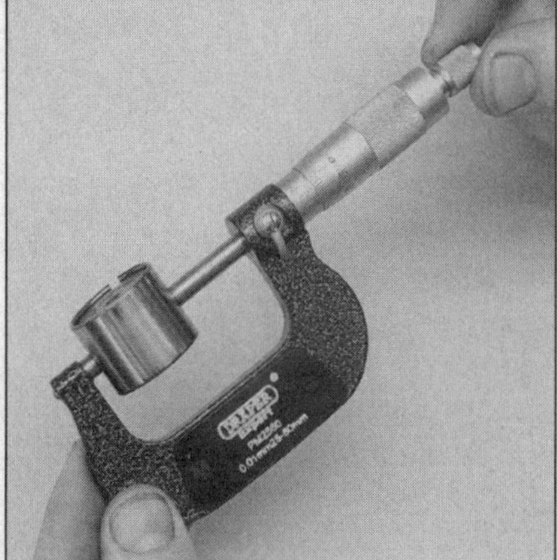
13.8 Use a micrometer to measure the diameter of the lifters

13.10 Check the cam lobes for pitting, wear and score marks - if scoring is excessive, as is the case here, replace the camshaft

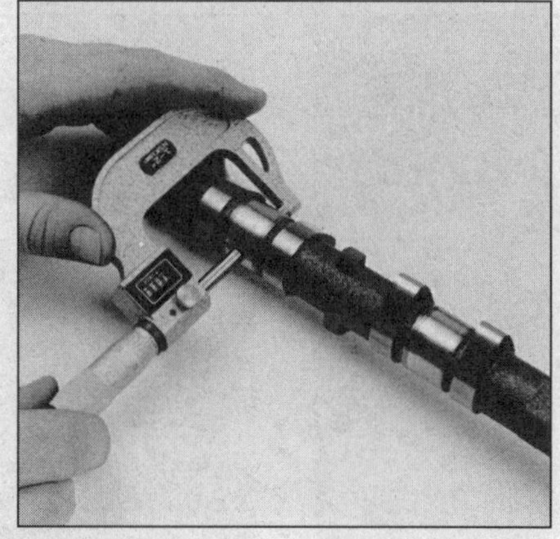
13.12 Measure each journal diameter with a micrometer - if any journal measures less than the specified limit, replace the camshaft

13.13a Lay a strip of Plastigage on each camshaft journal

8 Measure the outside diameter of each lifter **(see illustration)** - take measurements at the top and bottom of each lifter, then a second set at right-angles to the first; if any measurement is significantly different from the others, the lifter is tapered or oval (as applicable) and must be replaced. If the necessary equipment is available, measure the inside diameter of the corresponding cylinder head bore. Compare the measurements obtained to those given in the Specifications Section of this Chapter; if the lifters or the cylinder head bores are excessively worn, new lifters and/or a new cylinder head will be required.

9 On 1997 and earlier models, if the engine's valve components have sounded noisy, particularly if the noise persists after initial start-up from cold, there is reason to suspect a faulty hydraulic lifter. Only a good mechanic experienced in these engines can tell whether the noise level is typical, or if replacement of one or more of the lifters is warranted. If faulty lifters are diagnosed, and the engine's service history is unknown, it is always worth trying the effect of replacing the engine oil and filter (see Chapter 1), using *only* good-quality engine oil of the recommended viscosity and specification, before going to the expense of replacing any of the lifters.

10 Visually examine the camshaft lobes for score marks, pitting, galling (wear due to rubbing) and evidence of overheating (blue, discolored areas). Look for flaking away of the hardened surface layer of each lobe **(see illustration)**. If any such signs are evident, replace the component concerned.

11 Examine the camshaft bearing journals and the cylinder head bearing surfaces for signs of obvious wear or pitting. If any such signs are evident, replace the component concerned.

12 Using a micrometer, measure the diameter of each journal at several points **(see illustration)**. If the diameter of any one journal is less than the specified value, replace the camshaft.

13 To check the bearing journal running clearance, remove the hydraulic lifters, use a suitable solvent and a clean lint-free rag to clean all bearing surfaces, then install the camshafts and bearing caps with a strand of Plastigage across each journal **(see illustration)**. Tighten the bearing cap bolts to the specified torque (don't rotate the camshafts),

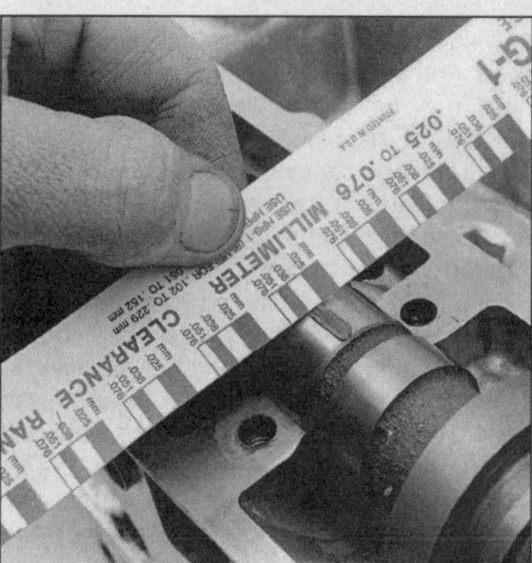

13.13b Compare the width of the crushed Plastigage to the scale on the envelope to determine the oil clearance

then remove the bearing caps and use the scale provided to measure the width of the compressed strands **(see illustration)**. Scrape off the Plastigage with your fingernail or the edge of a credit card - don't scratch or nick the journals or bearing caps.

14 If the running clearance of any bearing is found to be worn to beyond the specified

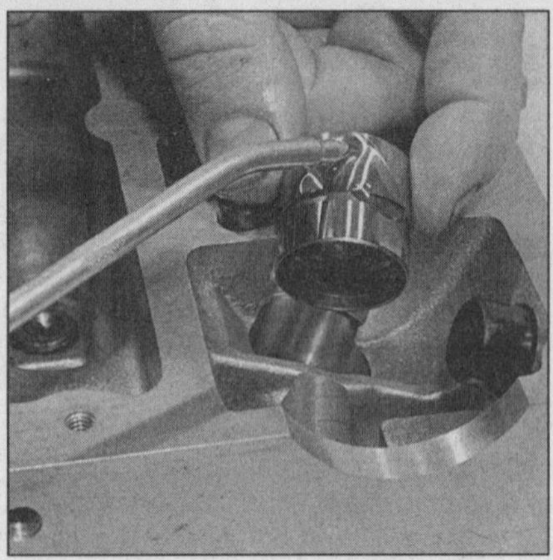
13.17 Oil the lifters liberally

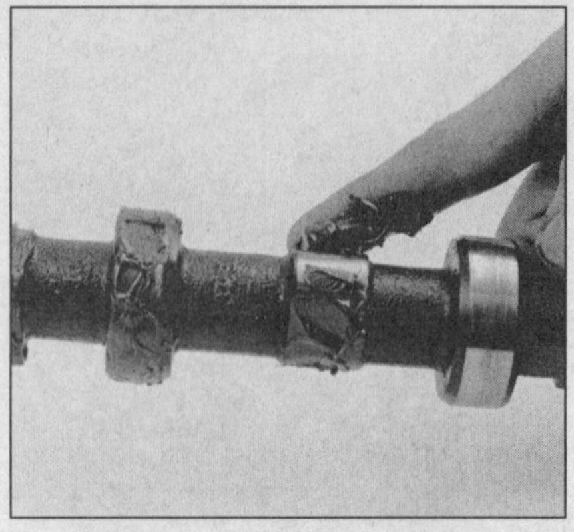
13.18a Apply camshaft installation lubricant or molybdenum disulfide-based grease to the cam lobes and journals before installing a camshaft

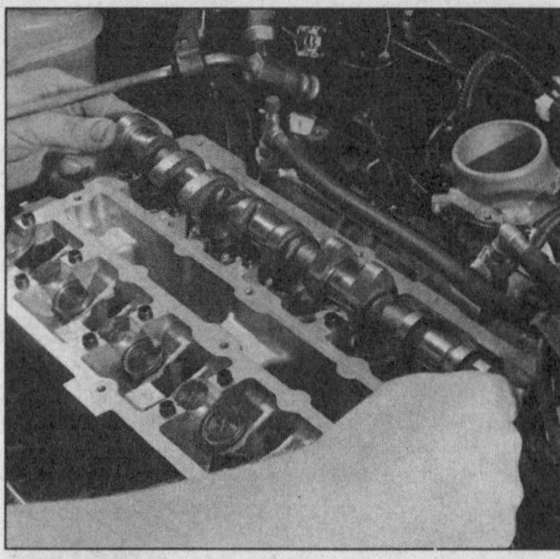
13.18b The intake camshaft has a camshaft position sensor lobe, which will identify it during installation

13.19 Apply sealant to the mating surface of the camshaft right-hand bearing caps

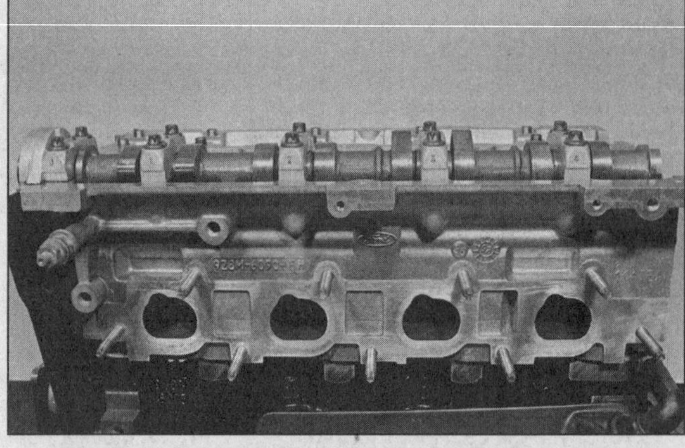
13.20 Etched marks on the camshaft bearing caps must be arranged as shown, and face out

service limits, and the camshaft journal diameters are within specifications, the cylinder head may have to be replaced. Consult an automotive machine shop for advice.

15 To check camshaft endplay, remove the lifters, clean the bearing surfaces carefully, and install the camshafts and bearing caps. Tighten the bearing cap bolts to the specified torque, then measure the endplay using a dial gauge mounted on the cylinder head so that its tip rests on the camshaft right-hand end.

16 Tap the camshaft fully towards the gauge, zero the gauge, then tap the camshaft fully away from the gauge and note the gauge reading. If the endplay measured is found to be at or beyond the specified service limit, install a new camshaft and repeat the check; if the clearance is still excessive, the cylinder head must be replaced.

Installation

Refer to illustrations 13.17, 13.18a, 13.18b, 13.19, 13.20, 13.21a, 13.21b and 13.21c

17 On reassembly, liberally oil the cylinder head lifter bores and the lifters **(see illustration)**. Note that if new lifters are being installed, they must be filled with clean engine oil before installation. Carefully install the lifters in the cylinder head, ensuring that each lifter is reinstalled in its original bore, and is the correct way up. Some care will be required to install the lifters squarely into their bores.

18 Liberally lubricate the camshaft bearings and lobes **(see illustration)**. On 1998 models, place a new gasket into the oil feed flange and install the oil feed flange on the exhaust camshaft. The oil feed flange must face up with its oil feed hole at the top and its locating tab positioned parallel to the camshaft. Ensuring that each camshaft is in its original location, install the camshafts, locating each so that the slot in its left-hand end is approximately parallel to, and just above, the cylinder head mating surface **(see illustration)**.

19 Ensure that the locating dowels are pressed firmly into their recesses, and check that all mating surfaces are completely clean, unmarked and free from oil. Apply a thin film of suitable sealant (the manufacturer recommends Loctite 518) to the mating surfaces of each camshaft's right-side bearing cap **(see illustration)**. Referring to Step 6 of Section 12, some owners may wish to install the new camshaft oil seals at this stage.

20 All camshaft bearing caps have a single-digit identifying number etched on them **(see illustration)**. The exhaust camshaft's bearing caps are numbered in sequence 0 (right-hand cap) to 4 (left-hand cap), the intake's 5 (right-hand cap) to 9 (left-hand cap); see **illustration 13.21b** for details. Each cap is to be installed so that its numbered side faces outward, to the front (exhaust) or to the rear (intake).

13.21a Keep the caps square to the cylinder head at all times when tightening them

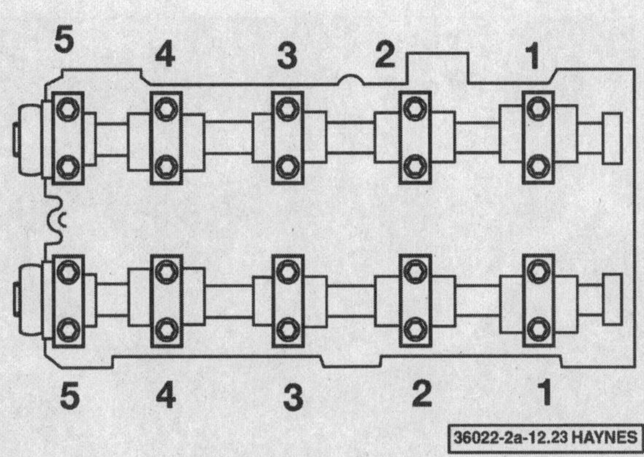

13.21b Camshaft bearing cap tightening sequence. Locate bearing caps according to etched numbers, aligned as described in text

13.21c Install the camshaft aligning tool to set TDC position

21 Ensuring that each cap is kept square to the cylinder head as it is tightened down, and working in the sequence shown, tighten the camshaft bearing cap bolts slowly and by one turn at a time, until each cap touches the cylinder head **(see illustrations)**. Next, go around again in the same sequence, tightening the bolts to the first stage torque specified, then once more, tightening them to the second stage setting. Work only as described, to impose gradually and evenly the pressure of the valve springs on the caps. Install the camshaft aligning tool; it should slip into place as described in Step 10 of Section 10 **(see illustration)**.

22 Wipe off all surplus sealant, so that none is left to find its way into any oilways. Follow the sealant manufacturer's instructions as to the time needed for curing; usually, at least an hour must be allowed between application of the sealant and starting the engine.

23 Install new oil seals to the camshafts as described in Step 5 of Section 12.

24 Using the marks and notes made on disassembly to ensure that each is reinstalled to its original camshaft, install the sprockets to the camshafts, tightening the retaining bolts loosely. Slip the timing belt back onto the pulleys (refer to Step 21 of Section 10) and tighten the bolts securely - use the forked holding tool described in Step 18 of Section 10.

25 The remainder of the reassembly procedure, including checking the camshaft alignment (valve timing) and setting the timing belt tension, is as described in Steps 17 to 27 of Section 10.

14 Cylinder head - removal and installation

Removal

Refer to illustrations 14.8a, 14.8b, 14.9, 14.13, 14.17, 14.18a, 14.18b and 14.22

Note: *The following text assumes that the cylinder head will be removed with both intake and exhaust manifolds attached; this simplifies the procedure, but makes it a bulky and heavy assembly to handle - an engine hoist will be required, to prevent the risk of injury, and to prevent damage to any delicate components as the assembly is removed and installed. If it is wished first to remove the manifolds, proceed as described in Sections 6 and 7 of this Chapter; amend the following procedure accordingly.*

1 Relieve the fuel system pressure (see Chapter 4).

2 With the vehicle parked on firm level ground, open the hood and disconnect the battery negative cable - see Chapter 5, Section 1.

3 Whenever you disconnect any vacuum lines, coolant and emissions hoses, wiring harness connectors, ground straps and fuel lines as part of the following procedure, always label them clearly, so that they can be correctly reassembled. Masking tape and/or a touch-up paint applicator work well for marking items. Take instant photos, or sketch the locations of components and brackets.

4 Disconnect the two electrical connectors, the vacuum hose (if so equipped) and the crankcase breather hose from the valve cover, then remove the complete air cleaner assembly with the mass airflow sensor, the resonator and the plenum chamber (see Chapter 4).

5 Equalize the pressure in the fuel tank by removing the filler cap, then undo the fuel feed and return lines connecting the engine to the chassis (see Chapter 4). Plug or cap all open fittings.

6 Disconnect the accelerator cable from the throttle linkage as described in Chapter 4 - if so equipped, disconnect also the cruise control actuator cable (see Chapter 12). Secure the cable(s) clear of the engine/transaxle.

7 Unbolt the power steering high-pressure tube from the cylinder head rear support plate/engine lifting eye, and from the front support plate/pump bracket. Releasing its wire clip, disconnect the power steering pressure switch electrical connector, then unbolt the ground lead from the cylinder head rear support plate/engine lifting eye.

8 Remove the three screws securing the wiring rail to the rear of the manifold. Releasing its wire clip, remove the large electrical connector (next to the fuel pressure regulator) to disconnect the engine wiring from the main harness **(see illustration)**. Remove the electrical connectors on each side of the ignition coil, and the single connector from beneath the front of the thermostat housing, to disconnect the coil and coolant temperature

14.8a Release the wire clip to disconnect the engine wiring harness connector from the intake manifold

14.8b Disconnect the ignition coil wire connectors (arrows)

14.9 Disconnect the vacuum hoses (arrows) as described in text

14.13 Disconnect all coolant hoses (arrows) from the thermostat housing

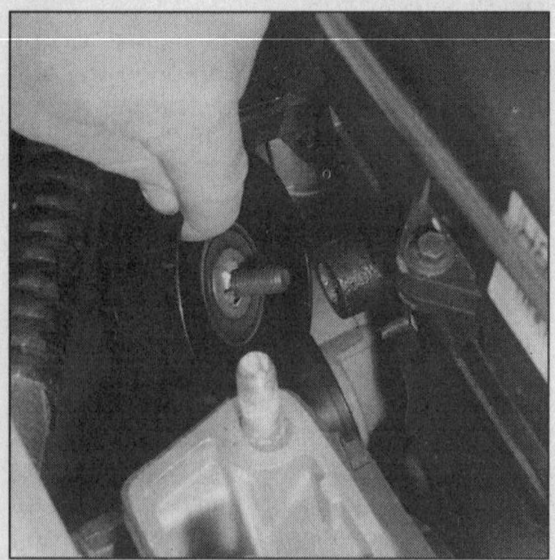

14.17 Unbolt the drivebelt idler pulley

14.18a Remove the cylinder head front . . .

14.18b . . . and rear support plates

gauge sending unit wiring **(see illustration)**.

9 Marking or labeling them as they are detached, disconnect the vacuum hoses as follows:

(a) *One from the rear of the throttle housing (only the one hose - there is no need to disconnect the second hose running to the fuel pressure regulator).*
(b) *One from the union on the intake manifold's left end* **(see illustration)**.
(c) *The power brake booster hose (see Chapter 9 for details).*
(d) *Disconnect all vacuum hoses from the Exhaust Gas Recirculation system components - one from the EGR valve and two from the EGR tube. (Note that these last two are of different sizes, as are their tube stubs, so they can only be connected the correct way.)*

10 Unbolt both parts of the exhaust manifold heat shield; unclip the coolant hose to allow the upper part to be removed. Either remove the dipstick and tube, or swing them out of the way.

11 Unscrew the single bolt securing the pulse-air filter housing to the engine/transaxle front mount bracket, then disconnect its vacuum hose.

12 Drain the cooling system (see Chapter 1).

13 Disconnect all coolant hoses from the thermostat housing **(see illustration)**.

14 Unscrew the two nuts to disconnect the exhaust system front pipe from the manifold (Chapter 4); disconnect the oxygen sensor wiring so that it isn't strained by the weight of the exhaust system.

15 Remove the drivebelt (see Chapter 1).

16 Support the weight of the engine/transaxle using a floor jack, with a wooden spacer to prevent damage to the oil pan.

17 Unscrew the six nuts securing the engine/transaxle right-hand mount bracket, then remove the bracket. Unbolt the drivebelt's idler pulley **(see illustration)**.

18 Unbolt the cylinder head front and rear support plates **(see illustrations)**.

19 Remove the timing belt and both camshafts (see Sections 10 and 13); if the cylinder head is to be disassembled, remove the hydraulic lifters.

20 Remove the timing belt inner shield (see Section 9).

21 Working in the *reverse* of the sequence shown in illustration 14.32c, loosen the ten cylinder head bolts progressively and by one turn at a time; a Torx bit (TX 55 size) will be required. Remove each bolt in turn, and ensure that new replacements are obtained for reassembly; these bolts are subjected to severe stresses and so must be replaced, regardless of their apparent condition, whenever they are disturbed.

22 Lift the cylinder head away; use assistance if possible, as it is a heavy assembly **(see illustration)**. Remove the gasket, noting the two dowels, and discard it.

Installation

Refer to illustrations 14.27, 14.30, 14.32a, 14.32b and 14.32c

23 The mating faces of the cylinder head and cylinder block must be perfectly clean before installing the head. Use a hard plastic or wood scraper to remove all traces of gasket and carbon; also clean the piston crowns. Take particular care, as the soft aluminum alloy is easily damaged. Also, make sure that the carbon isn't allowed to enter the oil and water passages - this is particularly important for the lubrication system, as carbon could block the oil supply to any of the engine's components. Using adhesive tape and paper, seal the water, oil and bolt holes in the cylinder block. Clean all the pistons in the same way. To prevent carbon entering the gap between the pistons and bores, smear a little

14.22 Using an engine hoist to lift off the cylinder head complete with the manifolds

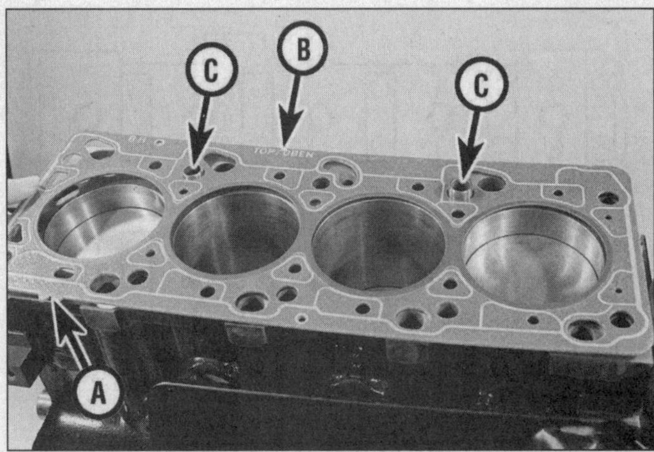

14.27 Ensuring the protruding tooth - or teeth - (A) are at the front and the marking (B) is facing up, locate the new cylinder head gasket on the dowels (C)

14.30 Installing the cylinder head - note the fabricated guide studs (arrows)

14.32a Tightening the cylinder head bolts (to the first and second stages) using a torque wrench . . .

grease in the gap. After cleaning each piston, use a small brush to remove all traces of grease and carbon from the gap, then wipe away the remainder with a clean rag.

24 Check the mating surfaces of the cylinder block and the cylinder head for nicks, deep scratches and other damage. If slight, they may be removed carefully with a file, but if excessive, machining may be the only alternative to replacement.

25 If warpage of the cylinder head gasket surface is suspected, use a straight edge to check it for distortion. Refer to Part C of this Chapter, Section 7, if necessary.

26 Wipe clean the mating surfaces of the cylinder head and cylinder block. Check that the two locating dowels are in position in the cylinder block, and that all cylinder head bolt holes are free from oil.

27 Position a new gasket over the dowels on the cylinder block surface, so that the TOP/OBEN mark is uppermost, and the tooth (or teeth, according to engine size) protruding from one edge point to the front of the vehicle **(see illustration)**.

28 Temporarily install the crankshaft pulley, and rotate the crankshaft counterclockwise so that No 1 cylinder's piston is lowered to approximately 13/16-inch before TDC, thus avoiding any risk of valve/piston contact and damage during reassembly.

29 As the cylinder head is such a heavy and awkward assembly to install with manifolds, it is helpful to make up a pair of guide studs from two 10 mm (thread size) studs approximately 3.5 inches long, with a screwdriver slot cut in one end - two old cylinder head bolts with their heads cut off would make a good starting point. Screw these guide studs, screwdriver slot upward, to permit removal, into the bolt holes at diagonally opposite corners of the cylinder block surface (or into those where the locating dowels are installed, as shown); ensure that approximately 2-3/4 inches of stud protrudes above the gasket.

30 Install the cylinder head, sliding it down the guide studs (if used) and locating it on the dowels **(see illustration)**. Unscrew the guide studs (if used) when the head is in place.

31 Install the new cylinder head bolts dry (*don't oil* their threads); carefully enter each into its hole and screw it in, by hand only, until finger-tight.

32 Working progressively and in the sequence shown, use first a torque wrench, then an ordinary socket extension bar and an angle gauge, to tighten the cylinder head bolts in the stages given in the Specifications Section of this Chapter **(see illustrations)**. **Note**: *Once tightened correctly, following this procedure, the cylinder head bolts don't require check-tightening, and must not be re-torqued.*

14.32b . . . and to the third stage using an angle gauge

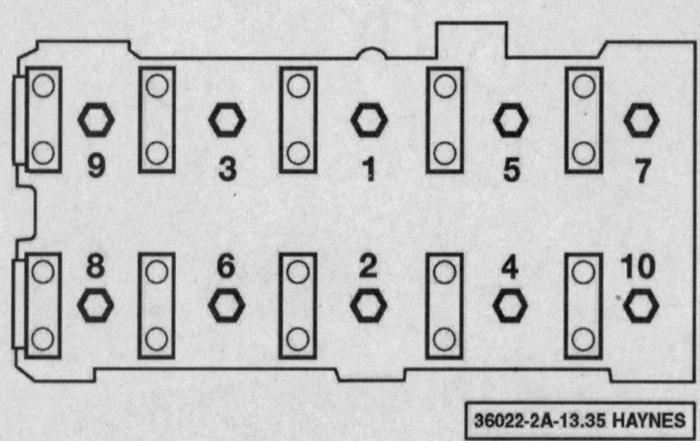

14.32c Cylinder head bolt tightening sequence

15.12 Equipment must be available to raise and support the engine/transaxle unit while the vehicle is raised, to allow oil pan removal

33 Install the hydraulic lifters (if removed), the camshafts, their oil seals and pulleys (see Sections 10, 11, 12 and 13, as appropriate). Temporarily install the crankshaft pulley, and rotate the crankshaft clockwise to return the pulley notches to the position described in Step 8 of Section 10.

34 Install the timing belt and covers, checking the camshaft alignment (valve timing) and setting the timing belt tension, as described in Section 10.

35 The remainder of reassembly is the reverse of the removal procedure, noting the following points:

(a) *Tighten all fasteners to the torque listed in this Chapter's Specifications.*

(b) *When reassembling the engine/transaxle right-hand mount, replace the self-locking nuts, and don't allow the mount to twist as the middle two of the bracket's six nuts are tightened.*

(c) *Refill the cooling system, and top-up the engine oil.*

(d) *Check all disturbed joints for signs of oil or coolant leakage, once the engine has been restarted and warmed-up to normal operating temperature.*

15 Oil pan - removal and installation

Removal

Refer to illustration 15.12

Note 1: *To perform this task with the engine/transaxle installed in the vehicle requires the assistance of at least one person, plus the equipment necessary to raise and support the front of the vehicle (high enough that the oil pan can be removed from underneath), and to lift and support the complete engine/transaxle unit 2 to 3 inches from its mounts while the vehicle is raised. Precise details of the procedure will depend on the equipment available - the following is typical.*

Note 2: *The full procedure outlined below must be followed, so that the mating surfaces can be cleaned and prepared to achieve an oil-tight joint on reassembly, and so that the oil pan can be aligned correctly; depending on your skill and experience, and the tools and facilities available, it may be that this task can be performed only with the engine removed from the vehicle.*

Note 3: *The oil pan gasket must be replaced whenever it is disturbed.*

1 With the vehicle parked on firm level ground, open the hood and disconnect the battery negative cable - see Chapter 5, Section 1.

2 Drain the engine oil, then clean and install the engine oil drain plug, tightening it to the specified torque. Although not strictly necessary as part of the disassembly procedure, owners are advised to remove and discard the oil filter, so that it can be replaced with the oil (see Chapter 1).

3 Drain the cooling system (see Chapter 1).

4 Disconnect the radiator bottom hose from the radiator union and from the (heater) coolant tube. Unbolt the coolant tube from the oil pan; if they will prevent oil pan removal, disconnect or release the coolant hoses from the oil cooler unions (if so equipped).

5 Unscrew the two bolts securing the power steering system tubes to the right-hand side of the subframe.

6 Remove the electrical connector(s) to disconnect the oxygen sensor and, if so equipped, the oil level sensor wiring - unclip the connectors to release the wiring where necessary.

7 If the vehicle is equipped with automatic transaxle, trace the fluid cooler lines from the transaxle to the radiator, and release them from any clips etc., so that they have as much movement as possible.

8 Remove the drivebelt cover (see Chapter 1).

9 Unscrew the nuts to disconnect the exhaust system front pipe from the manifold, then either unhook all the system's rubber mounts and remove the complete exhaust system from under the vehicle, or remove only the exhaust pipe/catalytic converter (see Chapter 4 for details).

10 Unscrew the oil pan-to-transaxle bolts, also any securing the engine/transaxle lower adapter plate.

11 Disconnect the two electrical connectors, the vacuum hose (if so equipped) and the crankcase breather hose from the valve cover, then remove the complete air cleaner assembly with the mass airflow sensor, the resonator and the plenum chamber (see Chapter 4).

12 Take the weight of the engine/transaxle unit using the lifting eyes provided on the cylinder head; bolt on additional lifting eyes where required **(see illustration)**. Remove completely the engine/transaxle front mount, unscrew the rear mount's center bolt, and unbolt the left-hand mount from the body. Unscrew the six nuts securing the right-hand mount bracket, and withdraw the bracket.

13 Being careful to watch the wiring, coolant hoses, fluid cooler tubes or gearshift linkage and transaxle support rods (where appropriate), and the radiator electric cooling fan, to ensure that nothing is trapped, stretched or damaged, lift the engine/transaxle unit by 2 to 3 inches and support it securely.

14 Progressively unscrew the oil pan retaining bolts. Break the oil pan loose by striking the oil pan with the palm of your hand or a rubber mallet, then lower the oil pan and remove it with the engine/transaxle lower adapter plate; note the presence of any shims between the oil pan and transaxle.

15 Remove and discard the oil pan gasket; this must be replaced as a matter of course whenever it is disturbed.

16 While the oil pan is removed, take the opportunity to remove the oil pump pick-up/strainer tube and to clean it (see Section 16).

Installation

Refer to illustrations 15.17, 15.18, 15.19a and 15.19b

17 On reassembly, thoroughly clean and degrease the mating surfaces of the cylinder block and oil pan, then use a clean rag to wipe out the oil pan and the engine's interior.

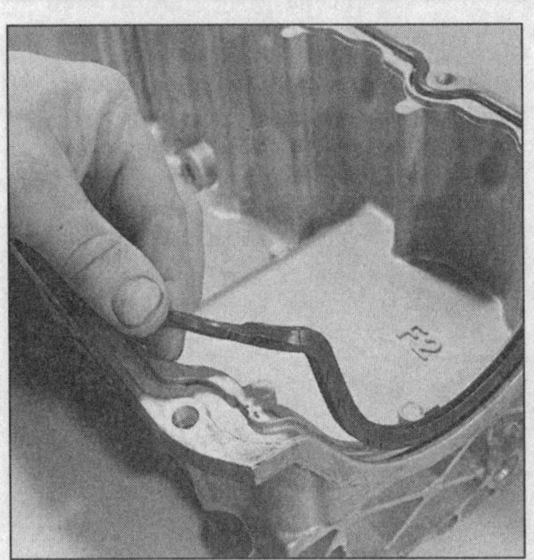
15.17 Ensure the gasket is located correctly in the oil pan groove

15.18 The engine/transaxle lower adapter plate must be installed with the oil pan

15.19a When installing the oil pan, apply sealant to the rear corners (arrow)

If the oil pump pick-up/strainer tube was removed, install a new gasket and install the tube, tightening its screws to the specified torque. Install the new gasket to the oil pan mating surface so that the gasket fits into the oil pan groove **(see illustration).**

18 If the oil pan is being installed with the engine/transaxle still connected and in the vehicle, proceed as follows:

(a) *Check that the mating surfaces of the oil pan, the cylinder block and the transaxle are absolutely clean. Any shims found on removal of the oil pan must be installed in their original locations.*

b) *Apply a thin film of sealant (the manufacturer recommends Hylosil 102) to the junctions of the cylinder block with the oil pump and the crankshaft rear main oil seal carrier. Immediately install the pan and tighten the oil pan bolts, lightly at first* **(see illustration).**

(c) *Ensuring that the engine/transaxle lower adapter plate is correctly located, firmly press the oil pan against the transaxle, and tighten the transaxle-to-oil pan (i.e., engine) bolts to the specified torque.*

(d) *Without disturbing the position of the oil pan, and working in a diagonal sequence from the center out, tighten the oil pan bolts to the specified torque.*

(e) *Proceed to Step 20.*

19 If the oil pan is being installed with the engine and transaxle separated (in or out of the vehicle), proceed as follows:

(a) *Apply a thin film of sealant (the manufacturer recommends Hylosil 102) to the junctions of the cylinder block rear main with the oil pump and the crankshaft rear main oil seal carrier* **(see illustration).** *Immediately install the pan and tighten the oil pan bolts, lightly at first* **(see illustration).**

(b) *Using a suitable straight edge to check alignment across the flat-machined faces of each, move the oil pan as necessary so that its left-hand face - including any shims found on removal - is flush with that of the cylinder block* **(see illustration).** *Without disturbing the position of the oil pan, and working in a diagonal sequence from the center outwards, tighten the oil pan bolts to the specified torque.*

15.19b Checking alignment of the oil pan to the cylinder block

(c) *Check again that both faces are flush before proceeding; if necessary, unbolt the oil pan again, clean the mating surfaces, and repeat the full procedure to ensure that the oil pan is correctly aligned.*

(d) *If it isn't possible to achieve exact alignment by moving the oil pan, shims are available in thickness of 0.25 mm (color-coded yellow) or 0.50 mm (color-coded black) to eliminate the discrepancy.*

20 The remainder of reassembly is the reverse of the removal procedure, noting the following points.

(a) *Tighten all fasteners to the torque listed in this Chapter's Specifications.*

(b) *Always replace any self-locking nuts disturbed on removal.*

(c) *Lower the engine/transaxle unit into place, and reassemble the rear, left-hand and right-hand mounts. Don't yet release the hoist; the weight of the engine/transaxle unit must not be taken by the mounts until all are correctly aligned.*

(d) *Refer to Part C, Section 4 of this Chapter for the transaxle mount installation procedure.*

(e) *Refill the cooling system (see Chapter 1).*

(f) *Refill the engine with oil, remembering that you are advised to install a new filter (see Chapter 1).*

(g) *Check for signs of oil or coolant leaks once the engine has been restarted and warmed-up to normal operating temperature.*

16 Oil pump - removal, inspection and installation

Removal

Refer to illustration 16.5

Note: *While this task is possible when the engine is in place in the vehicle, in practice, it requires so much preliminary disassembly, and is so difficult to perform due to the*

16.5 Unscrew the bolts (arrows) to remove the oil pump

16.6 Removing the oil pump inner rotor

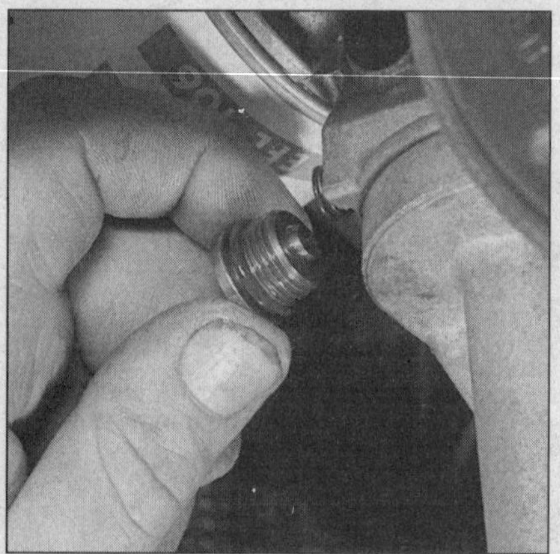

16.9a Unscrew the threaded plug - seen through the right-hand wheel inner fender . . .

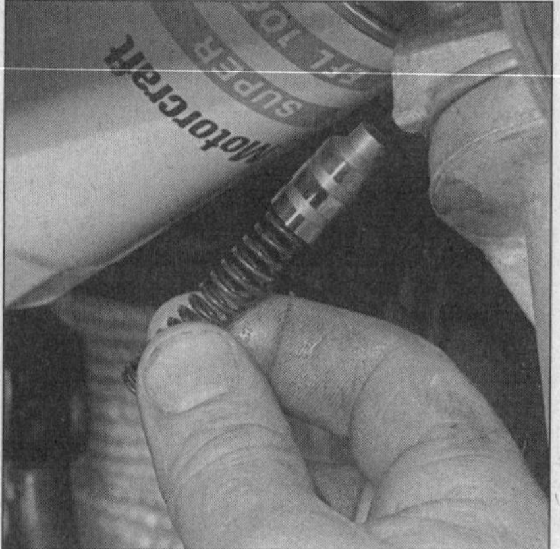

16.9b . . . to remove the oil pressure relief valve spring and plunger

16.12 Use a new gasket when installing the oil pump

restricted access, that owners are advised to remove the engine from the vehicle first. Note, however, that the oil pump pressure relief valve can be removed with the engine in place.

1 Remove the timing belt (see Section 10).

2 Remove the crankshaft sprocket and the thrust washer behind it, noting which way the thrust washer is installed (see Section 11).

3 Remove the oil pan (see Section 15).

4 Remove the screws securing the oil pump pick-up/strainer tube to the pump, then unscrew the nut and withdraw the oil pump pick-up/strainer tube. Discard the gasket.

5 Unbolt the pump from the cylinder block **(see illustration)**. Remove and discard the gasket, and remove the crankshaft right-hand oil seal. Thoroughly clean and degrease all components, particularly the mating surfaces of the pump, the oil pan, and the cylinder block.

Inspection

Refer to illustrations 16.6, 16.9a and 16.9b

6 Unscrew the Torx screws, and remove the pump cover plate; noting any identification marks on the rotors, remove the rotors **(see illustration)**.

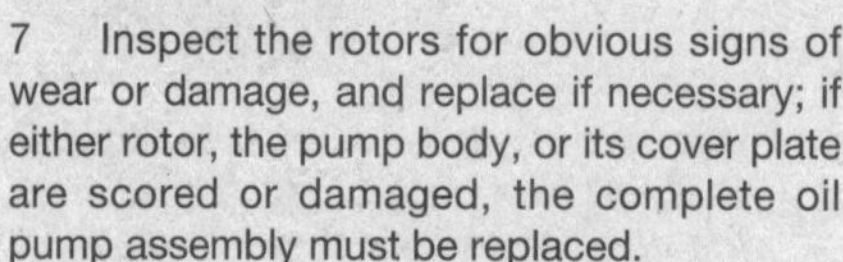

7 Inspect the rotors for obvious signs of wear or damage, and replace if necessary; if either rotor, the pump body, or its cover plate are scored or damaged, the complete oil pump assembly must be replaced.

8 The oil pressure relief valve can be disassembled, if required, without disturbing the pump. With the vehicle parked on firm level ground, apply the parking brake securely and raise its front end, supporting it securely on jackstands. Remove the front right-hand wheel and drivebelt cover (see Chapter 1) to provide access to the valve.

9 Unscrew the threaded plug, and recover the valve spring and plunger **(see illustrations)**. If the plug's sealing O-ring is worn or damaged, a new one must be obtained, to be installed on reassembly.

10 Reassembly is the reverse of the disassembly procedure; ensure the spring and valve are installed the correct way round, and tighten the threaded plug securely.

Installation

Refer to illustrations 16.12, 16.13 and 16.16

11 The oil pump must be primed on installation, by pouring clean engine oil into it, and rotating its inner rotor a few turns.

12 Using grease to stick the new gasket in place on the cylinder block/crankcase, and rotating the pump's inner rotor to align with the flats on the crankshaft, install the pump and insert the bolts, tightening them lightly at first **(see illustration)**.

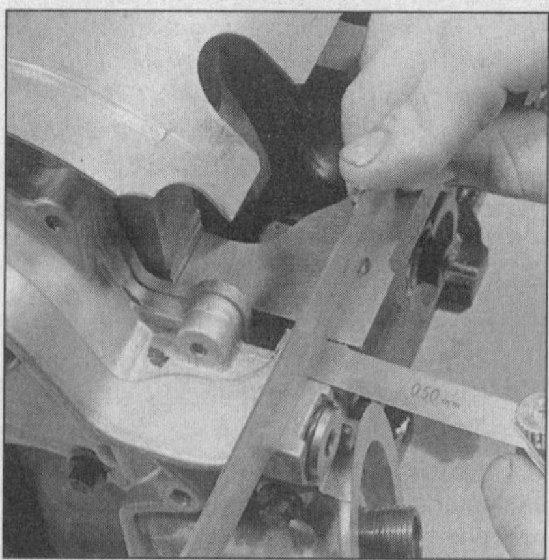

16.13 Check that the oil pump is positioned correctly

13 Using a suitable straight edge and feeler gauges, check that the pump is both centered *exactly* around the crankshaft, and aligned squarely so that its (oil pan) mating

16.16 Use a new gasket when installing the oil pick-up tube to the pump

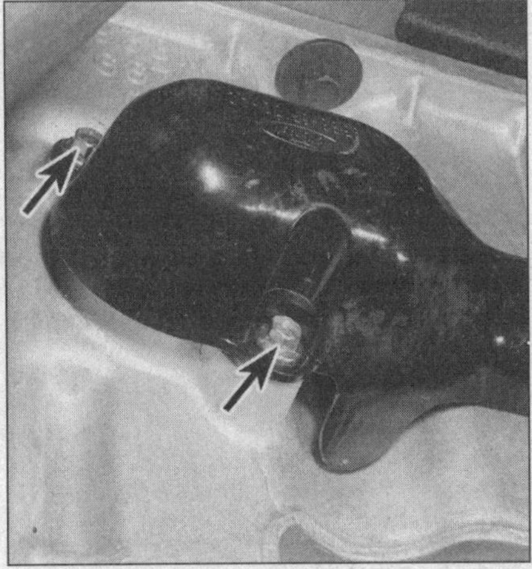
18.3 Remove the screws (arrows) to remove oil level sensor cover . . .

18.4 . . . then disconnect the wires from the sensor

surface is exactly the same amount - between 0.012 and 0.031 inch - below that of the cylinder block/crankcase on each side of the crankshaft. Being careful not to disturb the gasket, move the pump into the correct position and tighten its bolts to the torque listed in this Chapter's Specifications **(see illustration)**.

14 Check that the pump is correctly located; if necessary, unbolt it again, and repeat the full procedure to ensure that the pump is correctly aligned.

15 Install a new crankshaft rear oil seal (see Section 20).

16 Using grease to stick the gasket in place on the pump, install the pick-up/strainer tube, tightening its screws and nut to the torque listed in this Chapter's Specifications **(see illustration)**.

17 The remainder of reassembly is the reverse of the removal procedure.

17 Oil cooler - removal and installation

1 Drain the cooling system (see Chapter 1). Disconnect the coolant hoses from the oil cooler.

2 Unscrew the oil filter (see Chapter 1) - catch any escaping oil in a drip tray.

3 Unscrew the filter adapter from the oil pump, and remove the oil cooler; note how its unions are aligned, and be prepared for oil loss from the cooler.

4 Installation is the reverse of the removal procedure, noting the following points:

(a) *Replace all O-rings and seals disturbed on removal.*
(b) *Align the cooler's unions as noted on removal, and tighten the adapter to the specified torque.*
(c) *Refill the cooling system (see Chapter 1).*
(d) *Install the oil filter, then check the engine oil level, and top-up as necessary (see Chapter 1).*
(e) *Check for signs of oil or coolant leaks once the engine has been restarted and warmed-up to normal operating temperature.*

18 Oil level sensor - removal and installation

Refer to illustrations 18.3 and 18.4

1 With the vehicle parked on firm level ground, open the hood and disconnect the battery negative cable - see Chapter 5, Section 1.

2 Raise the front of the vehicle, and support it securely on jackstands.

3 Undo the two screws, and remove the sensor's cover from the front of the oil pan **(see illustration)**.

4 Disconnect the wiring from the sensor **(see illustration)**. Where necessary, remove the electrical connector to disconnect the sensor wiring, and unclip the connector to release the wiring from the vehicle.

5 Unscrew the sensor, and quickly plug the oil pan aperture to minimize oil loss; note the sensor's seal.

6 Installation is the reverse of the removal procedure; replace the sensor's seal if it is worn or damaged, and tighten the sensor to the specified torque. Check the engine oil level, and top-up as necessary (see Chapter 1) - check for signs of oil leaks once the engine has been restarted and warmed-up to normal operating temperature.

19 Oil pressure sending unit - removal and installation

Refer to illustration 19.1

1 The switch is screwed into the rear of the cylinder block, above the right-hand driveshaft's support bearing **(see illustration)**.

2 With the vehicle parked on firm level ground, open the hood and disconnect the battery negative cable - see Chapter 5, Section 1.

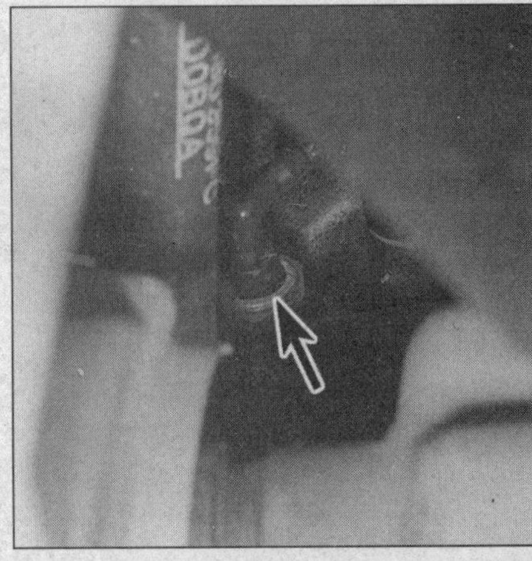
19.1 The oil pressure sending unit (arrow) is screwed into the rear of the cylinder block, above the right-hand driveshaft support bearing

3 Raise the front of the vehicle, and support it securely on jackstands.

4 Disconnect the wiring from the switch, and unscrew it; be prepared for some oil loss.

5 Installation is the reverse of the removal procedure; apply a thin smear of suitable sealant to the switch threads, and tighten it securely. Check the engine oil level, and top-up as necessary (see Chapter 1). Check for signs of oil leaks once the engine has been restarted and warmed-up to normal operating temperature.

20 Crankshaft oil seals - replacement

Note: *Don't try to pry these seals out without removing the oil pump or seal carrier - the seals are too soft, and the amount of space available is too small, for this to be possible*

20.2 Driving out the crankshaft front oil seal

20.5 A socket of the correct size can be used to install the new seal

20.6 Carefully tap the seal into place, exercising great care to prevent the seal from being damaged or distorted

20.12 Unscrew the bolts (arrows) to remove the crankshaft rear oil seal carrier . . .

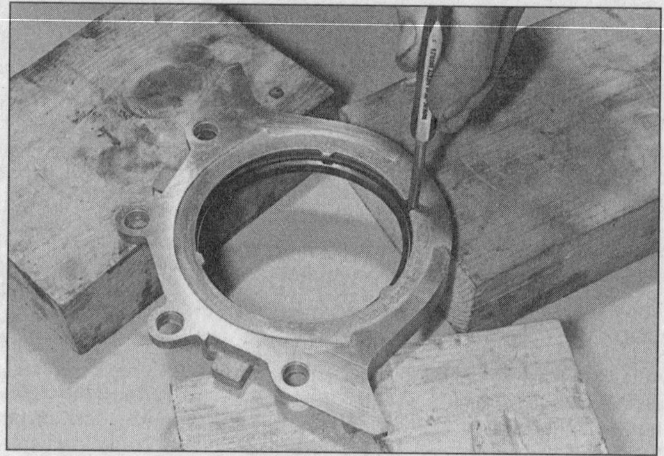
20.13 . . . and ensure the carrier is properly supported when driving out the used oil seal - note the notches provided for driving out the seal

without considerable risk of damage to the seal housing and/or the crankshaft journal. Follow exactly the procedure given below.

Front seal

Refer to illustrations 20.2, 20.6a and 20.6b

1 Remove the oil pump (see Section 16).

2 Drive the oil seal out of the pump from behind **(see illustration)**.

3 Clean the seal housing and crankshaft, polishing off any burrs or raised edges, which may have caused the seal to fail in the first place.

4 Install the oil pump (see Section 16).

5 Grease the lips and periphery of the new seal, to ease installation.

6 Press the seal squarely into place by hand; tap it in until it is flush with the pump housing, using a soft-faced mallet and a socket with an outside diameter only slightly smaller than the seal's **(see illustrations)**. This approach requires great care, to ensure that the seal is installed squarely, without distortion or damage.

7 Wash off any traces of oil. The remainder of reassembly is the reverse of the removal procedure, referring to the relevant text for details where required. Check for signs of oil leakage when the engine is restarted.

Rear main seal

Refer to illustrations 20.12, 20.13, 20.15, 20.16 and 20.18

8 Remove the transaxle (see the relevant Part of Chapter 7).

9 If equipped with a manual transaxle, remove the clutch (Chapter 8).

10 Unbolt the flywheel/driveplate (see Section 21).

11 Remove the oil pan (see Section 15).

12 Unbolt the oil seal carrier **(see illustration)**. Remove and discard its gasket.

13 Supporting the carrier evenly on wooden blocks, drive the oil seal out of the carrier from behind **(see illustration)**.

14 Clean the seal housing and crankshaft, polishing off any burrs or raised edges, which may have caused the seal to fail in the first place. Clean also the mating surfaces of the cylinder block/crankcase and carrier, using a scraper to remove all traces of the old gasket - be careful not to scratch or damage the material of either - then use a suitable solvent to degrease them.

15 Use grease to stick the new gasket in place on the cylinder block/crankcase, then install the carrier **(see illustration)**.

20.15 Use a new gasket when installing the rear oil seal carrier

20.16 Check that the oil seal carrier is correctly positioned

20.18 Using a guide made from a thin sheet of plastic to slide the oil seal lips over the crankshaft shoulder

21.11 Note the pawl (lower right corner of photo) used to lock the flywheel/driveplate while the bolts are tightened. This pawl is homemade

16 Using a straight edge and feeler gauges, check that the carrier is both centered *exactly* around the crankshaft, and aligned squarely so that its (oil pan) mating surface is exactly the same amount - between 0.012 and 0.031 inch - below that of the cylinder block/crankcase on each side of the crankshaft. Being careful not to disturb the gasket, move the carrier into the correct position, and tighten its bolts to the specified torque **(see illustration)**.

17 Check that the carrier is correctly located; if necessary, unbolt it again, and repeat the full procedure to ensure that the carrier is correctly aligned.

18 Make up a guide from a thin sheet of plastic or similar, lubricate the lips of the new seal and the crankshaft shoulder with grease, then install the seal, with the guide feeding the seal's lips over the crankshaft shoulder **(see illustration)**. Press the seal evenly into its housing by hand only, and use a soft-faced mallet to gently tap it into place until it is flush with the surrounding housing.

19 Wipe off any surplus oil or grease; the remainder of the reassembly procedure is the reverse of disassembly, referring to the relevant text for details where required. Check for signs of oil leakage when the engine is restarted.

21 Flywheel/driveplate - removal, inspection and installation

Removal

1 Remove the transaxle (see Chapter 7). Now is a good time to check components such as oil seals and replace them if necessary.

2 If equipped, remove the clutch (Chapter 8). Now is a good time to check or replace the clutch components and pilot bearing.

3 Use a center-punch or paint to make alignment marks on the flywheel/driveplate and crankshaft, to ensure correct alignment during installation.

4 Prevent the flywheel/driveplate from turning by locking the ring gear teeth, or by bolting a strap between the flywheel/driveplate and the cylinder block/crankcase. Loosen the bolts evenly until all are free.

5 Remove the bolts and ensure that new replacements are obtained for reassembly; these bolts are subjected to severe stresses, and so must be replaced, regardless of their apparent condition, whenever they are disturbed.

6 Noting the reinforcing plate (automatic transaxle-equipped models only), remove the flywheel/driveplate; don't drop it - it is very heavy.

Inspection

7 Clean the flywheel/driveplate to remove grease and oil. Inspect the surface for cracks, rivet grooves, burned areas and score marks. Light scoring can be removed with emery cloth. Check for cracked and broken ring gear teeth. Lay the flywheel/driveplate on a flat surface and use a straightedge to check for warpage.

8 Clean and inspect the mating surfaces of the flywheel/driveplate and the crankshaft. If the crankshaft rear seal is leaking, replace it (see Section 20) before installing the flywheel/driveplate.

9 While the flywheel/driveplate is removed, clean carefully its inboard (right-hand) face, particularly the recesses which serve as the reference points for the crankshaft speed/position sensor. Clean the sensor's tip, and check that the sensor is securely fastened.

Installation

Refer to illustration 21.11

10 On installation, ensure that the engine/transaxle adapter plate is in place (where necessary), then install the flywheel/driveplate to the crankshaft so that all bolt holes align - it will fit only one way - check this using the marks made on removal. Don't forget the reinforcing plate (if so equipped).

11 Lock the flywheel/driveplate by the method used on disassembly. Working in a diagonal sequence to tighten them evenly, and increasing to the final amount in two or three stages, tighten the new bolts to the specified torque **(see illustration)**.

12 The remainder of reassembly is the reverse of the removal procedure, referring to the relevant text for details where required.

22 Engine/transaxle mounts - inspection and replacement

General

1 The engine/transaxle mounts seldom require attention, but broken or deteriorated mounts should be replaced immediately, or the added strain placed on the driveline components may cause damage or wear.

2 While separate mounts may be removed and installed individually, if more than one is disturbed at a time - such as if the engine/transaxle unit is removed from its mounts - they must be reassembled and their fasteners tightened in a strict sequence.

3 Tighten the engine/transaxle mount fasteners to their specified torque, and in the sequence described in Part C of this Chapter, Section 4, Steps 49 and 50.

Inspection

4 During the check, the engine/transaxle unit must be raised slightly, to remove its weight from the mounts.

5 Raise the front of the vehicle, and support it securely on jackstands. Position a jack under the oil pan, with a large block of wood

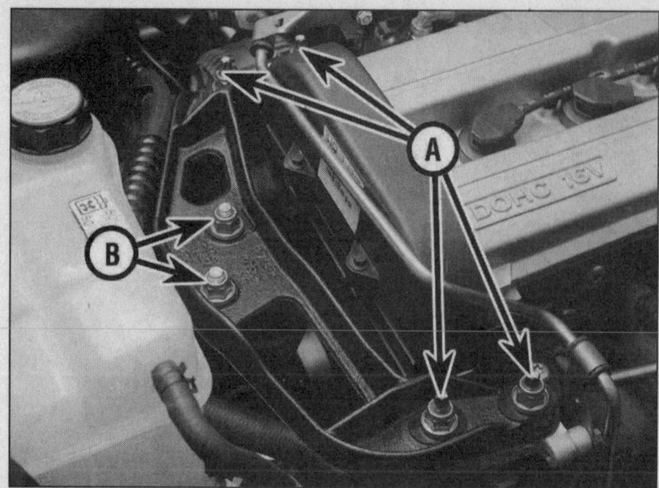

22.12 When reassembling the engine/transaxle right mount, tighten nuts (A) first, release the lifting equipment, then tighten the remaining nuts (B) - don't allow the mount to twist when doing so

22.15 The engine/transaxle left mount is secured by self-locking nuts (A) to the transaxle, by bolts (B) to the body

between the jack head and the oil pan, then carefully raise the engine/transaxle just enough to take the weight off the mounts. **Warning:** *DON'T place any part of your body under the engine when it is supported only by a jack!*

6 Check the mounts to see if the rubber is cracked, hardened or separated from the metal components. Sometimes the rubber will split right down the center.

7 Check for relative movement between each mount's brackets and the engine/transaxle or body (use a large screwdriver or lever to attempt to move the mounts). If movement is noted, lower the engine and check-tighten the mount fasteners.

Replacement

Front mount

8 Unbolt the resonator support bracket from the engine compartment front crossmember, loosen the two clamp screws securing the resonator to the mass airflow sensor and plenum chamber hoses, then swing the resonator up clear of the thermostat housing (see Chapter 4). Unbolt the pulse-air filter housing from the mount bracket, then unfasten the bolts/nuts securing the mount to the subframe, unscrew the center bolt and remove the mount; note the location of the wiring connector bracket. The mount's bracket can be unbolted from the transaxle if required.

9 On installation, ensure that the mount-to-transaxle bolts are securely tightened, then install the mount and wiring connector bracket. Tighten first the mount-to-subframe bolts/nuts, noting that these are to be tightened in two stages to the final specified torque. Finally tighten the mount's center bolt, again to the specified torque.

Right mount

Refer to illustration 22.12

10 Unscrew the nuts and remove the bracket; note that these nuts are self-locking, and must therefore be replaced whenever they are disturbed. Unbolt the mount from the body.

11 Where hydraulic-type mounts are used - they have only five nuts securing the bracket, and the mount is clearly identifiable from its shape - take care never to tilt these more than 5-degrees from vertical.

12 On installation, replace the self-locking nuts, then tighten all fasteners to the torque listed in this Chapter's Specifications. When tightening the nuts, tighten first the four bracket-to-engine nuts, then release the hoist or jack to allow the engine/transaxle's weight to rest on the mount. Don't allow the mount to twist as the last two of the nuts are tightened **(see illustration)**.

Left mount

Refer to illustrations 22.15 and 22.16

13 Disconnect the two electrical connectors, the vacuum hose (if so equipped) and the crankcase breather hose from the valve cover, then remove the complete air cleaner assembly with the mass airflow sensor, the resonator and the plenum chamber (see Chapter 4).

14 Unscrew the three nuts to release the mount from the transaxle, then unbolt it from the body. Note that the nuts are self-locking, and must therefore be replaced whenever they are disturbed. Unscrew the center bolt to disassemble the mount, if necessary to replace components.

15 On installation, replace the self-locking nuts, and don't allow the mount to twist as the nuts are tightened **(see illustration)**. Tighten all fasteners to the torque listed in this Chapter's Specifications.

Rear mount

16 If the vehicle is equipped with automatic transaxle, a separate damper may be installed beneath the subframe, which must be unbolted to reach the mount's fasteners **(see illustration)**.

17 Unbolt the mount from the subframe, then unscrew the mount's center bolt. If required, unbolt the mount's bracket from the transaxle.

18 On installation, ensure that the mount-to-transaxle bolts are securely tightened, then install the mount. Tighten first the mount-to-subframe bolts, noting that these are to be tightened in two stages to the final torque. Finally tighten the mount's center bolt, again to the specified torque.

23 Valve clearance check and adjustment (1998 and later models only)

Refer to illustrations 23.3 and 23.7

Note 1: *1997 and earlier models are equipped with hydraulic lifters that never require adjustment.*

Note 2: *This procedure is not recommended as a part of tune-up and maintenance. However, it should be performed whenever the camshafts are removed or if the valves become noisy (clattering).*

1 Disconnect the negative cable from the battery (see Chapter 5, Section 1).

2 Remove the valve cover (see Section 5).

3 Measure the clearance on each valve that has its camshaft lobe facing away from the lifter **(see illustration)**. Use a feeler gauge of the specified thickness (see this Chapter's Specifications) to start; if it does not fit, find the feeler gauge that does. Draw a diagram to keep track of which clearances you

22.16 If the vehicle is equipped with an automatic transaxle, an additional damper may be fastened to the underside of the engine/ transaxle rear mount, as shown

23.3 Measure the lifter-to-cam lobe clearance with a feeler gauge

already measured and the clearance measured at each one.

4 When you have measured all the valves that have the camshaft lobe facing away from the lifter, rotate the crankshaft until more can be measured. Repeat these operations until all clearances have been measured.

6 If any clearances are out of specification, it will be necessary to remove the camshafts (see Section 13) and lift each shim, one at a time, off the top of the lifter (a small screwdriver may help lift each shim off).

7 Measure the thickness of the shim with a micrometer **(see illustration)**. To calculate the correct thickness of a replacement shim that will place the valve clearance within the specified value, use the following formula:

N = T + (A – V)
T = thickness of the old shim
A = valve clearance measured
N = thickness of the new shim
V = desired valve clearance (see this Chapter's Specifications)

8 Select a shim with a thickness as close as possible to the valve clearance calculated. New shims are available from dealer service departments in a variety of thicknesses to correct any incorrect valve clearances. **Note:** *Through careful analysis of the shim sizes needed to bring the out-of-specification valve clearance within specification, it is often possible to simply move a shim that has to come out anyway to another lifter requiring a shim of that particular size, thereby reducing the number of new shims that must be purchased.*

9 Repeat this procedure until all the valves which are out of clearance have been corrected.

10 Installation of the components removed is the reverse of the removal procedure.

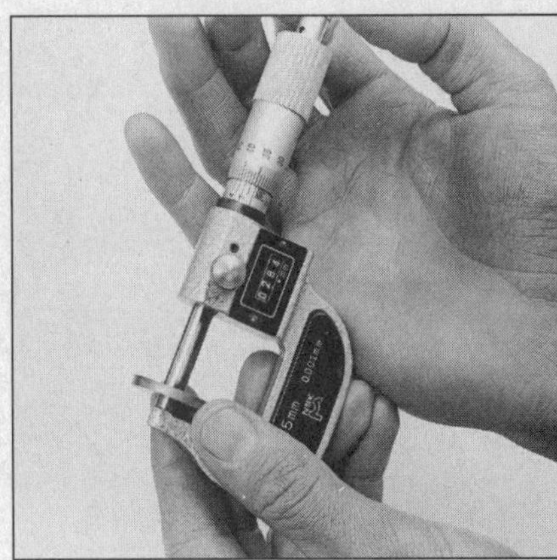

23.7 Measure the shim thickness with a micrometer

Notes

Chapter 2 Part B
V6 engine

Contents

Specifications

General

Engine type	V6, double overhead camshafts
Displacement:	153 cu. in. (2.5 liters)
Firing order	1-4-2-5-3-6
Compression pressure	Lowest reading cylinder must be within 75-percent of highest cylinder
Oil pressure at 1500 rpm (hot)	20 to 45 psi

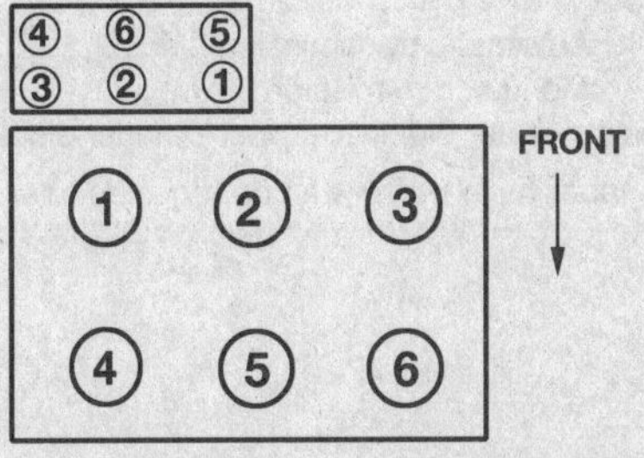

Cylinder and coil terminal locations

Camshafts and hydraulic lifters

Lobe lift (all)	0.188 inch
Camshaft endplay	0.001 to 0.0064 inch
Camshaft bearing clearance	
Standard	0.001 to 0.0029 inch
Service limit	0.0047 inch
Camshaft journal diameter	1.060 to 1.061 inches
Camshaft bearing inside diameter	1.062 to 1.063 inches
Lifter diameter	0.6290 to 0.6294 inch
Lifter-to-bore clearance	0.0007 to 0.0027 inch
Collapsed lifter gap	0.19 to 0.43 inch

Torque specifications

	Ft-lbs (unless otherwise indicated)
Valve cover bolts/studs	72 to 108 in-lbs
Oil pump-to-cylinder block bolts	72 to 108 in-lbs
Oil pan baffle fasteners	
1995 through 1998	15 to 22
1999 and later	
Step 1	44 in-lbs
Step 2	Tighten an additional 45 degrees
Oil pump screen cover and tube bolts	
1995 through 1998	72 to 108 in-lbs
1999 and later	
Step 1	44 in-lbs
Step 2	Tighten an additional 45 degrees
Oil pump screen cover and tube nuts	
1995 through 1998	72 to 108 in-lbs
1999 and later	
Step 1	44 in-lbs
Step 2	Tighten an additional 45 degrees
Cylinder head bolts*	
Stage 1	27 to 32
Stage 2	Rotate an additional 85 to 95-degrees
Stage 3	Loosen one full turn (minimum)
Stage 4	27 to 32
Stage 5	Rotate an additional 85 to 95-degrees
Stage 6	Rotate an additional 85 to 95-degrees
Camshaft journal cap bolts	72 to 108 in-lbs
Timing chain guide bolts	15 to 22
Timing chain tensioner bolts	15 to 22
Engine front cover bolts/studs	15 to 22
Drivebelt idler pulley bolt	15 to 22
Oil pan bolts	15 to 22
Oil pan-to-transaxle bolts	25 to 34
Oil pressure sensor adapter	15 to 22
Crankshaft pulley and damper bolt	
Stage 1	89
Stage 2	Loosen one full turn (minimum)
Stage 3	35 to 39
Stage 4	Rotate an additional 90-degrees
Camshaft rear seal retainer bolts	72 to 108 in-lbs
Intake manifold bolts (upper and lower)	72 to 108 in-lbs
Exhaust manifold nuts	13 to 16
Flywheel/driveplate bolts	54 to 64
Front subframe-to-body bolts	92 to 100
Upper front engine support bracket nuts	
Stage 1	84 in-lbs
Stage 2	Lower powertrain to load mount
Stage 3	52 to 70
Right front engine support mount-to-front subframe bolts	30 to 41
Left front engine support mount-to-front subframe bolts	
Stage 1	84 in-lbs
Stage 2	Verify front-to-rear alignment
Stage 3	30 to 41
Front engine support mount through-bolts (front and rear)	75 to 102
Engine/transmission support mount nuts	
Stage 1	84 in-lbs
Stage 2	Lower powertrain to load mount
Stage 3	
Automatic transmission	30 to 41
Manual transmission	52 to 70
Lower cylinder block-to-upper cylinder block bolts	See Part C of this chapter

** Cylinder head bolts must be replaced after each use.*

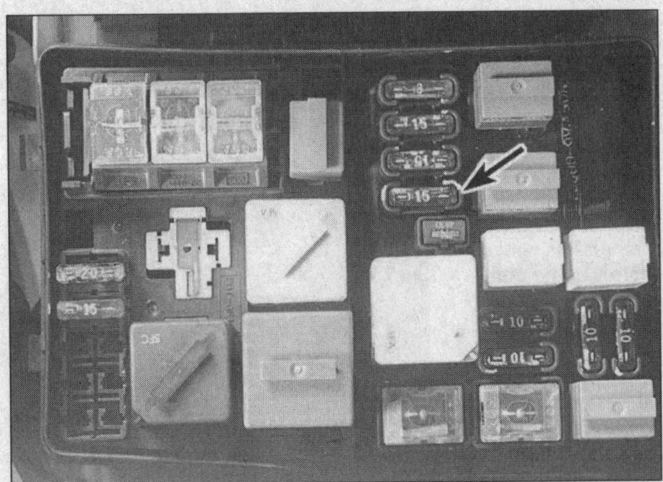

3.3 Remove the fuel pump fuse (arrow) to disable the electric fuel pump

3.4 To reach down the spark plug tunnels in the valve covers, a compression gauge with a long, slender hose is required for this engine

1 General information

This Part of Chapter 2 is devoted to repair procedures possible while the engine is still installed in the vehicle. Only the Specifications relevant to those procedures are included. Since these procedures are based on the assumption that the engine is installed in the vehicle, if the engine has been removed from the vehicle and mounted on a stand, some of the preliminary disassembly steps outlined won't apply.

During procedural steps in this chapter, "left" and "right" are frequently used to describe locations on the engine. These directions are in relation to the vehicle overall and also assume the perspective of sitting in the driver's seat. So, "left" means the driver's side of the vehicle and "right" means the passenger's side of the vehicle.

Information concerning engine/transmission removal and installation and engine overhaul can be found in Part C of this Chapter, which also includes the Specifications relevant to those procedures.

2 Repair operations possible with the engine in the vehicle

Many major repair operations can be accomplished without removing the engine from the vehicle.

Clean the engine compartment and the exterior of the engine with some type of pressure washer before any work is done. It will make the job easier and help keep dirt out of the internal areas of the engine.

It may help to remove the hood to improve access to the engine as repairs are performed (refer to Chapter 11 if necessary).

If vacuum, exhaust, oil or coolant leaks develop, indicating a need for gasket or seal replacement, the repairs can generally be made with the engine in the vehicle. The intake and exhaust manifold gaskets, timing cover gasket, oil pan gasket, crankshaft oil seals and cylinder head gaskets are all accessible with the engine in place.

Since the cylinder heads can be removed without pulling the engine, valve component servicing can also be accomplished with the engine in the vehicle. Replacement of the timing chain and sprockets is also possible with the engine in the vehicle.

In extreme cases caused by a lack of necessary equipment, repair or replacement of piston rings, pistons, connecting rods and rod bearings is possible with the engine in the vehicle. However, this practice is not recommended because of the cleaning and preparation work that must be done to the components involved.

3 Compression test

Refer to illustrations 3.3 and 3.4

1 A compression check will tell you the mechanical condition of your engine's upper end (pistons, rings, valves, head gasket). Specifically, it can tell you if the compression is down due to leakage caused by worn piston rings, defective valves and seats or a blown head gasket. **Note:** *The engine must be at normal operating temperature and the battery must be fully charged for this check.*

2 Begin by cleaning the area around the spark plugs before you remove them (compressed air should be used, if available, otherwise a small brush or even a bicycle tire pump will work). The idea is to prevent dirt from getting into the cylinders as the compression check is being done. Next, remove all of the spark plugs from the engine (see Chapter 1) and block the throttle wide open.

3 Disable the ignition system by unplugging the ignition coil electrical connectors (see Chapter 5) and remove the fuel pump fuse **(see illustration)** to disable the fuel pump.

4 Install the compression gauge in the spark plug hole **(see illustration)**.

5 Crank the engine over at least seven compression strokes and watch the gauge. The compression should build up quickly in a healthy engine. Low compression on the first stroke, followed by gradually increasing pressure on successive strokes, indicates worn piston rings. A low compression reading on the first stroke, which doesn't build up during successive strokes, indicates leaking valves or a blown head gasket (a cracked head could also be the cause). Deposits on the undersides of the valve heads can also cause low compression. Record the highest gauge reading obtained.

6 Repeat the procedure for the remaining cylinders and compare the results to this Chapter's Specifications.

7 Add some engine oil (about three squirts from a plunger-type oil can) to each cylinder, through the spark plug hole, and repeat the test.

8 If the compression increases after the oil is added, the piston rings are definitely worn. If the compression doesn't increase significantly, the leakage is occurring at the valves or head gasket. Leakage past the valves may be caused by burned valve seats and/or faces or warped, cracked or bent valves.

9 If two adjacent cylinders have equally low compression, there's a strong possibility that the head gasket between them is blown. The appearance of coolant in the combustion chambers or the crankcase would verify this condition.

10 If one cylinder is 20-percent lower than the others, and the engine has a slightly rough idle, a worn exhaust lobe on the camshaft could be the cause.

11 If the compression is unusually high, the combustion chambers are probably coated with carbon deposits. If that's the case, the cylinder head should be removed and decarbonized.

12 If compression is way down or varies greatly between cylinders, it would be a good idea to have a leak-down test performed by an automotive repair shop. This test will pinpoint exactly where the leakage is occurring and how severe it is.

4 Top Dead Center (TDC) for No 1 piston - locating

Refer to illustration 4.6

1 Top Dead Center (TDC) is the highest point in the cylinder that each piston reaches as it travels up-and-down when the crankshaft turns. Each piston reaches TDC on the compression stroke and again on the exhaust stroke, but TDC generally refers to piston position on the compression stroke. The timing marks on the vibration damper installed on the front of the crankshaft are referenced to the number one piston at TDC on the compression stroke.

2 Positioning the piston(s) at TDC is an essential part of procedures such as timing chain and sprocket replacement.

3 In order to bring any piston to TDC, the crankshaft must be turned using one of the methods outlined below. When looking at the front of the engine, normal crankshaft rotation is clockwise. **Warning:** *Before beginning this procedure, be sure to place the transmission in Neutral and remove the ignition key.*

- *a) The preferred method is to turn the crankshaft with a large socket and breaker bar attached to the vibration damper bolt threaded into the front of the crankshaft.*
- *b) A remote starter switch, which may save some time, can also be used. Attach the switch leads to the S (switch) and B (battery) terminals on the starter motor. Once the piston is close to TDC, use a socket and breaker bar as described in the previous paragraph.*
- *c) If an assistant is available to turn the ignition switch to the Start position in short bursts, you can get the piston close to TDC without a remote starter switch. Use a socket and breaker bar as described in Paragraph a) to complete the procedure.*

4 Disable the ignition system by disconnecting the primary electrical connectors at the ignition coil pack/modules (see Chapter 5).

5 Remove the spark plugs and install a compression gauge in the number one cylinder. Turn the crankshaft clockwise with a socket and breaker bar as described above.

6 When the piston approaches TDC, compression will be noted on the compression gauge. Continue turning the crankshaft until the keyway in the crankshaft damper is in the 11 o'clock position and the notch is aligned with the TDC mark on the front cover **(see illustration)**. At this point number one cylinder is at TDC on the compression stroke. If the marks aligned but there was no compression, the piston was on the exhaust stroke. Continue rotating the engine once more.

9 After the number one piston has been positioned at TDC on the compression stroke, TDC for any of the remaining cylinders can be located by turning the crankshaft and following the firing order (refer to the Specifications). Divide the crankshaft pulley into three equal sections with chalk marks at three points, each indicating 120-degrees of crankshaft rotation. Rotating the engine 120 degrees past TDC #1 will put the engine at TDC for cylinder #4.

4.6 To position the No. 1 piston at TDC, position the crankshaft pulley keyway (A) at 11 o'clock and align the mark on the pulley (B) with the mark (C) on the engine front cover

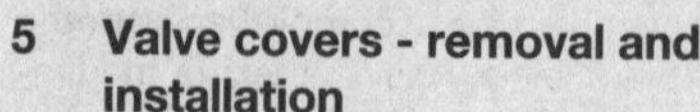

5 Valve covers - removal and installation

Refer to illustrations 5.1, 5.6, 5.7a, 5.7b and 5.10

Front valve cover

1 Disconnect the cable from the negative battery terminal (see Chapter 5, Section 1). Remove the plastic shield covering the front of the engine **(see illustration 6.2)**. Disconnect the crankcase ventilation tube from the front valve cover **(see illustration)**. Remove the tube from the vehicle.

2 Remove the upper intake manifold as described under Section 6.

3 Remove the fuel injector wiring brackets from the front valve cover studs. If necessary, disconnect the injector wires from the injectors. Move the wiring out of the way.

4 If so equipped, remove the intake manifold runner control actuator from the valve cover and lay it out of the way. Also, remove the intake manifold runner control actuator cable bridge from the two stud bolts located on the left end of the valve cover.

5 Disconnect the spark plug wires from the spark plugs on the front cylinder bank. Remove the spark plug wire bracket from the valve cover and lay them out of the way. If necessary, disconnect and remove the coolant expansion tank hose and wiring. Dis-

5.1 Disconnect the crankcase ventilation tube from the front valve cover (arrow)

5.6 Loosen the valve cover fasteners (arrows) gradually and evenly

5.7a Remove and discard the valve cover gasket - it must be replaced during assembly to prevent leakage

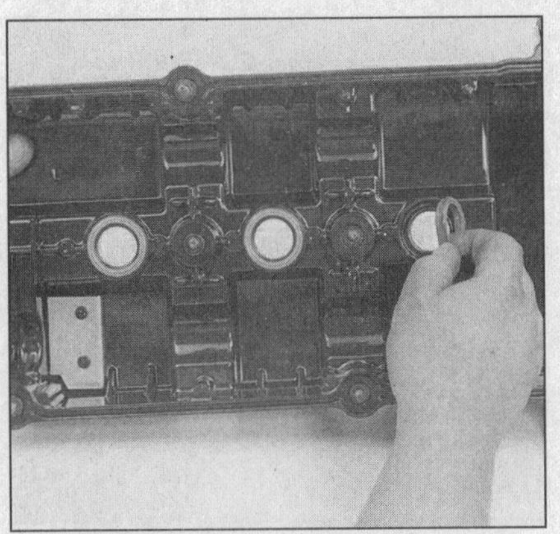

5.7b Remove and discard the gaskets from the valve cover at the spark plug holes

connect or remove any other wires, hoses or brackets that will interfere with valve cover removal.

6 Loosen the valve cover fasteners gradually **(see illustration)** and evenly until all are loose. Remove the valve cover fasteners and lift the valve cover off the engine.

7 Remove and discard the valve cover gaskets **(see illustrations)**. The gaskets must be replaced during assembly to prevent leakage.

8 Inspect the valve cover and cylinder head sealing surfaces for nicks or other damage. Clean the sealing surfaces with a clean solvent and a shop towel.

9 Install new valve cover gaskets into the cover. Make sure the gaskets are properly seated in their grooves.

10 Apply a 5/16-inch bead of RTV sealant at the locations shown **(see illustration)**.

11 Lower the valve cover into position making sure the gaskets are still in place. Install the cover fasteners. Tighten the fasteners gradually and evenly to the torque listed in this Chapter's Specifications.

12 Reconnect the coolant expansion tank hose and wiring. Attach the spark plug wire bracket to the valve cover and connect the spark plug wires to the spark plugs.

13 If so equipped, install the intake manifold runner control actuator and actuator cable bridge. Tighten the actuator and bridge fasteners to the torque listed in this Chapter's Specifications.

14 Install the upper intake manifold (Section 6).

15 Reconnect the crankcase ventilation tube to the valve cover.

Rear valve cover

16 Disconnect the negative battery cable from the battery (see Chapter 5, Section 1).

17 Remove the upper intake manifold (Section 6).

18 Disconnect the spark plug wires from the spark plugs and ignition coil. Remove the spark plug wire holding bracket.

19 Remove the ignition coil. See Chapter 5.

20 Disconnect the fuel injection wires from the injectors. Lay the injector wiring harness out of the way.

21 Remove or disconnect any other wires, hoses or brackets that will interfere with valve cover removal.

22 Loosen the valve cover fasteners gradually and evenly, until all fasteners are loose. Then, unscrew and remove the fasteners. Lift the valve cover off the cylinder head.

23 Inspect the valve cover and cylinder head sealing surfaces for nicks or other damage. Clean the sealing surfaces with clean solvent and a shop towel.

24 Remove and discard the valve cover gaskets - new gaskets must be installed during assembly to prevent leakage.

25 Apply a 5/16-inch bead of RTV sealant at the locations shown **(see illustration 5.10)**.

26 Install new gaskets on the valve cover. Make sure the gaskets are properly seated in their grooves. Lower the valve cover into place, making sure the gaskets are still in place.

27 Install the valve cover fasteners. Tighten the fasteners gradually and evenly to the torque listed in this Chapter's Specifications.

28 Reinstall all wiring harnesses and brackets.

29 Install the ignition coil (Chapter 5).

30 Reattach the spark plug wire holding bracket. Connect the spark plug wires to the spark plugs.

31 Install the upper intake manifold (Section 6). **Note:** *After the battery has been disconnected, the engine may exhibit some abnormal driveability symptoms. After driving 10 miles or more, however, the electronic engine management system will relearn its adaptive strategy and the engine will operate normally.*

6 Intake manifold - removal and installation

Warning: *Gasoline is extremely flammable, so take extra precautions when disconnecting any part of the fuel system. Don't smoke, or allow naked flames or bare light bulbs in or near the work area. Don't work in a garage where a natural gas appliance (such as a clothes dryer or water heater) is installed. If you spill gasoline on your skin, rinse it off immediately. Have a fire extinguisher rated for gasoline fires handy, and know how to use it.*

Upper intake manifold

Removal

Refer to illustrations 6.2, 6.3, 6.9a, 6.9b, 6.12, 6.13 and 6.16

1 Disconnect the negative battery cable from the battery (see Chapter 5, Section 1).

2 Remove the plastic shield covering the front of the engine **(see illustration)**.

3 Depress the locking tab and disconnect the connector from the mass airflow sensor **(see illustration)**.

4 Pry back the clips securing the air filter housing cover. Remove the air filter housing cover and lift out the filter element (Chapter 1).

5 Disconnect air bypass hose and PVC

2B

5.10 Apply 5/16-inch beads of RTV sealant to the locations shown (arrows) - be sure the new spark plug hole gaskets are securely in position before installing the cover

6.2 Remove these bolts (arrows) and lift off the plastic shield covering the front valve cover and water pump pulley

6.3 Unplug the connector from the mass airflow sensor

6.9a Pry off the throttle and speed control cable retaining clip . . .

6.9b . . . then disconnect the cables

hoses from the air cleaner duct.

6 Loosen the clamps and remove the air cleaner duct from the mass airflow sensor and throttle body inlet.

7 Disconnect the intake air temperature (IAT) sensor connector located on the side of the air filter housing.

8 Remove the fasteners securing the air filter housing and remove the housing.

9 Pry off the clip securing the throttle and speed control cables to the mounting bracket, then disconnect the cables **(see illustrations)**.

10 Remove the throttle cable mounting bracket.

11 Disconnect the vacuum hose from the exhaust gas recirculation (EGR) valve. Remove the two bolts securing the EGR valve and remove the valve (see Chapter 5). Remove and discard the EGR valve gasket. The EGR valve may be able to remain attached to the exhaust manifold tube. If not, remove the EGR valve from the tube.

12 Disconnect the idle air control (IAC) valve electrical connector **(see illustration)**.

13 Disconnect the two vacuum lines from the upper intake manifold **(see illustration)**. Unplug the electrical connector from the throttle position sensor (TPS).

14 Disconnect the vacuum hoses and electrical connector from the EGR vacuum regulator (EVR).

6.12 Disconnect the idle air control (IAC) electrical connector

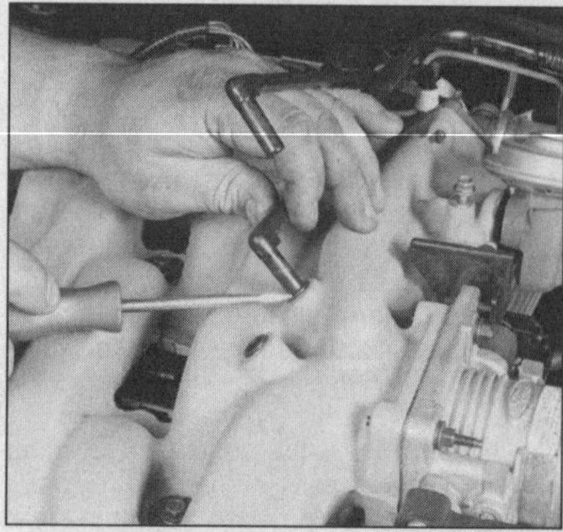
6.13 Disconnect the two vacuum lines from the intake manifold

15 Disconnect the PVC hose from the upper intake manifold (Chapter 1).

16 Loosen the upper intake manifold bolts in the sequence shown **(see illustration)**. Remove the upper intake manifold and discard the gaskets.

Installation

Refer to illustration 6.17

17 Installation is the reverse of the removal procedure, noting the following points:

(a) *When using a scraper and solvent to remove all traces of old gasket material and sealant from the manifold and cylinder head, be careful you don't scratch or damage the material of either; the intake manifold is made of aluminum alloy. If the gasket was leaking, have the mating surfaces checked for warpage at an automotive machine shop. The manifold must be replaced if it is found to be*

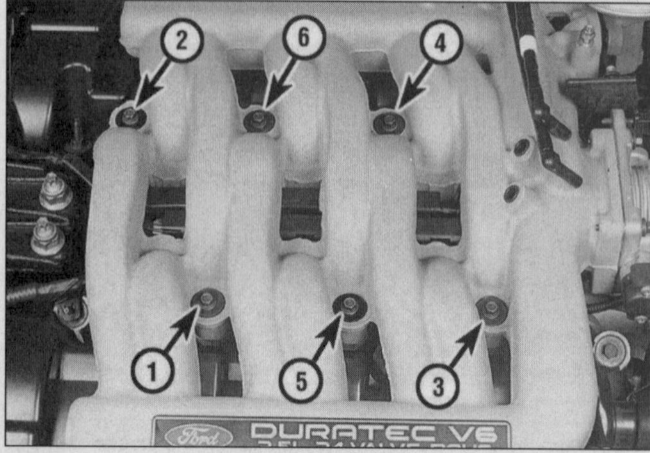

6.16 Loosen the upper intake manifold fasteners in the sequence shown

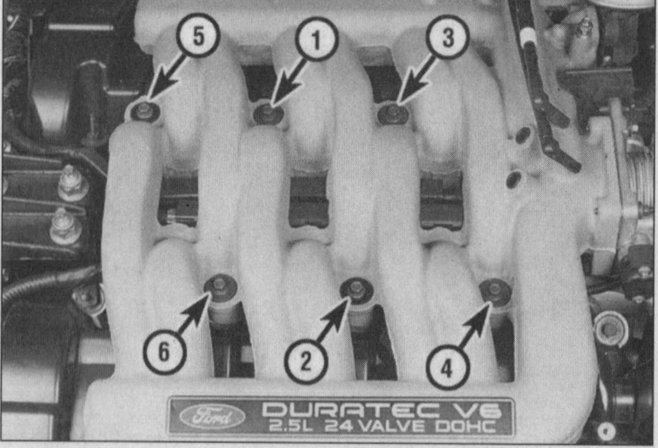

6.17 Tighten the upper intake manifold fasteners in the sequence shown

6.21 Remove the safety clip from the spring lock coupling

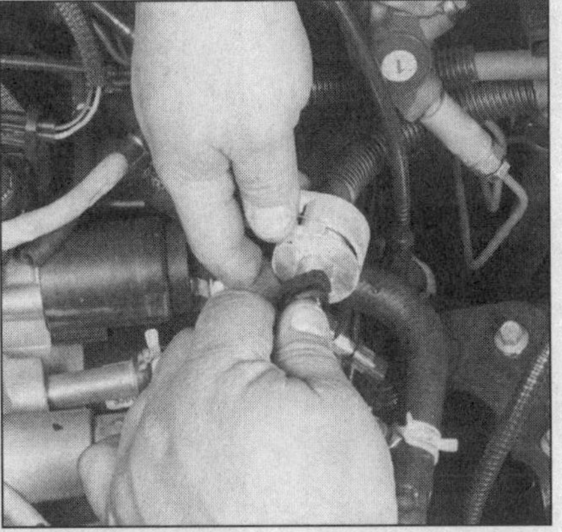

6.22 Disconnect the fuel line using a spring lock coupling disconnect tool

6.24 Disconnect the engine coolant temperature (ECT) sensor (it's located above the starter motor)

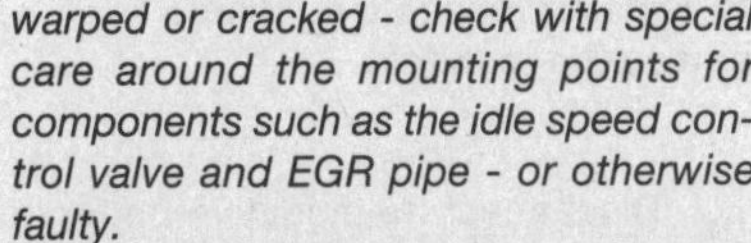

warped or cracked - check with special care around the mounting points for components such as the idle speed control valve and EGR pipe - or otherwise faulty.

(b) *Provided the mating surfaces are clean and flat, a new gasket will be sufficient to ensure the joint is gas-tight.* **Don't** *use any kind of silicone-based sealant on any part of the fuel system or intake manifold.*

(c) *Install a new gasket, then locate the upper manifold on the lower manifold install the fasteners. Tighten the fasteners in three or four steps in the sequence shown* **(see illustration)**.

(d) *Install the remaining parts in the reverse order of removal - tighten all fasteners to the torque wrench settings specified.*

(e) *Before starting the engine, check the accelerator cable for correct adjustment and the throttle linkage for smooth operation.*

(f) *When the engine is fully warmed up, check for signs of fuel, intake and/or vacuum leaks.*

Road test the vehicle, and check for proper operation of all disturbed components. **Note:** *After the battery has been disconnected, the engine may exhibit some abnormal driveability symptoms. After driving 10 miles or more, however, the electronic engine management system will relearn its adaptive strategy and the engine will operate normally.*

Lower intake manifold

Removal

Refer to illustrations 6.21, 6.22, 6.24, 6.25, 6.26, 6.27 and 6.28

Warning: *Gasoline is extremely flammable, so take extra precautions when disconnecting any part of the fuel system. Don't smoke, or allow naked flames or bare light bulbs in or near the work area. Don't work in a garage where a natural gas appliance (such as a clothes dryer or water heater) is installed. If you spill gasoline on your skin, rinse it off immediately. Have a fire extinguisher rated for gasoline fires handy, and know how to use it.*

18 Disconnect the negative battery cable from the battery. **Warning:** *The fuel system remains under considerable pressure even after the ignition switch has been switched off. To prevent personal injury, the fuel system pressure must be relieved prior to performing any service to fuel system components.*

19 Relieve the fuel pressure (Chapter 4).

20 Remove the upper intake manifold (see Step 1).

21 Remove the safety clip from the fuel line spring lock connector **(see illustration)**.

22 Place the spring lock coupling disconnect tool **(see illustration)** around the spring lock coupling. Close the tool and push it firmly into the open side of the coupling. Separate the coupling and remove the disconnect tool.

23 Disconnect the electrical connectors from the fuel injectors. Place the injector wiring harness aside.

24 Disconnect the engine coolant temperature (ECT) sensor **(see illustration)**. The sensor is located above the starter motor.

25 Disconnect the vacuum hose and electrical connector from the EGR back-pressure transducer **(see illustration)**.

26 Disconnect the vacuum hose from the fuel pressure regulator **(see illustration)**.

Caution: *Don't loosen, bend or damage the intake manifold runner control (IMRC) cable bracket when disconnecting the IMRC cable.*

27 Disconnect the intake manifold runner control (IMRC) actuator rod from the stud and bracket, if so equipped; or disconnect the vacuum hose from the IMRC vacuum solenoid **(see illustration)**.

28 To prevent warpage, loosen the eight lower manifold bolts gradually and evenly

6.25 Disconnect the electrical connector and vacuum hose (arrow) from the EGR back-pressure transducer

6.26 Disconnect the vacuum hose from the fuel pressure regulator (arrow)

6.27 Disconnect the vacuum hose (arrow) from the IMRC vacuum solenoid

6.28 Loosen the lower intake manifold bolts gradually and evenly until all are loose

7.4 Remove the exhaust manifold fasteners to remove the manifold

(see illustration) until all are loose. Then, remove the bolts.

29 Lift the lower intake manifold off the engine. Remove and discard the manifold gaskets.

30 Carefully clean all gasket material from the manifold and cylinder head mating surfaces. Don't nick, scratch or gouge the sealing surfaces. Inspect all components for cracks or other damage. If the manifold gaskets were leaking, have the mating surfaces checked for warpage at an automotive machine shop.

Installation

31 Install new lower intake manifold gaskets on the cylinder heads. Make sure the locating pins on the gaskets are facing down and are properly engaged with the locating holes in the cylinder heads.

32 Place the lower manifold into position on the cylinder heads. Make sure the gaskets are not dislodged.

33 Install the lower manifold bolts. Tighten the bolts gradually and evenly, in a crossing pattern, starting in the center and working outward.

34 Complete the remaining installation by reversing the removal procedure. Tighten the fasteners to the torque listed in this Chapter's Specifications. **Note:** *After the battery has been disconnected, the engine may exhibit some abnormal driveability symptoms. After driving 10 miles or more, however, the electronic engine management system will relearn its adaptive strategy and the engine will operate normally.*

7 Exhaust manifold - removal and installation

Front exhaust manifold

Removal and installation

Refer to illustration 7.4

Warning: *The engine and exhaust system must be completely cool before performing this procedure.*

1 Disconnect the negative battery cable from the battery (see Chapter 5, Section 1). Also disconnect the electrical connector for the oxygen sensor (see Chapter 6).

2 Remove the exhaust crossover tube.

3 If necessary for additional clearance, drain the cooling system and remove the radiator lower hose.

4 Remove the six nuts securing the exhaust manifold **(see illustration)**. Remove the manifold and discard the manifold gasket. Using a scraper, remove all traces of old gasket material and carbon deposits from the manifold and cylinder head mating surfaces. **Caution:** *When scraping, be careful not to gouge or scratch the cylinder head mating surface.* If the gasket was leaking, have the manifold checked for warpage at an automotive machine shop. If necessary, have the mating surfaces resurfaced.

5 Install a new manifold gasket over the cylinder head studs. Install the manifold and the nuts.

6 Tighten the nuts in three or four steps, in a circular pattern starting with the center fasteners. Tighten the nuts to the torque listed in this Chapter's Specifications.

7 Complete the remaining installation by reversing the removal procedure. If drained, refill the cooling system (Chapter 1). Start the engine and check for exhaust leakage. Repair any leakage before returning the vehicle to service. **Note:** *After the battery has been disconnected, the engine may exhibit some abnormal driveability symptoms. After driving 10 miles or more, however, the electronic engine management system will relearn its adaptive strategy and the engine will operate normally.*

Rear exhaust manifold

Removal and installation

Refer to illustrations 7.13 and 7.14

8 Disconnect the negative battery cable from the battery (see Chapter 5, Section 1).

9 Remove the alternator and alternator

7.13 Remove the bracket (A) from the driveshaft support bearing (B) and cylinder block (shown with engine removed for clarity)

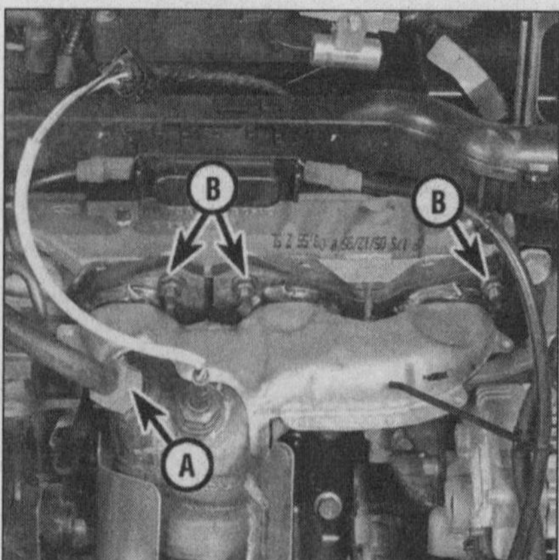

7.14 Disconnect the EGR tube (A) then remove the manifold mounting nuts (B) (the three bottom nuts are hidden in this photo)

8.5a To prevent the crankshaft from turning, engage the ring gear teeth with a large screwdriver or pry bar . .

mounting bracket (Chapter 5).

10 Remove the catalytic converter. Remove the exhaust crossover pipe (Y-pipe) from the exhaust manifold. See Chapter 4.

11 Disconnect and remove the oxygen sensor using a tool designed specifically for oxygen sensor removal/installation (see Chapter 6).

12 Loosen the right front wheel lug nuts. Raise the right front of the vehicle and support it securely with a jackstand. Remove the right front wheel.

13 Unbolt and remove the bracket that attaches the right driveshaft support bearing to the cylinder block **(see illustration)**. Remove the bracket from the support bearing and cylinder block.

14 Loosen and disconnect the EGR tube from the exhaust manifold. Then, remove the six exhaust manifold mounting nuts and remove the manifold from the engine **(see illustration)**. Remove and discard the manifold gasket.

15 Using a scraper, remove all traces of gasket material and carbon deposits from the exhaust manifold and cylinder head mating surfaces. If the gasket was leaking, have the manifold checked for warpage at an automotive machine shop. If necessary, have the manifold mating surface resurfaced. **Caution:** *When scraping, be very careful not to gouge or scratch the cylinder head mating surface.*

16 Install a new manifold gasket over the cylinder head studs. Install the manifold and the nuts.

17 Tighten the nuts in three or four steps, in a circular pattern starting with the center fasteners. Tighten the nuts to the torque listed in this Chapter's Specifications.

18 Complete the remaining installation by reversing the removal procedure. Start the engine and check for exhaust leakage. Repair any leakage before returning the vehicle to service. **Note:** *After the battery has been disconnected, the engine may exhibit some abnormal driveability symptoms. After driving 10 miles or more, however, the electronic engine management system will relearn its adaptive strategy and the engine will operate normally.*

8 Crankshaft pulley - removal and installation

Refer to illustrations 8.5a, 8.5b and 8.7

1 Loosen the right front wheel lug nuts. Raise the front of the vehicle and securely support it with jackstands.

2 Remove the right front wheel.

3 Remove the splash shield from the fender apron.

4 Remove the accessory drivebelt (Chapter 1).

5 The crankshaft must be secured to prevent its rotation while loosening the crankshaft pulley retaining bolt. **Caution:** *Turning the crankshaft counterclockwise can cause the timing chains to bind and result in timing chain, sprocket and timing chain tensioner damage. If it is necessary to turn the crankshaft, only turn it in a clockwise direction.*

a) *If the vehicle is equipped with a manual transmission, place the transmission in fifth gear and have an assistant firmly apply the brake.*

b) *If the vehicle is equipped with an automatic transmission, remove the small cover and hold the ring gear teeth using a large screwdriver or pry bar* **(see illustration)**.

c) *Attach a suitable holding tool (the manufacturer recommends using a strap-type tool) to the crankshaft pulley* **(see illustration)**. *Use care not to damage the crankshaft pulley.*

6 While holding the crankshaft from turning, loosen, then remove the crankshaft pulley bolt. Discard the bolt as a new torque-to-yield must be used during installation.

7 Attach a suitable puller to the crankshaft pulley using three bolts and washers **(see illustration)**. Remove the pulley from the crankshaft by turning the puller center bolt. Don't lose the Woodruff key; it may come off with the pulley or remain in the crankshaft keyway.

8 Clean the pulley seal surface and inside diameter using contact cleaner. Blow dry with compressed air.

9 Apply RTV sealant to the inner diameter of the crankshaft pulley at the keyway.

10 Install the pulley key into the keyway in the crankshaft. Install the crankshaft pulley onto the crankshaft. Install the pulley until fully seated. Use the old pulley bolt to draw the pulley into position. Make sure the key is still in place. **Caution:** *A new torque-to-yield crankshaft pulley bolt must be used during installation.*

11 Apply RTV sealant to the threads of the new crankshaft pulley bolt. Install the new pulley bolt and washer and tighten it to the torque listed in this Chapter's Specifications.

12 Complete the remaining assembly by reversing the removal procedure.

8.5b . . . or attach a suitable holding tool to the crankshaft pulley, then loosen and remove the crankshaft pulley bolt

8.7 Remove the crankshaft pulley using a bolt-type puller

9.7 With the engine properly supported, remove the nuts securing the engine support bracket to the engine and front engine mount

9.14a Remove the through-bolts from the front engine mount . . .

9 Front cover - removal and installation

Refer to illustrations 9.7, 9.14a, 9.14b, 9.15, 9.18, 9.19 and 9.23

Warning: *The engine must be raised and securely supported to provide sufficient clearance to remove the oil pan during this procedure. The manufacturer recommends using a three bar engine support to raise and support the engine. Don't attempt to complete this procedure unless the engine can be safely and securely supported.*

1 Disconnect the negative battery cable from the battery (see Chapter 5, Section 1).

2 Drain the engine oil (Chapter 1).

3 Remove the valve covers (Section 5).

4 Remove the alternator and alternator mounting bracket (Chapter 5).

5 Remove the crankshaft pulley (Section 8).

6 Install a suitable engine support fixture to the engine lifting eyes to support the engine when the front support bracket is removed. This type of support fixture can be obtained at most equipment rental yards.

7 Mark the mounting position of the right-side engine support bracket for installation reference. Then, remove the nuts that secure the support bracket to the engine and engine mount **(see illustration)**. Note the location of the ground wire attached to the lower stud. Remove the engine support bracket.

8 Disconnect the low coolant level sensor electrical connector. Then, remove the coolant expansion tank mounting fasteners and place the tank out of the way.

9 Remove the two bolts securing the rear mount to the subframe and remove the mount.

10 After removing the engine mount, place the coolant expansion tank back into position and install its fasteners loosely to hold it in place.

11 Loosen the bolts that secure the power steering pulley to the power steering pump. Don't remove the bolts yet.

12 Remove the accessory drivebelt (Chapter 1).

13 Remove the power steering pump pulley, power steering pump and pump mounting bracket. See Chapter 10.

14 Remove the through-bolts from the engine mounts **(see illustrations)**. Raise the engine sufficiently for oil pan removal. Make certain the engine is securely supported.

15 Disconnect the electrical connectors from the camshaft position (CMP) sensor and the crankshaft position (CKP) sensor **(see illustration)**.

16 Remove the oil pan (Section 14).

17 If necessary, loosen the air conditioning compressor mounting bolts and move the compressor aside as required to access the engine cover. Remove or disconnect any remaining wires, hoses, clamps or brackets that will interfere with engine cover removal.

Note: *Draw a sketch of the front cover and cover fasteners. Identify the location of all stud bolts for installation in their original locations.*

18 Loosen the front cover fasteners gradually and evenly, then remove the fasteners **(see illustration)**. Be sure to note the location of all stud bolts for reference during installation.

19 Remove the engine cover **(see illustration)**.

20 Remove and discard the cover-to-cylinder block gaskets.

9.14b . . . and the rear engine mount

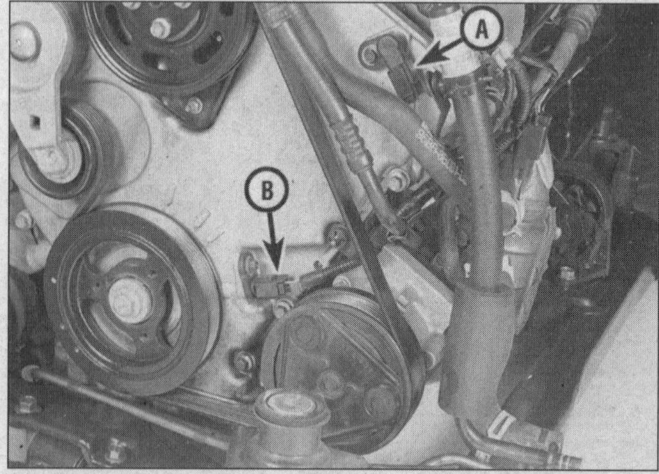

9.15 Disconnect the electrical connectors from the camshaft position sensor (A) and the crankshaft position sensor (B)

9.18 Remove the cover fasteners. Note the locations of all studs and bolts for installation reference

9.19 Lifting off the front cover

21 Carefully clean the engine and cover mating surfaces of all gasket material. Don't nick, gouge or scratch the mating surfaces or oil leakage will occur. After all gasket material is removed, clean the mating surfaces again using contact cleaner and a clean shop cloth. Make sure all traces of gasket material, grease, oil or other contamination are removed.

22 If necessary, replace the crankshaft seal in the front cover.

23 Apply a bead of sealant (part No. F4AZ-19562-B, or equivalent) approximately 1/8-inch wide and 1/2-inch long at the locations shown **(see illustration)**.

24 Install a new engine cover gasket on the cylinder block. Make sure the gasket fits properly over the alignment dowels.

25 Install the engine cover and cover fasteners. Make sure the fasteners are located in their original locations. Tighten the fasteners by hand until the cover is contacting the cylinder block and heads around its entire periphery.

26 Following a crossing pattern, tighten the cover fasteners to the torque listed in this Chapter's Specifications.

27 Install the drivebelt idler pulley and tighten to the torque listed in this Chapter's Specifications.

28 Install the oil pan (Section 14).

29 Install the crankshaft pulley (Section 8).

30 Connect the fuel injector wiring harness and connectors to the crankshaft position and camshaft position sensors. Secure the wiring harnesses with the correct clamps.

31 Install the power steering pump and hoses as described in Chapter 10.

32 Complete the remaining assembly by reversing the disassembly procedure.

33 Fill the crankcase with the recommended oil (Chapter 1). Fill the power steering reservoir with the recommended power steering fluid (Chapter 1).

34 Start the engine and warm to normal operating temperature. Check for leakage and correct as required. Check all fluid levels. **Note:** *After the battery has been disconnected, the engine may exhibit some abnormal driveability symptoms. After driving 10 miles or more, however, the electronic engine management system will relearn its adaptive strategy and the engine will operate normally.*

10 Timing chains, tensioners, and chain guides - removal, inspection, and installation

Note: *Because of a lack of clearance, this procedure is very difficult with the engine installed in the vehicle. If major engine work is being performed, it may be easier to remove the engine from the vehicle (see Chapter 2C).*

Removal

Refer to illustrations 10.2, 10.4a, 10.4b, 10.5, 10.6, 10.7, 10.8a, 10.8b and 10.10.

1 Remove the engine front cover (see Section 9). Slide the crankshaft position sensor trigger wheel off the crankshaft.

2 Install the crankshaft pulley retaining bolt into the crankshaft. Then use a wrench on the bolt to turn the crankshaft clockwise and place the crankshaft keyway at the 11 o'clock position. Verify TDC by observing the index marks on the backside of the camshaft sprockets. If the number 1 cylinder is at TDC, the index marks will be aligned **(see illustration)**. If not, turn the crankshaft exactly one full turn and again position the crankshaft keyway at 11 o'clock. **Caution:** *Turning the crankshaft counterclockwise can cause the timing chains to bind and damage the chains, sprockets and tensioners. Turn the crankshaft only clockwise.*

3 Recheck the marks on the sprockets; if they are aligned and the keyway is at 11 o'clock, the number 1 cylinder is at TDC on the compression stroke. Continue to turn the crankshaft clockwise until the keyway is at the 3 o'clock position, which will set the camshafts on the rear cylinder head in their

9.23 Apply beads of RTV sealant at the locations shown (at all the mating surface parting lines)

10.2 With the crankshaft keyway facing the 11 o'clock position and the marks on the back side of the timing sprockets aligned, the number 1 cylinder is at TDC

10.4a Remove the bolts securing the rear timing chain tensioner and remove the tensioner . . .

10.4b . . . then slide the tensioner arm off its pivot

10.5 Lift the rear timing chain off the sprockets and remove the chain

10.6 Remove the bolts securing the rear timing chain guide, then remove the guide

10.7 Remove the rear timing chain crankshaft sprocket

"neutral" position.

4 Remove the two bolts securing the timing chain tensioner for the rear chain. Remove the tensioner, then remove the tensioner arm **(see illustrations)**. Mark all parts that will be reused so they can be reinstalled in their original locations.

5 Lift the rear timing chain from the sprockets and remove the chain **(see illustration)**.

6 Remove the bolts securing the rear chain guide and remove the guide **(see illustration)**.

7 Slide the crankshaft sprocket for the rear timing chain off the crankshaft **(see illustration)**.

8 Rotate the crankshaft 1-2/3 turns clockwise, until the keyway is in the 11 o'clock position, setting the camshafts in the front cylinder head in their neutral position. Remove the front timing chain tensioner mounting bolts. Remove the tensioner and tensioner arm **(see illustrations)**.

9 Lift the front timing chain off the sprockets and remove the chain.

10 Remove the chain guide mounting bolts and remove the front chain guide **(see illustration)**. If necessary, slide the crankshaft sprocket for the front timing chain off the crankshaft.

Inspection

Note: *Do not mix parts from the front and rear timing chains and tensioners. Keep the parts separate.*

11 Clean all parts with clean solvent. Dry with compressed air.

12 Inspect the chain tensioners and tensioner arms for excessive wear or other damage.

13 Inspect the timing chain guides for deep grooves, excessive wear, or other damage.

14 Inspect the timing chain for excessive wear or damage.

15 Inspect the camshaft and crankshaft sprockets for chipped or broken teeth, excessive wear, or damage.

16 Replace any component that is in questionable condition.

Installation

17 The timing chain tensioners must be fully compressed and locked in place before chain installation. To prepare the chain tensioners for installation:

a) *Insert a small screwdriver into the access hole in the tensioner and release the pawl mechanism.*
b) *Compress the plunger into the tensioner housing until the plunger tip is below the plate on the pawl.*
c) *Hold the plunger in the compressed position and rotate the plunger one-half turn so the plunger can be removed. Remove the plunger and plunger spring.*
d) *Drain the oil from the tensioner housing and plunger.*

10.8a Remove the bolts that secure the front timing chain tensioner; remove the tensioner . . .

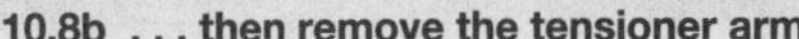

10.8b . . . then remove the tensioner arm

10.10 Remove the bolts securing the front timing chain guide and remove the guide

e) Lubricate the tensioner housing, spring and plunger with clean engine oil. Insert the plunger spring into the tensioner housing. Install the plunger into the housing and push it in until fully compressed. Then, turn the plunger 180 degrees and use a small screwdriver to push back the pawl mechanism into contact with the plunger.

f) With the plunger compressed, insert a 1/16-inch drill bit or a straightened paper clip into the small hole above the pawl mechanism to hold the plunger in place.

g) Repeat this procedure for the other tensioner.

18 If removed, install the crankshaft sprocket for the front timing chain. Make sure the crankshaft keyway is still at 11 o'clock.

19 Look at the index marks on the backside of the front bank exhaust and intake camshaft sprockets. The marks should be facing each other **(see illustration 10.2)**. If not, reposition the camshafts to align the index marks. **Caution:** *The timing chains have three links that are a different color than the rest of the links. When installed, the colored links on the chain must be aligned with the index marks on the camshaft and crankshaft sprockets* **(see illustration 10.32)**.

20 Install the front timing chain guide. Tighten the mounting bolts to the torque listed in this Chapter's Specifications.

21 Install the front timing chain around the camshaft and crankshaft sprockets. Make sure the index marks on the sprockets are aligned and the colored links of the chain are aligned with the marks on the camshaft and crankshaft sprockets.

22 Install the front tensioner arm over its pivot dowel. Seat the tensioner arm firmly on the cylinder head and block.

23 Install the front timing chain tensioner assembly **(see illustrations 10.8a and 10.8b)**. Be sure the tensioner plunger is fully compressed and locked in place. Tighten the tensioner mounting bolts to the torque listed in this Chapter's Specifications. Verify that the colored links of the timing chain are aligned with the index marks on the camshaft and crankshaft sprockets, the index marks on the camshaft sprockets are facing each other, and the crankshaft keyway is at 11 o'clock. If not, remove the timing chain and repeat the installation procedure.

24 Install the crankshaft sprocket for the rear timing chain on the crankshaft **(see illustration 10.7)**.

25 Rotate the crankshaft clockwise until the crankshaft keyway is in the 3 o'clock position. This will correctly position the pistons for installation of the rear timing chain.

26 Install the rear timing chain guide. Tighten the mounting bolts to the torque listed in this Chapter's Specifications.

27 Position the rear camshafts so the index marks on the sprockets are aligned with each other **(see illustration 10.2)**. **Caution:** *The timing chains have three links that are a different color than the rest of the links. When installed, the colored links on the chain must be aligned with the index marks on the camshaft and crankshaft sprockets* **(see illustration 10.32)**.

28 Install the rear timing chain around the camshaft and crankshaft sprockets **(see illustration 10.5)**. Make sure the index marks on the camshaft sprockets are facing each other and that the colored links of the chain are aligned with the index marks on the front of the camshaft and crankshaft sprockets.

29 Install the rear tensioner arm over its pivot dowel. Seat the tensioner arm firmly on the cylinder head and block.

30 Install the rear timing chain tensioner. Be sure the tensioner plunger is fully compressed and locked in place. Tighten the tensioner mounting bolts to specification **(see illustrations 10.4a and 10.4b)**. Verify that the colored links of the timing chain are aligned with the index marks on the camshaft and crankshaft sprockets, the index marks on the back of the camshaft sprockets are facing each other, and the crankshaft keyway is at 3 o'clock. If not, remove the timing chain and repeat the installation procedure.

31 Remove the drill bits or wires (locking pins) from the timing chain tensioners.

32 Rotate the crankshaft clockwise to the 11 o'clock position or the Number 1 TDC position. Verify the timing marks on the camshafts sprockets and the crankshaft sprocket with the paint marks on the links **(see illustration)**.

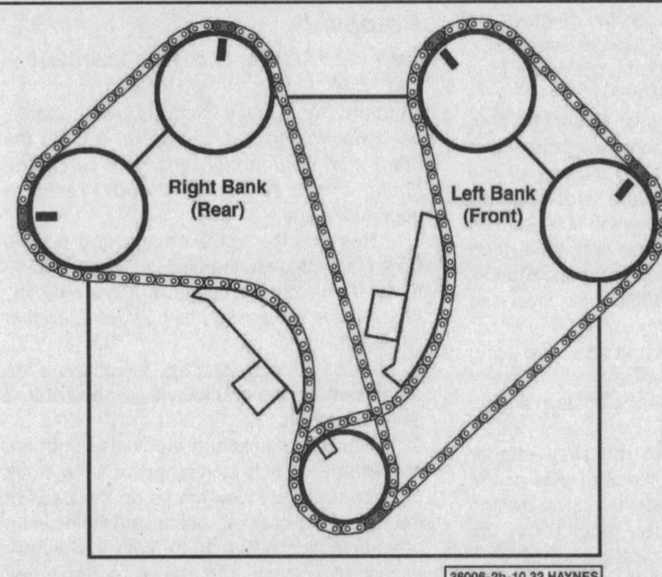

10.32 Location of the number 1 TDC with crankshaft keyway at 11 o'clock - although not visible, the painted link on the left bank (front) timing chain is located in the same position as the right bank (rear) timing chain

12.5 Remove the camshaft thrust caps first

12.6 On the rear camshafts, loosen the camshaft journal caps in several steps, following the sequence shown

33 Install the crankshaft position sensor trigger wheel on the crankshaft. Make sure the orange paint stripe on the trigger wheel is aligned with the crankshaft key.

34 Install the engine front cover (see Section 9).

35 Reinstall the remaining parts in the reverse order of removal.

36 Refer to Chapter 1 and fill the crankcase with the recommended oil; fill the power steering reservoir with the correct fluid; and refill and bleed the cooling system.

37 Connect the negative battery cable, start the engine and check for leaks. Check all fluid levels.

11 Camshaft oil seal - replacement

Note 1: *The front intake camshaft also drives the water pump via a pulley on the rear of the engine. Therefore, this camshaft is the only one equipped with a seal.*

1 Remove the water pump pulley cover.

2 Turn the water pump belt tensioner clockwise to release belt tension. Remove the drivebelt and carefully release the tensioner.

3 Remove the water pump pulley from the camshaft using a suitable puller.

4 Carefully pry the camshaft seal from its bore. Use extreme caution to not damage the seal retainer or the sealing surface of the camshaft. Discard the seal. **Note:** *If you encounter difficulty removing the seal, you can unbolt the seal retainer and remove it, then remove and install the seal on the workbench. This will require removal of the valve cover (see Section 5).*

5 Clean the camshaft and seal bore using a clean shop cloth.

6 Lubricate the new seal with clean engine oil.

7 Install the seal into the seal retainer using a seal driver or a piece of pipe of the proper diameter. Make sure the driver or pipe closely matches the outer diameter of the seal and will completely clear the camshaft.

8 If removed, install the seal retainer, using a new gasket. Tighten the bolts to the torque listed in this Chapter's Specifications. Install the valve cover (see Section 5).

Caution: *The water pump pulley must be pressed onto the camshaft using this tool. Don't attempt to drive the pulley onto the camshaft or engine damage will occur. If necessary, fabricate a tool that will thread into the camshaft and draw the pulley onto the camshaft.*

9 Install the water pump drive pulley onto the camshaft using a power steering pump pulley installer (available at most auto parts stores).

10 Rotate the water pump drive belt tensioner in a clockwise direction and install the water pump drive belt. Release the tensioner slowly. Install the water pump pulley shield to compete assembly.

12 Camshafts, lifters and rocker arms - removal, inspection and installation

Removal

Refer to illustrations 12.5, 12.6, 12.9, 12.10 and 12.14

Caution: *Don't rotate the crankshaft counterclockwise during this procedure. Turning the crankshaft counterclockwise will cause the timing chains to bind and could result in engine damage.*

1 Remove the valve covers and engine front cover as described in Sections 5 and 9. **Note:** *If only one camshaft requires removal, only remove the timing chain attached to that camshaft.*

2 Install the crankshaft pulley bolt into the crankshaft so the crankshaft can be rotated using a wrench.

3 Turn the crankshaft clockwise until the crankshaft keyway is facing the 11 o'clock position and the index marks on the back of the rear timing chain sprockets are facing each other **(see illustration 10.2)**. With the keyway facing 11 o'clock and the sprocket index marks aligned, the number 1 piston is at TDC. **Note:** *If the camshaft marks aren't aligned, turn the camshaft one complete revolution.*

4 Next, turn the crankshaft (clockwise) until the keyway is facing the three o'clock position. This locates the rear camshafts in the neutral position (base circle). Remove the rear timing chain as described in Section 10. **Caution 1:** *The camshaft journal caps and cylinder heads are marked with numbers to identify the locations of the caps. The caps MUST be installed in their original locations. Keep all parts from each camshaft together; never mix parts from one camshaft to another.* **Caution 2:** *The camshaft thrust caps must be removed prior to removing the journal caps to prevent damage to the thrust caps, camshaft or cylinder head.* **Note:** *The camshaft thrust caps and journal caps fit on dowels in the cylinder head. It may be necessary to lightly tap the caps using a soft-faced mallet to dislodge the caps.*

5 Remove the bolts securing the thrust caps **(see illustration)**. Note that the camshaft thrust caps are adjacent to the timing sprockets. Remove the thrust caps.

6 Following the sequence given **(see illustration)**, gradually loosen the bolts that secure the camshaft caps to the cylinder head. Loosen the bolts a little at a time, in several passes.

7 When all camshaft cap bolts are loose, finish removing the bolts and remove the caps. It may be necessary to lightly tap the caps with a soft-face mallet to dislodge the caps from the locating dowels.

8 Identify the camshafts (intake and exhaust). Lift the camshafts straight up and out of the cylinder head.

9 Remove the rocker arms **(see illustration)**. **Caution:** *Mark the position of the rocker arms so they can be reinstalled in their original locations.*

10 Place the rocker arms in a suitable container so they can be separated and identified **(see illustration)**.

11 If necessary, lift the valve lifters from their bores in the cylinder block. Identify and

12.9 Remove the rocker arms (arrows)

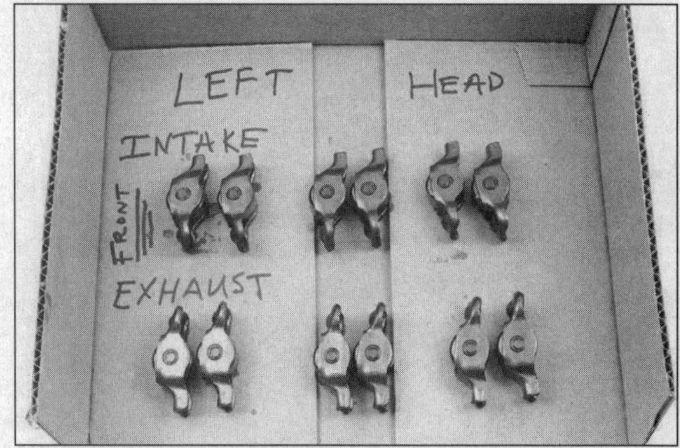

12.10 Place all components in a container so they can be separated and identified for installation in their original locations

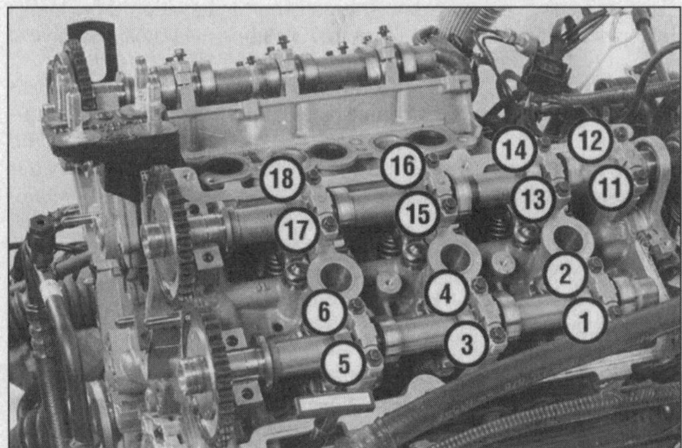

12.14 On the front camshafts, loosen the journal caps in several steps, in the sequence shown

12.18 Check the cam lobes for pitting, excessive wear and scoring. If scoring is excessive, as is the case here, replace the camshaft

separate the lifters so they can be reinstalled in their original locations.

12 To place the front camshafts in the neutral position (base circle) turn the crankshaft two turns (clockwise) until the crankshaft keyway is facing the 11 o'clock position and the index marks on the timing sprockets are facing directly toward each other.

13 Remove the front timing chain as described in Section 10.

14 Repeat Steps 5 to 11 to remove the front camshafts. Be sure to remove the camshaft thrust caps first, then loosen the journal caps on the front camshafts in the sequence shown **(see illustration)**.

Inspection

Refer to illustrations 12.18, 12.20, 12.21a, 12.21b, 12.28 and 12.33

15 With the camshafts and hydraulic lifters removed, check each for obvious wear (scoring, pitting out-of-round). Replace if necessary.

16 Measure the outside diameter of each lifter - take measurements at the top and bottom of each lifter, then a second set at right-angles to the first; if any measurement is significantly different from the others, the lifter is tapered or out-of-round (as applicable) and must be replaced. If the necessary equipment is available, measure the inside diameter of the corresponding cylinder head bore. Compare the measurements obtained to those given in the Specifications Section of this Chapter; if the lifters or the cylinder head bores are excessively worn, new lifters and/or a new cylinder head will be required.

17 If the valve train is noisy, particularly if the noise persists after initial start-up from cold, there is reason to suspect a faulty hydraulic lifter.

18 Visually examine the camshaft lobes for score marks, pitting, galling (wear due to rubbing) and evidence of overheating (blue, discolored areas). Look for flaking away of the hardened surface layer of each lobe **(see illustration)**. If any such wear is evident, replace the component concerned.

19 Examine the camshaft bearing journals and the cylinder head bearing surfaces for obvious wear or pitting. If any such wear is evident, replace the component concerned.

20 Using a micrometer, measure the diameter of each journal at several points **(see illustration)**. If the diameter of any one journal is less than the specified value, replace the camshaft.

21 To check the bearing journal oil clearance, remove the hydraulic lifters, use a suitable solvent and a clean lint-free rag to clean carefully all bearing surfaces, then install the camshafts and bearing caps with a piece of

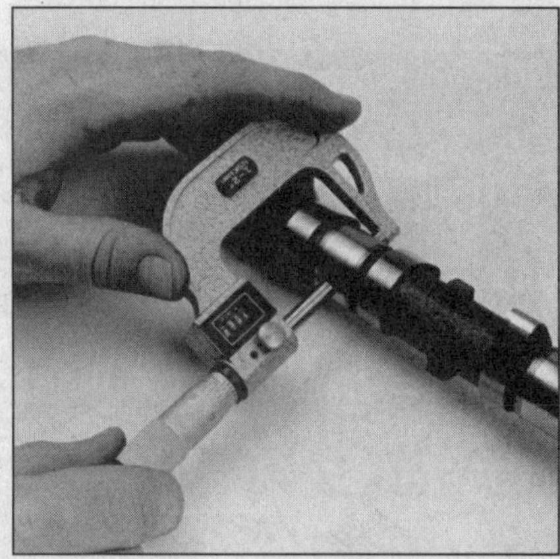

12.20 Measure each journal diameter using a micrometer. If any journal is less than the specified minimum, replace the camshaft

12.21a Lay a strip of Plastigage on each camshaft journal

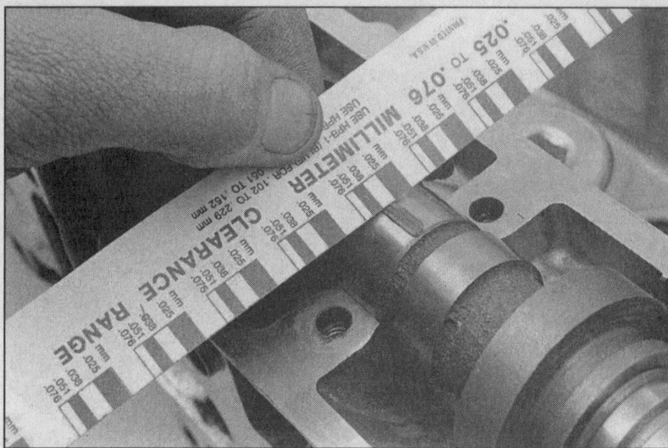

12.21b Compare the width of the crushed Plastigage to the scale on the package to determine the journal oil clearance

Plastigage across each journal **(see illustration)**. Tighten the bearing cap bolts to the specified setting (don't rotate the camshafts), then remove the bearing caps and use the scale provided to measure the width of the flattened Plastigage **(see illustration)**. Scrape off the Plastigage with your fingernail or the edge of a credit card - don't scratch or nick the journals or bearing caps.

22 If the oil clearance of any bearing is worn beyond the specified service limit, and the camshaft journal diameters are within specifications, the cylinder head may have to be replaced. Consult an automotive machine shop for advice before replacing the cylinder head.

23 To check camshaft endplay, remove the hydraulic lifters, clean the bearing surfaces carefully, and install the camshafts and bearing caps. Tighten the bearing cap bolts to the specified setting, then measure the endplay using a dial indicator mounted on the cylinder head so that its tip bears on the camshaft rear end.

24 Pry the camshaft fully toward the gauge, zero the gauge, then pry the camshaft fully away from the gauge, and note the gauge reading. If the endplay measured is at or beyond the specified service limit, install a new camshaft thrust cap and repeat the check. If the clearance is still excessive, the camshaft and/or cylinder head must be replaced.

Installation

25 Make sure the crankshaft keyway is still facing the 11 o'clock position.

26 Lubricate the front valve lifters and rocker arms with camshaft installation lube. Install the lifters into their original bores, then install the rocker arms in their correct locations.

27 Lubricate the front camshafts with camshaft installation lube. Install the camshafts in their correct locations. **Caution:** *The camshaft thrust caps must be installed after the journal caps are installed and tightened.*

28 Install the front camshaft journal caps in their correct locations. Install the journal cap bolts and tighten by hand until snug. Then, install the front camshaft thrust caps and bolts. Tighten the bolts in four to five steps, following the sequence shown **(see illustration)** to the torque listed in this Chapter's Specifications.

29 Install the front timing chain as described in Section 10.

30 Turn the crankshaft two full turns and position the crankshaft keyway at three o'clock.

31 Lubricate the rear valve lifters and rocker arms with camshaft installation lube. Install the lifters into their original bores, then install the rocker arms in their correct locations.

32 Lubricate the rear camshafts with camshaft installation lube. Install the camshafts in their correct locations. **Caution:** *The camshaft thrust caps must be installed after the journal caps are installed and tightened.*

33 Install the rear camshaft journal caps in their correct locations. Install the journal cap bolts and tighten by hand until snug. Then, install the front camshaft thrust caps and bolts. Tighten the bolts in four to five steps, following the sequence shown **(see illustration)** to the torque listed in this Chapter's Specifications.

34 Install the rear timing chain as described in Section 10.

35 Complete the remaining assembly by reversing the disassembly procedure.

13 Cylinder heads - removal and installation

Removal

Refer to illustrations 13.9, 13.10 and 13.11

Warning: *The engine must be raised and*

12.28 Tighten the camshaft bearing caps on the front cylinder head in several steps, following the sequence shown

12.33 Camshaft journal cap tightening sequence - rear cylinder head

13.9 Disconnect the electrical connector from the EGR valve back pressure transducer (arrow)

13.10 Remove the EGR tube from the rear exhaust manifold

securely supported to provide sufficient clearance to remove the oil pan during this procedure. The manufacturer recommends using a three bar engine support (to raise and support the engine. Don't attempt this procedure unless the engine can be safely and securely supported.

Note: *The following instructions describe the steps necessary to remove both cylinder heads. If only one cylinder head requires removal, disregard the steps pertaining to the other head.*

1 Disconnect the negative battery cable.

2 Drain the cooling system (see Chapter 1).

3 Remove the upper and lower intake manifold assemblies (see Section 6).

4 Drain the engine oil (see Chapter 1). Remove the oil pan (see Section 14) and engine front cover (see Section 9). **Note:** *If both cylinder heads must be removed, it is necessary to remove both timing chains, camshafts and rocker arms. If just the rear head requires removal, it is only necessary to remove the rear timing chain, camshafts and rocker arms from the rear cylinder head; the front can remain intact. However, if just the front head must be removed, it is still necessary to first remove the rear timing chain to access the front chain. In this case, the rear camshafts and rocker arms can remain installed. Rear cylinder head removal continues at Step 6. To remove the front cylinder head, continue at Step 14.*

5 Reinstall the engine front mount assembly (removed during front cover removal), lower the engine and remove the engine lifting device.

6 Remove the timing chain(s), camshafts and rocker arms as necessary.

7 If removing the rear cylinder head, remove the oxygen sensor from the rear exhaust manifold using a socket designed for this purpose (see Chapter 6).

8 Disconnect the EGR valve backpressure transducer hoses from the EGR valve-to-exhaust manifold tube.

9 Disconnect the electrical connector from the EGR valve back pressure transducer **(see illustration)**.

10 Remove the EGR valve tube from the rear exhaust manifold **(see illustration).**

11 Remove any hoses or electrical connectors from the coolant bypass assembly. Remove the two fasteners securing the coolant bypass assembly **(see illustration).** Remove the coolant bypass and place it aside. **Note:** *The rear cylinder head can be removed with the exhaust manifold and EGR valve back pressure transducer still attached.*

12 Loosen each head bolt, one turn at a time, following the reverse order of the sequence shown in **illustration 13.26a**. When all head bolts are completely loose, remove and discard the bolts. New cylinder head bolts must be used during installation.

13 Remove the cylinder head from the engine block and place it on a workbench. Remove and discard the head gasket. If necessary, remove the exhaust manifold from the head.

14 To remove the front cylinder head, remove the water pump (see Chapter 3). Remove the two nuts securing the tube attached to the lower radiator hose. Remove the tube from the front cylinder head.

15 If still installed, remove the coolant bypass assembly **(see illustration 13.11)**.

16 Remove the dipstick tube.

17 Loosen each head bolt, one turn at a time, following the reverse order of the sequence shown in illustration 13.26a. When all head bolts are completely loose, remove and discard the bolts. New cylinder head bolts must be used during installation.

18 Remove the cylinder head from the engine block and place it on a workbench. Remove and discard the head gasket. If necessary, remove the exhaust manifold from the head.

Installation

Refer to illustrations 13.26a and 13.26b

19 The mating surfaces of the cylinder head and cylinder block must be perfectly clean before installing the head. Use a scraper to clean the mating surfaces, but be very careful not to gouge the delicate aluminum surfaces.

20 Check the mating surfaces of the cylinder block and the cylinder head for nicks, deep scratches and other damage. If slight, they may be removed carefully with a file, but if excessive, machining may be the only alternative to replacement.

21 If warpage of the cylinder head gasket surface is suspected, use a straightedge to check it for distortion. Refer to Part C of this Chapter, if necessary.

22 Wipe clean the mating surfaces of the cylinder head and cylinder block.

23 Check that the two locating dowels are in position in the cylinder block, and that all cylinder head bolt holes are free of oil, corrosion or other contamination.

24 Install new cylinder head gaskets on the cylinder block and over the locating dowels. **Caution:** *The cylinder head bolts are the torque-to-yield type and are stretched during the tightening process. Therefore, the original bolts must be discarded and new bolts installed during assembly.*

25 Carefully install the cylinder head(s). Use

13.11 Remove the coolant bypass assembly from the engine and lay it aside

13.26a Cylinder head bolt TIGHTENING sequence (loosen the bolts in the reverse order)

13.26b An angle gauge is required to properly tighten the torque-to-yield cylinder head bolts

caution when lowering the head(s) onto the cylinder block to prevent damage to the head(s) or block. Make sure the heads fit properly over the locating dowels in the cylinder block.

26 Install new cylinder head bolts and turn down by hand until snug. Using a torque wrench and an angle gauge, tighten the head bolts in the recommended sequence to the torque listed in this Chapter's Specifications **(see illustrations)**.

27 Complete assembly by reversing the disassembly procedure. Tighten all remaining fasteners to the torque listed in this Chapter's specifications.

28 Refill the engine crankcase with oil and the cooling system with coolant (see Chapter 1).

29 Start the engine and warm to normal operating temperature. Check closely for oil or coolant leakage. Repair any leaks prior to returning the vehicle to service. **Note:** *After the battery has been disconnected, the engine may exhibit some abnormal driveability symptoms. After driving 10 miles or more, however, the electronic engine management system will relearn its adaptive strategy and the engine will operate normally.*

14 Oil pan - removal and installation

Removal

Refer to illustrations 14.3, 14.8, 14.10 and 14.12

Warning: *The engine must be raised and securely supported to provide sufficient clearance to remove the oil pan during this procedure. The manufacturer recommends using three bar engine support to raise and support the engine. Don't attempt this procedure unless the engine can be safely and securely supported. Precise details of the procedure depends on the equipment available, although the following is typical.*

1 Drain the engine oil (Chapter 1). Reinstall the oil pan drain plug and tighten to the torque listed in this chapter's specifications, using a new gasket if necessary.

2 Remove the water pump pulley shield.

3 Attach a suitable lifting device to the engine lifting eye **(see illustration)**.

4 Raise the front of the vehicle and support it with jackstands.

5 Remove the exhaust Y-pipe from the both exhaust manifolds. Also remove the bracket that supports the exhaust pipe from the oil pan on the right side.

6 Remove the two nuts that mount the air conditioning compressor heat shield to the oil pan.

7 Remove the flywheel/driveplate access cover.

8 Remove the two bolts that secure the oil pan to the transaxle **(see illustration)**.

9 Remove the through-bolts from the engine mounts. **Note:** *Mark the position of the front upper engine support bracket for reference during installation.*

10 Remove the nuts that hold the engine support bracket to the engine and engine mount **(see illustration)**. Note the location of the ground wire under one of the nuts. Remove the support bracket.

11 Using the engine support **(see illustration 14.3)**, raise the engine sufficiently to access the oil pan fasteners and remove the oil pan.

12 Note the location of any stud bolts. Also note the location of the two oil pan bolts in the recessed area adjacent to the transaxle **(see illustration)**. Remove the oil pan bolts and lower the pan from the vehicle. Remove and discard the oil pan gasket. If necessary,

14.3 To remove the oil pan, equipment must be available to raise and support the engine/transaxle assembly

14.8 Remove the two bolts (arrows) that secure the oil pan to the transaxle

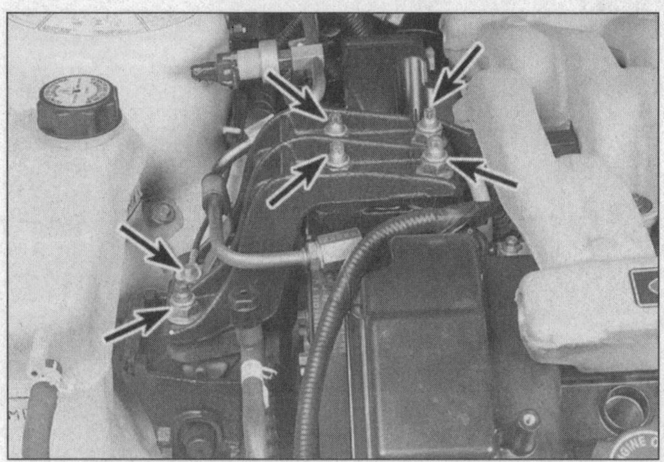
14.10 Remove the bolts (arrows) and remove the engine support bracket from the front of the engine

14.12 Be sure to remove the two oil pan bolts hidden in the recessed area next to the transaxle (arrow)

remove the fasteners that secure the oil screen and pickup tube and remove the screen/tube assembly.

13 Thoroughly clean the oil pan and cylinder block mating surfaces using lacquer thinner or acetone. The surfaces must be free of any residue that will inhibit the ability of the sealant to adhere properly. Clean the oil pan inside and out with solvent and dry with compressed air.

Installation

14 If removed, install a new O-ring seal onto the oil pickup tube. Install the tube and screen assembly and tighten the retaining fasteners to the torque listed in this Chapter's Specifications. Use a new self-locking nut to secure the pickup tube support bracket. Tighten the nut to the torque listed in this Chapter's Specifications.

15 Install a new gasket on the oil pan. Apply a 1/8-inch bead of RTV sealant to the oil pan gasket in the area of the engine front cover-to-cylinder block parting line.

16 Install the oil pan being careful not to dislodge the pan gasket. Install the pan bolts and tighten by hand. Be sure to install any stud bolts in the locations noted during removal. Install the two oil pan-to-transaxle bolts. Firmly push the oil pan against the transaxle and tighten the pan-to-transaxle bolts snugly. Then, following a cross pattern, tighten the oil pan bolts, gradually and evenly, to the torque listed in this chapter's specifications.

17 The remaining assembly is the reverse of disassembly, noting the following items:

(a) *Tighten all fasteners to the torque listed in this Chapter's Specifications.*

(b) *Always replace any self-locking nuts disturbed on removal.*

(c) *Lower the engine/transaxle unit into place, and reassemble the front engine support bracket. Don't yet release the hoist; the weight of the engine/transmission unit must be supported until all engine mount fasteners are installed.*

(d) *Refill the cooling system* (see Chapter 1).

(e) *Refill the engine with oil and install a new filter* (see Chapter 1).

(g) *Check for oil or coolant leaks once the engine has been started and warmed to normal operating temperature.*

15 Oil pump - removal, inspection and installation

2B

Refer to illustrations 15.3, 15.4 and 15.5

Note: *Because of the relatively low cost of the oil pump compared with the difficulty in accessing it for removal,*

Removal

1 Remove the oil pan and oil screen/pickup tube assembly (Section 14).

2 Remove the engine front cover (Section 9) and timing chains and crankshaft sprockets (Section 10).

3 Loosen each of the four oil pump mounting bolts one turn. Then, gradually and evenly, loosen each bolt in several steps. When all bolts are loose, remove the bolts and oil pump **(see illustration)**.

Inspection

4 Unscrew the Torx screws, and remove the pump cover plate **(see illustration)** from the pump body.

15.3 When all bolts are loose, remove the bolts (arrows) and lift off the oil pump

15.4 To disassemble the oil pump, remove the screws securing the pump cover to the pump body

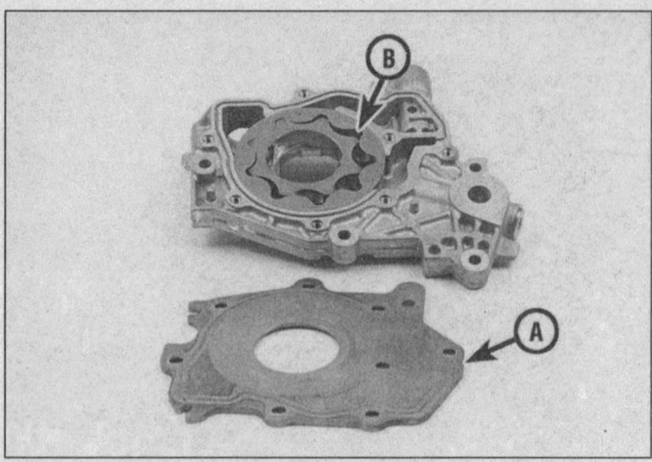

15.5 Remove the pump cover (A) and, noting any identification marks on the rotors, remove the inner and outer rotors (B) from the pump body

18.3 Install the crankshaft front seal (arrow) flush with the front cover surface

5 Noting any identification marks on the rotors, withdraw the inner and outer rotors from the pump body **(see illustration)**.

6 Clean all pump components with clean solvent and dry with compressed air. The pump internal parts must be absolutely clean upon assembly.

7 Inspect the rotors for obvious wear or damage. If either rotor, the pump body, or its cover plate are scored or damaged, the complete oil pump assembly must be replaced.

8 If all oil pump components are in acceptable condition, install the inner and outer rotors into the pump body. Install the rotors with any identification marks positioned as noted during disassembly. Install the pump cover and screws. Tighten the screws securely.

Installation

9 Rotate the oil pump inner rotor so it aligns with the flats on the crankshaft. Install the oil pump over the crankshaft and fit it firmly against the cylinder block.

10 Install the pump bolts and hand tighten until snug. Tighten the bolts gradually and evenly, to the torque listed in this chapter's specifications.

11 Complete the remaining assembly by reversing the disassembly procedure. Fill the crankcase with oil and install a new oil filter. Start the engine and warm to normal operating temperature while checking for leakage. Repair any leaks before returning the vehicle to service.

16 Oil cooler - removal and installation

Note: *Not all models are equipped with an oil cooler.*

1 Drain the cooling system (see Chapter 1). Disconnect the coolant hoses from the oil cooler. Remove the lower radiator shroud.

2 Unscrew the oil filter (see Chapter 1) - catch any escaping oil in a drip tray.

3 Unscrew the nut in the center of the filter adapter and withdraw the oil cooler. Note how its connections are aligned, and be prepared for oil loss from the cooler.

4 Installation is the reverse of the removal procedure, noting the following points:

(a) *Replace all O-rings and seals disturbed on removal.*

(b) *Align the cooler's unions as noted on removal, and tighten the adapter to the torque listed in this Chapter's Specifications.*

(c) *Refill the cooling system* (see Chapter 1).

(d) *Install the oil filter, then check the engine oil level, and top-up as necessary* (see Chapter 1).

(e) *Check for signs of oil or coolant leaks once the engine has been restarted and warmed-up to normal operating temperature.*

17 Oil pressure sending unit - removal and installation

1 This switch operates the oil pressure gauge or indicator on the dash. The switch is screwed into the rear of the cylinder block, adjacent to the oil filter.

2 With the vehicle parked on firm level ground, open the hood and disconnect the battery negative (ground) lead.

3 Raise the front of the vehicle, and support it securely on jack stands.

4 Unplug the wiring from the switch, and unscrew it; be prepared for some oil loss.

5 Installation is the reverse of the removal procedure. Apply a thin film of a suitable sealant to the switch threads and tighten it securely. Check the engine oil level, and top-up as necessary (see Chapter 1). Check for oil leaks once the engine has been started and warmed to normal operating temperature.

18 Crankshaft front oil seal - replacement

Refer to illustration 18.3

1 Remove the crankshaft pulley as described in Section 8 of this Chapter.

2 Using a seal removal tool or large screwdriver, pry the seal from the front cover. Use extreme caution to not damage the crankshaft sealing surface or the seal bore in the front cover. Discard the seal.

3 Lubricate the new seal's lip with clean engine oil. Using a seal driver or a large socket or piece of pipe with an outside diameter slightly smaller than the outside diameter of the seal, install the seal into the engine front cover until flush with the cover surface **(see illustration)**.

4 Complete the remaining assembly by reversing the disassembly procedure.

19 Rear main oil seal - replacement

Note: *A one-piece rear seal is used. The seal can be replaced without crankshaft removal, providing the correct special tools are available.*

1 Remove the transaxle (see Chapter 7).

2 Remove the flywheel/driveplate (Section 20).

3 Carefully drill two small holes in the seal casing and thread in two self-tapping screws. Pry on the screw heads to remove the seal. Thoroughly clean the crankshaft sealing surface and the seal bore in the cylinder block. Inspect the crankshaft for burrs or rough edges that can cause the new seal to fail.

4 Lubricate the seal lips of the new seal with clean engine oil. Install the seal using a seal driver. Make sure the seal is square with its bore during installation.

5 Install the flywheel/driveplate (Section 20) and transaxle (Chapter 7).

20 Flywheel/driveplate - removal, inspection and installation

Removal

1 Remove the transaxle (see the relevant Part of Chapter 7). Now is a good time to check components such as oil seals and replace them if necessary.

2 Where appropriate, remove the clutch (Chapter 8). Now is a good time to check or replace the clutch components and pilot bearing.

3 Use a center-punch or paint to make alignment marks on the flywheel/driveplate and crankshaft, to ensure correct alignment during installation.

4 Prevent the flywheel/driveplate from turning by locking the ring gear teeth, or by bolting a strap between the flywheel/driveplate and the cylinder block/crankcase. Loosen the bolts evenly until all are free.

5 Remove each bolt in turn, and ensure that new replacements are obtained for reassembly; these bolts are subjected to severe stresses, and so must be replaced, regardless of their apparent condition, whenever they are disturbed.

6 Noting the reinforcing plate (automatic transmission only), withdraw the flywheel/driveplate; do not drop it - it is very heavy.

Inspection

7 Clean the flywheel/driveplate to remove grease and oil. Inspect the surface for cracks, rivet grooves, burned areas and score marks. Light scoring can be removed with emery cloth. Check for cracked and broken ring gear teeth. Lay the flywheel/driveplate on a flat surface, and use a straight edge to check for warpage.

8 Clean and inspect the mating surfaces of the flywheel/driveplate and the crankshaft. If the crankshaft rear oil seal is leaking, replace it (see Section 19) before installing the flywheel/driveplate.

9 While the flywheel/driveplate is removed, carefully clean its inner surface, particularly the recesses which serve as the reference points for the crankshaft speed/position sensor. Clean the sensor's tip, and check that the sensor is securely fastened.

Installation

10 On installation, ensure that the engine/transmission adapter plate is in place (where necessary), then fit the flywheel/driveplate to the crankshaft so that all bolt holes align - it will fit only one way - check this using the marks made on removal. Do not forget the reinforcing plate (where fitted).

11 Lock the flywheel/driveplate by the method used on disassembly. Working in a diagonal sequence to tighten them evenly, alternating from bolt to bolt, to the torque listed in this Chapter's Specifications.

12 The remainder of reassembly is the reverse of the removal procedure, referring to the relevant text for details where required.

21.12 Remove the nuts securing the engine support bracket (A) to the engine and front mount (B)

21 Engine/transaxle mounts - inspection and replacement

General

1 The engine/transaxle mounts seldom require attention, but broken or deteriorated mounts should be replaced immediately, or the added strain placed on the driveline components may cause damage or wear.

2 While separate mounts may be removed and installed individually, if more than one is disturbed at a time - such as if the engine/transaxle unit is removed from its mounts - they must be reassembled and their fasteners tightened in sequence.

3 On reassembly, the weight of the engine/transmission unit must not be taken by the mounts until all are correctly aligned. Connect an engine hoist or support fixture tool in place of the front mount, then tighten the engine/transmission mounting fasteners to the specified torque, and in the sequence described in Part C of this Chapter.

Inspection

4 During the check, the engine/transaxle unit must be raised slightly, to remove its weight from the mounts.

5 Raise the front of the vehicle, and support it securely on axle stands. Position a jack under the oil pan, with a large block of wood between the jack head and the oil pan, then carefully raise the engine/transaxle just enough to take the weight off the mounts. **Warning:** *DO NOT place any part of your body under the engine when it is supported only by a jack!*

6 Check the mounts to see if the rubber is cracked, hardened or separated from the metal components. Sometimes the rubber will split right down the center.

7 Check for relative movement between each mounting's brackets and the engine/transaxle or body (use a large screwdriver or prybar to attempt to move the mounts). If movement is noted, lower the engine and check-tighten the mounting fasteners.

Replacement

Refer to illustration 21.12

Engine front support bracket and mount

8 Remove the water pump pulley cover.

9 To create clearance for support bracket removal, remove the coolant recovery tank and place it aside.

10 If necessary, disconnect the power steering discharge line from the power steering pump. Place a shop cloth under the line to keep power steering fluid off the engine mount.

11 Support the engine using a suitable lifting device or place a jack under the oil pan with a block of wood placed between the jack and pan. **Note:** *The support bracket nuts are the self-locking type. The manufacturer recommends using new self-locking nuts during assembly.*

12 Mark the position of the engine support bracket for correct installation. Remove the nuts securing the engine support bracket to the engine and front mount **(see illustration)**. Note the location of the ground wire under one of the nuts. Remove the engine support bracket.

13 If necessary, remove the three bolts that secure the engine front mount to the inner fender apron and remove the mount.

14 Reassemble the front mount and support bracket assembly by reversing the removal procedure. Replace the self-locking nuts and tighten all fasteners to the torque listed in this Chapter's Specifications.

Rear engine/transaxle mount

Note: *Self-locking nuts are used on the engine/transaxle mounts. It is recommended that the nuts be replaced during installation.*

15 Remove the battery (see Chapter 1).

16 Remove the air filter and filter housing.

17 Remove the water pump pulley shield.

18 Support the engine and transaxle with a suitable lifting device or place a jack under the oil pan with a block of wood placed between the jack and pan.

19 Remove the bolts securing the

engine/transaxle to the left-hand inner fender apron.

20 Remove the nuts securing the mount to the transaxle and remove the mount.

21 Reinstall the mount assembly by reversing the removal procedure. Replace all self-locking fasteners. Tighten all fasteners to the torque listed in this Chapter's Specifications.

Left-hand mount (front of vehicle)

22 Remove the bolts securing the front engine mount to the subframe

23 Remove the through-bolt securing the engine mount bracket to the engine mount.

24 Remove the engine mount from the subframe.

25 If necessary, remove the engine mount bracket form the engine.

26 During installation, ensure the mount bracket-to-transaxle bolts are securely tightened. Tighten the mount through bolt to the torque listed in this Chapter's Specifications.

Right-hand mount (rear of vehicle)

27 Unbolt the mount from the subframe, then unscrew the mounting's through-bolt. If required, unbolt the mount's bracket from the transaxle.

18 On installation, ensure that the mount-to-transaxle bolts are securely tightened, then install the mount. Tighten first the mount-to-subframe bolts, noting that these are to be tightened in two stages to the final specified torque setting. Finally tighten the mount's through-bolt, again to the specified torque setting.

Chapter 2 Part C
General engine overhaul procedures

Contents

Specifications

Four-cylinder engines

General

Oil pressure (with oil hot)	
1995 through 1997	20 to 45 psi at 1500 rpm
1998	35 to 65 at 2000 rpm
Cylinder head warpage limit	0.006 inch overall
Compression pressure	Lowest reading cylinder must be within 75 percent of highest cylinder

Valves

Valve lift	
1995 through 1997	
Intake	0.35 inch
Exhaust	0.31 inch
1998 and later	
Intake and exhaust	0.405 inch
Valve head diameter	
1995 through 1997	
Intake	1.26 inches
Exhaust	1.10 inches
1998 and later	
Intake	1.53 to 1.54 inches
Exhaust	1.33 to 1.34 inches

Valves (continued)

Valve stem diameter	
1995 through 1997	
Intake	0.2373 to 0.2379 inch
Exhaust	0.2366 to 0.2372 inch
1998 and later	
Intake	0.3159 to 0.3166 inch
Exhaust	0.3148 to 0.3156 inch
Valve stem-to-guide clearance	
1995 through 1997	
Intake	0.0007 to 0.0025 inch
Exhaust	0.0014 to 0.0032 inch
1998 and later	
Intake	0.0008 to 0.0027 inch
Exhaust	0.0018 to 0.0037 inch
1999 and later	0.0007 to 0.0025 inch
Maximum valve face runout	
1995 through 1997	0.0014 inch
1998 and later	0.002 inch
Valve spring free length	
1995 through 1997	1.70 inches
1998 and later	1.86 inches
Valve spring installed height	
1995 through 1997	1.35 inches
1998 and later	1.42 to 1.54 inches
Valve face angle	
1995 through 1997	91 degrees
1998 and later	45.6 degrees
Valve seat angle	
1995 through 1997	90 degrees
1998 and later	44.6 degrees

Cylinder block

Cylinder bore diameter	
Class 1	3.3386 to 3.3390 inches
Class 2	3.3390 to 3.3394 inches
Class 3	3.3394 to 3.3398 inches

Pistons and piston rings

Piston diameter	
Class 1	3.3374 to 3.3378 inches
Class 2	3.3378 to 3.3382 inches
Class 3	3.3382 to 3.3386 inches
Oversizes - all models	None available
Piston-to-cylinder bore clearance	0.0008 to 0.0016 inch
Piston ring end gap	
1995 through 1997	
Top compression ring	0.010 to 0.020 inch
Second compression ring	0.012 to 0.020 inch
Oil control ring	0.016 to 0.055 inch
1998	
Top and second compression rings	0.012 to 0.020 inch
Oil control ring	0.016 to 0.055 inch
1999 and later	
Top and second compression rings	0.010 to 0.011 inch
Oil control ring	0.0015 to 0.066 inch

Piston pin

Diameter	
White color code/piston crown marked (A)	0.8119 to 0.8120 inch
Red color code/piston crown marked (B)	0.8120 to 0.8121 inch
Blue color code/piston crown marked (C)	0.8121 to 0.8122 inch
Clearance in piston	0.0004 to 0.0006 inch
Connecting rod small-end bore internal diameter	0.8106 to 0.8114 inch

Crankshaft and bearings

Main bearing journal standard diameter	2.2827 to 2.2835 inches
Maximum allowable out-of-round and taper	0.0003 inch
Main bearing oil clearance	0.0004 to 0.0023 inch
Main bearing undersizes available	0.0008 inch, 0.010 inch
Connecting rod journal diameter	
1995 through 1998	1.8460 to 1.8468 inches
1999 and later	1.7279 to 1.7287 inches
Maximum allowable out-of-round and taper	0.0003 inch
Connecting rod bearing oil clearance	0.0006 to 0.0027 inch
Connecting rod bearing undersizes available	0.0008 inch, 0.010 inch
Crankshaft endplay	0.003 to 0.012 inch

Torque specifications

	Ft-lbs (unless specified otherwise)
Main bearing cap bolts and nuts	63
Connecting rod cap bolts*	
Stage 1	26
Stage 2	Tighten an additional 90 degrees
Piston-cooling oil jet/blanking plug Torx screws	84 in-lbs
Front suspension subframe bolts	96
Lower crankcase-to-cylinder block	
1998	16
1999	22

Note: *Refer to Part A of this Chapter for remaining torque specifications.*
**Once the bolts are removed, they must be discarded and replaced. See Section 17 for details.*

V6 engines

Cylinder head

Combustion chamber volume	43 to 46 cubic centimeters
Lifter diameter	0.6290 to 0.6294 inch
Lifter clearance to bore	0.0007 to 0.0027 inch
Collapsed lifter gap	0.019 to 0.043 inch
Rocker arm ratio	1.8:1

Cylinder bore

Bore diameter	
Grade 1	3.2440 to 3.2445 inches
Grade 2	3.2445 to 3.2449 inches
Grade 3	3.2449 to 3.2452 inches
Maximum allowable out-of-round	0.0008 inch
Maximum allowable taper	0.0002 inch

Valves and related components

Valve seat width	
Intake	0.043 to 0.055 inch
Exhaust	0.055 to 0.066 inch
Valve seat angle	44.75 degrees
Maximum allowable valve seat runout	0.001 inch
Valve face angle	45.5 degrees
Valve head diameter	
Intake	1.26 inches
Exhaust	1.02 inches
Maximum allowable valve face runout	0.001 inch
Valve stem diameter	
Intake	0.2350 to 0.2358 inch
Exhaust	0.2343 to 0.2350 inch
Valve stem clearance	
Intake	0.0007 to 0.0027 inch
Exhaust	0.0017 to 0.0037 inch
Valve spring free length	1.84 inches
Valve spring pressure	
Intake	
Valve opened	153 lbs at 1.18 inches
Valve closed	51 lbs at 1.57 inches
Exhaust	
Valve opened	153 lbs at 1.18 inches
Valve closed	51 lbs at 1.57 inches

Crankshaft and connecting rods

Crankshaft endplay	0.004 to 0.009 inch
Main bearing journal diameter	2.479 to 2.480 inches
Maximum allowable out-of-round	0.0006 inch
Maximum allowable taper	0.0004 inch
Main bearing oil clearance	
Desired	0.0010 to 0.0018 inch
Service limit	0.0019 inch
Connecting rod journal diameter	1.967 to 1.968 inches
Maximum allowable out-of-round	0.0006 inch
Maximum allowable taper	0.0004 inch
Connecting rod bearing oil clearance	0.001 to 0.0025 inch
Piston pin bore diameter (small end)	0.827 to 0.828 inch
Connecting rod bore diameter (big end)	2.0872 to 2.0879 inches
Length (center-to-center)	5.435 to 5.448 inches
Side clearance (installed)	
Standard	0.0039 to 0.012 inch
Service limit	0.014 inch

Pistons and rings

Piston diameter	
Grade 1	3.2436 to 3.244 inches
Grade 2	3.2440 to 3.2452 inches
Grade 3	3.2444 to 3.2452 inches
Piston-to-cylinder bore clearance	0.0005 to 0.0009 inch
Piston pin diameter	0.8272 to 0.8273 inch
Piston pin bore diameter (in piston)	0.8270 to 0.8272 inch
Piston pin-to-piston clearance	0.0001 to 0.00003 inch
Piston pin-to-connecting rod clearance	
Standard	0.0001 to 0.0007 inch
Service limit	0.0013 inch
Piston ring side clearance	
Top compression	0.0015 to 0.0029 inch
Service limit	0.0034 inch
Second compression	0.0015 to 0.0033 inch
Oil ring	Snug fit
Piston ring end gap	
Top compression	0.004 to 0.010 inch
Second compression	0.011 to 0.016 inch
Oil ring (steel rail)	0.006 to 0.025 inch

Torque specifications*

	Ft-lbs (unless specified otherwise)
Connecting rod cap bolts**	
Stage 1	17
Stage 2	32
Stage 3	Tighten an additional 90 degrees
Cylinder head bolts**	
Stage 1	29
Stage 2	Tighten an additional 90 degrees
Stage 3	Loosen one full turn
Stage 4	29
Stage 5	Tighten an additional 90 degrees
Stage 6	Tighten an additional 90 degrees
Camshaft cap bolts	84 in-lbs
Engine lifting eyes	83
Lower crankcase-to-cylinder block** **(see illustration 17.17, "tightening sequence")**	
Stage 1 - bolts 1 to 8	18
Stage 2 - bolts 9 to 16	30
Stage 3 - bolts 1 to 16	Tighten bolts 1 to 16 an additional 90 degrees
Stage 4 - bolts 17 to 22	18
Oil filter adapter	25
Oil pan baffle bolts	
Stage 1	44 in-lbs
Stage 2	Tighten an additional 45 degrees

***Note 1:** *Refer to Part A of this Chapter for remaining torque specifications.*

****Note 2:** *Once the bolts are removed, they must be discarded and new bolts installed. See Section 17 for details.*

1 General information

The information in this Chapter ranges from advice concerning preparation for an overhaul and the purchase of replacement parts, to detailed step-by-step procedures covering removal and installation of internal engine components and the inspection of parts.

The following Sections are written based on the assumption that the engine has been removed from the vehicle. For information concerning in-vehicle engine repair, as well as removal and installation of the external components necessary for the overhaul, see Part A of this Chapter and Section 5 of this Part.

When overhauling the engine, it is essential to first establish exactly what replacement parts are available. At the time of writing, components such as the piston rings are not available separately from the piston/connecting rod assemblies; pistons, wrist pins and valve guides are not available separately, and very few under- or oversized components are available for engine reconditioning. In most cases, it would appear that the easiest and most economically-sensible course of action is to replace a worn or damaged engine with an exchange unit.

2 Engine overhaul - general information

It's not always easy to determine when, or if, an engine should be completely overhauled, as a number of factors must be considered.

High mileage isn't necessarily an indication that an overhaul is needed, while low mileage doesn't preclude the need for an overhaul. Frequency of servicing is probably the most important consideration. An engine that's had regular and frequent oil and filter changes, as well as other required maintenance, will most likely give many thousands of miles of reliable service. Conversely, a neglected engine may require an overhaul very early in its life.

Excessive oil consumption is an indication that piston rings, valve seals and/or valve guides are in need of attention. Make sure that oil leaks aren't responsible before deciding that the rings and/or guides are worn. Perform a cylinder compression check (Part A of this Chapter, Section 3) to determine the extent of the work required.

Loss of power, rough running, knocking or metallic engine noises, excessive valve train noise and high fuel consumption may also point to the need for an overhaul, especially if they're all present at the same time. If a full service doesn't remedy the situation, major mechanical work is the only solution.

An engine overhaul involves restoring all internal parts to the specification of a new engine. **Note:** *Always check to determine what replacement parts are available before planning any overhaul operation. Refer to Section 1 of this Part. A good engine reconditioning specialist/automotive parts supplier may be able to suggest alternatives which will enable you to overcome the lack of replacement parts.*

During an overhaul, it is usual to replace the piston rings, and to rebore and/or hone the cylinders. The boring process is done by an automotive machine shop and new oversize pistons and rings installed - all these operations, of course, assume the availability of suitable replacement parts. The main and connecting rod (big-end) bearings are generally replaced and, if necessary, the crankshaft may be reground to restore the journals. Generally, the valves are also serviced, since they're usually in less-than-perfect condition at this point. While the engine is being overhauled, other components, such as the starter and alternator, can be replaced, or rebuilt, if the necessary parts can be found. The end result should be an as-new engine that will give many trouble-free miles. **Note:** *Critical cooling system components such as the hoses, drivebelt, thermostat and water pump MUST be replaced with new parts when an engine is overhauled. The radiator should be checked carefully, to ensure that it isn't clogged or leaking (see Chapter 3). Also, as a general rule, the oil pump should be replaced when an engine is rebuilt.*

Before beginning the engine overhaul, read through the entire procedure to familiarize yourself with the scope and requirements of the job. Overhauling an engine isn't difficult, but it is time-consuming. Plan on the vehicle being off the road for a minimum of two weeks, especially if parts must be taken to an automotive machine shop for repair or reconditioning. Check on availability of parts, and make sure that any necessary special tools and equipment are obtained in advance. Most work can be done with typical hand tools, although a number of precision measuring tools are required, for inspecting parts to determine if they must be replaced. Often, an automotive machine shop will handle the inspection of parts, and will offer advice concerning reconditioning and replacement. **Note:** *Always wait until the engine has been completely disassembled, and all components, especially the cylinder block/crankcase, have been inspected, before deciding what service and repair operations must be performed at an automotive machine shop. Since the block's condition will be the major factor to consider when determining whether to overhaul the original engine or buy a rebuilt one, never purchase parts or have machine work done on other components until the cylinder block/crankcase has been thoroughly inspected.* As a general rule, time is the primary cost of an overhaul, so it doesn't pay to install worn or substandard parts.

As a final note, to ensure maximum life and minimum trouble from a rebuilt engine, everything must be assembled with care in a spotlessly clean environment.

Engine rebuilding alternatives

The do-it-yourselfer is faced with a number of options when performing an engine overhaul. The decision to replace the engine block, piston/connecting rod assemblies and crankshaft depends on a number of factors, with the number one consideration being the condition of the block. Other considerations are cost, access to machine shop facilities, parts availability, time required to complete the project and the extent of prior mechanical experience on the part of the do-it-yourselfer.

Some of the rebuilding alternatives include:

Individual parts - If the inspection procedures reveal that the engine block and most engine components are in reusable condition, purchasing individual parts may be the most economical alternative. The block, crankshaft and piston/connecting rod assemblies should all be inspected carefully. Even if the block shows little wear, the cylinder bores should be surface honed.

Crankshaft kit - This rebuild package consists of a reground crankshaft and a matched set of pistons and connecting rods. The pistons will already be installed on the connecting rods. Piston rings and the necessary bearings will be included in the kit. These kits are commonly available for standard cylinder bores, as well as for engine blocks which have been bored to a regular oversize.

Short block - A short block consists of an engine block with a crankshaft and piston/connecting rod assemblies already installed. All new bearings are incorporated and all clearances will be correct. The existing cylinder head(s), camshaft, valve train components and external parts can be bolted to the short block with little or no machine shop work necessary.

Long block - A long block consists of a short block plus an oil pump, oil pan, cylinder head(s), valve cover(s), camshaft and valve train components, timing sprockets, belt or chain and timing cover. All components are installed with new bearings, seals and gaskets incorporated throughout. The installation of manifolds and external parts is all that is necessary.

Give careful thought to which alternative is best for you and discuss the situation with local automotive machine shops, auto parts dealers or parts store countermen before ordering or purchasing replacement parts.

3 Engine/transaxle removal - methods and precautions

If you've decided that the engine must be removed for overhaul or major repair work, several preliminary steps should be taken.

Locating a suitable place to work is extremely important. Adequate work space, along with storage space for the vehicle, will be needed. If a workshop or garage isn't

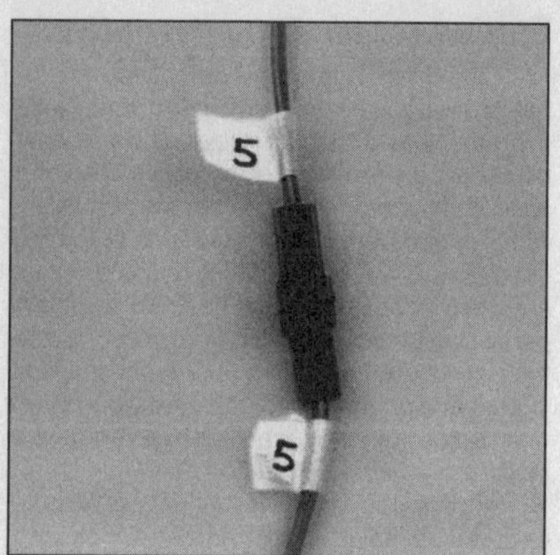

4.5 Label each wire and vacuum hose before disconnecting it

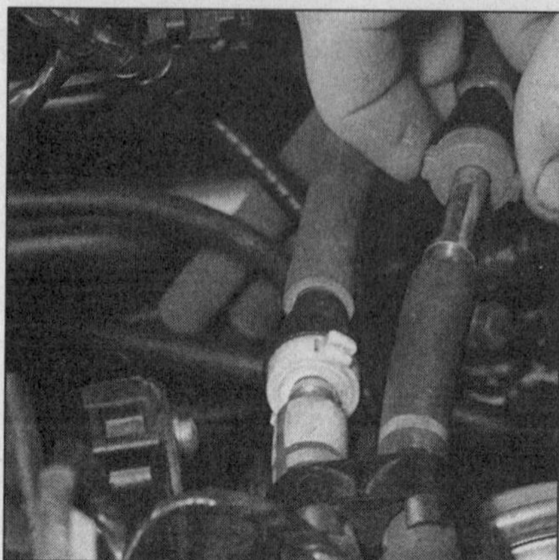

4.7 Note the color coding of the hoses when disconnecting the fuel delivery and return lines

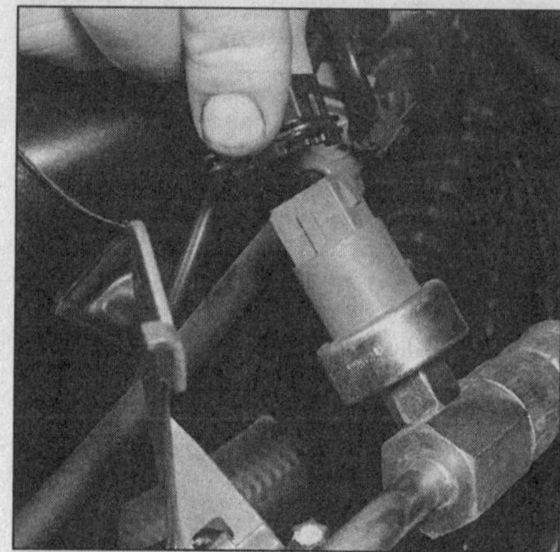

4.9a Disconnect the power steering pressure switch electrical connector . . .

available, at the very least, a flat, level, clean work surface made of concrete or asphalt is required.

Cleaning the engine compartment and engine/transaxle before beginning the removal procedure will help keep tools clean and organized.

The engine can only be withdrawn by removing it complete with the transaxle. The vehicle's body must be raised and supported securely, sufficiently high that the engine/transaxle can be unbolted as a single unit and lowered to the ground. The engine/transaxle unit can then be withdrawn from under the vehicle and separated. An engine hoist or A-frame will therefore be necessary. Make sure the equipment is rated in excess of the combined weight of the engine and transaxle. Safety is of primary importance, considering the potential hazards involved in removing the engine/transaxle from the vehicle.

If this is the first time you have removed an engine, a helper should be available. Advice and aid from someone more experienced would also be helpful. There are many instances when one person cannot simultaneously perform all of the operations required when removing the engine/transaxle from the vehicle.

Plan the operation ahead of time. Arrange for, or obtain, all of the tools and equipment you'll need prior to beginning the job. Some of the equipment necessary to perform engine/transaxle removal and installation safely, with relative ease, and which may have to be rented or borrowed, includes (in addition to the engine hoist) a heavy-duty floor jack, a strong pair of jackstands, some wooden blocks and an engine dolly (a low, wheeled platform capable of taking the weight off the engine/transaxle, so that it can be moved easily when on the ground). A complete set of wrenches and sockets (as described in the front of this manual) will be needed, together with plenty of rags and cleaning solvent for cleaning spilled oil, coolant and fuel. If the hoist is to be rented, make sure that you arrange for it in advance and perform all of the operations possible without it beforehand. This will save you money and time.

Plan for the vehicle to be out of use for quite a while. A machine shop will be required to perform some of the work which the do-it-yourselfer can't accomplish without special equipment. These establishments often have a busy schedule, so it would be a good idea to consult them before removing the engine, to accurately estimate the amount of time required to rebuild or repair components that may need work.

Always be extremely careful when removing and installing the engine/transaxle. Serious injury can result from careless actions. By planning ahead and taking your time, the job, although a major task, can be accomplished successfully.

4 Engine/transaxle - removal and installation

Warning: *Gasoline is extremely flammable, so take extra precautions when disconnecting any part of the fuel system. Don't smoke, or allow flames or bare light bulbs in or near the work area and don't work in a garage where a natural gas appliance (such as a clothes dryer or water heater) is installed. If you spill gasoline on your skin, rinse it off immediately. Have a fire extinguisher rated for gasoline fires nearby and know how to use it.*

Note: *Read through the entire Section in addition to the preceding Section, before beginning this procedure. The engine and transaxle are removed as a unit, lowered to the ground and removed from underneath, then separated outside the vehicle.*

Four-cylinder engine

Removal

Refer to illustrations 4.5, 4.7, 4.9a, 4.9b, 4.9c, 4.10a, 4.10b, 4.10c, 4.11, 4.13a, 4.13b, 4.13c, 4.25a, 4.25b, 4.30 and 4.35

1 Park the vehicle on firm, level ground, apply the parking brake firmly and loosen the nuts securing both front wheels.

2 Relieve the fuel system pressure (see Chapter 4).

3 Disconnect the battery negative (ground) lead - see Chapter 5, Section 1. For better access, the battery may be removed completely (see Chapter 5).

4 Place protective covers on the fenders and engine compartment front crossmember, then remove the hood (see Chapter 11).

5 Whenever you disconnect any vacuum lines, coolant and emissions hoses, wiring harness connectors, ground straps and fuel lines during the following procedure, always label them clearly, so that they can be correctly reassembled. Masking tape and/or a marking pen work well for marking items. Take instant photos or sketch the locations of components and brackets **(see illustration)**.

6 Remove the two electrical connectors, disconnect the vacuum hose (if equipped) and disconnect the crankcase breather hose from the valve cover, then remove the complete air cleaner assembly, with the mass airflow sensor, the resonator and the plenum chamber (see Chapter 4).

7 Equalize the pressure in the fuel tank by removing the filler cap, then undo the fuel feed and return lines connecting the engine to the chassis (see Chapter 4). Plug or cap all open attachments **(see illustration)**.

8 Disconnect the accelerator cable from the throttle linkage as described in Chapter 4 - if equipped, also disconnect the cruise control actuator cable (see Chapter 12). Secure the cable(s) clear of the engine/transaxle.

9 Releasing its wire clip, remove the power steering pressure switch electrical connector, then unbolt the power steering high-pressure line and the ground lead from the cylinder head rear support plate/engine lifting eye **(see illustrations)**.

10 Mark or label all components as they are disconnected (see paragraph 5 above). Disconnect the vacuum hoses as follows:

a) *One from the rear of the throttle housing (only the one hose - there is no need to disconnect the second hose running to the fuel pressure regulator)* **(see illustration)**.

4.9b . . . unbolt the power steering high-pressure line . . .

4.9c . . . and the ground lead from the cylinder head rear support plate/engine lifting eye

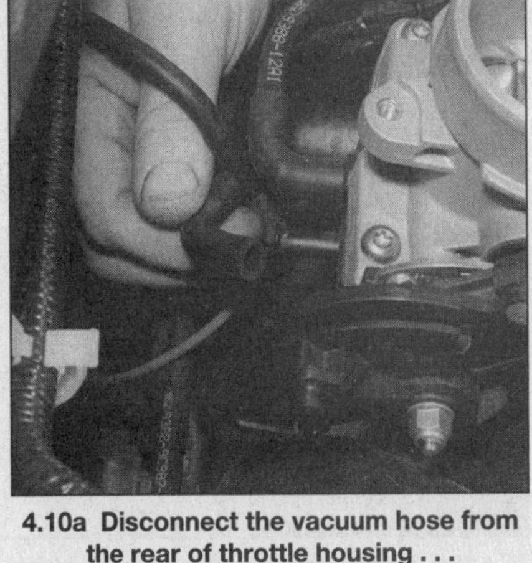

4.10a Disconnect the vacuum hose from the rear of throttle housing . . .

- b) *One from the fitting on the intake manifold's left-hand end* **(see illustration)**.
- c) *The braking system vacuum booster hose - from the intake manifold (see Chapter 9 for details).*
- d) *Also disconnect the vacuum hoses from the Exhaust Gas Recirculation system components - one from the EGR valve, two from the EGR tube (note that these last two are different sizes, as are their fittings, so that they can only be connected correctly).*
- e) *Trace the vacuum line from the pulse-air filter housing over the top of the transaxle and disconnect it by pulling the plastic tube out of the rubber hose just beneath the firewall-mounted pulse-air solenoid valve* **(see illustration)**.
- f) *Secure all these hoses so that they won't get damaged as the engine/transaxle is removed.*

11 Unbolt the engine/transaxle-to-body ground lead from the transaxle's top surface **(see illustration)**. Disconnect the speedometer drive cable (see Chapter 12) and secure it clear of the engine/transaxle.

12 If the vehicle is equipped with a manual transaxle, disconnect the hydraulic line from the clutch actuator (see Chapter 8). Plug the line to prevent leakage and contamination. For automatic transaxles, disconnect the selector cable (see Chapter 7, Part B).

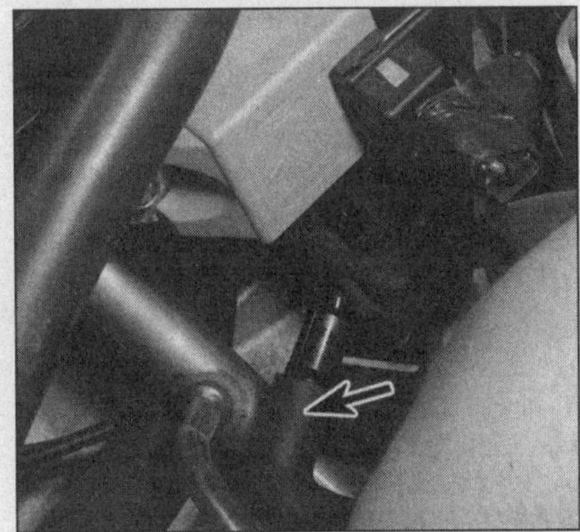

4.10b . . . the vacuum hose (arrow) from fitting on left-hand end of the intake manifold . . .

4.10c . . . and the brake booster hose (A), EGR valve hose (B), EGR pipe hoses (C) and pulse-air filter vacuum line (D)

13 Marking or labeling all components as they are disconnected (see paragraph 5 above), disconnect the engine wiring harness from the body as follows:

- a) *Starting at the left-hand side of the engine compartment, release and remove the three large electrical connectors clipped to the suspension mounts - note the wire clips attached to some connectors* **(see illustration)**.
- b) *Disconnect and/or release the battery-to-starter motor wiring, noting the single connector which must be disconnected.*
- c) *Remove the electrical connector(s) to disconnect the vehicle speed sensor,*

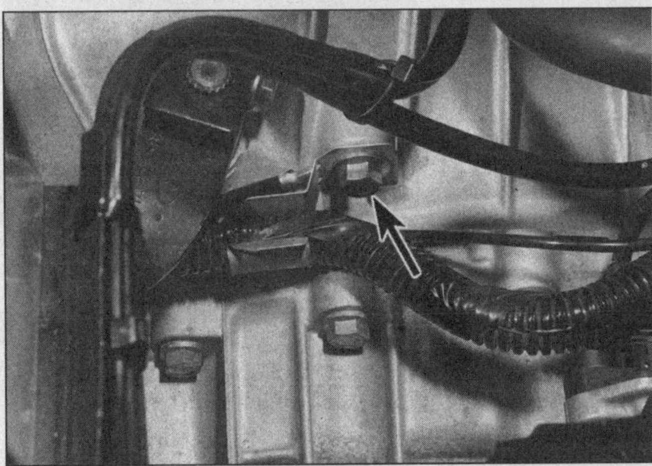

4.11 Unbolt the engine/transaxle-to-body ground connection (arrow)

4.13a Disconnect the three large electrical connectors at this location (arrow)

2C

4.13b Disconnect the engine wiring harness from the battery wiring and firewall components (arrows)

4.13c Disconnect the PCM wiring and ground lead (arrows) to release the engine wiring harness from the vehicle body

oxygen sensor and, if equipped, the oil level sensor wiring. Unclip the connectors to release the wiring where necessary.

d) *Work along the harness to the firewall, unclipping the harness and disconnecting the various firewall-mounted components connected into it, until you reach the right-hand side of the engine compartment* **(see illustration)**.

e) *Carefully pry the power steering fluid reservoir up and out of its clip on the suspension mounting, then unscrew the PCM connector's retaining bolt and remove the connector* **(see illustration)**.

f) *Unbolt the ground lead from the right-hand inner fender panel, release the engine wiring harness and install the power steering fluid reservoir.*

g) *Secure the engine wiring harness to the engine/transaxle so it cannot be damaged as the unit is removed from the vehicle.*

14 Unbolt both parts of the exhaust manifold heat shield; unclip the coolant hose to allow the upper part to be withdrawn.

15 Remove the drivebelt (see Chapter 1).

16 Unbolt the power steering pump (see Chapter 10); secure it as far as possible (without disconnecting the system's hoses) clear of the engine/transaxle.

17 Raise the vehicle and support it securely on jackstands, then remove the front wheels. Drain the cooling system and (if the engine is to be disassembled) drain the engine oil and remove the oil filter (see Chapter 1). Also drain the transaxle as described in the relevant Part of Chapter 7.

18 Withdraw the lower part of the exhaust manifold heat shield.

19 Unscrew the nuts to disconnect the exhaust system front exhaust pipe from the manifold, then unhook all the system's rubber hanger and withdraw the complete exhaust system from under the vehicle (see Chapter 4 for details).

20 If the vehicle is equipped with a manual transaxle, mark their positions, then disconnect the shift linkage and transaxle support rods from the rear of the transaxle. Unscrew the retaining nuts, then withdraw the shift linkage heat shield from the underbody. Unbolt the rear end of the linkage from the underbody, swivel the linkage around to the rear, and tie it to the underbody (see Chapter 7, Part A, for details).

21 Disconnect both stabilizer bar links from their respective suspension strut - note the flexible brake hose bracket attached to each link stud. Disconnect both tie-rod ends from their steering knuckles. Unfasten the clamp bolt securing each front suspension lower control arm balljoint to its steering knuckle (see Chapter 10 for details). Check that both balljoints can be released from the knuckle assemblies when required, but leave them in place for the time being, secured by the clamp bolts, if necessary.

22 If the vehicle is equipped with air conditioning, unbolt the accumulator/dehydrator from the subframe; secure it as far as possible (without disconnecting the system's hoses) clear of the engine/transaxle. **Warning:** *Don't disconnect the refrigerant hoses.*

23 Unbolt the steering gear from the subframe.

24 Unscrew the two bolts securing the power steering system lines to the right-hand side of the subframe.

25 Hold the radiator in its raised position, by inserting cotter pins through the holes in the rear of the engine compartment front crossmember and into the radiator's upper mounting extensions. Unbolt the radiator mounting brackets from the subframe. Note

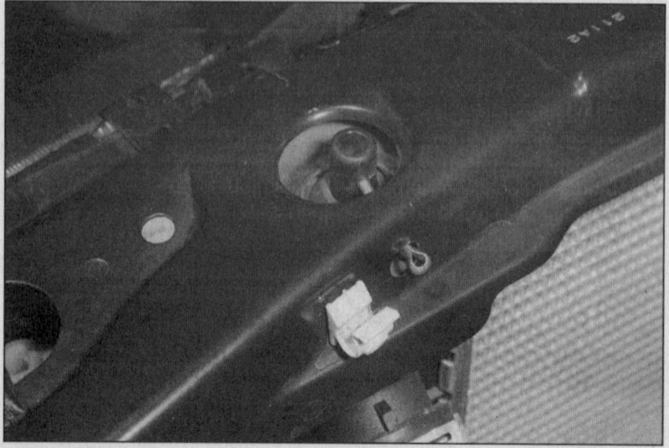
4.25a Use cotter pins as shown to secure the radiator in its raised position . . .

4.25b . . . and unbolt the bottom mounts (arrows) - do not lose the rubbers insulators

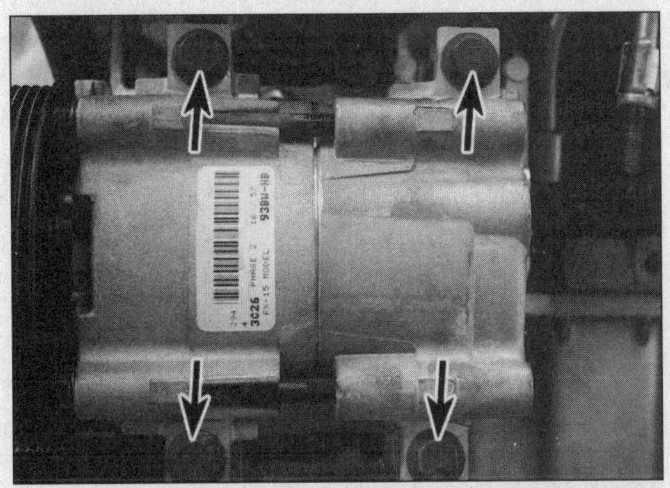

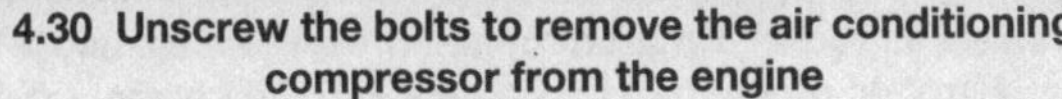
4.30 Unscrew the bolts to remove the air conditioning compressor from the engine

4.35 Lower the engine/transaxle unit out of the vehicle

that they are marked to ensure correct installation **(see illustrations)**. Note the direction of installation then remove and store the bottom mounts for safekeeping, noting which way up they are attached.

26 Unbolt the engine/transaxle rear mount from the subframe. If the vehicle is equipped with automatic transaxle, a separate damper may be attached beneath the subframe, which must be unbolted to reach the mount's fasteners. If the vehicle is equipped with a manual transaxle, also unscrew the mount center bolt, then unbolt the mounting bracket from the transaxle.

27 Unscrew the engine/transaxle front mount center bolt and unbolt the mount from the subframe, noting the location of the wiring connector bracket.

28 Use white paint or equivalent (don't use a sharp-pointed scriber, which might break the underbody protective coating and cause rusting) to mark the exact relationship of the subframe to the underbody. Unscrew the four mounting bolts from the subframe (note their different-sized washers - see also **illustration 4.47a**) and allow the subframe to hang down on the suspension lower control arm balljoints. Disconnect the balljoints one at a time from the steering knuckle assemblies (see Chapter 10) and lower the subframe to the ground. Withdraw the subframe from under the vehicle.

29 Mark or label all components as they are disconnected (see paragraph 5 above). Catch as much of the coolant as possible in a drain pan and disconnect the cooling system hoses and tube as follows - refer to Chapter 3 for further details, if required:

a) *Remove the radiator top hose.*
b) *Remove the heater hose running from the thermostat to the engine compartment firewall fitting.*
c) *Disconnect from the hose running to the coolant recovery tank - secure the hose clear of the working area.*
d) *Disconnect from the thermostat housing the coolant hose/tube which runs to the radiator bottom hose.*
e) *Disconnect the radiator bottom hose from the radiator. Secure the hose clear of the working area.*
f) *Unbolt the (heater) hose from the oil pan. Trace the hose to the engine compartment firewall fitting. If so equipped, disconnect the oil cooler hoses from the cooler fittings, then remove it.*
g) *Unless the vehicle has air conditioning, secure the radiator as far forward as possible while it is in its raised position. If equipped with air conditioning, remove the radiator completely* (see Chapter 3).

30 If the vehicle has air conditioning, remove the compressor's electrical connector, and unbolt the compressor from the engine **(see illustration)**. Secure it as far as possible (without disconnecting the system's hoses) clear of the engine/transaxle. **Warning:** *Don't disconnect the refrigerant hoses.*

31 If the vehicle has a manual transaxle, disconnect the driveshafts from the transaxle as follows, referring to Chapter 8 for further details when required:

a) *Unscrew the nuts securing the right-hand driveshaft support bearing and withdraw the heat shield.*
b) *Pull the right-hand driveshaft out of the transaxle. Be prepared to catch any spilled oil.*
c) *Secure the driveshaft clear of the engine/transaxle - remember that the unit is to be lowered out of the vehicle. Also ensure that the inner joint isn't turned more than 18 degrees.*
d) *Pry the left-hand driveshaft out of the transaxle - again, be prepared for oil spillage. Secure the driveshaft clear of the engine/transaxle, and ensure that its inner joint isn't turned more than 18 degrees.*

32 If the vehicle has an automatic transaxle, proceed as follows. Refer to Chapter 7, Part B and to Chapter 8 for further details when required:

a) *Unscrew its center bolt, then unbolt the engine/transaxle rear mounting bracket from the transaxle.*
b) *Disconnect the fluid cooler tube from the rear of the transaxle, and secure it clear of the unit.*
c) *Pry the left-hand driveshaft out of the transaxle. Be prepared to catch any spilled oil.*
d) *Secure the driveshaft clear of the engine/transaxle - remember that the unit is to be lowered out of the vehicle - and ensure that the inner joint isn't turned more than 18 degrees.*
e) *Unscrew the nuts securing the right-hand driveshaft support bearing, and withdraw the heat shield.*
f) *Pull the right-hand driveshaft out of the transaxle. Again, be prepared for oil spillage. Secure the driveshaft clear of the engine/transaxle, and ensure that its inner joint isn't turned more than 18 degrees.*
g) *Disconnect the fluid cooler tube from the front of the transaxle and secure it clear of the unit.*

33 The engine/transaxle unit should now be hanging on the right and left-hand mounts only, with all components which connect it to the rest of the vehicle disconnected or removed and secured well clear of the unit. Make a final check that this is the case, then ensure that the vehicle is securely supported, high enough to permit the withdrawal of the engine/transaxle unit from underneath. Allow for the height of the engine dolly, if used.

34 Take the weight of the engine/transaxle unit, using the lifting eyes provided on the cylinder head. Unscrew the six nuts securing the right-hand mounting bracket, then the three nuts securing the left-hand bracket. **Warning:** *Don't put any part of your body under the vehicle, or under the engine/transaxle unit, when they are supported only by a hoist or other lifting equipment.*

35 Lower the engine/transaxle to the ground, then withdraw it from under the vehicle **(see illustration)**.

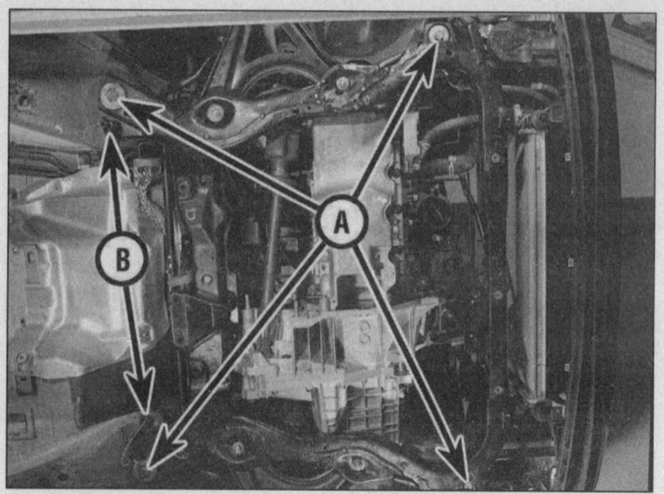

4.47 Tighten the subframe mounting bolts (A) while ensuring that alignment remains correct - alignment tools (B) shown in use here

4.49 A special tool is required to hold the engine/transaxle unit precisely so that mount can be tightened in the correct position

36 Referring to the relevant part of Chapter 7, separate the transaxle from the engine.

37 While the engine/transaxle is removed, check the mounts and replace them if they are worn or damaged. Also check the condition of all coolant and vacuum hoses and lines (see Chapter 1). Components that are normally hidden can now be checked properly and should be replaced if there is any question regarding their condition. If the vehicle has a manual transaxle, take the opportunity to overhaul the clutch components (see Chapter 8). It is regarded by many as good working practice to replace the clutch assembly as a matter of course, whenever major engine overhaul work is performed. Also check the condition of all components (such as the transaxle oil seals) disturbed on removal, and replace any that are damaged or worn.

Installation

Refer to illustrations 4.47, 4.49, 4.50a, 4.50b, 4.50c and 4.50d

38 Installation is the reverse of removal. Tighten all fasteners to the torque given. If a torque specification isn't listed in the Specifications Sections of the two Parts of this Chapter, refer to the Specifications Section of the relevant Chapter of this manual.

39 Always replace any circlips and self-locking nuts disturbed on removal.

40 Install new cable ties anywhere they were cut during removal.

41 With all overhaul operations completed, install the transaxle to the engine as described in Chapter 7.

42 Place the engine/transaxle unit under the vehicle, attach the hoist, and lift the unit into position until the right and left-hand mounts can be reassembled. Tighten the nuts only lightly at this stage. Don't yet release the hoist as the weight of the engine/transaxle unit must not be taken by the mounts until all are correctly aligned.

43 Using new circlips, and ensuring that the inner joints are not twisted through too great an angle (see Chapter 8), install the driveshafts. If the vehicle has a manual transaxle, the procedure is the reverse of that outlined in Step 31 above. If the vehicle has an automatic transaxle, proceed as follows, referring to Chapter 7, Part B and to Chapter 8 for further details when required:

a) *Install the left-hand driveshaft.*
b) *Reconnect the fluid cooler lines, first to the rear, then to the front, of the transaxle.*
c) *Install the right-hand driveshaft to the transaxle, install the heat shield and tighten the support bearing nuts to the specified torque.*
d) *Install the engine/transaxle rear mount bracket to the transaxle, tightening the bolts to the torque specified, then install the mount, tightening the center bolt only lightly at this stage.*

44 If the vehicle has air conditioning, install the compressor; tighten the bolts to the torque listed in this Chapter's Specifications and plug in its electrical connector.

45 Using the marks and notes made on removal, install the cooling system hoses. If they are left disconnected for the time being, don't forget to secure them at the appropriate moment during the reassembly procedure. Install the radiator (if removed), using cotter pins to secure it in the raised position.

46 Install the subframe one side at a time and hold it by securing the lower control arm balljoints to the steering knuckle assemblies. Install the subframe bolts, ensuring that the washers are installed correctly. Tighten the bolts only lightly at this stage.

47 The subframe must now be aligned on the underbody. The manufacturer specifies the use of a special tool, which is a pair of tapered guides with attachments to hold them in the subframe as it is installed. However, since the working diameter of these tools is one inch and since the corresponding aligning holes in the subframe and underbody are respectively 0.8 inch and 0.9 inch in diameter, there is a significant tolerance possible in the subframe's alignment, even if the correct tools are used. If these tools are not available, you can align the subframe by eye, centering the subframe aligning holes on those of the underbody, and using the marks made on removal for assistance. Alternatively, you can align the subframe using a tapered drift (such as a clutch-aligning tool), or even a deep socket wrench of suitable size **(see illustration)**.

48 Once the subframe is aligned as precisely as possible, tighten its bolts to the specified torque without disturbing its position. Recheck the alignment once all the bolts are securely tightened.

49 With the subframe aligned and securely fastened, the engine/transaxle unit must now be positioned precisely, before the mounts can be reassembled. The manufacturer specifies the use of a special tool. This is a fixture bolted to the subframe in place of the engine/transaxle front mount, so that when the mount's center bolt is installed, it is held 2.5 inches above the subframe's top surface, and offset 13/16 inch to the rear of the mount's subframe bolt holes (centers). DIY mechanics are advised to obtain the dealer tool. The only alternative is to fabricate one **(see illustration)**.

50 Fasten the tool to the subframe in place of the engine/transaxle front mount, and lightly tighten the mount's center bolt. Install the engine/transaxle mounts in the following sequence:

a) *Tighten the left-hand mount's nuts to the specified torque - don't allow the mount to twist as it is tightened* **(see illustration)**.
b) *Tighten the right-hand mount's four bracket-to-engine nuts to the specified torque.*
c) *Slowly release the hoist so that the weight of the engine/transaxle unit is taken by the mounts.*
d) *Tighten the right-hand mount's two bracket-to-mount nuts to the specified torque - don't allow the mount to twist as it is tightened* **(see illustration)**.

4.50a Do not allow the left mount to twist as its nuts (arrows) are tightened

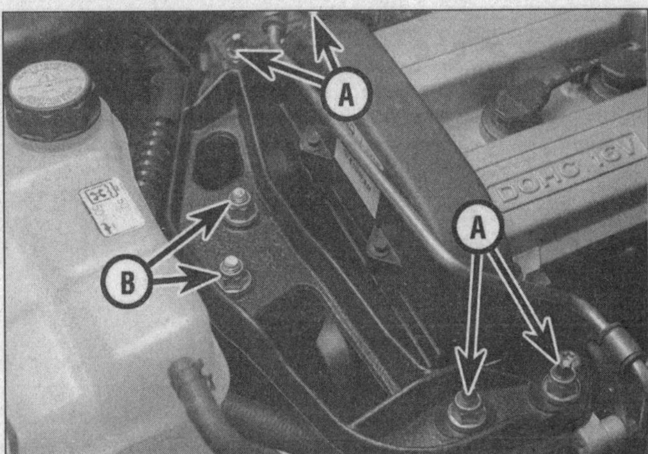

4.50b Tighten the right mount's four bracket-to-engine nuts (A), release the hoist, then tighten the two bracket-to-mount nuts (B). Do not allow mount to twist

e) *Reassemble the engine/transaxle rear mount, tightening the fasteners to the specified Torque; tighten the center bolt last.*

f) *Install the steering gear to the subframe (see Chapter 10).*

g) *Unbolt the special tool from the front mount, install the mount - don't forget the wiring connector bracket - and tighten first the mount's bolts/nuts, then its center bolt, to the correct* torque **(see illustrations)**.

51 Install the lower rubber mounts to the radiator. Ensure that both are installed correctly, then install the radiator mounting brackets to the subframe. Make sure that each is installed in its correct (marked) location. Tighten the bolts to the torque specified. Remove the cotter pins and secure the coolant hose connections (where necessary).

52 Install the air conditioning accumulator/dehydrator (where appropriate) to the subframe.

53 Tighten the two bolts securing the power steering system lines to the right side of the subframe.

54 Fasten each lower control arm balljoint and tie-rod end to their respective steering knuckles and both stabilizer bar links to their respective suspension strut. Note the flexible brake hose bracket attached to each link stud (see Chapter 10 for details).

55 If the vehicle has a manual transaxle, swivel the linkage around to the front, tighten its rear fasteners, then install the shift linkage heat shield. Reconnect the shift linkage and transaxle support rods to the transaxle. Adjust the linkage using the marks made during removal (see Chapter 7, Part A, for details).

56 Reinstall the remaining components and fasteners in the reverse order of removal.

57 Add coolant, engine oil and transaxle fluids as needed (see Chapter 1).

58 Start the engine and check for proper operation fluid leakage. Shut off the engine and recheck the fluid levels.

59 Remember that, since the front suspension subframe and steering gear have been disturbed, the wheel alignment and steering angles must be checked fully and carefully as soon as possible, with any necessary adjustments made. This operation is best performed by an experienced mechanic using the proper equipment. The vehicle should therefore be taken to a dealer or qualified person for attention.

V6 engine

Removal

Refer to illustrations 4.64, 4.70, 4.74a, 4.74b, 4.74c, 4.74d, 4.74e, 4.75a, 4.75b, 4.78a, 4.78b, 4.80 and 4.87

60 Park the vehicle on firm, level ground, apply the parking brake firmly and loosen the nuts securing both front wheels. Remove the hood (see Chapter 11).

61 Relieve the fuel system pressure (see Chapter 4).

62 Disconnect the battery negative (ground) lead - see Chapter 5, Section 1. For better access, the battery may be removed completely (see Chapter 5).

4.50c Unbolt the special tool . . .

4.50d . . . then install the front mount - do not forget the wiring connector bracket - tighten the mount's nuts first, then its center bolt

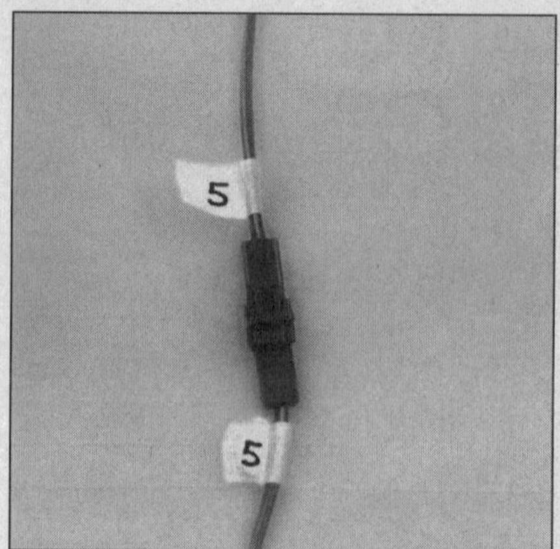

4.64 Label each wire or hose before disconnecting it

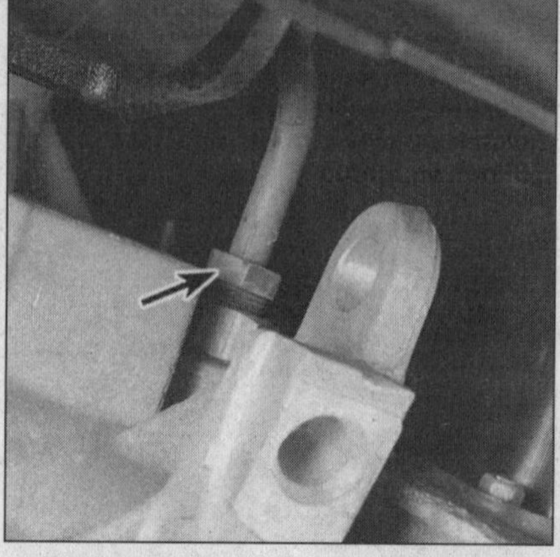

4.70 There are two transaxle cooler lines connected to the transaxle like this (arrow) - be sure to use a back-up wrench when disconnecting them and be ready for some fluid to spill

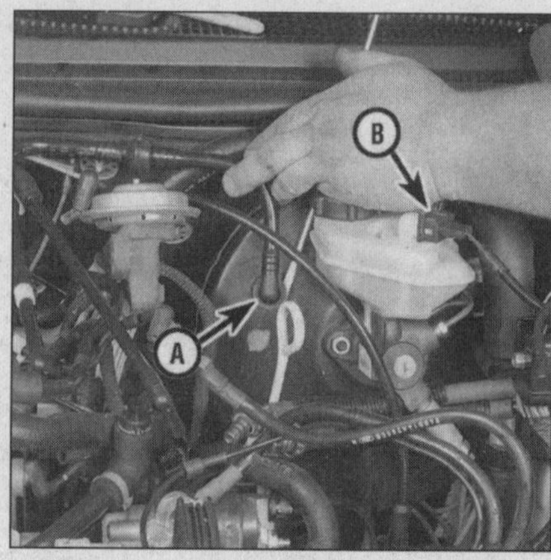

4.74a Disconnect the vacuum line from the brake booster (A), and the electrical connector from the master cylinder reservoir fill cap (B)

63 Place protective covers on the fenders and engine compartment front crossmember, then remove the hood (see Chapter 11).

64 Whenever you disconnect any vacuum lines, coolant and emissions hoses, wiring harness connectors, ground straps and fuel lines during the following procedure, always label them clearly, so that they can be correctly reassembled **(see illustration)**. Masking tape and/or a marking pen work well for marking items. Take instant photos or sketch the locations of components and brackets.

65 From inside the vehicle (driver's side passenger compartment), disconnect the steering column shaft from the flexible rack and pinion assembly joint (see Chapter 10).

66 Have the air conditioning system discharged at a dealership or qualified automotive air conditioning facility. See Chapter 3 for details. In most cases, the refrigerant can be reclaimed and stored for use to recharge the system. **Warning:** *The air conditioning system is under high pressure. Don't loosen any fittings or remove any components until after the system is discharged. Air conditioning refrigerant should be properly discharged into an approved type of container, at a dealership service department or an automotive air conditioning repair facility capable of handling R134a refrigerant. Cap or plug the lines as soon as they are disconnected to prevent moisture from entering the system. Always wear eye protection when disconnecting air conditioning system fittings.*

67 Disconnect the vacuum hoses and crankcase ventilation hoses and remove the complete air cleaner assembly, along with the mass airflow sensor and plenum chamber. See Chapter 1.

68 Raise the front of the vehicle and support is securely on jackstands. Remove the radiator lower shield. Drain the engine oil, transaxle and cooling system. Reinstall all drain plugs.

69 Disconnect the two power steering system cooler hoses from the metal cooler lines (located under the air conditioning compressor) and drain the fluid into a suitable container. Plug the hoses to prevent leakage and contamination.

70 Remove the transaxle cooling lines from the transaxle **(see illustration)**. Remove the transaxle cooling line mounting bracket from the left-hand side of the transaxle.

71 Remove the radiator lower hose.

72 Disconnect the electrical connector from the air conditioning compressor.

73 Disconnect the air conditioning compressor discharge line from the condenser.

74 Disconnect or remove the following items:

a) *Disconnect the electrical connectors from the oxygen sensors located in the front and rear exhaust manifolds.*
b) *Disconnect the fuel delivery lines* (Chapter 4).
c) *Disconnect the throttle and cruise control (if so equipped) cables from the throttle body (Chapter 4).*
d) *Disconnect the vacuum line from the brake booster and disconnect the electrical connector from the master cylinder fill cap* **(see illustration)**.

4.74b Disconnect the ground wire (A), then remove the screw (B) and disconnect the connector (C) from the powertrain control module (PCM)

4.74c Remove the nut (A) and remove the ground wire and steering line clamp from the right-hand engine support bracket. Disconnect the electrical connector from the power steering cutout switch (B), then separate the steering line at the fitting (C)

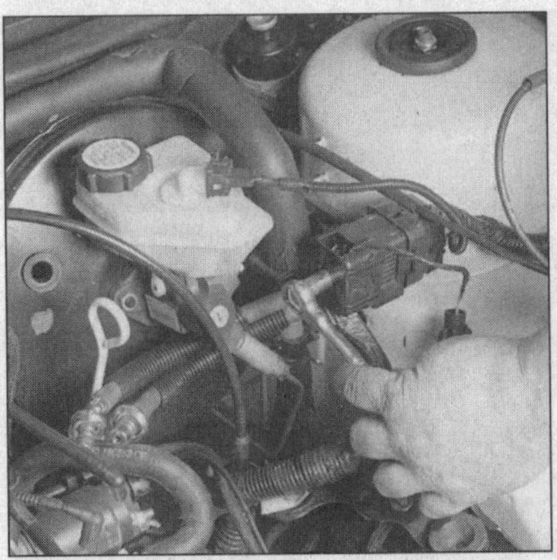

4.74d Remove the screw and separate the bulkhead connector halves

4.74e Disconnect the connector from the turbine shaft speed (TSS) sensor (arrow)

4.75a Remove the two bolts securing the shift cable bracket (arrows)

e) *Remove the ground wire, then remove the screw securing the connector to the powertrain control module (PCM)* **(see illustration)**.

f) *Remove the coolant hoses from the coolant recovery reservoir.*

g) *Remove the nut securing the ground wire and power steering line clamp to the right-hand engine support bracket* **(see illustration)**. *Remove the ground wire and power steering line from the support bracket. Disconnect the electrical connector from the power steering cutout switch and disconnect the power steering line. Separate the power steering line, plug the ends and position the line out of the way.*

h) *Disconnect the starter motor wiring* (Chapter 5).

i) *Remove the bolt securing the bulkhead connector halves. Separate the bulkhead connectors* **(see illustration)**.

j) *Disconnect the turbine shaft speed (TSS) sensor* **(see illustration)** *and any other electrical connector, vacuum hose or ground wire that will interfere with engine/transaxle removal.*

75 If equipped with an automatic transaxle, 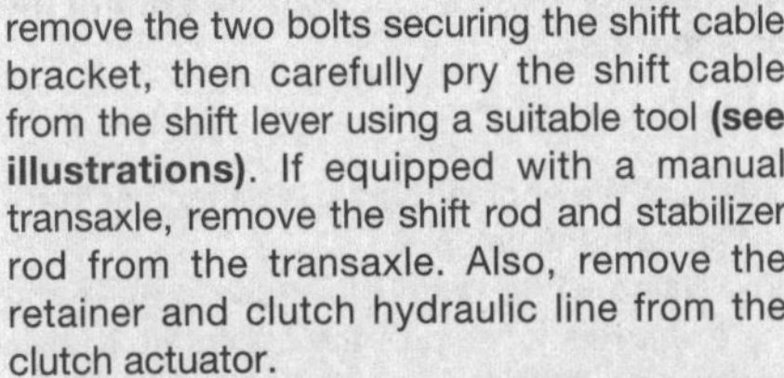
remove the two bolts securing the shift cable bracket, then carefully pry the shift cable from the shift lever using a suitable tool **(see illustrations)**. If equipped with a manual transaxle, remove the shift rod and stabilizer rod from the transaxle. Also, remove the retainer and clutch hydraulic line from the clutch actuator.

76 Remove the radiator upper hose from the radiator and engine. Next, disconnect the vacuum hose from the heater control valve.

77 If equipped with a manual transaxle, remove the nuts and disconnect the exhaust pipe from the rear of the catalytic converter. Remove the rubber hanger from the catalytic converter and disconnect the exhaust pipe from the converter. If equipped with an automatic transaxle, remove the flex pipe from the catalytic converter. Remove the rubber hanger from the catalytic converter. Remove the exhaust Y-pipe from the engine. See Chapter 4.

78 Hold the radiator, cooling motor and fan and fan shroud in the raised position by inserting cotter pins or wire through the holes in the rear of the engine compartment front crossmember and through the radiator's upper mounting extensions. Then, remove the two bolts from the right and left-hand radiator lower support brackets **(see illustrations)**.

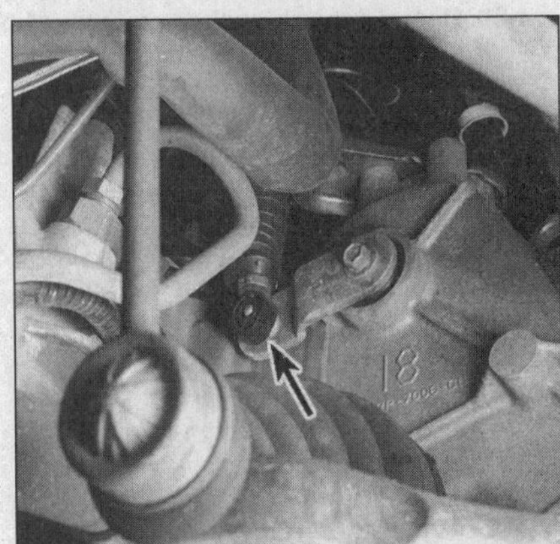

4.75b Carefully pry the shift cable (arrow) from the shift lever on the transaxle

79 Remove the splash shields from the right and left inner fenders.

80 **Note:** *This step is only necessary if the engine and transaxle will be separated after engine removal.* If equipped with an automatic transaxle, remove the driveplate

2C

4.78a Use cotter pins or wire as shown to secure the radiator, cooling fan motor and fan assembly in the raised position

4.78b Remove the bolts and the lower radiator support brackets (one on each side)

4.80 Remove the driveplate-to-torque converter nuts (arrow) if the automatic transaxle and engine will be separated after engine removal

4.87 Lowering the engine/transaxle assembly out of the vehicle

access cover and remove the four driveplate-to-torque converter *nuts* **(see illustration)**. Rotate the driveplate using a large screwdriver or prybar to access each nut.

81 Remove the front wheels and disconnect or remove the following suspension, steering and brake components:

a) *Disconnect the stabilizer bar from the right- and left-hand suspension struts. Place the stabilizer bars out of the way.*
b) *Remove the wire retainer, bolt and speed sensors from the right and left driveaxles.*
c) *Remove the brake calipers from the right and left sides* (See Chapter 9). *Don't allow the brake calipers to hang by their hydraulic hoses. Attach them to a suitable point using a length of wire (or equivalent).*
d) *Remove the pinch bolts and separate the steering knuckles from the lower control arm balljoints.* (Chapter 10).
e) *Remove the cotter pins and nuts and separate the tie-rod ends from the steering knuckles* (Chapter 10).
f) *Remove the driveaxle nuts and slide the steering knuckles off the driveaxles* (see Chapter 10).

82 Disconnect the air conditioning accumulator line using a spring lock coupling tool. Remove the accumulator mounting bolts and position it out of the way.

83 Remove the front and rear roll restrictor through-bolts.

84 Attach a suitable engine hoist. Raise the lift enough to remove the weight of the engine/transaxle assembly from the subframe. Remove the right and left engine support brackets.

85 All components that connect the engine/transaxle to the rest of the vehicle should now be disconnected or removed. Make a final check that this is the case and secure all wiring harness, hoses and lines out of the way. Ensure that the body is securely supported, high enough to permit the withdrawal of the engine/transaxle assembly from underneath the vehicle.

86 Using white paint (or equivalent), mark the exact relationship of the subframe to the underbody. With the engine hoist supporting the engine/transaxle, remove the bolts securing the subframe to the vehicle body. **Caution:** *Carefully check for interference between the engine/transaxle assembly and body while lowering the engine/transaxle from the vehicle. Also, make sure there is nothing still connected that will interfere with engine/transaxle removal.*

87 Carefully lower the engine/transaxle along with the subframe, driveaxles and rack and pinion steering gear to the ground. Withdraw the engine/transaxle assembly from under the vehicle **(see illustration)**.

88 While the engine/transaxle is removed, check the mounts and replace them if they are worn or damaged. Also check the condition of all coolant and vacuum hoses and lines (see Chapter 1). Components that are normally hidden can now be checked properly and should be replaced if there is any question regarding their condition. If the vehicle has a manual transaxle, take the opportunity to overhaul the clutch components (see Chapter 8). It is regarded by many as good working practice to replace the clutch assembly as a matter of course, whenever major engine overhaul work is performed. Also check the condition of all components (such as the transaxle oil seals) disturbed on removal, and replace any that are damaged or worn. Referring to the appropriate Section of Chapter 7, separate the transaxle from the engine, if necessary.

Installation

Refer to illustrations 4.93a and 4.93b

89 Installation is generally the reverse of the removal procedure, noting the following points. Tighten all fasteners to the specified torque. If a particular torque specification is not listed in this Chapter, refer to the specifications section of the relevant chapter.

90 Always replace any circlips or self-locking fasteners once they are removed.

91 Place the engine/transaxle, subframe and steering gear assembly under the vehicle, attach the hoist, and lift the unit into position. Install the subframe bolts, ensuring that the washers are installed correctly. Tighten the subframe bolts only lightly at this stage. Don't yet release the hoist as the weight of the engine/transaxle unit must not be held by the subframe until it is correctly aligned.

92 Using the marks and notes made on removal, install the cooling system hoses. If they are left disconnected for the time being, don't forget to secure them at the appropriate moment during the reassembly procedure. Install the radiator (if removed), using cotter pins to secure it in the raised position.

93 The subframe must now be aligned on the underbody. The manufacturer specifies the use of a special tool to do this. However, since the working diameter of these tools is one inch and since the corresponding aligning holes in the subframe and underbody are respectively 0.8 inch and 0.9 inch in diameter, there is a significant tolerance possible in the subframe's alignment, even if the correct tools are used. If these tools are not available, you can align the subframe by eye, centering the subframe aligning holes on those of the underbody, and using the marks made on removal for assistance. Alternatively, you can align the subframe using a tapered drift (such as a clutch-aligning tool), or even a deep socket wrench of suitable size **(see illustrations)**.

94 Once the subframe is aligned as precisely as possible, tighten its bolts to the specified torque without disturbing its position. Recheck the alignment once all the bolts are securely tightened.

95 With the subframe aligned and securely fastened, install the right and left engine support brackets. Refer to Chapter 2B, if necessary.

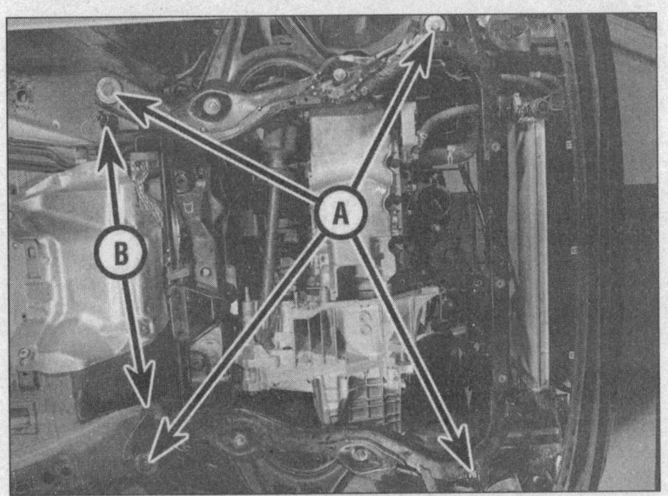

4.93a Tighten the subframe mounting bolts (A) while ensuring that alignment remains correct - service tools (B) are shown here . . .

4.93b . . . but an alternative method using ordinary hand tools can achieve acceptable alignment, if performed carefully

96 Install the radiator lower support brackets. Remove the cotter pins and secure the coolant hose connections (where necessary).

97 Install the air conditioning accumulator (where appropriate) to the subframe.

98 Fasten each lower control arm balljoint and tie rod end to their respective steering knuckles and both stabilizer bar links to their respective suspension strut. Note the flexible brake hose bracket attached to each link stud (see Chapter 10 for details).

99 If the vehicle has a manual transaxle, swivel the linkage around to the front, tighten its rear fasteners, then install the shift linkage heat shield. Reconnect the shift linkage and transaxle support rods to the transaxle. Connect the hydraulic line to the clutch actuator. Fill the clutch master cylinder and bleed the clutch system. See Chapter 8.

100 Reinstall the remaining components and fasteners in the reverse order of removal.

101 Add coolant, engine oil and transaxle fluids as needed (see Chapter 1). Charge the air conditioning system. See Chapter 3 for details.

102 Start the engine and check for proper and operation fluid leakage. Shut off the engine and recheck the fluid levels.

103 Since the front suspension subframe and steering gear have been disturbed, the wheel alignment and steering angles must be checked fully and carefully as soon as possible, with any necessary adjustments made. This operation is best performed by an experienced mechanic using the proper equipment. The vehicle should therefore be taken to a dealer or qualified person for attention.

5 Engine overhaul - disassembly sequence

1 It is much easier to disassemble and work on the engine if it is mounted on a portable engine stand. These stands can often be rented from a tool rent shop. Before the engine is mounted on a stand, the flywheel/driveplate should be removed (Part A of this Chapter) so that the stand bolts can be tightened into the end of the cylinder block/crankcase.

2 If a stand isn't available, it is possible to disassemble the engine with it mounted on blocks, on a sturdy workbench or on the floor. Be extra-careful not to tip or drop the engine when working without a stand.

3 If you are going to obtain a reconditioned engine, all external components must be removed first, to be transferred to the replacement engine (just as they will if you are doing a complete engine overhaul yourself). **Note:** *When removing the external components from the engine, pay close attention to details that may be helpful or important during installation. Note the installed position of gaskets, seals, spacers, pins, washers, bolts and other small items.* These external components include the following:

- a) *Alternator and brackets* (Chapter 5).
- b) *Spark plug wires and spark plugs* (Chapter 1).
- c) *Thermostat and housing* (Chapter 3).
- d) *Dipstick tube.*
- e) *Fuel injection system components* (Chapter 4).
- f) *All electrical switches and sensors - refer to the appropriate Chapter.*
- g) *Intake and exhaust manifolds (Part A of this Chapter).*
- h) *Oil filter* (Chapter 1).
- i) *Engine/transaxle mounting brackets (Part A of this Chapter, Section 22).*
- j) *Flywheel/driveplate (Part A of this Chapter, Section 21).*

4 If you are obtaining a short block (which consists of the engine cylinder block/crankcase, crankshaft, pistons and connecting rods all assembled), then the cylinder head, oil pan, oil pump and timing belt (four-cylinder) or chains (V6) will have to be removed also.

5 If you are planning a complete overhaul, the engine can be disassembled and the internal components removed in the following order.

- a) *Intake and exhaust manifolds (Part A of this Chapter).*
- b) *Timing belt (four-cylinder)or timing chains (V6), sprockets and tensioner(s), and timing belt inner cover (Part A or B of this Chapter).*
- c) *Cylinder head (s) (Part A or B of this Chapter).*
- d) *Flywheel/driveplate (Part A or Part B of this Chapter).*
- e) *Oil pan (Part A or Part B of this Chapter).*
- f) *Oil pump (Part A of this Chapter).*
- g) *Piston/connecting rod assemblies* (Section 9).
- h) *Crankshaft* (Section 10).

6 Before beginning the disassembly and overhaul procedures, make sure that you have all of the correct tools necessary. Refer to the introductory pages at the beginning of this manual for further information.

6 Cylinder head - disassembly

Refer to illustrations 6.1, 6.3a, 6.3b, 6.3c, 6.6a, 6.6b, 6.7 and 6.8

Note: *New and reconditioned cylinder heads are available from the manufacturers, and from engine overhaul specialists. Because some special tools are required for the disassembly and inspection procedures, and new components may not be readily available (refer to Section 1 of this Part), it may be more practical and economical for the home mechanic to purchase a reconditioned head, rather than to disassemble, inspect and recondition the original head.*

1 Remove the camshafts and hydraulic lifters (Part A or Part B of this Chapter), being careful to store the hydraulic lifters as described.

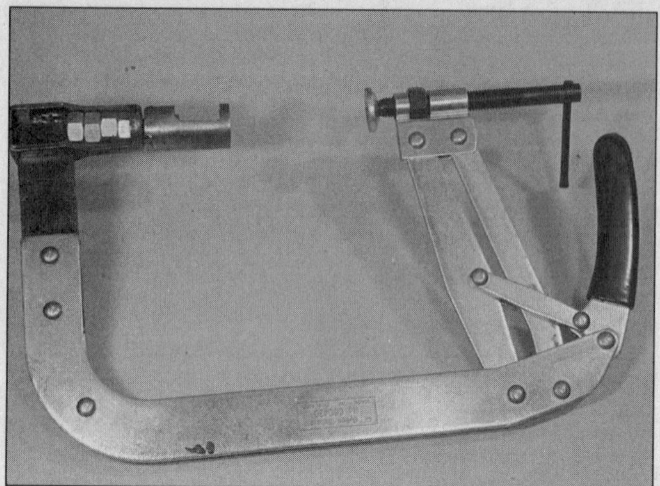
6.3a A standard valve spring compressor modified as shown . . .

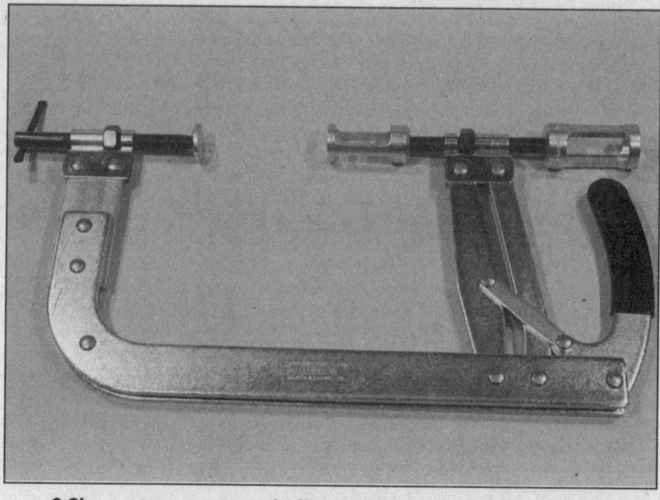
6.3b . . . or a purpose-built special version, is required to compress valve springs without damaging the cylinder head . . .

2 Remove the cylinder head (Part A or Part B of this Chapter).

3 Using a valve spring compressor, compress each valve spring until the keepers can be removed. A special valve spring compressor is required, to reach into the deep wells in the cylinder head without risk of damaging the hydraulic lifter bores. Such compressors are now widely available from most good auto parts stores. Release the compressor, and lift off the spring upper seat and spring **(see illustrations)**.

4 If, when the valve spring compressor is applied, the spring upper seat refuses to dislodge and expose the split keepers, gently tap the top of the tool, directly over the upper seat, with a light hammer. This will dislodge the seat.

5 Withdraw the valve through the combustion chamber. If it binds in the guide (won't pull through), push it back in, and deburr the area around the keeper groove with a fine file or whetstone; take care not to scratch the hydraulic lifter bores.

6 The manufacturer recommends the use of a special seal removal tool to extract the valve spring lower seat/stem oil seals; while this is almost indispensable if the seals are to be removed without risk of damage to the cylinder head, we found that a substitute can be made from a strong spring of suitable size. Screw on the tool or spring so that it bites into the seal, then pull the seal off the valve guide **(see illustrations)**.

7 It is essential that the valves are kept together with their keepers, spring seats and springs, and in their correct sequence (unless they are to be replaced). If they are going to be used again, place them in a labeled plastic bag or similar small container **(see illustration)**. Note that No 1 valve is nearest to the timing belt end of the engine.

8 If the oil-retaining valve is to be removed (to flush out the cylinder head oil galleries thoroughly), seek the advice of a machine shop as to how it can be extracted. The only course of action involves destroying the valve as follows. Screw a self-tapping screw into its vent hole and use the screw to pry or pull the valve out. A new valve must be purchased and pressed into place on reassembly **(see illustration)**.

7 Cylinder head and valve components - cleaning and inspection

Refer to illustrations 7.6, 7.12 and 7.14

1 Thorough cleaning of the cylinder head and valve components, followed by a detailed inspection, will enable you to decide how much valve service work must be performed

6.3c . . . so that both valve keepers can be removed from the valve's stem - a small magnetic pick-up tool prevents loss of small metal components on removal and installation

6.6a This special tool removes valve stem oil seals

6.6b Valve stem oil seals can be replaced with a home-made tool like this one (fabricated from a tightly-wound spring)

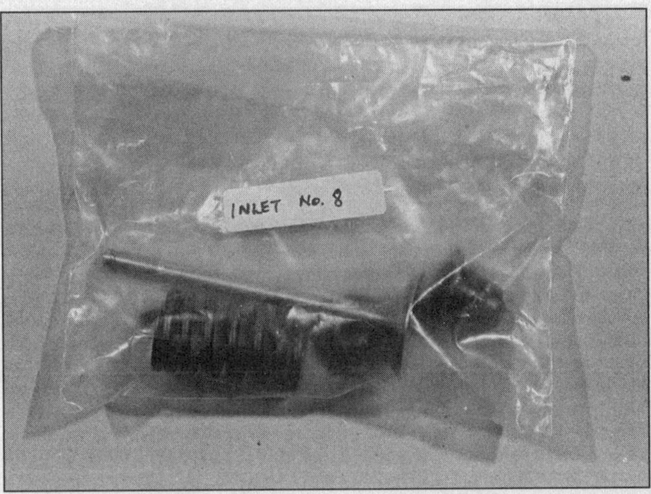

6.7 Use clearly marked containers to identify components and to keep matched assemblies together

during the engine overhaul. **Note:** *If the engine has been severely overheated, it is best to assume that the cylinder head is warped. Therefore, check carefully for warpage.*

Cleaning

2 Scrape away all traces of old gasket material and sealing compound from the cylinder head (see Part A or Part B of this Chapter).

3 Scrape away the carbon from the combustion chambers and ports, then wash the cylinder head thoroughly with a suitable solvent.

4 Scrape off any heavy carbon deposits that may have formed on the valves, then use a power-operated wire brush to remove deposits from the valve heads and stems.

Inspection

Note: *Be sure to perform all the following inspection procedures before concluding that the services of a machine shop or engine overhaul specialist are required. Make a list of all items that require attention.*

Cylinder head

5 Inspect the head very carefully for cracks, evidence of coolant leakage and other damage. If cracks are found, a new cylinder head should be obtained.

6 Use a straight edge and feeler gauge to check for cylinder head gasket warpage **(see illustration)**. If it is, it may be possible to resurface it.

7 Examine the valve seats in each of the combustion chambers. If they are severely pitted, cracked or burned, they must be replaced or reconditioned by an engine overhaul specialist. Minor pitting can be removed by grinding-in the valve heads and seats with fine valve-grinding compound, as described below.

8 If the valve guides are worn, indicated by a side-to-side motion of the valve, new guides must be installed. Measure the diameter of the existing valve stems (see below) and the bore of the guides, then calculate the clearance and compare the result with the specified value. If the clearance is excessive, replace the valves or guides as necessary.

9 The replacement of valve guides is best accomplished by an engine overhaul specialist or qualified machine shop.

10 If the valve seats are to be reconditioned, this must be done *only after* determining that the valve guides are in acceptable condition or after the guides have been replaced.

Valves

11 Examine the head of each valve for pitting, burning, cracks and general wear, and check the valve stem for scoring and wear ridges. Rotate the valve and check for any obvious runout. Look for pits and excessive wear on the tip of each valve stem. Replace any valve that is excessively worn or damaged.

12 If the valve appears satisfactory at this stage, measure the valve stem diameter at several points, using a micrometer **(see illustration)**. Any significant difference in the readings indicates wear of the valve stem. Should any of these conditions be apparent, the valve(s) must be replaced.

Valve components

13 Examine the valve springs for damage and discoloration. Also measure their free length by comparing each of the existing springs with a new component.

14 Stand each spring on a flat surface, and check it for squareness **(see illustration)**. If any of the springs are damaged, distorted, or have lost their tension, obtain a complete set of new springs.

15 Check the spring upper seats and keepers for obvious wear and cracks. Any questionable parts should be replaced, as extensive damage will occur if they fail during engine operation. Any damaged or excessively-worn parts must be replaced. The valve stem oil seals must be replaced as a matter of course whenever they are disturbed.

16 Check the hydraulic lifters as described in Part A or Part B of this Chapter.

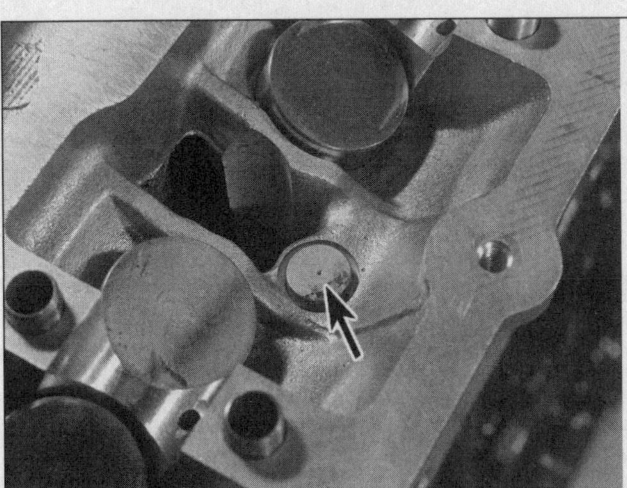

6.8 Cylinder head oil-retaining valve (arrow)

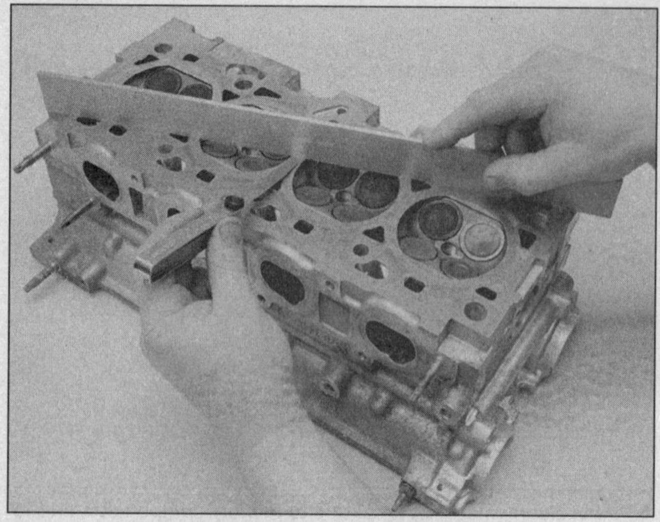

7.6 Check the cylinder head gasket surface for warpage, placing a precision straightedge across the head at various angles. Try to slip a feeler gauge under the straight edge (see the Specifications for the maximum distortion allowed and use a feeler gauge of that thickness)

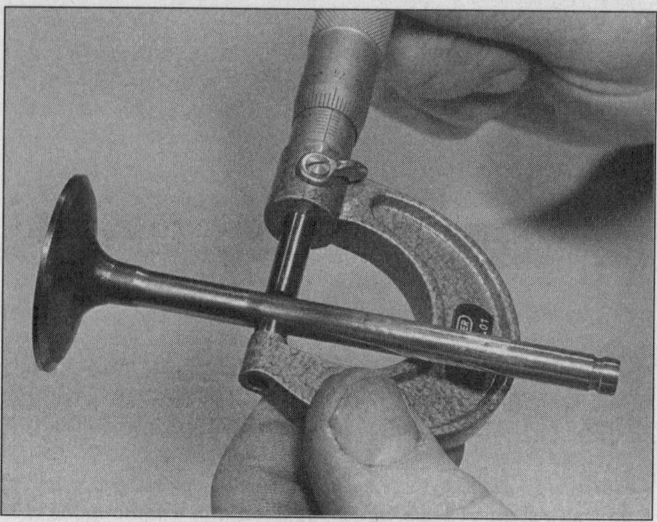

7.12 Measuring the diameter of a valve stem - if any significant difference is found in the measurements, excessive valve stem wear is indicated

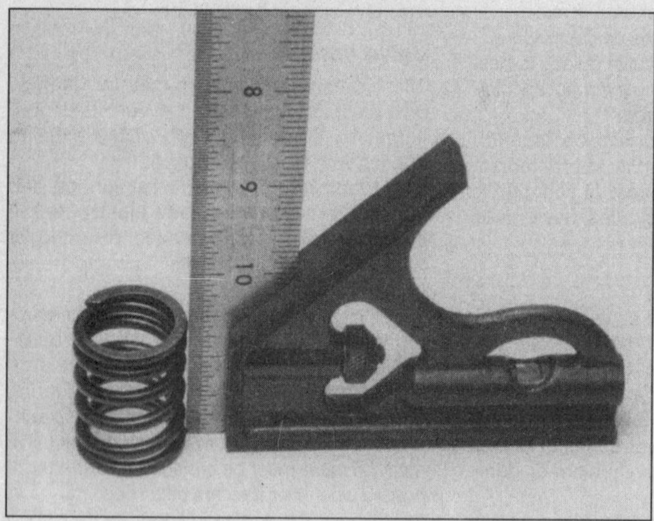

7.14 Check each valve spring for squareness

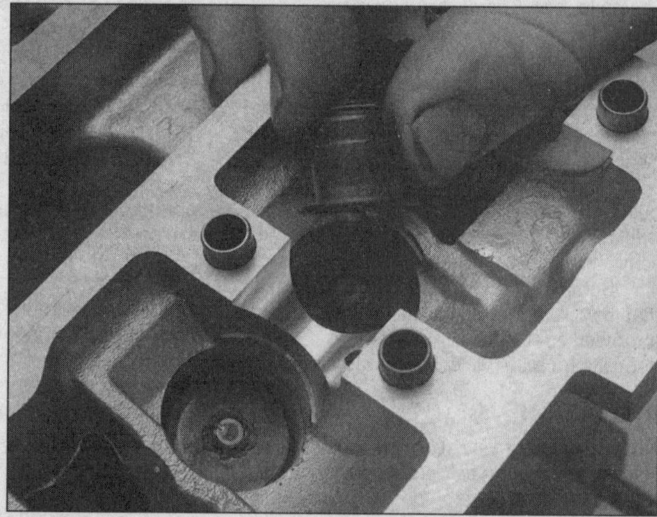

8.3 Valve spring pressure is sufficient to seat the valve stem seal

8 Cylinder head - reassembly

Refer to illustrations 8.3 and 8.5

1 Make sure the cylinder head is absolutely clean before beginning reassembly. Be sure to remove any metal particles and abrasive grit that may still be present from operations such as valve grinding or head resurfacing. Use compressed air, if available, to blow out all the oil holes and passages.

2 Beginning at one end of the head, lubricate and install the first valve. Apply moly-based grease or clean engine oil to the valve stem and install the valve. If the original valves are re-used, ensure that each is installed in its original guide. If new valves are being installed, insert them into the locations to which they have been lapped.

3 Install the plastic protector supplied with new valve stem oil seals to the end of the valve stem, then put the new seal squarely on top of the guide and leave it there. The action of installing the valve spring presses the oil seal into place **(see illustration)**.

4 Install the valve spring and upper seat.

5 Compress the spring with a valve spring compressor, then carefully install the keepers in the stem groove. Apply a small dab of grease to each keeper to hold it in place if necessary **(see illustration)**. Slowly release the compressor and make sure the keepers seat properly.

6 When the valve is installed, place the

8.5 Apply a small dab of grease to each keeper before installation - it will hold them in place on the valve stem until the spring is released

9.4 Remove the oil baffle (if so equipped) to provide access to the crankshaft and bearings

9.5 Each connecting rod and cap has a machined surface with the cylinder number stamped in it

cylinder head flat on the bench and, using a hammer and block of wood, tap the end of the valve stem gently, to settle the components.

7 Repeat the procedure for the remaining valves. Be sure to return the components to their original locations - don't mix them up!

8 Install the hydraulic lifters (Part A or Part B of this Chapter).

9 Piston/connecting rod assemblies - removal

Refer to illustrations 9.4, 9.5 and 9.6

Note: *While this task is theoretically possible when the engine is in place in the vehicle, in practice, it requires so much preliminary disassembly and is so difficult to perform due to the restricted access, that owners are advised to remove the engine from the vehicle first. In addition to the new gaskets and other replacement parts required, a hoist will be needed. Alternatively, an adjustable engine support fixture, having a hook which will engage the engine lifting eyes and allow the height of the engine to be adjusted, could be used. Lifting equipment such as this can be rented from most tool rental shops - be sure that any such equipment is rated well in excess of the combined weight of the engine/transaxle unit.*

1 Remove the cylinder head (Part A or Part B of this Chapter).

2 Bolt lifting eyes to suitable points on the engine and transaxle, then attach the lifting equipment so that the engine/transaxle unit is supported securely. Most models are already equipped with such lifting eyes.

3 Remove the oil pan (Part A or Part B of this Chapter). On 1998 four-cylinder models and all V6 models, remove the bolts securing the lower crankcase to the cylinder block and separate the lower crankcase from the block.

4 Remove the screws securing the oil pump pick-up/screen tube to the pump, then unscrew the four nuts and withdraw the oil pump pick-up/screen tube. If so equipped, also remove the oil baffle **(see illustration)**.

5 **Note:** *On 1998 four-cylinder models, the connecting rods and caps are of the cracked-cap design. During production, the connecting rod and cap are forged as a one-piece unit, then the cap is broken apart from the rod. Because of this design, the mating surfaces of each cap and rod is unique and, therefore, nearly impossible to mix up.* Temporarily install the crankshaft pulley, so the crankshaft can be rotated. Note that each piston/connecting rod assembly can be identified by its cylinder number (counting from the timing belt/chain end of the engine) etched into the flat-machined surface of both the connecting rod and its cap. Furthermore, each piston has an arrow stamped into its crown, pointing toward the timing belt/chain end of the engine. If no marks can be seen, make your own before removing any of the components, so that you can be certain of installing each piston/connecting rod assembly in its original location. **(see illustration)**.

6 Use your fingernail to feel if a ridge has formed at the upper limit of ring travel (about a quarter-inch down from the top of each cylinder). If carbon deposits or cylinder wear have produced ridges, they must be completely removed with a special tool called a ridge reamer **(see illustration)**. Follow the manufacturer's instructions provided with the tool. Failure to remove the ridges before attempting to remove the piston/connecting rod assemblies may result in piston ring breakage.

7 On 1998 four-cylinder models, remove the bolts that secure the lower crankcase to the cylinder block. Loosen the bolts gradually and evenly, following a crossing pattern. When all bolts are loose, remove the bolts and separate the lower crankcase from the cylinder block.

8 Loosen each of the connecting rod cap bolts one half turn at a time, until they can be removed by hand. Remove the No. 1 cap and bearing shell. Don't drop the shell out of the cap.

9 Remove the upper bearing shell, and push the connecting rod/piston assembly out through the top of the engine. Use a wooden hammer handle to push on the connecting

9.6 A ridge reamer may be required to remove the ridge from the top of each cylinder - do this before removing the pistons

rod's bearing recess. If resistance is felt, double-check that all of the ridge was removed from the cylinder.

10 Repeat the procedure for the remaining cylinders.

11 After removal, reassemble the rod caps and bearings on their respective connecting rods and install the bolts finger-tight. Leaving the old shells in place until reassembly will help prevent the bearing recesses from being accidentally nicked or gouged. New shells should be used on reassembly.

12 Don't attempt to separate the pistons from the connecting rods - see Section 12.

10 Crankshaft - removal

Refer to illustrations 10.1, 10.2, 10.3 and 10.4

Note: *The crankshaft can be removed only after the engine/transaxle has been removed from the engine. It is assumed that the transaxle and flywheel/driveplate, lower crankcase on 1998 four-cylinder models, timing belt, cylinder head, oil pan, oil pump pick-up/screen tube, oil baffle, oil pump and piston/connecting rod assemblies, have already*

10.1 Checking crankshaft endplay using a dial indicator

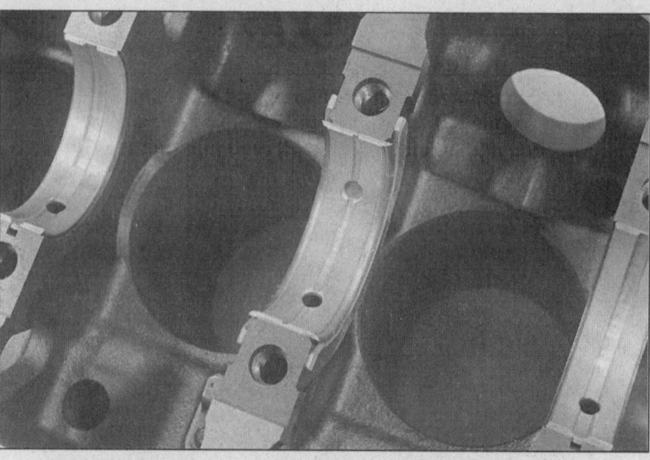
10.2 Thrustwashers integral with a main bearing control crankshaft endplay - on four-cylinder engines, the No 3 (center) bearing is the thrust bearing, while on V6 models, it is the No. 4 (rear) bearing

been removed. The crankshaft rear seal carrier must be unbolted from the cylinder block/crankcase before proceeding with crankshaft removal.

1 Before the crankshaft is removed, check the endplay. Mount a dial indicator with its plunger aligned with the crankshaft and just touching the crankshaft **(see illustration)**.

2 Pry the crankshaft fully away from the gauge, and zero it. Next, pry the crankshaft toward the gauge as far as possible, and check the reading on the dial indicator. The distance that the crankshaft moved is its endplay. If it is greater than specified, check the crankshaft thrust surfaces for wear. If no wear is evident, a new thrust control bearing should correct the endplay. On four-cylinder models, the thrust control bearing is part of the No. 3 (center) main bearing **(see illustration)**. On V6 models, the thrust control bearing consists of the No. 4 (rear) lower main bearing half and a washer that fits into the cylinder block.

3 If a dial indicator is not available, a feeler gauge can be used. Gently pry or push the crankshaft all the way toward the right-hand end of the engine. Slip a feeler gauge between the crankshaft and the face of the thrust bearing to determine the clearance **(see illustration)**.

4 On four-cylinder models, check the main bearing caps, to see if they are marked to indicate their locations **(see illustration)**. They should be numbered sequentially from the timing belt end of the engine - if not, mark them with number-stamping dies or a center-punch. The caps will also have an embossed arrow pointing to the timing belt end of the engine. Noting the different fasteners (for the oil baffle nuts) used on caps 2 and 4, loosen the cap bolts a quarter-turn at a time each, starting with the left and right end caps and working toward the center, until they can be removed by hand.

5 **Note:** *On V6 models, the lower crankcase holds the lower main bearing halves and the crankshaft in the cylinder block. Conventional main bearing caps are not used on V6 models. In addition, the interior lower crankcase bolts are the torque-to-yield design and must be replaced during assembly.* On V6 models, loosen the 22 lower crankcase-to-cylinder block. Loosen the bolts gradually and evenly following a cross-ing pattern. After all bolts are loose, remove them and separate the lower crankcase from the cylinder block. Note the position of the lower main bearing halves for reassembly reference.

6 On four-cylinder models, gently tap the caps with a soft-faced hammer, then separate them from the cylinder block/crankcase. If necessary, use the bolts as levers to remove the caps. Try not to drop the bearing shells if they come out with the caps.

7 Carefully lift the crankshaft out of the engine. It is a good idea to have an assistant available, since the crankshaft is heavy. With the main bearing halves in place in the cylinder block/crankcase and main bearing caps (four-cylinder) or lower crankcase (V6), return the caps to their respective locations on the block, or install the lower crankcase on the block and tighten the bolts finger-tight. Leaving the old bearings in place until reassembly will help prevent the bearing recesses from being accidentally nicked or gouged. New main bearings should be used on reassembly.

10.3 Checking crankshaft endplay with a feeler gauge

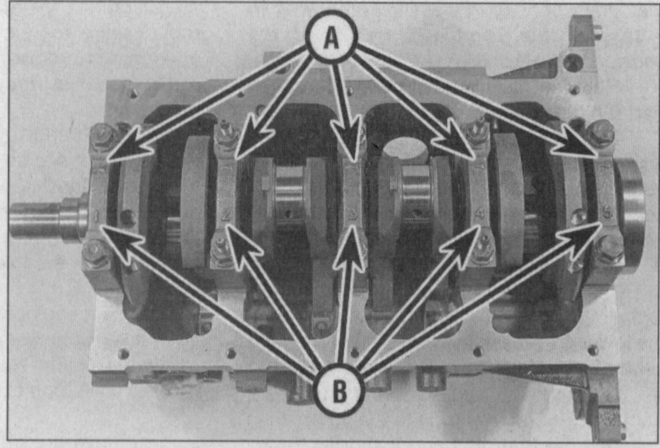

10.4 Before unbolting the crankshaft main bearing caps, note the arrows pointing to the timing belt end of the engine (A), and bearing numbers (B) from the timing belt end

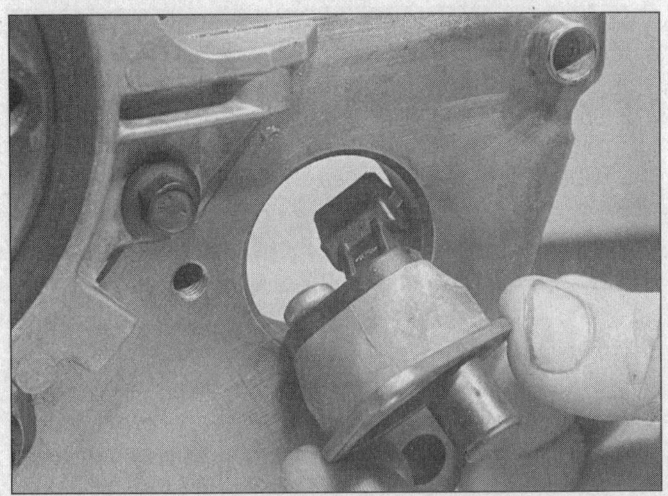
11.1a Remove all attached parts from the engine block - be especially careful with the crankshaft speed/position sensor

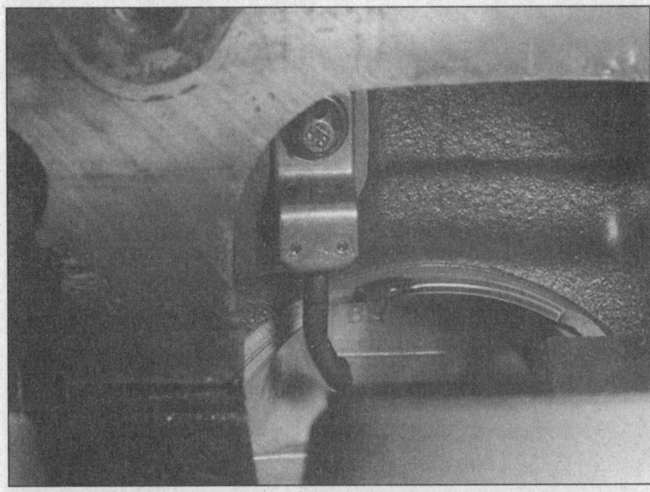
11.1b Remove the piston-cooling oil jets (if equipped) from the bottom of each cylinder, the manufacturer recommends you routinely replace these jets at overhaul time

11 Cylinder block/crankcase - cleaning and inspection

Refer to illustrations 11.1a, 11.1b, 11.1c, 11.2, 11.4, 11.8, 11.9 and 11.10

Cleaning

1 For complete cleaning, remove the water pump, all external components and all electrical switches/sensors. Unbolt the piston-cooling oil jets or plugs (as applicable). Note that the manufacturer states that the piston-cooling oil jets (if so equipped) must be replaced if the engine is disassembled for complete overhaul **(see illustrations)**.

2 Remove the main bearing caps (2.0 L models) or lower crankcase (V6 models) and separate the main bearings from the caps or lower crankcase and the cylinder block. Mark or label the bearings, indicating which crankshaft journal they were removed from and whether they were in the cylinder block or cap on four-cylinder models or lower crankcase on V6 models. Set them aside **(see illustration)**. Wipe the cylinder block and caps (or lower crankcase on V6 models) and inspect them for nicks, gouges and scratches.

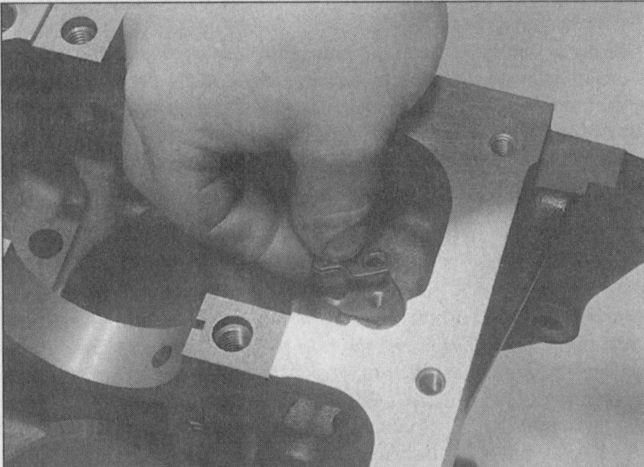
11.1c On four-cylinder models, these oil gallery plugs are used when no cooling oil jets are installed

3 Scrape all traces of gasket material from the cylinder block/lower crankcase, taking care not to damage the sealing surfaces.

4 Remove all oil gallery plugs (if equipped). The plugs are usually very tight - they may have to be drilled out and the holes retapped. Use new plugs when the engine is reassembled. Remove the core plugs by

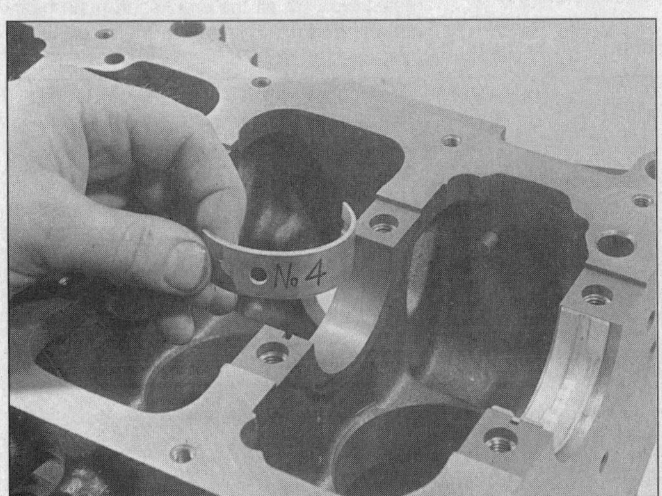

11.2 Use a felt marker pen to identify bearing inserts without damaging them

11.4 Use a hammer and punch to knock each core plug sideways in its bore

2C

11.8 All bolt holes in the block, especially the main bearing cap and cylinder head bolt holes, must be cleaned and restored with a tap (be sure to remove debris from the holes after this is done)

11.9 A large socket on an extension can be used to drive the new core plugs into their bores

knocking them sideways in their bores with a hammer and a punch, then grasping them with large pliers and pulling them back through their holes **(see illustration)**. **Caution:** *The core plugs (also known as freeze or soft plugs) may be difficult or impossible to retrieve if they are driven into the block coolant passages.*

5 If any of the castings are extremely dirty, they should be steam-cleaned.

6 After the castings are cleaned, clean all oil holes and oil galleries one more time. Flush all internal passages with warm water until the water runs clear, then dry thoroughly and apply a light film of oil to all machined surfaces to prevent rusting. If you have access to compressed air, use it to speed the drying process and to blow out all the oil holes and galleries. **Warning:** *Wear eye protection when using compressed air!*

7 If the castings are not very dirty, you can do an adequate cleaning job with hot soapy water (as hot as you can stand!) and a stiff brush. Take plenty of time, and do a thorough job. Regardless of the cleaning method used, be sure to clean all oil holes and galleries very thoroughly and to dry all components completely. Protect the machined surfaces as described above to prevent rusting.

8 All threaded holes must be clean and dry to ensure accurate torque application during reassembly. Clean and check the threads of all fasteners and threaded holes; however, note that some fasteners, such as the cylinder head, flywheel/driveplate bolts and lower crankcase bolts on V6 models must be replaced once they are removed. Run the proper-size tap into each of the holes to remove rust, corrosion, thread sealant or sludge and to restore damaged threads **(see illustration)**. If possible, use compressed air to clean the holes of debris produced by this operation. A good alternative is to spray an aerosol water-displacing lubricant into each hole using the long spout usually provided with the product. **Warning:** *Wear eye protection when cleaning out the holes using this technique. Also be sure to dry any excess liquid left in the holes.*

9 When all inspection and repair procedures are complete (see below) and the block is ready for reassembly, apply suitable sealant to the new oil gallery plugs and insert them into the holes in the block. Tighten them securely. After coating the sealing surfaces of the new core plugs with suitable sealant, install them in the cylinder block **(see illustration)**. Make sure they are driven straight and seated properly, or leakage could result. Special tools are available for this purpose, but a large socket with an outside diameter that will just slip into the core plug, used with an extension and hammer, will work just as well.

10 Install the blanking plugs or (new) piston-cooling oil jets (if so equipped), tightening their Torx screws securely **(see illustration)**. Also, install all other external components removed, referring to the relevant Chapter of this manual for further details where required. Install the main bearing caps (four-cylinder models) or lower crankcase (V6 models), and tighten the bolts finger-tight.

11 If the engine isn't going to be reassembled right away, cover it with a large plastic bag to keep it clean. Apply a thin coat of engine oil to all machined surfaces to prevent rust.

Inspection

Refer to illustrations 11.14a, 11.14b, 11.14c, 11.15, 11.23a and 11.23b

12 Inspect the castings for cracks, corrosion or other damage. Look for stripped threads in the threaded holes. If there has been any history of internal coolant leakage, it may be worthwhile to have the cylinder block checked for cracks with special equipment at a qualified machine shop. If defects are found, have them repaired, if possible, or replace the assembly.

13 Check each cylinder bore for scuffing and scoring.

14 Noting that the cylinder bores must be measured with all the crankshaft main bearing caps (four-cylinder models) or lower

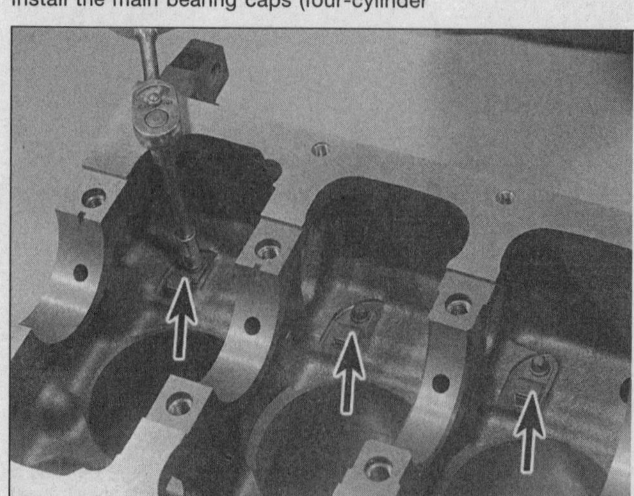

11.10 Don't forget to install all components, such as the oil gallery plugs (arrows)

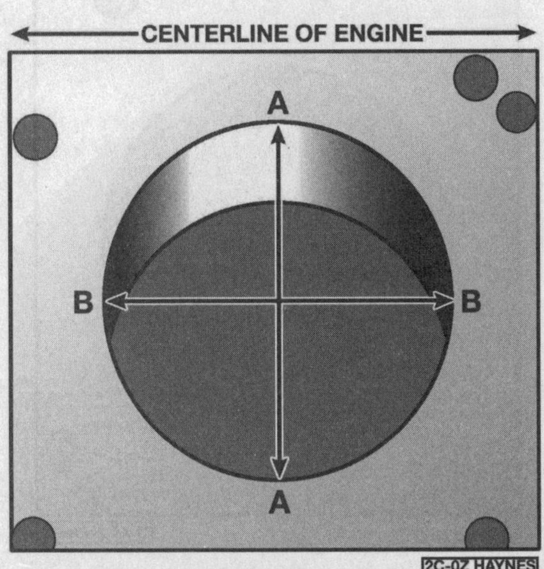

11.14a Measure the diameter of each cylinder at a right angle to the engine centerline (A) and parallel to the engine centerline (B) - out-of-round is the difference between A and B; taper is the difference between A and B at the top of the cylinder and A and B at the bottom of the cylinder

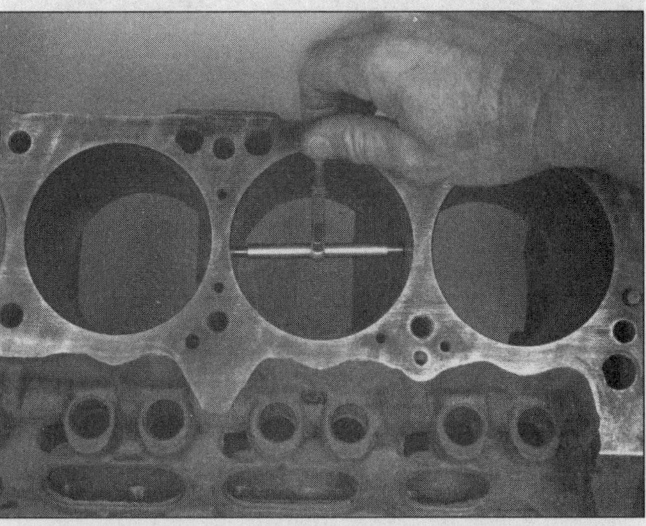

11.14b The ability to feel when the telescoping gauge is at the correct point will be developed over time, so work slowly, and repeat the check until you're satisfied that the bore measurement is accurate

crankcase (V6 models) bolted in place (without the crankshaft and bearing shells), to the specified torque, measure the diameter of each cylinder at the top (just under the ridge area), center and bottom of the cylinder bore, parallel to the crankshaft axis. Next, measure each cylinder's diameter at the same three locations across the crankshaft axis **(see illustrations)**. Record the measurements obtained.

15 Measure the piston diameter at a right-angle to the piston pin axis, just above the bottom of the skirt. Again, record the results **(see illustration)**.

16 To obtain the piston-to-bore clearance, measure the bore and piston skirt as described above, and subtract the skirt diameter from the bore measurement. If the precision measuring tools shown are not available, the condition of the pistons and bores can be determined, though not quite as accurately, by using a feeler gauge as follows. Select a feeler gauge of a thickness equal to the specified piston-to-bore clearance, then slip it into the cylinder along with the matching piston. The piston must be positioned exactly in its normal running position. The feeler gauge must be between the piston and cylinder on one of the thrust faces (at a right angle to the piston pin bore). The piston should slip through the cylinder (with the feeler gauge in place) with moderate pressure. If it falls through or slides through easily, the clearance is excessive and a new piston will be required. If the piston binds at the lower end of the cylinder and is loose toward the top, the cylinder is tapered. If tight spots are encountered as the piston/feeler gauge is rotated in the cylinder, the cylinder is out-of-round.

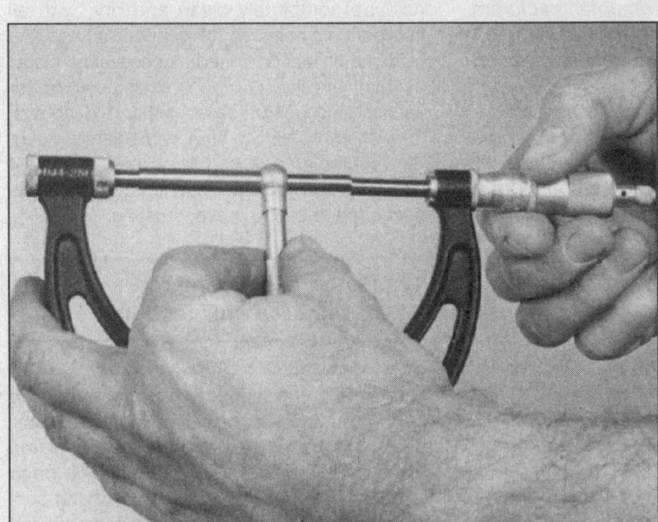

11.14c The gauge is then measured with a micrometer to determine the bore size

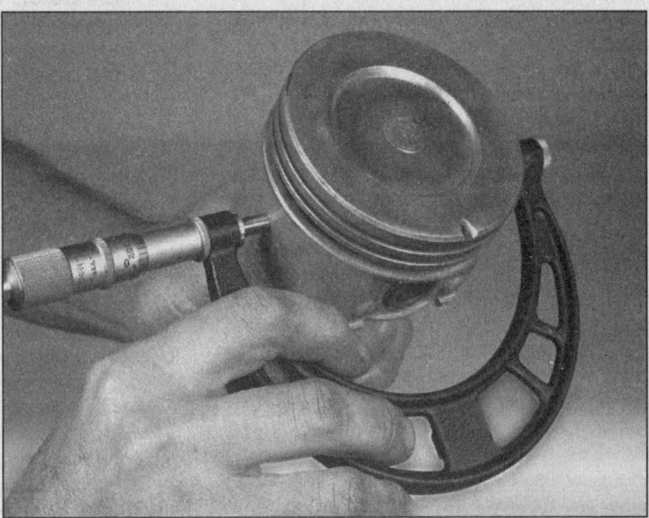

11.15 Measure the piston skirt diameter at a right-angle to the piston pin axis, just above the base of the skirt

11.23a A bead hone will produce better results if you have never honed cylinders before

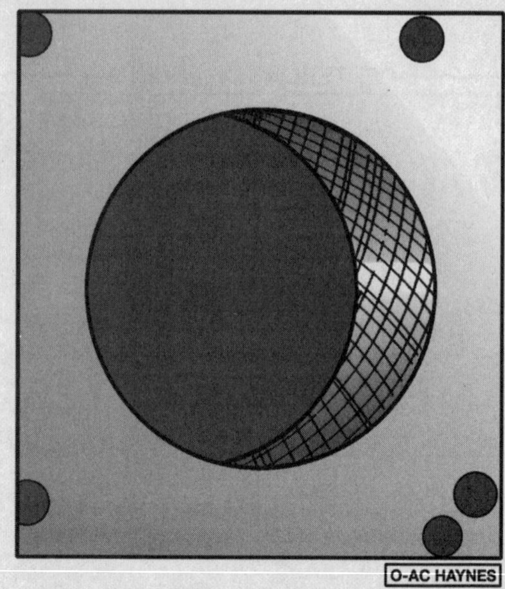

11.23b The cylinder hone should leave a smooth, cross-hatch pattern with the lines intersecting at approximately a 60-degree angle

17 Repeat these procedures for the remaining pistons and cylinder bores.

18 Compare the results with the Specifications at the beginning of this Chapter. If any measurement is beyond the dimensions specified for that class (check the piston crown marking to establish the class of piston installed), or if any bore measurement is significantly different from the others (indicating that the bore is tapered or out-of-round), the piston or bore is excessively worn.

19 Worn pistons must be replaced. Check with an auto parts store for availability.

20 If any of the cylinder bores are badly scuffed or scored or if they are excessively worn, out-of-round or tapered, the usual course of action would be to have the cylinder block/crankcase rebored, and to install new, oversize, pistons on reassembly. See a manufacturer parts department or machine shop for advice.

21 If the bores are in serviceable condition (not excessively worn, tapered or out-of-round). It may only be necessary to replace the piston rings.

22 If this is the case, the bores should be honed to allow the new rings to seat to the cylinders correctly and provide the best possible seal. Before honing the bores, install the main bearing caps (four-cylinder) or lower crankcase (V6) without the bearing inserts and tighten the bolts to the torque listed in this Chapter's Specifications. **Note:** *If you don't have the tools, or don't want to attempt the honing operation, most machine shops will do it for a reasonable fee.*

23 Two types of cylinder hones are commonly available - the flex hone (or bead hone) type, and the more traditional surfacing hone with spring-loaded stones. Both will do the job and are used with a power drill, but for the less-experienced mechanic, the bead hone will probably be easier to use. You will also need some honing oil (solvent) and rags. Proceed as follows:

a) *Mount the hone in the drill, compress the stones, and slip it into the first bore* **(see illustration)**. *Be sure to wear eye protection!*

b) *Lubricate the bore with plenty of honing oil, switch on the drill, and move the hone up and down the bore, at a pace that will produce a fine cross-hatch pattern on the cylinder walls. Ideally, the cross-hatch lines should intersect at approximately a 60-degree angle* **(see illustration)**. *Be sure to use plenty of lubricant, and don't remove any more material than is absolutely necessary to produce the desired finish.* **Note:** *Piston ring manufacturers may specify a different crosshatch angle - read and follow any instructions included with the new rings.*

c) *Don't withdraw the hone from the bore while it's running. Instead, switch off the drill and continue moving the hone up and down the bore until it comes to a complete stop, then compress the stones and withdraw the hone. If you're using a bead hone, switch off the drill, then turn the chuck in the normal direction of rotation while withdrawing the hone from the bore.*

d) *Wipe the oil out of the bore and repeat the procedure for the remaining cylinders.*

e) *When all the cylinder bores are honed, chamfer the top edges of the bores lightly with a small file so the rings won't catch when the pistons are installed. Be very careful not to nick the cylinder walls with the end of the file.*

f) *The entire cylinder block must be washed very thoroughly with warm, soapy water to remove all traces of the abrasive grit produced during the honing operation.* **Note:** *The bores can be considered clean when a lint-free white cloth - dampened with clean engine oil - used to wipe them out doesn't pick up any more honing residue, which will show up as gray areas on the cloth. Be sure to run a brush through all oil holes and galleries and flush them with running water.*

g) *When the cylinder block/crankcase is completely clean, rinse it thoroughly and dry it, then lightly oil all exposed machined surfaces to prevent rusting.*

24 The cylinder block/crankcase should now be completely clean and dry, with all components checked for wear or damage and repaired or reconditioned as necessary. Install as many ancillary components as possible, for safekeeping (see paragraphs 9 and 10 above). If reassembly isn't to start immediately, cover the block with a large plastic bag to keep it clean and protect the machined surfaces as described above to prevent rusting.

12 Piston/connecting rod assemblies - inspection

Refer to illustrations 12.4a and 12.4b

1 Before the inspection process can be performed, the piston/connecting rod assemblies must be cleaned and the original piston rings removed from the pistons. The rings should have smooth, polished working surfaces, with no dull or carbon-coated sections (showing that the ring isn't sealing correctly against the cylinder bore, allowing combus-

12.4a The piston ring grooves can be cleaned using a special tool, as shown here . . .

12.4b . . . or a section of a broken ring

13.3 Rubbing a penny lengthwise along each journal will reveal its condition - if copper rubs off and is embedded in the crankshaft, the journals should be reground

tion gases to blow by) and no traces of wear on their top and bottom surfaces. The end gaps should be clear of carbon, but not polished (indicating an insufficient end gap) and all the rings (including the elements of the oil control ring) should be free to rotate in their grooves, but without excessive up-and-down movement. If the rings appear to be in good condition, they are probably fit for further use. Check the end gaps (in an unworn part of the bore) as described in Section 16. If any of the rings appear to be worn or damaged, or have an end gap significantly different from the specified value, replace all of them as a set. **Note:** *While it is good practice to replace the piston rings when an engine is overhauled, they may be reused if in acceptable condition. If reusing the rings, make sure each ring is marked during removal to ensure that it is installed in its original ring groove, and in the same direction.*

2 Using a piston ring removal tool, carefully remove the rings from the pistons. Be careful not to nick or gouge the pistons in the process and mark or label each ring as it is removed, so its original top surface can be identified on reassembly, and so it can be returned to its original groove. Take care also with your hands - piston rings are sharp! If a piston ring removal tool isn't available, the rings can be removed by hand, expanding them over the top of the pistons. The use of two or three old feeler gauges are helpful for preventing the rings from dropping into empty grooves.

3 Scrape all traces of carbon from the top of the piston. A hand-held wire brush or a piece of fine emery cloth can be used, once the majority of the deposits have been scraped away. *Don't*, under any circumstances, use a wire wheel mounted in a drill motor to remove deposits from the pistons - the piston material is soft and may be eroded away by the wire wheel.

4 Use a piston ring groove-cleaning tool to remove carbon deposits from the ring grooves. If a tool isn't available, a piece broken off an old ring will do the job. Be very careful to remove only the carbon deposits - don't remove any metal, and don't nick or scratch the sides of the ring grooves **(see illustrations)**. Protect your fingers - piston rings are sharp!

5 Once the deposits have been removed, clean the piston/rod assemblies with solvent and dry them with compressed air (if available). Make sure the oil return holes in the back sides of the ring grooves, and the oil hole in the lower end of each rod, are clean.

6 If the pistons and cylinder walls aren't damaged or worn excessively - refer to Section 11 for details of inspection and measurement procedures - and if the cylinder block/crankcase isn't rebored, new pistons won't be necessary. Normal piston wear appears as even vertical wear on the piston thrust surfaces, and slight looseness of the top ring in its groove.

7 Carefully inspect each piston for cracks around the skirt, at the pin bosses and at the ring lands (between the ring grooves).

8 Look for scoring and scuffing on the thrust faces of the skirt, holes in the piston crown and burned areas at the edge of the crown. If the skirt is scored or scuffed, the engine may have been overheating and/or abnormal combustion, which caused excessively high operating temperatures. The cooling and lubrication systems should be checked thoroughly. A hole in the piston crown is an indication that abnormal combustion (pre-ignition) has occurred. Burned areas at the edge of the piston crown are usually evidence of spark knock (detonation). If any of the above problems are evident, the causes must be corrected or the damage will occur again. The causes may include intake (vacuum) leaks, incorrect fuel/air mixture, incorrect ignition timing or an EGR system malfunction.

9 Corrosion of the piston, in the form of small pits, indicates that coolant is leaking into the combustion chamber and/or the crankcase. Again, the cause must be corrected or the problem may persist in the rebuilt engine.

10 Check the piston-to-rod clearance by twisting the piston and rod in opposite directions. Any noticeable play indicates excessive wear, which must be corrected. The piston/connecting rod assemblies should be taken to a dealer or machine shop to have the pistons, piston pins and rods checked and new components installed as required.

11 Don't attempt to separate the pistons from the connecting rods. This is a task for a dealer or qualified machine shop, due to the special heating equipment, press, mandrels and supports required to do the job. If the piston/connecting rod assemblies do require this sort of work, have the connecting rods checked for bending and twisting, since only such engine repair specialists will have the facilities for this purpose.

12 Check the connecting rods for cracks and other damage. Temporarily remove the big-end bearing caps and the old bearing inserts, wipe the rod and cap bearing recesses clean and inspect them for nicks, gouges and scratches. After checking the rods, replace the old bearings, slip the caps into place, and tighten the bolts finger-tight.

13 Crankshaft - inspection

Refer to illustrations 13.3 and 13.5

1 Clean the crankshaft, and dry it with compressed air, if available. **Warning:** *Wear eye protection when using compressed air!* Be sure to clean the oil holes with a pipe cleaner or similar probe.

2 Check the main and connecting rod (big-end) bearing journals for uneven wear, scoring, pitting and cracking.

3 Rub a penny across each journal several times **(see illustration)**. If a journal picks up copper from the penny, it is too rough.

4 Remove all burrs from the crankshaft oil holes with a fine-cut file or scraper.

5 Using a micrometer, measure the diam-

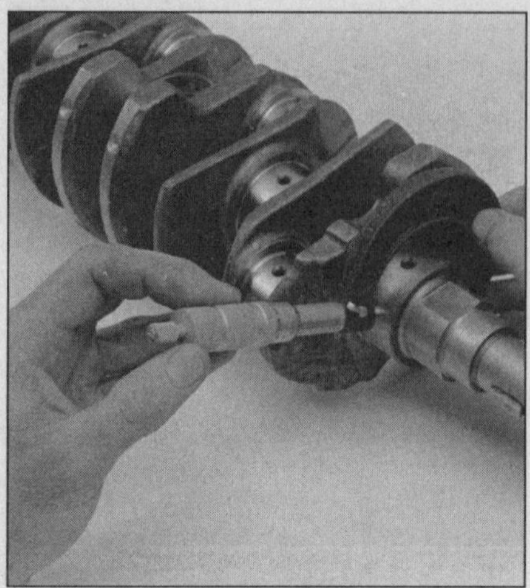

13.5 Measure the diameter of each crankshaft journal at several points to detect taper and out-of-round conditions

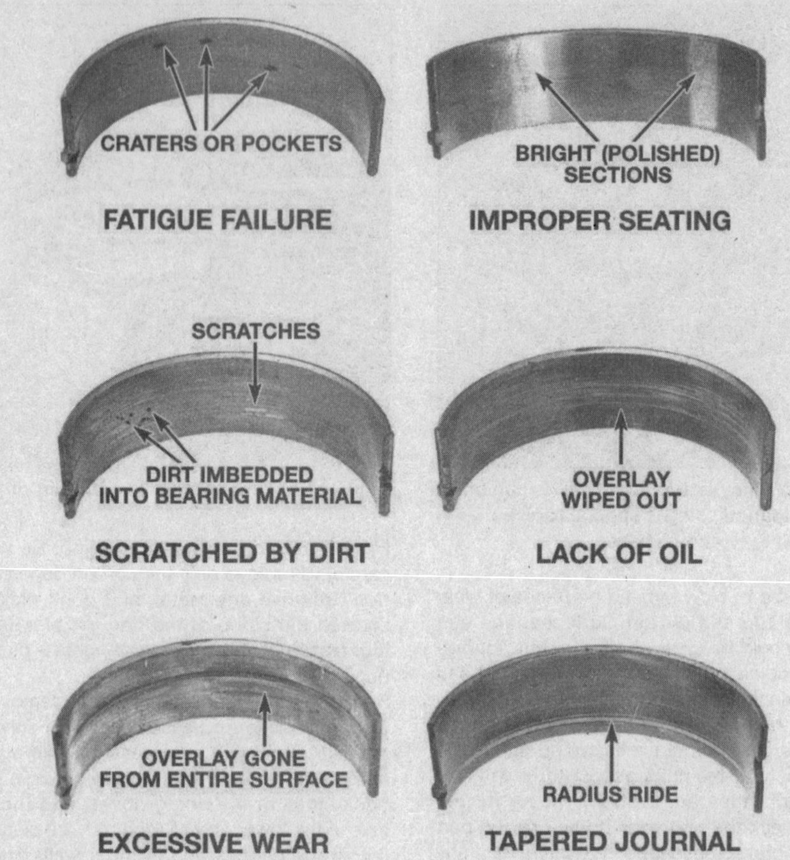

14.1 When inspecting the main and connecting rod bearings, look for these problems

eter of the main bearing and connecting rod journals, and compare the results with the Specifications at the beginning of this Chapter **(see illustration)**.

6 By measuring the diameter at a number of points around each journal's circumference, you'll be able to determine if the journal is out-of-round. Take the measurement at each end of the journal, near the webs, to determine if the journal is tapered.

7 If the crankshaft journals are damaged, tapered, out-of-round or worn beyond the limits specified in this Chapter, the crankshaft must be taken to a qualified machine shop who will regrind it, and who can supply the necessary undersize bearings.

8 Check the oil seal journals at each end of the crankshaft for wear and damage. If either seal has worn an excessive groove in its journal, consult a qualified machine shop, who will be able to advise whether a repair is possible, or whether a new crankshaft is necessary.

14 Main and connecting rod bearings - inspection

Refer to illustration 14.1

1 Even though the main and connecting rod bearings should be replaced during the engine overhaul, the old bearings should be retained for close inspection, as they may reveal valuable information about the condition of the engine **(see illustration)**.

2 Bearing failure occurs due to lack of lubrication, the presence of dirt or other foreign particles, overloading the engine and corrosion. Regardless of the cause of bearing failure, it must be corrected before the engine is reassembled to prevent it from happening again.

3 When inspecting the bearings, remove them from the cylinder block and main bearing caps (four-cylinder models) or lower crankcase (V6 models) and from the connecting rods and the rod caps, then lay them out on a clean surface in the same general position as their location in the engine. This will enable you to match any bearing problems with the corresponding crankshaft journal. *Don't* touch any bearing surface with your fingers while checking it, or the delicate surface may be scratched.

4 Dirt or other foreign material enters the engine in a variety of ways. It may be left in the engine during assembly or it may pass through filters or the crankcase ventilation system. It may get into the oil and from there into the bearings. Metal chips from machining operations and normal engine wear are often present. Abrasives are sometimes left in engine components after reconditioning, especially if parts are not cleaned thoroughly using the proper cleaning methods. Whatever the source, these foreign objects often end up embedded in the soft bearing material and are easily recognized. Large particles won't embed in the material, but will score or gouge the bearing and journal. The best prevention for this type of bearing failure is to clean all parts thoroughly and to keep everything absolutely clean during engine assembly. Frequent and regular engine oil and filter changes are also recommended.

5 Lack of lubrication (or lubrication breakdown) has a number of related causes. Excessive heat (which thins the oil), overloading (which squeezes the oil from the bearing face) and oil leakage (from excessive bearing clearances, worn oil pump or high engine speeds) all contribute to lubrication breakdown. Blocked oil passages, which usually are the result of misaligned oil holes in the bearing and journal, will also starve a bearing of oil and destroy it. If lack of lubrication is the cause of bearing failure, the bearing material is wiped or extruded from the steel backing of the bearing. Temperatures may increase to the point that the steel backing turns blue from overheating.

6 Driving habits can have a definite effect on bearing life. Full-throttle, low-speed operation (laboring the engine) puts very high loads on the bearings, which tends to squeeze out the oil film. These loads cause the bearings to flex, which produces fine cracks in the bearing face (fatigue failure). Eventually, the bearing material will loosen in pieces and separate from the steel backing. Short-distance driving leads to corrosion of bearings because insufficient engine heat is produced to evaporate condensed water and corrosive gases. These products collect in the engine oil, forming acid and sludge. As the oil is carried to the engine bearings, the acid attacks and corrodes the bearing material.

7 Incorrect bearing installing during engine assembly will lead to bearing failure as well. Tight-fitting shells leave insufficient

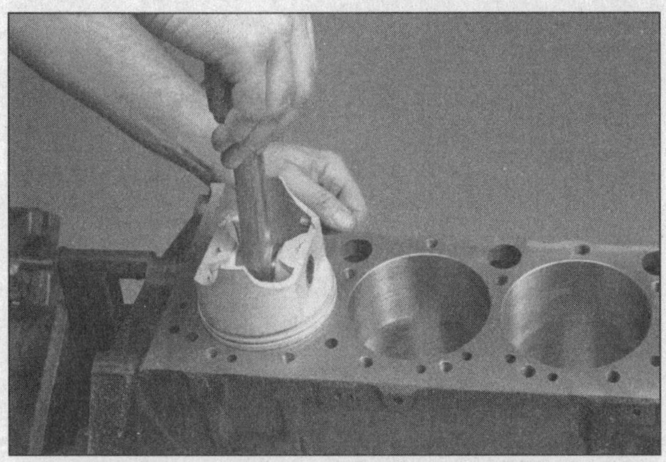

16.2 When checking the piston ring end gap, the ring must be square in the cylinder bore (this is done by pushing the ring down with the top of a piston)

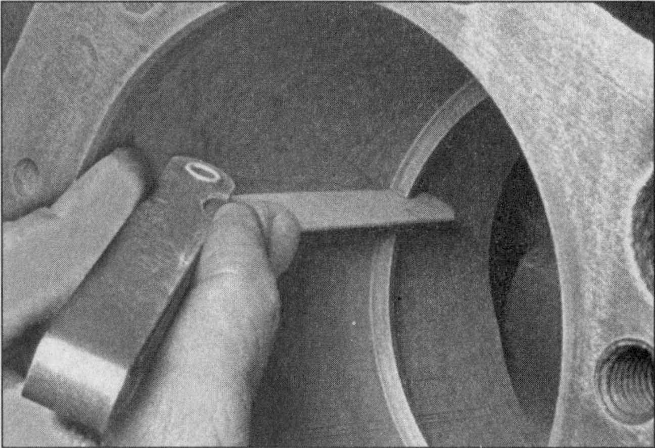

16.3 With the ring square in the bore, measure the end gap with a feeler gauge

bearing oil clearance and will result in oil starvation. Dirt or foreign particles trapped behind a bearing results in high spots on the bearing, which also lead to failure. *Don't* touch any bearing surface with your fingers during reassembly; there is a risk of scratching the delicate surface or of contaminating the surface with dirt.

15 Engine overhaul - reassembly sequence

Note: *The lower crankcase must be loosened in sequence to prevent warpage* **(see illustration 17.17).**

1 Before reassembly begins, ensure that all new parts have been obtained and that all necessary tools are available. Read through the entire procedure to familiarize yourself with the work involved and to ensure that all items necessary for reassembly of the engine are available. In addition to all normal tools and materials, suitable sealant will be required for certain seal surfaces. **Caution:** *Certain types of high-volatility RTV can foul the oxygen sensor and cause it to fail. Be sure that any RTV used is a low-volatility type and meets specifications for use on engines equipped with an oxygen sensor.* The manufacturer recommends using an RTV that meets specification WSE-M4G323-A6 for the oil pan-to cylinder block (or lower crankcase on 1998 four-cylinder and V6 models), the lower crankcase-to-cylinder block on 1998 four-cylinder and V6 models, oil pump/oil seal carrier joints, and the camshaft right-hand bearing cap on 1995 through 1997 four-cylinder models. In all other cases, provided the relevant mating surfaces are clean and flat, new gaskets will be sufficient to ensure the sealing surfaces are oil-tight. *Don't* use any kind of RTV sealant on any part of the fuel system or intake manifold and *never* use exhaust sealant upstream of the catalytic converter.

2 To save time and avoid problems, perform the engine reassembly in the following order:

a) Crankshaft (Section 17).
b) Piston/connecting rod assemblies (Section 18).
c) Oil pump (Part A or Part B of this Chapter).
d) Oil pan (Part A or Part B of this Chapter).
e) Flywheel/driveplate (Part A or Part B of this Chapter).
f) Cylinder head (Part A or Part B of this Chapter).
g) Timing belt inner cover, tensioner and sprockets, and timing belt (Part A or Part B of this Chapter).
h) Engine external components.

3 At this stage, all engine components should be absolutely clean and dry, with all faults repaired. All components should be neatly arranged on a completely-clean work surface or in individual containers.

16 Piston rings - installation

Refer to illustrations 16.2, 16.3, 16.6, 16.7a and 16.7b

1 Before installing new piston rings, check the end gaps. Lay out each piston ring set with a piston/connecting rod assembly and keep them together as a matched set from now on.

2 Insert the top compression ring into the first cylinder and square it up with the cylinder walls by pushing it in with the top of the piston **(see illustration)**. The ring should be near the bottom of the cylinder, at the lower limit of ring travel.

3 To measure the end gap, slip feeler gauges between the ends of the ring until a gauge equal to the gap width is found **(see illustration)**. The feeler gauge should slide between the ring ends with a slight drag. Compare the measurement to the value given in the Specifications Section of this Chapter. If the gap is larger or smaller than specified, double-check to make sure you have the correct rings before proceeding. If you are assessing the condition of used rings, have the cylinder bores checked and measured at a dealership service department or qualified machine shop, so that you can be sure of exactly which component is worn and seek advice as to the best course of action to take.

4 If the end gap is still too small, it must be enlarged by careful filing of the ring ends using a fine file. If it is too large, this isn't as serious, unless the specified limit is exceeded, in which case very careful inspection is required of all components, as well as of the new parts.

5 Repeat the procedure for each ring that will be installed in the first cylinder and for each ring in the remaining cylinders. Remember to keep the rings, pistons and cylinders matched up.

6 Install the piston rings as follows. If the original rings are being reused, use the marks or notes made on removal, to ensure that each ring is reinstalled in its original groove facing the same direction. New rings generally have their top surfaces identified by markings (often an indication of size, such as (STD), or the word (TOP) - the rings must be installed with such markings facing the top of the piston **(see illustration)**. **Note:** *Always*

16.6 Look for an etched marking (the STD shown here indicates a standard sized ring). The mark must face up when installed

16.7a Installing the spacer/expander in the oil control ring groove

16.7b DO NOT use a piston ring installation tool when installing the oil ring side rails

follow the instructions provided with the new rings - different manufacturers may require different approaches. Don't mix up the top and second compression rings, as they usually have different cross-sections.

7 The oil control ring (lowest one on the piston) is usually installed first. It is composed of three separate parts. Slip the spacer/expander into the groove **(see illustration)**. If an anti-rotation tang is used, make sure it is inserted into the drilled hole in the ring groove. Next, install the lower side rail. Don't use a piston ring installation tool on the oil ring side rails, as they may be damaged. Instead, place one end of the side rail into the groove between the spacer/expander and the ring land, hold it firmly in place and slide a finger around the piston while pushing the rail into the groove **(see illustration)**. Next, install the upper side rail using the same technique.

8 After the three oil ring components have been installed, check that both the upper and lower side rails can be turned smoothly in the ring groove.

9 The second compression (middle) ring is installed next, followed by the top compression ring - ensure their marks are facing the piston crown and be careful not to confuse them. Don't expand either ring any more than necessary to slide it over the top of the piston.

10 With all the rings in position, space the ring gaps (including the parts of the oil control ring) uniformly around the piston at 120° intervals. Repeat the procedure for the remaining pistons and rings.

17 Crankshaft - installation and main bearing oil clearance check

1 Crankshaft installation is the first major step in engine reassembly. It is assumed at this point that the cylinder block and crankshaft have been cleaned, inspected and repaired or reconditioned as necessary. Position the engine upside-down.

2 On four-cylinder models, remove the main bearing cap bolts and lift out the caps. Lay the caps out in the proper order, to ensure correct installation. On V6 models, remove the lower crankcase from the cylinder block.

3 If they're still in place, remove the old main bearings from the block and the main bearing caps or lower crankcase. Wipe the bearing recesses with a clean, lint-free cloth. They must be kept spotlessly-clean!

Main bearing oil clearance check

Refer to illustrations 17.4, 17.6, 17.7 and 17.10

4 Clean the backs of the new main bearings. Install the shells with an oil groove in each main bearing location in the block. On four-cylinder models, note the thrustwashers integral with the No 3 (center) upper main bearing. On V6 models, note the semi-circle shaped thrustwasher located adjacent to the No. 4 (transaxle end) upper main bearing. Install the main bearings in the rod caps on four-cylinder models or in the lower crankcase on V6 models. Make sure the tab on each bearing fits into the notch in the block, cap or lower crankcase. Also, the oil holes in the block must align with the oil holes in the bearings **(see illustration)**. **Caution:** *Don't hammer the shells into place and don't nick or gouge the bearing surfaces. No lubrication should be used at this time.*

5 Clean the bearing surfaces in the block and the crankshaft main bearing journals with a clean, lint-free cloth. Check or clean the oil

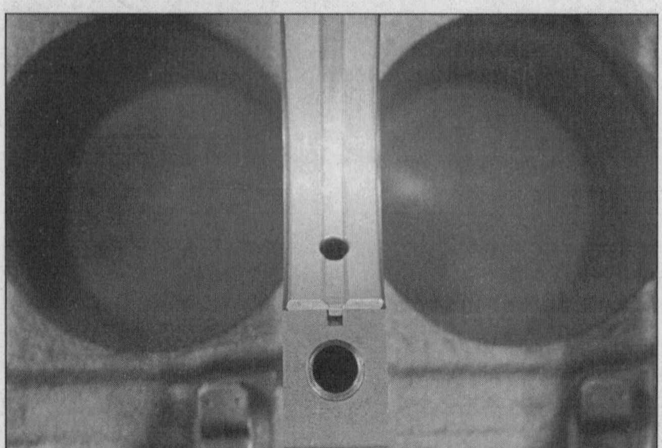

17.4 The tab on each bearing must engage with its associated notch and holes in the bearings should align with oil holes in the block

17.6 Lay the Plastigage strips on the main bearing journals (arrow), parallel to the crankshaft centerline

17.7 On four-cylinder models, install the main bearing caps and tighten the bolts as specified

17.10 Compare the width of the crushed Plastigage to the scale on the envelope to determine the main bearing oil clearance (always take the measurement at the widest point of the Plastigage). Be sure to use the correct scale; standard and metric scales are included

holes in the crankshaft, as any dirt here will go straight into the new bearings.

6 Once you're certain the crankshaft is clean, carefully lay it in position in the main bearings. Trim several pieces of the appropriate-size Plastigage (they must be slightly shorter than the width of the main bearings), and place one piece on each crankshaft main bearing journal, parallel with the crankshaft center-line **(see illustration)**.

7 Clean the bearing surfaces of the bearings in the caps (four-cylinder) or lower crankcase (V6). On four-cylinder models, install the caps in their respective positions (don't mix them up) with the arrows pointing to the timing belt end of the engine. Don't disturb the Plastigage **(see illustration)**. On V6 models, install the lower crankcase.

8 On four-cylinder models, working on one cap at a time, from the center main bearing outwards (and ensuring that each cap is tightened down squarely and evenly onto the block), tighten the main bearing cap bolts to the torque listed in this Chapter's Specifications. **Note:** *On V6 models, the interior bolts that secure the lower crankcase to the cylinder block are the torque-to-yield type and must be replaced during final assembly. It is acceptable, however, to perform the main bearing oil clearance check using the original bolts.* On V6 models, tighten the lower crankcase bolts as described under Final Installation, Step 17. Don't rotate the crankshaft at any time during this operation!

9 Remove the bolts and carefully lift off the main bearing caps (four-cylinder) or lower crankcase (V6). Don't disturb the Plastigage or rotate the crankshaft. If any of the main bearing caps are difficult to remove, tap them gently from side-to-side with a soft-faced mallet to loosen them.

10 Compare the width of the crushed Plastigage on each journal with the scale printed on the Plastigage envelope to obtain the main bearing oil clearance **(see illustration)**. Check the Specifications to make sure that the clearance is correct.

11 If the clearance isn't as specified, seek the advice of a qualified machine shop - if the crankshaft journals are in good condition (see Section 13), it may be possible simply to replace the main bearings to obtain the correct clearance. If this isn't possible, the crankshaft must be reground at a machine shop who can supply the necessary undersized bearings. First though, make sure that no dirt or oil was under the bearings during oil clearance measurement. If the Plastigage is noticeably wider at one end than the other, the journal may be tapered (see Section 13).

12 Carefully scrape all traces of the Plastigage material off the main bearing journals and the bearing surfaces. Be very careful not to scratch the bearing - use your fingernail or the edge of a credit card.

Final installation

Refer to illustrations 17.13, 17.15 and 17.17

13 Carefully lift the crankshaft out of the engine. Clean the bearing surfaces, then apply a thin, uniform layer of clean moly-based grease, engine assembly lubricant or clean engine oil to each surface **(see illustration)**. Coat the thrust control surfaces as well.

14 Lubricate the crankshaft oil seal journals with engine assembly lubricant or clean engine oil.

15 Make sure the crankshaft journals are clean, then lay the crankshaft back in place in the block **(see illustration)**.

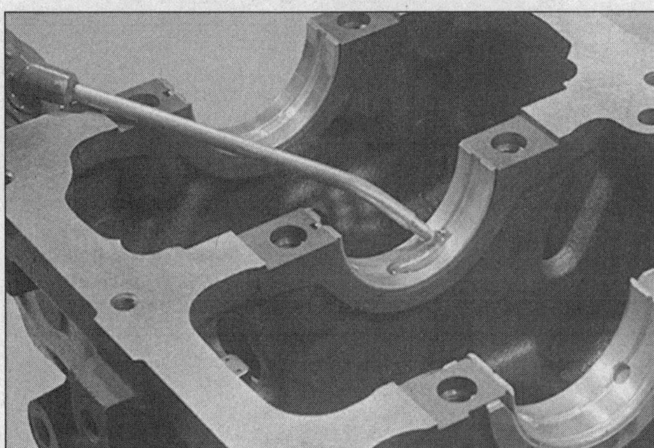

17.13 Ensure the bearing surfaces are absolutely clean and lubricate liberally . . .

17.15 . . . then install the crankshaft

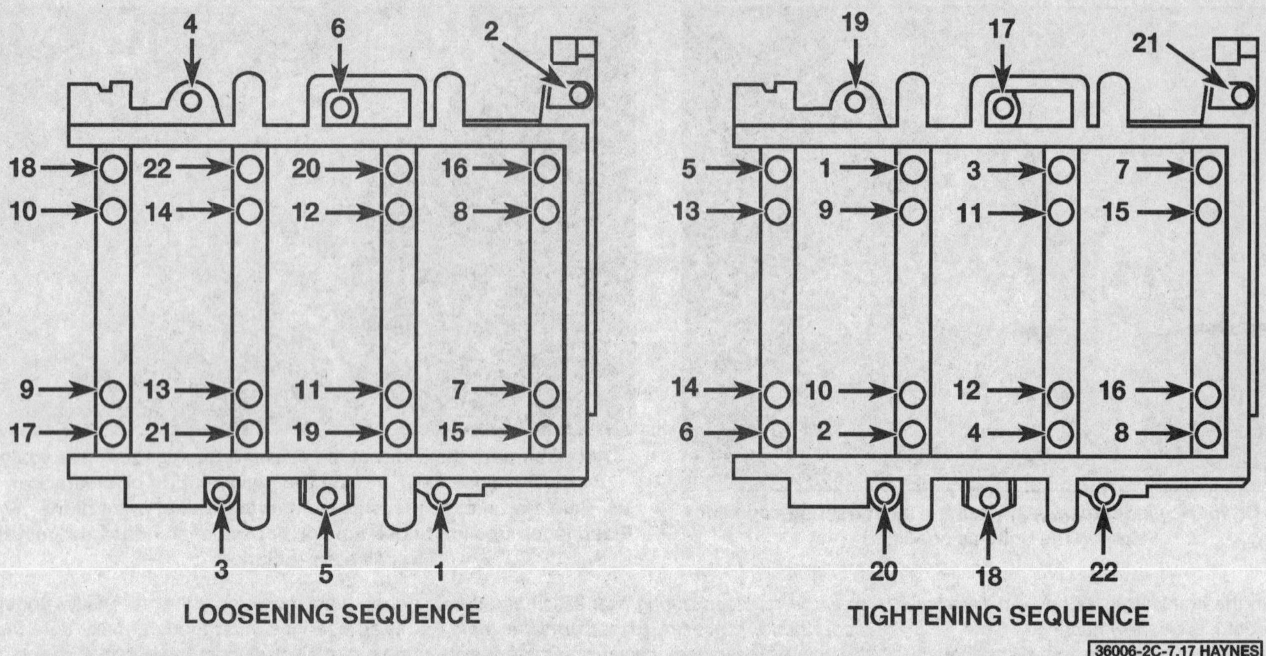

17.17 On V6 models, loosen or tighten the lower crankcase in the sequence shown, following the four-stage procedure in this Chapter's specifications - also note that bolts 1 to 16 in the tightening sequence are torque-to-yield bolts and not reusable

16 On four-cylinder models, install and tighten the main bearing caps as follows:

a) *Clean the bearing surfaces of the bearings in the caps, then lubricate them. Install the caps in their respective positions, with the arrows pointing to the timing belt end of the engine.*

b) *Working on one cap at a time, from the center main bearing outward (and ensuring that each cap is tightened squarely and evenly onto the block), tighten the main bearing cap bolts to the torque listed in this Chapter's Specifications.*

17 On V6 models, clean the bearing surfaces of the bearings in the lower crankcase. Lubricate the bearings. Note that the No. 4 bearing (transaxle end) is also the thrust control bearing.

a) *Apply a 1/8-inch bead of RTV to the cylinder block-to-lower crankcase mating surface. Do not apply the RTV within 1/8-inch of the crankshaft bore on each side.*

b) *Install the lower crankcase on the cylinder block.* **Note:** *Lower crankcase bolts 1 to 16* **(see illustration)** *are torque-to-yield bolts. The original bolts must be discarded and new ones installed during final assembly.*

c) *Install the lower crankcase bolts. Tighten the bolts in four stages in the sequence shown in* **illustration 17.17**, *following the procedure listed in this Chapter's Specifications.*

18 Rotate the crankshaft a number of times by hand, to check for any obvious binding.

19 Check the crankshaft endplay (see Section 10). It should be correct if the crankshaft thrust faces aren't worn or damaged and if the thrust control bearing(s) has been replaced.

20 On four-cylinder models, install the crankshaft rear oil seal carrier and install a new seal (see Part A of this Chapter, Section 20).

21 On V6 models, install a new rear seal (see Part B of this chapter).

18 Piston/connecting rod assemblies - installation and connecting rod bearing oil clearance check

1 Before installing the piston/connecting rod assemblies, the cylinder bores must be perfectly clean, the top edge of each cylinder must be chamfered and the crankshaft must be in place.

2 Remove the connecting cap from No. 1 cylinder connecting rod (refer to the marks noted or made during removal). Remove the original bearings and wipe the bearing recesses of the connecting rod and cap with a clean, lint-free cloth. They must be kept spotlessly clean!

Connecting rod bearing oil clearance check

Refer to illustrations 18.3, 18.9 and 18.11

3 Clean the back of the new upper bearing shell, install it to the connecting rod, then install the other shell of the bearing set to the big-end bearing cap. Make sure the tab on each shell fits into the notch in the rod or cap recess **(see illustration). Caution:** *Don't hammer the bearings into place and don't nick or gouge the bearing surface. Don't lubricate the bearing at this time.*

18.3 The tab on each connecting rod bearing must engage with notch in connecting rod or cap

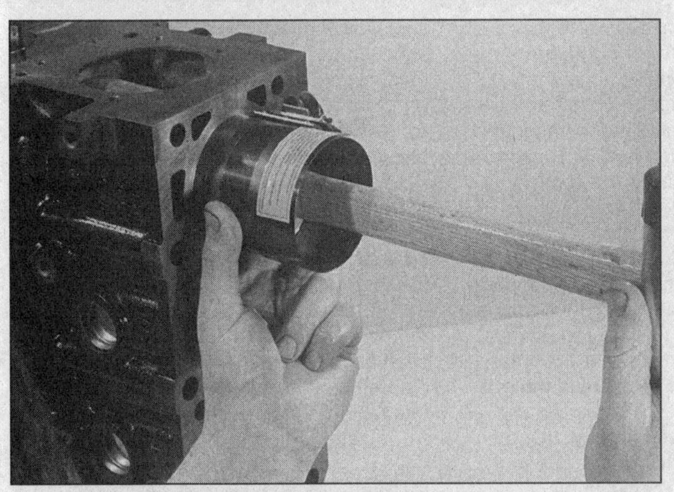

18.9 The piston can be driven gently into the cylinder bore with the end of a wooden or plastic hammer handle

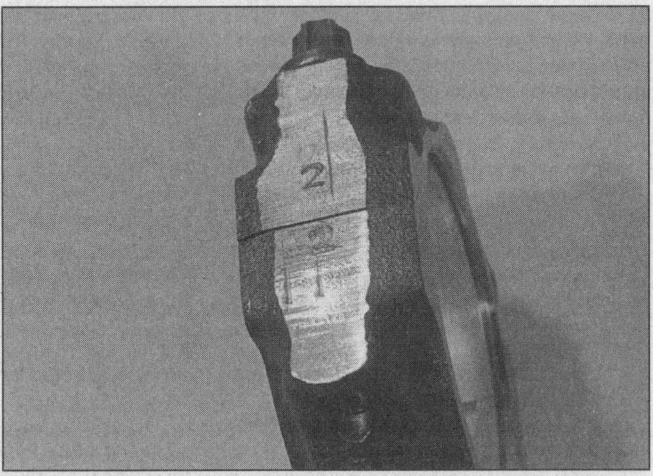

18.11 The connecting rod and its cap must have the same number and be opposite each other, as shown

4 It's critically important that all mating surfaces of the bearing components are perfectly clean and oil-free when they're assembled.

5 Position the piston ring gaps as described in Section 16, lubricate the piston and rings with clean engine oil and attach a piston ring compressor to the piston. Leave the skirt protruding about a quarter-inch, to guide the piston into the cylinder bore. The rings must be compressed until they're flush with the piston.

6 Rotate the crankshaft until No 1 connecting rod journal is at BDC (Bottom Dead Center), and apply a coat of engine oil to the cylinder walls.

7 Arrange the No 1 piston/connecting rod assembly so the arrow on the piston crown points to the timing belt (four-cylinder models) or timing chain (V6 models) end of the engine. Gently insert the assembly into the No 1 cylinder bore, and rest the bottom edge of the ring compressor on the cylinder block.

8 Tap the top edge of the ring compressor to make sure it's contacting the block around its entire circumference.

9 Gently tap on the top of the piston with the end of a wooden hammer handle **(see illustration)**, while guiding the connecting rod onto the connecting rod journal. The piston rings may try to pop out of the ring compressor just before entering the cylinder bore, so keep some pressure on the ring compressor. Work slowly and if any resistance is felt as the piston enters the cylinder, stop immediately. Find out what's binding, and fix it before proceeding. *Don't*, for any reason, force the piston into the cylinder - you might break a ring and/or the piston.

10 To check the connecting rod bearing oil clearance, cut a piece of the appropriate-size Plastigage slightly shorter than the width of the connecting rod bearing, and lay it in place on the No 1 connecting rod journal, parallel with the crankshaft center-line **(see illustration 17.6)**.

11 Clean the connecting rod-to-cap mating surfaces, and install the rod caps cap. Make sure the etched number on the cap is on the same side as that on the rod **(see illustration)**. **Note:** *On V6 models, the connecting rod bolts are torque-to-yield bolts. During final assembly, the original bolts must be discarded and new ones installed. It is acceptable, however, to use the original bolts during the oil clearance check.* Tighten the cap bolts evenly. First use a torque wrench to tighten the bolts to the initial torque listed in this Chapter's Specifications, then use an ordinary socket extension bar and an angle gauge to tighten the bolts further to the specified (second stage) angle. Use a thin-walled socket to avoid erroneous torque readings that can result if the socket is wedged between the cap and nut or bolt. If the socket tends to wedge itself between the nut (or bolt) and the cap, lift up on it slightly until it no longer contacts the cap. Don't rotate the crankshaft at any time during this operation!

12 Unscrew the bolts and detach the cap, being very careful not to disturb the Plastigage.

13 Compare the width of the crushed Plastigage to the scale printed on the Plastigage envelope, to obtain the oil clearance **(see illustration 17.10)**. Compare it to the Specifications, to make sure the clearance is correct.

14 If the clearance isn't as specified, seek the advice of a qualified machinist - if the crankshaft journals are in good condition (see Section 13), it may be possible simply to replace the bearings to obtain the correct clearance. If this isn't possible, the crankshaft must be reground by a machine shop, who can also supply the necessary undersized bearings. First though, make sure that no dirt or oil was trapped under the bearings during oil clearance measurement. Also, recheck the connecting rod journal diameter. If the Plastigage is wider at one end than the other, the connecting rod journal may be tapered (see Section 13).

15 Carefully scrape all traces of the Plastigage material off the journal and the bearing surface. Be very careful not to scratch the bearing - use your fingernail or the edge of a credit card.

Final piston/connecting rod installation

16 Make sure the bearing surfaces are perfectly clean, then apply a uniform layer of clean moly-based grease, engine assembly lubricant or clean engine oil to both of them. You'll have to push the piston into the cylinder to expose the connecting rod bearing surface.

17 Slide the connecting rod back into place on the connecting rod journal, install the bearing cap and then tighten the bolts in three stages, as described above.

18 Repeat the entire procedure for the remaining piston/connecting rod assemblies.

19 The important points to remember are:

a) *Keep the backs of the bearings and the recesses of the connecting rods and caps perfectly clean when assembling them.*
b) *Make sure you have the correct piston/rod assembly for each cylinder - use the etched cylinder numbers to identify the and its cap.*
c) *The arrow on the piston crown must face the timing belt (four-cylinder) or timing chain (V6) end of the engine.*
d) *Lubricate the cylinder bores with clean engine oil.*
e) *Lubricate the bearing surfaces when installing the connecting rod caps after the oil clearance has been checked.*

20 After all the piston/connecting rod assemblies have been properly installed, rotate the crankshaft a number of times by hand, to check for any obvious binding.

21 On 1998 four-cylinder models, install, install a new lower crankcase-to-cylinder block gasket. Install the lower crankcase to the cylinder block, install the bolts and tighten finger-tight.

22 Place a straightedge across the transaxle mating surface of the cylinder block and lower crankcase to check lower crankcase-to-cylinder block alignment. The lower crankcase should be flush with the cylinder block. If not flush, the alignment should be within:

a) A 0.004 inch overlap to a 0.010 inch gap on models equipped with a manual transaxle.

b) No overlap to a 0.010 inch gap on models equipped with an automatic transaxle.

23 Once the alignment is within specification, tighten the lower crankcase bolts to the torque listed in this Chapter's Specifications.

19 Engine - initial start-up after overhaul

1 With the engine installed in the vehicle, double-check the engine oil and coolant levels. Make a final check to determine if everything is reconnected, and that there are no tools or rags left in the engine compartment.

2 With the spark plugs removed and the ignition system disabled by disconnecting the ignition coil's electrical connector, remove fuse 14 to disable the fuel pump. Crank the engine with the starter until the oil pressure warning light goes out.

3 Install the spark plugs, and connect all the spark plug wires (Chapter 1). Reconnect the ignition coil wiring, install the fuel pump fuse, then switch on the ignition and listen for the fuel pump. It will run for a little longer than usual, due to the lack of pressure in the system.

4 Start the engine, noting that this also may take a little longer than usual, due to the fuel system components being empty.

5 While the engine is idling, check for fuel, coolant and oil leaks. Don't be alarmed if there are some odd smells and smoke from parts getting hot and burning off oil deposits. If the hydraulic lifters have been disturbed, some valve gear noise may be heard at first; although this should disappear as the oil circulates throughout the engine, and normal pressure is restored in the lifters.

6 Keep the engine idling until hot water is felt circulating through the radiator upper hose. Check that it idles reasonably smoothly at the usual speed, then switch it off.

7 After a few minutes, recheck the oil and coolant levels, and top-up as necessary (Chapter 1).

8 If they were tightened as described, there is no need to retighten the cylinder head bolts once the engine has first run after reassembly - in fact, the manufacturer states that the bolts *must not* be retightened.

9 If new components such as pistons, rings or crankshaft bearings have been installed, the engine must be broken-in for the first 500 miles (800 km). Don't operate the engine at full-throttle or allow it to labor in any gear during this period. It is recommended that the oil and filter be changed at the end of this period.

Chapter 3
Cooling, heating, and air conditioning systems

Contents

3

Specifications

Coolant

Mixture type .... See Chapter 1
Cooling system capacity .... See Chapter 1

System pressure

Recovery tank filler cap pressure rating .... 13 to 18 psi
Pressure test .... 20 psi - should hold this pressure for at least 10 seconds

Thermostat

Starts to open .... 189 to 194 degrees F
Fully open .... 216 degrees F

Radiator electric cooling fan

Switches on at
- First stage .... 100°C
- Second stage .... 103°C

Switches off at
- First stage .... 93°C
- Second stage .... 100°C

Coolant temperature sensor

Resistance
- At 68 degrees F .... 35.0 to 40.0 K-ohms
- At 212 degrees F .... 1.9 to 2.5 K-ohms
- At 248 degrees F .... 1.0 to 1.3 K-ohms

Air conditioning system

Refrigerant type R134a
Refrigerant capacity .... 24.5 to 27.5 ounces

Torque specifications

	Ft-lbs (unless otherwise indicated)
Lower radiator support bolts	71 to 97 in-lbs
Automatic transaxle cooler lines	15 to 19
Thermostat housing-to-cylinder head bolts (four-cylinder)	78 in-lbs
Water outlet-to-thermostat housing bolts	
Four-cylinder	78 in-lbs
V6	156 in-lbs
Coolant temperature gauge sender	
Four-cylinder	62 to 89 in-lbs
V6	13 to 18
Engine coolant temperature sensor	89 to 124 in-lbs
Water pump bolts	156 in-lbs
Water pump pulley bolts (four-cylinder)	89 to 124 in-lbs
Air conditioning condenser mounting bolts	24 to 48 in-lbs
Air conditioning compressor mounting bolts	
Four-cylinder	
1995 through 1997	15 to 22
1998 and later	65
V6	15 to 22
Fan shroud-to-radiator	24 to 28 in-lbs
Water crossover retainers (V6)	71 to 106 in-lbs
Right-hand engine support bracket (1998 Four-cylinder models)	
Nuts	59
Bolts	37

1 General information

All vehicles covered in this manual are equipped with a pressurized cooling system with thermostatically-controlled coolant circulation. On four-cylinder models, a water pump is mounted on the drivebelt end of the cylinder block and is driven by the camshaft drivebelt from the crankshaft pulley. On V6 models, the water pump is mounted on the transaxle end of the engine and is driven by a pulley attached to the front intake camshaft. Hot coolant from the engine circulates through the radiator and is cooled by the air passing through the radiator core. The coolant then circulates through the thermostat housing, to the water pump. On four-cylinder models, the water pump delivers coolant to the cylinder head and cylinder block. On V6 models, the water pump delivers the coolant to the cylinder block, then the cylinder heads. Coolant exits the engine through the thermostat housing on four-cylinder models or the water crossover on V6 models, and circulates back to the radiator.

A wax pellet type thermostat is located in a housing at the transaxle end of the engine. During warm-up, the closed thermostat prevents coolant from circulating through the radiator. Instead, it returns through the coolant metal pipe running across the front of the engine to the radiator bottom hose and the water pump. The supply to the heater is made from the rear of the thermostat housing. As the engine nears normal operating temperature, the thermostat opens and allows hot coolant to travel through the radiator, where it is cooled before returning to the engine.

The cooling system is sealed by a pressure-type filler cap in the expansion tank. The pressure in the system raises the boiling point of the coolant, and increases the cooling efficiency of the radiator. When the engine is at normal operating temperature, the coolant expands, and the surplus is displaced into the expansion tank. When the system cools, the surplus coolant is automatically drawn back from the tank into the radiator. **Warning 1:** *DO NOT attempt to remove the expansion tank filler cap, or to disturb any part of the cooling system, while it or the engine is hot, as there is a very great risk of scalding. If the expansion tank filler cap must be removed before the engine and radiator have fully cooled down (even though this is not recommended) the pressure in the cooling system must first be released. Cover the cap with a thick layer of cloth, to avoid scalding, and slowly unscrew the filler cap until a hissing sound can be heard. When the hissing has stopped, showing that pressure is released, slowly unscrew the filler cap further until it can be removed; if more hissing sounds are heard, wait until they have stopped before unscrewing the cap completely. At all times, keep well away from the filler opening.* **Warning 2:** *Do not allow antifreeze to come in contact with your skin, or with the painted surfaces of the vehicle. Rinse off spills immediately with plenty of water. Never leave antifreeze lying around in an open container, or in a puddle in the driveway or on the garage floor. Children and pets are attracted by its sweet smell, but antifreeze is fatal if ingested.* **Warning 3:** *If the engine is hot, the electric cooling fan may start rotating even if the engine is not running, so be careful to keep hands, hair and loose clothing well clear when working in the engine compartment.*

Heating system

The heating system consists of a blower fan and heater core (radiator) located in the heater unit, with hoses connecting the heater core to the engine cooling system. Hot engine coolant is circulated through the heater core. When the heater temperature control on the dash is operated, a flap door opens to expose the heater box to the passenger compartment. When the blower control is operated, the blower fan forces air through the unit according to the setting selected.

2 Antifreeze - general information

Warning: *Do not allow antifreeze to come in contact with your skin, or with the painted surfaces of the vehicle. Rinse off spills immediately with plenty of water. Antifreeze is highly toxic if ingested. Never leave antifreeze lying around in an open container, or in puddles on the floor; children and pets are attracted by its sweet smell, and may drink it. Check with local authorities about disposing of used antifreeze - many have collection centers which will see that antifreeze is disposed of safely.*

The cooling system should be filled with a water/ethylene glycol-based antifreeze solution, of a strength which will prevent freezing down to at least -20°F, or lower if the local climate requires it. Antifreeze also provides protection against corrosion, and increases the coolant boiling point.

The cooling system should be maintained according to the schedule described in Chapter 1. If antifreeze is used that does not meet the manufacturers specification, old or contaminated coolant mixtures are likely to cause damage, and encourage the formation of corrosion and scale in the system. Use distilled water with the antifreeze, if available - if not, be sure to use only soft water. Clean rainwater is suitable.

Before adding antifreeze, check all hoses and hose connections, because antifreeze tends to leak through very small openings. Engines don't normally consume coolant, so if the level goes down, find the cause and correct it.

The exact mixture of antifreeze-to-water which you should use depends on the relative weather conditions. The mixture should contain at least 40% antifreeze, but not more than 70%. Consult the mixture ratio chart on the antifreeze container before adding coolant. Hydrometers are available at most automotive accessory shops to test the coolant. Use antifreeze which meets the vehicle manufacturer's specifications.

3

3 Cooling system hoses - disconnection and replacement

Air conditioning system

Note: *Refer to the warnings given in Section 1 of this Chapter before starting work.*

1 If the checks described in Chapter 1 reveal a faulty hose, it must be replaced as follows.

2 First drain the cooling system (see Chapter 1); if the antifreeze is not due for replacement, the drained coolant may be re-

4.5 Unbolt water outlet to withdraw thermostat

4.7 On V6 models the thermostat housing is hidden under the battery and air intake duct (arrow)

used, if it is collected in a clean container.

3 To disconnect any hose, use a pair of pliers to release the spring clamps (or a screwdriver to loosen screw-type clamps), then move them along the hose clear of the fitting. Carefully work the hose off its stubs. The hoses can be removed with relative ease when new - on an older car, they may have stuck.

4 If a hose proves stubborn, try to release it by rotating it on its unions before attempting to work it off. Gently pry the end of the hose with a blunt instrument (such as a flat-bladed screwdriver), but do not apply too much force, and take care not to damage the pipe stubs or hoses. Note in particular that the radiator hose unions are fragile; do not use excessive force when attempting to remove the hoses. If all else fails, cut the hose with a sharp knife, then slit it so that it can be peeled off in two pieces. While expensive, this is preferable to buying a new radiator.

5 When installing a hose, first slide the clamps onto the hose, then work the hose onto its unions. If the hose is stiff, use soap (or washing-up liquid) as a lubricant, or soften it by soaking it in boiling water, but take care to prevent scalding.

6 Work each hose end fully onto its fitting, then check that the hose is settled correctly and is properly routed. Slide each clip along the hose until it is behind the fitting flared end, before tightening it securely.

7 Refill the system with coolant (see Chapter 1).

8 Check carefully for leaks as soon as possible after disturbing any part of the cooling system.

4 Thermostat - removal, testing and installation

Warning: *the engine must be completely cool when performing this procedure. Never under any circumstances remove the coolant recovery tank cap while the engine is running or cooling system/engine damage and/or personal injury could result.*

Note: *Do not run the vehicle without a thermostat installed. The engine management system will stay in open loop causing the emissions and fuel economy to suffer.*

Removal

Four-cylinder models

Refer to illustration 4.5

1 Disconnect the cable from the negative terminal of the battery (see Chapter 5, Section 1).

2 If necessary, unbolt the resonator support bracket from the engine compartment front crossmember. Loosen the two clamp screws securing the resonator to the mass airflow sensor and plenum chamber hoses, then swing the resonator up clear of the thermostat housing (see Chapter 4).

3 Drain the cooling system (see Chapter 1). If the coolant is relatively new or in good condition, drain it into a clean container and reuse it.

4 Disconnect the recovery tank coolant hose and the radiator top hose from the thermostat housing's water outlet.

5 Unbolt the water outlet and withdraw the thermostat **(see illustration)**. Note the position of the air bleed valve and how the thermostat is installed (which end is facing outward).

Removal

V6 models

Refer to illustration 4.7

6 Drain the cooling system (see Chapter 1). If the coolant is relatively new or in good condition, drain it into a clean container for reuse.

7 Remove the battery to gain access to the thermostat housing **(see illustration)**. If necessary, remove the air intake duct from the air cleaner housing and mass airflow sensor to create additional room.

8 Loosen the clamps and disconnect the coolant hoses from the thermostat housing. Remove the housing.

9 Remove the two bolts securing the water outlet to the thermostat housing and remove the thermostat. Note the installation direction of the thermostat for reference during installation.

Testing

General check

10 Before assuming the thermostat is causing a cooling system problem, check the coolant level, drivebelt tension and condition (see Chapter 1) and temperature gauge operation.

11 If the engine seems to be taking a long time to warm up (based on heater output or temperature gauge operation), the thermostat is probably stuck open. If so, replace the thermostat.

12 If the engine runs hot, use your hand to check the temperature of the radiator top hose. If the hose isn't hot, but the engine is, the thermostat is probably stuck closed, preventing the coolant from exiting the engine and circulating to the radiator - replace the thermostat. **Caution:** *Don't drive the vehicle without a thermostat. The lack of a thermostat will slow warm-up time. The engine management system's PCM will then stay in warm-up mode for longer than necessary, causing emissions and fuel economy to suffer.*

13 If the radiator top hose is hot, it means that the coolant is circulating and the thermostat is open. Consult the *Troubleshooting* section at the front of this manual to assist in tracing possible cooling system faults.

Thermostat test

14 If the thermostat remains in the open position at room temperature, it is faulty and must be replaced.

15 To test it fully, suspend the (closed) thermostat on a length of string in a container of cold water, with a thermometer beside it. Ensure that neither touches the side of the container.

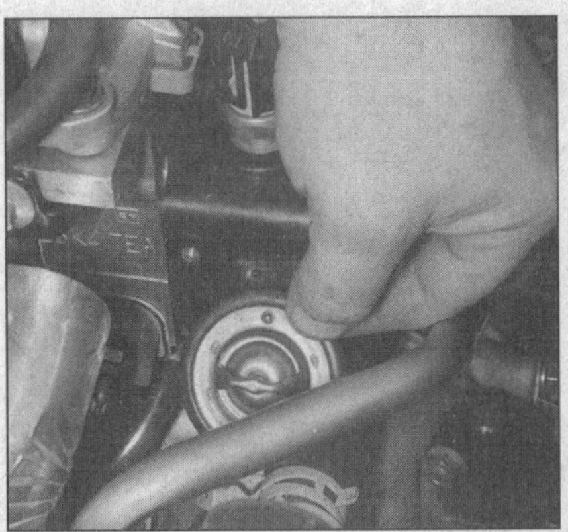
4.18 Ensure thermostat is reinstalled as shown

16 Heat the water, and check the temperature at which the thermostat begins to open. Compare this value with the value listed in this Chapter's Specifications. Continue to heat the water until the thermostat is fully open. The temperature at which this should happen is stamped in the thermostat. Remove the thermostat and allow it to cool and confirm that it closes fully.

17 If the thermostat does not open and close as described, if it sticks in either position, or if it does not open at the specified temperature, it must be replaced.

5.10a Fan shroud is secured at top by mounting nut (A), at bottom by clip (B) . . .

Installation

All models

Refer to illustration 4.18

18 Installation is the reverse of the removal procedure. Clean the mating surfaces carefully, replace the thermostat's gasket if it is worn or damaged, then install the thermostat with its air bleed valve facing toward the water outlet **(see illustration)**. Tighten the water outlet bolts to the torque listed in this Chapter's Specifications.

19 Refill the cooling system (see Chapter 1).

20 Start the engine and allow it to reach normal operating temperature, then check for leaks and proper thermostat operation.

5 Radiator electric cooling fan(s) - testing, removal and installation

Note: *Refer to the warnings given in Section 1 of this Chapter before starting work.*

Testing

1 The radiator cooling fan is controlled by the engine management system's ECU, acting on the information received from the coolant temperature sensor. Where twin fans or two-speed fans are installed, control is through a resistor assembly, secured to the bottom left-hand corner of the fan shroud - this can be replaced separately if faulty.

2 First, check the relevant fuses and relays (see Chapter 12).

3 To test the fan motor, disconnect the electrical connector, and use fused jumper wires to connect the fan directly to the battery. If the fan still does not work, replace the motor.

4 If the motor proved sound, the fault lies in the coolant temperature sensor (see Section 6 for testing details), in the wiring harness (see Chapter 12 for testing details) or in the engine management system (see Chapter 6).

Removal and installation

Refer to illustrations 5.10a, 5.10b and 5.11

5 Disconnect the cable from the negative battery terminal (see Chapter 5, Section 1).

6 Unbolt the resonator support bracket from the engine compartment front crossmember. Loosen the two clamp screws securing the resonator to the mass airflow sensor and plenum chamber hoses, then swing the resonator up clear of the thermostat housing (see Chapter 4).

7 Drain the cooling system (see Chapter 1).

8 Remove the radiator top hose completely. Disconnect the metal coolant pipe/hose from the thermostat, and unbolt the coolant pipe from the exhaust manifold heat shield.

9 Disconnect the cooling fan electrical connector(s), then release all wiring and hoses from the fan shroud.

10 Unscrew the two nuts securing the fan shroud, then lift the assembly to disengage it from its bottom mountings and from the radiator top edge **(see illustrations)**.

11 Withdraw the fan and shroud as an assembly **(see illustration)**.

12 At the time of writing, the fan, motor and shroud are available only as a complete assembly, and must be replaced together if faulty.

13 Installation is the reverse of the removal procedure. Ensure that the shroud is settled correctly at all four mounting points before installing and tightening the nuts.

3

6 Cooling system electrical switches and sensors - testing, removal and installation

Note: *Refer to the warnings given in Section 1 of this Chapter before starting work.*

Coolant temperature gauge sender

Testing

1 If the coolant temperature gauge is inoperative, check the fuses first (see Chapter 12).

2 If the gauge indicates Hot at any time, consult the *"Troubleshooting"* section at the front of this manual, to assist in tracing possible cooling system faults.

5.10b . . . and is hooked over radiator top edge

5.11 Removing radiator electric cooling fan and shroud assembly

6.9a On four-cylinder models the coolant temperature gauge sender is located on the thermostat housing

6.9b On V6 models, the coolant temperature gauge sender is located in the water crossover

3 If the gauge indicates Hot shortly after the engine is started from cold, disconnect the coolant temperature sender's electrical connector. If the gauge reading now drops, replace the sender. If the reading remains high, the wire to the gauge may be shorted to ground, or the gauge is faulty.

4 If the gauge fails to indicate after the engine has been warmed up (approximately 10 minutes) and the fuses are known to be sound, switch off the engine. Disconnect the sender's electrical connector, and use a jumper wire to connect the white/red wire to a clean ground point (bare metal) on the engine. Switch on the ignition without starting the engine. If the gauge now indicates Hot, replace the sender.

5 If the gauge still does not work, the circuit may be open, or the gauge may be faulty. See Chapter 12 for additional information.

Removal

Refer to illustrations 6.9a and 6.9b

6 On four-cylinder models, unbolt the resonator support bracket from the engine compartment front crossmember. Loosen the two clamp screws securing the resonator to the mass airflow sensor and plenum chamber hoses, then swing the resonator up clear of the thermostat housing (see Chapter 4). On V6 models, remove air inlet duct from the air cleaner housing and mass airflow sensor.

7 Drain the cooling system (see Chapter 1).

8 On four-cylinder models, disconnect the recovery tank coolant hose and the radiator top hose from the thermostat housing's water outlet, then disconnect the metal tube/hose from the thermostat.

9 Disconnect the electrical connector from the sender located on the thermostat housing on four-cylinder models or the water crossover on V6 models **(see illustrations)**.

10 Unscrew the sender and remove it.

Installation

11 Clean as thoroughly as possible the opening in the thermostat housing (four-cylinder) or water crossover (V6), then apply a light coat of sealant to the sender's threads. Screw in the sender and tighten it to the torque listed in this Chapter's Specifications. Plug in its electrical connector.

12 Complete the remaining installation by reversing the removal procedure. Fill the cooling system (see Chapter 1) and run the engine to check for leakage.

Coolant temperature sensor

Testing

Refer to illustrations 6.15a and 6.15b

13 Disconnect the cable from the negative battery terminal (see Chapter 5, Section 1).

14 On four-cylinder models, unbolt the resonator support bracket an loosen the screws securing the resonator to the mass airflow sensor and plenum chamber hoses, then swing the resonator up clear of the thermostat housing (see Chapter 4). On V6 models, remove the inlet air duct from the air cleaner housing and mass airflow sensor.

15 Disconnect the electrical connector from the sensor **(see illustrations)**.

16 Using an ohmmeter, measure the resistance between the sensor terminals. Depending on the temperature of the sensor tip, the

6.15a Location of the Engine Coolant Temperature (ECT) sensor (arrow) on four-cylinder models

6.15b On V6 models, the Engine Coolant Temperature (ECT) sensor (arrow) is located in the water crossover

resistance measured will vary, but should be within the limits given in this Chapter's Specifications. If the sensor's temperature is varied by removing it (see below) and cooling it or warming it gently, its resistance should alter accordingly.

17 If the results indicate that the sensor is defective, replace it.

18 On completion, plug in the connector and reinstall the resonator.

Removal

19 Disconnect the cable from the negative battery terminal (see Chapter 5, Section 1).

20 Remove the inlet air duct from the air cleaner housing and mass airflow sensor.

21 With the engine *completely cool*, remove the coolant recovery tank cap to release any pressure, then reinstall the cap. Provided you work swiftly and plug the opening as soon as the sensor is unscrewed, coolant loss will thus be minimized; this will avoid the draining of the complete cooling system which would otherwise be necessary (see Chapter 1).

22 Disconnect the electrical connector from the sensor.

23 Unscrew the sensor and withdraw it. If the cooling system has not been drained, plug the opening as quickly as possible.

Installation

24 Apply a light coat of sealant to the sensor's threads. Remove the plug from the sensor hole (where applicable), and quickly install the sensor to prevent coolant loss. Tighten the sensor to the torque listed in this chapter's specifications, and connect its electrical connector.

25 Reinstall the air inlet duct, fill the cooling system (see Chapter 1) and run the engine to check for leakage.

Coolant low level switch

Testing

26 The switch is a reed-type unit mounted in the bottom of the cooling system expansion tank, activated by a magnetic float. If the coolant level falls to the "MIN" level or less, the appropriate bulb lights in the warning display.

27 If the bulb fails to light during the 5-second bulb test, check the bulb, and replace if necessary as described in Chapter 12.

28 To check the switch itself, disconnect its electrical connector, and use an ohmmeter to measure the resistance across the switch terminals. With the float up, a resistance of 90 ohms should be measured; when it is down, the resistance should increase to approximately 150 K-ohms.

29 If the results obtained from the check are significantly different from those expected, the switch is faulty, and must be replaced.

30 If the switch and bulb are proven to be sound, the fault must be in the wiring or in the auxiliary warning control assembly (see Chapter 12).

Removal

31 Disconnect the battery negative (ground) lead (see Chapter 5, Section 1).

32 Remove the expansion tank (see Section 7).

33 Disconnect the switch electrical connector.

34 Release the switch by twisting its retainer counterclockwise, then withdraw it.

Installation

35 Installation is the reverse of the removal procedure. Refill the cooling system (see Chapter 1). Start the engine, and check for coolant leaks when it is fully warmed-up.

7 Radiator and coolant recovery tank - removal, inspection and installation

Note: *Refer to the warnings given in Section 1 of this Chapter before starting work.*

Radiator

Removal

Refer to illustration 7.5

Warning: *The engine must be completely cool before performing this procedure.*

Note: *If leakage is the reason for removing the radiator, bear in mind that minor leaks can often be cured using a radiator sealant with the radiator in place.*

1 Remove the radiator fan and shroud assembly (see Section 5).

2 Disconnect the bottom hose from the radiator.

3 If the vehicle is equipped with an automatic transaxle, disconnect the fluid cooler lines, and plug the lines and fittings.

4 If the vehicle is equipped with air conditioning, unscrew the condenser mounting nuts or bolts, detach the condenser from the radiator, and tie it to the engine compartment front crossmember. On 1998 models, disconnect the electrical connector from the air conditioning compressor. Also, disconnect the connector from the air conditioning low-pressure switch.

5 Unbolt the radiator mounting brackets from the subframe; note that they are different, and are marked to ensure correct installation **(see illustration)**. Collect the bottom rubber insulators, noting which way up they are installed, and store them carefully.

6 Carefully lower the radiator from the vehicle, and withdraw it.

7 With the radiator removed, it can be inspected for leaks and damage. If it needs repair, have a radiator specialist or dealer service department perform the work, as special techniques are required.

8 Insects and dirt can be removed from the radiator with a garden hose or a soft brush. Don't bend the cooling fins as this is done.

Installation

9 Installation is the reverse of the removal procedure. Be sure the insulators are seated properly at the base of the radiator.

7.5 Radiator mounting bracket-to-subframe bolts (A), air conditioning system condenser mounting bolt (B)

10 After installation, refill the cooling system with the proper mixture of antifreeze and water (see Chapter 1).

11 Start the engine, and check for leaks. Allow the engine to reach normal operating temperature, indicated by the radiator top hose becoming hot. Recheck the coolant level, and add more if required.

12 If working on a vehicle with automatic transaxle, check and add transaxle fluid as needed (see Chapter 1).

Coolant recovery tank

13 With the engine *completely cool*, remove the expansion tank filler cap to release any pressure, then reinstall the cap.

14 Disconnect the hoses from the tank, upper hose first. As each hose is disconnected, drain the tank's contents into a clean container. If the antifreeze is not due for replacement, the drained coolant may be re-used, if it is kept clean.

15 Unscrew the tank's two mounting bolts and withdraw it, unplugging the coolant low level switch electrical connector (if equipped).

16 Wash out the tank, and inspect it for cracks and chafing - replace it if damaged.

17 Installation is the reverse of the removal procedure. Refill the cooling system with the proper mixture of antifreeze and water (see Chapter 1), then start the engine and allow it to reach normal operating temperature, indicated by the radiator top hose becoming hot. Recheck the coolant level and add more if required, then check for leaks.

8 Water pump - check, removal and installation

Warning: *Refer to the warnings given in Section 1 of this Chapter before starting work.*

Check

1 A failure in the water pump can cause serious engine damage due to overheating.

8.8 Power steering system pump should be removed to reach water pump hose fitting

8.9 Unscrew bolts . . .

8.10 . . . to remove water pump - always replace gasket and clean all mating surfaces carefully

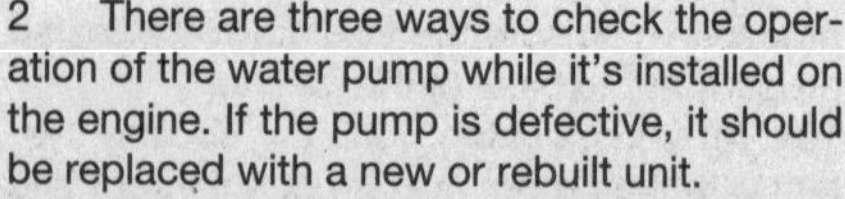

2 There are three ways to check the operation of the water pump while it's installed on the engine. If the pump is defective, it should be replaced with a new or rebuilt unit.

3 With the engine running at normal operating temperature, squeeze the radiator top hose. If the water pump is working properly, a pressure surge should be felt as the hose is released. **Warning:** *Keep your hands away from the radiator electric cooling fan blades!*

4 On four-cylinder models, remove the timing belt covers (see Chapter 2, Part A). On V6 models, remove the water pump pulley shield (see Chapter 2, Part B) The water pump is equipped with vent hole. If a failure occurs in the pump seal, coolant will leak from the hole. In most cases you'll need a flashlight to find the hole on the water pump from underneath to check for leaks.

5 If the water pump shaft bearings fail, there may be a howling sound from the area of the water pump while it's running. Shaft wear can be felt if the water pump pulley is rocked up and down. Don't mistake drivebelt slippage, which causes a squealing sound, for water pump bearing failure.

Removal and installation

Warning: *The engine must be completely cool before performing this procedure.*

1995 through 1997 four-cylinder models

Refer to illustrations 8.8, 8.9 and 8.10

6 Remove the timing belt and tensioner (see Chapter 2, Part A). As noted in Chapter 2, if the belt is fouled with coolant, it must be replaced as a matter of course.

7 Drain the cooling system (see Chapter 1).

8 Disconnect the radiator bottom hose from the pump. It is easier to reach the hose if the power steering pump is unbolted and moved aside as described in Chapter 10 **(see illustration).** Do not disconnect any of the power steering system hoses.

9 Unbolt and remove the water pump **(see illustration).** If the pump is being replaced, unbolt the timing belt guide pulleys, and transfer them to the new pump.

10 Clean the mating surfaces carefully; the gasket must be replaced whenever it is disturbed **(see illustration).**

11 On installation, use grease to stick the new gasket in place, reinstall the pump, and tighten the pump bolts to the torque listed in this Chapter's Specifications.

12 The remainder of the reassembly procedure is the reverse of removal. Note that a new tensioner spring and retaining pin must be installed if the timing belt has been removed for the first time. Tighten all fasteners to the torque listed in this Chapter's Specifications. Refill the system with coolant as described in Chapter 1.

1998 four-cylinder models

13 Disconnect the cable from the negative battery terminal (see Chapter 5, Section 1).

14 Drain the cooling system (see Chapter 1).

15 Raise the front of the vehicle and support it securely with a jackstands. Remove the front right-hand wheel, then remove the four bolts that secure the right-hand inner fender splash shield. Remove the shield.

16 Remove the coolant recovery tank as described in this chapter.

17 **Warning:** *The engine must be supported securely for the remainder of this procedure to prevent personal injury.* Support the engine with a suitable support fixture or a floor jack placed under the oil pan. Be sure to place a wooden block on the jack to protect the oil pan from damage. When the engine is supported securely, remove the nuts and bolts securing the right-hand engine support bracket.

18 Loosen the water pump pulley bolts and remove the accessory drivebelt. Remove the water pump pulley.

19 Remove the water pump mounting bolts and separate the pump from the engine. Rotate the pump 180 degrees to provide clearance for removal. Remove the pump.

20 Clean the mating surface(s) carefully and thoroughly. Install the pump using a new gasket. Tighten the pump mounting bolts to the torque listed in this Chapter's Specifications.

21 The remaining assembly is the reverse of the disassembly procedure. Fill the cooling system, start the engine and check for leakage.

V6 models

22 Disconnect the cable from the negative battery terminal (see Chapter 5, Section 1).

23 Remove the water pump pulley shield.

24 Rotate the water pump drivebelt tensioner clockwise to relieve tension on the belt. Remove the belt.

25 Drain the cooling system (see Chapter 1).

26 Remove the clamps and disconnect the coolant hoses from the water pump. Remove the three bolts that secure the water pump housing to the cylinder head. Remove the water pump assembly from the engine. If necessary, separate the water pump from the pump housing.

27 Carefully clean all gasket material from the mating surface(s).

28 Install the water pump on the pump housing using a new gasket. Install the mounting bolts and tighten them to the torque listed in this Chapter's Specifications.

29 The remaining reassembly is the reverse of the disassembly procedure. Fill the cooling system and start the engine and check for leakage.

9 Heater/ventilation components - removal and installation

Warning: *All models are equipped with airbags. Always disable the airbag system before working in the vicinity of the steering column or instrument panel to avoid the possibility of accidental deployment of the airbag, which could cause personal injury (see Chapter 12).*

Heater blower motor

Removal

Refer to illustration 9.5

1 Disconnect the cable from the negative battery terminal (see Chapter 5, Section 1).

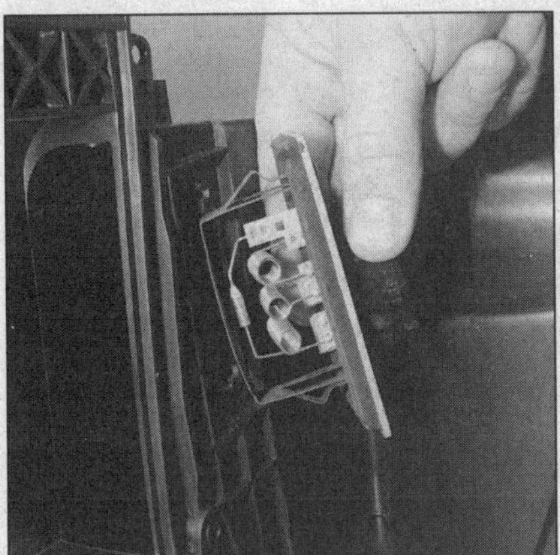
9.5 Heater blower motor control resistor can be pried out of heater unit

9.6 Ensure blower motor retaining lug engages securely in heater unit on reassembly

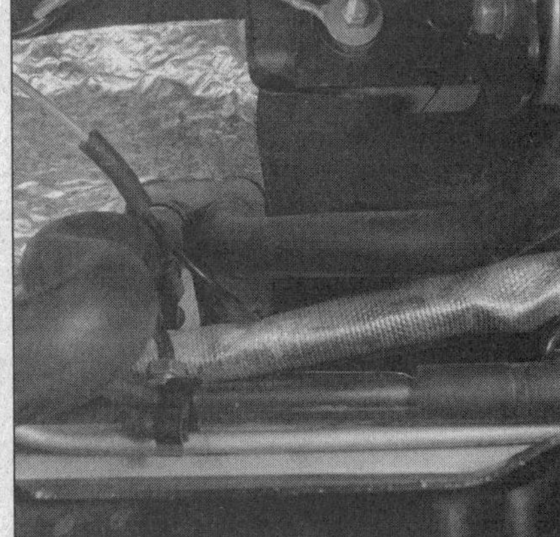
9.9a Coolant pipes to heater core must be disconnected . . .

Disable the airbag system (see Chapter 12).
2 Release the four clips (by pulling them out) securing the passenger side footwell upper trim panel, then withdraw the panel.
3 Disconnect the motor's electrical connector.
4 Lift the motor's retaining lug slightly, twist the motor counterclockwise (seen from beneath) through approximately 30 degrees, then withdraw the assembly.
5 The motor's control resistor can be removed by sliding a slim screwdriver into the slot provided in one end. Press the screwdriver in approximately 1/4-inch against spring pressure, and pry the resistor out **(see illustration)**.

9.9b . . . but can be reached best from beneath vehicle

Installation

Refer to illustration 9.6

6 Installation is the reverse of the removal procedure. Reinstall the motor, and twist it clockwise until the retaining lug engages securely **(see illustration)**.

Heater core

Removal

Refer to illustrations 9.9a, 9.9b, 9.11, 9.12, 9.13 and 9.14

7 Disconnect the cable from the negative battery terminal (see Chapter 5, Section 1). Disable the airbag system (see Chapter 12).
8 Drain the cooling system (see Chapter 1).
9 Disconnect the coolant hoses from the heater core tubes protruding through the engine compartment firewall **(see illustrations)**.
10 Working inside the passenger compartment, remove the trim panels from each footwell, just in front of the center console. Each panel is secured by two screws. If additional clearance is required, the center console can be removed as well (see Chapter 11), but this is not essential. If so equipped, remove the screws securing the airbag diagnostic monitor and place it aside.
11 Remove the single screw to release the air duct in the base of the heater unit **(see illustration)**.
12 Remove the three screws securing the air outlet to the heater unit bottom cover, then release the clips. There is a single plastic clip on each side, and additional metal clips may be found. Push the duct up to retract it, and withdraw the air outlet **(see illustration)**.
13 Release the clips (there are two plastic clips on each side, and additional metal clips may be found) then withdraw the heater unit's bottom cover, complete with the core **(see illustration)**.

3

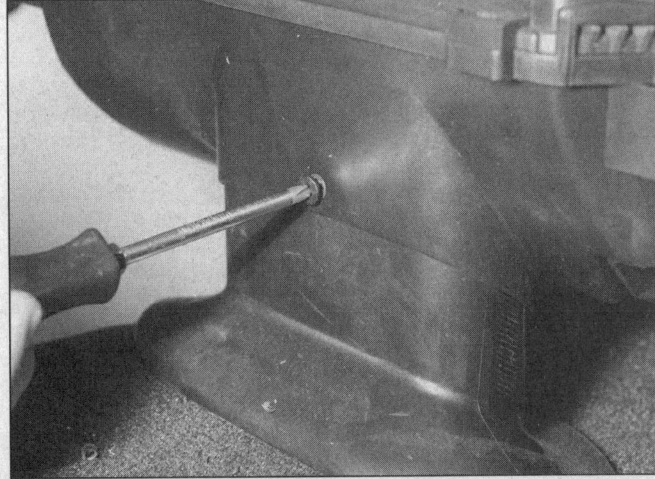
9.11 Remove screw to allow air duct to be retracted into air distributor at base of heater unit . . .

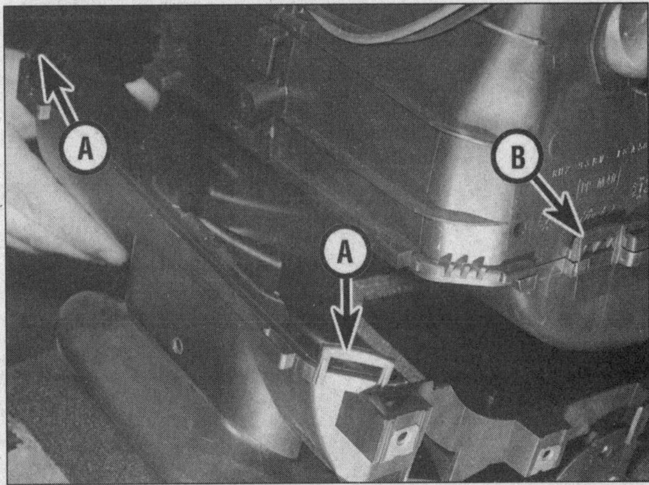

9.12 . . . release clips (A) to free air distributor from base of heater unit - note clips (B) securing . . .

9.13 . . . heater unit's bottom cover, complete with core

9.14 Remove clamp (one screw) to separate core from heater unit's bottom cover

14 Remove the screw and withdraw the clamp to separate the heater core from the bottom cover **(see illustration)**.

Installation

15 Installation is the reverse of the removal procedure. Additional metal clips may be required to secure the heater unit's bottom cover and the air outlet. Ensure that the duct is lowered from the air outlet and secured with its screw.

16 Refill the cooling system with the proper mixture of antifreeze and water (see Chapter 1). Start the engine and allow it to reach normal operating temperature, indicated by the radiator top hose becoming hot. Recheck the coolant level and add more if required, then check for leaks. Check the operation of the heater.

10 Heater/air conditioning controls - removal and installation

Warning: *All models are equipped with airbags. Always disable the airbag system before working in the vicinity of the steering column or instrument panel to avoid the possibility of accidental deployment of the airbag, which could cause personal injury (see Chapter 12).*

Blower/air conditioning control

Removal

Refer to illustration 10.4

1 Disconnect the battery negative (ground) lead (see Chapter 5, Section 1).

2 Remove the ashtray. Referring to the relevant Sections of Chapter 11, undo the two upper screws from the center console and pull out the cassette storage compartment, then remove the radio/cassette player.

3 Pull the heater control/radio bezel out of the three clips securing its top edge, pull it forwards and disconnect the switch electrical connector (if equipped).

4 Pull off the heater control knobs, and remove the screw securing each end of the heater control unit **(see illustration)**. Pull the control unit out of the dash.

5 Disconnect the two electrical connectors from the blower/air conditioning control. Remove the retaining screw and withdraw the control, twisting it to release it from the panel.

Installation

6 Installation is the reverse of the removal procedure. Check the operation of the control on completion.

Temperature control

Removal

Refer to illustration 10.8

7 Remove the heater control unit as described in paragraphs 1 to 4 above.

8 On vehicles without air conditioning, unhook the operating cable from the temperature control **(see illustration)**; where air conditioning is installed, disconnect the control's electrical connector. Undo the retaining screw, and withdraw the control.

Installation

9 Installation is the reverse of the removal procedure; check the operation of the control on completion.

Air distribution control

Removal

Refer to illustration 10.10

10 Remove the heater control unit as described in paragraphs 1 to 4 above. Disconnect the electrical connectors, and unhook the operating cable (if equipped) to withdraw the unit **(see illustration)**.

11 Use a pair of slim screwdrivers to release the clips on each side of the control, then withdraw the control from the unit.

10.4 Remove screws securing each end of heater control unit

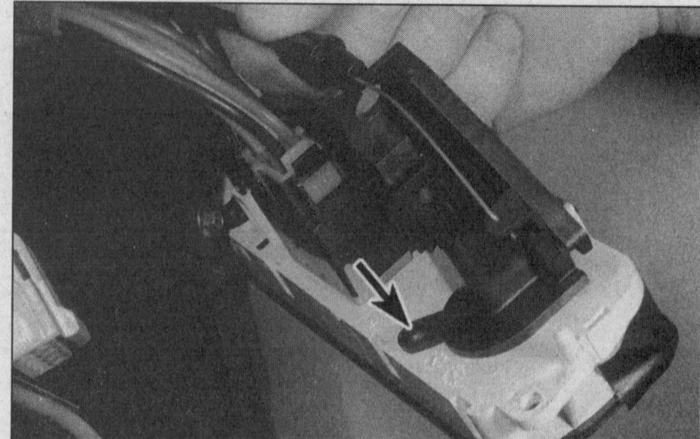

10.8 Unhooking operating cable from temperature control - note retaining screw (arrow)

Installation

12 Installation is the reverse of the removal procedure. Check the operation of the controls on completion.

11 Air conditioning system - general information and precautions

General information

The air conditioning system consists of a condenser mounted in front of the radiator, an evaporator mounted adjacent to the heater core, a compressor mounted on the engine, an accumulator/dehydrator, and the plumbing connecting all of the above components - this contains a choke (or "venturi") mounted in the inlet to the evaporator, which creates the drop in pressure required to produce the cooling effect.

A blower fan forces the warmer air of the passenger compartment through the evaporator core (rather like a radiator in reverse), transferring the heat from the air to the refrigerant. The liquid refrigerant boils off into low-pressure vapor, taking the heat with it when it leaves the evaporator.

Precautions

Warning: *The air conditioning system is under high pressure. Do not loosen any fittings or remove any components until after the system has been discharged. Air conditioning refrigerant should be properly discharged into an approved type of container, at a dealer service department or an automotive air conditioning repair facility capable of handling R134a refrigerant. Always wear eye protection when disconnecting air conditioning system fittings.*

When an air conditioning system is installed, it is necessary to observe the following special precautions whenever dealing with any part of the system, its associated components, and any items which necessitate disconnection of the system:

a) *While the refrigerant used - R134a - is less damaging to the environment than the previously-used R12, it is still a very dangerous substance. It must not be allowed into contact with the skin or eyes, or there is a risk of frostbite. It must also not be discharged in an enclosed space - while it is not toxic, there is a risk of suffocation. The refrigerant is heavier than air, and so must never be discharged over a pit.*

b) *The refrigerant must not be allowed to come in contact with a naked flame, otherwise a poisonous gas will be created - under certain circumstances, this can form an explosive mixture with air. For similar reasons, smoking in the presence of refrigerant is highly dangerous, particularly if the vapor is inhaled through a lighted cigarette.*

c) *Never discharge the system to the atmosphere - R134a is not an ozone-depleting chlorofluorocarbon (CFC) as is R12, but is instead a hydrofluorocarbon, which causes environmental damage by contributing to the "greenhouse effect" if released into the atmosphere.*

d) *R134a refrigerant must **not** be mixed with R12; the system uses different seals (now green-colored, previously black) and has different fittings requiring different tools, so that there is no chance of the two types of refrigerant becoming mixed accidentally.*

e) *If for any reason the system must be disconnected, entrust this task to your dealer or a refrigeration engineer.*

f) *It is essential that the system be professionally discharged prior to using any form of heat - welding, soldering, brazing, etc. - in the vicinity of the system, before having the vehicle oven-dried at a temperature exceeding 70°C after repainting, and before disconnecting any part of the system.*

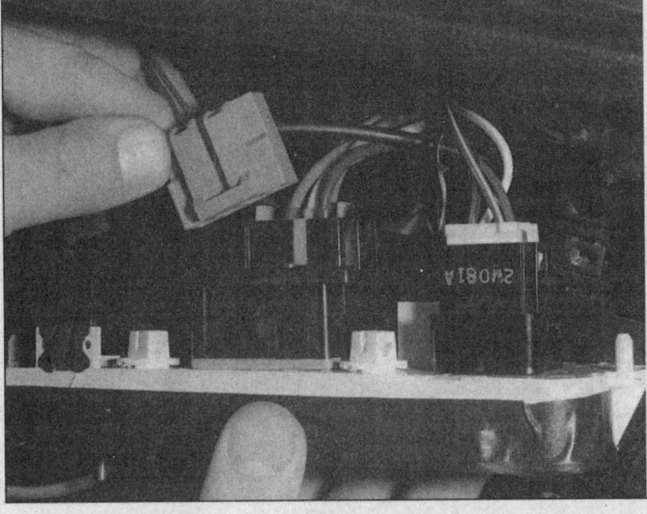

10.10 Unplugging electrical connectors from rear of heater control unit

12 Air conditioning system components - removal and installation

Warning: *The air conditioning system is under high pressure. Do not loosen any fittings or remove any components until after the system has been discharged. Air conditioning refrigerant should be properly discharged into an approved type of container, at a dealer service department or an automotive air conditioning repair facility capable of handling R134a refrigerant. Cap or plug the pipe lines as soon as they are disconnected, to prevent the entry of moisture. Always wear eye protection when disconnecting air conditioning system fittings.*

Note: *This Section refers to the components of the air conditioning system itself - refer to Sections 9 and 10 for details of components common to the heating/ventilation system.*

Condenser

1 Have the refrigerant discharged at a dealer service department or an automotive air conditioning repair facility.

2 Disconnect the battery negative (ground) lead (see Chapter 5, Section 1).

3 Remove the radiator undershield (see Chapter 1).

4 Using a spring-lock coupling tool (available at most auto parts stores), disconnect the refrigerant lines from the condenser. Immediately cap the openings, to prevent the entry of dirt and moisture.

5 Unbolt the condenser **(see illustration 7.5)** and lift it out of the vehicle. Store it upright, to prevent oil loss.

6 Installation is the reverse of removal.

7 If a new condenser was installed, add 20 cc of refrigerant oil to the system.

8 Have the system evacuated, charged and leak-tested by the specialist who discharged it.

Evaporator

9 The evaporator is mounted with the heater core. Apart from the need to have the refrigerant discharged, and to use a spring-lock coupling tool (available at most auto parts stores) to disconnect the lines, the procedure is as described in Section 9 of this Chapter.

10 On reassembly, if a new evaporator was installed, add 20 cc of refrigerant oil to the system.

11 Have the system evacuated, charged and leak-tested by the specialist who discharged it.

Compressor

12 Have the refrigerant discharged at a dealer service department or an automotive air conditioning repair facility.

13 Disconnect the battery negative (ground) lead (see Chapter 5, Section 1).

14 Remove the radiator undershield (see Chapter 1).

15 Remove the drivebelt (see Chapter 1).

16 Unbolt the compressor from the cylinder block/crankcase, press it to one side, and unscrew the clamping bolt to disconnect the refrigerant lines. Plug the line connections,

12.23 Disconnect pressure-cycling switch electrical connector

12.33 Disconnect pressure-regulating switch electrical connector

swing the compressor upright, disconnect its electrical connector, then withdraw the compressor from the vehicle. **Note:** *Keep the compressor level during handling and storage. If the compressor has seized, or if you find metal particles in the refrigerant lines, the system must be flushed out by an air conditioning technician, and the accumulator/dehydrator must be replaced.*

17 Prior to installation, turn the compressor clutch center six times, to disperse any oil that has collected in the head.

18 Reinstall the compressor in the reverse order of removal; replace all seals disturbed.

19 If you are installing a new compressor, refer to the compressor manufacturer's instructions for adding refrigerant oil to the system.

20 Have the system evacuated, charged and leak-tested by the specialist that discharged it.

Accumulator/dehydrator

Refer to illustration 12.23

21 Have the refrigerant discharged at a dealer service department or an automotive air conditioning repair facility.

22 Disconnect the battery negative (ground) lead (see Chapter 5, Section 1).

23 The accumulator/dehydrator, which acts as a reservoir and filter for the refrigerant, is located in the left-hand front corner of the engine compartment. Using a spring-lock coupling tool (available at most auto parts stores), disconnect the refrigerant line next to the accumulator/dehydrator from the compressor. Immediately cap the openings, to prevent the entry of dirt and moisture, then disconnect the pressure-cycling switch electrical connector **(see illustration)**.

24 Remove the radiator undershield (see Chapter 1).

25 Unbolt the accumulator/dehydrator from the front suspension subframe.

26 Using a spring-lock coupling tool (available at most auto parts stores), disconnect the lower refrigerant line from the accumulator/dehydrator. It may be necessary to unscrew the pressure-cycling switch to allow the use of the tool. Immediately cap the openings, to prevent the entry of dirt and moisture.

27 Withdraw the accumulator/dehydrator.

28 Reinstall the accumulator/dehydrator in the reverse order of removal; replace all seals disturbed.

29 If you are installing a new accumulator/dehydrator, refer to the manufacturer's instructions for adding refrigerant oil to the system.

30 Have the system evacuated, charged and leak-tested by the specialist that discharged it.

Pressure-cycling and pressure-regulating switches

Refer to illustration 12.33

31 Have the refrigerant discharged at a dealer service department or an automotive air conditioning repair facility.

32 Disconnect the battery negative (ground) lead (see Chapter 5, Section 1).

33 Disconnect the switch electrical connector, and unscrew it **(see illustration)**.

34 Installation is the reverse of the removal procedure; there is no need to top-up the refrigerant oil.

35 Have the system evacuated, charged and leak-tested by the specialist that discharged it.

Chapter 4
Fuel and exhaust systems

Contents

Specifications

Fuel pressure (at idle)	
Pressure regulator vacuum hose connected	27.5 to 33.5 psi
Pressure regulator vacuum hose disconnected	36 to 42 psi
Fuel system hold pressure	26 psi
Fuel injector resistance	13.7 to 15.2 ohms
Idle speed control valve resistance	6 to 14 ohms
Idle-increase solenoid valve resistance	50 to 120 ohms

Torque specifications

	Ft-lbs (unless otherwise indicated)
Plenum chamber-to-intake manifold fasteners	35 in-lbs
Throttle body-to-intake manifold bolts	88 in-lbs
Idle air control valve bolts	88
Fuel injector retainer bolts (V6 models)	71 to 106 in-lbs
Fuel pressure regulator bolts	
Four-cylinder engine	35 in-lbs
V6 engine	
1995 through 1997	66
1998	53 in-lbs
1999 and later	60 in-lbs
Fuel rail-to-intake manifold bolts	88 in-lbs
Fuel feed and return line threaded couplings at fuel rail	17 to 22
All exhaust system nuts and bolts	30 to 33

1 General information and precautions

This Chapter is concerned with those features of the engine management system that supply clean fuel and air to the engine. Since the emission control sub-systems modify the functions of both the fuel and exhaust sub-systems, all of which are integral parts of the whole engine management system, there are many cross-references to Chapters 5 and 6. Information on the electronic control system, its troubleshooting, sensors and actuators, is given in Chapter 6.

The air intake system consists of several plastic components designed to eliminate induction roar as much as possible. The air intake tube (opening behind the direction indicator/headlight assembly) is connected, via small and large resonators located under the front left-hand fender, to the air cleaner assembly in the engine compartment. Once it has passed through the filter element and the mass airflow sensor, the air enters the plenum chamber mounted above the throttle body and intake manifold; the resonator mounted in the engine compartment further reduces noise levels.

The fuel system consists of a plastic tank (mounted under the body, beneath the rear seats), combined metal and plastic fuel hoses, an electric fuel pump mounted in the fuel tank, and an electronic fuel injection system.

On four-cylinder models, the exhaust system consists of an exhaust manifold, the front exhaust pipe and catalytic converter and a rear section incorporating two or three mufflers and the tailpipe. On V6 models, the exhaust system consists of two exhaust manifolds, the Y-pipe, catalytic converter and the tailpipe. The service replacement exhaust system consists of three or four sections: the front exhaust pipe or Y-pipe, catalytic converter, the intermediate pipe and front muffler and the tailpipe and rear muffler. On some versions, the tailpipe is in two pieces, with two rear mufflers. The system is suspended throughout

4

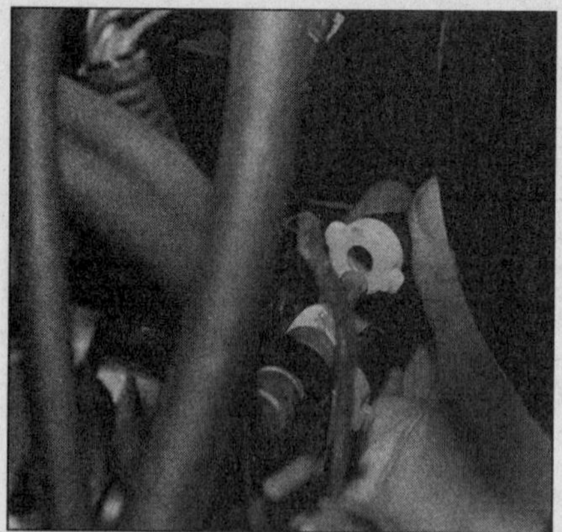

3.3 Disconnect fuel line quick-release couplings by squeezing together the protruding locking lugs and pulling the coupling apart

3.7a If the spring lock couplings are equipped with safety clips, pry them off with a small screwdriver

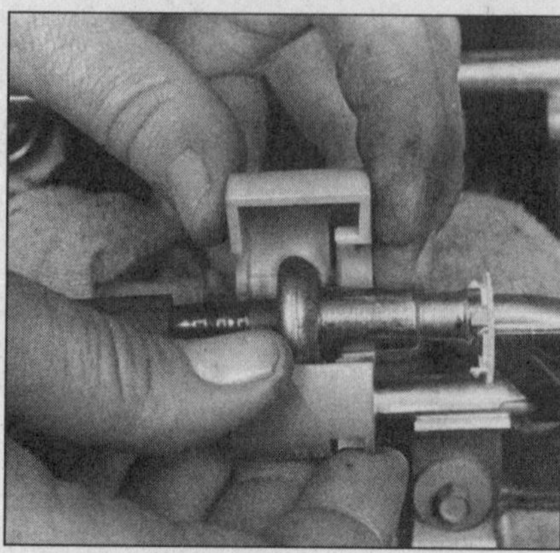

3.7b Open the spring-loaded halves of the spring lock coupling tool and place it in position around the coupling, then close it

its entire length by rubber hangers.

Extreme caution should be exercised when dealing with either the fuel or exhaust systems. Fuel is a primary element for combustion. Be very careful! The exhaust system is an area for exercising caution, as it operates at very high temperatures. Serious burns can result from even momentary contact with any part of the exhaust system, and the fire risk is ever-present. The catalytic converter in particular runs at very high temperatures - refer to the information in Chapter 6. **Warning:** *Many of the procedures in this Chapter require the removal of fuel lines and connections, which may result in some fuel spillage. Gasoline is extremely flammable, so take extra precautions when you work on any part of the fuel system. Don't smoke, or allow open flames or bare light bulbs, near the work area. Don't work in a garage where a natural gas-type appliance (such as a water heater or clothes dryer) with a pilot light is present. If you spill any fuel on your skin, rinse it off immediately with soap and water. When you perform any kind of work on the fuel system, wear safety glasses, and have a Class B type fire extinguisher on hand. Before carrying out any operation on the fuel system, refer also to the precautions given in "Safety first!" at the beginning of this manual, and follow them implicitly. Gasoline is a highly dangerous and volatile liquid, and the precautions necessary when handling it cannot be overstressed.*

2 Fuel pressure relief

Warning: *Gasoline is extremely flammable, so take extra precautions when you work on any part of the fuel system. Don't smoke or allow open flames or bare light bulbs near the work area, and don't work in a garage where a natural gas-type appliance (such as a water heater or a clothes dryer) with a pilot light is present. Since gasoline is carcinogenic, wear latex gloves when there's a possibility of being exposed to fuel, and, if you spill any fuel on your skin, rinse it off immediately with soap and water. Mop up any spills immediately and do not store fuel-soaked rags where they could ignite. The fuel system is under constant pressure, so, if any fuel lines are to be disconnected, the fuel pressure in the system must be relieved first. When you perform any kind of work on the fuel system, wear safety glasses and have a Class B type fire extinguisher on hand.*

Caution: *After the fuel pressure has been relieved, it's a good idea to lay a shop towel over any fuel connection to be disassembled, to absorb the residual fuel that may leak out when servicing the fuel system.*

1 The fuel system referred to in this Chapter is defined as the fuel tank and tank-mounted fuel pump/fuel gauge sender unit, the fuel filter, the fuel injectors and the pressure regulator in the injector rail, and the metal pipes and flexible hoses of the fuel lines between these components. All these contain fuel, which will be under pressure while the engine is running and/or while the ignition is switched on.

2 The pressure will remain for some time after the ignition has been switched off, and must be relieved before any of these components is disturbed for servicing work.

3 The simplest method is simply to disconnect the fuel pump's electrical supply while the engine is running - either by removing the fuel pump fuse (number 14), or by lifting the red button on the fuel cut-off switch (see Section 13) - and to allow the engine to idle until it dies through lack of fuel pressure. Turn the engine over once or twice on the starter to ensure that all pressure is released, then switch off the ignition; do not forget to install the fuse (or depress the red button, as appropriate) when work is complete.

4 The manufacturer's method of depressurization is to attach a fuel pressure gauge equipped with a bleed hose to the fuel rail pressure test/release fitting - a Schrader-type valve with a plastic cap, located on the fitting of the fuel feed line and the fuel rail - to release the pressure, using a suitable container and wads of rag to catch the spilled fuel. Do not simply depress the valve core to release fuel pressure - fuel will spray out, with a consequent risk of fire, and of personal

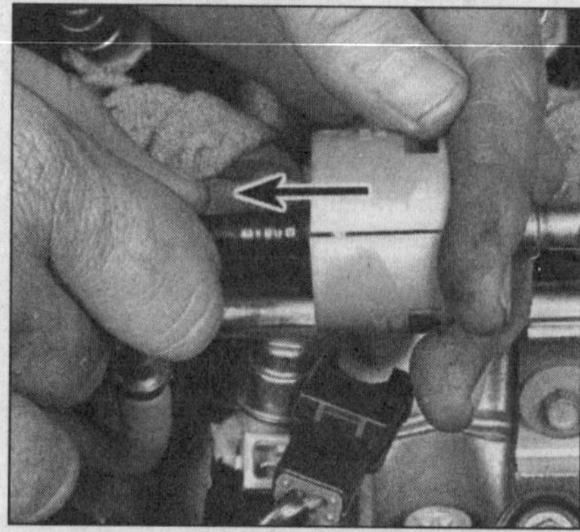

3.7c To disconnect the coupling, push the tool into the cage opening to expand the garter spring and release the female fitting, then pull the male and female fittings apart

injury through fuel getting into your eyes. **Warning:** *Either procedure will merely relieve the increased pressure necessary for the engine to run. Remember that fuel will still be present in the system components, and take precautions accordingly before disconnecting any of them.*

5 Note that, once the fuel system has been depressurized and drained (even partially), it will take significantly longer to restart the engine - perhaps several seconds of cranking - before the system is refilled and pressure restored.

3 Fuel lines and fittings - general information

Warning: *Gasoline is extremely flammable, so take extra precautions when you work on any part of the fuel system. See the* **Warning** *in Section 2.*

Disconnecting and connecting quick-release couplings

Refer to illustration 3.3

1 Quick-release couplings are used on many of the fuel feed and return lines.

4.2 On V6 models, disconnect the Intake Air Temperature (IAT) sensor

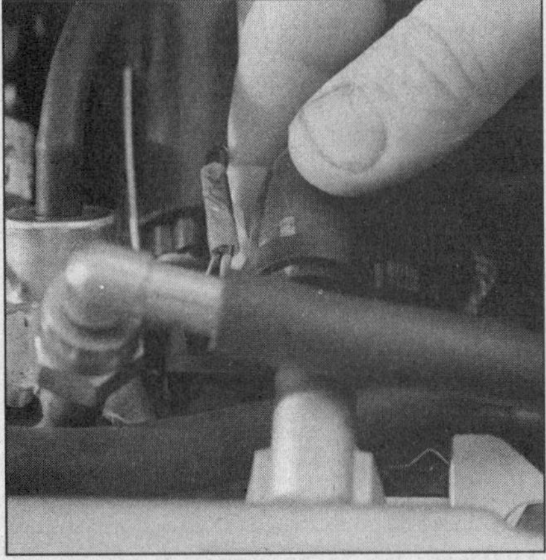
4.3 Disconnecting the crankcase breather hose from the valve cover

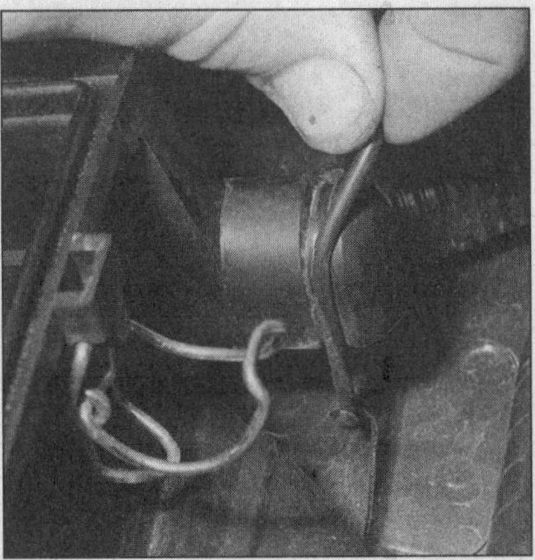
4.4 Remove the rubber retaining band to withdraw the air cleaner assembly

2 Before disconnecting any fuel system component, relieve the residual pressure in the system (see Section 2), and equalize tank pressure by removing the fuel filler cap. **Warning:** *This procedure will merely relieve the increased pressure necessary for the engine to run - remember that fuel will still be present in the system components, and take precautions accordingly before disconnecting any of them.*

3 Release the protruding locking lugs on each fitting, by squeezing them together and carefully pulling the coupling apart **(see illustration).** Use a rag to soak up any spilled fuel. Where the unions are color-coded, the lines cannot be confused. Where both unions are the same color, note carefully which line is connected to which, and ensure that they are correctly reconnected on installation.

4 To reconnect one of these couplings, press them together until the locking lugs snap into their groove. Switch the ignition on and off five times to pressurize the system, and check for any sign of fuel leakage around the disturbed coupling before attempting to start the engine.

Spring lock couplings - disconnecting and connecting

Refer to illustrations 3.7a, 3.7b and 3.7c

5 The fuel supply and return lines used on SEFI engines utilize spring lock couplings at the engine fuel rail end instead of plastic push-connect fittings. The male end of the spring lock coupling, which is girded by two O-rings, is inserted into a female flared end engine fitting. The coupling is secured by a garter spring which prevents disengagement by gripping the flared end of the female fitting. A cup-tether assembly provides additional security.

6 To disconnect the 1/2-inch spring lock coupling supply fitting, you will need to obtain a spring lock coupling tool, available at most auto parts sales stores. Be aware that 1/2- inch and 3/8-inch fittings require different tools.

7 Study the accompanying illustrations carefully before detaching either spring lock coupling fitting **(see illustrations).**

Checking

8 Checking procedures for the fuel lines are included in Chapter 1.

Component replacement

9 If you must replace any damaged sections, use original-equipment replacement hoses or lines, constructed from exactly the same material as the section you are replacing. Do not install substitutes constructed from inferior or inappropriate material, or you could cause a fuel leak or a fire.

10 Before detaching or disconnecting any part of the fuel system, note the routing of all hoses and lines, and the orientation of all clamps and clips. Replacement sections must be installed in exactly the same manner.

11 Before disconnecting any part of the fuel system, be sure to relieve the fuel system pressure (see Section 2), and equalize tank pressure by removing the fuel filler cap. Also disconnect the battery negative (ground) lead - see Chapter 5, Section 1. Cover the part being disconnected with a rag, to absorb any fuel that may spray out.

4 Air cleaner assembly and air intake components - removal and installation

Refer to illustrations 4.2, 4.3, 4.4 and 4.5

Air cleaner assembly

1 Disconnect the cable from the negative battery terminal - see Chapter 5, Section 1.

2 Disconnect the mass airflow sensor from the air cleaner cover (see Chapter 6). On V6 models, disconnect the intake air temperature (IAT) sensor **(see illustration).**

3 Disconnect the crankcase breather hose, either from the air cleaner housing or from the valve cover **(see illustration).**

4 Remove the rubber retaining band **(see illustration).** Withdraw the air cleaner assembly, lifting it upwards out of its grommets, and releasing it from the rubber connector sleeve in the inner fender panel.

4.5 Ensure the air filter housing intake mouth is fully engaged inside the connector sleeve

4

5 Installation is the reverse of the removal procedure. Ensure that the housing pegs seat correctly in their grommets, and that the intake mouth is fully engaged inside the connector sleeve **(see illustration).**

Air intake components

Note: *Depending on the reason for removal, these components can be removed either individually, or as one assembly. For example, disconnecting the two electrical connectors and disconnecting the vacuum hose (if equipped), will allow the air cleaner assembly cover to be removed with the mass airflow sensor, the resonator and the plenum chamber.*

Mass airflow sensor

6 Refer to Section 4 of Chapter 6.

Intake air resonator (1995 through 1997 four-cylinder models)

Refer to illustration 4.7

7 Unbolt the resonator support bracket from the engine compartment front crossmember. Loosen the two clamp screws securing the resonator to the mass airflow sensor and plenum chamber hoses. Swing the resonator clear of the thermostat housing

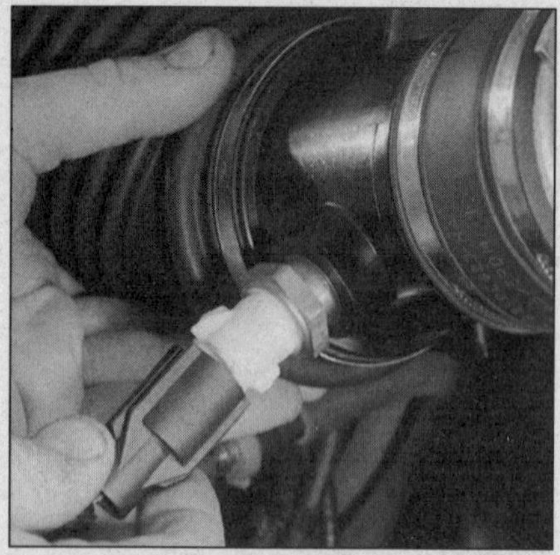

4.7 Unplugging the intake air temperature sensor's electrical connector (four-cylinder models)

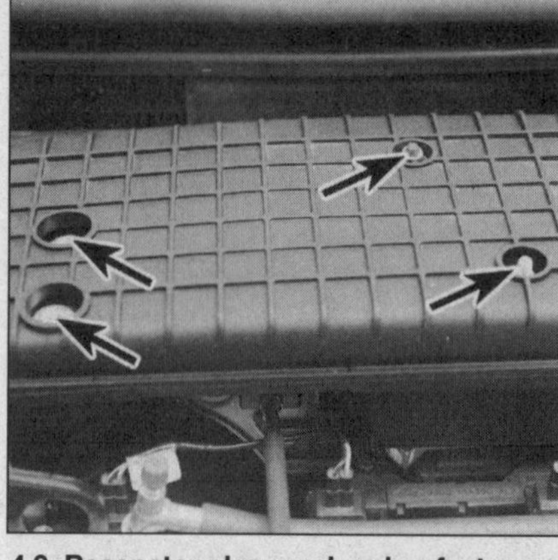

4.9 Resonator plenum chamber fasteners - four shown here, some models may only have three

4.10a Lift the plenum chamber and (if equipped) disconnect the vacuum hose - note the two rubber spacers . . .

4.10b . . . and the sealing O-ring in the chamber's mouth

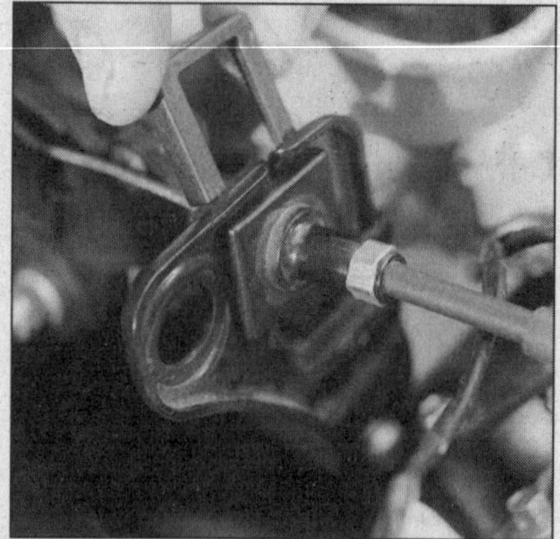

5.3 Removing the clip securing the accelerator cable to throttle body bracket

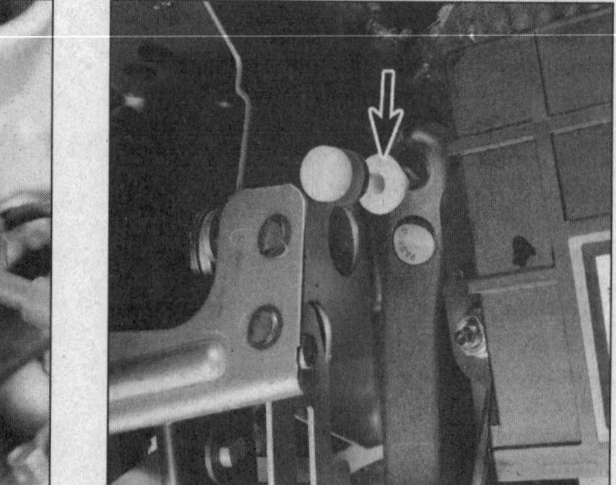

5.4 Pull the accelerator cable end fitting out of the pedal

and disconnect the intake air temperature sensor's electrical connector **(see illustration)**. Withdraw the resonator.

8 Installation is the reverse of the removal procedure.

Resonator plenum chamber (four-cylinder models)

Refer to illustrations 4.9, 4.10a and 4.10b

9 Prying out the rubber plugs covering them, remove the chamber's fasteners **(see illustration)**. Loosen the clamp screw securing the chamber to the air inlet duct.

10 Lift the chamber and (if equipped) disconnect the vacuum hose from its underside. Withdraw the chamber - note the two rubber spacers (one on each throttle body stud) and the sealing O-ring in the chamber's mouth **(see illustrations)**.

11 Installation is the reverse of the removal procedure. Ensure that the O-ring and spacers are correctly seated.

Under fender components

12 Remove the left-hand wheel inner fender liner.

13 Unbolt and withdraw the air intake tube and both resonators as required.

14 Installation is the reverse of the removal procedure.

5 Accelerator cable (models without traction control)- removal, installation and adjustment

Removal

Refer to illustrations 5.3 and 5.4

1 Disconnect the cable from the negative terminal of the battery - see Chapter 5, Section 1.

2 On four-cylinder models, remove the plenum chamber (see Section 4).

3 Remove the clip securing the cable to the throttle body bracket **(see illustration)**. Disconnect the cable end from the throttle linkage, and release the cable from any securing clips or ties.

4 Working in the passenger compartment, reach up to the top of the accelerator pedal. Pull the end attachment and collar out of the pedal, then release the cable inner wire through the slot in the pedal **(see illustration)**. Tie a length of string to the end of the cable.

5 Returning to the engine compartment, pull the cable through the firewall until the string can be untied and the cable removed.

Installation

6 Installation is the reverse of the removal procedure; use the string to draw the cable through the firewall.

7 Adjust the cable as described below.

5.9 Location of the accelerator cable adjuster - remove the metal clip to enable adjustment to be made

Adjustment

Refer to illustration 5.9

8 Remove the plenum chamber (see Section 4).

9 Find the cable adjuster - this is either at the throttle body bracket, or two-thirds along the length of the cable, clipped to the right front strut tower **(see illustration)**. Remove

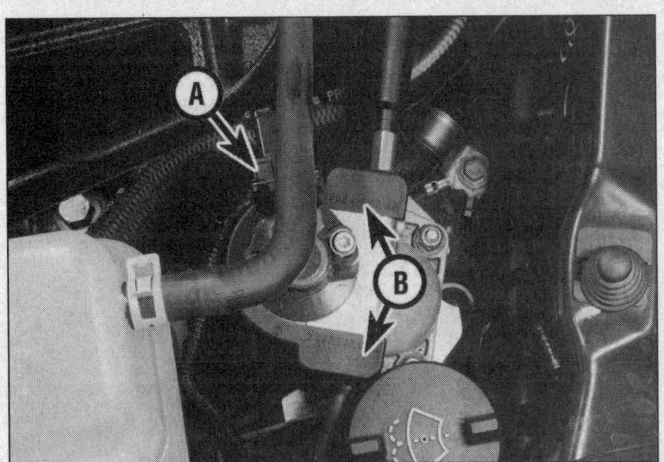

6.4 Disconnect the TCS throttle actuator's electrical connector (A) and pry off its cover at two points (B)

6.11 Location of the TCS throttle actuator-to-throttle body cable adjuster

the metal clip and lubricate the adjuster's grommet with soapy water.

10 Remove any slack by pulling the cable outer housing as far as possible out of the adjuster. Have an assistant depress the accelerator pedal fully - the cable housing will move back into the adjuster - and hold it there while the clip is reinstalled.

11 Verify that the throttle valve moves smoothly and easily from the fully closed to the fully open position and back again, as the assistant depresses and releases the accelerator pedal. Re-adjust the cable if required.

12 When the setting is correct, install the resonator plenum chamber (see Section 4).

6 Accelerator cable (models with traction control) - removal, installation and adjustment

Removal

Refer to illustration 6.4

Note: *While the following procedure deals with the complete cable, the pedal-to-actuator and actuator-to-throttle body sections of the cable are available separately and can be removed and reinstalled individually. If doing this, modify the procedure as required.*

1 Disconnect the cable from the negative terminal of the battery - see Chapter 5, Section 1.

2 Remove the resonator plenum chamber (see Section 4).

3 Remove the clip securing the cable to the throttle body bracket, then pull the cable's grommet out of the bracket. Disconnect the cable end from the throttle linkage, and release the cable from any securing clips or ties.

4 Disconnect the TCS throttle actuator's electrical connector, and pry off its cover **(see illustration)**.

5 Noting which cable section is connected to which pulley, disconnect the first cable end from the throttle actuator's upper pulley, then slide the cable casing upwards out of the actuator housing. Disconnect the second cable in the same way from the actuator's lower pulley.

6 Working in the passenger compartment, reach up to the top of the accelerator pedal. Pull the end fitting and collar out of the pedal, then release the cable inner wire through the slot in the pedal. Tie a length of string to the end of the cable.

7 Returning to the engine compartment, pull the cable through the firewall until the string can be untied and the pedal-to-actuator cable removed.

Installation

8 Installation is the reverse of the removal procedure. Use the string to draw the pedal-to-actuator cable through the firewall. Ensure that each cable end is connected to the correct actuator pulley.

9 Adjust both cables as described below.

Adjustment

Refer to illustration 6.11

Note: *Both sections of the cable must be adjusted together, even if only one has been disturbed.*

10 Remove the plenum chamber (see Section 4).

11 Remove the metal clip from the adjuster of each cable section **(see illustration)**, and lubricate the adjusters' grommets with soapy water.

12 Remove any slack by pulling both cables out as far as possible out of their respective adjusters.

13 Disconnect the TCS throttle actuator's electrical connector, and pry off its cover. Lock both pulleys together by pushing a locking pin (a pin punch or a similar tool of suitable size) into their alignment holes. Disconnect the actuator-to-throttle body cable end from the throttle linkage.

14 Have an assistant depress the accelerator pedal fully. The pedal-to-actuator cable casing will move back into the adjuster; hold it there, and install the clip.

15 Connect the actuator-to-throttle body cable end to the throttle linkage, and check that the cable grommet is correctly secured in the housing bracket.

16 Again have the assistant depress the accelerator pedal fully. The actuator-to-throttle body cable casing will move back into the adjuster; hold it there, and install the clip.

17 Remove the locking pin from the pulleys. Check that the throttle valve moves smoothly and easily from the fully closed to the fully open position and back again, as the assistant depresses and releases the accelerator pedal. Re-adjust the cable(s) if required.

18 When the setting is correct, install the TCS throttle actuator's cover and electrical connector, then install the resonator plenum chamber (see Section 4).

4

7 Accelerator pedal - removal and installation

Refer to illustration 7.2

1 Disconnect the cable from the pedal - see Section 5 or 6, as appropriate.

2 Remove the retaining nuts and bolt, then withdraw the pedal assembly **(see illustration)**.

3 Installation is the reverse of the removal procedure. Adjust the cable(s) as described in Section 5 or 6.

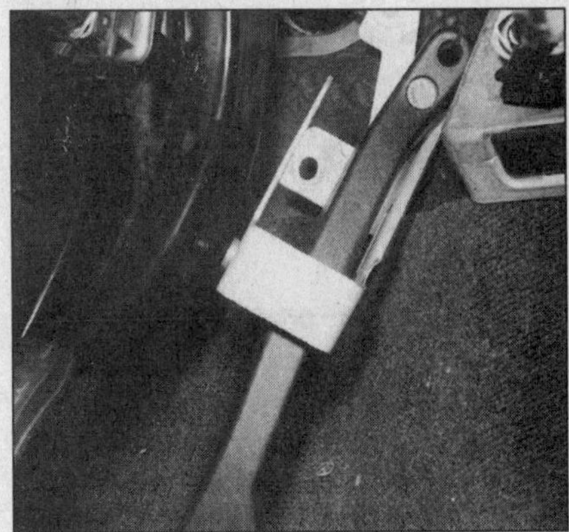

7.2 Removing the accelerator pedal assembly

8.4 A fuel pressure gauge, equipped with an adapter to fit the Schrader-type valve on the fuel rail pressure test/release fitting, is needed to check fuel pressure

9.4 Unplugging the fuel pump/fuel gauge sender unit electrical connector

8 Fuel pump/fuel pressure - check

Warning: *Gasoline is extremely flammable, so take extra precautions when you work on any part of the fuel system. See the* **Warning** *in Section 2.*

Fuel pump operation check

1 Switch on the ignition and listen for the fuel pump (the sound of an electric motor running, audible from beneath the rear seats). Assuming there is sufficient fuel in the tank, the pump should start and run for approximately one or two seconds, then stop, each time the ignition is switched on. **Note:** *If the pump runs continuously all the time the ignition is switched on, the electronic control system is running in the backup (or "limp-home") mode referred to by the manufacturer as "Limited Operation Strategy" (LOS). This almost certainly indicates a fault in the PCM itself, and the vehicle should therefore be taken to a dealer or other qualified repair shop for a full test of the complete system, using the correct diagnostic equipment; do not waste time trying to test the system without such facilities.*

2 Listen for fuel return noises from the fuel pressure regulator. It should be possible to feel the fuel pulsing in the regulator and in the feed hose from the fuel filter.

3 If the pump does not run at all, check the fuse, relay and wiring (see Chapter 6).

Fuel pressure check

Refer to illustration 8.4

3 A fuel pressure gauge, equipped with an adapter to fit the Schrader-type valve on the fuel rail pressure test/release fitting (identifiable by its blue plastic cap, and located on the fitting of the fuel feed line and the fuel rail) is required for the following procedure.

4 If using a pressure gauge with a bleed-off valve, ensure that its tap is turned fully counterclockwise, then attach it to the valve **(see illustration)**.

5 Start the engine and allow it to idle. Note the gauge reading as soon as the pressure stabilizes, and compare it with the pressure listed in this Chapter's Specifications.

(a) *If the pressure is high, check for a restricted fuel return line. If the line is clear, replace the pressure regulator.*

(b) *If the pressure is low, pinch the fuel return line. If the pressure now goes up, replace the fuel pressure regulator. If the pressure does not increase, check the fuel feed line, the fuel pump and the fuel filter.*

6 Detach the vacuum hose from the fuel pressure regulator; the pressure shown on the gauge should increase. Note the increase in pressure, and compare it with that listed in this Chapter's Specifications. If the pressure increase is not as specified, check the vacuum hose and pressure regulator.

7 Reconnect the regulator vacuum hose, and switch off the engine. Verify that the fuel pressure stays at the specified level for five minutes after the engine is turned off.

8 Carefully disconnect the fuel pressure gauge. Be sure to cover the fitting with a rag before loosening it. Mop up any spilled gasoline.

9 Run the engine, and check that there are no fuel leaks.

9 Fuel pump/fuel gauge sender unit - removal and installation

Refer to illustrations 9.4, 9.5, 9.6, 9.7a and 9.7b

Warning: *Gasoline is extremely flammable, so take extra precautions when you work on any part of the fuel system. See the* **Warning** *in Section 2.*

1 Relieve the residual pressure in the fuel system (see Section 2), and equalize tank pressure by removing the fuel filler cap.

2 Disconnect the battery negative (ground) lead - see Chapter 5, Section 1.

3 Unbolt or fold forwards (as appropriate) the rear seat base cushion (see Chapter 11). Withdraw from the vehicle's floor the grommet covering the fuel pump/sender unit. Wash off any dirt from the tank's top surface, and dry it; use a vacuum cleaner to clean the immediate surroundings of the vehicle's interior, to reduce the risk of introducing water, dirt and dust into the tank while it is open.

4 Disconnect the fuel pump/sender unit's electrical connector **(see illustration)**.

5 To disconnect the fuel feed and return pipes from the unit, release each pipe's coupling by squeezing together the protruding locking lugs on each fitting and carefully pulling the coupling apart. Use a rag to soak up any spilled fuel. Where the couplings are difficult to separate, use a pair of pliers and a block of wood as shown, to lever the pipe out of the fitting. Considerable force may be required, but be as careful as possible to avoid damaging any of the components **(see illustration)**.

6 Release the fuel pump/sender unit's retaining ring by turning it counterclockwise **(see illustration)**.

7 Withdraw the fuel pump/fuel gauge sender unit, taking care not to bend the float arm. The float arm is mounted on a spring-loaded extension, to hold it closely against the bottom of the tank. Note the sealing ring; this must be replaced whenever it is disturbed **(see illustrations)**.

8 On installation, use a new sealing ring, and ensure that the gauze filter over the base of the pump pick-up is clean.

9 Align the pump/sender unit with the tank opening, and install it, ensuring that the float arm is not bent. Insert the unit so that the float arm slides correctly up the extension, until the unit's top mounting plate can be aligned with the tank opening and pressed onto the sealing ring. This may require a considerable amount of pressure; if so, be care-

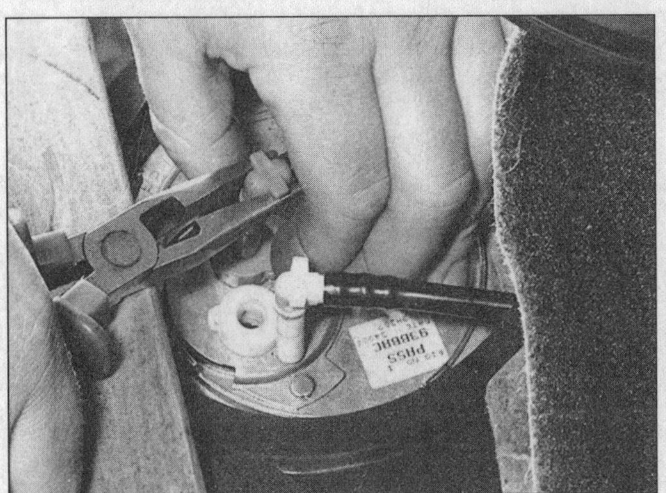

9.5 If fuel couplings are difficult to release, use pliers and a block of wood as shown to pry the pipe end out of the fitting - be careful not to damage the pipes or unions

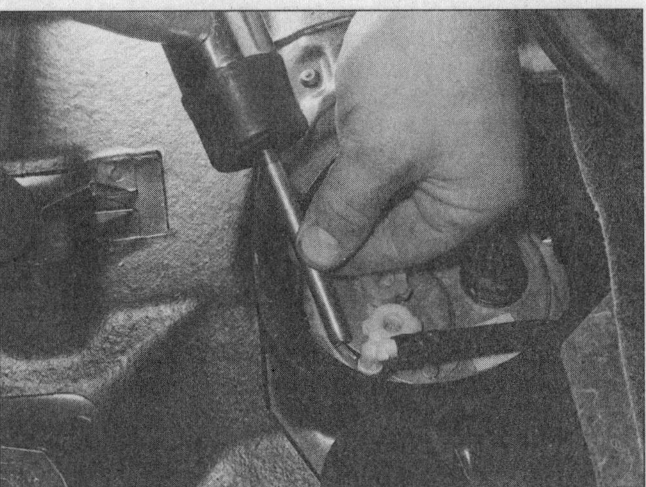

9.6 Fuel pump/fuel gauge sender unit's retaining ring can be released using ordinary tools as shown. Correct service tool will probably be required on installation

9.7a Removing the fuel pump/fuel gauge sender unit - take care not to bend the float arm, and note how it is fitted on the spring-loaded extension

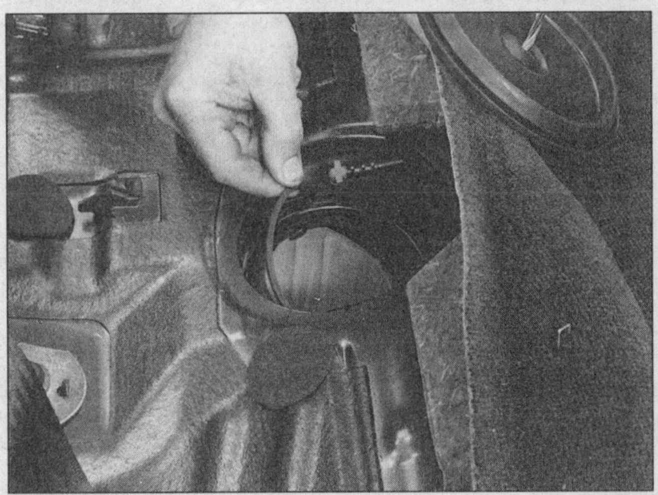

9.7b Fuel pump/fuel gauge sender unit's sealing ring must be replaced whenever it is disturbed

ful to avoid damaging any of the components.

10 Maintain the pressure while an assistant installs and engages the retaining ring. When the ring is engaged in the tank lugs, turn it clockwise to tighten it until it is secured.

11 The remainder of the installation procedure is the reverse of removal. Observe the color-coding to ensure that the fuel pipes are reconnected to the correct unions.

10 Fuel tank - removal and installation

Refer to illustrations 10.6, 10.7, 10.8 and 10.11

Warning 1: *Gasoline is extremely flammable, so take extra precautions when you work on any part of the fuel system. See the* **Warning** *in Section 2.*

Warning 2: *Before disconnecting or opening any part of the fuel system, relieve the residual pressure* (see Section 2), *and equalize tank pressure by removing the fuel filler cap. Also disconnect the battery negative (ground) lead - see Chapter 5, Section 1.*

1 A fuel tank drain plug is not provided; it is therefore preferable to carry out the removal operation when the tank is nearly empty. Before proceeding, disconnect the battery negative (ground) lead, and siphon or hand-pump the remaining fuel from the tank. **Warning:** *Don't start the siphoning action by mouth - use a siphoning kit (available at most auto parts stores). Alternatively, disconnect the feed pipe from the fuel filter* (see Chapter 1), *and connect a spare length of hose to this so that when the ignition is switched on, the fuel pump will empty the tank into a clean container. If this approach is adopted, ensure that the container is large enough to take all the fuel in the tank, and be careful to take all suitable precautions to prevent the risk of fire.*

2 Unbolt (as appropriate) the rear seat base cushion (see Chapter 11). Withdraw from the vehicle's floor the grommet covering the fuel pump/sender unit. Disconnect the fuel pump/sender unit's electrical connector, and disconnect the fuel return pipe (coded red) from the unit (see Section 9).

3 Raise the rear of the vehicle, and support it securely on jackstands. Get underneath and familiarize yourself with the layout of the fuel tank assembly before proceeding. **Warning:** *Do not place any part of your body under a vehicle when it's supported only by a jack!*

4 Either remove the fuel filter, or disconnect its outlet pipe (see Chapter 1).

5 Unhook the exhaust system rubber mountings. Lower the system onto a suitable support, so that the front downpipe-to-exhaust manifold fitting is not strained, or remove it completely (see Section 17).

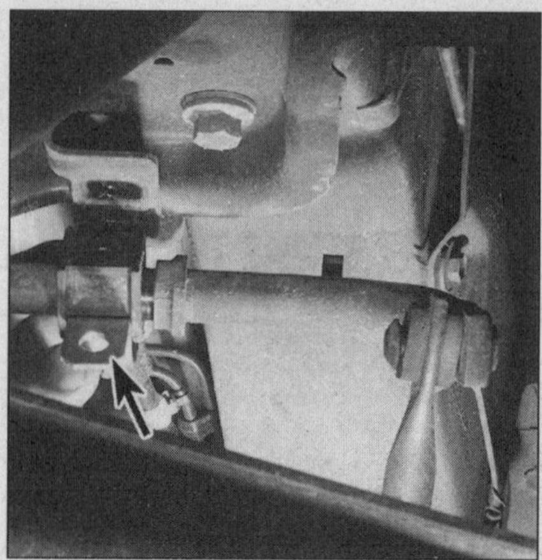

10.6 Unbolt rear stabilizer bar mounting clamps (one arrow) when preparing to remove the fuel tank

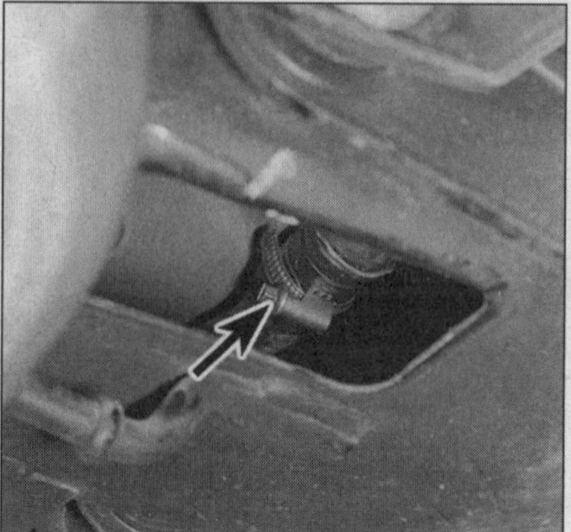

10.7 Fuel filler vent hose clamp is accessible through the right-hand side aperture in the rear suspension crossmember

10.8 Exhaust system must be lowered and the heat shield removed to enable fuel tank removal - arrows show location of retaining strap front bolts

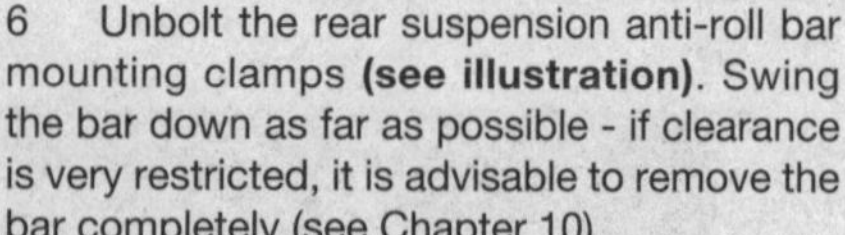

6 Unbolt the rear suspension anti-roll bar mounting clamps **(see illustration)**. Swing the bar down as far as possible - if clearance is very restricted, it is advisable to remove the bar completely (see Chapter 10).

7 Disconnect the flexible vent hose from the molded plastic fuel tank filler neck as follows: Reach up into the right-hand side aperture in the rear suspension crossmember, loosen the clamp, and work the hose off the filler neck stub. This is a job for someone with small hands, good tools and a lot of patience! **(see illustration)**.

8 Unscrew the six retaining nuts and withdraw the exhaust system's rear heat shield from the underbody **(see illustration)**.

9 Support the tank with a floor jack. Place a sturdy plank between the support and the tank, to protect the tank.

10 Unscrew the bolt at the front of each retaining strap, and pivot them down until they are hanging out of the way. Note the ground lead under the left-hand strap's bolt - clean the mating surfaces before the tank is reinstalled, so that clean, metal-to-metal contact is ensured.

11 Lower the tank enough to unclip the fuel return pipe (coded red) from its top surface, then disconnect the charcoal canister's vapor hose from the fitting at the top rear of the tank **(see illustration)**. If you have any doubts, clearly label the fuel lines and hoses, and their respective unions. Plug the hoses, to prevent leakage and contamination of the fuel system.

12 Remove the tank from the vehicle, releasing it from the filler neck stub. While the tank is removed, unhook the retaining straps (twist them 90-degrees to do so), and check that they and their locations in the underbody are in good condition.

13 With the fuel tank removed, the filler neck can be withdrawn. It is secured by a single screw in the filler opening, and by two bolts to the underbody.

14 Installation is the reverse of the removal procedure.

11 Fuel tank cleaning and repair - general information

Warning: *Gasoline is extremely flammable, so take extra precautions when you work on any part of the fuel system. See the* **Warning** *in Section 2.*

1 Any repairs to the fuel tank or filler neck should be carried out by a professional who has experience in this critical and potentially dangerous work. Even after cleaning and flushing of the fuel system, explosive fumes can remain and ignite during repair of the tank.

2 If the fuel tank is removed from the vehicle, it should not be placed in an area where sparks or open flames could ignite the fumes coming out of the tank. Be especially careful inside garages where a natural gas-type appliance is located, because the pilot light could cause an explosion.

12 Roll-over valves - removal and installation

Warning: *Gasoline is extremely flammable, so take extra precautions when you work on any part of the fuel system. See the* **Warning** *in Section 2.*

1 Remove the fuel tank (see Section 10).

2 Pry the two valves out of the tank, and remove the anti-trickle fill valve from its mounting. Take care not to damage the valves or the tank. Pry out the rubber seals from the tank openings, and replace then if they are worn, distorted, or if either has been leaking.

3 If either valve is thought to be faulty, seek the advice of a dealer as to whether they can be replaced individually. If not, the complete valve and pipe assembly must be replaced.

4 Installation is the reverse of the removal procedure. Ensure that both roll-over valves are pressed securely into their seals, so that there can be no fuel leaks.

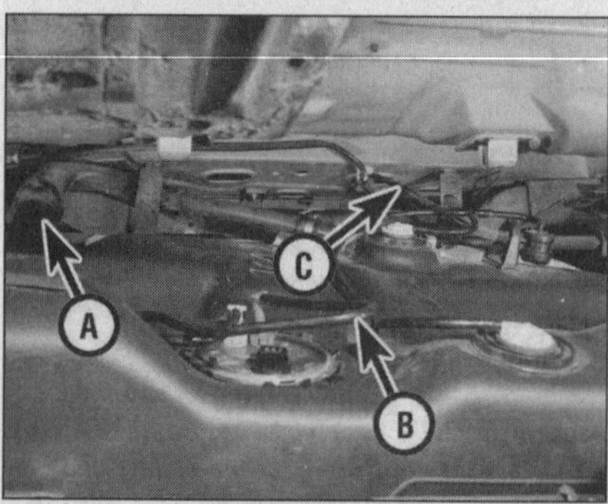

10.11 Lower the fuel tank - do not distort the filler neck stub (A) - and unclip the (red-coded) fuel return pipe (B), then disconnect the charcoal canister's vapor hose (C)

13 Fuel cut-off switch - removal and installation

Refer to illustration 13.3

1 Disconnect the battery negative (ground) cable - see Chapter 5, Section 1.

2 Remove the trim panel from the left-hand footwell.

3 Peel back the sound-insulating material from the switch, and remove its two retaining screws **(see illustration)**.

4 Disconnect the switch electrical con-

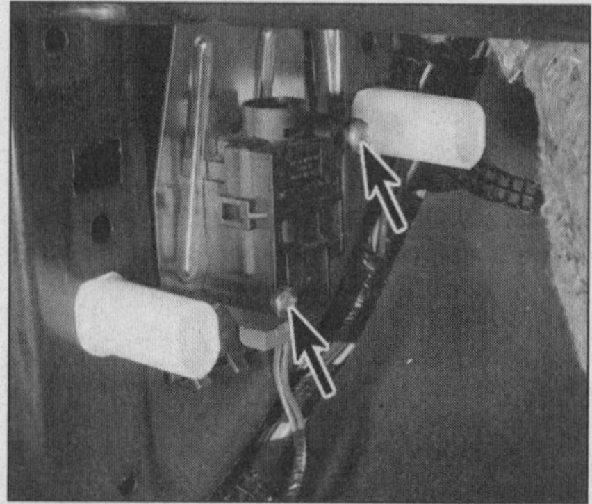

13.3 Fuel cut-off switch retaining screws

nector, and withdraw the switch.

5 Installation is the reverse of the removal procedure. Ensure that the switch is reset by depressing its red button.

14 Fuel injection system/engine management system - general information

These models are equipped with a Sequential Electronically controlled Fuel Injection (SEFI) system. The system is composed of three basic sub-systems: fuel system, air induction system and electronic control system. **Note:** *Refer to Chapter 6 for further information on the components of the system.*

Fuel system

An electric fuel pump located inside the fuel tank supplies fuel under pressure to the fuel rail, which distributes fuel evenly to all injectors. A filter between the fuel pump and the fuel rail protects the components of the system. A pressure regulator controls the system pressure in relation to manifold vacuum. From the fuel rail, fuel is injected into the intake ports, just above the intake valves, by a fuel injector. The system also includes features such as the flushing of fresh (i.e., cold) fuel around each injector on start-up, thus improving hot starts.

The amount of fuel supplied by the injectors is precisely controlled by an Electronic Control Unit (ECU). The ECU uses the signals derived from the engine speed/crankshaft position sensor and the camshaft position sensor, to trigger each injector separately in cylinder firing order (sequential injection), with benefits in terms of better fuel economy and lower exhaust emissions.

Air induction system

The air induction system consists of an air filter housing, a mass airflow sensor, an intake resonator and plenum chamber (four-cylinder models) and a throttle body. The mass airflow sensor is an information gathering device for the PCM; it uses a heated wire system to send the PCM a constantly varying (analog) voltage signal corresponding to the volume of air passing into the engine. Another sensor measures intake air temperature. The PCM uses these signals to calculate the mass (density) of air entering the engine.

The throttle valve inside the throttle body is controlled by the driver, through the accelerator pedal. As the valve opens, the amount of air that can pass through the system increases. The throttle position sensor opens further, the mass airflow sensor's signal alters and the PCM opens each injector for a longer duration, to increase the amount of fuel delivered to the inlet ports.

Electronic control system

The PCM controls the fuel injection system, as well as the other sub-systems which make up the entire engine management system. It receives signals from a number of information sensors, which monitor such variables as intake air mass and temperature, coolant temperature, engine speed and position, acceleration/deceleration, and exhaust gas oxygen content. These signals help the PCM determine the injection duration necessary for the optimum air/fuel ratio. These sensors and associated PCM-controlled relays are located throughout the engine compartment. For further information regarding the PCM and its control of the engine management system, see Chapter 6.

Idle speed and mixture adjustment - general

Both the idle speed and mixture are under the control of the PCM, and cannot be adjusted. Not only can they not be adjusted, they cannot even be checked, except with the use of special diagnostic equipment (see Chapter 6) - this makes it a task for a specialist. *Do not* attempt to "adjust" these settings in any way without such equipment.

If the idle speed and mixture are thought to be incorrect, take the vehicle to a dealer service department or other repair shop for the complete system to be tested.

On models equipped with a heated windshield, an idle-increase solenoid valve is used, which raises the idle speed to compensate for the increased load on the engine when the heated windshield is switched on. When the valve is open, air from the plenum chamber bypasses the throttle body and idle speed control valve, passing directly into the intake manifold through the union on its left end. The system is active only for the four minutes that the heated windshield circuit is live, and is supplementary to the main (PCM-controlled) idle speed regulation.

15 Fuel injection system/engine management system - check

Warning: *Gasoline is extremely flammable, so take extra precautions when you work on any part of the fuel system. See the* **Warning** *in Section 2.*

Note: *This is an initial check of the fuel delivery and air induction sub-systems of the engine management system, to be carried out in conjunction with the operational check of the fuel pump* (see Section 8)*, and as part of the preliminary checks of the complete engine management system* (see Section 3 of Chapter 6).

1 Check the ground wire connections for tightness. Check all wiring and electrical connectors that are related to the system. Loose electrical connectors and poor grounds can cause many problems that resemble more serious malfunctions.

2 Verify that the battery is fully charged. The PCM and sensors depend on an accurate supply voltage to properly meter the fuel.

3 Check the air filter element - a dirty or partially blocked filter will severely impede performance and economy (see Chapter 1).

4 If a blown fuse is found, replace it and see if it blows again. If it does, search for a short-circuited wire in the harness related to the system (see Chapter 6).

5 Check the air intake duct from the intake to the intake manifold for leaks, which will result in an excessively lean mixture. Also check the condition of the vacuum hoses connected to the intake manifold.

6 On four-cylinder models, remove the plenum chamber from the throttle body. On V6 models, remove the intake duct from the throttle body. Check the throttle valve for dirt, carbon or other residue build-up. If it's dirty, seek the advice of a dealer service department or other qualified repair shop - since the electronic control system is designed to compensate for factors such as the build-up of dirt in the throttle body, it may well be best to leave it dirty, unless the deposits are extensive. **Caution:** *A label on the throttle body states specifically that the housing bore and the throttle valve have a special coating, and must not be cleaned using carburetor cleaner, as this may damage it.*

7 With the engine running, place a screwdriver or a stethoscope against each injector, one at a time. Listen through the screwdriver handle or stethoscope for a distinct clicking sound, indicating operation.

8 If an injector isn't operating (or sounds different from the others), turn off the engine, and disconnect the electrical connector from the injector. Check the resistance across the terminals of the injector and compare your reading with the resistance value listed in this Chapter's Specifications. If the resistance isn't as specified, replace the injector.

9 A rough idle, diminished performance and/or increased fuel consumption could also be caused by clogged or fouled fuel injectors. Fuel additives that can sometimes clean fouled injectors are available at car accessory shops.

10 The remainder of the system checks should be left to a dealer service department or other qualified repair specialist, as there is a chance that the PCM may be damaged if tests are not performed properly.

16 Fuel system components - check and replacement

Warning: *Gasoline is extremely flammable, so take extra precautions when you work on any part of the fuel system. See the* **Warning** *in Section 2.*

Throttle body

Check

1 Remove the plenum chamber (four-cylinder engine) or inlet air duct (V6 engine) (see Section 4), and verify that the throttle linkage operates smoothly.

2 If the housing bore and valve are dirty enough for you to think that this might be the

16.8 Unscrew the bolts (arrows) to remove throttle housing

16.15 Remove the throttle body fasteners and separate the body from the intake manifold

cause of a fault, seek the advice of a dealer. *Do not* clean the housing (see the notes in the checking procedure given in Section 15).

Replacement

Four-cylinder models

Refer to illustration 16.8

3 Disconnect the cable from the negative battery terminal - see Chapter 5, Section 1.

4 Remove the plenum chamber (see Section 4).

5 Disconnect the accelerator cable from the throttle linkage (see Section 5 or 6, as appropriate). If equipped, also disconnect the cruise control actuator cable.

6 Releasing its wire clip, disconnect the large electrical connector (next to the fuel pressure regulator). Similarly release and disconnect the Throttle Position Sensor's electrical connector.

7 Clearly label, then detach, all vacuum hoses from the throttle body.

8 Remove the throttle body mounting screws **(see illustration)**, then detach the throttle body and gasket from the intake manifold. Discard the gasket - this must be replaced whenever it is disturbed.

9 Using a soft brush and carburetor cleaner, thoroughly clean the exterior of the throttle body, then blow out all passages with compressed air. **Caution:** *Do not clean the throttle body's bore, the throttle valve, or the throttle position (TP) sensor, either by scraping or with a solvent. Just wipe them carefully with a clean soft cloth.*

10 Installation is the reverse of the removal procedure. Install a new throttle body gasket and tighten the screws to the torque listed in this Chapter's specifications.

V6 models

Refer to illustration 16.15

11 Disconnect the cable from the negative battery terminal - see Chapter 5, Section 1.

12 Remove the air cleaner and air inlet duct (see Section 4). Also remove the water pump pulley shield.

13 Disconnect the Throttle Position Sensor electrical connector. Detach the wiring from the stud and lay it aside.

14 Disconnect the accelerator and speed control (if so equipped) cables from the throttle body. Lay the cables out of the way.

15 Remove the throttle body mounting bolts and nut **(see illustration)**. Remove the throttle body. Remove and discard the throttle body gasket - a new gasket must be used during installation.

16 Using a soft brush and carburetor cleaner, thoroughly clean the exterior of the throttle body, then blow out all passages with compressed air. **Caution:** *Do not clean the throttle body's bore, the throttle valve, or the throttle position sensor, either by scraping or with a solvent. Just wipe them carefully with a clean soft cloth. If scraping is necessary to remove the throttle body gasket, use extreme caution to prevent damage to the mating surfaces. Also, do not allow any gasket material to fall into the intake manifold.*

17 Installation is the reverse of the removal procedure. Install a new throttle body gasket and tighten the fasteners to the torque listed in this Chapter's Specifications.

Fuel rail and injectors

Check

18 Refer to the procedure in the fuel system check (see Section 15).

Replacement

Four-cylinder models

Refer to illustrations 16.25 and 16.26a and 16.26b

Note: *For simplicity, and to ensure absolute cleanliness on reassembly, the following procedure describes the removal of the fuel rail assembly, complete with the injectors and pressure regulator, so that the injectors can be serviced individually on a clean work surface. Be careful not to allow any dirt to enter the system.*

19 Relieve the pressure in the fuel system (see Section 2), and equalize tank pressure by removing the fuel filler cap.

20 Disconnect the cable from the negative battery terminal - see Chapter 5, Section 1.

21 Remove the plenum resonance chamber (see Section 4).

22 If the additional clearance is required, disconnect the accelerator cable from the throttle linkage (see Section 5 or 6, as appropriate). If equipped, also disconnect the cruise control actuator cable (see Chapter 12).

23 Releasing the wire clips, disconnect the four fuel injector electrical connectors.

24 Disconnect the fuel feed and return lines at the quick-release couplings next to the power brake booster, then unclip the fuel hoses from the intake manifold; use rag to soak up any spilled fuel. **Note:** *Do not disturb the threaded couplings at the fuel rail unions unless absolutely necessary; these are sealed at the factory. The quick-release couplings will suffice for all normal service operations.*

25 Disconnect the crankcase breather hose from the valve cover union, and the vacuum hose from the fuel pressure regulator **(see illustration)**.

26 Unscrew the three bolts securing the fuel rail, and withdraw the rail, carefully prying it out of the intake manifold, and draining any remaining fuel into a suitable clean container **(see illustrations)**. Note the seals between the rail noses and the manifold. These must be replaced whenever the rail is removed.

27 Clamping the rail carefully in a vise fitted with soft jaws, unscrew the two bolts securing each injector, and withdraw the injectors. Place each in a clean, clearly labeled storage container.

28 If you are replacing the injector(s), discard the old injector, the nose seal and the O-rings. If you are simply replacing leaking injector O-rings, and intend to re-use the same injectors, remove the old nose seal and O-rings, and discard them.

29 Further testing of the injector(s) is beyond the scope of the home mechanic. If you are in doubt as to the status of any injector(s), it can be tested at a dealer service department.

30 Installation is the reverse of the removal procedure, noting the following points:

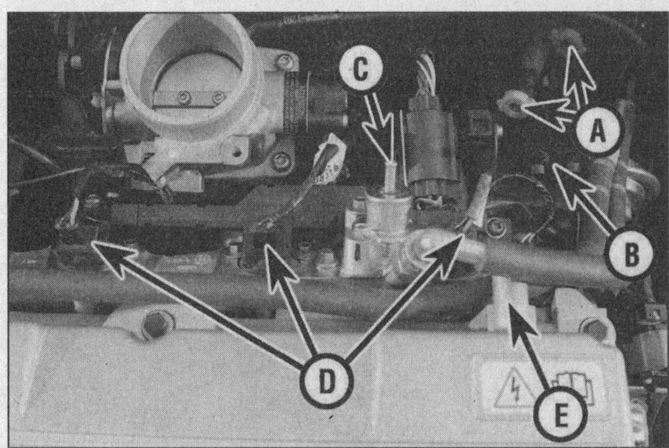

16.25 Injector removal - disconnect the fuel lines at the quick-release couplings (A), unclip the hoses (B), disconnect the vacuum hose from the regulator (C), unplug the electrical connectors (D) - three of four shown - and disconnect the breather hose from union (E)

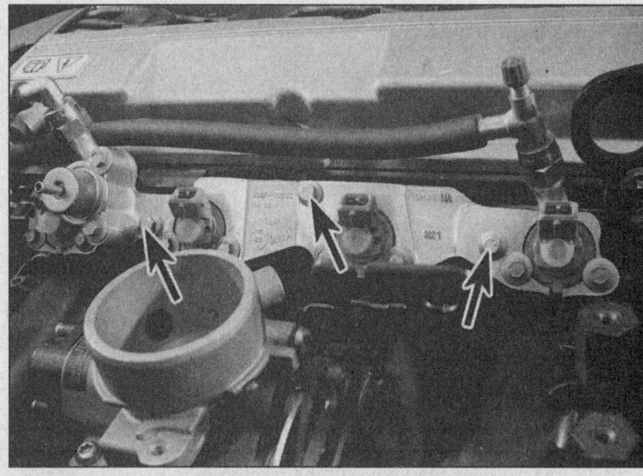

16.26a Unscrew the bolts . . .

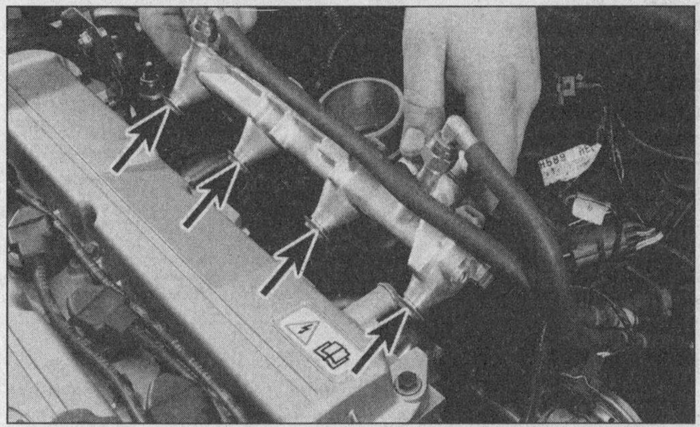

16.26b . . . and withdraw the fuel rail with the injectors and pressure regulator - renew the nose seals whenever the rail is disturbed

16.34 Disconnect the injection harness from the injectors

(a) Lubricate each nose seal and O-ring with clean engine oil on installation.

(b) Locate each injector carefully in the fuel rail recess, ensuring that the locating tab on the injector head fits into the slot provided in the rail.

(c) Install a new seal to each fuel rail nose, and ensure the seals are not displaced as the rail is reinstalled. Ensure that the fuel rail is settled fully in the manifold before tightening the three bolts evenly and to the torque listed in this Chapter's specifications.

(d) Fasten the fuel feed and return quick-release couplings as described in Section 3.

(e) Ensure that the breather hose, vacuum hose and wiring are routed correctly, and secured on reconnection by any clips or ties provided.

(f) On completion, switch the ignition on and off five times, to activate the fuel pump and pressurize the system, without cranking the engine. Check for fuel leaks around all disturbed fittings and connections before attempting to start the engine.

16.35 Remove the fuel rail mounting bolts and lift the fuel rail and injectors from the engine as an assembly

V6 models

Refer to illustrations 16.34 and 16.35

31 Relieve the residual pressure in the fuel system (see Section 2), and equalize tank pressure by removing the fuel filler cap.

32 Disconnect the cable from the negative battery terminal - see Chapter 5, Section 1.

33 Remove the upper intake manifold (see Part B of Chapter 2).

34 Disconnect all interfering wiring connectors and harnesses. Label them as you proceed. Disconnect the injector harnesses from the injectors **(see illustration)**. Lift the harness straight up and off the injectors.

35 Disconnect the fuel hoses from the fuel rail. Next, remove the fuel rail mounting bolts **(see illustration)**. Carefully disengage the injectors from the lower intake manifold and

16.43 Disconnect the vacuum hose, remove the screws and remove the fuel pressure regulator (four-cylinder models)

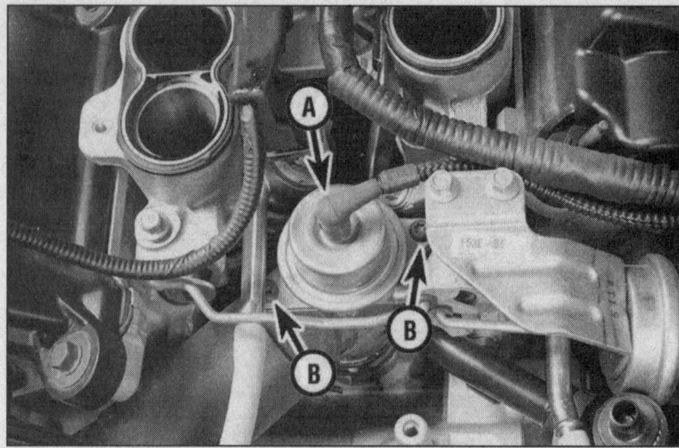

16.44 Remove the vacuum hose (A) from the regulator, remove the two screws (B) and remove the fuel pressure regulator (V6 models)

lift the rail and all six injectors from the engine as an assembly.

36 If you are replacing the injector(s), discard the old injector, the nose seal and the O-rings. If you are simply replacing leaking injector O-rings, and intend to re-use the same injectors, remove the old nose seal and O-rings, and discard them.

37 Further testing of the injector(s) is beyond the scope of the home mechanic. If you are in doubt as to the status of any injector(s), it can be tested at a dealer service department.

38 Installation is the reverse of the removal procedure, noting the following points:

(a) *Lubricate each nose seal and O-ring with clean engine oil on installation.*

(b) *Locate each injector carefully in the fuel rail recess, ensuring that the locating tab on the injector head fits into the slot provided in the rail.*

(c) *Install a new seal to each fuel rail nose, and ensure the seals are not displaced as the rail is reinstalled. Ensure that the fuel rail is settled fully in the manifold before tightening the fuel rail bolts evenly and to the torque listed in this Chapter's Specifications.*

(d) *Fasten the fuel feed and return quick-release couplings as described in Section 3.*

(e) *Ensure that the breather hose, vacuum hose and wiring are routed correctly, and secured on reconnection by any clips or ties provided.*

(f) *On completion, switch the ignition on and off five times, to activate the fuel pump and pressurize the system, without cranking the engine. Check for fuel leaks around all disturbed fittings and connections before attempting to start the engine.*

Fuel pressure regulator

Check

39 Refer to the fuel pump/fuel pressure check procedure (see Section 8).

Replacement

Refer to illustrations 16.43 and 16.44

40 Relieve the residual pressure in the fuel system (see Section 2), and equalize tank pressure by removing the fuel filler cap.

41 Disconnect the cable from the negative battery terminal - see Chapter 5, Section 1.

42 On four-cylinder models, remove the resonator plenum chamber (see Section 4). On V6 engines, remove the upper intake manifold.

43 On four-cylinder models, disconnect the vacuum hose from the regulator. Remove the two regulator mounting screws and remove the regulator **(see illustration)**. Soak up spilled fuel using a clean rag.

44 On V6 models, disconnect the vacuum hose from the regulator. Remove the two regulator screws and remove the regulator **(see illustration)**. Soak up spilled fuel using a clean rag.

45 Installation is the reverse of the removal procedure, noting the following points:

(a) *Replace the regulator sealing O-ring whenever the regulator is disturbed. Lubricate the new O-ring with clean engine oil on installation.*

(b) *Locate the regulator carefully in the fuel rail recess and tighten the bolts to the torque listed in this Chapter's specifications.*

(c) *On completion, switch the ignition on and off five times, to activate the fuel pump and pressurize the system, without cranking the engine. Check for fuel leaks around all disturbed connections before attempting to start the engine.*

Idle Air Control (IAC) valve

Check

Refer to illustrations 16.48a and 16.48b

46 Disconnect the cable from the negative battery terminal - see Chapter 5, Section 1.

47 Raise the front of the vehicle, and support it securely on jackstands. **Warning:** *Do not place any part of your body under a vehicle when it's supported only by a jack!*

48 Disconnect the valve's electrical connector **(see illustrations)**.

49 Connect a 12-volt battery across the valve's terminals - positive (+) to terminal 37 (the green/yellow wire) and negative (-) to terminal 21 (the black/yellow wire). **Caution:** *It is*

16.48a On four-cylinder models, access the idle air control valve from under the vehicle - disconnect the electrical connector to test the valve

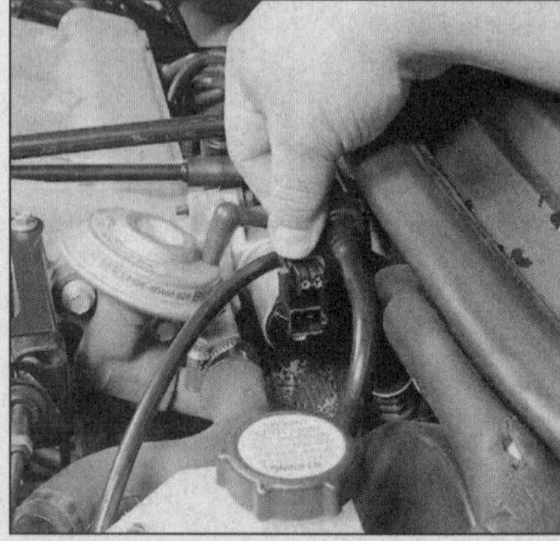

16.48b On V6 models, the idle air control valve is located next to the firewall - disconnect the electrical connector to test the valve

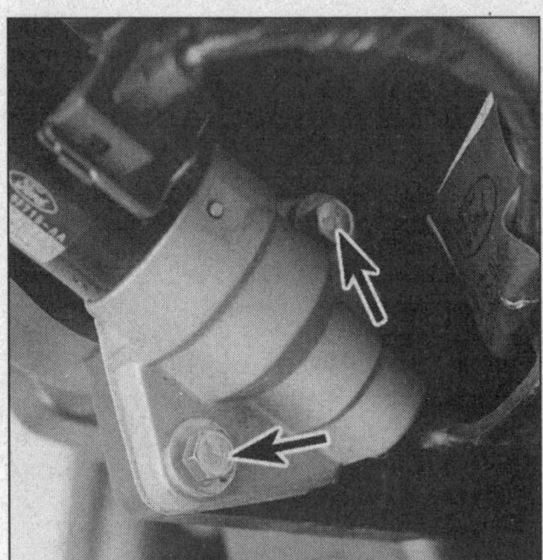

16.55a On four-cylinder models, remove the bolts to remove the idle air control valve

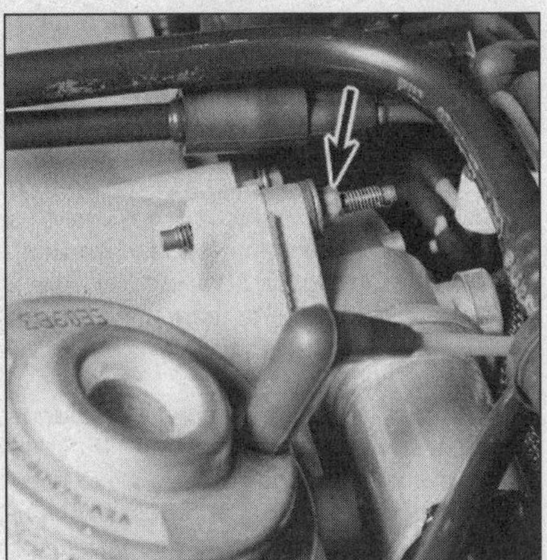

16.55b On V6 models, remove the mounting nuts (arrow, other nut not visible) and remove the Idle Air Control valve

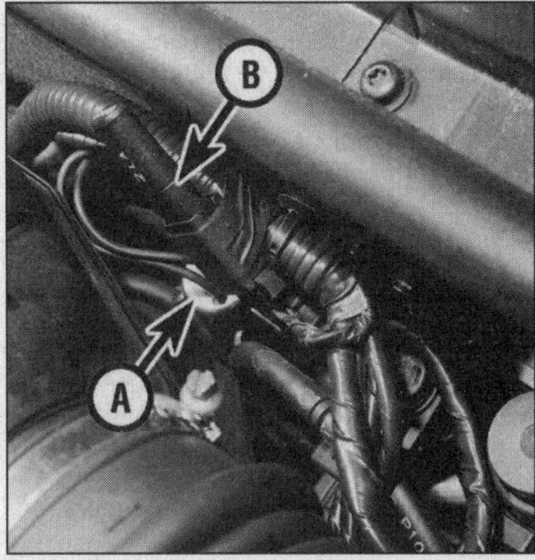

16.58 Location of idle-increase solenoid valve (A) and diode (B)

essential that the correct polarity is observed or the diode in the valve may be damaged.

50 A distinct click should be heard each time contact is made and broken. If not, measure the resistance between the terminals. If the resistance is as specified, the valve is okay (but there may be a problem with the wiring or the PCM). If the resistance is not as specified, replace the valve (see below).

51 Plug in the valve's electrical connector.

Replacement

Refer to illustrations 16.55a and 16.55b

52 Disconnect the battery negative (ground) lead - see Chapter 5, Section 1.

53 On four-cylinder models, raise the front of the vehicle, and support it securely on jackstands. **Warning:** *Do not place any part of your body under a vehicle when it's supported only by a jack!*

54 Disconnect the valve's electrical connector.

55 Unscrew the two retaining bolts (four-cylinder) or nuts (V6), and withdraw the valve from the intake manifold **(see illustrations)**.

56 Since the valve's individual components are not available separately, and the complete assembly must be replaced if it is diagnosed to be faulty, there is nothing to be lost by attempting to flush out the passages, using carburetor cleaner or similar solvent. This won't take much time or effort, and may well cure the fault, although it should be noted that the manufacturer recommends against cleaning the valve with any type of solvent.

57 Installation is the reverse of the removal procedure, noting the following points:

(a) *Clean the mating surfaces carefully, and always install a new gasket whenever the valve is disturbed.*

(b) *Tighten the bolts evenly to the torque listed in this Chapter's Specifications.*

(c) *Once the wiring and battery are reconnected, start the engine and allow it to idle. When it has reached normal operating temperature, confirm that the idle speed is stable and that no air leaks are evident. Switch on all electrical loads (headlights, heated rear window, etc.), and make sure that the idle speed is still correct.*

Idle-increase solenoid valve

Check

Refer to illustration 16.58

58 If this valve is thought to be faulty, disconnect its electrical connector and disconnect its vacuum hoses, then connect a battery directly across the valve's terminals. Check that air can flow through the valve's passages when the solenoid is energized, and that nothing can pass when the solenoid is not energized. Alternatively, connect an ohmmeter to measure the resistance between the valve's terminals, and compare this reading to that listed in the Specifications Section at the beginning of this Chapter. Replace the valve if it is faulty **(see illustration)**.

59 The solenoid is equipped with a diode to control any voltage spikes which might occur as the solenoid is switched off. A faulty diode would not, therefore, necessarily interfere with the operation of the valve. If the diode is thought to be faulty, however, it can be checked by disconnecting it and connecting an ohmmeter across its terminals to check that continuity exists in one direction only. If continuity is found in both directions, or in neither, the diode is faulty and must be replaced.

Replacement

60 If better access is required, remove the plenum chamber (see Section 4).

61 Disconnect the battery negative (ground) lead - see Section 1 of Chapter 5.

62 Disconnect the valve's electrical connector. Unclip the valve from the firewall, then disconnect its vacuum hoses and withdraw it.

63 Installation is the reverse of the removal procedure.

17 Exhaust system - general information

Refer to illustration 17.5

Warning: *Inspection and repair of exhaust system components should be done only after allowing the exhaust components to cool completely. This applies particularly to the catalytic converter, which operates at very high temperatures. Also, when working under the vehicle, make sure it is securely supported on jackstands.*

1 On four-cylinder models, the exhaust system is composed of an exhaust manifold, the front exhaust pipe, flex pipe and catalytic converter, and a rear section incorporating a rear muffler. The exhaust system on V6 models is essentially the same except it has two exhaust manifolds and a Y-type exhaust pipe at the engine. The exhaust system on all models is suspended throughout its entire length by rubber hangers.

2 If any of these parts are damaged or deteriorated, excessive noise and vibration will occur.

3 Conduct regular inspections of the exhaust system, to keep it safe and quiet. Look for any damaged or bent parts, open seams, holes, loose connections, excessive corrosion, or other defects which could allow exhaust fumes to enter the vehicle. Deteriorated exhaust system components should not be repaired - they should be replaced with new parts.

4 If the exhaust system components are extremely corroded or rusted together, they will probably have to be cut from the exhaust system. The most convenient way of accomplishing this is to have it performed at a shop specializing in exhaust repair. If, however, you want to save money by doing it yourself (and you don't have an oxy/acetylene cutting torch), simply cut off the old components using a hacksaw. If you have compressed air, special pneumatic cutting chisels can also be used. If you do decide to perform the job at

home, be sure to wear eye protection to protect your eyes from metal chips and work gloves to protect your hands.

5 Here are some simple guidelines to apply when repairing the exhaust system: **Warning:** *The catalytic converter operates at very high temperatures and takes a long time to cool. Wait until it's completely cool before attempting to remove the converter. Failure to do so could result in a serious burn.*

- (a) *Work from the back to the front when removing exhaust system components.*
- (b) *Apply penetrating fluid to the exhaust system component fasteners, to make them easier to remove.*
- (c) *Use new gaskets, rubber hangers and clamps when installing exhaust system components.*
- (d) *Apply anti-seize compound to the threads of all exhaust system fasteners during reassembly.*
- (e) *Note that on some models, the exhaust pipe is secured to the manifold by two coil springs, spring seats and self-locking nut on each. If so equipped, tighten the nuts until they stop on the bolt shoulders; the pressure of the springs will then be sufficient to make a leakproof connection* **(see illustration)**. *Do not overtighten the nuts to cure a leak - the bolts or studs will shear. Replace the gasket and the springs if a leak is found.*
- (f) *Be sure to allow sufficient clearance between newly installed parts and all points on the underbody, to avoid overheating the floorpan, and possibly damaging the interior carpet and insulation. Pay particularly close attention to the catalytic converter and its heat shield.*

17.5 Tighten exhaust system front downpipe-to-manifold nuts as described - do not overtighten them

Chapter 5
Engine electrical systems

Contents

5

Specifications

Battery

Type	Lead-acid
Rating - Cold cranking amps	540 to 650 CCA

Ignition timing

Nominal	10° ± 2° BTDC

Note: *Ignition timing is under control of PCM - it may vary constantly at idle speed, and is not adjustable.*

Ignition coil

Output	37.0 kilovolts (minimum)
Primary resistance - measured at coil connector terminal pins	0.50 ± 0.05 ohms

Alternator

Output	130 amps
Minimum brush length - all types	7/32 inch
Regulated voltage @ 2000 (engine) rpm	13.0 to 15.0 volts

Starter motor

Type	Permanent magnet, gear reduction
Minimum brush length - all types	11/32 inch
Commutator minimum diameter	1.29 inches
Maximum commutator runout	0.005 inch
Armature endplay	0.012 inch

Torque specifications — **Ft-lbs** (unless otherwise indicated)

Torque specifications	Ft-lbs (unless otherwise indicated)
Crankshaft position sensor bolt	
2.0L	53 to 108 in-lbs
V6	71 to 106 in-lbs
Ignition coil bracket-to-cylinder head screws (1995 through 1997 2.0L)	13 to 17
Ignition coil mounting screws	
1998 2.0L	53 in-lbs
V6	40 to 61 in-lbs
Alternator mounting bolts	
1995 through 1997	15 to 22
1998	33
Alternator mounting bracket bolts	15 to 22
Alternator pulley nut	33
Alternator output terminal nut	80 to 97 in-lbs
Starter motor mounting bolts	15 to 20
Solenoid bolts	45 to 89 in-lbs
Starter motor mounting bracket	
Bolts	18
Nuts	150 in-lbs
Starter through-bolts	45 to 89 in-lbs

1 General information, precautions and battery disconnection

General information

The engine electrical systems include all ignition, charging and starting components. Because of their engine-related functions, these components are discussed separately from body electrical devices such as the lights, the instruments, etc. (which are included in Chapter 12).

Precautions

Refer to illustration 1.2

Always observe the following precautions when working on the electrical system:

(a) *Be extremely careful when servicing engine electrical components. They are easily damaged if checked, connected or handled improperly.*
(b) *Never leave the ignition switched on for long periods of time when the engine is not running.*
(c) *Don't disconnect the battery cables while the engine is running.*
(d) *Maintain correct polarity when connecting a battery cable from another vehicle during jump starting - see the "Booster battery (jump) starting" section at the front of this manual.*
(e) *Always disconnect the negative lead first, and reconnect it last, or the battery may be shorted by the tool being used to loosen the lead clamps* **(see illustration)**.

It's also a good idea to review the safety-related information regarding the engine electrical systems located in the *"Safety first!"* section at the front of this manual, before beginning any operation included in this Chapter.

Battery disconnection

Several systems installed to the vehicle require battery power to be available at all times, either to ensure their continued operation (such as the clock) or to maintain control unit memories (such as that in the engine management system's ECU) which would be wiped if the battery were to be disconnected. Whenever the battery is to be disconnected therefore, first note the following, to ensure that there are no unforeseen consequences of this action:

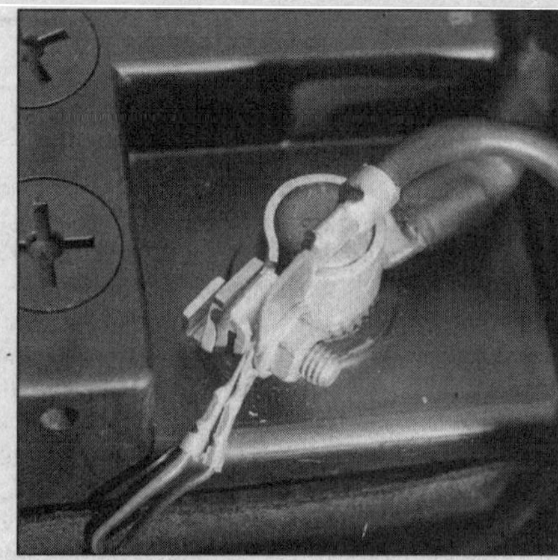

1.2 Always disconnect battery - negative (ground) lead first - to prevent the possibility of short-circuits

(a) *First, on any vehicle with central locking, it is a wise precaution to remove the key from the ignition, and to keep it with you, so that it does not get locked in if the central locking should engage accidentally when the battery is reconnected!*
(b) *The engine management system's ECU will lose the information stored in its memory - referred to by the manufacturer as the "KAM" (Keep-Alive Memory) - when the battery is disconnected. This includes idling and operating values, and any fault codes detected - in the case of the fault codes, if it is thought likely that the system has developed a fault for which the corresponding code has been logged, the vehicle must be taken to a dealer for the codes to be read, using the special diagnostic equipment necessary for this (see Chapter 6). Whenever the battery is disconnected, the information relating to idle speed control and other operating values will have to be reprogrammed into the unit's memory. The ECU does this by itself, but until then, there may be surging, hesitation, erratic idle and a generally inferior level of performance. To allow the ECU to relearn these values, start the engine and run it as close to idle speed as possible until it reaches its normal operating temperature, then run it for approximately two minutes at 1200 rpm. Next, drive the vehicle as far as necessary - approximately 5 miles of varied driving conditions is usually sufficient - to complete the relearning process.*
(c) *If the battery is disconnected while the alarm system is armed or activated, the alarm will remain in the same state when the battery is reconnected. The same applies to the engine immobilizes system (if equipped).*
(d) *If a trip computer is in use, any information stored in memory will be lost.*
(e) *If a "Keycode" audio unit is in-stalled, and the unit and/or the battery is disconnected, the unit will not function again on reconnection until the correct security code is entered. Details of this procedure, which varies according to the unit and model year, are given in the "Ford Audio Systems Operating Guide" supplied with the vehicle when new, with the code itself being given in a "Radio Passport" and/or a "Keycode Label" at the same time. Ensure you have the correct code before you disconnect the battery. For obvious security reasons, the procedure is not given in this manual. If you do not have the code or details of the correct procedure, but can supply proof of ownership and a legitimate reason for wanting this information, the vehicle's selling dealer may be able to help.*

2.2a Unscrew hold-down nuts (one of two arrows) . . .

2.2b . . . and withdraw hold-down clamp to release battery

Devices known as "memory-savers" (or "code-savers") can be used to avoid some of the above problems. Precise details vary according to the device used. Typically, it is plugged into the cigarette lighter, and is connected by its own wires to a spare battery; the vehicle's own battery is then disconnected from the electrical system, leaving the "memory-saver" to pass sufficient current to maintain audio unit security codes and ECU memory values, and also to run permanently-live circuits such as the clock, all the while isolating the battery in the event of a short-circuit occurring while work is carried out. **Warning:** *Some of these devices allow a considerable amount of current to pass, which can mean that many of the vehicle's systems are still operational when the main battery is disconnected. If a "memory-saver" is used, ensure that the circuit concerned is actually "dead" before carrying out any work on it!*

2 Battery - removal and installation

Refer to illustration 2.2a and 2.2b

Note: *See also the relevant Sections of Chapter 1.*

1 Disconnect the battery cables, negative (ground) cable first - see Section 1.

2 Remove the battery hold-down clamp **(see illustrations)**.

3 Lift out the battery. Be careful - it's heavy.

4 While the battery is out, inspect the tray for corrosion (see Chapter 1).

5 If you are replacing the battery, make sure that you get one that's identical, with the same dimensions, amperage rating, cold cranking rating, etc. Dispose of the old battery in a responsible fashion. Most local authorities have facilities for the collection and disposal of such items - batteries contain sulfuric acid and lead, and should not be simply thrown out with the household rubbish!

6 Installation is the reverse of the removal procedure.

3 Battery cables - check and replacement

Note: *See also the relevant Sections of Chapter 1.*

1 Periodically inspect the entire length of each battery cable for damage, cracked or burned insulation, and corrosion. Poor battery cable connections can cause starting problems and decreased engine performance.

2 Check the cable-to-terminal connections at the ends of the cables for cracks, loose wire strands and corrosion. The presence of white, fluffy deposits under the insulation at the cable terminal connection is a sign that the cable is corroded and should be replaced. Check the terminals for distortion, missing clamp bolts, and corrosion.

3 When removing the cables, always disconnect the negative lead first, and reconnect it last (see Section 1). Even if only the positive cable is being replaced, be sure to disconnect the negative cable from the battery first (see Chapter 1 for further information regarding battery cable removal).

4 Disconnect the old cables from the battery, then trace each of them to their opposite ends, and detach them from the starter solenoid and ground terminals. Note the routing of each cable, to ensure correct installation.

5 If you are replacing either or both of the old cables, take them with you when buying new cables. It is vitally important that you replace the cables with identical parts. Cables have characteristics that make them easy to identify: positive cables are usually red, larger in cross-section, and have a larger-diameter battery post clamp; ground cables are usually black, smaller in cross-section and have a slightly smaller-diameter clamp for the negative post.

6 Clean the threads of the solenoid or ground connection with a wire brush to remove rust and corrosion. Apply a light coat of battery terminal corrosion inhibitor, or petroleum jelly, to the threads, to prevent future corrosion.

7 Attach the cable to the solenoid or ground connection, and tighten the mounting nut/bolt securely.

8 Before connecting a new cable to the battery, make sure that it reaches the battery post without having to be stretched.

9 Connect the positive cable first, followed by the negative cable.

4 Ignition system - general information and precautions

General

The ignition system includes the ignition switch, the battery, the crankshaft speed/position sensor, the coil, the primary (low tension/LT) and secondary (high tension/HT) wiring circuits, and the spark plugs. On models with automatic transaxle, a separate ignition module is also installed, its functions being incorporated in the ECU on models with manual transaxle. The ignition system is controlled by the engine management system's Electronic Control Unit (ECU). Using data provided by information sensors which monitor various engine functions (such as engine speed and piston position, intake air mass and temperature, engine coolant temperature, etc.), the ECU ensures a perfectly-timed spark under all conditions (see Chapter 6). **Note:** *The ignition timing is under the full control of the ECU, and cannot be adjusted - see Section 8 for further details.*

Precautions

When working on the ignition system, take the following precautions:

(a) *Do not keep the ignition switch on for more than 10 seconds if the engine will not start.*

(b) *If a separate tachometer is ever required for servicing work, consult a dealer service department before buying a tachometer for use with this vehicle - some tachometers may be incompatible with this ignition system - and always connect it in accordance with the equipment manufacturer's instructions.*

(c) *Never connect the ignition coil terminals to ground. This could result in damage to the coil and/or the ECU or ignition module (whichever is installed).*

(d) *Do not disconnect the battery when the engine is running.*

(e) *Make sure that the ignition module (if equipped) is properly grounded.*

(f) *Refer to the warning at the beginning of the next Section concerning HT voltage.*

5 Ignition system - testing

Warning: *Because of the high voltage generated by the ignition system, extreme care should be taken whenever an operation is*

6.9 Disconnect coil electrical connector (A), suppressor connector (B), and spark plug/Spark plug wires (C), remove screws (D), then undo Torx-type screws (E) to release ignition coil assembly

6.14 To remove the ignition coil on V6 models, disconnect the primary ignition connector (A), remove the spark plug wires and remove the mounting screws (B) - note the ground wire under one mounting screw

performed involving ignition components. This not only includes the ignition module/ECU, coil and spark plug (HT) leads, but related components such as electrical connectors, tachometer and other test equipment also.

Note: *This is an initial check of the "ignition part" of the main engine management system, to be carried out as part of the preliminary checks of the complete engine management system (see Chapter 6).*

1 If the engine turns over but won't start, disconnect the (HT) lead from any spark plug, and attach it to a calibrated tester (available at most automotive accessory shops). Connect the clip on the tester to a good ground - a bolt or metal bracket on the engine. If you're unable to obtain a calibrated ignition tester, have the check carried out by a dealer service department or similar. Any other form of testing (such as jumping a spark from the end of an Spark plug wire to ground) is not recommended, because of the risk of personal injury, or of damage to the ECU/ignition module (see notes above and in Section 4).

2 Crank the engine and watch the end of the tester to see if bright blue, well-defined sparks occur.

3 If sparks occur, sufficient voltage is reaching the plug to fire it. Repeat the check at the remaining plugs, to ensure that all leads are sound and that the coil is serviceable. However, the plugs themselves may be fouled or faulty, so remove and check them as described in Chapter 1.

4 If no sparks or intermittent sparks occur, the spark plug wire(s) may be defective - check them as described in Chapter 1.

5 If there's still no spark, check the coil's electrical connector, to make sure it's clean and tight. Check for full battery voltage to the coil at the connector's center terminal. The coil is grounded through the ECU - *do not* attempt to check this. Check the coil itself (see Section 6). Make any necessary repairs, then repeat the check again.

6 The remainder of the system checks should be left to a dealer service department or other qualified repair facility, as there is a chance that the ECU may be damaged if tests are not performed properly.

6 Ignition coil - removal and installation

Warning: *Because of the high voltage generated by the ignition system, extreme care should be taken whenever an operation is performed involving ignition components. This not only includes the ignition module/ECU, coil and spark plug (HT) leads, but related components such as electrical connectors, tachometer and other test equipment also.*

Check

1 Having checked that full battery voltage is available at the center terminal of the coil's electrical connector (see Section 5), disconnect the battery negative (ground) lead - see Section 1.

2 Disconnect the coil's electrical connector, if not already disconnected.

3 Using an ohmmeter, measure the resistance of the coil's primary windings, connecting the meter between the coil's terminal pins as follows. Measure first from one outer pin to the center pin, then from the other outer pin to the center. Compare your readings with the coil primary resistance listed in the Specifications Section at the beginning of this Chapter.

4 Disconnect the spark plug (HT) leads - note their connections or label them carefully, as described in Chapter 1. Use the meter to check that there is continuity (i.e., a resistance corresponding to that of the coil secondary winding) between each pair of (HT) lead terminals; On four-cylinder models, coil terminals No. 1 and 2 are connected by their secondary windings as are terminals No. 3 and 4. On V6 models, terminals No. 1 and 5 are connected, terminals No. 3 and 4 are connected and terminals No. 2 and 6 are connected. Now switch to the highest resistance scale, and check that there is no continuity between either pair of terminals and the other - i.e., there should be infinite resistance between terminals 1 and 2, or 4 and 3 - and between any terminal and ground.

5 If either of the above tests provide resistance values outside the specified amount, or results other than those described, replace the coil. Any further testing should be left to a dealership service department or other qualified repair facility.

Removal and installation

Four-cylinder models

Refer to illustration 6.9

Note: *On four-cylinder models, the ignition coil is mounted to a bracket located at the rear of the cylinder head.*

6 Disconnect the cable from the negative battery terminal (see Section 1).

7 Remove the mass airflow sensor and resonator (see Chapter 4).

8 Disconnect the electrical connector from each side of the coil, then disconnect the spark plug (HT) leads - note their connections or label them carefully, as described in Chapter 1.

9 On 1995 through 1997 models, remove the two screws securing the EGR pipe to the coil bracket. Remove the coil mounting screws. Withdraw the coil assembly from the cylinder head **(see illustration)**.

10 The radio frequency interference capacitor can be unbolted from the mounting bracket, if required.

11 Installation is the reverse of the removal procedure. Ensure that the spark plug (HT) leads are connected correctly and tighten the coil screws securely.

V6 models

Refer to illustration 6.14

Note: *On V6 models, the ignition coil is mounted on the rear valve cover.*

12 Disconnect the cable from the negative battery terminal (see Section 1).

13 Disconnect any wiring harnesses attached to the ignition coil. If necessary, remove the EGR valve vacuum regulator solenoid from the upper intake manifold.

14 Disconnect the spark plug (HT) leads from the ignition coil. Squeeze their locking tabs, and carefully twist and lift the wires off the coil. Label the wires for reference during installation. Disconnect the coil primary connector, then remove the mounting screws and remove the coil **(see illustration)**. If replacing the coil, remove the radio frequency interference capacitor from the ignition coil and install it onto the new coil.

15 Installation is the reverse of removal. Make sure the ground wire is attached to one of the coil mounting screws. Also, ensure that the spark plug (HT) leads are connected correctly.

7 Ignition timing - checking

As noted in Section 4, the ignition timing is controlled entirely by the ECU (acting with the ignition module, on models with automatic transaxle), and cannot be adjusted. The value quoted in the Specifications Section of this Chapter is for reference only, and may vary significantly if "checked" by simply connecting a timing light to the system and running the engine at idle speed.

Not only can the ignition timing not be adjusted, it cannot be checked either, except with the use of special diagnostic equipment (see Chapter 6) - this makes it a task for a dealer service department.

8 Crankshaft speed/position sensor - checking, removal and installation

Checking

1 See Section 4 of Chapter 6.

Removal and installation

Refer to illustrations 8.4a and 8.4b

2 Disconnect the cable from the negative battery terminal (see Section 1).

3 Raise the front of the vehicle, and support it securely on jackstands. **Warning**: *Do not place any part of your body under a vehicle if it's supported only by a jack!* On four-cylinder models, remove the splash shield from the left-hand inner fender. On V6 models, remove the splash shield from the right-hand inner fender, if necessary, to gain access to the sensor.

4 Disconnect the sensor's electrical connector **(see illustrations)**.

5 Remove the sensor's retaining screw and withdraw the sensor.

6 Installation is the reverse of the removal procedure.

9 Charging system - general information and precautions

General information

The charging system includes the alternator, an internal voltage regulator, a no-charge (or "ignition") warning light, the battery, and the wiring between all the components. The charging system supplies electrical power for the ignition system, the lights, the radio, etc. The alternator is driven by the drivebelt at the front (right-hand end) of the engine.

The purpose of the voltage regulator is to limit the alternator's voltage to a preset value. This prevents power surges, circuit overloads, etc., during peak voltage output.

The charging system doesn't ordinarily require periodic maintenance. However, the drivebelt, battery and wires and connections should be inspected at the intervals outlined in Chapter 1.

The dashboard warning light should come on when the ignition key is turned to positions "II" or "III", then should go off immediately the engine starts. If it remains on, or if it comes on while the engine is running, there is a malfunction in the charging system (see Section 10). If the light does not come on when the ignition key is turned, and the bulb is sound (see Chapter 11), there is a fault in the alternator.

Precautions

Be very careful when making electrical circuit connections to a vehicle equipped with an alternator, and note the following:

(a) *When reconnecting wires to the alternator from the battery, be sure to note the polarity.*
(b) *Before using arc-welding equipment to repair any part of the vehicle, disconnect the wires from the alternator and the battery terminals.*
(c) *Never start the engine with a battery charger connected.*
(d) *Always disconnect both battery cables before using a battery charger.*
(e) *The alternator is driven by an engine drivebelt which could cause serious injury if your hand, hair or clothes become entangled in it with the engine running.*
(f) *Because the alternator is connected directly to the battery, it could arc or cause a fire if overloaded or shorted-out.*
(g) *Wrap a plastic bag over the alternator, and secure it with rubber bands, before steam-cleaning or pressure-washing the engine.*
(h) *Never disconnect the alternator terminals while the engine is running.*

10 Charging system - testing

1 If a malfunction occurs in the charging circuit, don't automatically assume that the alternator is causing the problem. First check the following items:

(a) *Check the tension and condition of the drivebelt - replace it if it is worn or deteriorated (see Chapter 1).*
(b) *Ensure the alternator mounting bolts and nuts are tight.*
(c) *Inspect the alternator wiring harness and the electrical connections at the alternator; they must be in good condition, and tight.*
(d) *Check the large (Mega fuse) in the engine harness located at the back of the engine compartment between the firewall and engine or check the main fuses in the engine compartment (see Chapter 12). If any is blown, determine the cause, repair the circuit and replace the fuse (the vehicle won't start and/or the accessories won't work if the fuse is blown).*
(e) *Start the engine and check the alternator for abnormal noises - for example, a shrieking or squealing sound may indicate a badly-worn bearing or brush.*
(f) *Make sure that the battery is fully-charged - one bad cell in a battery can cause overcharging by the alternator.*
(g) *Disconnect the battery cables (negative first, then positive). Inspect the battery*

5

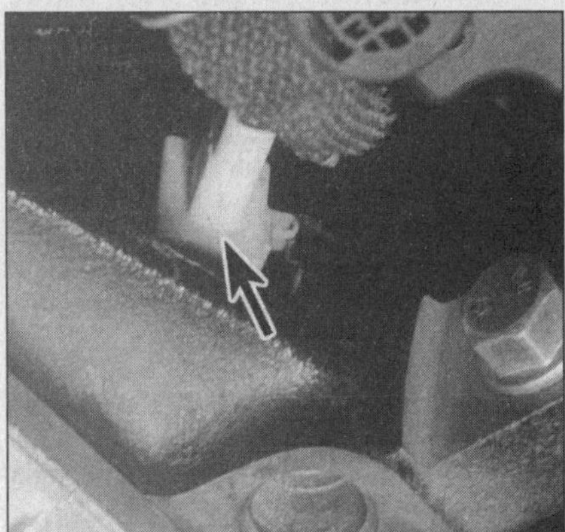

8.4a Location of crankshaft speed/position sensor - connector - in front of cylinder block/crankcase

8.4b Location of crankshaft position sensor (arrow) - V6 engine

posts and the lead clamps for corrosion. Clean them thoroughly if necessary (see Section 3 and Chapter 1). Reconnect the cable to the positive terminal.

(h) With the ignition and all accessories switched off, insert a test light between the battery negative post and the disconnected negative cable clamp:

(1) If the test light does not come on, reattach the clamp and proceed to the next step.

(2) If the test light comes on, there is a drain in the electrical system of the vehicle. The short must be repaired before the charging system can be checked.

(3) To find the drain, disconnect the alternator wiring harness:

(a) If the light goes out, the alternator is at fault.

(b) If the light stays on, remove each fuse until it goes out - this will tell you which component is causing the drain.

2 Using a voltmeter, check the battery voltage with the engine off. It should be approximately 12 volts.

3 Start the engine and check the battery voltage again. Increase engine speed until the voltmeter reading remains steady; it should now be approximately 13.5 to 14.6 volts.

4 Switch on as many electrical accessories (e.g. the headlights, heated rear window and heater blower) as possible, and check that the alternator maintains the regulated voltage at around 13 to 14 volts. The voltage may drop and then come back up; it may also be necessary to increase engine speed slightly, even if the charging system is working properly.

5 If the voltage reading is greater than the specified charging voltage, replace the voltage regulator (see Section 12).

6 If the voltmeter reading is less than that specified, the fault may be due to worn brushes, weak brush springs, a faulty voltage regulator, a faulty diode, a severed phase winding, or worn or damaged slip rings. The brushes and slip rings may be checked (see Section 12), but if the fault persists, the alternator should be replaced or taken to an auto-electrician for testing and repair.

11 Alternator - removal and installation

Four-cylinder models

Refer to illustration 11.3

1 Disconnect the cable from the negative battery terminal (see Section 1).

2 Remove the resonator chamber (see Chapter 4).

3 Unscrew the nuts to disconnect the wiring from the alternator **(see illustration)**. If additional working clearance is required, remove the right-hand of the three screws securing the wiring harness to the rear of the intake manifold.

11.3 Disconnecting the alternator wiring on four-cylinder models

4 Raise and support the front right-hand corner of the vehicle with a jackstand. On 1998 models, remove the right front wheel and splash shield from the right-hand inner fender. Remove the drivebelt and the engine oil filter - soak up the spilled oil using a shop towel (see Chapter 1). Rather than reinstall a used filter, you are advised to drain the engine oil, then to install a new filter and refill the engine with clean oil on reassembly. Where an engine oil cooler is installed, it may be necessary to remove this as well, to provide the clearance necessary to remove the alternator (see Chapter 2, Part A).

5 Unscrew the two bolts securing the power steering system lines to the right-hand side of the front suspension subframe.

6 Remove the mounting bolts. Lift the alternator clear of the engine. There is limited space to remove he alternator, so do not damage any hoses or wiring. Do not drop the alternator; it is fragile.

7 If you are replacing the alternator, take the old one with you when purchasing a replacement unit. Make sure that the new or rebuilt unit is identical to the old alternator. Look at the terminals - they should be the same in number, size and location as the terminals on the old alternator. Finally, look at the identification markings - they will be stamped in the housing or printed on a tag affixed to the housing. Make sure that these numbers are the same on both alternators.

8 Many new/rebuilt alternators do not have a pulley installed, so you may have to switch the pulley from the old unit to the new/rebuilt one. When buying an alternator, ask about the installation of pulleys - some auto-electrical specialists will perform this service free of charge.

9 Installation is the reverse of the removal procedure, referring where necessary to the relevant Chapters of this manual. Tighten all fasteners to the torque listed in this Chapter's Specifications and the other relevant chapters.

10 Check the charging voltage to verify proper operation of the alternator (see Section 10).

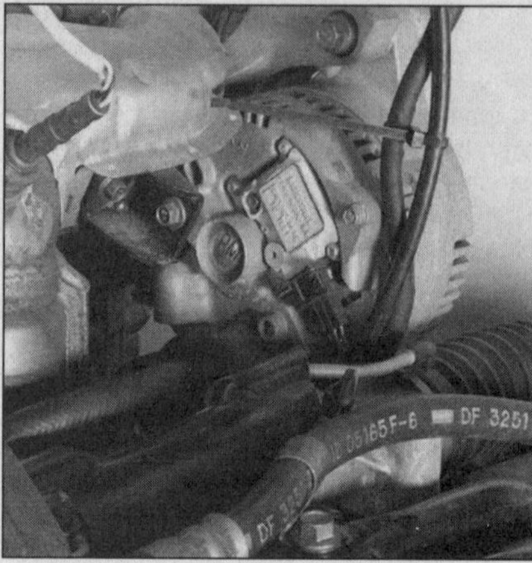

11.16 Disconnect the alternator wiring from the back of the alternator

V6 models

Refer to illustration 11.16

11 Disconnect the cable from the negative terminal of the battery.

12 Raise the vehicle and support it securely on jackstands. Remove the right front wheel. Remove the splash shield from the right-hand inner fender.

13 Remove the drivebelt (see Chapter 1).

14 Remove the right-hand driveaxle (see Chapter 8). Disconnect the right-hand outer tie-rod end from the steering knuckle.

15 Unbolt the exhaust Y-pipe from the exhaust manifolds and lower it away from the engine.

16 Disconnect the alternator wiring from the back of the alternator **(see illustration)**.

17 Remove the alternator rear support bracket bolt from the cylinder block, the upper and lower mounting bolts and remove the alternator though the fender opening.

18 If you are replacing the alternator, take the old one with you when purchasing a replacement unit. Make sure that the new or rebuilt unit is identical to the old alternator. Look at the terminals - they should be the same in number, size and location as the terminals on the old alternator. Finally, look at the identification markings - they will be stamped in the housing or printed on a tag affixed to the housing. Make sure that these numbers are the same on both alternators.

19 Many new/rebuilt alternators do not have a pulley installed, so you may have to switch the pulley from the old unit to the new/rebuilt one. When buying an alternator, ask about the installation of pulleys - some auto-electrical specialists will perform this service free of charge.

20 Installation is the reverse of the removal procedure, referring where necessary to the relevant Chapters of this manual. Tighten all fasteners to the torque listed in this Chapter's Specifications and the other relevant chapters.

21 Check the charging voltage to verify proper operation of the alternator (see Section 10).

12.3 To detach the voltage regulator/brush holder assembly, remove the four screws

12 Alternator brushes and voltage regulator - replacement

Refer to illustrations 12.3, 12.4, 12.5 and 12.9

Note: *The voltage regulator is an integral part of the alternator. The regulator and brushes can be replaced if necessary. If other service to the alternator is required, replace the alternator as an assembly.*

1 Remove the alternator (see Section 11).

2 Set the alternator on a clean workbench.

3 Remove the four voltage regulator mounting screws **(see illustration)**.

4 Detach the voltage regulator **(see illustration)**.

5 Detach the rubber plugs (if used) and remove the brush lead retaining screws and nuts to separate the brush leads from the holder **(see illustration)**. Note that the screws have Torx heads and require a special screwdriver.

6 After noting the relationship of the brushes to the brush holder assembly, remove both brushes. Don't lose the springs.

7 If you're installing a new voltage regulator, insert the old brushes into the brush holder of the new regulator. If you're installing new brushes, insert them into the brush holder of the old regulator. Make sure the springs are properly compressed and the brushes are properly inserted into the recesses in the brush holder.

8 Install the brush lead retaining screws and nuts.

9 Insert a short section of wire, like a straightened paper clip, through the hole in the voltage regulator **(see illustration)** to hold the brushes in the retracted position during regulator installation. New brushes are provided with the pin installed to ease installation.

10 Carefully install the regulator. Make sure the brushes don't hang up on the rotor.

11 Install the voltage regulator screws and tighten them securely.

12 Remove the wire or paper clip.

13 Install the alternator (see Section 12).

12.4 Lift the assembly from the alternator

13 Starting system - general information and precautions

General information

The sole function of the starting system is to crank the engine quickly enough to allow it to start.

The starting system consists of the battery, the starter motor, the starter solenoid, and the wires connecting them. The solenoid is mounted directly on the starter motor.

The solenoid/starter motor assembly is installed on the rear upper part of the engine, next to the transmission bellhousing.

When the ignition key is turned to Start position, the starter solenoid is actuated through the starter control circuit. The starter solenoid then connects the battery to the starter. The battery supplies the current to the starter motor, which does the actual work of cranking the engine.

The starter motor on a vehicle equipped with automatic transaxle can be operated only when the selector lever is in Park or Neutral. If equipped with a manual transaxle, the starter will only operate when the clutch is depressed completely.

If the alarm system is armed or activated (if so equipped), the starter motor cannot be operated.

Precautions

Always observe the following precautions when working on the starting system:

(a) *Excessive cranking of the starter motor can overheat it and cause serious damage. Never operate the starter motor for more than 15 seconds at a time without pausing to allow it to cool for at least two minutes. Excessive starter operation will also risk unburned fuel collecting in the catalytic converter, causing it to overheat when the engine does start.*

(b) *The starter is connected directly to the battery and could arc or cause a fire if mishandled, overloaded or shorted to ground.*

12.5 To remove the brushes from the voltage regulator/brush holder, detach the rubber plugs from the two brush lead screws and remove the both screws (arrows)

12.9 Before installing the voltage regulator/brush holder, insert a paper clip as shown to hold the brushes in place during installation - after installation, simply pull the paper clip out (new brushes already have a pin installed to ease installation)

(c) *Always detach the lead from the negative terminal of the battery before working on the starting system (see Section 1).*

14 Starting system - testing

Note: *Before troubleshooting a starter malfunction, make sure that the battery is fully-charged, and the alarm system is not activated.*

1 If the starter motor does not operate all, make sure that, on automatic transmission models, the selector lever is in Park or Neutral.

2 Make sure that the battery is fully-charged and that all leads, both at the battery and starter solenoid terminals, are clean and secure.

3 If the starter motor spins but the engine

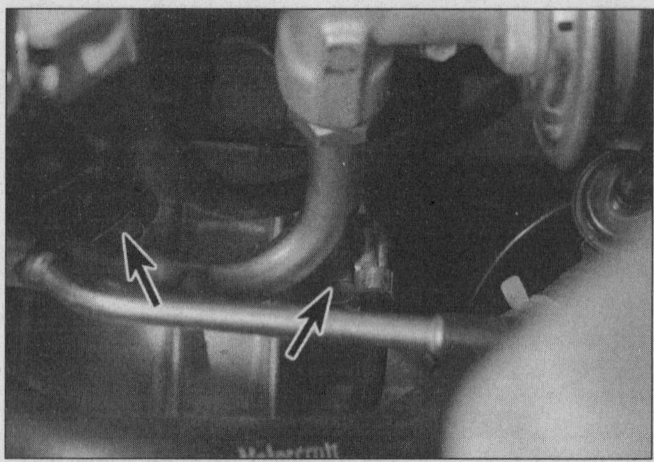

15.3 Unscrew the upper two starter motor mounting bolts (arrows) from above (four-cylinder models)

15.6 Disconnect the starter motor wiring (A), then remove the remaining mounting bolts (B) and remove the starter motor from under the vehicle (four-cylinder models)

is not cranking, the overrunning clutch or (when applicable) the reduction gears in the starter motor may be slipping, in which case the starter motor must be overhauled or replaced. (Other possibilities are that the starter motor mounting bolts are very loose or that teeth are missing from the flywheel/driveplate ring gear.)

4 If, when the switch is actuated, the starter motor does not operate at all but the solenoid clicks, then the problem lies with either the battery, the main solenoid contacts, or the starter motor itself (or the engine is seized).

5 If a distinct click cannot be heard from the solenoid when the switch is actuated, the battery is faulty or the solenoid itself is defective.

6 To check the solenoid, connect a fused jumper lead between the battery (+) and the ignition switch terminal (the small terminal) on the solenoid. If the starter motor now operates, the solenoid is good, and the problem is in the ignition switch, selector lever position sensor (automatic transmission) or in the wiring.

7 If the starter motor still does not operate, remove it (see Section 15). The brushes and commutator may be checked (see Section 16), but if the fault persists, the motor should be replaced or taken to a dealership service department or a qualified electrical shop for testing and repair.

8 If the starter motor cranks the engine at an abnormally-slow speed, first make sure that the battery is fully charged and that all terminal connections are clean and tight. If the engine is partially seized, or has the wrong viscosity oil in it, it will crank slowly.

9 Run the engine until normal operating temperature is reached, then switch it off and disable the ignition system by disconnecting the ignition coil's primary ignition electrical connector. Also, remove fuse 14 to disconnect the fuel pump.

10 Connect a voltmeter positive lead to the battery positive terminal, and connect the negative lead to the negative terminal.

11 Crank the engine, and note the voltmeter reading as soon as a steady value is indicated. Do not allow the starter motor to turn for more than 15 seconds at a time. A reading of 10.5 volts or more, with the starter motor turning at normal cranking speed, is normal. If the reading is 10.5 volts or more but the cranking speed is slow, the solenoid contacts are burned, the motor is faulty, or there is a bad connection. If the reading is less than 10.5 volts and the cranking speed is slow, the starter motor is faulty, excessive resistance is present in the starting circuit or there is a problem with the battery.

15 Starter motor - removal and installation

Four-cylinder models

Refer to illustrations 15.3 and 15.6

1 Disconnect the cable from the negative battery terminal (see Section 1).

2 Remove the air cleaner and mass airflow sensor (see Chapter 4).

3 Unscrew the upper two starter motor mounting bolts, noting that one also secures an engine/transaxle ground wire **(see illustration)**.

4 Raise the front of the vehicle, and support it securely on jackstands. **Warning**: *Do not place any part of your body under a vehicle when it's supported only by a jack!*

5 Unscrew the nuts to disconnect the wiring from the starter/solenoid terminals.

6 Remove the remaining starter motor mounting bolt **(see illustration)**. Remove the starter.

7 Installation is the reverse of the removal procedure. Tighten the bolts to the torque listed in this Chapter's Specifications.

V6 models

Refer to illustration 15.11

8 Disconnect the cable from the negative battery terminal (see Section 1).

15.11 On V6 models, disconnect the starter electrical connectors and support bracket (arrows)

9 Remove the air cleaner and air cleaner mounting bracket.

10 Raise the front of the vehicle and support it securely on jackstands.

11 Disconnect the starter motor electrical connectors. Also remove the two nuts and bolt securing the support bracket to the starter motor and transaxle housing **(see illustration)**. Remove the bracket.

12 On models equipped with an automatic transaxle, remove the shift cable bracket from the transaxle housing and disconnect the cable from the transaxle.

13 Remove the fuel lines from the fuel line support bracket located on the accelerator cable mounting bracket. Remove the fuel line support bracket.

14 Remove the two starter motor mounting bolts from the top of the starter motor. Disengage the starter motor from the alignment pins on the transaxle housing and remove the starter.

15 Installation is the reverse of removal. Tighten the fasteners to the torque listed in this Chapter's Specifications.

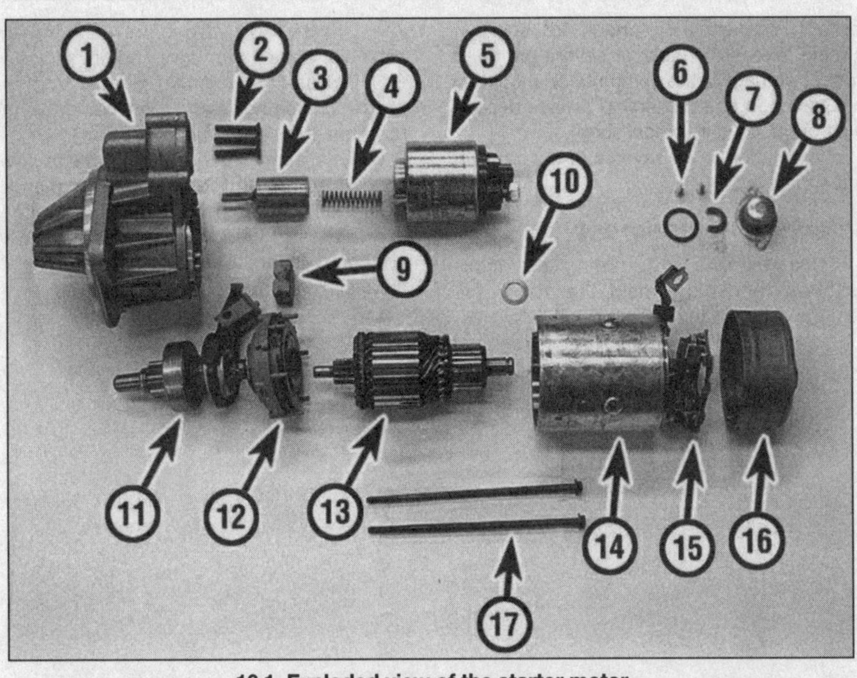

16.1 Exploded view of the starter motor

1 *Drive end housing*
2 *Solenoid screws*
3 *Solenoid switch plunger*
4 *Spring*
5 *Solenoid switch*
6 *Dust cap seal and screws*
7 *Circlip*
8 *Dust cover cap*
9 *Rubber sealing block*
10 *Armature thrust washer*
11 *Drive assembly and fork lever*
12 *Planetary drive*
13 *Armature*
14 *Pole housing*
15 *Field coil*
16 *Commutator end cover*
17 *Through-bolts*

16.2a Remove the two screws to release the end cap. Withdraw the gasket and pry out the C-clip, noting any shims installed to control armature endplay

16.2b Remove the two through-bolts . . .

16 Starter motor - brush and solenoid replacement

Refer to illustrations 16.1, 16.2a, 16.2b, 16.2c 16.2d, 16.2e and 16.2f

1 Remove the starter motor from the vehicle (see Section 16) **(see illustration)**.

Brush replacement

2 Remove the brushes as shown **(see illustrations)**.

3 In some cases, the brushes will have wear limit marks, in the form of a groove etched along one face of each brush. If the brushes are worn down to these marks, they must be replaced. If no marks are provided, measure the length of each brush, and compare it with the minimum length given in this Chapter's Specifications. If any brush is worn below this limit, replace the brushes as a set. If the brushes are still serviceable, clean them with a cloth moistened with electrical contact cleaner. Verify that the spring pressure is equal for all brushes, and holds the brushes securely against the commutator. If in doubt about the condition of the brushes and springs, compare them with new components.

4 Clean the commutator with electrical

16.2c . . . and withdraw the end housing or cap

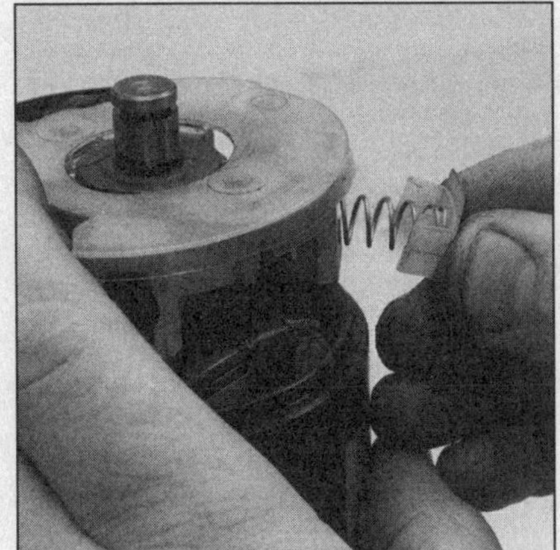

16.2d Unclip the brush holders and springs

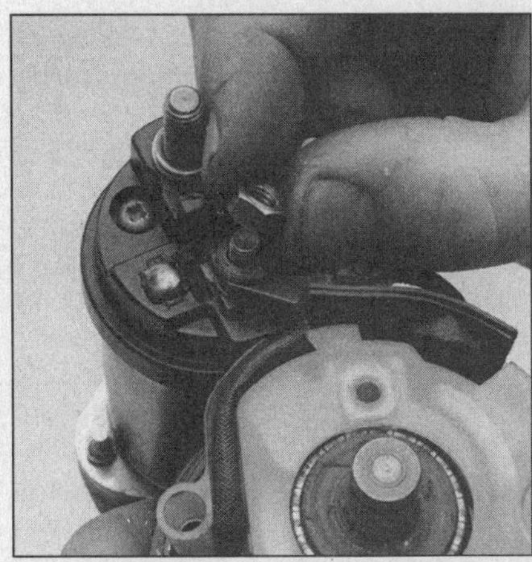

16.2e Unscrew the nut securing the solenoid link . . .

16.2f . . . and withdraw the holder and brushes

contact cleaner, then check for scoring, burning, excessive wear or severe pitting. If worn or damaged, the commutator should be reconditioned at a dealership service department or qualified electrical shop.

5 Installation is the reverse of the removal procedure.

Solenoid replacement

6 Unscrew the nut, noting the lock-washer(s), and disconnect the motor link from the solenoid terminal.

7 Unscrew the two bolts securing the solenoid to the motor drive end housing.

8 Release the solenoid plunger from the starter engaging lever, then withdraw the solenoid, noting the spring.

9 Installation is the reverse of the removal procedure. Clean the solenoid, its plunger and the motor/solenoid mating surfaces carefully, and lubricate the plunger/starter engaging lever surfaces with a smear of grease.

Chapter 6
Emissions and engine control systems

Contents

Specifications

Crankshaft position sensor

Resistance	200 to 450 ohms

Camshaft position sensor

Resistance	200 to 900 ohms

Intake air temperature sensor

Resistance:	
At 68 degrees F	37.30 kOhms ± 15%
At 194 degrees F	3.84 kOhms ± 15%

Throttle position sensor

Resistance (see text)	400 to 6000 ohms

Power steering pressure switch

Operating pressures	
Contacts open - infinite resistance	456 to 460 psi
Contacts close - 0 to 2.5 ohms resistance	Between 196 and 348 psi

Charcoal canister-purge solenoid valve

Resistance	50 to 120 ohms

Pulse-air solenoid valve

Resistance	50 to 120 ohms

Torque Specifications

	Ft-lbs (unless otherwise indicated)
Camshaft position sensor screw	
Four-cylinder	
1995 through 1997	156 to 204 in-lbs
1998 and later	66 in-lbs.
V6	
1995 through 1997	71 to 106 in-lbs
1998 and later	84 in-lbs

6

Torque Specifications (continued)	Ft-lbs (unless otherwise indicated)
Intake air temperature sensor	17
Oxygen sensor	44
Exhaust Gas Recirculation (EGR) system components:	
Four-cylinder	
Valve-mounting bolts	62 to 97 in-lbs
Valve to exhaust manifold and coil bracket bolts	62 to 97 in-lbs
Valve to exhaust manifold tube nuts	44
V6	
Valve mounting bolts	15 to 22
Valve to exhaust manifold tube nuts	26 to 33
Air injection system components:	
Filter housing mounting bolt	35
Piping-to-exhaust manifold sleeve nuts	24
Idle air control valve	
Four-cylinder	
1995 through 1997	71 to 97 in-lbs
1998 and later	84 in-lbs
V6	
1995 through 1997	71 to 106 in-lbs
1998 and later	84 in-lbs
Engine coolant temperature sensor	
Four-cylinder	
1995 through 1997	89 to 120 in-lbs
1998 and later	156 in-lbs
V6	
1995 through 1997	120 to 168 in-lbs
1998 and later	17
Throttle position sensor-to-throttle body screws	27 in-lbs
Knock sensor	
Four-cylinder	
1995 through 1997	132 to 180 in-lbs
1998 and later	177 in-lbs
V6	
1995 through 1997	21 to 29
1998 and later	40

1 General information

To minimize pollution of the atmosphere from incompletely-burned and evaporating gases, and to maintain good driveability and fuel economy, a number of emission control systems are used on these vehicles. They include the following:

(a) *The engine management system (comprising both fuel and ignition sub-systems) itself.*
(b) *Positive Crankcase Ventilation (PCV) system.*
(c) *Evaporative Emissions Control (EVAP) system.*
(d) *Exhaust Gas Recirculation (EGR) system.*
(e) *Catalytic converter.*

The Sections of this Chapter include general descriptions, checking procedures within the scope of the home mechanic, and component replacement procedures (when possible) for each of the systems listed above.

Before assuming an emissions control system is malfunctioning, check the fuel and ignition systems carefully (see Chapters 4 and 5). The diagnosis of some emission control devices requires specialized tools, equipment and training. If checking and servicing become too difficult, or if a procedure is beyond the scope of your skills, consult your dealer service department or other specialist.

This doesn't mean, however, that emission control systems are particularly difficult to maintain and repair. You can quickly and easily perform many checks, and do most of the regular maintenance, at home with common tune-up and hand tools. **Note:** *The most frequent cause of emissions problems is simply a loose or broken electrical connector or vacuum hose, so always check the electrical connectors and vacuum hoses first.*

Pay close attention to any special precautions outlined in this Chapter. It should be noted that the illustrations of the various systems may not exactly match the system installed on your vehicle, due to changes made by the manufacturer during production or from year-to-year.

Vehicles sold in some areas will carry a Vehicle Emissions Control Information (VECI) label, and a vacuum hose diagram located in the engine compartment. These contain important specifications and setting procedures for the various emissions control systems, with the vacuum hose diagram identifying emissions control components. When servicing the engine or emissions systems, the VECI label in your particular vehicle should always be checked for up-to-date information.

2 Electronic control system - description and precautions

Description

The EEC-IV engine management system controls fuel injection by means of a microcomputer known as the PCM (Powertrain control module).

The PCM receives signals from various sensors, which monitor changing engine operating conditions such as intake air mass (i.e., intake air volume and temperature), coolant temperature, engine speed, acceleration/deceleration, exhaust oxygen content, etc. These signals are used by the PCM to determine the correct injection duration.

The system is analogous to the central nervous system in the human body - the sensors (nerve endings) constantly relay signals to the PCM (brain), which processes the data and, if necessary, sends out a command to change the operating parameters of the engine (body) by means of the actuators (muscles).

Here's a specific example of how one portion of this system operates. An oxygen sensor, located in the exhaust downpipe, constantly monitors the oxygen content of the exhaust gas. If the percentage of oxygen in the exhaust gas is incorrect, an electrical signal is sent to the PCM. The PCM processes this information, and then sends a command to the fuel injection system, telling it to change the air/fuel mixture; the end result is an air/fuel mixture ratio which is constantly maintained at a predetermined ratio, regardless of driving conditions. This happens in a fraction of a second, and goes on almost all the time while the engine is running - the exceptions are that the PCM cuts out the system and runs the engine on values pre-programmed ("mapped") into its memory both while the oxygen sensor is reaching its normal operating temperature after the engine has been started from cold, and when the throttle is fully open for full acceleration.

In the event of a sensor malfunction, a back-up circuit will take over, to provide driveability until the problem is identified and fixed.

Precautions

(a) *Always disconnect the power by uncoupling the battery terminals* - see Section 1 of Chapter 5 - *before removing any of the electronic control system's electrical connectors.*
(b) *When installing a battery, be particularly careful to avoid reversing the positive and negative battery leads.*
(c) *Do not subject any components of the system (especially the PCM) to severe impact during removal or installation.*
(d) *Do not be careless during troubleshooting. Even slight terminal contact can invalidate a testing procedure, and damage one of the numerous transistor circuits.*
(e) *Never attempt to work on the PCM, to test it (with any kind of test equipment), or to open its cover.*
(f) *If you are inspecting electronic control system components during rainy weather, make sure that water does not enter any part. When washing the engine compartment, do not spray these parts or their electrical connectors with water.*

3 Diagnosis system - general information

General

The various components of the fuel, ignition and emissions control systems (not forgetting the same PCM's control of subsystems such as the radiator cooling fan, air conditioning and automatic transaxle, where appropriate) are so closely interlinked that diagnosis of a fault in any one component is virtually impossible using traditional methods. Working on simpler systems in the past, the experienced mechanic may well have been able to use personal skill and knowledge immediately to pinpoint the cause of a fault, or quickly to isolate the fault, by elimination; however, with an engine management system integrated to this degree, this is not likely to be possible in most instances, because of the number of symptoms that could arise from even a minor fault.

So that the causes of faults can be quickly and accurately traced and rectified, the PCM is provided with a built-in self-diagnosis facility, which detects malfunctions in the system's components. When a fault occurs, three things happen: the PCM identifies the fault, stores a corresponding code in its memory, and (in most cases) runs the system using back-up values pre-programmed ("mapped") into its memory; some form of driveability is thus maintained, to enable the vehicle to be driven to a garage for attention.

Any faults that may have occurred are indicated in the form of three-digit codes when the system is connected (via the built-in diagnosis or self-test connectors, as appropriate) to special diagnostic equipment - this points the user in the direction of the faulty circuit, so that further tests can pinpoint the exact location of the fault.

Given below is the procedure that would be followed by a technician to trace a fault from scratch. Should your vehicle's engine management system develop a fault, read through the procedure and decide how much you can attempt, depending on your skill and experience and the equipment available to you, or whether it would be simpler to have the vehicle attended to by your local dealer. If you are concerned about the apparent complexity of the system, however, remember the comments made in the fourth paragraph of Section 1 of this Chapter; the preliminary checks require nothing but care, patience and a few minor items of equipment, and may well eliminate the majority of faults.

(a) Preliminary checks
*(b) Fault code read-out **
*(c) Check ignition timing and base idle speed. Recheck fault codes to establish whether fault has been cured or not **
*(d) Carry out basic check of ignition system components. Recheck fault codes to establish whether fault has been cured or not **
*(e) Carry out basic check of fuel system components. Recheck fault codes to establish whether fault has been cured or not **
*(f) If fault is still not located, carry out system test **

Note: *Operations marked with an asterisk require special test equipment.*

Preliminary checks

Refer to illustration 3.11

Note: *When carrying out these checks to trace a fault, remember that if the fault has appeared only a short time after any part of the vehicle has been serviced or overhauled, the first place to check is where that work was carried out, however unrelated it may appear, to ensure that no carelessly-reinstalled components are causing the problem.*

If you are tracing the cause of a "partial" engine fault, such as lack of performance, in addition to the checks outlined below, check the compression pressures (see Part A of Chapter 2) and bear in mind the possibility that one of the hydraulic tappets might be faulty, producing an incorrect valve clearance. Check also that the fuel filter has been replaced at the recommended intervals.

If the system appears completely dead, remember the possibility that the alarm/inhibitor system may be responsible.

1 The first check for anyone without special test equipment is to switch on the ignition, and to listen for the fuel pump (the sound of an electric motor running, audible from beneath the rear seats); assuming there is sufficient fuel in the tank, the pump should start and run for approximately one or two seconds, then stop, each time the ignition is switched on. If the pump runs continuously all the time the ignition is switched on, the electronic control system is running in the back-up (or "limp-home") mode referred to by the manufacturer as "Limited Operation Strategy" (LOS). This almost certainly indicates a fault in the PCM itself, and the vehicle should therefore be taken to a dealer for a full test of the complete system using the correct diagnostic equipment; do not waste time trying to test the system without such facilities.

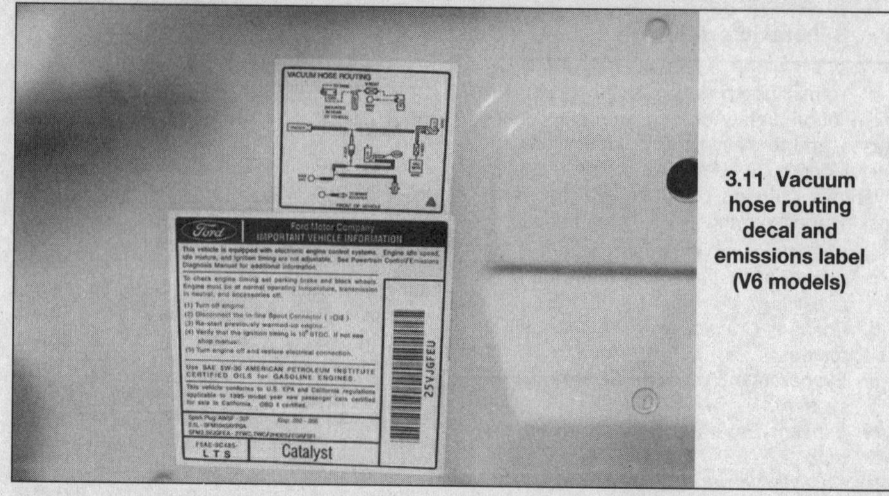

3.11 Vacuum hose routing decal and emissions label (V6 models)

2 If the fuel pump is working correctly (or not at all), a considerable amount of troubleshooting is still possible without special test equipment. Start the checking procedure as follows.

3 Open the hood and check the condition of the battery connections - remake the connections or replace the leads if a fault is found (Chapter 5). Use the same techniques to ensure that all ground points in the engine compartment provide good electrical contact through clean, metal-to-metal joints, and that all are securely fastened. (In addition to the ground connection at the engine lifting eye and that from the transaxle to the body/battery, there is one ground connection behind each headlight assembly, and one below the power steering fluid reservoir.)

4 Referring to the information given in Chapter 12 and in the wiring diagrams at the back of this manual, check that all fuses protecting the circuits related to the engine management system are in good condition. Install new fuses if required; while you are there, check that all relays are securely plugged into their sockets.

5 Next work methodically around the engine compartment, checking all visible wiring, and the connections between sections of the wiring harness. What you are looking for at this stage is wiring that is obviously damaged by chafing against sharp edges, or against moving suspension/transaxle components and/or the drivebelt, by being trapped or crushed between carelessly-reinstalled components, or melted by being forced into contact with hot engine castings, coolant or EGR pipes, etc. In almost all cases, damage of this sort is caused in the first instance by incorrect routing on reassembly after previous work has been carried out (see the note at the beginning of this sub-Section).

6 Obviously wires can break or short together inside the insulation so that no visible evidence betrays the fault, but this usually only occurs where the wiring harness has been incorrectly routed so that it is stretched taut or kinked sharply; either of these conditions should be obvious on even a casual inspection. If this is thought to have happened and the fault proves elusive, the suspect section of wiring should be checked very carefully during the more detailed checks which follow.

7 Depending on the extent of the problem, damaged wiring may be repaired by rejoining the break or splicing-in a new length of wire, using solder to ensure a good connection, and remaking the insulation with adhesive insulating tape or heat-shrink tubing, as desired. If the damage is extensive, given the implications for the vehicle's future reliability, the best long-term answer may well be to replace that entire section of the harness, however expensive this may appear.

8 When the actual damage has been repaired, ensure that the wiring harness is rerouted correctly, so that it is clear of other components, is not stretched or kinked, and is secured out of harm's way using the plastic clips, guides and ties provided.

9 Check all electrical connectors, ensuring that they are clean, securely fastened, and that each is locked by its plastic tabs or wire clip, as appropriate. If any connector shows external signs of corrosion (accumulations of white or green deposits, or streaks of "rust"), or if any is thought to be dirty, it must be disconnected and cleaned using electrical contact cleaner. If the connector pins are severely corroded, the connector must be replaced; note that this may mean the replacement of that entire section of the harness - see your local dealer for details.

10 If the cleaner completely removes the corrosion to leave the connector in a satisfactory condition, it would be wise to pack the connector with a suitable material which will exclude dirt and moisture, and prevent the corrosion from occurring again; a dealer may be able to recommend a suitable product. **Note:** *The system's connectors use gold-plated pins, which must **not** be mixed with the older tin-plated types (readily identifiable from the different color) if a component is replaced, nor must the lithium grease previously used to protect tin-plated pins be used*

on gold-plated connectors.

11 Working methodically around the engine compartment, check carefully that all vacuum hoses and pipes are securely fastened and correctly routed, with no signs of cracks, splits or deterioration to cause air leaks, or of hoses that are trapped, kinked, or bent sharply enough to restrict air flow **(see illustration)**. Check with particular care at all connections and sharp bends, and replace any damaged or deformed lengths of hose.

12 Working from the fuel tank, via the filter, to the fuel rail (and including the feed and return), check the fuel lines, and replace any that are found to be leaking, trapped or kinked.

13 Check that the accelerator cable is correctly secured and adjusted; replace the cable if there is any doubt about its condition, or if it appears to be stiff or jerky in operation. Refer to the relevant Sections of Chapter 4 for further information, if required.

14 If there is any doubt about the operation of the throttle, remove the plenum chamber from the throttle body, and check that the throttle valve moves smoothly and easily from the fully-closed to the fully-open position and back again, as an assistant depresses the accelerator pedal. If the valve shows any sign of stiffness, sticking or otherwise-inhibited movement (and the accelerator cable is known from the previous check to be in good condition), spray the throttle linkage with penetrating lubricant, allow time for it to work, and repeat the check; if no improvement is obtained, the complete throttle body must be replaced (Chapter 4).

15 Unclip the air cleaner cover, and check that the air filter element and the crankcase ventilation system filter are not clogged or soaked. (A clogged air filter will obstruct the intake air flow, causing a noticeable effect on engine performance; a clogged crankcase ventilation system filter will inhibit crankcase "breathing"). Replace or clean the filter(s) as appropriate; refer to the relevant Sections of Chapter 1 for further information, if required. Before installation the air cleaner cover, check that the air intake (located under the front left-hand fender, opening behind the direction indicator/headlight assembly) is clear. It should be possible to blow through the intake, or to probe it (carefully) as far as the rear of the direction indicator light.

16 Start the engine and allow it to idle.

Note: *Working in the engine compartment while the engine is running requires great care if the risk of personal injury is to be avoided; among the dangers are burns from contact with hot components, or contact with moving components such as the radiator cooling fan or the drivebelt. Refer to "Safety first!" at the front of this manual before starting, and ensure that your hands, and long hair or loose clothing, are kept well clear of hot or moving components at all times.*

17 Working from the air intake junction at the inner fender panel, via the air cleaner assembly and mass airflow sensor, to the resonator, plenum chamber, throttle body and intake manifold (and including the various vacuum hoses and pipes connected to these), check for air leaks. Usually, these will be revealed by sucking or hissing noises, but minor leaks may be traced by spraying a solution of soapy water on to the suspect fitting; if a leak exists, it will be shown by the change in engine note and the accompanying air bubbles (or sucking-in of the liquid, depending on the pressure difference at that point). If a leak is found at any point, tighten the fastening clamp and/or replace the faulty components, as applicable.

18 Similarly, work from the cylinder head, via the manifold (and not forgetting the related EGR and pulse-air system components) to the tailpipe, to check that the exhaust system is free from leaks. The simplest way of doing this, if the vehicle can be raised and supported safely and with complete security while the check is made, is to temporarily block the tailpipe while listening for the sound of escaping exhaust gases; any leak should be evident. If a leak is found at any point, tighten the fastening clamp bolts and/or nuts, replace the gasket, and/or replace the faulty section of the system, as necessary, to seal the leak.

19 It is possible to make a further check of the electrical connections by wiggling each electrical connector of the system in turn as the engine is idling; a faulty connector will be immediately evident from the engine's response as contact is broken and remade. A faulty connector should be replaced to ensure the future reliability of the system; note that this may mean the replacement of that entire section of the harness - see your local dealer for details.

20 Switch off the engine. If the fault is not yet identified, the next step is to check the ignition voltages, using an engine analyzer with an oscilloscope - without such equipment, the only tests possible are to remove and check each spark plug in turn, to check the spark plug (HT) lead connections and resistances, and to check the connections and resistances of the ignition coil. Refer to the relevant Sections of Chapters 1 and 5.

21 The final step in these preliminary checks would be to use an exhaust gas analyzer to measure the CO level at the exhaust tailpipe. This check cannot be made without special test equipment - see your local dealer for details.

Fault code read-out

Refer to illustrations 3.26 and 3.45

Note: *The fault codes listed in this section apply to 1995 models only. 1996 and later models are equipped with the second generation On-Board Diagnostic system (OBD-II). OBD-II fault codes are different than those listed and obtainable only with specialized equipment.*

22 As noted in the general comments at the beginning of this Section, the preliminary checks outlined above should eliminate the majority of faults from the engine management system. If the fault is not yet identified, the next step is to connect a fault code reader to the PCM, so that its self-diagnosis facility can be used to identify the faulty part of the system; further tests can then be made to identify the exact cause of the fault.

23 In their basic form, fault code readers are simply hand-held electronic devices, which take data stored within an PCM's memory and display it when required as two- or three-digit fault codes. The more sophisticated versions now available can also control sensors and actuators, to provide more effective testing; some can store information, so that a road test can be carried out, and any faults encountered during the test can be displayed afterwards.

24 The manufacturer specifies the use of their STAR (Self-Test Automatic Readout) tester; most dealers should have such equipment, and the staff trained to use it effectively. The only alternatives are as follows:

(a) *To obtain one of those proprietary readers which can interpret EEC-IV three-digit codes - at present, such readers are too expensive for the DIY enthusiast, but are becoming more popular with smaller specialist garages.*

(b) *To use an analog voltmeter, whereby the stored codes are displayed as sweeps of the voltmeter needle. This option limits the operator to a read-out of any codes stored - i.e., there is no control of sensors and/or actuators - but can still be useful in pinpointing the faulty part of the engine management system. The display is interpreted as follows. Each code (whether fault code or command/separator) is marked by a three-to-four second pause - code "538" would therefore be shown as long (3 to 4 seconds) pause, five fast sweeps of the needle, slight (1 second) pause, three fast sweeps, slight pause, eight fast sweeps, long pause.*

(c) *Owners without access to such equipment must take the vehicle to a dealer, or to an expert who has similar equipment and the skill to use it.*

25 Because of the variations in the design of fault code readers, it is not possible to give exact details of the sequence of tests; the manufacturer's instructions must be followed, in conjunction with the codes given below. The following ten paragraphs outline the procedure to be followed using a version of the dealer STAR tester, to illustrate the general principles, as well as notes to guide the owner using only a voltmeter.

26 The vehicle must be prepared by applying the parking brake, switching off the air conditioning (if equipped) and any other electrical loads (lights, heated rear window, etc.), then selecting neutral (manual transaxle) or the "P" position (automatic transaxle). Where the engine is required to be running, it must be fully warmed-up to normal operating temperature before the test is started. Using any adapters required, connect the fault code

reader to the system via the (triangular, three-pin) self-test connector on the right-hand end of the engine compartment firewall **(see illustration)**. If a voltmeter is being used, connect its positive lead to the battery positive terminal, and its negative lead to the self-test connector's output terminal, pin 17. Have a pen and paper ready to write down the codes displayed.

27 Set the tester in operation. For the dealer STAR tester, a display check will be carried out and the test mode requirements must be entered. If a voltmeter is being used, connect a spare length of wire to ground the self-test connector's input terminal, pin 48. Be very careful to ensure that you ground the correct terminal - the one with the white/green wire. The first part of the test starts, with the ignition switched on, but with the engine off. On pressing the "Mem/test" button, the tester displays "TEST" and the ready code "000", followed by a command code "010" - the accelerator pedal must be fully depressed within 10 seconds of the command code appearing, or fault codes "576" or "577" will appear when they are called up later. If a voltmeter is being used, code "000" will not appear (except perhaps as a flicker of the needle) and "010" will appear as a single sweep - to ensure correct interpretation of the display, watch carefully for the interval between the end of one code and the beginning of the next, otherwise you will become confused and misinterpret the read-out.

28 The tester will then display the codes for any faults in the system at the time of the test. Each code is repeated once; if no faults are present, code "111" will be displayed. If a voltmeter is being used, the pause between repetitions will vary according to the equipment in use and the number of faults in the system, but was found to be approximately 3 to 4 seconds - it may be necessary to start again, and to repeat the read-out until you are familiar with what you are seeing.

29 Next the tester will display code "010" (now acting as a separator), followed by the codes for any faults stored in the PCM's memory; if no faults were stored, code "111" will be displayed.

30 When prompted by the tester, the operator must next depress the accelerator pedal fully; the tester then checks several actuators. Further test modes include a "wiggle test" facility, whereby the operator can check the various connectors as described in paragraph 19 above (in this case, any fault will be logged and the appropriate code will be displayed), a facility for recalling codes displayed, and a means for clearing the PCM's memory at the end of the test procedure when any faults have been rectified.

31 The next step when using the STAR tester is to conduct a test with the engine running. With the tester set in operation (see paragraph 26 above) the engine is started and allowed to idle. On pressing the "Mem/test" button, the tester displays "TEST", followed by one of two codes, as follows.

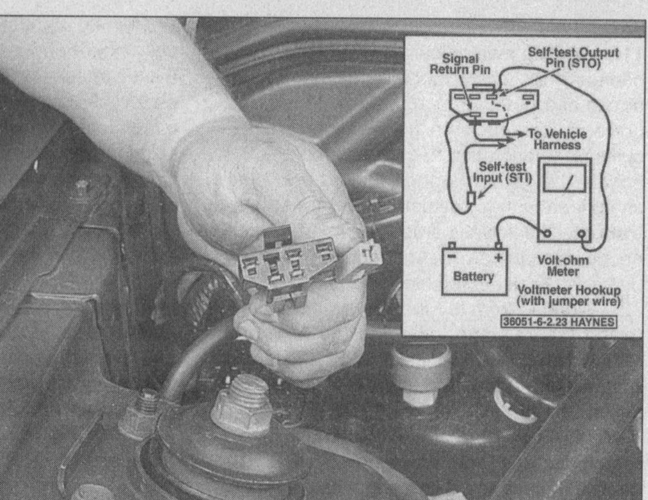

3.26 Typical location of diagnostic Test connector - to read a stored trouble code, connect a voltmeter to the Diagnostic Test connector, then connect a jumper wire between the self test input and pin number 2 on the larger connector - turn the ignition switch ON and watch the voltmeter needle or CHECK ENGINE light

32 If warning code "998" appears, followed by the appropriate fault code, switch off and check as indicated the coolant temperature sensor, the intake air temperature sensor, the mass airflow sensor, the throttle position sensor and/or their related circuits, then restart the test procedure.

33 If command code "020" appears, carry out the following procedure within ten seconds:

(a) Depress the brake pedal fully.
(b) Turn the steering to full-lock (either way) and center it again, to produce a signal from the power steering pressure switch - if no signal is sent, fault code "521" will be displayed.
(c) If automatic transaxle is installed, switch the overdrive cancel button on and off, then do the same for the "Economy/Sport" mode switch.
(d) Wait for separator code "010" to be displayed, then within 10 seconds, depress the accelerator pedal fully, increasing engine speed rapidly above 3000 rpm - release the pedal.

34 Any faults found in the system will be logged and displayed. Each code is repeated once; if no faults are present, code "111" will be displayed.

35 When the codes have been displayed for all faults logged, the PCM enters its "Service Adjustment Program", as follows:

(a) The program lasts for 2 minutes.
(b) The idle speed control valve is deactivated, and the idle speed is set to its pre-programmed (unregulated) value. If the appropriate equipment is connected, the base idle speed can be checked (note, however, that it is not adjustable).
(c) The ignition timing can be checked if a timing light is connected (note, however, that it is not adjustable).
(d) Pressing the accelerator pedal fully at any time during this period will execute a cylinder balance test. Each injector in turn is switched off, and the corresponding decrease in engine speed is logged - code "090" will be displayed if the test is successful.
(e) At the end of the 2 minutes, the completion of the program is shown by the engine speed briefly rising, then returning to normal idling speed as the idle speed control valve is reactivated.

36 As with the engine-off test, further test modes include a "wiggle test" facility, whereby the operator can check the various connectors as described in paragraph 19 above (in this case, any fault will be logged and the appropriate code will be displayed), a facility for recalling codes displayed, and a means for clearing the PCM's memory at the end of the test procedure when any faults have been rectified. If equipment other than the STAR tester is used, the PCM's memory can be cleared by disconnecting the battery - if this is not done, the code will reappear with any other codes in the event of subsequent trouble, but remember that other systems with memory (such as the clock and audio equipment) will also be affected. Should it become necessary to disconnect the battery during work on any other part of the vehicle, first check to see if any fault codes have been logged.

37 Given below are the possible codes, their meanings, and where relevant, the action to be taken as a result of a code being displayed.

Code	Circuit or system	Corrective action
000	Ready for test	
010	Command/separator code	Depress accelerator pedal fully, then release
020	Command code	Depress brake pedal fully, then release
10	Cylinder No. 1 low	During cylinder balance test
20	Cylinder No. 2 low	During cylinder balance test
30	Cylinder No. 3 low	During cylinder balance test
40	Cylinder No. 4 low	During cylinder balance test
90	Cylinder balance test successful	
111	No faults found	
112 to 114	Intake air temperature sensor	Check component (Section 4 of this Chapter)
116 to 118	Coolant temperature sensor - normal operating temperature not reached	If fault still exists on reaching normal operating temperature, check component (Chapter 3)
121 to 125	Throttle position sensor	Check component (Section 4 of this Chapter)
129	Incorrect response from air mass meter while conducting test	Repeat test
136, 137	Oxygen sensor	Check component (Section 4 of this Chapter)
139	Oxygen sensor	Check component (Section 4 of this Chapter)
144	Oxygen sensor	Check component (Section 4 of this Chapter)
157 to 159	Mass airflow sensor	Check component (Section 4 of this Chapter)
167	Incorrect response from throttle potentiometer while conducting test	Repeat test
171	Oxygen sensor	Check component (Section 4 of this Chapter)
172	Oxygen sensor - mixture too weak	Check component (Section 4 of this Chapter)
173	Oxygen sensor - mixture too rich	Check component (Section 4 of this Chapter)
174, 175	Oxygen sensor	Check component (Section 4 of this Chapter)
176	Oxygen sensor - mixture too weak	Check component (Section 4 of this Chapter)
177	Oxygen sensor - mixture too rich	Check component (Section 4 of this Chapter)
178	Oxygen sensor	Check component (Section 4 of this Chapter)
179	Fuel system - mixture too weak	Check EGR valve (Section 6 of this Chapter)
181	Fuel system - mixture too rich	Check EGR valve (Section 6 of this Chapter)
182	Idle mixture too weak	Check idle speed control valve (Chapter 4)
183	Idle mixture too rich	If mixture OK, check fuel system (see below)
184, 185	Mass airflow sensor	Check component (Section 4 of this Chapter)
186	Injector opening time (pulse width) too long	Carry out system test (see below)
187	Injector opening time (pulse width) too short	Carry out system test (see below)
188	Oxygen sensor - mixture too weak	Check component (Section 4 of this Chapter)
189	Oxygen sensor - mixture too rich	Check component (Section 4 of this Chapter)
191	Idle mixture too weak	Check EGR valve (Section 6 of this Chapter) and idle speed control valve (Chapter 4)
192	Idle mixture too rich	Check EGR valve (Section 6 of this Chapter) and idle speed control valve (Chapter 4)
194, 195	Oxygen sensor	Check component (Section 4 of this Chapter)

Code	Circuit or system	Corrective action
211	No ignition signal to PCM	Carry out system test (see below)
212	Tachometer circuit	Carry out system test (see below)
213	No ignition signal from PCM	Carry out system test (see below)
214	Camshaft position sensor	Check component (Section 4 of this Chapter)
215 to 217	Ignition coil	Carry out system test (see below)
218, 222	Tachometer circuit	Carry out system test (see below)
226	PCM/ignition module pulse	Carry out system test (see below)
227	Crankshaft speed/position sensor	Check component (Chapter 5)
228	Ignition module/ignition coil winding 1	Carry out system test (see below)
229	Ignition module/ignition coil winding 2	Carry out system test (see below)
231	Ignition module/ignition coil winding 3	Carry out system test (see below)
232	Ignition coil primary windings	Carry out system test (see below)
233	Ignition module	Carry out system test (see below)
234 to 237	Ignition coil primary windings	Carry out system test (see below)
238	Ignition module/ignition coil primary windings	Carry out system test (see below)
239	No ignition signal to PCM on cranking	Carry out system test (see below)
241	Incorrect response from PCM and/or ignition module while conducting test	Repeat test
243	Ignition coil failure	Carry out system test (see below)
311 to 316	Pulse-air system	Carry out system test (see below)
326	EGR system exhaust gas pressure differential sensor	Check component (Section 6 of this Chapter)
327	EGR system exhaust gas pressure differential sensor or solenoid valve	Check components (Section 6 of this Chapter)
328	EGR system solenoid valve	Check component (Section 6 of this Chapter)
332	EGR valve not opening	Check component (Section 6 of this Chapter)
334	EGR system solenoid valve	Check component (Section 6 of this Chapter)
335	EGR system exhaust gas pressure differential sensor	Check component (Section 6 of this Chapter)
336	Exhaust gas pressure too high	Check system (Section 6 of this Chapter)
337	EGR system exhaust gas pressure differential sensor or solenoid valve	Check components (Section 6 of this Chapter)
338, 339	Coolant temperature sensor	Carry out system test (see below)
341	Service connector grounded	Disconnect connector and repeat test - reconnect on completion
411	Engine speed too low during test	Check for air leaks, then repeat test
412	Engine speed too high during test	Check for air leaks, then repeat test
413 to 416	Idle speed control valve	Check component (Chapter 4, Section 16)
452	Vehicle speed sensor	Check component (Section 4 of this Chapter)
511, 512	PCM memory	Check whether battery was disconnected, then check fuse 11 - if fault still exists, replace PCM (Section 6 of this Chapter)
513	PCM reference voltage	Carry out system test (see below)
519, 521	Power steering pressure switch not operated during test	Check component is installed and connected, then repeat test - if fault still exists, carry out system test (see below)

Code	Circuit or system	Corrective action
522, 523	Selector lever position sensor	Check component (Chapter 7, Part B)
536	Brake on/off switch not activated during test	Repeat test
538	Operator error during test	Repeat test
539	Air conditioning switched on during test	Switch off and repeat test
542, 543	Fuel pump circuit	Carry out system test (see below)
551	Idle speed control valve circuit	Carry out system test (see below)
552	Pulse-air system circuit	Carry out system test (see below)
556	Fuel pump circuit	Check fuel pump relay - if fault still exists, carry out system test (see below)
558	EGR system solenoid valve circuit	Carry out system test (see below)
563	Radiator (high-speed) electric cooling fan relay and/or circuit	Carry out system test (see below)
564	Radiator electric cooling fan relay and/or circuit	Carry out system test (see below)
565	Charcoal canister-purge solenoid valve	Check component (Section 5 of this Chapter)
573	Radiator electric cooling fan relay and/or circuit	Carry out system test (see below)
574	Radiator (high-speed) electric cooling fan relay and/or circuit	Carry out system test (see below)
575	Fuel pump and/or fuel cut-off switch circuits	Carry out system test (see below)
576, 577	Accelerator pedal not depressed fully during test procedure - automatic transaxle kickdown not activated	Repeat test
621	Automatic transaxle shift solenoid 1 circuit	Refer to Chapter 7, Part B
622	Automatic transaxle shift solenoid 2 circuit	Refer to Chapter 7, Part B
624	Automatic transaxle electronic pressure control solenoid	Refer to Chapter 7, Part B
625	Automatic transaxle electronic pressure control solenoid circuit	Refer to Chapter 7, Part B
629	Automatic transaxle torque converter clutch solenoid	Refer to Chapter 7, Part B
634	Selector lever position sensor circuit	Check component (Chapter 7, Part B)
635, 637	Automatic transaxle fluid temperature sensor	Refer to Chapter 7, Part B
639	Automatic transaxle speed sensor	Refer to Chapter 7, Part B
645	Automatic transaxle 1st speed	Refer to Chapter 7, Part B
646	Automatic transaxle 2nd speed	Refer to Chapter 7, Part B
647	Automatic transaxle 3rd speed	Refer to Chapter 7, Part B
648	Automatic transaxle 4th speed	Refer to Chapter 7, Part B
653	Automatic transaxle overdrive cancel button and "Economy/Sport" mode switch not operated during test	Repeat test
998	Warning code	Check fault(s) indicated by subsequent code(s)

Ignition timing and base idle speed check

Note: *The following procedure is a check only, essentially of the PCM. Both the ignition timing and the base idle speed are controlled by the PCM. The ignition timing is not adjustable at all; the base idle speed is set in production, and should not be altered.*

38 If the fault code read-out (with any checks resulting from it) has not eliminated the fault, the next step is to check the PCM's control of the ignition timing and the base idle speed. This task requires the use of a STAR tester (a proprietary fault code reader can be used only if it is capable of inducing the PCM to enter its "Service Adjustment Program"), coupled with an accurate tachometer and a good-quality timing light. Without this equipment, the task is not possible; the vehicle must be taken to a dealer for attention.

39 To make the check, apply the parking brake, switch off the air conditioning (if equipped) and any other electrical loads (lights, heated rear window, etc.), then select neutral (manual transaxle) or the "P" position (automatic transaxle). Start the engine, and warm it up to normal operating temperature. The radiator electric cooling fan must be running continuously while the check is made; this should be activated by the PCM, when prompted by the tester. Switch off the engine, and connect the test equipment as directed by the manufacturer - refer to paragraph 26 above for details of STAR tester connection.

40 Raise and support the front of the vehicle securely, and remove the drivebelt cover (see Chapter 1). Emphasize the two pairs of notches in the inner and outer rims of the crankshaft pulley, using white paint. Note that an ignition timing reference mark is not provided on the pulley - in the normal direction of crankshaft rotation (clockwise, seen from the right-hand side of the vehicle) the first pair of notches are irrelevant to the vehicles covered in this manual, while the second pair indicate Top Dead Center (TDC) when aligned with the rear edge of the raised mark on the oil pan; when checking the ignition timing, therefore, the (rear edge of the) oil pan mark should appear just before the TDC notches (see Part A of Chapter 2, Section 4, for further information if required).

41 Start the engine and allow it to idle. Work through the engine-running test procedure until the PCM enters its "Service Adjustment Program" - see paragraph 35 above.

42 Use the timing light to check that the timing marks appear approximately as outlined above at idle speed. Do not spend too much time on this check; if the timing appears to be incorrect, the system may have a fault, and a full system test must be carried out (see below) to establish its cause.

43 Using the tachometer, check that the base idle speed is as given in the Specifications Section of Chapter 4.

44 If the recorded speed differs significantly from the specified value, check for air leaks, as described in the preliminary checks (paragraphs 15 to 18 above), or any other faults which might cause the discrepancy.

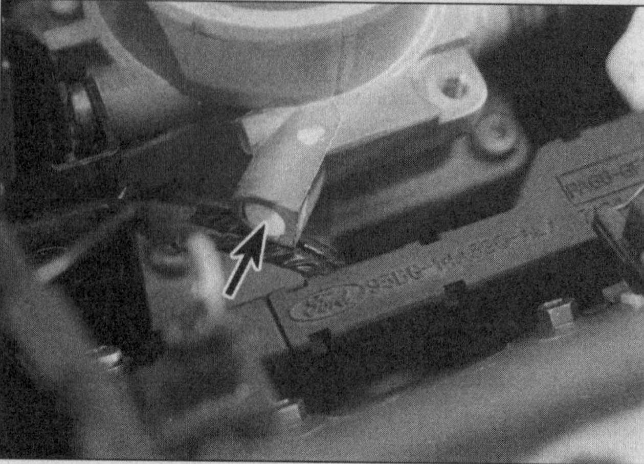

3.45 Throttle housing air bypass screw is sealed on production with a white tamperproof plug

45 The base idle speed is set in production by means of an air bypass screw (located in the front right-hand corner of the throttle body) which controls the amount of air that is allowed to pass through a bypass passage, past the throttle valve when it is fully closed in the idle position; the screw is then sealed with a white tamperproof plug **(see illustration)**. In service, the idle speed is controlled by the PCM, which has the ability to compensate for engine wear, build-up of dirt in the throttle body, and other factors which might require changes in idle speed. The air bypass screw setting should not, therefore, be altered. If any alterations are made, a blue tamperproof plug must be installed, and the engine should be allowed to idle for at least five minutes on completion, so that the PCM can re-learn its idle values.

46 When both checks have been made and the "Service Adjustment Program" is completed, follow the tester instructions to return to the fault code read-out, and establish whether the fault has been cured or not.

Basic check of ignition system

47 If the checks so far have not eliminated the fault, the next step is to carry out a basic check of the ignition system components, using an engine analyzer with an oscilloscope - without such equipment, the only tests possible are to remove and check each spark plug in turn, to check the spark plug (HT) lead connections and resistances, and to check the connections and resistances of the ignition coil. Refer to the relevant Sections of Chapters 1 and 5.

Basic check of fuel system

48 If the checks so far have not eliminated the fault, the next step is to carry out a basic check of the fuel system components.

49 Assuming that the preliminary checks have established that the fuel pump is operating correctly, that the fuel filter is unlikely to be blocked, and also that there are no leaks in the system, the next step is to check the fuel pressure (see Chapter 4). If this is correct, check the injectors (see Chapter 4) and the Positive Crankcase Ventilation system (see Chapter 1).

System test

50 The final element of the testing procedure is to carry out a system test, using a break-out box - this is a device that is connected between the PCM and its electrical connector, so that the individual circuits indicated by the fault code read-out can be tested while connected to the system, if necessary with the engine running. In the case of many of the system's components, this enables their output voltages to be measured - a more accurate means of testing.

51 In addition to the break-out box and the adapters required to connect it, several items of specialist equipment are needed to complete these tests. This puts them quite beyond the scope of many smaller dealers, let alone the DIY owner; the vehicle should be taken to a dealer for attention.

4 Information sensors - general information, testing, removal and installation

Note: *This Section is concerned principally with the sensors which give the PCM the information it needs to control the various engine management sub-systems - for further details of those systems and their other components, refer to the relevant Chapter of this manual.*

General information

Powertrain Control Module (PCM)

1 This component is the heart of the entire engine management system, controlling the fuel injection, ignition and emissions control systems. It also controls sub-systems such as the radiator cooling fan, air conditioning and automatic transaxle, where appropriate. Refer to Section 2 of this Chapter for an illustration of how it works.

Mass airflow sensor (MAF)

2 This uses a "hot-wire" system, sending the PCM a constantly-varying (analog) voltage signal corresponding to the mass of air passing into the engine. Since air mass varies with temperature (cold air being denser than warm), measuring air mass provides the PCM with a very accurate means of determining the correct amount of fuel required to achieve the ideal air/fuel mixture ratio.

Crankshaft position sensor (CKP)

3 This is an inductive pulse generator bolted to the cylinder block. On four-cylinder models the sensor scans the ridges between 36 holes machined in the inboard (right-hand) face of the flywheel/driveplate. As each ridge passes the sensor tip, a signal is generated, which is used by the PCM to determine engine speed. On V6 models, the crankshaft is mounted on the right-hand engine cover and is triggered by a pulse wheel with 36 teeth mounted on the crankshaft (inside the engine cover).

4 The ridge between the 35th and 36th holes (corresponding to 90-degrees BTDC) is missing - this step in the incoming signals is used by the PCM to determine crankshaft (piston) position.

Camshaft position sensor (CMP)

5 On four-cylinder models the camshaft position sensor is bolted to the rear left-hand end of the cylinder head, and is triggered by a high-point mark lobe on the intake camshaft. On V6 models, the camshaft position sensor is mounted on the right-hand side of the front cylinder head and is triggered by a high-point on the front intake camshaft. The camshaft position sensor functions in the same way as the crankshaft position sensor, producing a series of pulses (corresponding to No. 1 cylinder at 46-degrees ATDC). This gives the PCM a reference point, to enable it to determine the firing order, and operate the injectors in the appropriate sequence.

Engine coolant temperature sensor (ECT)

6 This component, which is screwed into the top of the thermostat housing on four-cylinder models or into the water crossover on V6 models, is an NTC (Negative Temperature Coefficient) thermistor - that is, a semiconductor whose electrical resistance decreases as its temperature increases. It provides the PCM with a constantly-varying (analog) voltage signal, corresponding to the temperature of the engine coolant. This is used to refine the calculations made by the PCM, when determining the correct amount of fuel required to achieve the ideal air/fuel mixture ratio.

Intake air temperature sensor (IAT)

7 On 1995 through 1997 four-cylinder models, the IAT is screwed into the underside of the air intake resonator. On 1998 four-cylinder models, the IAT is located in the air inlet duct. The IAT is located in the air cleaner cover on all V6 models. The IAT is also an NTC thermistor - see the previous paragraph - providing the PCM with a signal corresponding to the temperature (density) of air passing into the engine. This is used to refine the calculations made by the PCM, when determining the correct amount of fuel required to achieve the ideal air/fuel mixture ratio.

Throttle position sensor (TP)

8 This is mounted on the end of the throttle valve shaft, to provide the PCM with a constantly-varying (analog) voltage signal corresponding to the throttle opening. This allows the PCM to register the engine load when determining the amount of fuel required by the engine.

Vehicle speed sensor (VSS)

9 This component is a Hall-effect generator, mounted on the transaxle's speedometer drive. It supplies the PCM with a series of pulses corresponding to the vehicle's road speed, enabling the PCM to control features such as the fuel shut-off on the overrun, and to provide information for the trip computer, adaptive damping and cruise control systems (if equipped).

Power steering pressure switch

10 This is a pressure-operated switch, screwed into the power steering system's high-pressure line. Its contacts are normally closed, opening when the system reaches the specified pressure. On receiving this signal, the PCM increases the idle speed, to compensate for the additional load on the engine.

Exhaust gas pressure differential sensor

11 This component measures the difference in pressure of the exhaust gases across a venturi (restriction) in the Exhaust Gas Recirculation (EGR) system's tube, and sends the PCM a voltage signal corresponding to the pressure difference.

Oxygen sensor (O2S)

12 The oxygen sensor(s) in the exhaust system provides the PCM with constant feedback - "closed-loop" control - which enables it to adjust the mixture to provide the best possible conditions for the catalytic converter to operate.

13 The sensor has a built-in heating element which is controlled by the PCM, to bring the sensor's tip to an efficient operating temperature as rapidly as possible. The sensor's tip reacts to the oxygen content in the exhaust stream and sends the PCM a varying voltage depending on the amount of oxygen in the exhaust gases. Optimum combustion efficiency occurs at a air/fuel ratio of 14.7:1 (stoichiometric ratio) If the air/fuel ratio is excessively lean, the oxygen sensor inputs a low-voltage signal to the PCM. If the mixture is excessively rich, the sensor inputs a high-voltage signal.

Air conditioning system

14 Two pressure-operated switches and the compressor clutch solenoid are connected to the PCM, to enable it to determine how the system is operating. The PCM can increase idle speed or switch off the system, as necessary, so normal vehicle operation and driveability are not impaired. See Chapter 3 for further details, but note that diagnosis and repair should be left to a dealer service department or qualified air conditioning specialist.

Automatic transaxle

15 In addition to the driver's controls, the transaxle has a speed sensor, a fluid temperature sensor (built into the solenoid valve unit) and a selector lever position sensor. All of these are connected to the PCM, to enable it to control the transaxle through the solenoid valve unit. See Part B of Chapter 7 for further details.

Testing

Powertrain control module

16 **Do not** attempt to test the PCM with any kind of equipment. If it is thought to be defective, take the vehicle to a dealership service department for the entire electronic control system to be checked using the proper diagnostic equipment. Only if all other possibilities have been eliminated should the PCM be considered at fault, and replaced. It is important to note that under normal conditions, the PCM is very reliable. Generally if a PCM fails, something caused it to fail, such as a poor ground circuit or a voltage spike.

Mass airflow sensor

17 Testing of this component is beyond the scope of the DIY mechanic and should be left to a dealership service department.

Crankshaft speed/position sensor

18 Disconnect the electrical connector from the sensor.

19 Using an ohmmeter, measure the resistance between the sensor terminals. Compare this reading to the one listed in this Chapter's Specifications. If the indicated resistance is not within the specified range, replace the sensor.

20 Connect the sensor's electrical connector on completion.

Camshaft position sensor

21 The procedure is as described in paragraphs 18 to 20 above.

Coolant temperature sensor

22 Refer to Chapter 3.

4.36a Unclip and lift the power steering fluid reservoir out of the way - take care not to spill the fluid

4.36b Remove the bolt (arrow) to release the PCM electrical connector

Intake air temperature sensor

23 Disconnect the electrical connector from the sensor.

24 Using an ohmmeter, measure the resistance between the sensor terminals. Depending on the temperature of the sensor tip, the resistance measured will vary, but it should be within the limits listed in this Chapter's Specifications. If the sensor's temperature is varied - by cooling it, or by warming it gently - its resistance should alter accordingly.

25 If the results obtained show the sensor to be faulty, replace it.

Throttle position sensor

26 Remove the plenum chamber (see Chapter 4) and disconnect the sensor's electrical connector.

27 Using an ohmmeter, measure the resistance between the sensor's terminals - first between the center terminal and one of the outer two, then from the center to the remaining outer terminal. The resistance should be within the limits given in the Specifications Section of this Chapter, and should alter *smoothly* as the throttle valve is moved from the fully-closed (idle speed) position to fully open and back again.

28 If the resistance measured is significantly different from the specified value, if there are any breaks in continuity, or if the reading fluctuates erratically as the throttle is operated, the sensor is faulty, and must be replaced.

Vehicle speed sensor

29 Testing of this component is beyond the scope of the DIY mechanic, and should be left to a dealer service department.

Power steering pressure switch

30 Disconnect the electrical connector from the sensor.

31 Using an ohmmeter, measure the resistance between the switch terminals. With the engine switched off or idling with the wheels in the straight-ahead position, continuity (little or no resistance) should be indicated. With the engine running and the steering turned to full-lock, the pressure increase in the system should open the switch contacts and no continuity (infinity) should be noted.

32 Replace the switch if it doesn't function as described.

Exhaust gas pressure differential sensor

33 Testing of this component is beyond the scope of the DIY mechanic, and should be left to a dealer service department.

Oxygen sensor

34 Testing of this component can be done only by attaching special diagnostic equipment to the sensor wiring and confirming that the voltage varies from low to high values

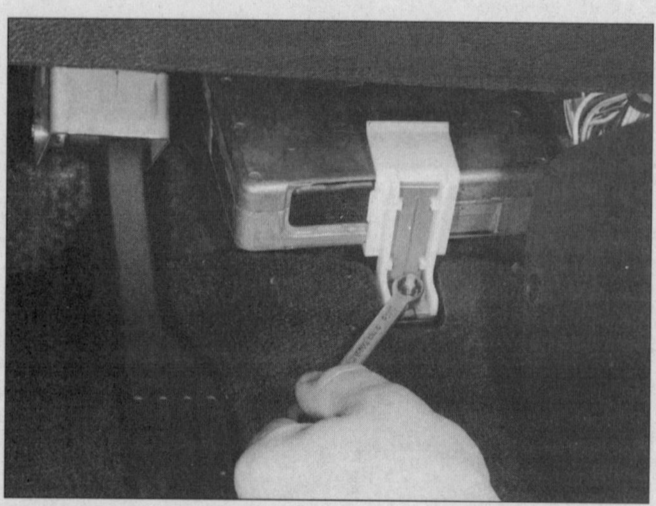
4.37 Unscrew the retaining bolt and remove the PCM mounting bracket . . .

4.38 . . . then lift the PCM to disengage it

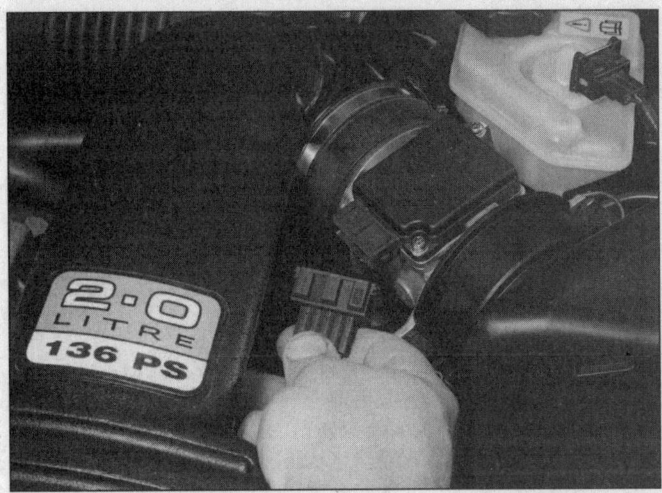

4.40 Disconnect the mass air flow sensor's electrical connector . . .

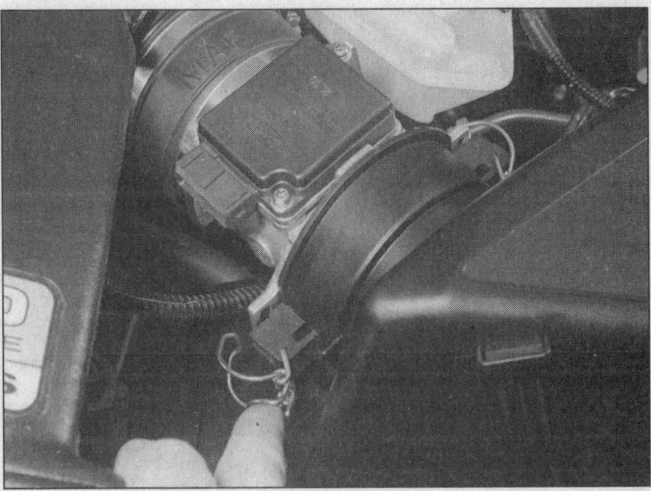

4.41a . . . and release the clips to separate the sensor from the air cleaner cover - four-cylinder model shown

while the engine is running. *Do not* attempt to test any part of the system with anything other than the correct test equipment. This is beyond the scope of the DIY mechanic, and should be left to a dealer service department.

Removal and installation

35 Before disconnecting any of these components, always disconnect the power by disconnecting the cable from the negative terminal of the battery (see Section 1 of Chapter 5).

Powertrain control module

Refer to illustrations 4.36a, 4.36b, 4.37 and 4.38

Note: *The PCM is fragile. Take care not to drop it or subject it to any other kind of impact and do not subject it to extremes of temperature or allow it to get wet.*

36 Carefully pry the power steering fluid reservoir upward out of its clip on the suspension mounting. Unscrew the PCM connector's retaining bolt and disconnect the connector **(see illustrations)**.

37 Working in the passenger compartment, unscrew the retaining bolt and withdraw the mounting bracket **(see illustration)**.

38 Lifting the PCM to release it from the firewall carrier bracket, withdraw the unit **(see illustration)**.

39 Installation is the reverse of the removal procedure. Whenever the PCM (or battery) is disconnected, the information relating to idle speed control and other operating values will be lost from its memory until the unit has reprogrammed itself. Until then, there may be surging, hesitation, erratic idle and a generally-poor level of performance. To allow the PCM to re-learn these values, start the engine and run it as close to idle speed as possible until it reaches its normal operating temperature, then run it for approximately two minutes at 1200 rpm. Next, drive the vehicle as far as necessary - approximately 5 miles of varied driving conditions is usually sufficient to complete the re-learning process.

Mass airflow sensor

Refer to illustrations 3.40, 4.41a and 4.41b

40 Releasing its wire clip, disconnect the meter's electrical connector **(see illustration)**.

41 Release the clips and lift the air cleaner cover. On four-cylinder models, release the two smaller clips and detach the meter from the cover **(see illustrations)**. On V6 models, remove the four bolts and remove the sensor

6

4.41b Remove the bolts (arrows) to remove the mass air flow sensor on V6 models (three of four shown)

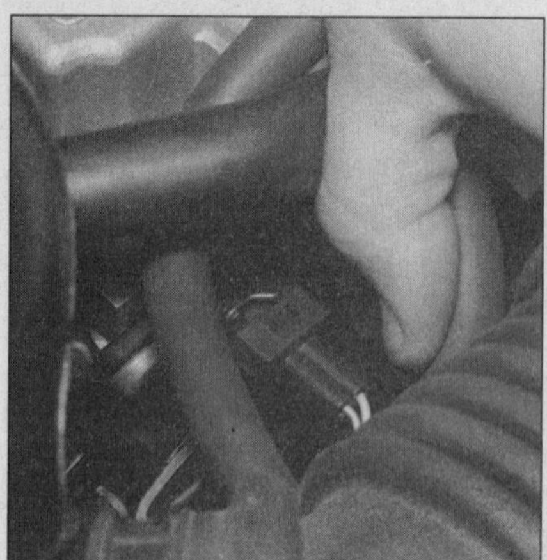

4.45 On four-cylinder models, the camshaft position sensor is located at the left-hand rear of the cylinder head

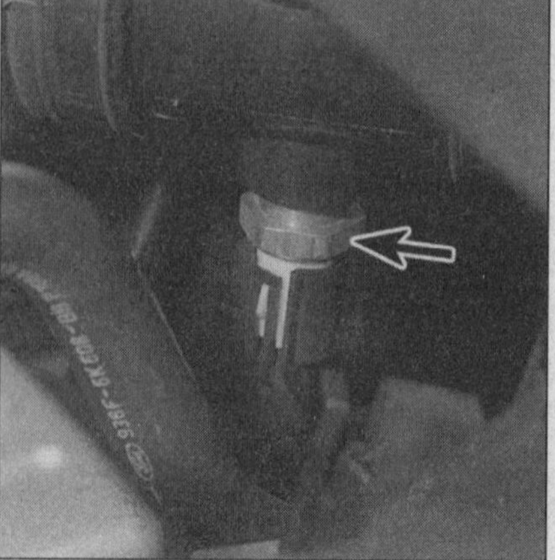

4.49a On 1995 through 1997 four-cylinder models, the intake air temperature sensor (arrow) is screwed into the bottom of the intake resonator - on 1998 four-cylinder models, the sensor is located in the air inlet duct

4.49b On V6 models, the air intake sensor is located in the air cleaner housing

from the cover.

42 Loosen the clamp securing the sensor to the air inlet duct and withdraw the sensor.

43 Installation is the reverse of the removal procedure. Ensure that the sensor and air cleaner cover are seated correctly and securely fastened, so that there are no air leaks.

Crankshaft position sensor

44 Refer to Chapter 5.

Camshaft position sensor

Refer to illustration 4.45

45 Remove the mass airflow sensor and on four-cylinder models, the resonator (refer to Chapter 4) to gain access to the sensor **(see illustration)**. Release the fuel feed and return hoses from their clip.

46 **Note:** *On four-cylinder models, the camshaft sensor is located at the left-hand rear of the cylinder head. On V6 models, the sensor is located on the right-hand end of the front cylinder head.* Release the wire clip and disconnect the sensor's electrical connector. Remove the retaining screw, and withdraw the sensor from the cylinder head; be prepared for slight oil loss.

47 Installation is the reverse of the removal procedure, noting the following points:

(a) *Apply petroleum jelly or clean engine oil to the sensor's O-ring.*

(b) *Locate the sensor fully in the cylinder head, and wipe off any surplus lubricant before securing it.*

(c) *Tighten the screw to the torque listed in this Chapter's Specifications.*

Coolant temperature sensor

48 Refer to Chapter 3, Section 6.

Intake air temperature sensor

Refer to illustrations 4.49a and 4.49b

49 Remove the mass airflow sensor and resonator, on four-cylinder models, (refer to Chapter 4) to gain access to the sensor **(see illustrations)**.

50 Releasing its clip, disconnect the sensor's electrical connector, then remove the sensor from the resonator, air inlet duct or air cleaner housing.

51 Installation is the reverse of the removal procedure. Tighten the sensor to the torque listed in this Chapter's Specifications. If it is overtightened, its tapered thread may crack the resonator, duct or air cleaner housing.

Throttle position sensor

Refer to illustration 4.53

52 On four-cylinder models, remove the plenum chamber (see Chapter 4). On V6 models, remove the water pump pulley shield. If necessary, remove the PCV hose from the air inlet duct.

53 Disconnect the sensor's electrical connector. Remove the retaining screws, and withdraw the unit from the throttle body **(see illustration)**. *Do not* force the sensor's center to rotate past its normal operating range; the unit will be seriously damaged.

54 Installation is the reverse of the removal procedure, noting the following points:

(a) *Ensure that the sensor is correctly orientated, by locating its center on the D-shaped throttle shaft (throttle closed), and aligning the sensor body so the bolts pass easily into the throttle body.*

(b) *Tighten the screws evenly to the torque listed in this Chapter's Specifications (but do not overtighten them, or the sensor body will be cracked).*

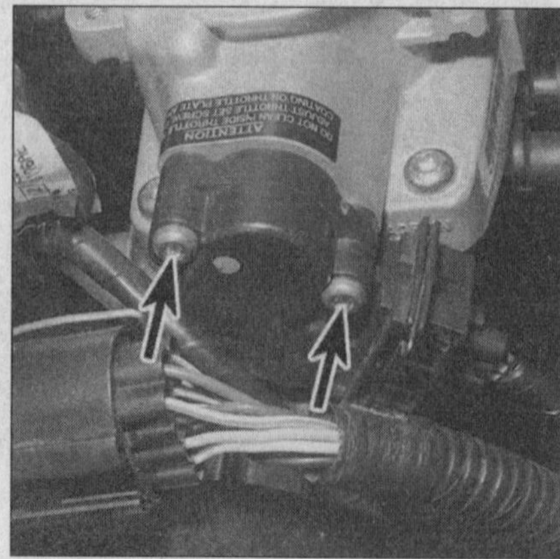

4.53 The throttle position sensor is secured by two screws (arrows)

Vehicle speed sensor

Refer to illustration 4.55

55 The sensor is mounted at the base of the speedometer drive cable, and is removed with the speedometer drive pinion **(see illustration)**. Refer to the relevant Section of Chapter 7, Part A or B, as applicable.

Power steering pressure switch

Refer to illustrations 4.56a and 4.56b

56 Disconnect the switch's electrical connector, then unscrew the switch **(see illustrations)**. Place a shop towel under the switch to catch any spilled fluid. If a sealing washer is installed, replace it if it is worn or damaged.

57 Installation is the reverse of the removal procedure; tighten the switch securely, then top-up the fluid reservoir (see Chapter 1) to replace any fluid lost from the system and

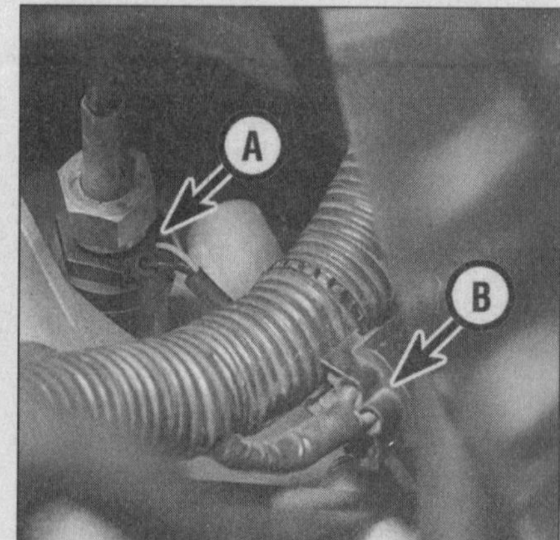

4.55 The vehicle speed sensor (A) and electrical connector (B)

4.56a On four-cylinder models, the power steering switch is located in the power steering line at the right-hand rear end of the engine

bleed out any trapped air (see Chapter 10, Section 33).

Exhaust gas pressure differential sensor

Note: *See Section 6, illustration 6.26.*

58 On four-cylinder models, if better access is required, remove the resonator (see Chapter 4).

59 Disconnect the sensor's electrical connector. Remove the two retaining screws, withdraw the unit from the firewall mounting bracket on four-cylinder models, or the left-hand rear cylinder head on V6 models, then disconnect the two vacuum hoses. Note that the hoses are of different sizes to ensure that they cannot be mixed up on reconnection.

60 Check the condition of both hoses and replace them if necessary (see Chapter 1).

61 Installation is the reverse of the removal procedure. Ensure that the hoses are securely connected to the correct fittings.

Oxygen sensor

Refer to illustrations 4.62a, 4.62b and 4.64

Note: *The sensor is delicate and will not work if it is dropped or knocked, if its power supply is disrupted or if any cleaning materials are used on it.*

62 Disconnect the electrical connector the sensor **(see illustrations)**.

63 Raising and supporting the front of the vehicle if required to remove the sensor from underneath, unscrew the sensor from the exhaust pipe on four-cylinder models or from each exhaust manifold on V6 models. Retrieve the gasket (if equipped).

64 On installation, clean the gasket (if equipped) and replace it if it is damaged or worn. Apply anti-seize compound to the sensor's threads to prevent it from seizing to the exhaust pipe or exhaust manifold(s). Install the sensor and tighten it to the torque listed in this Chapter's Specifications. A special slotted socket is required to do this **(see illustration)**. Reconnect the wiring and install the connector plug.

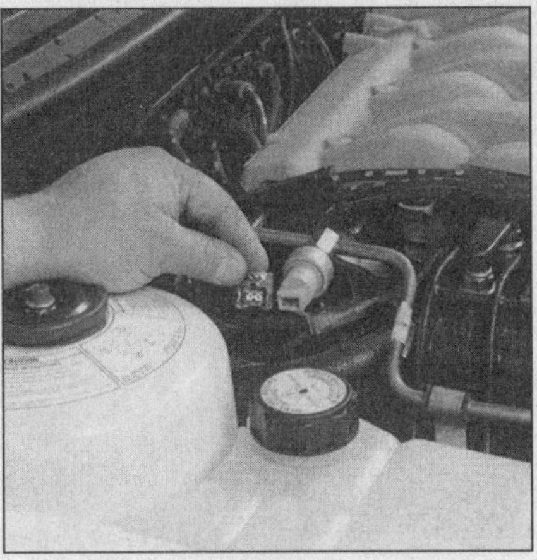
4.56b On V6 models, the power steering switch is located in the power steering line at the upper right-hand end of the engine

4.62b On V6 models, an oxygen sensor is located in the front and rear exhaust manifolds

5 Evaporative emissions control (EVAP) system - general information, checking and component replacement

General information

1 This system is designed to minimize the escape of unburned hydrocarbons into the atmosphere. The fuel tank filler cap is sealed and a charcoal canister is mounted underneath the tank, to collect and store gasoline vapor generated in the tank when the vehicle is parked. When the engine is running, the vapor is cleared from the canister (under the control of the PCM via the canister-purge solenoid valve) into the inlet tract, to be burned by the engine during normal combustion **(see illustration 2.1a)**.

2 To ensure that the engine runs correctly when it is cold and/or idling, and to protect the catalytic converter from the effects of an excessively mixture, the canister-purge solenoid valve is not opened by the PCM until the engine is at normal operating temperature

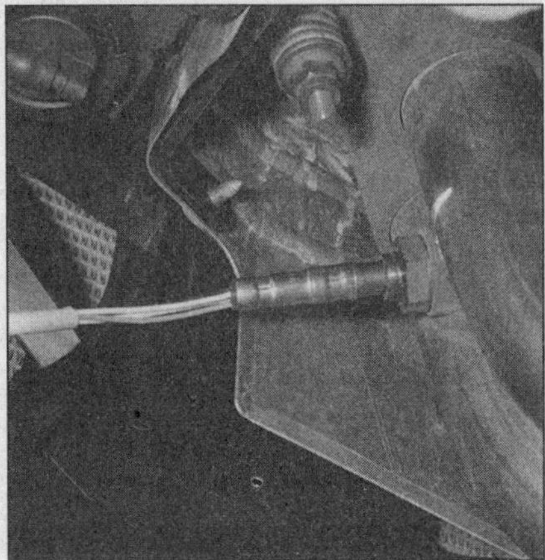
4.62a The oxygen sensor is screwed into the exhaust pipe on four-cylinder models

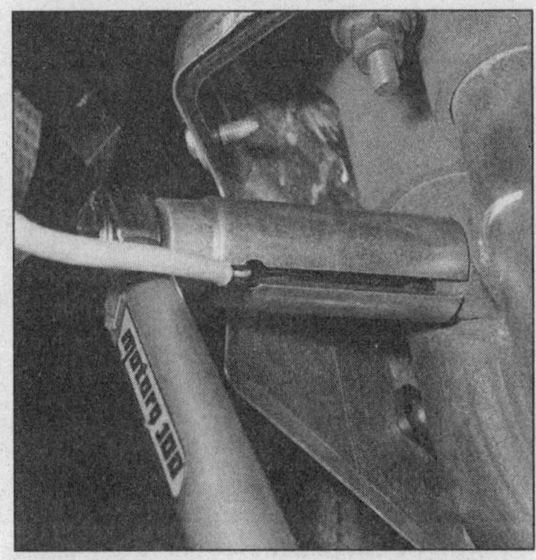
4.64 A slotted socket will be required to tighten the sensor with a torque wrench

6

and running under load. The solenoid valve is then switched on and off to allow the stored vapor to pass into the inlet.

Checking

3 Poor idle, stalling and poor driveability can be caused by an inoperative canister-purge solenoid valve, a damaged canister, split or cracked hoses or hoses connected to the wrong attachments. Check the fuel filler cap for a damaged or deformed gasket.

4 Fuel loss or fuel odor can be caused by liquid fuel leaking from fuel lines, a cracked or damaged canister, an inoperative canister-purge solenoid valve, and disconnected, misrouted, kinked or damaged vapor or control hoses.

5 Inspect each hose attached to the canister for kinks, leaks and cracks along its entire length. Repair or replace as necessary.

6 Inspect the canister. If it is cracked or damaged, replace it. Look for fuel leaking from the bottom of the canister. If fuel is leaking, replace the canister, and check the hoses and hose routing.

7 If the canister-purge solenoid valve is thought to be faulty, disconnect its electrical connector and disconnect its vacuum hoses.

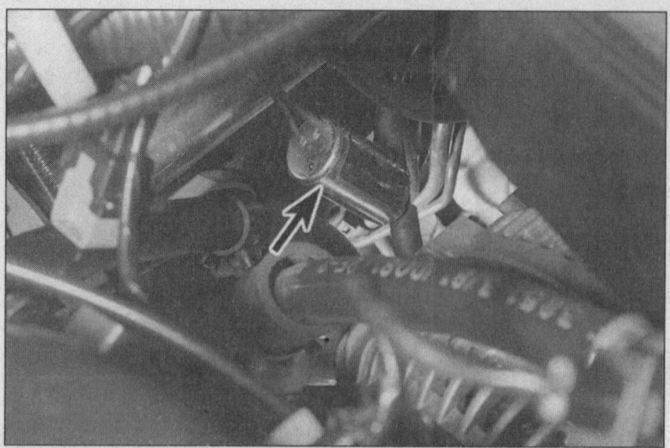

5.10 Charcoal canister purge solenoid valve (arrow) is clipped to the firewall behind the engine

5.13 On 1995 through 1997 models, remove the canister bracket bolt - on 1998 models, remove the canister front bolt and loosen the two rear bolts

5.14 Disconnect the vapor hose(s) and remove the canister and bracket

5.16 On 1995 through 1997 models, release the clip and drive out the pin to separate the canister from the mounting bracket

Connect a 12-volt battery directly across the valve terminals. Check that air can flow through the valve passages when the solenoid is energized and that air cannot pass when the solenoid is not energized. Alternatively, connect an ohmmeter to measure the resistance across the solenoid terminals and compare this reading to the one listed in this Chapter's Specifications. Replace the solenoid valve if it is faulty.

8 Further testing should be left to a dealer service department.

Component replacement

Charcoal canister-purge solenoid valve

Refer to illustration 5.10

9 Disconnect the cable from the negative terminal of the battery (see Chapter 5, Section 1). If better access is required on four-cylinder models, remove the plenum chamber (see Chapter 4). On V6 models, remove the ignition coil (see Chapter 5).

10 Disconnect the valve's electrical connector **(see illustration)**. Unclip the valve from the firewall, then disconnect its vacuum hoses and withdraw it.

11 Installation is the reverse of the removal procedure.

Charcoal canister

Refer to illustrations 5.13, 5.14 and 5.16

12 Disconnect the cable from the negative battery terminal (see Chapter 5, Section 1). Raise the vehicle and support it securely on jackstands.

13 On 1995 through 1997 models, remove the canister bracket bolt. On 1998 models, remove the front canister bracket bolt and loosen the two canister rear bracket bolts **(see illustration)**.

14 Lower the canister and bracket and disconnect the vent solenoid electrical connector. Disconnect the vapor tube and remove the canister and bracket **(see illustration)**.

15 If necessary, remove the vent solenoid from the canister.

16 On 1995 through 1997 models, release the clip and drive out the pin and separate the canister from the bracket, if necessary **(see illustration)**.

17 On 1998 models, pry the canister bracket away from the canister and remove the canister.

18 Install by reversing the removal procedure.

6 Exhaust Gas Recirculation (EGR) system - general information, checking and component replacement

General information

Note: *The EGR valve and related components are not used on 1998 four-cylinder models.*

1 To reduce oxides of nitrogen (NO_x) emissions, some of the exhaust gases are recirculated through the EGR valve to the intake manifold. This has the effect of lowering combustion temperatures.

2 The system consists of the EGR valve, the EGR exhaust gas pressure differential sensor, the EGR solenoid valve, the PCM, and various sensors **(see illustration 2.1a)**. The PCM is programmed to produce the ideal EGR valve lift for each operating condition.

Checking

EGR valve

Refer to illustration 6.4

3 Start the engine and allow it to idle.

6.4 To test the EGR valve, attach a hand vacuum pump to the valve

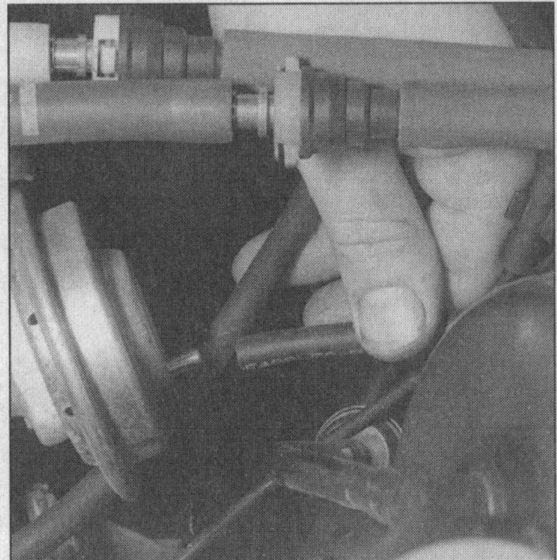
6.9a Location of EGR vacuum hose on four-cylinder models

6.9b EGR valve mounting bolts (arrows) - four-cylinder models

4 Detach the vacuum hose from the EGR valve and attach a hand vacuum pump in its place **(see illustration)**.

5 Apply vacuum to the EGR valve. Vacuum should remain steady and the engine should run poorly or stall.

(a) If the vacuum doesn't remain steady and the engine doesn't run poorly, replace the EGR valve and recheck it.

(b) If the vacuum remains steady but the engine doesn't run poorly, remove the EGR valve and check the valve and the intake manifold for blockage. Clean or replace parts as necessary, and recheck.

EGR system

6 Any further checking of the system requires special tools and test equipment. Take the vehicle to a dealer service department for checking.

Component replacement

Note: *These components will be very hot when the engine is running. Always allow the engine to cool down fully before starting work, to prevent the possibility of burns.*

EGR valve

Refer to illustrations 6.9a, 6.9b and 6.9c

7 Disconnect the cable from the negative terminal of the battery - see Section 1 of Chapter 5.

8 Remove the mass airflow sensor, and on four-cylinder models, the resonator - refer to Chapter 4. On V6 models, remove the idle air control valve.

9 Detach the vacuum hose, unscrew the EGR tuber nut securing the EGR tube to the valve, remove the two valve mounting bolts, and withdraw the valve from the intake manifold **(see illustrations)**. Ensure that the tube of the pipe is not damaged or distorted as the valve is withdrawn and note the valve's gasket; this must be replaced whenever the valve is disturbed.

10 Note that the metal pipe from the valve to the manifold itself should not be disturbed - it is not available separately from the manifold. However, check whenever the manifold is removed that the tube is securely fastened.

11 Check the valve for sticking and heavy carbon deposits. If such is found, clean the valve or replace it.

12 Installation is the reverse of the removal procedure. Apply anti-seize compound to the sleeve nut threads, install a new gasket and tighten the valve bolts to the torque listed in this Chapter's Specifications.

EGR tube

Four-cylinder models

Refer to illustrations 6.15 and 6.16

13 Disconnect the cable from the negative battery terminal (see Section 1 of Chapter 5).

14 Remove the mass airflow sensor and resonator - refer to Chapter 4.

15 Unbolt the exhaust manifold heat shield and remove both parts, or move them aside as required to reach the end of the EGR tube. Unscrew the tube nut securing the tube to the exhaust manifold **(see illustration)**.

16 Remove the two screws securing the tube to the ignition coil bracket, then disconnect the two vacuum hoses - note that these are of different sizes, to ensure that they cannot be mixed up on reconnection. Unscrew the sleeve nut securing the EGR tube to the valve **(see illustration)**. Withdraw the tube.

17 Check the condition of both hoses and replace them if necessary (see Chapter 1). Note that if the exhaust gases have been backfiring excessively, due to a blocked exhaust system, both hoses must be

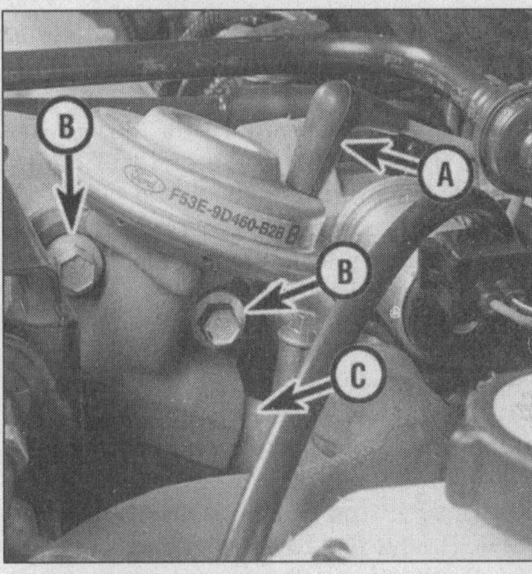

6.9c Location of EGR vacuum hose (A), EGR valve mounting bolts (B) and EGR tube (C) on V6 models

6

6.15 Remove the exhaust manifold heat shield and unscrew the tube nut (arrow) and separate the EGR tube from the exhaust manifold

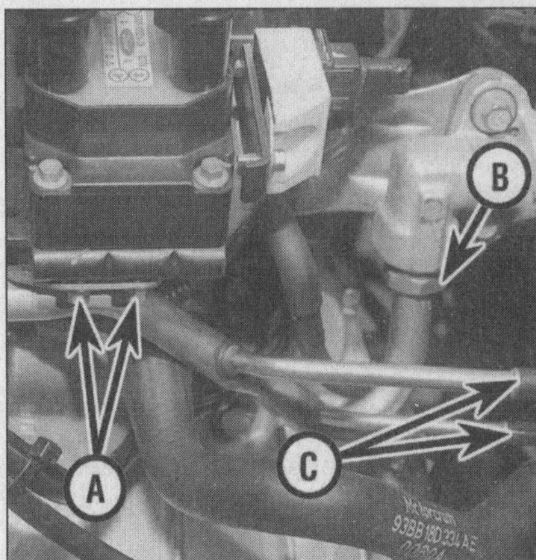

6.16 Remove the screws (A) and tube nut (B), then disconnect the hoses (C) to release the EGR pipe

6.22 Remove the EGR tube nut from the rear exhaust manifold - V6 models

6.26 EGR solenoid valve (A) and EGR exhaust gas pressure differential sensor (B) located on firewall mounting bracket - four-cylinder model shown, V6 similar

replaced and their connections on the tube must be cleaned thoroughly.

18 Installation is the reverse of the removal procedure. Ensure that the hoses are securely connected to the correct fittings. Apply anti-seize compound to the sleeve nut threads, tighten the nuts securely and tighten the two screws to the torque listed in this chapter's specifications.

V6 models

Refer to illustration 6.22

19 Disconnect the idle air control valve tube from the air cleaner and upper intake manifold.

20 Unscrew the EGR tube sleeve nut from the EGR valve and disconnect the tube.

21 Raise the vehicle and support it securely on jackstands. Remove left front wheel and the splash shield from the left-hand inner fender.

22 Remove the EGR tube nut from the rear exhaust manifold and remove the tube **(see illustration)**.

23 Installation is the reverse of removal. Apply anti-seize compound to the nuts on both ends of the tube.

EGR exhaust gas pressure differential sensor

24 Refer to Section 4 of this Chapter.

EGR solenoid valve

Refer to illustration 6.26

Note: *This component can be identified by its larger top and its two fastening screws. Do not confuse it with the adjacent air injection solenoid valve (if equipped), especially when reconnecting vacuum hoses.*

25 Disconnect the cable from the negative battery terminal (see Section 1 of Chapter 5).

26 Remove the mass airflow sensor and, on four-cylinder models, the resonator (see Chapter 4). If better access is required, remove the plenum chamber also **(see illustration)**.

27 Releasing its wire clip, disconnect the electrical connector from the valve. Remove the two retaining screws, and withdraw the valve from the firewall mounting bracket, then label and disconnect the two vacuum hoses.

28 Installation is the reverse of the removal procedure; ensure that the hoses are correctly reconnected.

7 Air injection system - general information, checking and component replacement

Note: *Not all models are equipped with an air injection system.*

General information

1 This system consists of the pulse-air-air solenoid valve, the injection-air valve itself, contained in the filter housing and the tubing **(see illustration 2.1a)**. It injects filtered air directly into the exhaust ports, using the pressure variations in the exhaust gases to draw air through from the filter housing; air will flow into the exhaust only when its pressure is below atmospheric. The pulse-air valve can allow gases to flow only one way so there is no risk of hot exhaust gases flowing back into the filter.

2 The system's primary function is raise exhaust gas temperature on start-up, thus reducing the amount of time taken for the oxygen sensor and catalytic converter to reach operating temperature.

3 To ensure that the system does not upset the smooth running of the engine under normal driving conditions, it is linked by the pulse-air solenoid valve to the PCM, so that it only functions during engine warm-up, when the oxygen sensor is not influencing the air/fuel mixture ratio.

Checking

4 Poor idle, stalling, backfiring and poor driveability can be caused by a fault in the system.

5 Inspect the vacuum tube/hose connected between the filter housing and the solenoid valve for kinks, leaks and cracks along its entire length. Repair or replace as necessary.

6 Inspect the filter housing and tubing. If either is cracked or damaged, replace it.

7 If the pulse-air solenoid valve is thought to be faulty, disconnect its electrical connector and disconnect its vacuum hoses. Connect a battery directly across the valve terminals, and confirm that air can flow through the valve passages when the solenoid is thus energized, but not when the solenoid is not energized. Alternatively, connect an ohmmeter to measure the resistance across the valve terminals, and compare this reading to the one listed in the Specifications Section at the beginning of this Chapter. Replace the solenoid valve if it is faulty.

8 Further testing should be left to a dealer service department.

Component replacement

Pulse-air solenoid valve

Refer to illustration 7.10

Note: *This component can be identified by its smaller top and its clip fastening. Do not confuse it with the adjacent EGR solenoid valve, especially when reconnecting vacuum hoses.*

9 Disconnect the cable from the negative battery terminal (see Section 1 of Chapter 5).

10 Remove the mass airflow sensor and resonator (see Chapter 4). If better access is

7.10 Pulse-air solenoid valve (arrow) is located on the firewall mounting bracket. It can be identified by its smaller top and its clip fastener

7.13 Disconnect the vacuum hose from the base of pulse-air filter housing

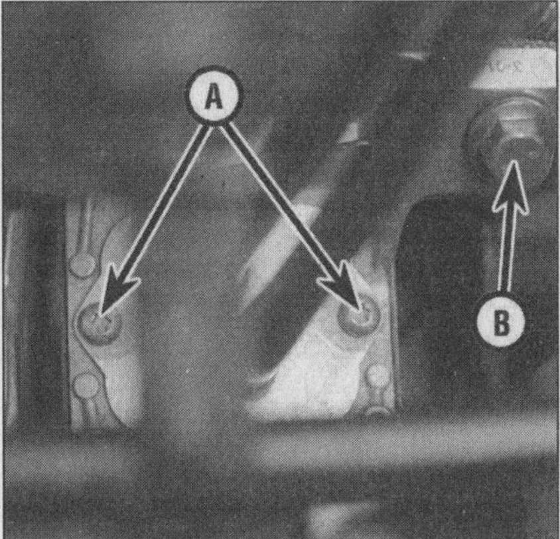

7.16 Remove the screws (A) to disconnect the tubing from the housing, and mounting bolt (B) to release the housing

7.17a Remove four screws to release the filter housing top from the base . . .

7.17b . . . and withdraw the foam filter for cleaning, if required - note the valve in the base of the housing

7.23 Removing the pulse-air tubing - do not bend or distort it

required, remove the plenum chamber also **(see illustration)**.

11 Releasing its wire clip, disconnect the electrical connector, then use a small screwdriver to release the clip securing the valve to the firewall mounting bracket. Withdraw the valve, then label and disconnect the two vacuum hoses.

12 Installation is the reverse of the removal procedure; ensure that the hoses are correctly reconnected.

Pulse-air filter housing

Refer to illustrations 7.13, 7.16, 7.17a and 7.17b

Note: *This component, and those around it, will be very hot when the engine is running. Always allow the engine to cool down fully before starting work, to prevent the possibility of burns.*

13 Raise the front of the vehicle, and support it securely on jackstands. Disconnect the vacuum hose from the base of the filter housing **(see illustration)**.

14 Disconnect the battery negative (ground) lead - see Section 1 of Chapter 5.

15 Unbolt the resonator support bracket from the engine compartment front crossmember, loosen the two clamp screws securing the resonator to the mass airflow sensor and plenum chamber hoses, then swing the resonator up clear of the thermostat housing (see Chapter 4).

16 Remove the screws securing the filter housing to the tubing, unscrew the mounting bolt, then withdraw the housing **(see illustration)**.

17 To disassemble the filter housing, undo the four screws and separate the top from the base of the housing; extract the foam filter, and clean it in a suitable solvent **(see illustrations)**. If any of the housing's components are worn or damaged, the assembly must be replaced.

18 Installation is the reverse of the removal procedure.

Pulse-air tubing

Refer to illustration 7.23

Note: *This component, and those around it, will be very hot when the engine is running. Always allow the engine to cool down fully before starting work, to prevent the possibility of burns.*

19 Disconnect the cable from the negative battery terminal (see Section 1 of Chapter 5).

20 Remove the mass airflow sensor and resonator (see Chapter 4).

21 Unbolt the exhaust manifold heat shield; unclip the coolant hose to allow the upper part to be withdrawn. Apply penetrating oil to the EGR tube sleeve nut and to the pulse-air system sleeve nuts.

22 Remove the EGR tube (see Section 6).

23 Remove the screws securing the filter housing to the tubing **(see illustration 7.16)**. Unscrew the four sleeve nuts securing the tubes to the exhaust manifold, and remove the tubing as an assembly, taking care not to distort it **(see illustration)**.

24 Carefully clean the tubing, particularly its threads and those of the manifold, removing all traces of corrosion which might prevent them seating properly, causing air leaks when the engine is restarted.

25 On installation, insert the tubing carefully into the cylinder head ports, taking care not to bend or distort it. Apply anti-seize compound to the threads and tighten the retaining sleeve nuts while holding each tube firmly in its port. If a suitable wrench is available, tighten the sleeve nuts to the torque listed in this Chapter's Specifications.

26 The remainder of the installation procedure is the reverse of removal.

Pulse-air filter housing and tubing assembly

Refer to illustration 7.31

Note: *These components, and those around them, will be very hot when the engine is running. Always allow the engine to cool down fully before starting work, to prevent the possibility of burns.*

27 Disconnect the cable from the negative battery terminal (see Chapter 5, Section 1). Unbolt the resonator support bracket from the engine compartment front crossmember. Loosen the two clamp screws securing the resonator to the mass airflow sensor and plenum chamber hoses, then swing the resonator up clear of the thermostat housing (see Chapter 4).

28 Drain the cooling system (see Chapter 1) and disconnect the coolant hose and the coolant tube/hose from the thermostat housing.

29 Unbolt the exhaust manifold heat shield.

7.31 Remove the mounting bolt (arrow) to remove the complete pulse-air assembly - do not bend or distort the tubing

Apply penetrating oil to the EGR tube sleeve nut, and to the pulse-air system sleeve nuts.

30 Remove the EGR tube (see Section 6).

31 Unscrew the filter housing mounting bolt. Unscrew the four sleeve nuts securing the tubes into the exhaust manifold and remove the assembly, taking care not to distort it **(see illustration)**.

32 Clean the tubing, particularly its threads and those of the manifold, removing all traces of corrosion, which might prevent them seating properly, causing air leaks when the engine is restarted.

33 On installation, insert the tubing carefully into the cylinder head ports, taking care not to bend or distort it. Apply anti-seize compound to the threads, and tighten the retaining sleeve nuts while holding each tube firmly in its port; if a suitable wrench is available, tighten the sleeve nuts to the torque listed in this Chapter's Specifications.

34 The remainder of the installation procedure is the reverse of removal. Refill the cooling system (see Chapter 1). Run the engine, check for exhaust leaks and check the coolant level

8 Positive Crankcase Ventilation (PCV) system - general information, checking and component replacement

General information

1 The crankcase ventilation system main components are the oil separator mounted on the front (radiator) side of the cylinder block/crankcase, and the Positive Crankcase Ventilation (PCV) valve set in a rubber grommet in the separator's left-hand upper end. The associated tubes/hoses consists of a crankcase breather tube and two flexible hoses connecting the PCV valve to a union on the left-hand end of the intake manifold, and a crankcase breather hose connecting the valve cover to the air cleaner assembly. A small foam filter in the air cleaner prevents dirt from being drawn directly into the engine.

2 The function of these components is to reduce the emission of unburned hydrocarbons from the crankcase and to minimize the formation of oil sludge. By ensuring that a vacuum is created in the crankcase under most operating conditions, especially at idle, and by positively inducing fresh air into the system, the oil vapor and blow-by gases collected in the crankcase are drawn from the crankcase, through the oil separator, into the inlet tract, to be burned by the engine during normal combustion.

Checking

3 Checking procedures for the system components are included in Chapter 1.

Component replacement

Cylinder head-to-air cleaner hose

4 See Chapter 1.

Positive Crankcase Ventilation (PCV) valve

5 The valve is plugged into the oil separator. Depending on the tools available, access to the valve may be possible once the pulse-air assembly has been removed (see Section 7). If this is not feasible, proceed as outlined in paragraph 6 below.

Oil separator

6 Remove the exhaust manifold (see Chapter 2, Part A or Part B). The Positive Crankcase Ventilation (PCV) valve can now be disconnected and flushed, or replaced, as required, as described in Chapter 1.

7 Unbolt the oil separator from the cylinder block, and withdraw it. Remove and discard the gasket.

8 Flush out or replace the oil separator, as required (see Chapter 1).

9 On reassembly, install a new gasket, and tighten the fasteners to the torque listed in Chapter 2, Part A or Part B Specifications.

10 The remainder of the installation procedure is the reverse of removal. Refill the cooling system (see Chapter 1). Run the engine, check for exhaust leaks and check the coolant level after the engine reaches normal operating temperature.

9 Catalytic converter - general information, checking and component replacement

General information

1 The exhaust gases of any gasoline engine (however efficient or well-tuned) consist largely (approximately 99%) of nitrogen (N_2), carbon dioxide (CO_2), oxygen (O_2), other inert gases and water vapor (H_2O). The remaining 1 % is made up of the noxious materials which are currently seen (CO_2 apart) as the major polluters of the environment: carbon monoxide (CO), unburned hydrocarbons (HC), oxides of nitrogen (NO_x) and some solid particulate matter.

2 Left to themselves, most of these pollutants are thought to eventually break down naturally (CO and NO_x, for example, break down in the upper atmosphere to release CO_2) having first caused ground-level environmental problems. The massive increase world-wide in the use of motor vehicles and the current popular concern for the environment has caused the introduction in most countries of legislation, in varying degrees of severity, to combat the problem.

3 The device most commonly used to clean up vehicle exhausts is the catalytic converter. It is installed into the vehicle's exhaust system and uses precious metals (platinum and palladium or rhodium) as catalysts to speed up the reaction between the pollutants and the oxygen in the vehicle's exhaust gases.

4 The converter consists of an element (or substrate) of ceramic honeycomb, coated with a combination of precious metals in such a way as to produce a vast surface area over which the exhaust gases must flow. The element is mounted in a stainless-steel box. A simple oxidation (or two-way) catalytic converter can deal with CO and HC only, while a reduction (or three-way) catalytic converter can deal with CO, HC and NO_x. Three-way catalytic converters are further sub-divided into open-loop (or uncontrolled) converters which can remove 50 to 70 % of pollutants and closed-loop (also known as controlled or regulated) converters which can remove over 90% of pollutants.

5 The catalytic converter installed to the vehicles covered in this manual is of the three-way closed-loop type.

6 The catalytic converter is a reliable and simple device which needs no maintenance in itself, but there are some facts of which an owner should be aware if the converter is to function properly for its full service life.

(a) *Always keep the ignition and fuel systems well-maintained in accordance with the manufacturer's schedule (Chapter 1) - particularly, ensure that the air filter element, the fuel filter and the spark plugs are replaced at the correct intervals. If the intake air/fuel mixture is allowed to become too rich due to neglect, the unburned surplus will enter and burn in the catalytic converter, overheating the element and eventually destroying the converter.*

(b) *If the engine develops a misfire, do not drive the vehicle at all (or at least as little as possible) until the fault is cured - the misfire will allow unburned fuel to enter the converter, which will result in its overheating, as noted above. For the same reason, do not persist if the engine refuses to start - either trace the problem and repair it yourself, or have the vehicle checked immediately at a dealer-*

ship service department or by a qualified mechanic.

(c) Avoid allowing the vehicle to run out of gasoline.

(d) DO NOT push- or tow-start the vehicle unless no other alternative exists, especially if the engine and exhaust are at normal operating temperature. Starting the engine in this way may soak the catalytic converter in unburned fuel, causing it to overheat when the engine does start - see (b) above.

(e) DO NOT switch off the ignition at high engine speeds, in particular, do not "blip" the throttle immediately before switching off. If the ignition is switched off at anything above idle speed, unburned fuel will enter the (very hot) catalytic converter, with the possible risk of its igniting on the element and damaging the converter.

(f) Avoid repeated successive cold starts followed by short journeys. If the converter is never allowed to reach its proper operating temperature, it will gather unburned fuel, allowing some to pass into the atmosphere and the rest to soak in the element, causing it to overheat when a long trip is made - see (b) above.

(g) DO NOT use fuel or engine oil additives - these may contain substances harmful to the catalytic converter. Similarly, DO NOT use silicone-based sealants on any part of the engine or fuel system, unless they are specifically formulated for use in vehicles equipped with a catalytic converter. Also do not use exhaust sealants on any part of the exhaust system upstream of the catalytic converter. Even if the sealant itself does not contain additives harmful to the converter, pieces of it may break off and foul the element, causing local overheating.

(h) DO NOT continue to use the vehicle if the engine burns oil to the extent of leaving a visible trail of blue smoke. Unburned carbon deposits will plug the converter passages and reduce its efficiency. In severe cases, the element will overheat.

(i) Remember that the catalytic converter operates at very high temperatures - hence the heat shields on the vehicle underbody - and the casing will become hot enough to ignite combustible materials which brush against it. DO NOT, therefore, park the vehicle in dry undergrowth, over long grass or piles of dead leaves.

(j) Remember that the catalytic converter is FRAGILE. Do not strike it with tools during servicing work and take great care when working on the exhaust system (see Chapter 4). *Ensure that the converter is well clear of any jacks or other lifting gear used to raise the vehicle.*

(k) In some cases, particularly when the vehicle is new and/or is used for stop/start driving, a sulfurous smell (like that of rotten eggs) may be noticed from the exhaust. This is common to many catalytic converter-equipped vehicles, and seems to be due to the small amount of sulfur found in some gasses reacting with hydrogen in the exhaust, to produce hydrogen sulfide (H^2S) gas. While this gas is toxic, it is not produced in sufficient amounts to be a problem. Once the vehicle has covered a few thousand miles, the problem should disappear - meanwhile, a change of driving style, or of the brand of gasoline used, may improve the exhaust smell.

(l) The catalytic converter on a well-maintained and well-driven vehicle should last for 50,000 to 100,000 miles. From this point on, careful checks should be made at regular intervals to ensure that the converter is still operating efficiently. If the converter is no longer effective, it must be replaced.

Checking

7 Checking the operation of a catalytic converter requires expensive and sophisticated diagnostic equipment, starting with a high-quality exhaust gas analyzer. If the level of CO in the exhaust gases is too high, a complete inspection check of the engine management system must be performed (see Section 3 of this Chapter) to eliminate all other possibilities before the converter is suspected of being faulty.

8 The vehicle should be taken to a dealer for this work to be performed using the correct diagnostic equipment; do not waste time trying to test the system without such facilities.

Component replacement

9 On four-cylinder models the catalytic converter is part of the exhaust system front exhaust pipe; on V6 models, the catalytic converters are part of the exhaust manifolds - see Chapter 4 for details of removal and installation.

Notes

Chapter 7 Part A
Manual transaxle

Contents

Specifications

Manufacturer's code

Manual transaxle	MTX-75

Gear ratios

1st	3.42:1
2nd	2.14:1
3rd	1.45:1
4th	1.03:1
5th	0.77:1
Reverse	3.42:1

Final drive ratios

Four-cylinder models	3.84:1
V6 models	4.06:1

Torque specifications

	Ft-lbs (unless otherwise indicated)
Transaxle to engine	30
Shift linkage support rod	41
Shift linkage clamp bolt	144 in-lbs
Shift assembly rear mounting	32
Shift linkage to selector shaft	17

1 General information

The vehicles covered by this manual are equipped with either a 5-speed manual or a 4-speed automatic transaxle. This Part of Chapter 7 contains information on the manual transaxle. Service procedures for the automatic transaxle are contained in Part B.

The manual transaxle is a compact, two-piece, lightweight aluminum alloy housing, containing both the transaxle and differential assemblies. The manual transaxle code name is MTX-75, MT standing for *Manual Transaxle*, X for transaxle (front-wheel-drive), and 75 being the distance between the input and output shafts in mm.

Because of the complexity, possible unavailability of replacement parts and special tools necessary, internal repair procedures for the manual transaxle are not recommended for the home mechanic. For readers who wish to tackle a transaxle rebuild, exploded views and brief notes on overhaul are provided. The bulk of the information in this Chapter is devoted to removal and installation procedures.

2 Shift linkage - adjustment

Note: *A special tool will be required in order to carry out the following adjustment. This tool is simply a slotted ring which locks the shift lever in the neutral position during adjustment. If the tool is not available, adjustment is still possible by proceeding on a trial-and-error basis, preferably with the help of an assistant to hold the shift lever in the neutral position.*

1 Remove the center console as described in Chapter 11.

3.1 View of the top of the shift lever assembly with the center console removed

2 Apply the parking brake, jack up the front of the vehicle and support it on jackstands. Move the shift lever to the neutral position.
3 Working beneath the vehicle, loosen the clamp bolt on the shift linkage located behind the transaxle.
4 With the shift lever still in neutral, fit the special tool over the shift lever, and locate it in the recess in the lever retaining housing on top of the transaxle. Twist the tool clockwise to lock the lever in the neutral position. Take care during the adjustment not to move the shift lever or displace the adjustment tool.
5 Check that the front part of the shift linkage from the transaxle is in neutral. It will be necessary to move the linkage slightly forwards and backwards to determine that it is in the correct position.
6 Recheck that the adjustment tool is still correctly fitted to the shift lever, then tighten the clamp bolt on the shift linkage.
7 Remove the adjustment tool from the shift lever.
8 Lower the vehicle to the ground, then install the center console with reference to Chapter 11.

3 Shift linkage and shift lever - removal and installation

Removal

Refer to illustration 3.1 and 3.6

1 Remove the center console as described in Chapter 11 **(see illustration)**.
2 Apply the parking brake, jack up the front of the vehicle and support it on jackstands. Move the shift lever to its neutral position.
3 Working beneath the vehicle, unscrew the bolt and disconnect the shift linkage from the selector shaft on the rear of the transaxle.
4 Mark the position of the shift linkage front and rear sections in relation to each other. Loosen the clamp bolt and remove the front section.
5 Unscrew the bolt securing the shift support rod to the bracket on the rear of the transaxle.
6 Remove the heat shield. Support the weight of the shift linkage assembly, unscrew the nuts from the rear mounting bracket, and lower the assembly from the underbody **(see illustration)**.

3.6 Shift linkage assembly rear mounting

7 Remove the insulator rubber from the rear of the assembly.
8 Examine the insulator rubber and the stabilizer bar mounting rubber for wear and deterioration, and if necessary obtain new ones.

Installation

9 Installation is a reversal of the removal procedure, but adjust the linkage as described in Section 2.

4 Speedometer drive pinion - removal and installation

Removal

1 Access to the speedometer drive pinion may be gained from the top of the engine (after removing the mass airflow sensor and air ducting - see Chapter 4), or from below by raising the front of the vehicle and reaching up over the top of the transaxle. If the latter method is used, make sure that the vehicle is supported adequately on jackstands.
2 Unscrew the nut and disconnect the speedometer cable from the vehicle speed sensor on the transaxle. Use two spanners to loosen the nut - one to counterhold the sensor, and the other to unscrew the cable nut.
3 Disconnect the wiring from the vehicle speed sensor, then unscrew the sensor from the top of the drive pinion.
4 Using a pair of grips, pull out the drive pinion retaining roll pin from the transaxle casing.
5 Withdraw the speedometer drive pinion and bearing from the top of the transaxle.
6 Using a small screwdriver, pry the O-ring from the groove in the bearing; obtain a new one for reassembly.
7 Wipe clean the drive pinion and bearing, also the seating bore in the transaxle casing.

Installation

8 Installation is a reversal of the removal procedure, but lightly oil the new O-ring before inserting the assembly in the transaxle casing. Drive in the retaining roll pin using a hammer.

5 Oil seals - replacement

1 Oil leaks frequently occur due to wear or deterioration of the differential side gear seals and/or the shift selector shaft oil seal and speedometer drive pinion O-ring. Replacement of these seals is relatively easy, since the repairs can be performed without removing the transaxle from the vehicle.

Differential side gear oil seals

Refer to illustrations 5.4a and 5.4b

2 The differential side gear oil seals are located at the sides of the transaxle, where the driveaxles enter the transaxle. If leakage at the seal is suspected, raise the vehicle and support it securely on jackstands. If the seal is leaking, oil will be found on the side of the transaxle below the driveaxle.
3 Refer to Chapter 8 and remove the appropriate driveaxle. If removing the right driveaxle, it will be necessary to remove the intermediate shaft as well.
4 Using a large screwdriver or lever, carefully pry the oil seal out of the transaxle casing, taking care not to damage the transaxle casing **(see illustrations)**.
If an oil seal is reluctant to move, it is some-

5.4a Pry out the oil seal with a suitable lever

5.4b Removing the oil seal from the transaxle casing

times helpful to carefully drive it *into* the transaxle a little way, applying the force at one point only. This will have the effect of swiveling the seal out of the casing, and it can then be pulled out. If the oil seal is particularly difficult to remove, an oil seal removal tool may be obtained from a garage or accessory shop.

5 Wipe clean the oil seal seating in the transaxle casing.

6 Dip the new oil seal in clean oil, then press it a little way into the casing by hand, making sure that it is square to its seating.

7 Using suitable tubing or a large socket, carefully drive the oil seal fully into the casing until it contacts the seating.

8 Install the driveaxle with reference to Chapter 8.

Shift selector shaft oil seal

9 Apply the parking brake, jack up the front of the vehicle and support it on jackstands.

10 Unscrew the bolt securing the shift linkage to the shaft on the rear of the transaxle. Pull off the linkage and remove the rubber trunk.

11 Using a suitable tool or grips, pull the oil seal out of the transaxle casing. Technicians use a slide hammer, with an end fitting which locates over the oil seal extension. In the absence of this tool, if the oil seal is particularly tight, drill one or two small holes in the oil seal, and screw in self-tapping screws. The oil seal can then be removed from the casing by pulling on the screws.

12 Wipe clean the oil seal seating in the transaxle.

13 Dip the new oil seal in clean oil, then press it a little way into the casing by hand, making sure that it is square to its seating.

14 Using suitable tubing or a large socket, carefully drive the oil seal fully into the casing.

15 Locate the rubber trunk over the selector shaft.

16 Install the shift linkage to the shaft on the rear of the transaxle, and tighten the bolt.

17 If necessary, adjust the shift linkage as described in Section 2 of this Chapter.

Speedometer drive pinion oil seal

18 The procedure is covered in Section 4 of this Chapter.

6 Back-up light switch - removal and installation

Removal

1 Remove the air cleaner and the mass airflow sensor as described in Chapter 4.

2 Disconnect the wiring leading to the back-up light switch on the top of the transaxle.

3 Unscrew the mounting bolts, and remove the back-up light switch from the cover housing on the transaxle.

Installation

4 Installation is a reversal of the removal procedure.

7 Manual transaxle - removal and installation

Note: *Read through this procedure before starting work to see what is involved, particularly in terms of lifting equipment. Depending on the facilities available, the home mechanic may prefer to remove the engine and transaxle together, then separate them on the bench, as described in Chapter 2.*

Removal

Refer to illustrations 7.3, 7.6, 7.7, 7.10, 7.11, 7.13, 7.23, 7.24, 7.25, 7.26, 7.27a, 7.27b, 7.30a, 7.30b, 7.31a, 7.31b, 7.32a, 7.32b, 7.33, 7.34a, 7.34b, 7.34c, 7.35, 7.43 and 7.51

1 Disconnect the cable from the negative battery terminal (see Chapter 5, Section 1). For better access, the battery may be removed completely.

2 If necessary, the hood may be removed as described in Chapter 11, Section 8 for better access, and for fitting the engine lifting hoist.

3 Hold the radiator in its raised position by inserting cotter pins through the holes in the upper mounting extensions **(see illustration)**. This is necessary to retain the radiator when the subframe is removed.

4 Remove the mass airflow sensor and air inlet duct with reference to Chapter 4. On V6 models, remove the water pump pulley cover.

5 Remove the air cleaner assembly as described in Chapter 4.

6 Disconnect the wiring from the back-up light switch on the transaxle **(see illustration)**.

7 Unscrew the bolt, and remove the wiring harness bracket from the top of the transaxle **(see illustration)**.

8 Detach the ground cable located between the transaxle and the body. On V6 models, disconnect the accelerator and speed control cables. Also on V6 models, Disconnect the power steering discharge line from the power steering pump, disconnect the power steering pressure switch, then remove the power steering line from the clamp at the right engine support bracket and lay the steering line aside.

9 Disconnect the clutch release cylinder hydraulic line from the release cylinder by removing the clip securing the line.

10 Unscrew and remove the three upper bolts securing the transaxle to the engine. Also unscrew the mounting bolt with the

7.3 Use cotter pins to hold the radiator in its raised position

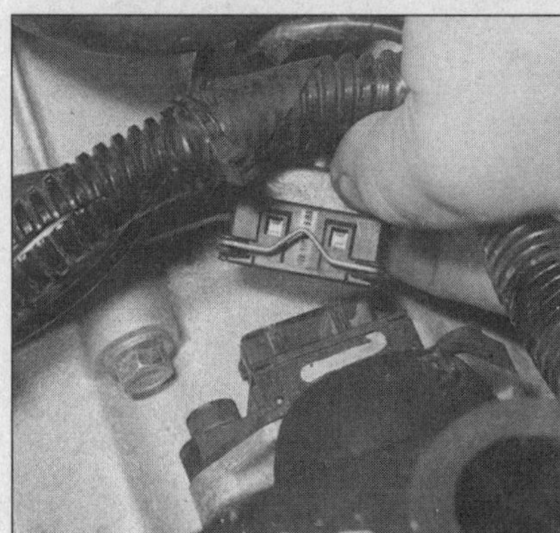

7.6 Disconnecting the wiring multi-plug from the back-up light switch

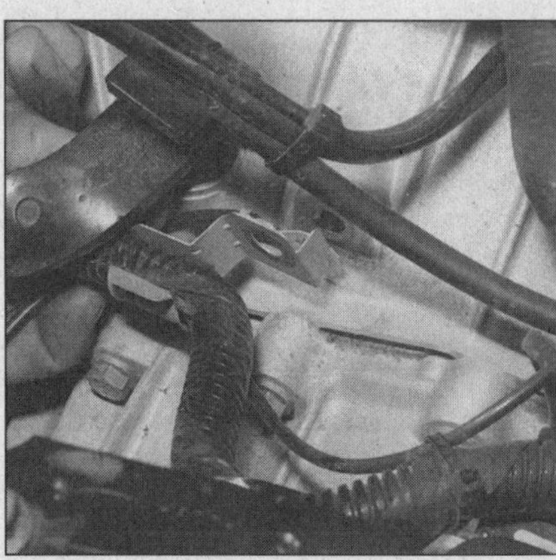

7.7 Removing the wiring harness bracket from the top of the transaxle

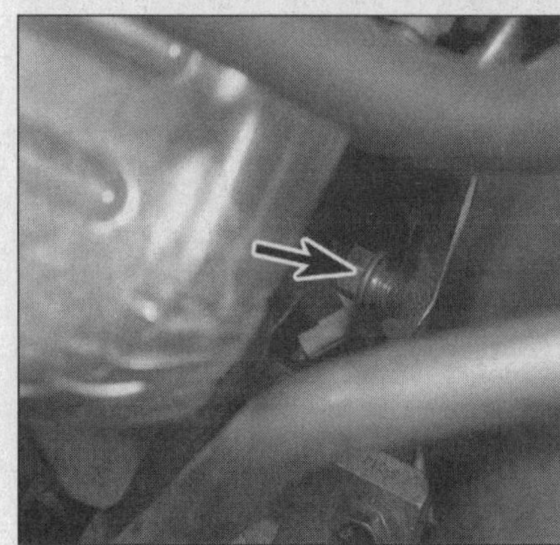

7.10 Mounting bolt with ground lead located beneath the exhaust manifold

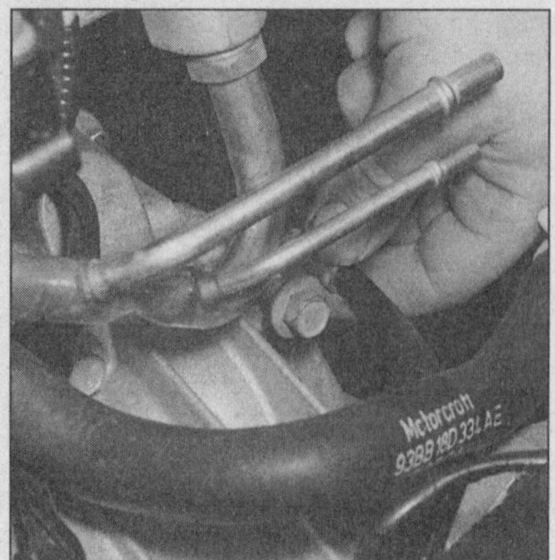

7.11 Removing the starter motor bolt with the ground cable

7.13 Radiator front lower cover removal

7.23 Unscrew the bolt securing the shift linkage rod to the shaft on the rear of the transaxle

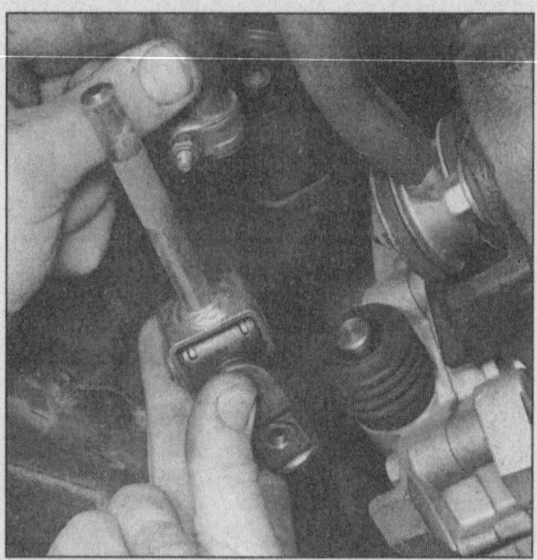

7.24 Removing the shift linkage front section

7.25 Unscrewing the bolt securing the shift support rod to the bracket on the rear of the transaxle

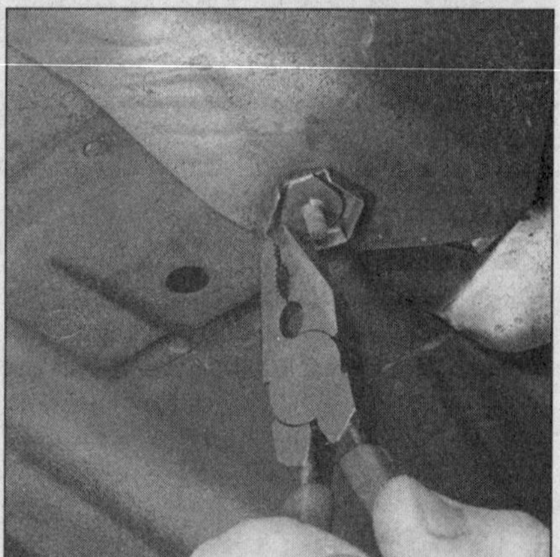

7.26 Removing the gear linkage heat shield

ground lead, located beneath the exhaust manifold **(see illustration)**.

11 On four-cylinder models, unscrew and remove the starter motor upper mounting bolt, noting that an ground cable is attached to it **(see illustration)**. On V6 models, remove the starter motor (see Chapter 5).

12 Apply the parking brake, raise the front of the vehicle and support it on jackstands. Remove the front wheels.

13 Remove the front lower cover from under the radiator by prying out the side clips and unscrewing the retaining bolts **(see illustration)**.

14 Remove the inner fender liner from the right side of the vehicle as described in Chapter 11.

15 Unscrew the bolts and remove the drivebelt cover.

16 Working on each side of the vehicle in turn, unscrew the nut and disconnect the stabilizer bar link from the strut, noting that the flexible brake hose bracket is attached to the link stud.

17 Extract the cotter pins, then unscrew the nuts securing the tie-rod ends to the steering knuckles on each side. Release the balljoints from the steering knuckle arms, using a balljoint separator tool.

18 Working on each side in turn, note which way round the front suspension lower arm balljoint clamp bolt is fitted, then unscrew and remove it from the knuckle assembly. Lever the balljoint down from the knuckle - if it is tight, pry the joint open carefully using a large flat-bladed tool. Take care not to damage the balljoint seal during the separation procedure.

19 Disconnect the cooling fan multi-plug on the subframe behind the radiator, and unclip the plug from the bracket.

20 Disconnect the multi-plug from the wiring leading to the oxygen sensor, then unclip the wiring from the engine rear mounting.

21 Disconnect the vacuum hose from the pulse-air system filter (if equipped).

22 Remove the complete exhaust system as described in Chapter 4.

23 Unscrew the bolt securing the shift linkage to the selector shaft on the rear of the transaxle **(see illustration)**.

24 Mark the position of the shift linkage front and rear sections, then unscrew the clamp bolt. Disconnect the linkage from the selector shaft on the rear of the transaxle, and separate the front and rear sections of the linkage **(see illustration)**.

7.27a Unscrew the gear linkage rear mounting bolts . . .

25 Unscrew the mounting bolt, and disconnect the shift linkage support rod from the bracket on the rear of the transaxle **(see illustration)**.

26 Remove the shift linkage heat shield from the underbody by unscrewing the nuts **(see illustration)**.

27 Unscrew and remove the shift linkage

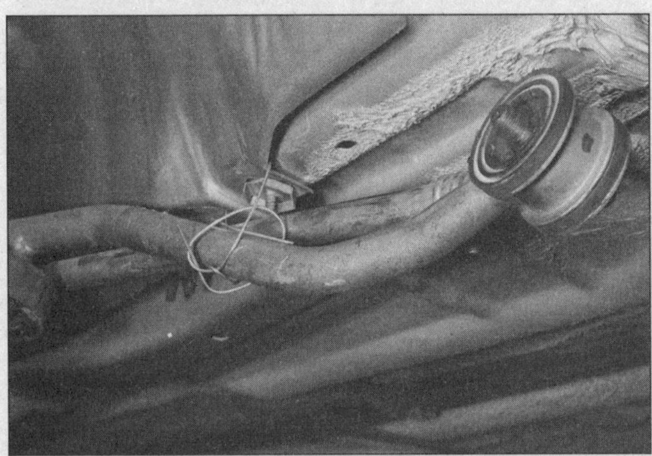
7.27b ... swivel the linkage around, and tie it to the underbody

7.30a Remove the center bolt from the rear mounting ...

7.30b ... then unbolt the mounting from the subframe and remove it

7.31a Unscrew the nut and bolt ...

7.31b ... and remove the transaxle support rod bracket

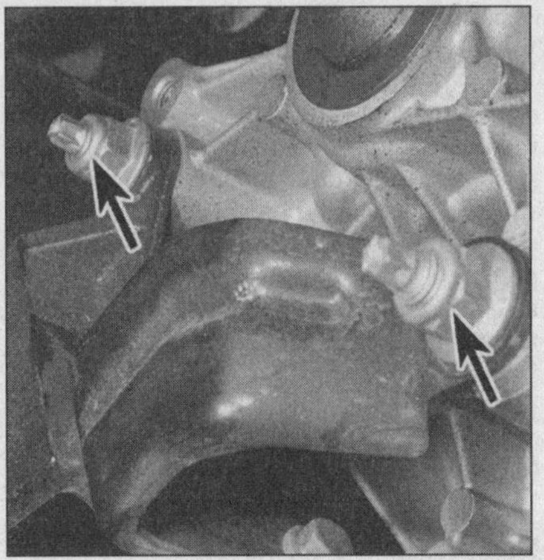
7.32a Nuts securing the rear mounting bracket to the transaxle

7.32b Removing the rear mounting bracket

rear mounting bolts, swivel the linkage around to the rear, and tie it to the underbody **(see illustrations)**.

28 On models equipped with air conditioning, unscrew and remove the mounting bolts securing the accumulator/drier to the subframe, and tie it to one side.

29 Unscrew and remove the bolts securing the steering gear to the subframe. The bolts are difficult to reach using normal wrenches. If possible, the special tool should be obtained (see Chapter 10).

30 Unscrew and remove the center bolt from the engine/transaxle rear mounting (roll restrictor), then unbolt the mount from the subframe **(see illustrations)**.

31 Unscrew the nut and bolt, and remove the support rod bracket from the rear of the transaxle **(see illustrations)**.

32 Unscrew the nuts and bolts, and remove the engine/transaxle rear mounting bracket from the transaxle **(see illustrations)**.

33 Unscrew and remove the center bolt from the engine front mount, and detach the

7.33 Removing the bolt from the engine front mounting bracket

7.34a Removing the power steering fluid cooler pipes from the subframe

7.34b Unscrewing the subframe front . . .

7.34c . . . and rear mounting bolts

7.35 Unscrewing the transaxle oil drain plug

pulse-air filter from the bracket on the mounting (if equipped) **(see illustration)**.

34 With the help of an assistant, support the weight of the subframe, using floor jacks if possible. Unscrew the bolts securing the power steering fluid cooler lines to the subframe, then unscrew the subframe mounting bolts, and lower the subframe to the ground **(see illustrations)**.

35 Position a suitable container beneath the transaxle, then unscrew the drain plug and drain the oil **(see illustration)**. Install and tighten the plug on completion.

36 Unscrew the bolts securing the right driveaxle center bearing to the cylinder block. Remove the heat shield, then pull out the right strut so that the intermediate shaft is removed from the transaxle differential gears. Be prepared for oil spillage.

37 Support the right driveaxle on jackstands, making sure that the inner tripod joint is not turned through more than 18° (damage may occur if the joint is turned through too great an angle).

38 Insert a suitable prybar between the left driveaxle inner joint and the transaxle case (with a thin piece of wood against the case), then pry the joint free from the differential. If it is difficult to remove, strike the prybar firmly with the palm of the hand. Be careful not to damage the adjacent components, and be prepared for oil spillage. As the right driveaxle has already been removed, it is possible to release the left driveaxle by inserting a forked drift from the right side, but care must be taken to prevent damage to the differential gears.

39 Support the left driveaxle on jackstands, making sure that the inner tripod joint is not turned through more than 18° (damage may occur if the joint is turned through too great an angle).

40 Disconnect the multi-plug from the wiring leading to the vehicle speed sensor.

41 Unscrew the cable nut, and disconnect the speedometer cable from the top of the vehicle speed sensor. Hold the sensor with a wrench while the cable nut is loosened.

42 If necessary, the vehicle may be lowered to the ground at this stage, to connect an engine hoist. If an engine support bar which locates over the engine compartment is used, then the vehicle may be left in its raised position.

43 Attach the hoist to diagonally-opposite positions on the engine, and take the weight of the engine and transaxle **(see illustration)**.

44 Unscrew the nuts from the engine right mounting bracket. Note that, where a hydraulic mount is installed (see Chapter 2A, Section 22), the mount must never be tilted by more than 5°.

45 Unscrew the retaining nuts and remove the engine/transaxle left mount from the transaxle.

46 On models fitted with air conditioning, lower the engine until the compressor is below the right side member.

47 On models without air conditioning, lower the transaxle until it is opposite the opening on the left side of the engine compartment.

48 Support the weight of the transaxle on a floor jack. Use safety chains or a cradle to steady the transaxle on the jack.

49 On four-cylinder models, remove the remaining starter motor mounting bolts.

50 Unscrew and remove the lower bolts

7.43 Supporting the engine with a hoist

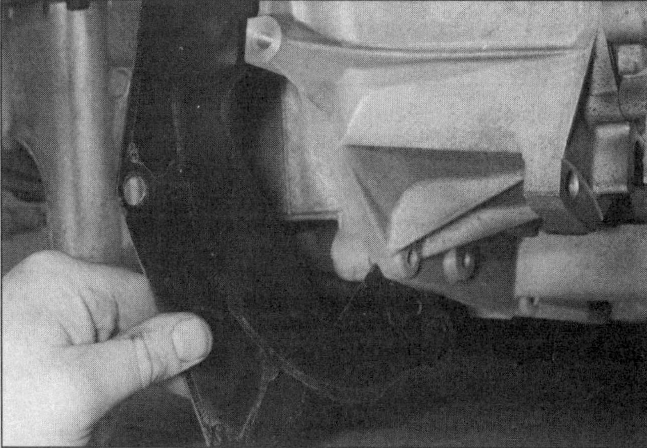

7.51 Removing the lower cover plate

securing the transaxle to the engine. Also unscrew the bolts securing the lower cover plate to the transaxle.

51 With the help of an assistant, withdraw the transaxle squarely from the engine, taking care not to allow its weight to hang on the clutch friction disc. As the transaxle is being withdrawn, remove the lower cover plate located between the transaxle and engine **(see illustration)**. Lower the transaxle to the ground.

52 The clutch components can now be inspected with reference to Chapter 8, and replaced if necessary. Unless they are virtually new, it is worth replacing the clutch components as a matter of course, even if the transaxle has been removed for some other reason.

Installation

53 If removed, install the clutch components (see Chapter 8).

54 With the transaxle secured to the floor jack as on removal, raise it into position, then carefully slide it onto the rear of the engine, at the same time engaging the input shaft with the clutch friction disc splines. Do not use excessive force to install the transaxle - if the input shaft does not slide into place easily, readjust the angle of the transaxle so it is level, and/or turn the input shaft so that the splines engage properly with the disc. If problems are still experienced, check that the clutch friction disc is correctly centered (Chapter 8).

55 Install the lower bolts securing the transaxle to the engine, and tighten moderately at this stage.

56 On four-cylinder models, insert and tighten the starter mounting bolts, noting that an ground cable is attached to one of them. On V6 models, install the starter (see Chapter 5).

57 Raise the transaxle to its normal position.

58 Install the engine/transaxle left mounting, and tighten the nuts.

59 Install the engine right mounting bracket, and tighten the nuts.

60 If previously lowered, raise the front of the vehicle, and support on jackstands.

61 Install the speedometer cable to the vehicle speed sensor, and tighten the cable nut.

62 Reconnect the wiring to the speed sensor.

63 Insert the left driveaxle into the transaxle, making sure that it is fully engaged with the internal snap-ring.

64 Install the right driveaxle and intermediate shaft, and tighten the bolts.

65 Install and align the subframe, with reference to Chapter 2B, Section 4. Tighten the mounting bolts to the specified torque.

66 Install the pulse-air filter (if equipped). Tighten the center bolt in the engine front mounting.

67 Install the engine rear mounting bracket, and tighten the bolts.

68 Install the transaxle support rod and bracket, and tighten the bolts and nut.

69 Install the engine rear mounting to the subframe, and tighten the bolts.

70 Install the steering gear to the subframe, and tighten the mounting bolts.

71 On models with air conditioning, install the accumulator/drier to the subframe, and tighten the mounting bolts.

72 Install the shift linkage and heat shield (see Section 3).

73 Install the transaxle shift support rod to the rear of the transaxle, and tighten the bolt. Adjust the shift linkage if necessary, with reference to Section 2.

74 Install the exhaust system (see Chapter 4.

75 Reconnect the vacuum hose to the pulse-air system filter (if equipped).

76 Reconnect the oxygen sensor wiring.

77 Reconnect and secure the cooling fan multi-plug.

78 Install the front suspension lower arm balljoints to the knuckle assemblies (see Chapter 10).

79 Install the tie-rod ends to the steering knuckles on each side (see Chapter 10).

80 Install the stabilizer bar links to the struts, and tighten the nuts.

81 Install the drivebelt cover and the inner fender liner.

82 Install the front lower cover beneath the radiator.

83 Install the wheels, and lower the vehicle to the ground.

84 Insert the upper bolts securing the transaxle to the engine.

85 Reconnect the clutch hydraulic line and bleed the clutch (see Chapter 8). Reconnect the power steering line on V6 models. Make sure the steering line is securely clamped in position on the right engine support bracket. Note that a ground wire is also located under one of the nuts on the support bracket. Reconnect the power steering pressure switch electrical connector.

86 Install the ground cable between the transaxle and the body.

87 Install the wiring harness bracket to the top of the transaxle.

88 Reconnect the wiring to the back-up light switch.

89 Tighten all transaxle mounting bolts fully.

90 Install the air cleaner assembly, mass airflow sensor and air inlet duct (see Chapter 4).

91 Remove the cotter pins holding the radiator in its raised position.

92 If removed, install the hood.

93 If removed, install the battery and reconnect the leads.

94 Fill the transaxle with oil, and check the level as described in Chapter 1.

95 Make a final check that all connections have been made, and all bolts tightened fully.

96 Road test the vehicle to check for proper transaxle operation, then check the transaxle visually for leakage of oil.

8 Manual transaxle mounting - checking and replacement

This procedure is covered in Chapter 2A, Section 22.

9 Manual transaxle overhaul - general

1 Overhauling a manual transaxle is a difficult job for the do-it-yourselfer. It involves the dismantling and reassembly of many small parts. Numerous clearances must be precisely measured and, if necessary, changed with selected spacers and circlips. As a result, if transaxle problems arise, while the unit can be removed and installed by a competent do-it-yourselfer, overhaul should be left to a transaxle specialist. Rebuilt transaxles may be available - check with your dealer parts department, motor factors, or transaxle specialists. At any rate, the time and money involved in an overhaul is almost sure to exceed the cost of a rebuilt unit.

2 Nevertheless, it's not impossible for an inexperienced mechanic to rebuild a transaxle, providing the special tools are available, and the job is done in a deliberate step-by-step manner so nothing is overlooked.

3 The tools necessary for an overhaul include: internal and external snap-ring pliers, a bearing puller, a slide hammer, a set of pin punches, a dial test indicator, and possibly a hydraulic press. In addition, a large, sturdy workbench and a vise or transaxle will be required.

4 During dismantling of the transaxle, make careful notes of how each part comes off, where it fits in relation to other parts, and what holds it in place. Actually noting how they are fitted when you remove the parts will make it much easier to get the transaxle back together.

5 Before taking the transaxle apart for repair, it will help if you have some idea what area of the transaxle is malfunctioning. Certain problems can be closely tied to specific areas in the transaxle, which can make component examination and replacement easier. Refer to the *"Troubleshooting"* section at the end of this manual for information regarding possible sources of trouble.

Chapter 7 Part B
Automatic transaxle

Contents

Specifications

Torque specifications

	Ft-lbs (unless otherwise indicated)
Selector cable support bracket	15 to 19
Torque converter-to-driveplate	25 to 29
Automatic transaxle to engine	
1995 through 1997	41 to 50
1998	30
Oil cooler lines	
1995 through 1997	17
1998 and later	27 to 32
Selector lever to floor	84 in-lbs
Speed sensor	44 in-lbs
Transaxle drain plug	19 to 21
Selector lever position sensor	88 in-lbs

1 General information

The CD4E automatic transaxle is controlled electronically by the engine management electronic control unit. There are two operational modes (Economy and Sport), and a driver-operated overdrive inhibit switch prevents the 4th gear from operating when required during certain conditions. With the Economy mode selected, gear changes occur at low engine speeds, whereas with the Sport mode selected, the changes occur at high engine speeds.

The transaxle incorporates a chain drive between the planetary gearsets and the final drive. The transaxle fluid is cooled by a cooler located within the radiator.

There is no kickdown switch, as kickdown is controlled by the throttle position sensor in the engine management system.

The electronic control system has a fail-safe mode, which gives the transaxle limited operation in order to drive the vehicle home or to a repair shop.

The gear selection includes the normal P, R, N, D, 2, and 1 positions. As a safety measure, it is necessary for the ignition to be switched on and for the brake pedal to be depressed in order to move the selector from position P. If the vehicle battery is discharged, the selector lever release solenoid will not function; if it is required to move the vehicle in this state, insert a pen or a similar small instrument into the aperture on the left side of the center console. Push the locking lever rearwards to allow the selector lever to be moved.

2 Troubleshooting - general

1 In the event of a fault occurring on the transaxle, first check that the fluid level is correct (see Chapter 1). If there has been a loss of fluid, check the oil seals as described in Section 7. Also check the hoses to the fluid cooler in the radiator for leaks. The only other checks possible for the home mechanic are the adjustment of the selector cable (Section 3) and the selector lever position sensor (Section 6).

2 If the fault still persists, it is necessary to determine whether it is of an electrical, mechanical or hydraulic nature; to do this, special test equipment is required. It is therefore essential to have the work carried out by an automatic transaxle specialist or dealer if a

3.6 Selector lever on the side of the transaxle

3.7 Cable support bracket bolts

transaxle fault is suspected.

3 Do not remove the transaxle from the vehicle for possible repair before professional troubleshooting has been carried out, since most tests require the transaxle to be in the vehicle.

3 Selector cable - removal, installation and adjustment

Removal

Refer to illustrations 3.6 and 3.7

1 Loosen the left front wheel lug nuts. Apply the parking brake, jack up the front of the vehicle and support it on jackstands. Remove the wheel.

2 Remove the mass airflow sensor and ducting (Chapter 4) in order to gain access to the selector cable, which is located on the left side of the transaxle.

3 Working beneath the vehicle, remove the heat shield for access to the bottom of the selector lever assembly.

4 Disconnect the inner cable from the bottom of the selector lever assembly.

5 Turn the outer cable locking ring counterclockwise by 90-degrees to unlock it from the selector lever plate on the bottom of the selector lever assembly. Hold the collar while turning the locking ring.

6 Working in the engine compartment, pull the inner cable end fitting outwards from the lever on the side of the transaxle **(see illustration)**.

7 Unbolt the cable support bracket from the transaxle **(see illustration)**.

8 Detach the remaining cable supports, and withdraw the cable assembly from the vehicle.

Installation and adjustment

9 Installation is a reversal of the removal procedure, but adjust the cable as follows.

10 Inside the vehicle, move the selector lever to position "D".

11 With the inner cable disconnected from the lever on the side of the transaxle, check that the lever is in the "D" position. To do this, it will be necessary to move the lever slightly up and down until it is positioned correctly. A further check can be made by observing that the "D" mark on the selector lever position sensor is correctly aligned.

12 Check that the cable locking ring beneath the vehicle is still unlocked (i.e. turned counterclockwise by 90-degrees).

13 With both the selector levers inside the vehicle and on the side of the transaxle in position "D", install the cable end fitting to the transaxle lever, then turn the locking ring 90-degrees clockwise to lock it.

14 Install the heat shield to the underbody.

15 Install the mass airflow sensor and ducting.

16 Install the left front wheel, then lower the vehicle to the ground. Tighten the lug nuts to the torque listed in the Chapter 1 Specifications.

17 Road test the vehicle to check the operation of the transaxle.

4 Selector assembly - removal and installation

Removal

1 Remove the center console as described in Chapter 11.

2 Apply the parking brake, then jack up the front of the vehicle and support it securely on jackstands.

3 Working beneath the vehicle, remove the heat shield, then disconnect the selector cable end fitting from the bottom of the selector lever assembly.

4 Unscrew the mounting nuts securing the selector cable plate to the bottom of the lever assembly.

5 Disconnect the wiring multi-plugs, then withdraw the selector lever assembly from inside the vehicle. Recover the gasket.

6 If necessary, the selector lever and position indicator may be unbolted from the top of the assembly.

Installation

7 Installation is a reversal of the removal procedure, but adjust the selector cable as described in Section 3.

5 Speedometer drive pinion - removal and installation

Removal

1 The speedometer drive pinion is located on the right rear side of the transaxle. First apply the parking brake, then jack up the front of the vehicle and support it on jackstands.

2 Unscrew the nut, and disconnect the speedometer cable from the vehicle speed sensor on the transaxle. Use two wrenches to loosen the nut - one to counterhold the sensor, and the other to unscrew the cable nut.

3 Disconnect the wiring from the vehicle speed sensor.

4 Unscrew the clamp bolt, and remove the clamp plate securing the drive pinion and vehicle speed sensor in the transaxle.

5 Pull out the speedometer drive pinion and bearing assembly, together with the vehicle speed sensor.

6 Unscrew the vehicle speed sensor from the drive pinion bearing.

7 Remove the pinion from the bearing.

8 Using a small screwdriver, pry the rubber O-ring from the groove in the bearing; obtain a new one for reassembly.

9 Wipe clean the drive pinion and bearing, also the seating bore in the transaxle casing.

Installation

10 Installation is a reversal of the removal procedure. Lightly oil the new O-ring before inserting the assembly in the transaxle casing. Tighten the clamp bolt.

6.2 Multi-plug for the selector lever position sensor

6.7 With "D" selected, "D" mark (A) on the selector lever position sensor should align with cut-outs (B) in shaft's plastic insert (shown here with "P" selected)

6 Selector lever position sensor - removal, installation and adjustment

Removal

Refer to illustration 6.2

1 Remove the mass airflow sensor and ducting (Chapter 4) in order to gain access to the selector lever position sensor, which is located on top of the transaxle.

2 Disconnect the wiring multi-plug **(see illustration)**.

3 Unscrew the mounting bolts, and remove the sensor.

Installation and adjustment

Refer to illustration 6.7

4 Installation is a reversal of the removal procedure, but check the alignment of the sensor as follows before fully tightening the mounting bolts.

5 Move the selector lever to position "N".

6 The tool for aligning the sensor consists of a metal plate, with pegs to engage with the cut-outs in the sensor and shaft. A similar tool may be made up, or alternatively, a straight edge may be used to check the alignment.

7 Twist the sensor on the shaft until the slots in the sensor housing and the plastic insert in the shaft are correctly aligned. With the sensor correctly aligned, tighten the bolts, then remove the alignment tool. As a further check, move the selector lever to position "D", and check that the "D" mark on the sensor is aligned with the slots in the shaft's plastic insert **(see illustration)**.

7 Oil seals - replacement

Differential side gear oil seals

1 The procedure is the same as that for the manual transaxle (refer to Chapter 7A, Section 5).

Speedometer drive pinion oil seal

2 The procedure is covered in Section 5 of this Chapter.

8 Automatic transaxle - removal and installation

Note: *Read through this procedure before starting work, to see what is involved, particularly in terms of lifting equipment. Depending on the facilities available, the home mechanic may prefer to remove the engine and transaxle together, then separate them on the bench, as described in Chapter 2.*

Removal

Refer to illustrations 8.6, 8.7a, 8.7b, 8.28 and 8.34

1 Disconnect the battery negative cable (refer to Chapter 5, Section 1). For better access, the battery may be removed completely.

2 If necessary, remove the hood (Chapter 11) for better access, and for attaching the engine lifting hoist.

3 Raise the radiator, and hold it in the raised position by inserting cotter pins through the holes in the upper mounting extensions. This is necessary to retain the radiator when the subframe is removed.

4 Remove the mass airflow sensor and ducting (Chapter 4).

5 Remove the air cleaner assembly (Chapter 4).

6 Detach the battery ground lead from the transaxle **(see illustration)**.

7 Disconnect the wiring multi-plugs from the inhibitor switch, control unit, transaxle speed sensor and turbine sensor **(see illustrations)**.

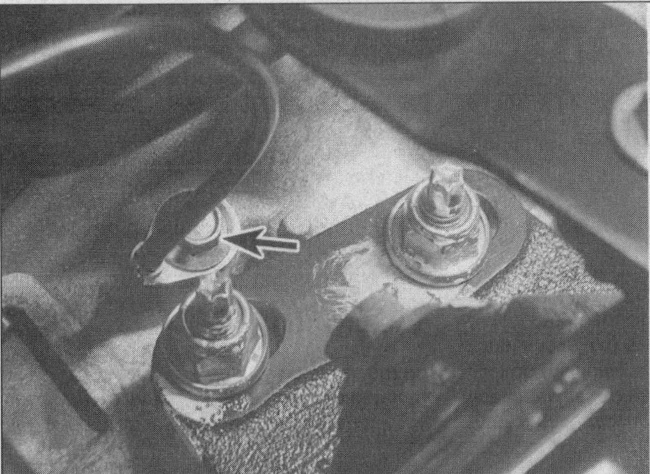

8.6 Ground lead attachment on the transaxle

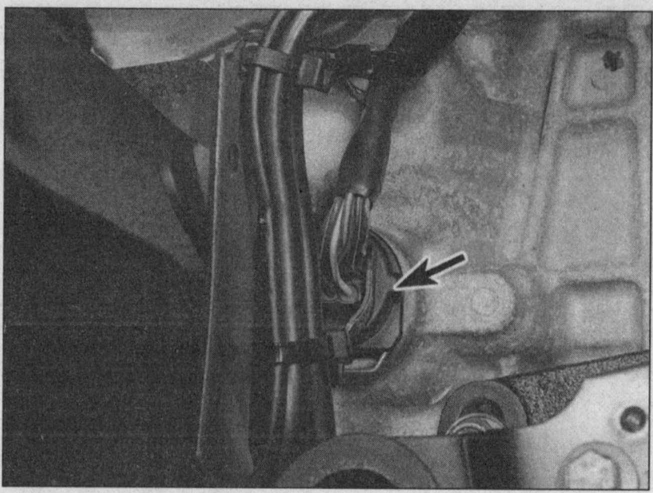

8.7a Inhibitor switch multi-plug on the top of the transaxle

8.7b Turbine sensor multi-plug on the side of the transaxle

8 Pull the selector cable end fitting from the lever on the side of the transaxle, then unbolt the support bracket.

9 Loosen the front wheel lug nuts. Apply the parking brake, jack up the front of the vehicle and support it on jackstands. Remove the front wheels.

10 Remove the wheel arch liner from the right side of the vehicle (Chapter 11).

11 Remove the drivebelt cover (see Chapter 1).

12 Working on each side of the vehicle in turn, unscrew the nut and disconnect the stabilizer bar link from the strut, noting that the flexible brake hose bracket is attached to the link stud.

13 Extract the cotter pins, then unscrew the nuts securing the tie-rod ends to the steering knuckles on each side. Release the tie-rod ends from the steering knuckle arms, using a balljoint separator tool.

14 Working on each side in turn, note which way the front suspension lower arm balljoint clamp bolt is attached, then unscrew and remove it from the knuckle assembly.

15 Lever the balljoint down from the knuckle - if it is tight, pry the fitting open carefully using a large flat-bladed tool. Take care not to damage the balljoint seal during the separation procedure.

16 Remove the front lower cover from under the radiator, by prying out the side clips and unscrewing the retaining bolts.

17 Drain the cooling system as described in Chapter 1.

18 Disconnect the multi-plug from the wiring leading to the oxygen sensor, then unclip the wiring from the engine rear mounting.

19 Remove the complete exhaust system (Chapter 4).

20 On models with air conditioning, unscrew and remove the mounting bolts securing the receiver-drier to the subframe, and tie it to one side.

21 Unscrew and remove the bolts securing the steering gear to the subframe. The bolts are difficult to reach using normal wrenches, and if possible the special cranked tool should be obtained (see Chapter 10).

22 Unbolt the engine/transaxle rear mounting from the subframe.

23 Unscrew and remove the center bolt from the engine front mount.

24 Unbolt the radiator bracket from the subframe.

25 With the help of an assistant, support the weight of the subframe, using floor jacks if possible. Unscrew the bolts securing the power steering fluid cooler pipes to the subframe, then unscrew and remove the subframe mounting bolts, and lower the subframe to the ground.

26 Unscrew and remove the center bolt from the engine/transaxle rear mount, then unbolt the mount from the transaxle.

27 Unscrew the fitting nut securing the automatic transaxle fluid cooler pipe to the left side of the transaxle. Unclip the pipe, and move it to one side. Plug the end of the pipe, to prevent dust and dirt entering the hydraulic system.

28 Position a suitable container beneath the transaxle, then unscrew the drain plug and drain the fluid **(see illustration)**. Install and tighten the plug on completion.

29 Insert a lever between the left driveaxle inner CV joint and the transaxle case (with a thin piece of wood against the case), then pry free the joint from the differential. If it proves reluctant to move, strike the lever firmly with the palm of the hand. Be careful not to damage the adjacent components, and be prepared for fluid spillage.

30 Support the left driveaxle on jackstands, making sure that the inner fitting is not turned more than 18-degrees (damage may occur if the fitting is turned through too great an angle).

31 Unscrew the bolts securing the right driveaxle center bearing to the cylinder block, remove the heat shield, then pull out the right strut so that the intermediate shaft is removed from the transaxle differential gears. Be prepared for fluid spillage.

32 Support the right driveaxle on jackstands, again making sure that the inner fitting is not turned more than 18-degrees (damage may occur if the fitting is turned through too great an angle).

33 At the front of the transaxle, unscrew the fitting nut and disconnect the fluid cooler pipe. Plug the end of the pipe, to prevent dust and dirt entering the hydraulic system.

34 Unscrew the bolts and remove the cover plate from the bottom of the transaxle, for access to the torque converter retaining bolts **(see illustration)**.

35 Unscrew and remove the torque converter retaining bolts. It will be necessary to turn the engine, using the crankshaft pulley bolt, so that each of the four bolts can be unscrewed through the aperture.

36 If necessary, the vehicle may be lowered to the ground at this stage, in order to connect an engine support hoist. If an engine support bar which mounts over the engine compartment is to be used, then the vehicle may be left in its raised position.

37 Attach the hoist or engine support bar to diagonally opposite positions on the engine, and take the weight of the engine and transaxle.

38 At the top of the engine, disconnect the two wiring multi-plugs from the thermostat housing.

39 Disconnect the radiator hoses from the thermostat housing.

40 Unscrew the mounting bolts, and remove the thermostat housing.

41 Unscrew and remove the upper mounting bolts securing the automatic transaxle to the engine.

42 Unscrew the nuts from the engine right mounting bracket. Note that, where a hydraulic mount is installed (see Chapter 2A, Section 22), the mount must never be tilted by more than 5-degrees.

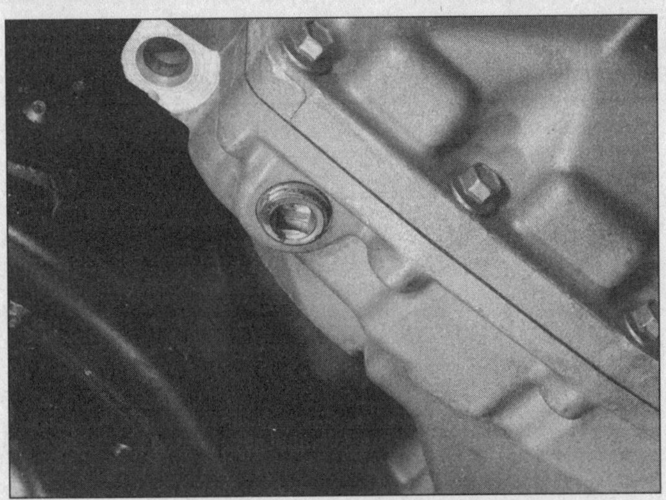

8.28 Automatic transaxle fluid drain plug

8.34 Removing the cover plate from the bottom of the transaxle

43 Unscrew the retaining nuts, and remove the engine/transaxle left mount from the transaxle.
44 On models with air conditioning, lower the engine until the compressor is below the right side subframe member.
45 On models without air conditioning, lower the transaxle until it is opposite the aperture on the left side of the engine compartment.
46 Support the weight of the transaxle on a floor jack. Use safety chains or make up a cradle to steady the transaxle on the jack.
47 Unscrew and remove the starter motor mounting bolts.
48 Unscrew and remove the lower bolts securing the transaxle to the engine.
49 With the help of an assistant, withdraw the transaxle squarely from the engine, making sure that the torque converter comes away with the transaxle, and does not stay in contact with the driveplate. If this precaution is not taken, there is a risk of the torque converter falling out and being damaged.
50 Lower the transaxle to the ground.

Installation

Refer to illustration 8.52

51 Clean the contact surfaces of the driveplate and torque converter.
52 Check that the torque converter is fully entered in the transaxle. To do this, place a straight-edge on the transaxle flange, and check that the torque converter hub is flush with the straight-edge **Caution:** *This procedure is important, to ensure that the torque converter is engaged with the fluid pump. If it is not fully engaged, serious damage will occur.*
53 With the help of an assistant, raise the transaxle, and locate it on the rear of the driveplate. The torque converter must remain in full engagement during the installation procedure.
54 Install and tighten the transaxle-to-engine bolts.
55 Install and tighten the starter motor mounting bolts.
56 Remove the floor jack.
57 Install the engine/transaxle left and right mounts, but do not fully tighten them at this stage.
58 Install the thermostat housing, and tighten the bolts.
59 Reconnect the radiator hoses to the thermostat housing.
60 Reconnect the two wiring multi-plugs to the thermostat housing.
61 Insert and tighten all of the torque converter retaining bolts to the specified torque. Turn the engine as required to bring each of the bolts into view. **Note:** *Install all of the bolts before tightening any of them.*
62 Install the cover plate to the bottom of the transaxle, and tighten the bolts.
63 Install the fluid cooler pipe to the front of the transaxle, and tighten the fitting nut.
64 Install the right driveaxle and intermediate shaft, together with the heat shield (refer to Chapter 8 if necessary).
65 Install the left driveaxle (refer to Chapter 8 if necessary).
66 Install the fluid cooler pipe to the left side of the transaxle, making sure that it engages with the clips correctly. Tighten the fitting nut.
67 Install the engine/transaxle rear mount to the transaxle, but do not fully tighten the center bolt at this stage.
68 Install the subframe, and align it as described in Chapter 2B, Section 4. Tighten the mounting bolts to the specified torque.
69 Install the power steering fluid cooler pipes to the subframe, and tighten the bolts.
70 Install the radiator bracket to the subframe, and tighten the bolts.
71 Insert the center bolt in the engine front mounting, and hand-tighten it.
72 Secure the engine/transaxle rear mounting to the subframe.
73 Remove the hoist from the engine.
74 Align and tighten the engine mounting bolts, with reference to Chapter 2A, Section 22.
75 Install the steering gear to the subframe, and tighten the bolts.
76 On models with air conditioning, install the receiver-drier to the subframe, and tighten the bolts.
77 Install the complete exhaust system, with reference to Chapter 4.
78 Reconnect the oxygen sensor multiplug, then clip the wiring to the engine rear mounting.
79 Install the front lower cover under the radiator.
80 Install both of the front suspension lower arm balljoints, and tighten the clamp bolts. Refer to Chapter 10 if necessary.
81 Install the tie-rod ends to the steering knuckles on both sides. Refer to Chapter 10 if necessary.
82 Install the stabilizer bar links to the struts on both sides.
83 Install the drivebelt cover and the right side wheel arch liner.
84 Install the front wheels and lower the vehicle to the ground. Tighten the lug nuts to the torque listed in the Chapter 1 Specifications.
85 Install the selector cable and bracket, and tighten the bolts.
86 Reconnect the wiring multi-plugs for the inhibitor switch and control switch.
87 Install the battery ground lead to the transaxle, and tighten the bolt.
88 Install the air cleaner assembly as described in Chapter 4.
89 Install the mass airflow sensor and air inlet duct, with reference to Chapter 4.
90 Remove the cotter pins holding the radiator in its raised position.
91 If removed, install the hood with reference to Chapter 11.
92 Reconnect the battery negative cable.
93 Adjust the selector cable as described in Section 3.

94 Adjust the selector lever position sensor as described in Section 6.
95 Fill the transaxle with the correct quantity of fluid, through the dipstick/filler tube (see Chapter 1).
96 Refill the cooling system with reference to Chapter 1.
97 After running the engine, recheck the transaxle fluid level, and top-up if necessary (refer to Chapter 1).
98 Road test the vehicle to check the transaxle for correct operation.

9 Automatic transaxle mounts - check and replacement

This procedure is covered in Chapter 2A, Section 22.

10 Automatic transaxle overhaul - general information

1 Overhaul of the automatic transaxle should be left to an automatic transaxle specialist or a dealer. Refer to the information given in Section 2 before removing the unit.
2 Note that, if the vehicle is still within the warranty period, in the event of a fault it is important to take it to a dealer, who will carry out a comprehensive diagnosis procedure using specialist equipment. Failure to do this will invalidate the warranty.

Chapter 8
Clutch and driveaxles

Contents

Specifications

Clutch

Recommended fluid	Dot 3 brake fluid
Maximum pressure plate runout	0.028 inch
Disc lining minimum thickness (to rivet heads)	1/32-inch
Maximum flywheel runout	0.008 inch

Torque specifications

	Ft-lbs (unless otherwise indicated)
Bleed screw	61 to 87 in-lbs
Driveaxle support bearing bracket-to-cylinder block bolts	17 to 22
Driveaxle/hub retaining nut	
1995 through 1997	251
1998 and later	200
Release cylinder bolts	
1995 through 1997	84 to 168 in-lbs
1998 and later	88 in-lbs
Release cylinder hydraulic fitting	124 in-lbs
Clutch master cylinder nuts	88 in-lbs
Pressure plate-to-flywheel bolts	
1995 through 1997	13 to 18
1998 and later	21

1 General information

The information in this Chapter deals with the components from the engine flywheel to the front wheels, except for the transaxle, which is covered in Chapter 7, Parts A and B. For the purposes of this Chapter, these components are grouped into the two categories, clutch (for manual transaxle models) and driveaxles (for manual and automatic transaxle models). Separate Sections within this Chapter offer general descriptions and inspection procedures for each group.

Since many of the procedures covered in this Chapter involve working under the vehicle, make sure that it is securely supported on jackstands placed on a firm, level floor.

2 Clutch - description and check

1 All manual transaxle models are equipped with a hydraulically operated single dry plate clutch assembly. The cover assembly consists of a steel cover (doweled and bolted to the rear face of the flywheel), the pressure plate and a diaphragm spring.

2 The clutch disc is free to slide along the transaxle input shaft, and is held in position between the flywheel and the pressure plate by the pressure of the diaphragm spring. Friction lining material is riveted to the clutch disc (driven plate), which has a spring-cushioned hub, to absorb transaxle shock.

3 The clutch is actuated by a hydraulic release cylinder/release bearing assembly, controlled by the clutch master cylinder. The master cylinder shares a common fluid reservoir with the brake master cylinder. The clutch release mechanism consists of the release cylinder/release bearing assembly. Depressing the clutch pedal actuates the release cylinder/release bearing by means of the master cylinder. The release bearing pushes against the diaphragm fingers, moving the center of the pressure plate diaphragm spring inward. As the center of the spring is pushed inward, the outside of the spring pivots outward, moving the pressure plate backward and disengaging its grip on the clutch disc.

4 When the pedal is released, the diaphragm spring forces the pressure plate back into contact with the friction linings on the clutch disc. The disc is now firmly held between the pressure plate and the flywheel, thus transmitting engine power to the transaxle.

5 Because of the hydraulic design, the clutch is self-adjusting.

6 The following checks may be performed to diagnose a clutch problem.

(a) *First check the entire length of the hydraulic line between the clutch master cylinder and release cylinder for fluid leakage. Confirm that the hydraulic line is located correctly, without any sharp turns.*

(b) *To check clutch spin down time, run the engine at normal idle speed with the transaxle in Neutral (clutch pedal up). Disengage the clutch (pedal down), wait several seconds, then engage reverse. No grinding noise should be heard. A grinding noise would most likely indicate a problem in the pressure plate or the clutch disc. Remember, however, that the transaxle reverse gear is a synchromesh design, so the probable symptom of a clutch fault would be a slight rearward movement (or attempted movement) of the vehicle. If the check is made on level ground with the parking brake released, the movement would be more noticeable.*

(c) *To check for complete clutch release, run the engine at idle, and hold the clutch pedal approximately half an inch from the floor. Shift between 1st gear and reverse several times. If the shift is not smooth, or if the vehicle attempts to move forward or backward, component failure is indicated. Check the clutch master cylinder fluid level.*

(d) *Check the clutch pedal for excessive wear of the bushings and for any obstructions which may restrict the pedal movement.*

3 Clutch adjustment - check

Because of it's hydraulic design, clutch adjustment is not possible or required. Any wear of the clutch disc is compensated for by the clutch master cylinder and fluid.

4 Clutch master cylinder - removal and installation and hydraulic system bleeding

Warning: *Do not allow brake fluid to enter your eyes or contact your skin. If brake fluid contacts the skin or enters the eyes, flush immediately with clean water.*

Caution: *Brake fluid will damage painted or plastic surfaces. If the fluid contacts a plastic or painted surface, wash the area immediately with clean water.*

Master cylinder removal and installation

1 Disconnect the cable from the negative battery terminal (see Chapter 5, Section 1).

2 Depress the locking tab and lower the storage compartment door above the clutch pedal.

3 Remove the three screws and remove the lower instrument panel. Depress the locking tab and open the central junction box. Disconnect the electrical from the upper and lower central junction box. Remove the four nuts that secure the central junction box and remove it.

4 Disconnect the fluid delivery line from the fluid reservoir from the clutch master cylinder. Use a shop towel to prevent hydraulic (brake) fluid from spilling on the carpet.

5 Remove the clip that secures the discharge line to the master cylinder and disconnect the line.

6 Remove the clip that secures the master cylinder piston to the brake pedal. Then remove the two master cylinder mounting nuts and remove the master cylinder.

7 Installation is the reverse of removal. Make sure the hydraulic lines are securely attached to the master cylinder. Check the fluid level (Chapter 1) and bleed the system.

Bleeding hydraulic system

8 Fill the brake fluid reservoir with clean DOT 3 brake fluid.

9 Push the clutch pedal to the floor completely at least 30 times to force air into the release cylinder.

10 Attach a transparent hose to the bleed screw on the release cylinder. Submerse the other end of the hose in a container partially filled with clean brake fluid. While an assistant holds the clutch pedal to the floor, open the bleed screw and note any air bubbles in the hose.

11 Close the bleed valve, then release the clutch pedal. **Note:** *Make sure the fluid reservoir doesn't run dry during the bleeding process, or additional air will be drawn into the system.*

12 Repeat the process until air bubbles are no longer present in the hose. Check the fluid level in the reservoir and add fluid as necessary (see Chapter 1).

5 Clutch components - removal, inspection and installation

Warning: *Dust created by clutch wear and deposited on the clutch components may contain asbestos, which is a health hazard. DO NOT blow it out with compressed air, and do not inhale any of it. DO NOT use gasoline or petroleum-based solvents to clean off the dust. Brake system cleaner should be used to flush the dust into a suitable receptacle. After the clutch components are wiped clean with rags, dispose of the contaminated rags and cleaner in a sealed, marked container.*

Removal

Refer to illustrations 5.1, 5.2, 5.3 and 5.4

1 Access to the clutch may be gained in one of two ways. The engine/transaxle unit can be removed, as described in Chapter 2B, and the transaxle separated from the engine on the bench. Alternatively, the engine may be left in the vehicle and the transaxle removed independently, as described in Chapter 7A. If the latter course of action is taken, note that the transaxle need only be moved to the left of the engine compartment - it is not necessary to remove it completely **(see illustration)**.

5.1 Clutch is accessible with the transaxle moved to one side

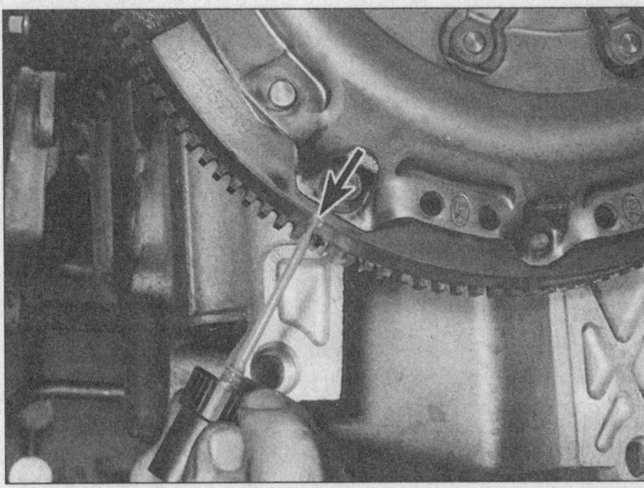

5.2 Marking the pressure plate and flywheel with a dab of paint

2 Having separated the transaxle from the engine, check if there are any marks identifying the relation of the pressure plate to the flywheel. If not, make your own marks using a dab of paint or a scriber **(see illustration)**. These marks will be used if the original cover is reinstalled, and will help to maintain the balance of the unit. A new cover may be installed in any position allowed by the locating dowels.

3 Unscrew and remove the six pressure plate retaining bolts, working in a diagonal sequence, and loosening the bolts only a turn at a time **(see illustration)**. If necessary, the flywheel may be held stationary using a wide-bladed screwdriver, inserted in the teeth of the starter ring gear and resting against part of the cylinder block.

4 Ease the pressure plate off its locating dowels. Be prepared to catch the clutch disc, which will drop out as the cover is removed **(see illustration)**. Note which way the disc is installed.

Inspection

5 The most common problem which occurs in the clutch is wear of the clutch disc (driven plate). However, all the clutch components should be inspected at this time, particularly if the engine has covered a high mileage. Unless the clutch components are known to be virtually new, it is worth replacing them all as a set (disc, pressure plate and release bearing). Replacing a worn clutch disc by itself is not always satisfactory, especially if the old disc was slipping and causing the pressure plate to overheat.

6 Examine the linings of the clutch disc for wear and loose rivets, and the disc hub and rim for distortion, cracks, broken torsion springs, and worn splines. The surface of the friction linings may be highly glazed, but as long as the friction material pattern can be clearly seen, and the rivet heads are at least 1 mm below the lining surface, this is satisfactory. If there is any sign of oil contamination, indicated by shiny black discoloration, the disc must be replaced, and the source of the contamination traced and rectified. This will be a leaking crankshaft oil seal or transaxle input shaft oil seal. The replacement procedure for the former is given in Chapter 2; replacement of the transaxle input shaft oil seal should be entrusted to a dealer or other qualified repair shop, as it involves dismantling the transaxle, and the replacement of the clutch release bearing guide tube, using a press. The disc must also be replaced if the lining thickness has worn down to, or just above, the level of the rivet heads.

7 Inspect the flywheel for cracks, heat checking, score marks and other damage. If the imperfections are slight, a machine shop can resurface it to make it flat and smooth. Refer to Chapter 2 for the flywheel removal procedure. Check the machined face of the pressure plate. If it is grooved, or heavily scored, replacement is necessary. The pressure plate must also be replaced if any cracks are apparent, or if the diaphragm spring is damaged or its pressure suspect. Pay particular attention to the tips of the spring fingers, where the release bearing acts upon them.

8 With the transaxle removed, it is also advisable to check the condition of the release bearing, as described in Section 7. Having got this far, it is almost certainly worth replacing it.

5.3 Unscrewing the pressure plate bolts

5.4 Removing the pressure plate and disc

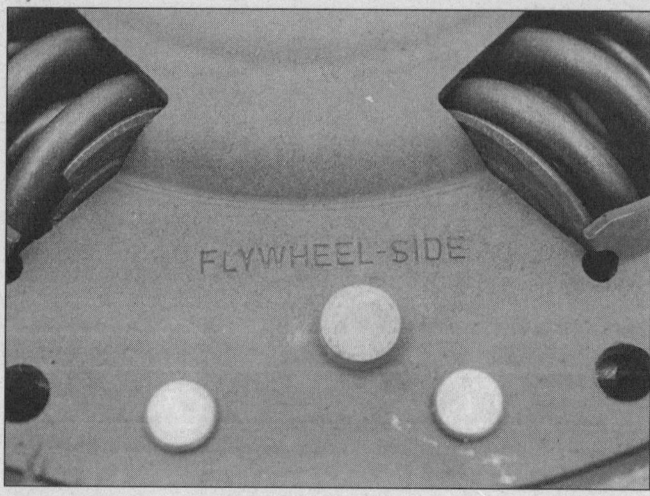

5.11 "FLYWHEEL-SIDE" marking on the clutch disc

5.15 Using a clutch-aligning tool to centralize the clutch disc

Installation

Refer to illustrations 6.11 and 6.15

9 It is important that no oil or grease is allowed to come into contact with the friction material of the clutch disc or the pressure plate and flywheel faces. To ensure this, it is advisable to install the clutch assembly with clean hands, and to wipe down the pressure plate and flywheel faces with a clean dry rag before assembly begins.

10 Technicians use a special tool for aligning the clutch disc at this stage. The tool holds the disc centrally on the pressure plate, and locates in the middle of the diaphragm spring fingers. If the tool is not available, it will be necessary to align the disc after assembling the pressure plate loosely on the flywheel, as described in the following paragraphs.

11 Place the clutch disc against the flywheel, ensuring that it is facing the correct direction. It should be marked FLYWHEEL SIDE, but if not, position it so that the raised hub with the cushion springs is facing away from the flywheel **(see illustration)**.

12 Place the pressure plate over the dowels. Install the retaining bolts, and tighten them finger-tight so that the clutch disc is gripped lightly, but can still be moved.

13 The clutch disc must now be aligned so when the engine and transaxle are mated, the splines of the transaxle input shaft will pass through the splines in the center of the clutch disc hub.

14 Clutch alignment can be performed by inserting a round bar through the hole in the center of the clutch disc, so that the end of the bar rests in the hole in the rear of the crankshaft. Move the bar sideways or up and down to move the clutch disc in whichever direction is necessary to achieve the correct alignment. Alignment can then be checked by removing the bar and viewing the clutch disc hub in relation to the diaphragm spring fingers, or by viewing through the side openings of the pressure plate and verifying that the disc is aligned in relation to the outer edge of the pressure plate.

15 An alternative and more accurate method of alignment is to use a commercially available clutch-aligning tool, obtainable from most automotive retail parts stores **(see illustration)**.

16 Once the clutch is properly aligned, progressively tighten the pressure plate bolts in a diagonal sequence to the torque listed in this Chapter's Specifications.

17 Confirm that the input shaft splines, clutch disc splines and release bearing guide sleeve are clean. Apply a thin coat of high melting-point grease to the input shaft splines and the release bearing guide sleeve.

18 Install the transaxle to the engine.

6 Clutch release cylinder/release bearing - removal, inspection and installation

Removal

1 Separate the engine and transaxle as described in the previous Section.

2 Disconnect the master cylinder-to-release cylinder hydraulic line from the release cylinder.

3 Remove the three release cylinder/release bearing assembly retaining bolts and slide the release cylinder off the transaxle input shaft splines.

Inspection

4 Inspect the release cylinder/release bearing for fluid leakage and excessively worn pressure plate contact area. Replace the release cylinder/release bearing assembly if there is any question regarding its condition.

Installation

5 Installation of the clutch release cylinder/release bearing is a reversal of the removal procedure. Install the clutch hydraulic line and bleed the clutch hydraulic system (see Section 4).

7 Driveaxles - description

Drive is transmitted from the transaxle differential to the front wheels by means of two driveaxles. The right driveaxle is in two sections, and incorporates a support bearing.

Each driveaxle consists of three main components: the sliding (tripod type) inner joint, the actual driveaxle, and the outer CV (constant velocity) joint. The inner (male) end of the left tripod joint is secured in the differential side gear by the engagement of a snap-ring. The inner (female) end of the right driveaxle is held on the intermediate shaft by the engagement of a snap-ring. The intermediate shaft is held in the transaxle by the support bearing, which in turn is supported by a bracket bolted to the rear of the cylinder block. The outer CV joint on both driveaxles is of ball-bearing type, and is secured in the front hub by the hub nut.

8 Driveaxles - removal and installation

Removal

Refer to illustrations 8.10a and 8.10b

1 Remove the wheel cover from the wheel, apply the parking brake, and engage 1st gear or "P". Loosen the hub nut about half a turn. This nut is very tight.

2 Loosen the front wheel retaining nuts.

3 Apply the parking brake, jack up the front of the vehicle and support it on jackstands. Remove the wheel.

4 Remove the front brake disc as described in Chapter 9.

5 Completely unscrew and remove the hub/driveaxle retaining nut. Note that the nut is of special laminated design, and should only be re-used a maximum of 5 times. (It is a good idea to file a small notch in the nut every time it is removed.) Obtain a new nut if necessary.

8.10a Using a puller on the hub flange . . .

8.10b . . . to press the driveaxle out of the front hub and steering knuckle

6 Retain the suspension strut piston with an Allen key, then loosen the strut support mounting nut and unscrew it five complete turns. It is not necessary to remove the nut at this stage, but note that a new one will be required on installation. Where necessary, detach the ABS wiring from the strut.

7 Unscrew the nut securing the stabilizer bar link to the front suspension strut, and position the link to one side.

8 Extract the cotter pin from the tie-rod end balljoint nut. Unscrew the nut, and detach the rod from the arm on the steering knuckle using a conventional balljoint removal tool. Take care not to damage the balljoint seal.

9 Note which way the front suspension lower arm balljoint clamp bolt is installed, then unscrew and remove it from the knuckle assembly. Lever the balljoint down from the knuckle; if it is tight, carefully pry the clamp open using a large flat-bladed tool. Take care not to damage the balljoint seal during the separation procedure.

8.11 Removing the left driveaxle from the transaxle

10 Using a universal puller located on the hub flange, press the driveaxle through the front hub and steering knuckle by pulling the knuckle outwards **(see illustrations)**. When the driveaxle is free, support it on an jack-stand, making sure that the inner tripod joint is not turned through more than 18° (damage may occur if the joint is turned through too great an angle).

Left side

Refer to illustration 8.11

11 Insert a lever between the inner CV joint and the transaxle case, with a thin piece of wood against the case. Pry free the inner joint from the differential **(see illustration)**. If it proves reluctant to move, strike the lever firmly with the palm of the hand. Be careful not to damage the adjacent components, and be prepared for oil spillage. Note that if the right driveaxle has already been removed, it is possible to release the left driveaxle by inserting a forked drift from the right side. However, care must be taken to prevent damage to the differential gears, particularly if the special tool is not used.

12 Withdraw the driveaxle from under the vehicle.

13 Extract the circlip from the groove on the inner end of the driveaxle, and obtain a new one.

8.16 Removing the heat shield from the right driveaxle support bearing

8.17 Removing the complete right-hand driveaxle

Right side

Refer to illustration 8.16 and 8.17

14 The right driveaxle may either be removed complete with the intermediate shaft from the transaxle, or it may be disconnected from the outer end of the intermediate shaft. If the latter course of action is taken, use a soft-faced mallet to sharply tap the inner CV joint housing from the intermediate shaft. The internal circlip will be released, and the driveaxle may be withdrawn from the splines.

15 Extract the circlip from the groove on the outer end of the intermediate shaft. Obtain a new circlip for use when installation.

16 If the complete driveaxle is to be removed, proceed as follows. Unscrew the bolts securing the driveaxle support bearing bracket to the rear of the cylinder block, and remove the heat shield **(see illustration)**.

17 Withdraw the complete driveaxle from the transaxle and from the bearing bracket, and remove it from under the vehicle **(see illustration)**. Be prepared for oil spillage.

Both sides

Refer to illustration 8.36

18 Check the condition of the transaxle oil seals, and if necessary replace them as described in Chapter 7A (manual transaxle) or Chapter 7B (automatic transaxle). Check the support bearing, and if necessary replace it as described in Section 11 of this Chapter.

Installation

Right side

19 If the intermediate shaft has not been removed, proceed to paragraph 22. Otherwise, proceed as follows.

20 Carefully install the complete driveaxle in the support bearing and into the transaxle, taking care not to damage the oil seal. Turn the driveaxle until it engages the splines on the differential gears.

21 Tighten the bolts securing the support bearing to the bracket on the cylinder block to the specified torque. Proceed to paragraph 26.

22 Locate the new circlip in the groove on the outer end of the intermediate shaft, then smear 6 to 8 grams of grease over the entire circumference of the intermediate shaft splines. This grease prevents frictional corrosion.

23 Locate the right driveaxle on the intermediate shaft splines, and push it on until the internal circlip is heard to engage with the groove in the shaft.

Left side

24 Locate the new circlip in the groove on the inner end of the driveaxle.

25 Insert the driveaxle into the transaxle, making sure that the circlip is fully engaged.

Both sides

26 Pull the knuckle outwards, and insert the outer end of the driveaxle through the hub. Turn the driveaxle to engage the splines in the hub, and fully push on the hub. The manufacturer uses a special tool to draw the driveaxle into the hub, but it is unlikely that the splines will be tight. However, if they are, it will be necessary to obtain the tool, or to use a similar home-made tool.

27 Screw on the hub nut finger-tight.

28 Locate the front suspension lower arm balljoint stub in the bottom of the knuckle. Insert the clamp bolt in the previously noted position, screw on the nut, and tighten it to the specified torque.

29 Install the tie-rod end balljoint to the steering knuckle, and screw on the nut. Tighten the nut to the specified torque.

30 Check that the balljoint nut cotter pin holes are aligned. If not, re-position the nut, but make sure that it is still tightened within the tolerance of the torque wrench setting. Insert a new cotter pin, and bend its legs back to secure it.

31 Locate the stabilizer bar link on the front suspension strut, and tighten the nut to the specified torque.

32 Remove the suspension strut upper mounting nut and install the new nut, tightening it to the specified torque (Chapter 10). Where necessary, install the ABS wiring to the strut bracket.

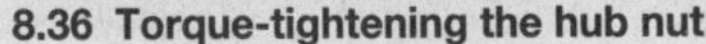

8.36 Torque-tightening the hub nut

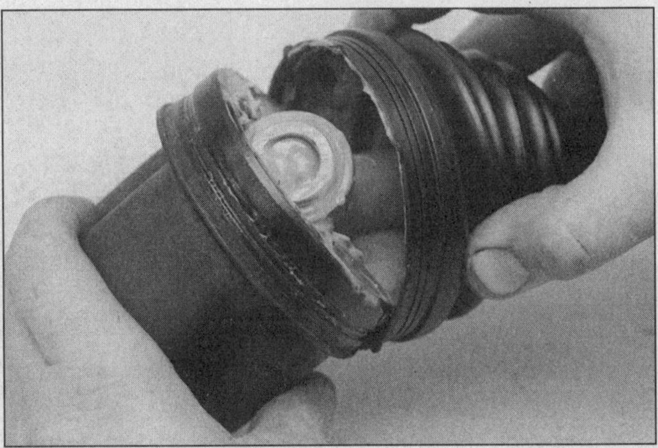

9.29 Removing the boot from the inner joint housing

33 Install the front brake disc with reference to Chapter 9.

34 Check the transaxle oil level, and top-up if necessary as described in Chapter 1.

35 Install the wheel and lug nuts, and lower the vehicle to the ground. Tighten the lug nuts to the torque listed in the Chapter 1 Specifications.

36 Fully tighten the hub nut to the specified torque **(see illustration)**. Finally, install the wheel cover.

9 Driveaxle inner CV joint boot - replacement

1 The inner CV joint boot is replaced by disconnecting the driveaxle from the inner CV joint housing at the transaxle (left side) or intermediate shaft (right side). The work can be carried out either with the driveaxle removed from the vehicle, or with it *in place*. If it is wished to fully remove the driveaxle, refer to Section 9 first. Note that if both the inner and outer boots are being replaced at the same time, the outer boot can be removed from the inner end of the driveaxle.

Replacement without removing the driveaxle

2 Loosen the front wheel nuts on the appropriate side. Apply the parking brake, jack up the front of the vehicle and support it on jackstands. Remove the wheel.

3 Unscrew the nut securing the stabilizer bar link to the front suspension strut, and position the link to one side.

4 Extract the cotter pin from the tie-rod end balljoint nut. Unscrew the nut, and detach the rod from the arm on the steering knuckle using a conventional balljoint removal tool. Take care not to damage the balljoint seal.

5 Note which way the front suspension lower arm balljoint clamp bolt is installed, then unscrew and remove it from the knuckle assembly. Lever the balljoint down from the knuckle; if it is tight, pry the clamp open carefully using a large flat-bladed tool. Take care not to damage the balljoint seal during the separation procedure.

6 Mark the driveaxle in relation to the joint housing, to ensure correct installation.

7 Note the installed location of both of the inner joint boot retaining clamps. Release the clamps from the boot, and slide the boot back along the driveaxle (away from the transaxle) a little way.

8 Pull the front suspension strut outwards, while guiding the tripod joint out of the joint housing. As the tripod is being withdrawn from the housing, be prepared for some of the bearing rollers to fall out. Identify them for position with a dab of paint. Support the inner end of the driveaxle on a jackstand.

9 Remove the support ring from the joint housing.

10 Remove the remaining bearing rollers from the tripod, and identify them for position with a dab of paint.

11 Check that the inner end of the driveaxle is marked in relation to the splined tripod hub. If not, carefully center-punch the two items, to ensure correct installation. Alternatively, use dabs of paint on the driveaxle and one end of the tripod.

12 Extract the snap-ring retaining the tripod on the driveaxle.

13 Using a suitable puller, remove the tripod from the end of the driveaxle, and slide off the boot.

14 If the outer boot is also to be replaced, remove it with reference to Section 12.

15 Clean the driveaxle, and obtain a new tripod retaining snap-ring. The boot retaining clamps and the steering tie-rod end cotter pin must also be replaced.

16 Slide the new boot on the driveaxle, together with new clamps. Also locate the support ring on the joint housing.

17 Install the tripod on the driveaxle splines, if necessary using a soft-faced mallet to drive it fully onto the splines. It must be installed with the chamfered edge leading (towards the driveaxle), and with the previously made marks aligned. Secure it in position using the new snap-ring. Ensure that the snap-ring is fully engaged in its groove.

18 Locate the bearing rollers on the tripod in their previously noted positions, using grease to hold them in place.

19 With the front suspension strut pulled outwards, guide the tripod joint into the housing, making sure that the previously made marks are aligned. Pack the joint with 180 grams of CV joint grease.

20 Slide the boot along the driveaxle, and locate it on the support ring located on the joint housing. The small-diameter end of the boot must be located in the groove on the driveaxle.

21 Ensure that the boot is not twisted or distorted, then insert a small screwdriver under the lip of the boot at the housing end. This will allow trapped air to escape during the next step.

22 Push the tripod fully into the housing, then pull it out by 20 mm. Remove the screwdriver, then install the retaining clamps and tighten them.

23 Reconnect the front suspension lower arm balljoint to the knuckle assembly. Install and tighten the clamp nut and bolt.

24 Reconnect the tie-rod end balljoint to the steering knuckle, and tighten the nut to the specified torque. Check that the cotter pin holes are correctly aligned; if necessary, reposition the nut, making sure that it is still tightened within the torque tolerance. Insert a new cotter pin, and bend its legs back to secure it.

25 Install the stabilizer bar link to the front suspension strut, and tighten the nut to the specified torque.

26 Install the wheel, and lower the vehicle to the ground. Tighten the wheel nuts.

Replacement with the driveaxle on the bench

Refer to illustrations 9.29, 9.31, 9.32, 9.34, 9.35, 9.38, 9.40a, 9.40b and 9.45

27 Mount the driveaxle in a vise.

28 Mark the driveaxle in relation to the joint housing, to ensure correct installation.

29 Note the installed location of both of the inner joint boot retaining clamps, then release the clamps from the boot, and slide the boot back along the driveaxle a little way **(see illustration)**.

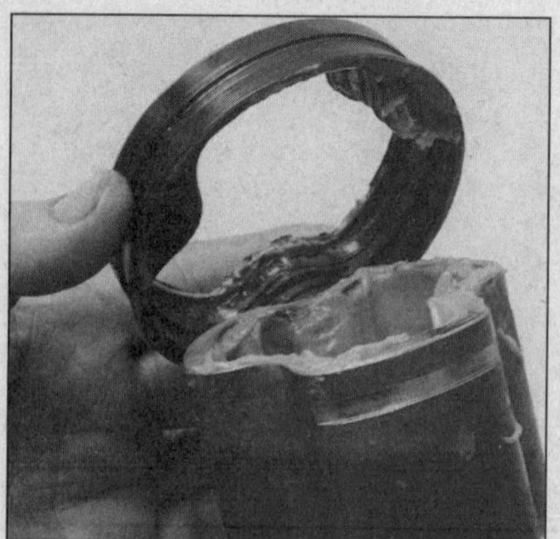

9.31 Removing the support ring from the joint housing

9.32 Removing the bearing rollers

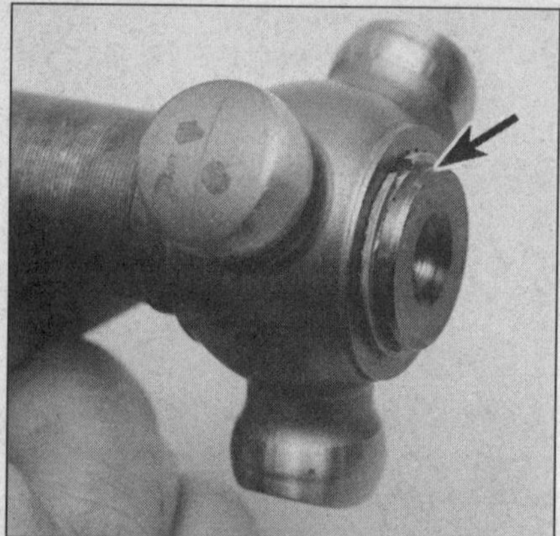

9.34 Snap-ring retaining the tripod on the driveaxle

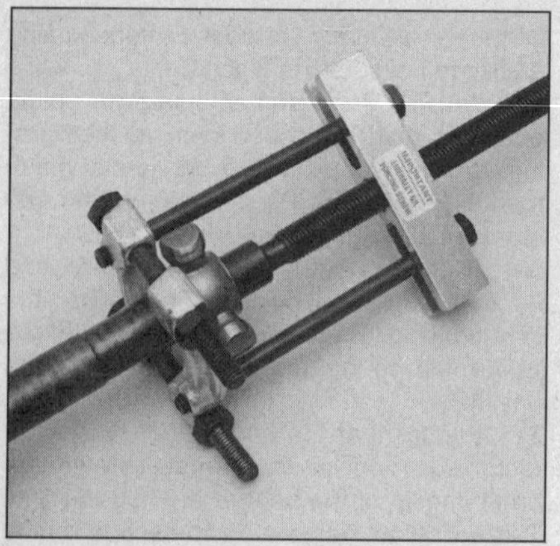

9.35 Using a puller to remove the tripod

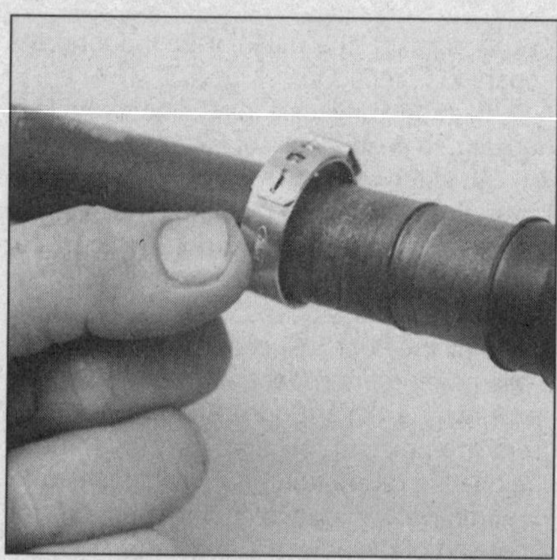

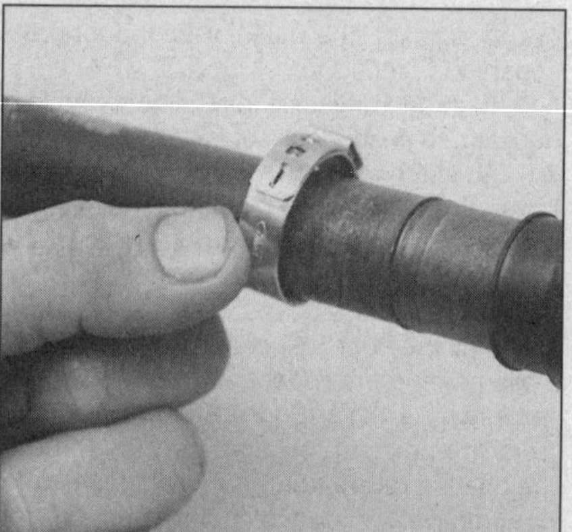

9.38 Slide the boot and clamps onto the driveaxle

9.40a Locate the tripod on the splines . . .

30 Remove the inner joint housing from the tripod. As the housing is being removed, be prepared for some of the bearing rollers to fall out. Identify them for position with a dab of paint.

31 Remove the support ring from the joint housing **(see illustration)**.

32 Remove the remaining bearing rollers from the tripod, and identify them for position with a dab of paint **(see illustration)**.

33 Check that the inner end of the driveaxle is marked in relation to the splined tripod hub. If not, carefully center-punch the two items, to ensure correct installation. Alternatively, use dabs of paint on the driveaxle and one end of the tripod.

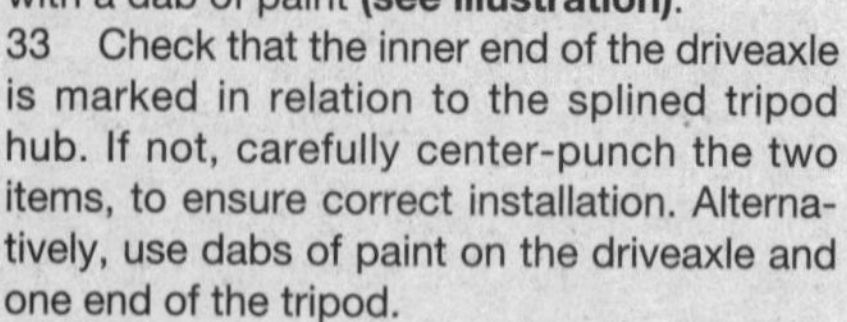

34 Extract the snap-ring retaining the tripod on the driveaxle **(see illustration)**.

35 Using a puller, remove the tripod from the end of the driveaxle, and slide off the boot **(see illustration)**.

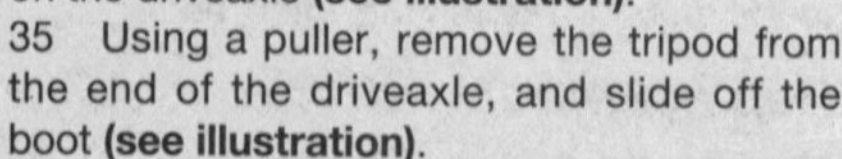

36 If the outer boot is also to be replaced, remove it with reference to Section 10.

37 Clean the driveaxle, tripod and joint housing and obtain a new joint retaining snap-ring. The boot retaining clamps must also be replaced.

38 Slide the new boot on the driveaxle, together with new clamps **(see illustration)**.

39 Locate the support ring on the CV joint housing.

40 Install the tripod on the driveaxle splines, if necessary using a soft-faced mallet and a suitable socket to drive it fully onto the splines. It must be installed with the chamfered edge leading (towards the driveaxle), and with the previously made marks aligned. Secure it in position using a new snap-ring. Ensure that the snap-ring is fully engaged in its groove **(see illustrations)**.

41 Locate the bearing rollers on the tripod in their previously noted positions, using grease to hold them in place.

9.40b . . . and drive it fully onto the driveaxle

42 Guide the joint housing onto the tripod joint, making sure that the previously made marks are aligned. Pack the joint with 180 grams of new CV joint grease.

43 Slide the boot along the driveaxle, and locate it on the support ring on the CV joint housing. The small-diameter end of the boot must be located in the groove on the driveaxle.

44 Ensure that the boot is not twisted or distorted, then insert a small screwdriver under the lip of the boot at the housing end.

9.45 Using a clamp crimping tool to tighten the retaining clamps

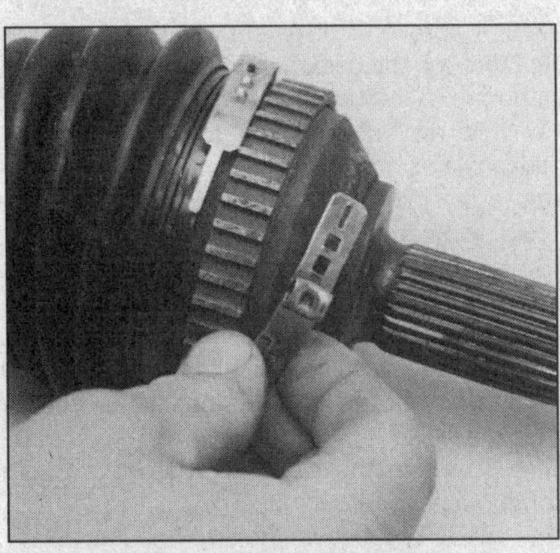
10.4a Release the clamps . . .

10.4b . . . and remove the boot

10.5a Drive off the outer CV joint hub . . .

10.5b . . . and remove the joint from the driveaxle

10.6 Circlips installed on the outer end of the driveaxle

This will allow trapped air to escape during the next step.

45 Push the housing fully on the tripod, then pull it out by 20 mm. Remove the screwdriver, then install the retaining clamps and tighten them **(see illustration)**.

10 Driveaxle outer CV joint boot - replacement

Refer to illustrations 10.4a, 10.4b, 10.5a, 10.5b, 10.6, 10.9 and 10.11

1 The outer CV joint boot can be replaced by removing the inner boot first as described in Section 10, or after removing the driveaxle as described in Section 8. If the driveaxle is removed, then the inner boot need not necessarily be removed. It is impractical to replace the outer boot by dismantling the outer joint with the driveaxle in position in the vehicle. The following paragraphs describe replacement of the boot on the bench.

2 Mount the driveaxle in a vise.

3 Mark the driveaxle in relation to the CV joint housing, to ensure correct installation.

4 Note the installed location of both of the boot retaining clamps, then release the clamps from the boot, and slide the boot back along the driveaxle a little way **(see illustrations)**.

5 Using a brass drift or a copper mallet, carefully drive the outer CV joint hub from the splines on the driveaxle. Initial resistance will be felt until the internal circlips are released. Take care not to damage the bearing cage **(see illustrations)**.

6 Extract the outer circlip from the end of the driveaxle **(see illustration)**.

7 Slide the boot over the remaining circlip, and remove it together with the clamps.

8 Clean the driveaxle, and obtain new joint retaining circlips. The boot retaining clamps must also be replaced.

9 Slide the new boot (together with new clamps) onto the driveaxle and over the inner circlip **(see illustration)**.

10 Install a new outer circlip to the groove in the driveaxle.

11 Scoop out all of the old grease, then pack the joint with 100 grams of new CV joint grease **(see illustration)**.

12 Locate the CV joint on the driveaxle so that the splines are aligned, then push the joint until the internal circlips are fully engaged.

10.9 Installing the new boot and clamps on the driveaxle

10.11 Packing the outer CV joint with new grease

13 Move the boot along the driveaxle, and locate it over the joint and onto the outer CV joint housing. The small-diameter end of the boot must be located in the groove on the driveaxle.

14 Ensure that the boot is not twisted or distorted, then insert a small screwdriver under the lip of the boot at the housing end, to allow any trapped air to escape.

15 Remove the screwdriver, install the retaining clamps in their previously noted positions, and tighten them **(see illustration 9.45)**.

11 Driveaxles - inspection and joint replacement

1 If any of the checks described in Chapter 1 reveal apparent excessive wear or play in any driveaxle joint, first remove the wheel cover, and check that the hub nut (driveaxle outer nut) is tightened to the specified torque. Repeat this check on the hub nut on the other side.

2 Road test the vehicle, and listen for a metallic clicking from the front, as the vehicle is driven slowly in a circle on full-lock. If a clicking noise is heard, this indicates wear in the outer constant velocity joint, which means that the joint must be replaced; reconditioning is not possible.

3 To replace an outer CV joint, remove the driveaxle as described in Section 8, then separate the joint from the driveaxle with reference to Section 10. In principle, the boot can be left on the driveaxle, provided that it is in good condition; in practice, it makes sense to replace the boot in any case, having got this far.

4 If vibration, consistent with road speed, is felt through the car when accelerating, there is a possibility of wear in the inner tripod joints.

5 To replace an inner joint, remove the driveaxle as described in Section 8, then separate the joint from the driveaxle with reference to Section 9.

6 Continual noise from the right driveaxle, increasing with road speed, may indicate wear in the support bearing. To replace this bearing, the driveaxle and intermediate shaft must be removed, and the bearing extracted using a puller.

7 Remove the bearing dust cover, and obtain a new one.

8 Drive or press on the new bearing, applying the pressure to the inner race only. Similarly drive or press on the new dust cover.

Chapter 9 Brakes

Contents

Specifications

General

Fluid type	See Chapter 1

Front brakes

Type	Ventilated disc, with single-piston floating caliper
Disc thickness	
New	0.95 inch
Minimum*	0.87 inch
Maximum disc run-out	0.006 inch
Maximum disc thickness variation	0.0006 inch
Maximum front hub face runout	0.002 inch

**Refer to the dimension cast into the disc (it supersedes the information printed here).*

Rear drum brakes

Type	Leading and trailing shoes, with automatic adjusters
Drum diameter	
New	9.0 inches
Maximum diameter*	9.04 inches

**Refer to the dimension cast into the drum (it supersedes the information printed here).*

Rear disc brakes

Type	Solid disc, with single-piston floating caliper
Disc thickness	
New	0.787 inch
Minimum*	0.71 inch
Maximum disc run-out (equipped)	0.006 inch
Maximum disc thickness variation	0.0006 inch
Maximum rear hub face runout	0.002 inch

**Refer to the dimension cast into the disc (it supersedes the information printed here).*

Torque specifications	**Ft-lbs** (unless otherwise indicated)
Front caliper bracket	89
Rear caliper bracket	89
Front caliper guide bolts	21
Rear caliper guide bolts	30
Rear drum brake back plate	37
Vacuum booster unit	30
Master cylinder	17
ABS hydraulic unit to bracket	180 in-lbs
Wheel lug nuts	See Chapter 1
Wheel cylinder bolts	108 in-lbs

1 General information

The braking system is of dual-circuit design, with ventilated discs at the front, and drum or disc brakes (according to model) at the rear. The front calipers are of floating single-piston design, using asbestos-free pads. The rear drum brakes are of the leading and trailing shoe type. They are self-adjusting during normal brake operation. The rear brake shoe linings are of different thicknesses, in order to allow for the different proportional rates of wear.

Pressure-control relief (PCR) valves are attached to the rear brakes, to prevent rear wheel lock-up under hard braking. The valves are sometimes referred to as pressure-conscious reducing valves. On non-ABS models, they are installed in the master cylinder rear brake outlet ports; on ABS models, they are located on the ABS unit.

When rear disc brakes are installed, the rear brake caliper is located on the front of the knuckle.

The parking brake is cable-operated, and acts on the rear brakes. On rear drum brake models, the cables operate on the rear trailing brake shoe operating levers, and on rear disc brake models, they operate on levers on the rear calipers. The parking brake lever incorporates an automatic adjuster, which removes any slack from the cables when the lever is disengaged. Parking brake lever movement remains consistent at all times, and no adjustment is necessary or possible.

If equipped, the anti-lock braking system (ABS) is of the four-channel low-pressure type. It uses the basic conventional brake system, together with a Bendix ABS hydraulic unit installed between the master cylinder and the four wheel brakes. The hydraulic unit consists of a hydraulic actuator, an ABS brake pressure pump, an ABS module with built-in relay box, and two pressure-control relief valves. Braking at each of the four wheels is controlled by separate solenoid valves in the hydraulic actuator. If wheel lock-up is detected on a wheel when the vehicle speed is above 3 mph, the valve opens, releasing pressure to the relevant brake, until the wheel regains a rotational speed corresponding to the speed of the vehicle. The cycle can be repeated many times a second. In the event of a fault in the ABS system, the conventional braking system is not affected. Diagnosis of a fault in the ABS system requires the use of special equipment, and this work should therefore be left to a dealer. Diagnostic connectors are located on the side of the left front suspension tower.

The traction control system (TCS) is installed as an option to some models, and uses the basic ABS system, with an additional pump and valves installed to the hydraulic actuator. If wheel spin is detected at a speed below 30 mph, one of the valves opens, to allow the pump to pressurize the relevant brake, until the spinning wheel slows to a rotational speed corresponding to the speed of the vehicle. This has the effect of transferring torque to the wheel with most traction. At the same time, the throttle plate is closed slightly, to reduce the torque from the engine. At speeds above 30 mph, the TCS operates by throttle plate adjustment only.

2.3a Pry the retaining clip from the caliper. Hold it with a pair of pliers, to avoid personal injury. On models equipped with pad wear sensors, it will be necessary to disconnect the wiring

2 Front brake pads - replacement

Refer to illustrations 2.3a, 2.3b, 2.3c, 2.3d, 2.3e, 2.3f and 2.3g

Warning: *Disc brake pads must be replaced on both front wheels at the same time - never replace the pads on only one wheel, as uneven braking may result. Although genuine linings are asbestos-free, the dust created by wear of non-genuine pads may contain asbestos, which is a health hazard. Never blow it out with compressed air, and don't inhale any of it. DO NOT use petroleum-based solvents to clean brake parts; use brake cleaner or rubbing alcohol only. DO NOT allow any brake fluid, oil or grease to contact the brake pads or disc. Also refer to the warning at the start of Section 15 concerning brake fluid.*

1 Apply the parking brake. Loosen the front wheel nuts, jack up the front of the vehicle and support it on jackstands.

2 Remove the front wheels. Work on one brake assembly at a time, using the assembled brake for reference if necessary.

3 Follow the accompanying photos, beginning with **illustration 2.3a**, for the pad removal procedure. Be sure to stay in order, and read the caption under each illustration.

4 Inspect the front brake disc for scoring and cracks. If a detailed inspection is necessary, refer to Section 4.

2.3b Pry the plastic covers from the ends of the two guide pins

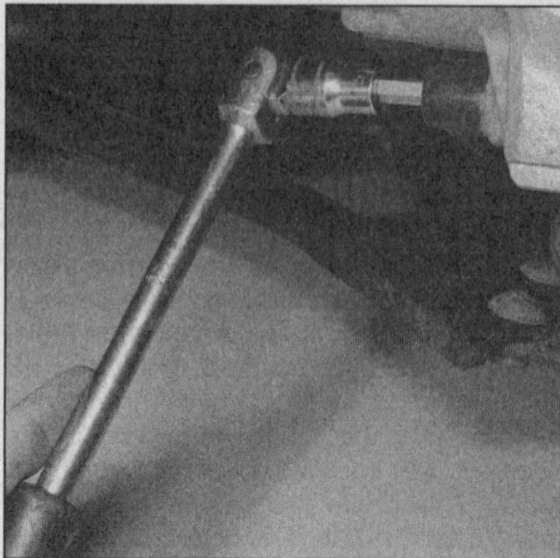
2.3c Using a 7 mm Allen key, unscrew . . .

2.3d . . . and remove the guide bolts securing the caliper to the carrier bracket

2.3e Withdraw the caliper from the disc, and support it on a jackstand to avoid straining the hydraulic hose. The outer pad will normally remain in position against the disc, but the inner pad will stay attached to the piston in the caliper

2.3f Pull the inner pad from the piston in the caliper

2.3g Remove the outer pad from the caliper frame. Brush all dust and dirt from the caliper, pads and disc, but do not inhale it, as it may be harmful to health. Scrape any corrosion from the disc

5 The piston must be pushed back into the caliper bore, to provide room for the new brake pads. A C-clamp can be used to accomplish this. As the piston is depressed to the bottom of the caliper bore, the fluid in the master cylinder will rise slightly. Make sure that there is sufficient space in the brake fluid reservoir to accept the displaced fluid, and if necessary, siphon some off first.

6 Install the new pads using a reversal of the removal procedure, but tighten the guide bolts to the torque wrench setting given in the Specifications at the beginning of this Chapter.

7 On completion, firmly depress the brake pedal a few times, to bring the pads to their normal working position. Check the level of the brake fluid in the reservoir, and top-up if necessary.

8 Give the vehicle a short road test, to make sure that the brakes are functioning correctly, and to bed-in the new linings to the contours of the disc. New linings will not provide maximum braking efficiency until they have bedded-in; avoid heavy braking as far as possible for the first hundred miles or so.

3 Front brake caliper - removal, overhaul and installation

Note: *Refer to the warning at the beginning of the previous Section before proceeding.*

Removal

Refer to illustrations 3.2, 3.3 and 3.6

1 Apply the parking brake. Loosen the front wheel nuts, jack up the front of the vehicle and support it on jackstands. Remove the appropriate front wheel.

2 Install a brake hose clamp to the flexible hose leading to the front brake caliper. This will minimize brake fluid loss during subsequent operations **(see illustration)**.

3 Loosen (but do not completely unscrew) the fitting on the caliper end of the flexible

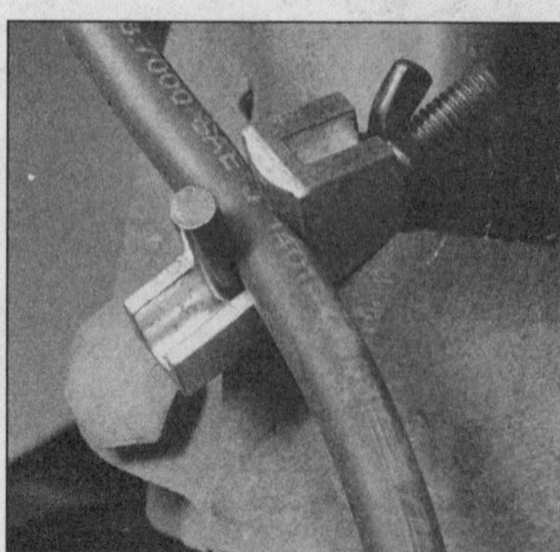
3.2 Brake hose clamp attached to the front flexible brake hose

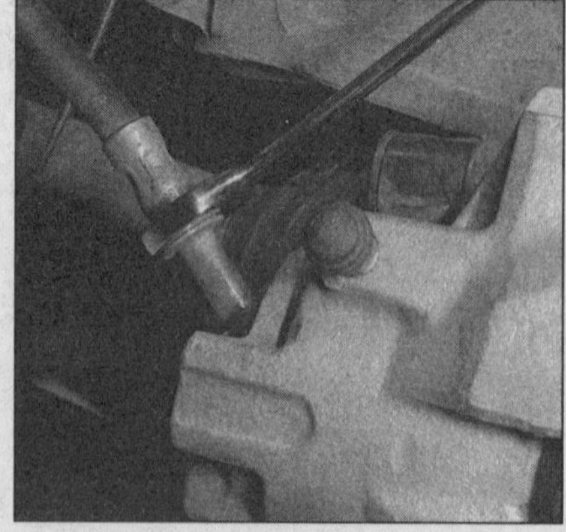
3.3 Loosening the flexible brake hose at the caliper

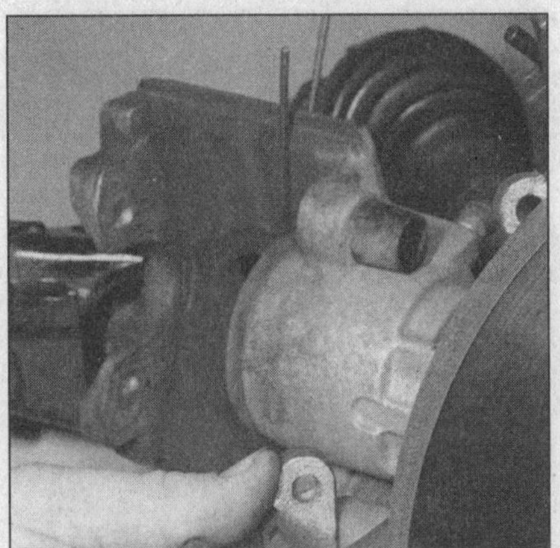
3.6 Removing the caliper carrier bracket

brake hose **(see illustration)**.

4 Remove the front brake pads as described in Section 2.

5 Support the caliper in one hand, and prevent the hydraulic hose from turning with the other hand. Unscrew the caliper from the hose, making sure that the hose is not twisted unduly or strained. Once the caliper is detached, plug the open hydraulic unions in the caliper and hose, to keep out dust and dirt.

6 If required, the caliper carrier bracket can be unbolted and removed from the steering knuckle **(see illustration)**.

Overhaul

7 With the caliper on the bench, brush away all traces of dust and dirt, but take care not to inhale any dust, as it may be injurious to health.

8 Pull the dust-excluding rubber seal from the end of the piston.

9 Apply low air pressure to the fluid inlet fitting, and eject the piston. Only low air pressure is required for this, such as is produced by a foot-operated tire pump. **Caution:** *The piston may be ejected with some force.* Position a thin piece of wood between the piston and the caliper body, to prevent damage to the end face of the piston, in the event of it being ejected suddenly.

3.15 Tightening the carrier bracket mounting bolts

10 Using a suitable blunt instrument (for instance a knitting needle or a crochet hook), pry the piston seal from the groove in the cylinder bore. Take care not to scratch the surface of the bore.

11 Clean the piston and caliper body with rubbing alcohol, and allow to dry. Examine the surfaces of the piston and cylinder bore for wear, damage and corrosion. If the piston alone is unserviceable, a new piston must be obtained, along with seals. If the cylinder bore is unserviceable, the complete caliper must be replaced. The seals must be replaced, regardless of the condition of the other components.

12 Coat the piston and seals with clean brake fluid, then manipulate the piston seal into the groove in the cylinder bore.

13 Push the piston squarely into its bore.

14 Install the dust-excluding rubber seal onto the piston and caliper, then depress the piston fully.

Installation

Refer to illustration 3.15

15 Install the caliper, and where applicable the carrier bracket, by back-up the removal operations. Make sure that the flexible brake hose is not twisted. Tighten the mounting bolts and wheel nuts to the specified torque **(see illustration)**.

16 Bleed the brake circuit according to the procedure given in Section 14, remembering to remove the brake hose clamp from the flexible hose. Make sure there are no leaks from the hose connections. Test the brakes carefully before returning the vehicle to normal service.

4 Front brake disc - inspection, removal and installation

Note: *To prevent uneven braking, BOTH front brake discs should be replaced or reground at the same time.*

Inspection

Refer to illustrations 4.4a, 4.4b, 4.5, 4.10a and 4.10b

1 Apply the parking brake. Loosen the relevant wheel nuts, jack up the front of the vehicle and support it on jackstands. Remove the wheel.

2 Remove the front brake caliper and carrier bracket with reference to Section 3, but do not disconnect the flexible hose. Support the caliper on a jackstand, or suspend it out of the way with a piece of wire, taking care to avoid straining the flexible hose.

3 Temporarily install two of the wheel nuts to diagonally-opposite studs, with the flat sides of the nuts against the disc. Tighten the nuts progressively, to hold the disc firmly.

4 Scrape any corrosion from the disc. Rotate the disc, and examine it for deep scoring, grooving or cracks. Using a micrometer, measure the thickness of the disc in several places. The minimum thickness is stamped on the disc hub **(see illustrations)**. Light wear and scoring is normal, but if excessive, the disc should be removed, and either reground by a specialist, or replaced. If regrinding is undertaken, the minimum thickness must be maintained. Obviously, if the disc is cracked, it must be replaced.

5 Using a dial gauge or a flat metal block and feeler gauges, check that the disc run-out 10 mm from the outer edge does not exceed the limit given in the Specifications. To do this, fix the measuring equipment, and

4.4a Using a micrometer to measure the thickness of the front brake disc

4.4b Disc minimum thickness marking

4.5 Measuring the disc run-out with a dial gauge

9

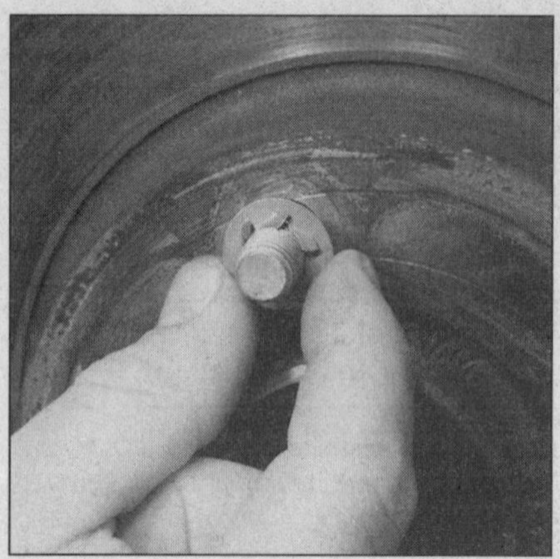

4.10a Remove the special washers . . .

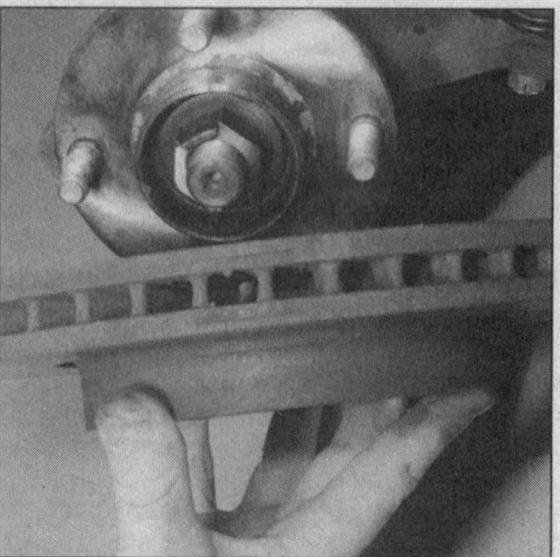

4.10b . . . and withdraw the disc

5.2a Releasing the automatic adjuster mechanism with a screwdriver inserted through the small hole in the back plate

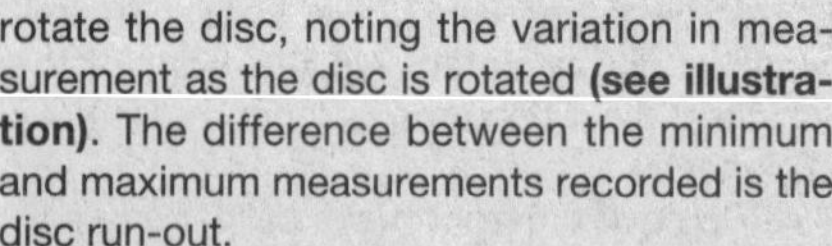

rotate the disc, noting the variation in measurement as the disc is rotated **(see illustration)**. The difference between the minimum and maximum measurements recorded is the disc run-out.

6 If the run-out is greater than the specified amount, check for variations of the disc thickness as follows. Mark the disc at eight positions 45° apart, then using a micrometer, measure the disc thickness at the eight positions, 15 mm in from the outer edge. If the variation between the minimum and maximum readings is greater than the specified amount, the disc should be replaced.

7 The hub face run-out can also be checked in a similar way. First remove the disc as described later in this Section, fix the measuring equipment, then slowly rotate the hub, and check that the run-out does not exceed the amount given in the Specifications. If the hub face run-out is excessive, this should be corrected (by replacing the hub bearings - see Chapter 10) before rechecking the disc run-out.

Removal

8 With the wheel and caliper removed, remove the wheel nuts which were temporarily installed in paragraph 3.

9 Mark the disc in relation to the hub, if it is to be installed.

10 Remove the two special washers (if equipped), and withdraw the disc over the wheel studs **(see illustrations)**.

Installation

11 Make sure that the disc and hub mating surfaces are clean, then locate the disc on the wheel studs. Align the previously-made marks if the original disc is being installed.

12 Install the two special washers, if equipped.

13 Install the brake caliper and carrier bracket with reference to Section 3.

14 Install the wheel, and lower the vehicle to the ground.

15 Test the brakes carefully before returning the vehicle to normal service.

5 Rear brake drum - removal, inspection and installation

Note: *To prevent uneven braking, BOTH rear brake drums should be replaced at the same time.*

Removal

Refer to illustrations 5.2a and 5.2b

1 Chock the front wheels, release the parking brake and engage 1st gear (or "P"). Loosen the relevant wheel nuts, jack up the rear of the vehicle and support it on jackstands. Remove the wheel.

2 Remove the two special clips (if equipped), and withdraw the brake drum over the wheel studs. If the drum will not pass over the shoes, it is possible to release the automatic adjuster mechanism by prying out the small rubber grommet near the center of the back plate, and inserting a screwdriver through the small hole. The self-adjusting ratchet can then be rotated, so that the brake shoes move to their lowest setting **(see illustrations)**. Install the rubber grommet before proceeding.

3 With the brake drum removed, clean the dust from the drum, brake shoes, wheel cylinder and back plate, using brake cleaner or rubbing alcohol. *Take care not to inhale the dust, as it may contain asbestos.*

Inspection

4 Clean the inside surfaces of the brake drum, then examine the internal friction surface for signs of scoring or cracks. If it is cracked, deeply scored, or has worn to a diameter greater than the maximum given in the Specifications, then it should be replaced, together with the drum on the other side.

5 Regrinding of the brake drum is not recommended.

Installation

6 Locate the brake drum over the wheel studs. Make sure that the drum contacts the hub flange.

5.2b Removing a rear brake drum

7 Install the wheel, then check the remaining rear drum.

8 Lower the vehicle to the ground, and tighten the wheel nuts to the specified torque. Depress the brake pedal several times, in order to operate the self-adjusting mechanism and set the shoes at their normal operating position.

9 Test the brakes carefully before returning the vehicle to normal service.

6 Rear brake shoes - replacement

Refer to illustrations 6.2a through 6.2o

Warning: *Drum brake shoes must be replaced on both rear wheels at the same time - never replace the shoes on only one wheel, as uneven braking may result. Also, the dust created by wear of the shoes may contain asbestos, which is a health hazard. Never blow it out with compressed air, and don't inhale any of it. An approved filtering mask should be worn when working on the brakes. DO NOT use petroleum-based solvents to clean brake parts; use brake cleaner or rubbing alcohol only.*

1 Remove the rear brake drums as described in Section 5. Work on one brake

6.2a Note the correct position of the springs and the adjuster strut, then clean the components with brake cleaner, and allow to dry. Position a tray beneath the back plate, to catch the fluid and residue

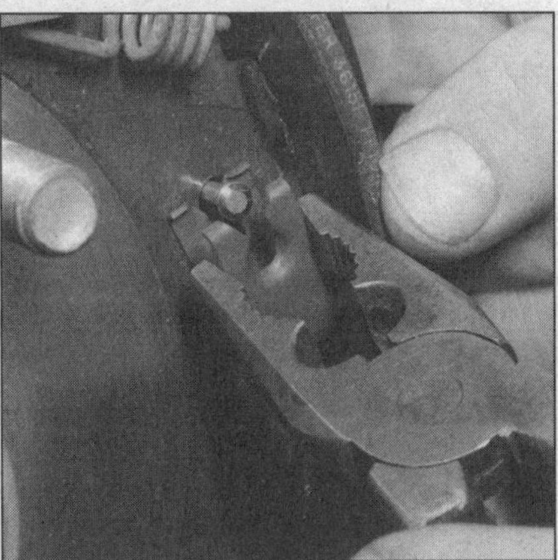

6.2b Remove the two shoe hold-down springs, using a pair of pliers to depress the upper ends so that they can be withdrawn downwards off the pins

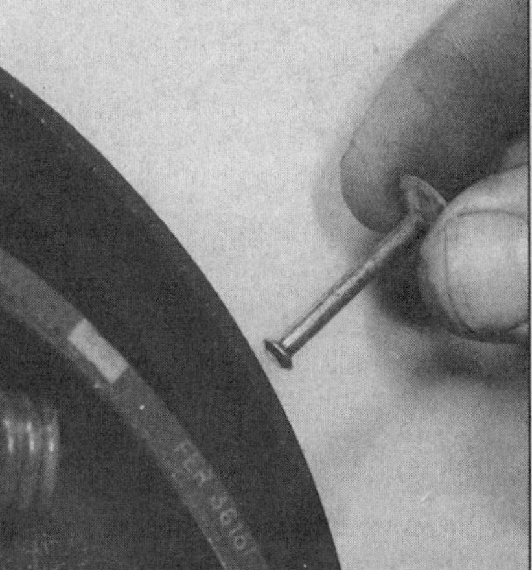

6.2c Remove the hold-down pins from the back plate

6.2d Pull the bottom end of the leading (front) brake shoe from the bottom anchor (use pliers or an adjustable wrench over the edge of the shoe to lever it away)

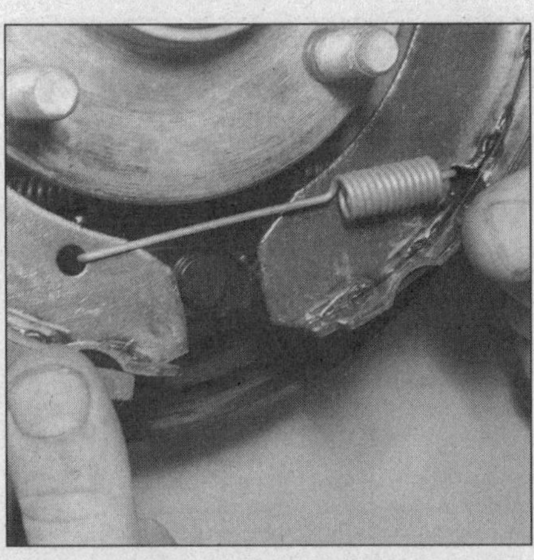

6.2e Release the trailing (rear) brake shoe from the anchor, then move the bottom ends of both shoes towards each other

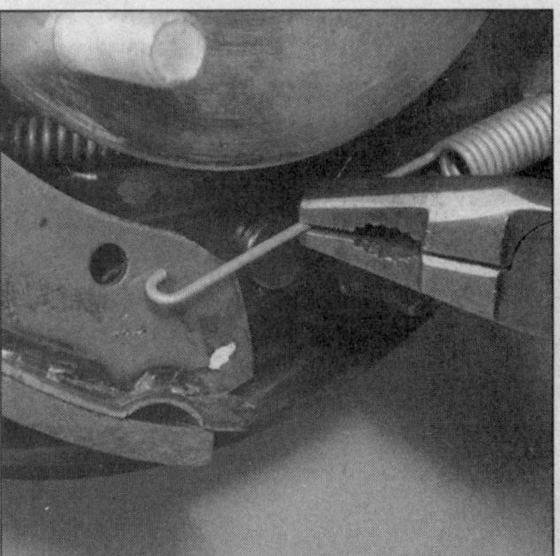

6.2f Unhook the lower return spring from the shoes, noting the location holes

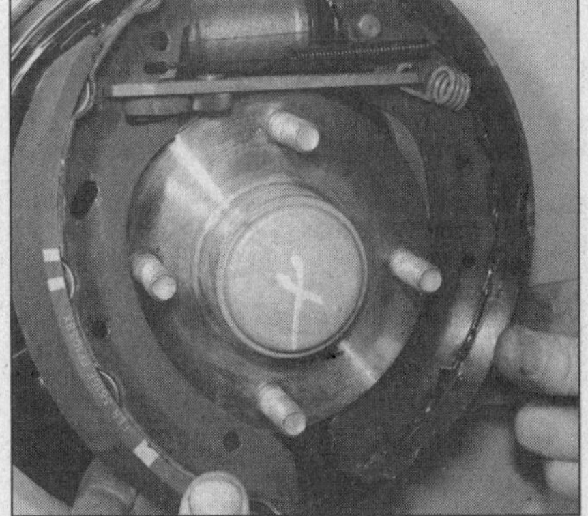

6.2g Move the bottom ends of the brake shoes together, and disconnect the top ends of the shoes from the wheel cylinder, taking care not to damage the rubber boots

6.2h Unhook the upper return spring from the shoes . . .

6.2i . . . and withdraw the leading shoe from the back plate

assembly at a time, using the assembled brake for reference if necessary.

2 Follow the accompanying illustrations for the brake shoe replacement procedure **(see illustrations 6.2a to 6.2o)**. Be sure to stay in order, and read the caption under each illustration.

3 If the wheel cylinder shows signs of fluid leakage, or if there is any reason to suspect it of being defective, inspect it now, as described in the next Section.

4 Install the new brake shoes using a reversal of the removal procedure, but set the eccentric cam at its lowest position before assembling it to the trailing shoe.

5 Before installing the brake drum, it should be checked as described in Section 5.

6 With the drum in position, install the wheel, then carry out the replacement proce-

9

6.2j To prevent the wheel cylinder pistons from being accidentally ejected, place a suitable elastic band or wire lengthwise over the cylinder/pistons. Don't press the brake pedal while the shoes are removed

6.2k Pull the parking brake cable spring back from the operating lever on the rear of the trailing shoe. Unhook the cable end from the cut-out in the lever, and remove the shoe

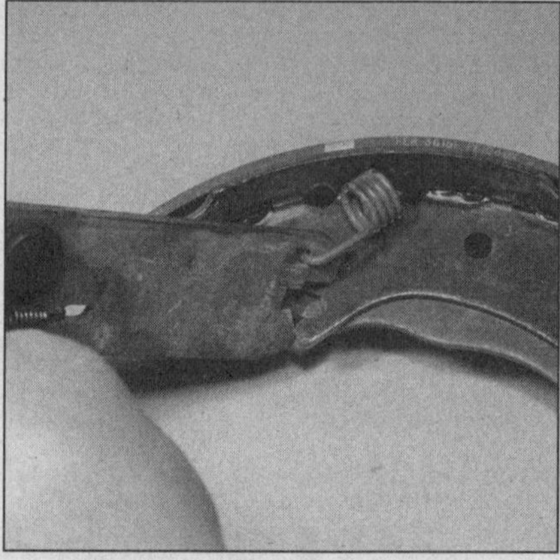

6.2l Unhook the automatic adjustment strut from the trailing brake shoe . . .

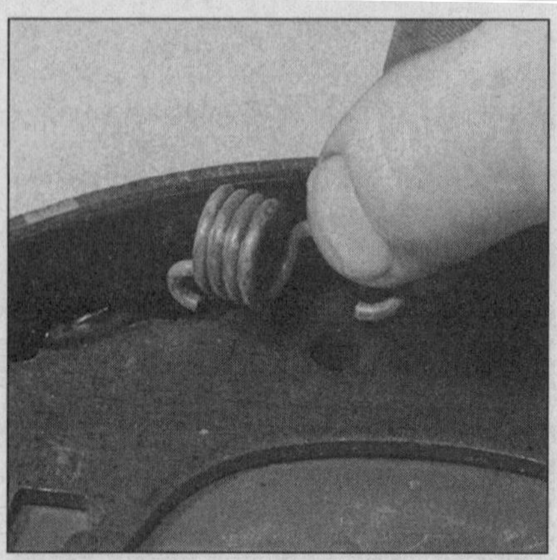

6.2m . . . and remove the small spring

6.2n Clean the back plate, and apply small amounts of high-melting-point brake grease to the brake shoe contact points. Be careful not to get grease on any friction surfaces

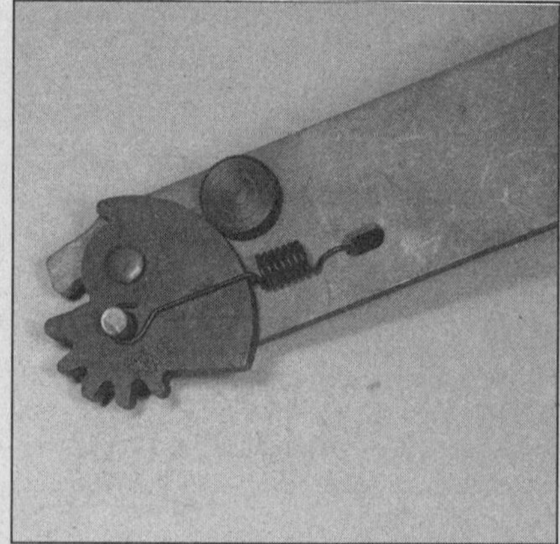

6.2o Lubricate the sliding components of the automatic adjuster with a little high-melting-point brake grease, but leave the serrations on the eccentric cam shown here clean

dure on the remaining rear brake.

7 Lower the vehicle to the ground, and tighten the wheel nuts.

8 Depress the brake pedal several times, in order to operate the self-adjusting mechanism and set the shoes at their normal operating position.

9 Make several forward and reverse stops, and operate the parking brake fully two or three times. Give the vehicle a road test, to make sure that the brakes are functioning correctly, and to bed-in the new linings to the contours of the disc. Remember that the new linings will not give full braking efficiency until they have bedded-in.

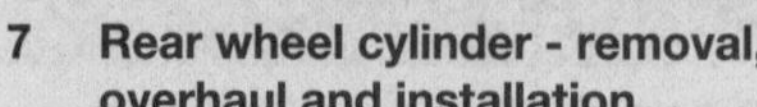

7 Rear wheel cylinder - removal, overhaul and installation

Note: *Before starting work, check on the availability of parts (overhaul kit of seals). Also bear in mind that if the brake shoes have been contaminated by fluid leaking from the wheel cylinder, they must be replaced. In principle, the shoes on BOTH sides of the vehicle must be replaced, even if they are only contaminated on one side.*

Removal

Refer to illustration 7.5

1 Remove the brake drum as described in Section 5.

2 Minimize fluid loss either by removing the master cylinder reservoir cap, and then tightening it down onto a piece of cellophane to obtain an airtight seal, or by using a brake hose clamp, a C-clamp, or similar tool, to clamp the flexible hose at the nearest convenient point to the wheel cylinder.

3 Pull the brake shoes apart at their top ends, so that they are just clear of the wheel cylinder. The automatic adjuster will hold the shoes in this position, so that the cylinder can be withdrawn.

4 Wipe away all traces of dirt around the hydraulic fitting at the rear of the wheel cylinder, then undo the fitting nut.

5 Unscrew the two bolts securing the wheel cylinder to the back plate **(see illustration)**.

6 Withdraw the wheel cylinder from the back plate so that it is clear of the brake shoes. Plug the open hydraulic unions, to prevent the entry of dirt, and to minimize further fluid loss while the cylinder is detached.

7.5 Bolts securing the wheel cylinder to the back plate. Hydraulic fitting nut and bleed screw cover are also visible

Overhaul

7 Clean the external surfaces of the cylinder, and unscrew the bleed screw.

8 Carefully pry off the dust cover from each end of the cylinder.

9 Tap the wheel cylinder on a block of wood to eject the pistons and seals, keeping them identified for location. Finally remove the spring.

10 Clean the pistons and the cylinder by washing in rubbing alcohol or fresh hydraulic fluid. Do not use gasoline, paraffin or any other mineral-based fluid. Remove and discard the old seals, noting which way round they are installed.

11 Examine the surfaces of the pistons and the cylinder bores, and look for any signs of rust or scoring. If such damage is evident, the complete wheel cylinder must be replaced.

12 Reassemble by lubricating the first piston in clean hydraulic fluid, then manipulating a new seal into position, so that its raised lip faces away from the brake shoe bearing face of the piston.

13 Insert the piston into the cylinder. As the seal enters the bore, twist the piston back and forth so that the seal lip is not trapped.

14 Insert the spring, then install the remaining piston and seal, again making sure that the seal lip is not trapped as it enters the bore.

15 Install new dust covers to the grooves in the pistons and wheel cylinder body.

16 Install the bleed screw.

Installation

17 Wipe clean the back plate, and remove the plug from the end of the hydraulic pipe. Install the cylinder onto the back plate, and screw in the hydraulic fitting nut by hand, being careful not to cross-thread it.

18 Tighten the mounting bolts, then fully tighten the hydraulic fitting nut.

19 Retract the automatic brake adjuster mechanism, so that the brake shoes engage with the pistons of the wheel cylinder. To do this, pry the shoes apart slightly, turn the automatic adjuster to its minimum position, and release the shoes.

20 Remove the clamp from the flexible brake hose, or the cellophane from the master cylinder (as applicable).

21 Install the brake drum with reference to Section 5.

22 Bleed the brake hydraulic system as described in Section 14. Providing suitable precautions were taken to minimize loss of fluid, it should only be necessary to bleed the relevant rear brake.

23 Test the brakes carefully before returning the vehicle to normal service.

8 Rear brake pads - replacement

Warning: *Disc brake pads must be replaced on BOTH rear wheels at the same time - never replace the pads on only one wheel, as uneven braking may result. Although genuine linings are asbestos-free, the dust created by wear of non-genuine pads may contain asbestos, which is a health hazard. Never blow it out with compressed air, and don't inhale any of it. DO NOT use petroleum-based solvents to clean brake parts; use brake cleaner or rubbing alcohol only. DO NOT allow any brake fluid, oil or grease to contact the brake pads or disc.*

1 Chock the front wheels, and engage 1st gear (or "P"). Loosen the rear wheel nuts, jack up the rear of the vehicle and support it on jackstands.

2 Remove the rear wheels. Work on one brake assembly at a time, using the assembled brake for reference if necessary.

3 Inspect the rear brake disc as described in Section 10.

4 Extract the spring clip, and pull out the retaining pin securing the caliper to the carrier bracket.

5 Swivel the caliper away from the carrier bracket, to expose the brake pads.

6 Disconnect the pad wear warning light wire (when equipped) at the connector. Also unbolt the brake hose bracket from the rear suspension strut, to avoid straining the flexible hose.

7 If necessary, the caliper may be completely removed by prying off the cap and unscrewing the pivot guide bolt. Support the caliper on a jackstand, or tie it to one side with wire.

8 Remove the pads from the carrier bracket.

9 Brush all dust and dirt from the caliper, pads and disc, but do not inhale it, as it may be harmful to health. Scrape any corrosion from the disc.

10 Before installing the new pads, screw the caliper piston fully into its bore, at the same time pressing the piston fully to the bottom of the bore. Proprietary tools are available for this operation in a pinch, it may be possible to use long-nosed pliers engaged with the cut-outs in the piston. Brake fluid will be displaced into the master cylinder reservoir, so check first that there is enough space to accept the fluid. If necessary, siphon off some of the fluid.

11 Install the new pads using a reversal of the removal procedure. On completion, firmly depress the brake pedal a few times, to bring the pads to their normal working position. Check the level of the brake fluid in the reservoir, and top-up if necessary.

12 Give the vehicle a road test, to make sure that the brakes are functioning correctly, and to bed-in the new linings to the contours of the disc. Remember that full braking efficiency will not be obtained until the new linings have bedded-in.

9 Rear brake caliper - removal, overhaul and installation

Removal

1 Chock the front wheels, and engage 1st gear (or "P"). Loosen the rear wheel nuts, jack up the rear of the vehicle and support it on jackstands. Remove the appropriate rear wheel.

2 Install a brake hose clamp to the flexible hose leading to the rear brake caliper. This will minimize brake fluid loss during subsequent operations.

3 Loosen (but do not completely unscrew) the fitting on the caliper end of the flexible hose.

4 Remove the rear brake pads, and free the caliper as described in Section 8.

5 Disconnect the parking brake cable from the caliper.

6 Support the caliper and disconnect the hydraulic hose, making sure that the hose is not twisted or strained unduly. Once the caliper is detached, place it to one side, and plug the open hydraulic unions to keep dust and dirt out.

7 If necessary, unbolt the carrier bracket from the knuckle.

Overhaul

8 Before proceeding check the availability of replacement parts. In principle, the overhaul information given for the front brake caliper will apply, noting that it will be necessary to unscrew the piston from the parking brake mechanism (see Section 8, paragraph 10) before being able to expel the piston from the caliper. On reassembly, push the piston fully into the caliper, and screw it back onto the parking brake mechanism. **Do not** attempt to disassemble the parking brake mechanism; if the mechanism is faulty, the complete caliper assembly must be replaced.

Installation

9 Install the caliper, and where applicable the carrier bracket, by reversing the removal operations. Tighten the mounting bolts and wheel nuts to the specified torque, and do not forget to remove the brake hose clamp from the flexible brake hose.

10 Bleed the brake circuit according to the procedure given in Section 14. Make sure there are no leaks from the hose connections. Test the brakes carefully before returning the vehicle to normal service.

10 Rear brake disc - inspection, removal and installation

Refer to Section 4 (front disc inspection). Once the rear caliper is removed, the procedure is the same.

11.1 Brake fluid reservoir and low level warning light multi-plug

11 Master cylinder - removal and installation

Removal

Refer to illustration 11.1

1 Disconnect the low fluid level warning light multi-plug from the fluid reservoir filler cap **(see illustration).** Unscrew and remove the cap (note that the filler cap should not be inverted). Draw off the hydraulic fluid from the reservoir, using an old battery hydrometer or a poultry baster. *Do not* siphon the fluid by mouth; it is poisonous. Any brake fluid spilled on paintwork should be washed off with clean water, without delay - *brake fluid is also a highly-effective paint-stripper!*

2 Identify the locations of each brake pipe on the master cylinder. On non-ABS models, there are four pipes; the two rear brake pipes are attached to PCR (pressure-conscious relief) valves on the master cylinder. On ABS models, there are only two pipes, which lead to the ABS hydraulic unit.

3 Place rags beneath the master cylinder to catch spilled hydraulic fluid.

4 Clean around the hydraulic fitting nuts. Unscrew the nuts, and disconnect the hydraulic lines from the master cylinder. A flare nut wrench should be used in preference to an open-ended wrench. Plug or cap open unions, to keep dust and dirt out.

5 Unscrew the mounting nuts, and withdraw the master cylinder from the studs on the front of the brake booster.

6 Recover the gasket from the master cylinder.

7 If the master cylinder is faulty, it must be replaced. At the time of writing, no overhaul kits were available.

Installation

8 Clean the contact surfaces of the master cylinder and brake booster.

9 Locate a new gasket on the master cylinder.

10 Position the master cylinder on the studs on the brake booster. Install and

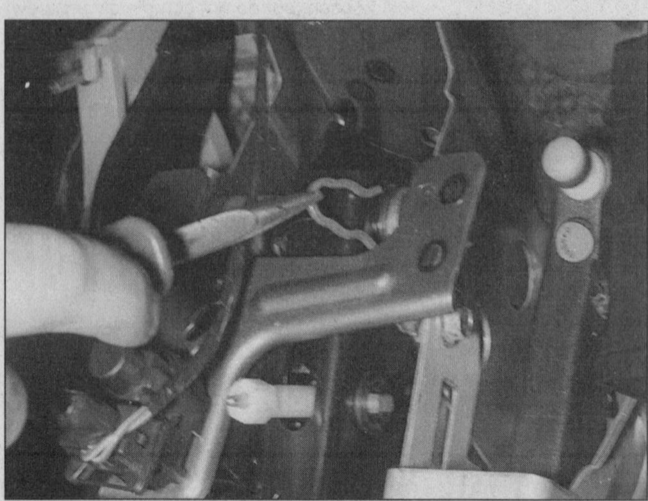

12.3 Removing the hairpin clip from the end of the brake pedal pivot shaft

12.4a Unscrew the nut securing the pedal trunnion to the pushrod . . .

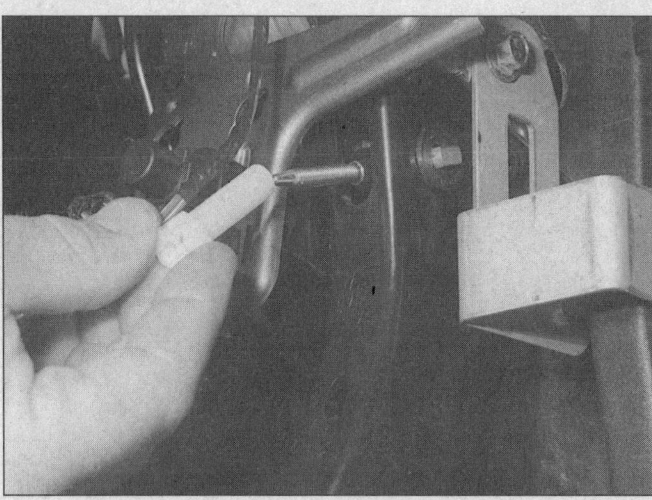

12.4b . . . and remove the tube from the pushrod

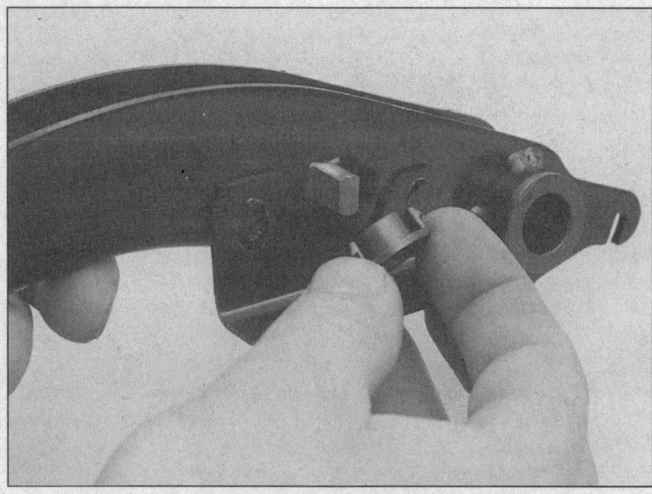
12.6a Pry out the bushings . . .

tighten the nuts to the specified torque.
11 Carefully insert the hydraulic lines in the apertures in the master cylinder, then tighten the fitting nuts. Make sure that the nuts enter their threads correctly.
12 Fill the reservoir with fresh brake fluid.
13 Bleed the hydraulic system as described in Section 14.
14 Install the reservoir filler cap, and reconnect the multi-plug for the low fluid level warning light.
15 Test the brakes carefully before returning the vehicle to normal service.

12 Brake pedal - removal and installation

Removal

Refer to illustrations 12.3, 12.4a, 12.4b, 12.5a, 12.5b, 12.6a, 12.6b and 12.6c

1 Working inside the vehicle, move the driver's seat fully to the rear, to allow maximum working area.
2 Remove the ashtray, then unscrew the screws and remove the lower dash panel.
3 Pry the hairpin clip from the end of the pedal pivot shaft, and remove the washer **(see illustration)**.
4 Unscrew the nut securing the pedal trunnion to the pushrod. The nut is located near the top of the pedal **(see illustrations)**.
5 Press the pedal pivot shaft to the left, through the mounting bracket, just far enough to allow the pedal to be withdrawn. On manual transaxle models, leave the blue nylon spacer (located between the clutch and brake pedals) on the pivot shaft **(see illustration)**. On automatic transaxle models, the shaft can be removed completely **(see illustration)**.
6 With the pedal removed, pry out the bushings from each side. If necessary, also remove the pushrod trunnion and the rubber pad. Replace the components as necessary **(see illustrations)**.

Installation

7 Prior to installing the pedal, apply a little grease to the pivot shaft, pedal bushings and trunnion.
8 Installation is a reversal of the removal procedure, but make sure that the pedal bushings are correctly located, and that the pedal shaft "D" section locates in the side of the pedal bracket. Also make sure that the hairpin clip is correctly located.

13 Hydraulic pipes and hoses - inspection, removal and installation

Inspection

1 Jack up the front and rear of the vehicle, and support on jackstands.
2 Check for signs of leakage at the pipe unions, then examine the flexible hoses for signs of cracking, chafing and fraying.

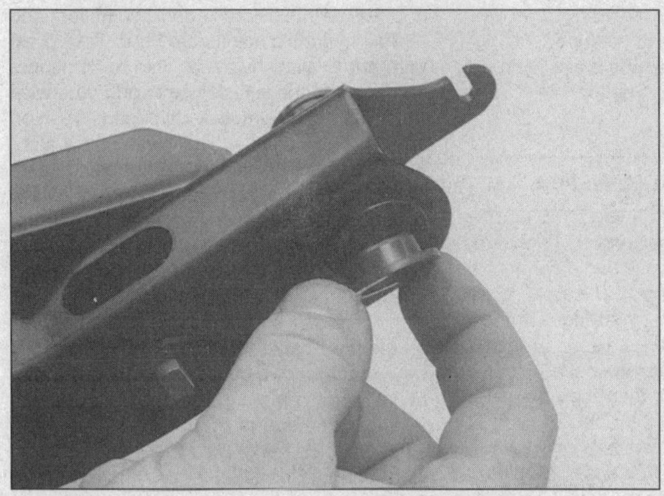
12.6b . . . from each side of the pedal . . .

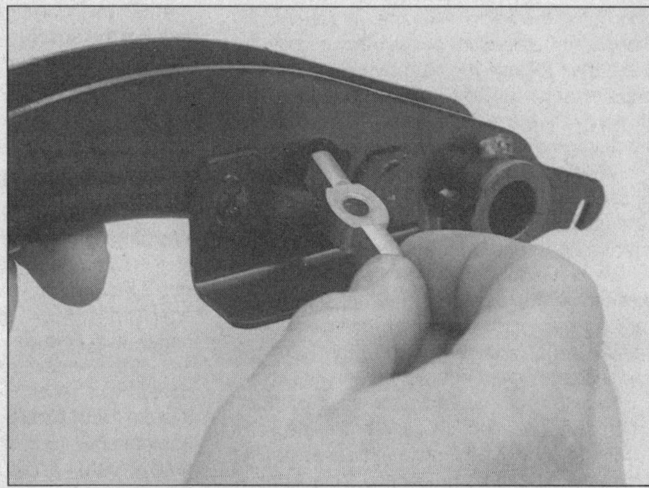
12.6c . . . and remove the pushrod trunnion

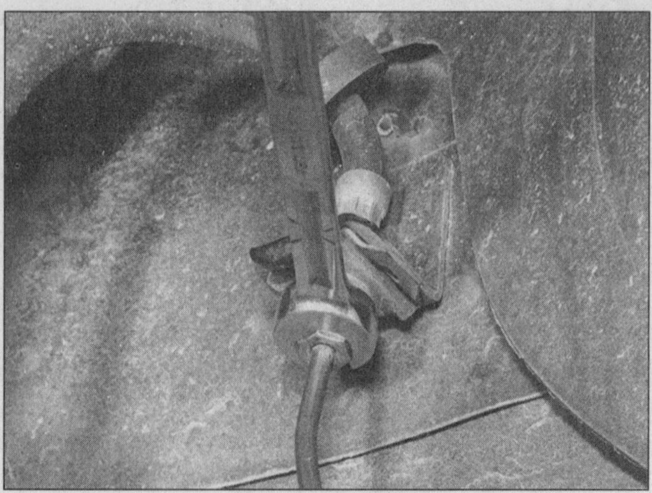

13.6a Unscrewing a brake pipe fitting nut using a flare nut wrench

13.6b Pulling out a brake pipe mounting clip

3 The brake pipes should be examined carefully for signs of dents, corrosion or other damage. Corrosion should be scraped off, and if the depth of pitting is significant, the pipes replaced. This is particularly likely in those areas underneath the vehicle body where the pipes are exposed and unprotected.
4 Replace any defective brake pipes and/or hoses.

Removal

Refer to illustrations 13.6a and 13.6b

5 If a section of pipe or hose is to be removed, loss of brake fluid can be reduced by unscrewing the filler cap, and completely sealing the top of the reservoir with cellophane or adhesive tape. Alternatively, the reservoir can be emptied (see Section 11). If any brake fluid is spilled onto the bodywork, it must be washed off without delay - *brake fluid is also a highly-effective paint-stripper!*
6 To remove a section of pipe, hold the adjoining hose fitting nut with a wrench to prevent it from turning, then unscrew the fitting nut at the end of the pipe, and release it. Repeat the procedure at the other end of the pipe, then release the pipe by pulling out the clips attaching it to the body **(see illustrations)**. Where the fitting nuts are exposed to the full force of the weather, they can sometimes be quite tight. If an open-ended wrench is used, rounding of the flats on the nuts is not uncommon, and for this reason, it is preferable to use a flare nut (brake) wrench, which will engage all the flats. If such a wrench is not available, self-locking grips may be used as a last resort; these may well damage the nuts, but if the pipe is to be replaced, this does not matter.
7 To further minimize the loss of fluid when disconnecting a flexible brake line from a rigid pipe, clamp the hose as near as possible to the pipe to be detached, using a brake hose clamp or a pair of self-locking grips with protected jaws.
8 To remove a flexible hose, first clean the ends of the hose and the surrounding area, then unscrew the fitting nuts from the hose ends. Recover the spring clip, and withdraw the hose from the serrated mounting in the support bracket. Where applicable, unscrew the hose from the caliper.
9 Brake pipes supplied with flared ends and fitting nuts can be obtained individually, or in sets from dealers or accessory shops. The pipe is then bent to shape, using the old pipe as a guide, and is ready for installing. Be careful not to kink or crimp the pipe when bending it; ideally, a proper pipe-bending tool should be used.

Installation

10 Installation of the pipes and hoses is a reversal of removal. Make sure that all brake pipes are securely supported in their clips, and ensure that the hoses are not kinked. Check also that the hoses are clear of all suspension components and underbody attachments, and will remain clear during movement of the suspension and steering.
11 On completion, bleed the brake hydraulic system as described in Section 14.

14 Hydraulic system - bleeding

Warning: *Brake fluid is poisonous. Take care to keep it off bare skin, and in particular not to get splashes in your eyes. The fluid also attacks paintwork - wash off spillages immediately with cold water.*

1 If the master cylinder has been disconnected and reconnected, then the complete system (both circuits) must be bled of air. If a component of one circuit has been disturbed, then only that particular circuit need be bled.
2 Bleeding should commence on one front brake, followed by the diagonally-opposite rear brake. The remaining front brake should then be bled, followed by its diagonally-opposite rear brake.
3 There are a variety of do-it-yourself "one-man" brake bleeding kits available from auto parts stores, and it is recommended that one of these kits be used wherever possible, as they greatly simplify the brake bleeding operation. Follow the kit manufacturer's instructions in conjunction with the following procedure. If a pressure-bleeding kit is obtained, then it will not be necessary to depress the brake pedal in the following procedure.
4 During the bleeding operation, do not allow the brake fluid level in the reservoir to drop below the minimum mark. If the level is allowed to fall so far that air is drawn in, the whole procedure will have to be started again from scratch. Only use new fluid for topping-up, preferably from a freshly-opened container. *Never re-use fluid bled from the system.*
5 Before starting, check that all rigid pipes and flexible hoses are in good condition, and that all hydraulic unions are tight. Take great care not to allow hydraulic fluid to come into contact with the vehicle paintwork, otherwise the finish will be seriously damaged. Wash off any spilled fluid immediately with cold water.
6 If a brake bleeding kit is not being used, gather together a clean jar, a length of plastic or rubber tubing which is a tight fit over the bleed screw, and a new can of the specified brake fluid (see Chapter 1 Specifications). The help of an assistant will also be required.
7 Clean the area around the bleed screw on the front brake unit to be bled (it is important that no dirt be allowed to enter the hydraulic system), and remove the dust cap. Connect one end of the tubing to the bleed screw, and immerse the other end in the jar, which should be filled with sufficient brake fluid to keep the end of the tube submerged.

8 Open the bleed screw by one or two turns, and have the assistant depress the brake pedal to the floor. Tighten the bleed screw at the end of the downstroke, then have the assistant release the pedal. Continue this procedure until clean brake fluid, free from air bubbles, can be seen flowing into the jar. Finally tighten the bleed screw with the pedal in the fully-depressed position.
9 Remove the tube, and install the dust cap. Top-up the master cylinder reservoir if necessary, then repeat the procedure on the diagonally opposite rear brake.
10 Repeat the procedure on the remaining circuit, starting with the front brake, and followed by the diagonally-opposite rear brake.
11 Check the feel of the brake pedal - it should be firm. If it is spongy, there is still some air in the system, and the bleeding procedure should be repeated.
12 When bleeding is complete, top-up the master cylinder reservoir and install the cap.

15 Vacuum booster unit - testing, removal and installation

Testing

1 To test the operation of the brake booster, depress the brake pedal four or five times to dissipate the vacuum, then start the engine while keeping the brake pedal depressed. As the engine starts, there should be a noticeable "give" in the brake pedal as vacuum builds up. Allow the engine to run for at least two minutes, and then switch it off. If the brake pedal is now depressed again, it should be possible to hear a hiss from the brake booster when the pedal is depressed. After four or five applications, no further hissing should be heard, and the pedal should feel harder.
2 Before assuming that a problem exists in the brake booster itself, inspect the non-return valve as described in the next Section.

Removal

3 Refer to Section 11 and remove the master cylinder.
4 Disconnect the vacuum hose adapter at the brake booster by pulling it free from the rubber grommet. If it is reluctant to move, pry it free, using a screwdriver with its blade inserted under the flange.
5 Unscrew the four nuts securing the brake booster to the mounting brackets on the firewall in the engine compartment.
6 Unscrew the nut securing the pedal trunnion to the brake booster pushrod inside the passenger compartment. The nut is located near the top of the pedal, and is accessible through an access hole. For improved access, remove the lower dash panel first.
7 Withdraw the brake booster from the firewall, and remove it from the engine compartment. Take care not to damage the firewall rubber grommet as the pushrod passes through it.
8 Note that the brake booster cannot be disassembled for repair or overhaul and, if faulty, must be replaced.

Installation

9 Installation is a reversal of the removal procedure. Refer to Section 11 for details of installing the master cylinder.

16.2 Removing the plastic adapter from the brake booster

16 Vacuum booster unit vacuum hose and non-return valve - removal, testing and installation

Removal

Refer to illustration 16.2

1 Depress the brake pedal four or five times, to dissipate any remaining vacuum from the brake booster.
2 Disconnect the vacuum hose adapter at the brake booster, by pulling it free from the rubber grommet **(see illustration)**. If it is reluctant to move, pry it free, using a screwdriver with its blade inserted under the flange.
3 Detach the vacuum hose from the intake manifold connection, pressing in the collar to disengage the tabs, then withdrawing the collar slowly.
4 If the hose or the fixings are damaged or in poor condition, they must be replaced.

Testing

5 Examine the non-return valve for damage and signs of deterioration, and replace it if necessary. The valve may be tested by blowing through its connecting hoses in both directions. It should only be possible to blow from the brake booster end towards the intake manifold.

Installation

6 Installation is a reversal of the removal procedure. If installing a new non-return valve, ensure that it is installed in the correct direction.

17 Pressure-control relief valve (non-ABS models) - removal and installation

Removal

1 On non-ABS models, the two pressure-control relief valves (sometimes referred to as pressure-conscious reducing valves) are located on the master cylinder outlets to the rear brake line circuits.
2 Unscrew and remove the fluid reservoir filler cap, and draw off the fluid - see Section 11.
3 Position some rags beneath the master cylinder, to catch any spilled fluid.
4 Clean around the valve to be removed. Hold the PCR valve stationary with one wrench, and unscrew the hydraulic pipe fitting nut with another wrench. Pull out the pipe, and bend it slightly away from the valve.
5 Unscrew the PCR valve from the master cylinder.
6 Note that the primary and secondary PCR valves have different thread diameters, to prevent improper installation. The primary valve has a 12 mm diameter thread, and the secondary valve has a 10 mm diameter thread.

Installation

7 Installation is a reversal of the removal procedure. On completion, bleed the hydraulic system as described in Section 14.

18 Pressure-control relief valve (ABS models) - removal and installation

Removal

1 On ABS models, the pressure-control relief valves are located on the ABS hydraulic unit.

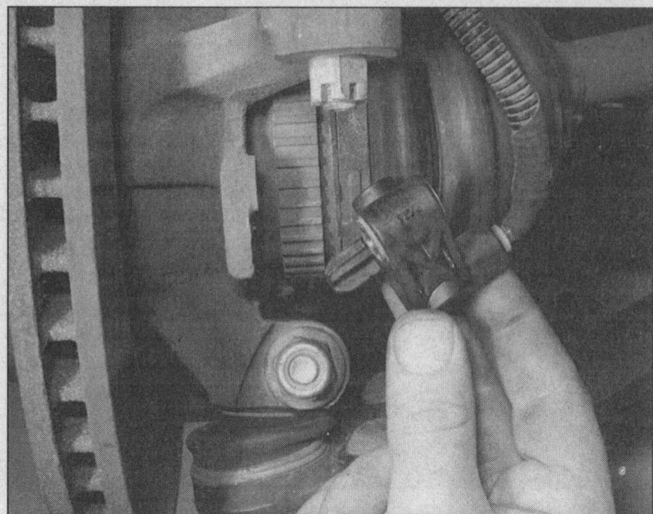

20.4 Unscrew the mounting bolt and remove the ABS sensor

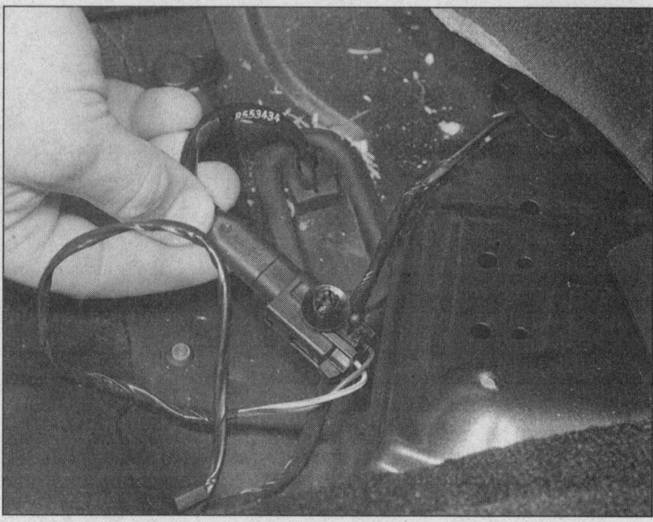

20.12 Rear ABS sensor wiring multi-plug located beneath the rear seat

2 Disconnect the battery negative (ground) lead (Chapter 5, Section 1).

3 Remove the air cleaner assembly as described in Chapter 4.

4 Remove the engine air inlet duct and air plenum chamber.

5 Disconnect the low fluid level warning multi-plug from the brake fluid reservoir.

6 Unscrew and remove the brake fluid reservoir filler cap, and completely seal the top of the reservoir using cellophane or adhesive tape. This will reduce loss of fluid when the PCR valve is removed.

7 Unscrew the master cylinder mounting nuts, and carefully withdraw the cylinder from the brake booster, leaving the brake pipes still connected to it. Move the master cylinder over to the left side of the engine compartment, to rest against the left suspension tower. (Throughout this manual, left and right are as seen from the driver's seat.)

8 Unscrew the brake booster mounting nuts, and move the unit to one side.

9 Position some rags beneath the ABS unit, to catch spilled fluid.

10 Clean around the valve to be removed. Hold the PCR valve stationary with one wrench, and unscrew the hydraulic pipe fitting nut with another wrench. Pull out the pipe, and bend it slightly away from the valve.

11 Unscrew the PCR valve from the ABS unit.

Installation

12 Installation is a reversal of the removal procedure. On completion, bleed the hydraulic system as described in Section 14.

19 ABS hydraulic unit - removal and installation

Note: *If any part of the ABS hydraulic unit is defective, it must be replaced as an assembly. Apart from the relay box (Section 21), individual replacement parts are not available.*

Removal

1 Remove both pressure-control relief valves as described in Section 18.

2 Identify the location of the remaining brake hydraulic pipes on the ABS hydraulic unit, then unscrew the fitting nuts and pull out the pipes. Carefully bend the pipes away from the hydraulic unit, to allow the unit to be removed.

3 Disconnect the multi-plugs from the hydraulic unit. To disconnect the main 22-pin multi-plug, push the lock tab, then swivel the multi-plug outwards and unhook it.

4 Unscrew the nut securing the pedal trunnion to the brake booster pushrod inside the passenger compartment. The nut is located near the top of the pedal, and is accessible through an access hole. For improved access, remove the lower dash panel first.

5 Remove the vacuum booster unit, together with the pushrod, from the engine compartment. Take care not to damage the rubber grommet in the firewall.

6 Unscrew the pump mounting nut.

7 Raise the side of the ABS hydraulic unit, then swivel the unit out of the right-side mounting. Take care not to lose the bracket studs and insulator ring.

Installation

8 Locate the insulator ring on the pump end, and install the stud cap to the insulator ring.

9 Lower the ABS hydraulic unit into position, right end first.

10 Install the right bracket studs onto the insulators.

11 Lower the left end of the ABS hydraulic unit onto the bracket, then install and tighten the pump mounting nut.

12 Install the vacuum booster unit and pushrod on the firewall bracket, taking care not to damage the rubber grommet.

13 Insert the pushrod in the pedal trunnion, and tighten the nut.

14 Install the lower dash panel if it was removed.

15 Reconnect the multi-plugs to the hydraulic unit.

16 Reconnect the brake pipes to the hydraulic unit, and tighten the fitting nuts.

17 Install both pressure-control relief valves, with reference to Section 18.

20 ABS wheel sensor - testing, removal and installation

Testing

1 Checking of the sensors is done before removal, connecting a voltmeter to the disconnected sensor multi-plug. Using an analog (moving coil) meter is not practical, since the meter does not respond quickly enough. A digital meter having an AC facility may be used to check that the sensor is operating correctly. To do this, raise the relevant wheel then disconnect the wiring to the ABS sensor and connect the meter to it. Spin the wheel and check that the output voltage is between 1.5 and 2.0 volts, depending on how fast the wheel is spun. Alternatively, an oscilloscope may be used to check the output of the sensor - an alternating current will be traced on the screen, of magnitude depending on the speed of the rotating wheel.

2 If the sensor output is low or zero, replace the sensor.

Removal

Front wheel sensor

Refer to illustration 20.4

3 Apply the parking brake, jack up the front of the vehicle and support it on jackstands. Remove the relevant wheel.

4 Unscrew the sensor mounting bolt located on the steering knuckle, and withdraw the sensor **(see illustration)**.

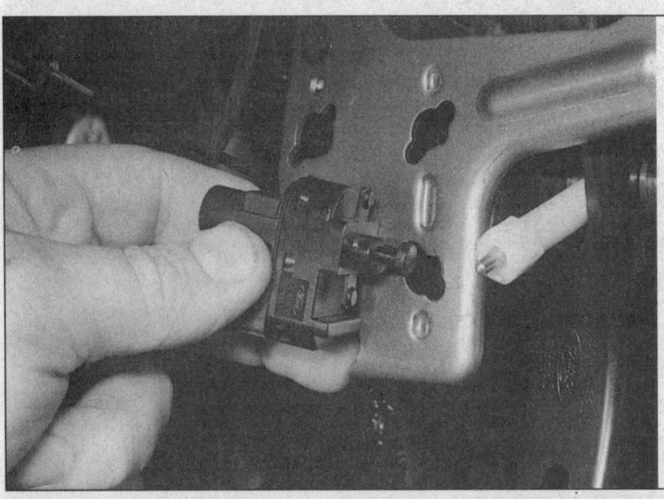
24.4 Removing the brake light switch

5 Remove the sensor wiring harness from the support brackets on the front suspension strut and wheel arch.

6 Pry out the stud clips, and remove the Torx screws and screw clips holding the wheel arch liner in position. Withdraw the liner.

7 Disconnect the multi-plug, and withdraw the sensor and wiring harness.

Rear wheel sensor

Refer to illustration 20.12

8 Chock the front wheels, and engage 1st gear (or "P"). Jack up the rear of the vehicle and support it on jackstands. Remove the relevant wheel.

9 Unscrew the sensor mounting bolt, located on the brake back plate (drum brakes) or rear suspension knuckle (disc brakes), and withdraw the sensor.

10 On disc brake models, pry out the stud clips, and remove the Torx screws and screw clips holding the wheel arch liner in position. Withdraw the liner.

11 Disconnect the sensor wiring harness from the supports on the rear suspension strut (or knuckle) and wheel arch.

12 Working inside the vehicle, lift the rear seat cushion, then disconnect the multi-plug for the sensor wiring harness **(see illustration)**.

13 Withdraw the sensor and wiring harness through the rubber grommet in the rear floor.

Installation

Front and rear wheel sensors

14 Installation is a reversal of the removal procedure.

21 ABS relay box - removal and installation

Removal

1 Disconnect the battery negative (ground) cable (Chapter 5, Section 1).

2 Detach the vacuum hose from the intake manifold connection, pressing in the collar to disengage the tabs, then withdrawing the collar slowly.

3 To improve access, free the heater hose from its retaining clips, and position it clear of the relay box.

4 Disconnect the wiring connector(s) from the relay box and, where necessary, the speed sender unit.

5 Loosen and remove the four Torx retaining screws, and withdraw the relay box from the hydraulic unit.

Installation

6 Installation is a reversal of the removal procedure. Do not overtighten the relay box retaining screws, as the plastic is easily cracked.

22 TCS inhibitor switch - removal and installation

Removal

1 Disconnect the battery negative (ground) cable (Chapter 5, Section 1).

2 Using a small screwdriver and a suitable pad (to protect the dash), pry out the TCS inhibitor switch from the dash.

3 Disconnect the multi-plug from the switch, and withdraw the switch.

Installation

4 Installation is a reversal of the removal procedure.

23 TCS throttle actuator - removal and installation

Removal

1 The TCS throttle actuator is located in the front right corner of the engine compartment. First disconnect the battery negative (ground) cable (Chapter 5, Section 1).

2 Disconnect the wiring multi-plug at the TCS actuator.

3 Pry off the motor cover.

4 Turn the upper throttle control segment, to provide some play in the accelerator cable leading to the throttle body, then disconnect the cable by unhooking the end stop. Release the cable from the motor housing support.

5 Turn the lower accelerator control segment, to provide play in the accelerator cable from the accelerator pedal, then disconnect the cable by unhooking the end stop. Release the cable from the motor housing support.

6 Unscrew the mounting bolts, and lift out the TCS throttle actuator.

Installation

7 Installation is a reversal of the removal procedure. Adjust the accelerator cables as described in Chapter 4.

24 Brake light switch - removal and installation

Removal

Refer to illustration 24.4

1 Disconnect the battery negative (ground) cable (Chapter 5, Section 1).

2 Remove the lower dash panel, with reference to Chapter 11.

3 Disconnect the wiring multi-plug from the switch.

4 Rotate the switch counterclockwise by a quarter-turn, and withdraw it from the pedal bracket **(see illustration)**.

Installation and adjustment

5 With the switch removed, reset it by fully extending its plunger.

6 Depress the brake pedal until the distance between the pedal and mounting bracket is approximately one inch.

7 Hold the pedal in this position, and install the brake light switch to the mounting bracket .

8 With the switch securely clipped in position, release the brake pedal, and gently pull it fully back to the at-rest position. This will automatically set the adjustment of the brake light switch.

9 Reconnect the wiring connector and the battery, and check the operation of the switch prior to installing the lower dash panel (Chapter 11).

25 Parking brake lever - removal and installation

Removal

Refer to illustration 25.6

1 Raise the front and rear of the vehicle, and support it on jackstands. Fully release the parking brake lever.

2 Remove the center console as described in Chapter 11.

3 Working beneath the vehicle, release the exhaust system from the rubber mountings.

25.6 Parking brake lever mounting bolts

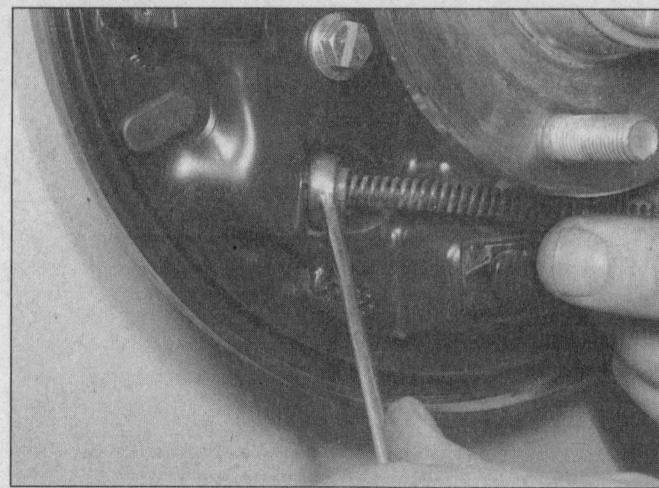
26.8 Using a ring wrench to compress the retaining lugs securing the outer cable to the back plate

Lower the exhaust system as far as possible, supporting it on blocks or more jackstands.
4 Detach the exhaust heat shield from the underbody.
5 Unhook the secondary (rear) parking brake cables from the equalizer bar.
6 Working inside the vehicle, unscrew and remove the two mounting bolts securing the parking brake lever to the floor **(see illustration)**.
7 Turn the parking brake lever upside-down, then disconnect the primary cable end from the segment.
8 Withdraw the parking brake from inside the vehicle.

Installation

9 Installation is a reversal of the removal procedure, making sure that the primary cable is correctly located in the segment. Check the operation of the parking brake before returning the vehicle to normal service.

26 Parking brake cables - removal and installation

Removal

Primary (front)

1 Remove the parking brake lever as described in Section 26.
2 Pry the grommet from the underbody, and withdraw the cable from beneath the vehicle.

Secondary (rear)

Refer to illustrations 26.8, 26.10a and 26.10b
3 Chock the front wheels, and engage 1st gear (or "P"). Jack up the rear of the vehicle and support it on jackstands. Fully release the parking brake lever.
4 Remove the relevant rear wheel.
5 Working beneath the vehicle, release the exhaust system from the rubber mountings. Lower the exhaust system as far as possible, supporting it on blocks or more jackstands.
6 Unbolt the exhaust heat shield from the underbody.
7 Unhook the relevant cable from the equalizer bar **(see illustration)**.
8 On drum brake models, remove the rear brake shoes on the relevant side as described in Section 6, then remove the outer cable from the back plate by compressing the three retaining lugs (use a suitable ring wrench) and pushing the cable through **(see illustration)**.
9 On disc brake models, unhook the end of the cable from the parking brake operating arm on the rear caliper.
10 Release the lugs securing the outer cable to the underbody brackets, then release the cable from the clips, and withdraw it from under the vehicle **(see illustrations)**.

Installation

All cables

11 Installation is a reversal of the removal procedure, but make sure that the cable end fittings are correctly located. Check the operation of the parking brake before returning the vehicle to normal service.

26.10a Release the lugs using a ring wrench . . .

26.10b . . . and remove the outer cable from the underbody brackets

Chapter 10
Suspension and steering systems

Contents

Specifications

Torque specifications

Ft-lbs (unless otherwise indicated)

Front suspension

	Ft-lbs
Front subframe	96
Lower arm balljoint to lower arm (service replacement, bolted on)	43
Lower arm balljoint-to-steering knuckle pinch bolt	
1995 through 1997	40
1998 and later	62
Lower arm to subframe	62
Stabilizer bar	18
Stabilizer bar link	26
Suspension strut-to-steering knuckle pinch-bolt	62
Suspension strut upper mounting nut	34
Suspension strut thrust bearing retaining nut	44
Driveaxle/hub retaining nut	See Chapter 8

Torque specifications

	Ft-lbs
Rear suspension	
Crossmember mounting bolts	75 to 102
Front lower arm to knuckle and to crossmember	52 to 72
Rear lower arm to knuckle	75 to 102
Rear lower arm to crossmember	52 to 72
Stabilizer bar	14 to 19
Stabilizer bar link	22 to 30
Suspension strut to knuckle	52 to 72
Drum brake backing plate	33 to 40
Disc brake splash shield	66
Hub nut	214
Tie-bar and tie-bar bracket	75 to 102
Suspension strut upper mounting bolts	17 to 22
Suspension strut upper nut	30 to 43
Steering	
Steering gear mounting bolts	101
Tie-rod end to steering knuckle	18 to 22
Tie-rod end locknut	25 to 35
Steering wheel	33 to 41
Flexible coupling-to-pinion shaft clamp bolt	17 to 24
Power steering pipe unions to valve body	20 to 26
Steering column-to-coupling clamp bolt	168 to 240 in-lbs
Steering column mounting bolts	168 to 240 in-lbs
Steering pump mounting bolts	180 to 252 in-lbs
Steering pump pressure line	42 to 54
Wheel lug nuts	95

1.5 The power steering system fluid cooler is located in front of the radiator

1.6a Adaptive damping switch located near the parking brake lever

1 General information

Refer to illustrations 1.5, 1.6a and 1.6b

The independent front suspension is of MacPherson strut type, incorporating coil springs, integral telescopic shock absorbers, and an stabilizer bar. The struts are attached to steering knuckles at their lower ends, and the knuckles are in turn attached to the lower suspension arm by balljoints. The stabilizer bar is bolted to the rear of the subframe, and is connected to the front suspension struts by links.

The independent rear suspension is of "Quadralink" type, having four mounting points on each side of the vehicle. The two lower arms are attached to the rear suspension knuckle at their outer ends, and to the rear crossmember at their inner ends. A tie-bar, positioned between the bottom of the knuckle and the floor, locates the suspension longitudinally. A rear stabilizer bar is installed on all models.

A variable-ratio type rack-and-pinion steering gear is installed, together with a conventional column and telescopic coupling, incorporating two universal joints. Power-assisted steering is installed on all models. A power steering system fluid cooler is installed, in front of the cooling system radiator on the crossmember **(see illustration)**. On models with adaptive damping, a steering position sensor with sensor disc is located above the upper universal joint.

On models with adaptive damping, it is possible to select a hard or soft setting for the front and rear shock absorbers. The system is computer-controlled; a switch is provided near the parking brake lever for selection of "Sport" or "Normal" mode. With this system, a solenoid valve is installed to each suspension strut. When the valve is open, the hydraulic oil inside the shock absorber is routed through a bypass channel, making the action "softer". When the solenoid valve is closed, the shock absorber action becomes "harder". The system takes into consideration the speed of the vehicle; at high speeds, the shock absorbers are automatically set to "hard". The adaptive damping computer module is located in the luggage compartment, behind the rear seat, and incorporates a self-test function **(see illustrations)**.

When working on the suspension or steering, you may come across nuts or bolts which seem impossible to loosen. These nuts and bolts on the underside of the vehicle are continually subjected to water, road grime, mud, etc., and can become rusted or seized, making them extremely difficult to remove. In order to unscrew these stubborn nuts and bolts without damaging them (or other components), use lots of penetrating oil, and allow it to soak in for a while. Using a wire brush to clean exposed threads will also ease removal of the nut or bolt, and will help to prevent damage to the threads. Sometimes, a sharp blow with a hammer and punch will break the bond between a nut and bolt, but care must be taken to prevent the punch from slipping off and ruining the threads. Heating the nut or bolt and surrounding area with a torch sometimes helps too, but this is not recommended, because of the obvious dangers associated with fire. Extension bars or pipes will increase leverage, but never use one on a ratchet, as the internal mechanism could be damaged. Actually *tightening* the nut or bolt first may help to break it loose. Nuts or bolts which have required drastic measures to remove them should always be replaced.

Since most of the procedures dealt with in this Chapter involve jacking up the vehicle and working underneath it, a good pair of jackstands will be needed. A hydraulic floor jack is the preferred type of jack to lift the vehicle, and it can also be used to support certain components during removal and installation operations. **Warning:** *Never, under any circumstances, rely on a jack to support the vehicle while working beneath it. When jacking up the vehicle, do not lift or support it beneath the front or rear subframes.*

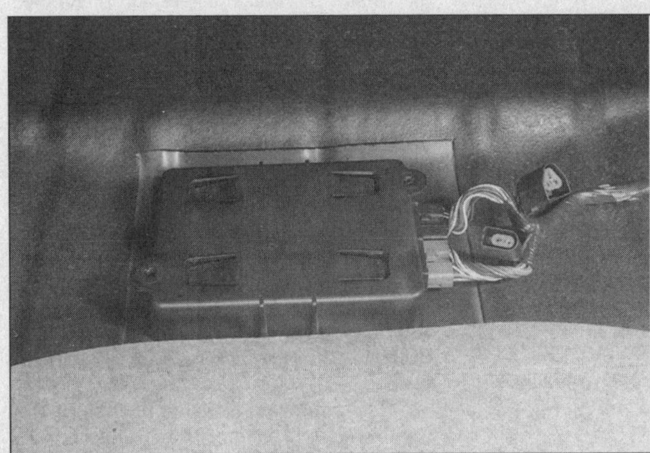

1.6b Adaptive damping computer module located in the luggage compartment

4.2 Removing the brake hose support bracket from the front of the front suspension strut

4.6 Removing the stabilizer bar link and ABS sensor wiring bracket

2 Steering knuckle and hub assembly - removal and installation

Removal

1 Apply the parking brake. Remove the wheel cover from the relevant front wheel, and loosen (but do not remove) the driveaxle/hub nut. This nut is very tight.

2 Loosen the front wheel nuts, jack up the front of the vehicle and support it on jackstands. Remove the front wheel.

3 Extract the cotter pin from the tie-rod end balljoint nut. Unscrew the nut, and detach the rod from the arm on the steering knuckle using a conventional balljoint removal tool. Take care not to damage the balljoint seal.

4 Remove the ABS sensor (when equipped) as described in Chapter 9.

5 Remove the brake caliper and brake disc as described in Chapter 9, but do not disconnect the flexible hose from the caliper. Suspend the caliper from a suitable point under the wheel arch, taking care not to strain the hose.

6 Unscrew and remove the driveaxle/hub nut. Note that the nut is of special laminated design, and should only be re-used a maximum of 5 times. (It is a good idea to file a small notch on the nut every time it is removed.) Obtain a new nut if necessary.

7 Note which way the lower arm balljoint clamp bolt is installed, then unscrew and remove it from the knuckle assembly. Lever the balljoint down from the knuckle; if it is tight, pry the clamp open using a large flat-bladed tool. Take care not to damage the balljoint seal during the separation procedure.

8 Remove the pinch-bolt securing the steering knuckle assembly to the front suspension strut. Pry open the clamp using a wedge-shaped tool, and release the knuckle from the strut. If necessary, tap the knuckle downwards with a soft-headed mallet to separate the two components. Support the knuckle on an jackstand.

9 Pull the steering knuckle and hub assembly from the driveaxle splines. If it is tight, connect a universal puller to the hub flange, and withdraw it from the driveaxle. When the driveaxle is free, support it on an jackstand, or suspend it from a suitable point under the wheel arch, making sure that the inner constant velocity joint is not turned through more than 18°. (Damage may occur if the joint is turned through too great an angle.)

Installation

10 Lift the steering knuckle and hub assembly onto the driveaxle splines, and support the assembly on an jackstand.

11 Locate the assembly on the front suspension strut. Insert the pinch-bolt with its head facing forwards. Install the nut and tighten it to the specified torque.

12 Install the lower arm balljoint to the knuckle assembly, and insert the clamp bolt with its head facing forwards. Install the nut and tighten it to the specified torque.

13 Install the driveaxle/hub nut, and tighten it moderately at this stage. Final tightening of the nut is made with the vehicle lowered to the ground.

14 Install the brake caliper and brake disc as described in Chapter 9.

15 If equipped, install the ABS sensor as described in Chapter 9.

16 Reconnect the tie-rod end balljoint to the steering arm, and tighten the nut to the specified torque. Check that the cotter pin holes are aligned; if necessary, turn the nut to the nearest alignment, making sure that the torque wrench setting is still within the specified range. Insert a new cotter pin, and bend it back to secure.

17 Install the front wheel, and lower the vehicle to the ground. Tighten the wheel nuts to the torque listed in the Chapter 1 Specifications.

18 Tighten the driveaxle/hub nut to the specified torque, and install the wheel cover.

3 Front hub and bearings - inspection and replacement

Inspection

1 The front hub bearings are non-adjustable, and are supplied already greased.

2 To check the bearings for excessive wear, apply the parking brake, jack up the front of the vehicle and support it on jackstands.

3 Grip the front wheel at top and bottom, and attempt to rock it. If excessive movement is noted, it may be that the hub bearings are worn. Do not confuse wear in the driveaxle outer joint or front suspension lower arm balljoint with wear in the bearings. Hub bearing wear will show up as roughness or vibration when the wheel is spun; it will also be noticeable as a rumbling or growling noise when driving.

Replacement

4 Remove the steering knuckle and hub assembly as described in Section 2.

5 The hub must now be removed from the bearing inner races. It is preferable to use a press to do this, but it is possible to drive out the hub using a length of metal tube of suitable diameter.

6 Part of the inner race will remain on the hub, and this should be removed using a puller.

7 Note that if this procedure is being used to replace the hub only (i.e. it is not intended to replace the bearings), then it is important to check the condition of the bearing balls and races, to see if they are install for re-use. It is difficult to be sure that no damage has occurred, especially if makeshift methods have been used during removal; in practice, it is probably false economy not to replace the bearings in any case, having got this far.

8 Using snap-ring pliers, extract the inner and outer snap-rings securing the hub bearing in the steering knuckle.

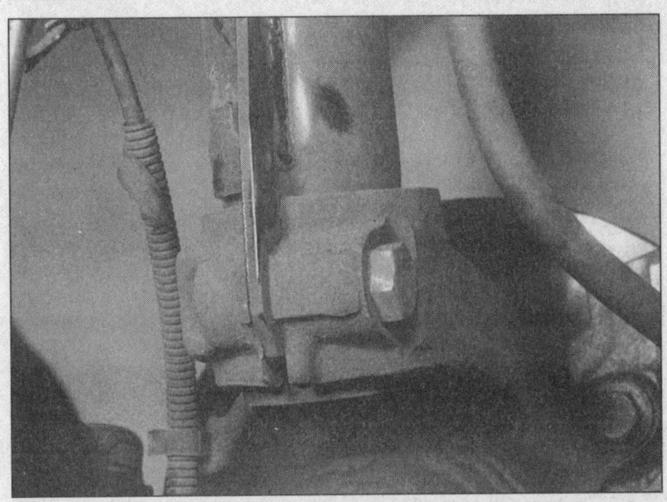

4.9 Front suspension strut upper mounting nut

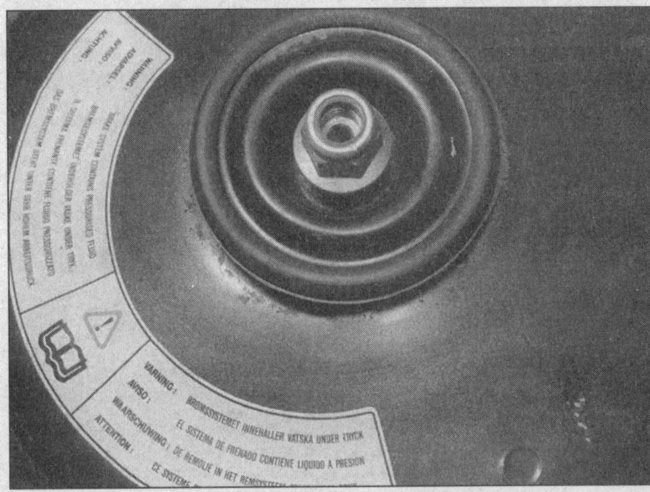

4.7 Steering knuckle-to-strut pinch-bolt

9 Press or drive out the bearing, using a length of metal tubing of diameter slightly less than the bearing outer race.

10 Clean the bearing seating faces in the steering knuckle.

11 Locate one of the snap-rings in the outer groove of the knuckle.

12 Press or drive the new bearing into the knuckle until it contacts the snap-ring, using a length of metal tube of diameter slightly less than the outer race. Do not apply any pressure to the inner race.

13 Locate the remaining snap-ring in the inner groove of the knuckle.

14 Support the inner race on a length of metal tube, then press or drive the hub fully into the bearing.

15 Install the steering knuckle and hub assembly as described in Section 2.

4 Front suspension strut - removal and installation

Removal

Refer to illustrations 4.2, 4.6, 4.7 and 4.9

1 Loosen the wheel lug nuts. Apply the parking brake, then jack up the front of the vehicle and support it on jackstands. Remove the appropriate front wheel.

2 Unbolt the brake hose support bracket from the front of the suspension strut **(see illustration)**.

3 Remove the brake caliper as described in Chapter 9, but do not disconnect the flexible hydraulic hose from the caliper. Suspend the caliper from a suitable point under the wheel arch, taking care not to strain the hose.

4 Extract the cotter pin from the tie-rod end balljoint nut. Unscrew the nut, and detach the rod from the arm on the steering knuckle using a conventional balljoint removal tool. Take care not to damage the balljoint seal.

5 Remove the ABS sensor (when equipped) from the steering knuckle, as described in Chapter 9.

6 Remove the nut and disconnect the stabilizer bar link from the strut. Note that, on models installed with ABS, the ABS wheel sensor wiring support bracket is located beneath the nut **(see illustration)**.

7 Unscrew the strut-to-knuckle pinch bolt **(see illustration)** down off the strut; if it is tight, pry the clamp open carefully using a large flat-bladed tool.

8 Where applicable, disconnect the adaptive damping wiring multi-plug at the strut, and unclip the wire.

9 Working inside the engine compartment, remove the strut cap (if equipped). Unscrew and remove the strut upper mounting nut, holding the piston rod stationary with an 8 mm Allen key **(see illustration)**.

10 Lower the suspension strut from under the wheel arch. Support the lower arm with a floor jack to prevent it from hanging down excessively.

Installation

Refer to illustration 4.20

11 Locate the suspension strut in its upper mount, and loosely screw on the nut.

12 With the clamp pried open, locate the front suspension strut on the steering knuckle, and install the pinch-bolt. Tighten the bolt to the specified torque.

13 Where applicable, reconnect the adaptive damping multi-plug, and install the wire in the clip.

14 Reconnect the stabilizer bar link to the strut, and tighten the nut to the specified torque. On models installed with ABS, do not forget to locate the sensor wiring support bracket beneath the nut.

15 If equipped, install the ABS sensor as described in Chapter 9.

16 Install the tie-rod end balljoint to the steering knuckle, and tighten the nut to the specified torque. Check that the cotter pin holes are aligned; if necessary, turn the nut to the nearest alignment, making sure that the torque wrench setting is still within the specified range. Insert a new cotter pin, and bend it back to secure.

17 Install the brake caliper as described in Chapter 9.

18 Install the brake hose support bracket to the strut, and tighten the bolt.

19 Install the wheel, and lower the vehicle to the ground. Tighten the wheel nuts to the torque listed in the Chapter 1 Specifications.

20 Tighten the suspension strut upper mounting nut to the specified torque, while holding the piston rod with an 8 mm Allen key. If the adapter needed to do this is not available, the nut can be tightened initially with a box-end wrench while the piston rod is held. Final tightening can then be carried out using a torque wrench and a conventional socket **(see illustration)**.

5 Front suspension strut - overhaul

Refer to illustrations 5.3, 5.4, 5.5a, 5.5b and 5.5c

Warning: *Before attempting to disassemble the front suspension strut, a tool to hold the coil spring in compression must be obtained. Do not attempt to use makeshift methods. Uncontrolled release of the spring could cause damage and personal injury. Use a high-quality spring compressor, and carefully follow the tool manufacturer's instructions provided with it. After removing the coil spring with the compressor still installed, place it in a safe, isolated area.*

1 If the front suspension struts exhibit signs of wear (leaking fluid, loss of damping capability, sagging or cracked coil springs) then they should be disassembled and overhauled as necessary. The struts themselves cannot be serviced, and should be replaced if faulty, but the springs and related components can be replaced. To maintain balanced characteristics on both sides of the vehicle, the components on both sides should be replaced at the same time.

2 With the strut removed from the vehicle, clean away all external dirt, then mount it in a vise.

4.20 Final tightening of the front suspension strut upper mounting nut

5.3 Coil spring compressor tools equipped to the coil spring

5.4 Unscrewing the nut from the top of the strut

5.5a Removing the top mounting from the strut

3 Install the coil spring compressor tools (ensuring that they are fully engaged), and compress the spring until all tension is relieved from the upper mounting **(see illustration)**.

4 Hold the strut piston with an Allen key, and unscrew the thrust bearing retaining nut with a box-end wrench **(see illustration)**.

5 Withdraw the top mounting, thrust bearing, upper spring seat and spring, followed by the boot and the bump stop **(see illustrations)**.

6 If a new spring is to be installed, the original spring must now be carefully released from the compressor. If it is to be re-used, the spring can be left in compression.

7 With the strut assembly now completely disassembled, examine all the components

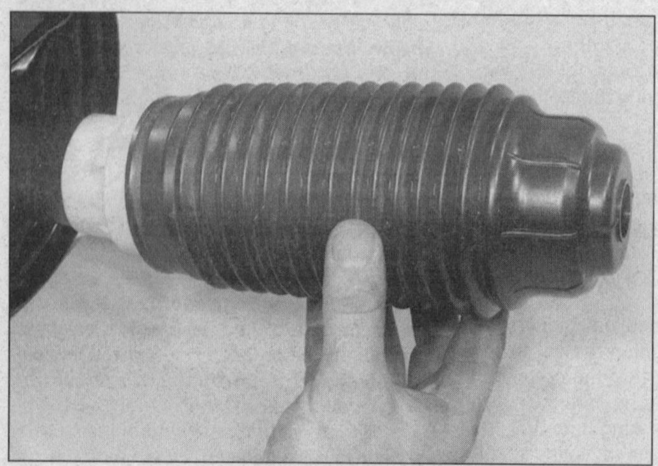
5.5b Removing the boot

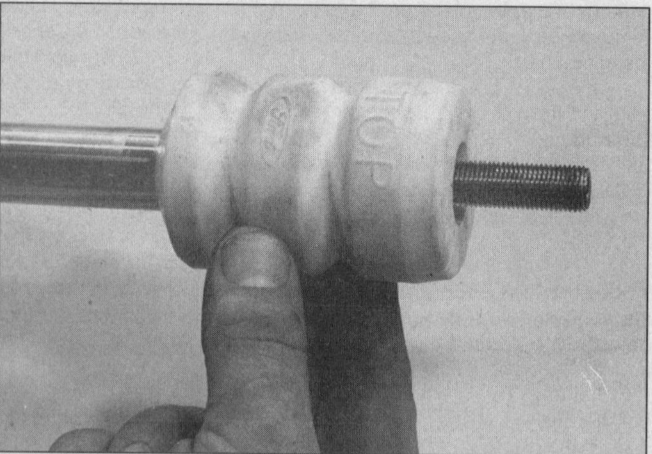
5.5c Removing the bump stop

6.2a Unscrew the nut . . .

6.2b . . . and disconnect the stabilizer bar link and (on ABS models) the sensor wiring support bracket

for wear and damage, and check the bearing for smoothness of operation. Replace components as necessary.

8 Examine the strut for signs of fluid leakage. Check the strut piston for signs of pitting along its entire length, and check the strut body for signs of damage. Test the operation of the strut, while holding it in an upright position, by moving the piston through a full stroke, and then through several short strokes. In both cases, the resistance felt should be smooth and continuous. If the resistance is jerky, uneven, or if there is any visible sign of wear or damage to the strut, replacement is necessary.

9 Reassembly is a reversal of dismantling, noting the following points:

a) *Make sure that the coil spring ends are correctly located in the upper and lower seats before releasing the compressor.*
b) *Check that the bearing is correctly installed to the piston rod seat.*
c) *Tighten the thrust bearing retaining nut to the specified torque.*

6 Front stabilizer bar and links - removal and installation

Removal

Refer to illustrations 6.2a and 6.2b

1 Apply the parking brake, jack up the front of the vehicle and support it on jackstands. Remove both front wheels.

2 Unscrew the nuts, and disconnect the stabilizer bar links from the front suspension struts on both sides of the vehicle. Note that, on models with ABS, the wheel sensor wiring support brackets are located beneath the nuts **(see illustrations)**.

3 Unscrew and remove the stabilizer bar mounting bolts from the engine subframe on both sides of the vehicle.

4 Withdraw the stabilizer bar from one side of the vehicle, taking care not to damage the surrounding components.

5 If necessary, unscrew the nuts and remove the links from the stabilizer bar.

Installation

6 Installation is a reversal of the removal procedure. Tighten the fasteners to torque values listed in this Chapter's Specifications.

7 Front suspension lower arm - removal and installation

Removal

Right lower arm

Refer to illustrations 7.3a and 7.3b

1 Apply the parking brake. Loosen the right front wheel lug nuts, raise the front of the vehicle and support it securely on jackstands. Remove the wheel.

2 Remove the inner fender splash shield, if necessary, for access to the lower arm pivot bolts.

3 Remove the balljoint pinch bolt and separate the lower arm balljoint from the steering knuckle **(see illustrations).**

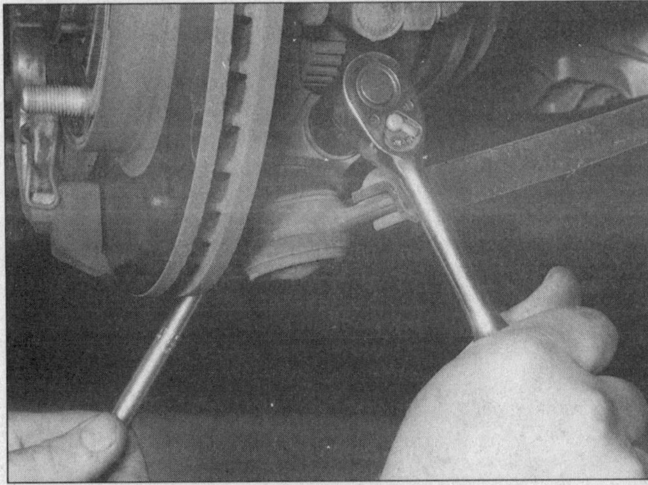

7.3a Unscrew the lower arm balljoint pinch bolt . . .

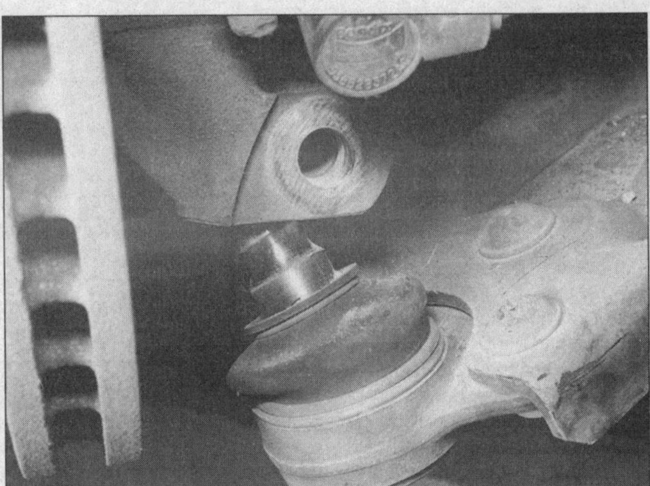

7.3b . . . and disconnect the balljoint from the knuckle

8.0 Original riveted front suspension lower arm balljoint

4 Unscrew the four lower arm-to-subframe bolts/nuts and detach the lower arm from the subframe.

Left lower arm

5 Disconnect the cable from the negative terminal of the battery (see Chapter 5, Section 1).

6 Attach an engine support fixture or an engine hoist to the engine/transaxle lift eyes.

7 Support the radiator as shown in **illustration 20.7**.

8 Apply the parking brake. Loosen the lug nuts on both front wheels, raise the front of the vehicle and support it securely on jackstands. Remove the wheels. If an engine hoist is being used to support the engine/transaxle assembly, raise it to take up the slack in the chain.

9 Detach the exhaust system from the exhaust manifold(s) (see Chapter 4). The exhaust system must be able to hang down about four inches to allow the subframe to be lowered an equal amount. if necessary, completely remove the exhaust system from the vehicle.

10 Remove the pinch bolt and detach the steering column shaft from the steering gear (see Section 18).

11 If the vehicle is equipped with a manual transaxle, detach the shift rod from the transaxle.

12 Remove the cover underneath the radiator, then remove the radiator lower mounts (see illustration 4.25b in Chapter 2 Part C).

13 Remove the pinch bolts from both lower control arm balljoints and separate the lower arms from the steering knuckles **(see illustrations 7.3a and 7.3b)**.

14 Locate the power steering cooler lines at the front of the subframe and disconnect them. Plug the hoses to prevent excessive fluid loss and contamination.

15 Separate the stabilizer links from each side of the stabilizer bar.

16 Remove the nuts from the four lower arm mounting bolts.

17 Support the subframe with two floor jacks (one at the front and one at the rear). Unbolt the engine/transmission front and rear mounts from the subframe (see Chapter 2 Part C). Remove the subframe mounting bolts (see illustration 4.47 in Chapter 2 Part C). Slowly lower the subframe far enough to remove the four lower arm mounting bolts.

18 Remove the bolts and detach the lower arm from the subframe.

Installation

19 Installation is the reverse of the removal procedure, with the following points:

a) *When installing the control arm-to-subframe bolts, insert them from the top of the subframe (bolt heads pointing up).*
b) *Tighten the control arm-to-subframe bolts/nuts to the torque listed in this Chapter's Specifications.*
c) *Tighten the balljoint pinch bolts to the torque listed in this Chapter's Specifications.*
d) *If the left control arm was removed, align the subframe as described in Chapter 2C, Section 4, and be sure to tighten the subframe mounting bolts to the torque listed in the Chapter 2 Part C Specifications.*
e) *Tighten the stabilizer bar links to the torque listed in this Chapter's Specifications.*
f) *Tighten the steering shaft pinch bolt to the torque listed in this Chapter's Specifications.*
g) *Check the power steering fluid and add some, if necessary, to bring it to the appropriate level (see Chapter 1).*
I) *Install the drivebelt cover, if removed.*
i) *Tighten the wheel lug nuts to the torque listed in the Chapter 1 Specifications.*

8 Front suspension lower arm balljoint - replacement

Refer to illustration 8.0

Note: *If the lower arm balljoint is worn, either the complete lower arm or the balljoint alone can be replaced. If the balljoint has already been replaced, it will be bolted in position; if the original balljoint is being replaced, then it will be riveted in position* **(see illustration).** *This Section describes the replacement of a riveted balljoint.*

1 Remove the pinch bolt and separate the lower arm balljoint from the steering knuckle (see Section 7).

2 Use a 1/8-inch drill to make a pilot hole through each of the three rivets. Now use a 11/32-inch drill to drill the rivets to a depth of 1/2-inch, then use a punch to drive the rivets out of the arm. **Caution:** *When drilling, take extreme care not to enlarge the holes in the control arm.*

3 Clean any rust or dirt from the rivet holes.

4 The new balljoint is supplied with a protective plastic cover over the rubber boot and stub, and it is recommended that this remains in position until it is time to connect the balljoint to the steering knuckle.

5 Locate the new balljoint on the lower arm, and use three new bolts to secure it, inserting the bolts from the top of the arm. Tighten the nuts to the torque specified in the instructions that came with the balljoint. Make sure that the location lug on the balljoint engages the hole in the lower arm.

6 Connect the front suspension lower arm to the steering knuckle as described in Section 7.

9 Rear hub and bearings - inspection and replacement

Note: *Removal of the rear hub damages the bearings, and renders them unserviceable for future use. The hub and bearing assembly* ***must*** *always be replaced if it is removed.*

Inspection

1 The rear hub bearings are non-adjustable, and are supplied complete with the hub. It is not possible to replace the bearings separately from the hub.

2 To check the bearings for excessive wear, chock the front wheels, then jack up the rear of the vehicle and support it on jackstands. Fully release the parking brake.

3 Grip the rear wheel at the top and bottom, and attempt to rock it. If excessive movement is noted, or if there is any roughness or vibration felt when the wheel is spun, it is indicative that the hub bearings are worn.

Replacement

4 Remove the rear wheel.

5 On models equipped with rear brake drums, remove the rear brake drum as described in Chapter 9.

6 On models equipped with rear brake discs, remove the rear brake disc as described in Chapter 9.

7 On all models, tap off the dust cap and unscrew the hub nut. Note that the nut is of special laminated design, and should only be re-used a maximum of 5 times. It is a good idea to mark the nut with a file every time it is removed. Obtain a new one if necessary.

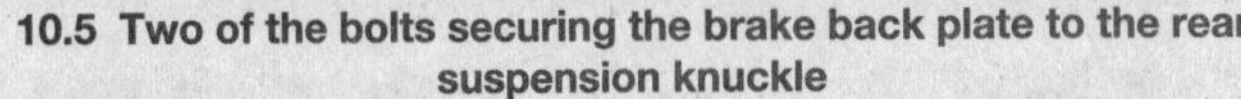

10.5 Two of the bolts securing the brake back plate to the rear suspension knuckle

11.3 Unclipping the ABS sensor wiring from the strut

8 Using a suitable puller, draw the hub and bearing assembly off the stub axle. Note that this procedure renders the bearings unserviceable for future use.

9 Locate the new rear hub and bearing assembly on the stub axle, then install the hub nut and tighten it to the specified torque.

10 Tap the dust cap fully onto the hub.

11 Install the rear brake disc or drum as applicable, as described in Chapter 9.

12 Install the rear wheel, and lower the vehicle to the ground.

10 Rear suspension knuckle - removal and installation

Note: *Removal of the rear hub from the knuckle damages the bearings, and renders them unserviceable for future use. The hub and bearing assembly* ***must*** *always be replaced if it is removed.*

Removal

Refer to illustration 10.5

1 Chock the front wheels, then jack up the rear of the vehicle and support it on jackstands. Remove the appropriate rear wheel.

2 When applicable, remove the ABS sensor from the knuckle as described in Chapter 9.

3 Remove the rear hub and bearing assembly as described in Section 9.

Drum brake models

4 Install a brake hose clamp to the flexible brake hose, then release the clip and detach the flexible hose from the strut. Unscrew the fitting nut, and detach the rigid brake pipe from the wheel cylinder. If preferred (to eliminate any bleeding procedure during installation) the rigid brake pipe may remain attached to the wheel cylinder, provided that care is taken to prevent damage to both the rigid and flexible brake pipes.

5 Unbolt the back plate from the rear suspension knuckle **(see illustration)**, and support it to one side on an jackstand. The brake shoes and parking brake cable can remain attached.

Disc brake models

6 Unbolt the splash shield from the rear suspension knuckle.

All models

7 Unscrew and remove the bolt securing the tie-bar to the bottom of the knuckle, and move the tie-bar downwards.

8 Unscrew and remove the bolts securing the front and rear lower arms to the knuckle, and move the arms to one side.

9 Support the knuckle on an jackstand, then unscrew and remove the clamp bolt securing the knuckle to the strut.

10 Pry the top of the knuckle apart carefully using a large flat-bladed tool, and withdraw the knuckle downwards from the strut. Withdraw the knuckle from under the rear wheel arch.

Installation

11 Locate the knuckle fully on the strut, then insert the clamp bolt and tighten to the specified torque.

12 Install the front and rear lower arms to the knuckle, and insert the bolts finger-tight at this stage.

13 Install the tie-bar to the bottom of the knuckle, and insert the bolt finger-tight at this stage.

14 Install the back plate (or splash shield, as applicable) to the rear suspension knuckle, and tighten the bolts to the specified torque.

Drum brake models

15 Reconnect the rigid brake pipe to the wheel cylinder (if disconnected), and tighten the fitting nut.

16 Attach the flexible hose to the strut, install the clip, and remove the hose clamp.

All models

17 Install a new rear hub and bearing assembly as described in Section 9.

18 Where applicable, install the ABS sensor as described in Chapter 9.

19 Install the wheel, and lower the vehicle to the ground.

20 With the weight of the vehicle on the suspension, fully tighten the mounting bolts for the tie-bar and lower arms.

21 Where applicable, bleed the hydraulic brake circuit as described in Chapter 9.

11 Rear suspension strut - removal and installation

Warning: *Before attempting to remove the rear suspension strut, a tool to hold the coil spring in compression must be obtained. Careful use of conventional coil spring compressors will prove satisfactory.*

Removal

Refer to illustrations 11.3, 11.8a, 11.8b, 11.8c, 11.9a, 11.9b, 11.10a, 11.10b, 11.11, 11.12, 11.13 and 11.14

1 In order to remove the rear suspension strut, the coil spring must be temporarily compressed. This will enable the piston rod to be retracted into the strut, and will provide additional room for releasing the strut from the bump stop on top of the rear suspension crossmember. **Warning:** *It is important to only use a high-quality spring compressor; carefully follow the tool manufacturer's instructions provided with it.*

2 Chock the front wheels, then jack up the rear of the vehicle and support it on jackstands. Remove the appropriate wheel.

3 If equipped, unclip the ABS sensor wiring from the strut, and remove the sensor from the knuckle as described in Chapter 9 **(see illustration)**.

11.8a Tie-bar mounting bolt on knuckle

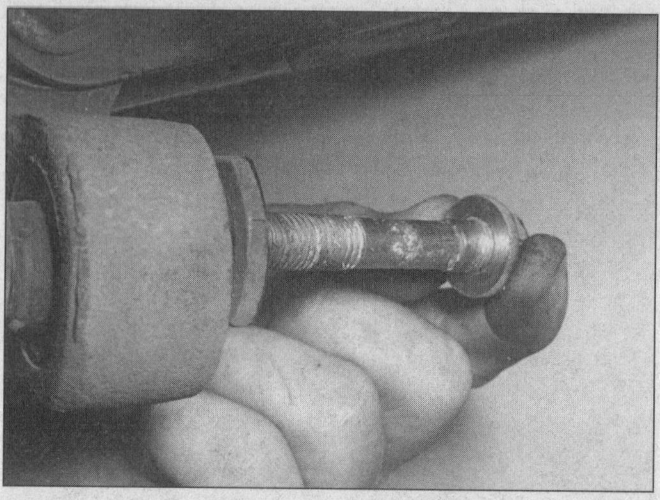
11.8b Remove the bolt . . .

11.8c . . . and move the tie-bar downwards

11.9a Unscrew the bolt . . .

4 On models equipped with adaptive damping, unclip the wiring from the strut and disconnect the multi-plug.

5 On drum brake models, install a brake hose clamp to the rear flexible brake hose, then unscrew the fitting nut securing the rigid brake pipe to the flexible hose on the strut. Extract the clip, and disconnect the flexible hose from the strut.

6 On models equipped with rear disc brakes, unbolt the caliper from the knuckle as described in Chapter 9, but leave the

11.9b . . . and remove the rear lower arm from the knuckle

11.10a Support the knuckle on a floor jack . . .

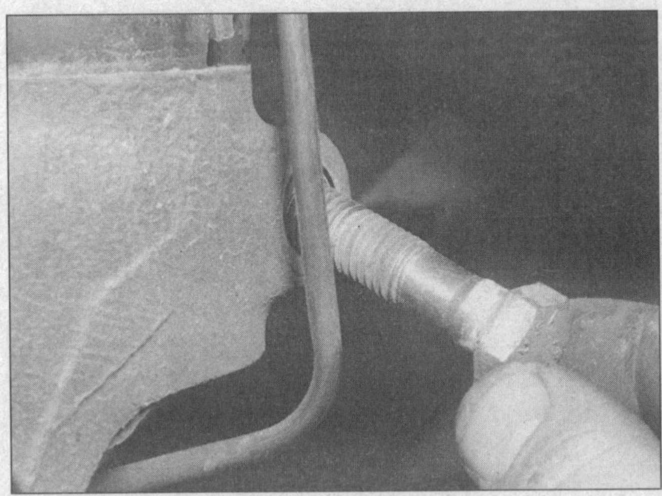
11.10b . . . and remove the knuckle-to-strut clamp bolt

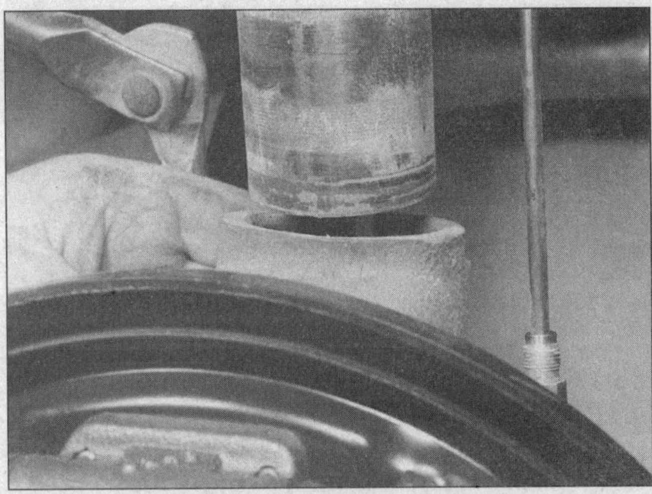
11.11 Separating the knuckle from the strut

11.12 Compressor tools attached to the rear coil spring

11.13 Bolts securing the strut upper mounting to the underbody

hydraulic hose attached. Support the caliper on an jackstand, making sure that the flexible hose is not strained.

7 Unscrew the nut securing the rear stabilizer bar link to the front lower arm on the appropriate side. Hold the actual link with an adjustable wrench or locking pliers while unscrewing the nut, to prevent damage to the link joint.

8 Unscrew and remove the bolt securing the tie-bar to the bottom of the knuckle. Move the tie-bar downwards **(see illustrations)**.

9 Unscrew and remove the bolts securing the front and rear lower arms to the knuckle, and move the arms to one side **(see illustrations)**.

10 Support the knuckle on a floor jack, then unscrew and remove the clamp bolt securing the knuckle to the strut **(see illustrations)**.

11 Pry the clamp on the knuckle apart using a large flat-bladed tool. Disconnect the knuckle from the strut, and lower it on the floor jack as far as possible, taking care not to damage the parking brake cable **(see illustration)**.

12 Install the coil spring compressor tool (ensuring that it is fully engaged), and compress the coil spring until all tension is relieved from the upper and lower mountings **(see illustration)**. This will also release the bracket on the strut from the bump stop rubber on the top of the rear crossmember.

13 Support the strut, then reach up under the wheel arch, and unscrew the two bolts securing the upper mounting to the underbody **(see illustration)**.

14 Slightly lift the strut, to force the piston into the shock absorber and release the strut bracket from the bump stop on the crossmember. Lower the strut assembly and withdraw it from under the vehicle **(see illustration)**.

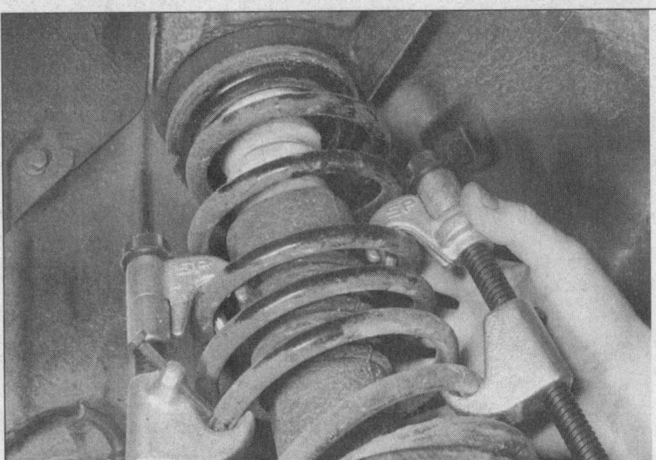
11.14 Removing the rear suspension strut

10

12.1a Rear strut dismantling - unscrew the upper mounting nut . . .

12.1b . . . remove the cup . . .

Installation

15 Locate the strut assembly (together with the coil spring compressor tool) under the wheel arch, and locate the bracket on the bump stop on the rear suspension crossmember. Insert the two bolts securing the upper mounting to the underbody tower, and tighten them to the specified torque.

16 Carefully release the coil spring compressor tool, making sure that the spring locates correctly in the upper and lower seats, and that the strut bracket locates on the crossmember bump stop. The bump stop is tapered inwards, and the strut bracket should be fully engaged with it before releasing the coil spring.

17 Raise the knuckle and engage it with the strut, then insert the clamp bolt and tighten to the specified torque.

18 Reconnect the front and rear lower arms to the knuckle, and finger-tighten the bolts at this stage.

19 Reconnect the tie-bar to the bottom of the knuckle, and finger-tighten the bolt at this stage.

20 Install the stabilizer bar link to the lower arm, and tighten the nut to the specified torque.

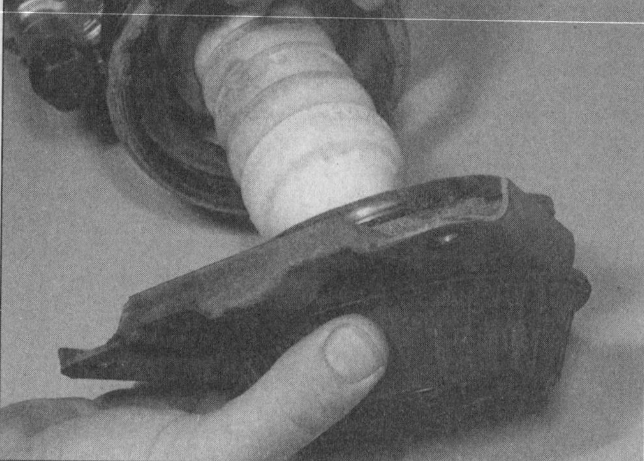
12.1c . . . upper mounting bracket and seat . . .

21 On disc brake models, install the caliper bracket to the knuckle, and tighten the mounting bolts to the specified torque (see Chapter 9). Make sure that the flexible brake hose is not twisted.

22 On drum brake models, connect the flexible hose to the strut, insert the clip, then insert the rigid brake line and tighten the fitting nut. Remove the brake hose clamp, then bleed the hydraulic brake circuit as described in Chapter 9.

23 Where applicable, reconnect the wiring multi-plug for the adaptive damping, and clip the wiring to the strut.

24 Where applicable, install the ABS sensor as described in Chapter 9, and clip the wiring to the strut.

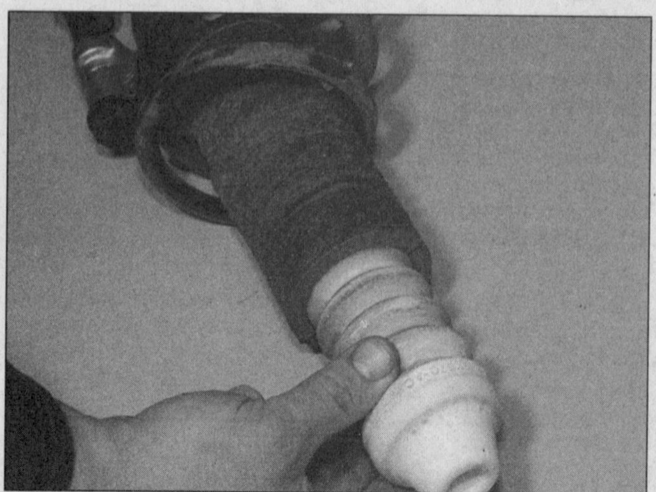
12.1d . . . boot and bump stop . . .

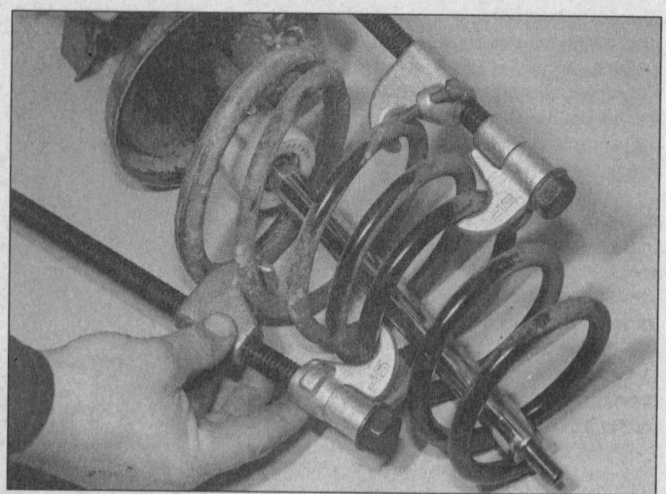
12.1e . . . and coil spring

25 Install the wheel, and lower the vehicle to the ground.

26 With the weight of the vehicle on the rear suspension, fully tighten the lower arm and tie-bar mounting bolts.

12 Rear suspension strut - overhaul

Refer to illustrations 12.1a, 12.1b, 12.1c, 12.1d and 12.1e

1 The procedure is similar to that for the front suspension strut, and reference should be made to Section 5. Note that the spring compressor tools will already be in position on the coil spring following the removal operation. Refer also to the accompanying illustrations for details of the separate components **(see illustrations)**.

13 Rear stabilizer bar and links - removal and installation

Removal

Refer to illustrations 13.2a, 13.2b, 13.2c and 13.3

1 Chock the front wheels, then jack up the rear of the vehicle and support it on jackstands. Remove both rear wheels.

2 Unscrew the nuts securing the stabilizer bar links to the front lower arms on both sides. Hold the upper part of the links with a wrench while loosening the nuts. Recover the rubber bushings **(see illustrations)**.

3 Unscrew the bolts securing the stabilizer bar mounting clamps to the rear suspension crossmember, then unhook the clamps and withdraw the stabilizer bar from under the vehicle **(see illustration)**.

4 Examine the rubber bushings for the mounting clamps and links, and if necessary replace them. The links are available individually.

Installation

5 Locate the stabilizer bar on the rear crossmember, hook the mounting clamps in position, and insert the bolts. Tighten the bolts to the specified torque.

6 Locate the stabilizer bar links in the front lower arms on both sides, making sure that the rubber bushings are in position. Install the nuts and tighten them to the specified torque.

7 Install the rear wheels, and lower the vehicle to the ground.

13.2a Loosen the nut . . .

13.2b . . . remove the nut and rubber bushing . . .

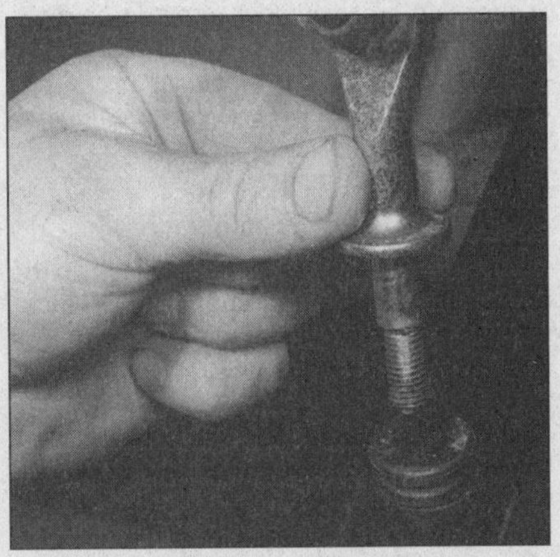

13.2c . . . and remove the stabilizer bar link from the lower arm

13.3 Rear stabilizer bar mounting clamp

14.9 Bolt securing the rear lower arm to the crossmember

14 Rear suspension lower arms - removal and installation

Removal

1 Chock the front wheels, then jack up the rear of the vehicle and support it on jackstands. Remove the appropriate rear wheel.

Front lower arm

2 To remove the front lower arm, it is necessary to remove the fuel tank first. Refer to Chapter 4 for details.

3 Unscrew the nut and disconnect the stabilizer bar link from the lower arm. Hold the actual link with an adjustable wrench or grips while unscrewing the nut, to prevent damage to the link joint. Recover the rubber bushing.

4 Unscrew and remove the bolt securing the front lower arm to the knuckle.

5 Unscrew and remove the bolt securing the front lower arm to the crossmember.

6 Withdraw the front lower arm from under the vehicle.

Rear lower arm

Refer to illustration 14.9

7 Unscrew and remove the bolt securing the rear lower arm to the knuckle.

8 The bolt securing the rear lower arm to the crossmember has an eccentric head and spacer, which are used to adjust the rear toe setting. Before removing this bolt, mark its position, using a scriber or similar sharp instrument through the aperture in the crossmember.

9 Unscrew and remove the bolt securing the rear lower arm to the crossmember **(see illustration)**. The bolt may be removed through the aperture in the crossmember. Recover the eccentric spacer.

10 Withdraw the rear lower arm from under the vehicle.

Installation

Refer to illustration 14.11

11 Installation is a reversal of the removal procedure, but the arm mounting bolts should be finger-tightened initially, and only

14.11 "TOP" marking on the rear lower arm

15.4 Tie-bar bracket on the underbody

fully tightened after the vehicle is lowered to the ground, so that its weight is on the rear suspension. Note that the rear lower arm is marked "TOP" for correct installation **(see illustration)**. The rear toe setting should be checked, and if necessary adjusted, at the earliest opportunity.

15 Rear suspension tie-bar - removal and installation

Removal

Refer to illustration 15.4

1 Chock the front wheels, then jack up the rear of the vehicle and support it on jackstands. Remove the appropriate rear wheel.

2 Disconnect the parking brake cable from the tie-bar bracket on the underbody.

3 Unscrew and remove the bolt securing the tie-bar bracket to the rear suspension knuckle **(see illustration 11.8a)**.

4 Unscrew the bolts securing the tie-bar bracket to the underbody, and withdraw the bracket from the vehicle **(see illustration)**.

5 Mount the bracket in a vise, then unscrew and remove the bolt, and remove the tie-bar from the bracket.

6 It is not possible to replace the rubber bushings - if they are worn excessively, the tie-bar should be replaced complete.

Installation

7 Installation is a reversal of the removal procedure. The bracket-to-underbody bolts should be fully tightened to the specified torque before lowering the vehicle. The bolts securing the tie-bar to the bracket and knuckle should be finger-tightened initially, and only fully tightened after the vehicle is lowered to the ground, so that its weight is on the rear suspension.

16 Rear suspension crossmember - removal and installation

Note: *Before attempting to remove the rear suspension crossmember, tools to hold the coil springs in compression must be obtained. Careful use of conventional coil spring compressors will prove satisfactory.*

Removal

Refer to illustration 16.8

1 Chock the front wheels, then jack up the rear of the vehicle and support it on jackstands. Remove both rear wheels.

2 Remove the complete exhaust system as described in Chapter 4.

3 Unscrew and remove the bolts securing the tie-bars to the rear suspension knuckles, and disconnect the tie-bars.

4 Unscrew the nuts securing the rear stabilizer bar links to the front lower arms. Hold the actual links stationary while the nuts are being unscrewed, to prevent damage to the joints. Swivel the stabilizer bar upwards, and recover the rubber bushings.

5 Where applicable, remove the ABS wheel sensor from the rear suspension knuckle as described in Chapter 9.

6 Unscrew and remove the bolts, and disconnect both lower arms from the rear suspension knuckle.

7 To allow the rear suspension struts to be released from the rubber stops on the top of the crossmember, it is necessary to install coil spring compressor tools to both of the rear coil springs, and compress them until all tension is removed from the upper and lower mountings. **Warning:** *It is important to only use high-quality spring compressors, and to carefully follow the tool manufacturer's instructions provided with them.* With the compressor tools installed, support the struts to one side.

8 Support the rear suspension crossmember on a floor jack, then unscrew the four mounting bolts from the underbody **(see illustration)**.

9 Lower the crossmember to the ground.

10 Unscrew the bolts securing the stabilizer bar clamps to the crossmember, then remove the clamps and withdraw the stabilizer bar.

11 Remove the lower arms from the crossmember as described in Section 14.

16.8 One of the rear suspension crossmember mounting bolts

Installation

12 Installation is a reversal of the removal procedure. The manufacturer specifies the use of a special tool (tool number 15-097) to accurately align the crossmember onto the underbody before tightening the mounting bolts. This tool should be obtained if possible, since inaccurate alignment would result in bad handling and excessive tire wear. The tie-bar and arm mounting bolts should be finger-tightened initially, and only fully tightened after the vehicle is lowered to the ground, so that its weight is on the rear suspension. The rear toe setting should be checked, and if necessary adjusted, at the earliest opportunity.

17 Steering wheel - removal and installation

Warning: *All models are equipped with an air bag system. Make sure that the safety recommendations given in Chapter 12 are followed, to prevent personal injury.*

Removal

Refer to illustrations 17.6 and 17.7

1 Disconnect the battery negative (ground)

17.6 Removing the steering wheel retaining bolt

17.7 Feeding the horn and air bag wiring through the hole in the steering wheel hub

cable (refer to Chapter 5, Section 1).

2 **Warning:** *Before proceeding, wait a minimum of 15 minutes, as a precaution against accidental firing of the air bag unit. This period ensures that any stored energy in the back-up capacitor is dissipated.*

3 Turn the steering wheel so that the front wheels are in the straight-ahead position.

4 Unscrew the screws, and remove the steering column upper and lower shrouds.

5 From the rear of the steering wheel, unscrew the air bag module mounting screws. Carefully lift the module from the steering wheel, and disconnect the air bag multi-plug and horn wiring connections. **Warning:** *Carry the airbag module with the trim side facing away from your body. Place the air bag module in a safe place, with the mechanism facing downwards as a precaution against accidental operation.*

6 Make sure that the steering lock is not engaged. Unscrew the retaining bolt from the center of the steering wheel **(see illustration)**.

7 Remove the steering wheel from the top of the column, while feeding the horn and air bag wiring through the hole in the steering wheel hub **(see illustration)**.

Installation

Refer to illustration 17.9

8 Make sure that the front wheels are still facing straight-ahead, then locate the steering wheel on the top of the steering column.

9 Install the retaining bolt, and tighten it to the specified torque while holding the steering wheel **(see illustration)**. Do not tighten the bolt with the steering lock engaged, as this may damage the lock.

10 Reconnect the horn wiring connections and air bag multi-plug.

11 Locate the air bag module/horn contact on the steering wheel, then insert the mounting screws and tighten them.

12 Install the steering column upper and lower shrouds. Insert and tighten the screws.

13 Reconnect the battery negative (ground) cable.

18 Steering column - removal, inspection and installation

Warning: *All models are equipped with an air bag system. Make sure that the safety recommendations given in Chapter 12 are followed, to prevent personal injury.*

Removal

Refer to illustrations 18.4a, 18.4b, 18,4c, 18.4d, 18.4e, 18.6a, 18.6b, 18.7a, 18.7b, 18.7c and 18.8

1 Disconnect the battery negative (ground) lead (refer to Chapter 5, Section 1). **Warning:** *Before proceeding, wait a minimum of 15 minutes, as a precaution against accidental firing of the air bag unit. This period ensures that any stored energy in the back-up capacitor is dissipated.*

2 Turn the steering wheel so that the front wheels are in the straight-ahead position.

3 Remove the ignition key, then turn the steering wheel slightly as necessary until the steering lock engages.

4 Unscrew the screws, and remove the steering column lower and upper shrouds. As the lower shroud is being removed, it will be necessary to remove the rubber ring from the ignition switch/steering lock **(see illustrations)**.

17.9 Tightening the steering wheel retaining bolt

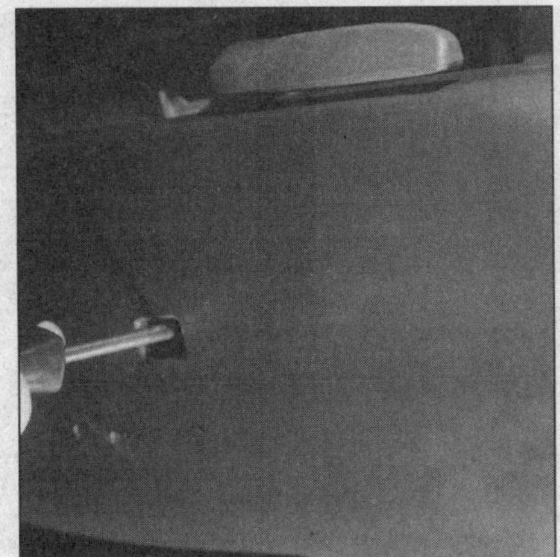
18.4a Unscrew the screws from the lower shroud . . .

18.4b . . . remove the rubber ring . . .

10

18.4c . . . and remove the lower shroud

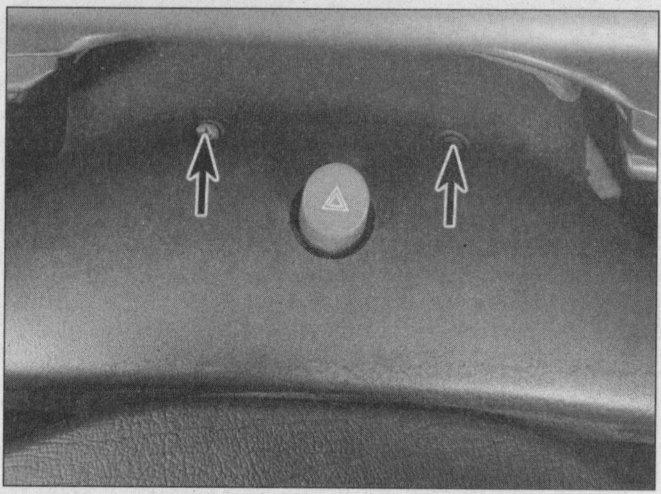
18.4d Upper shroud retaining screws

18.4e Removing the upper shroud

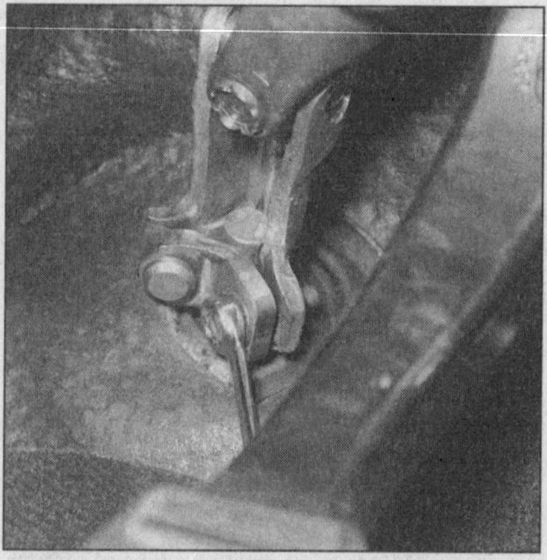
18.6a Unscrew the clamp plate bolt . . .

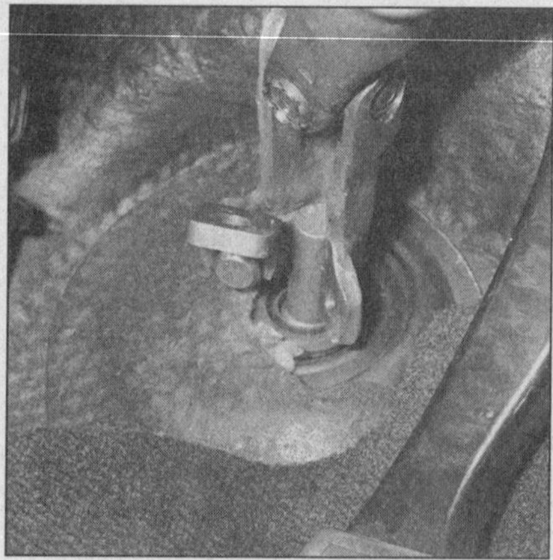
18.6b . . . and swivel the clamp plate around

5 Remove the driver's side lower dash panel (see Chapter 11).

6 Unscrew the clamp plate bolt securing the steering column shaft to the flexible coupling. Swivel the clamp plate around, and disengage it from the flexible coupling stub **(see illustrations)**.

7 Release the cable tie from the wiring harness at the steering column, and disconnect the multi-plugs **(see illustrations)**.

8 Unscrew and remove the steering column mounting bolts, then slide the column upwards to disengage the retaining tab from the groove in the cross-beam bracket, and withdraw it from inside the vehicle **(see illustration)**.

Inspection

Refer to illustration 18.9 and 18.10

9 With the steering column removed, check the universal joints for wear, and examine the column upper and lower shafts for any signs of damage or distortion **(see illustration)**. Where evident, the column should be replaced complete.

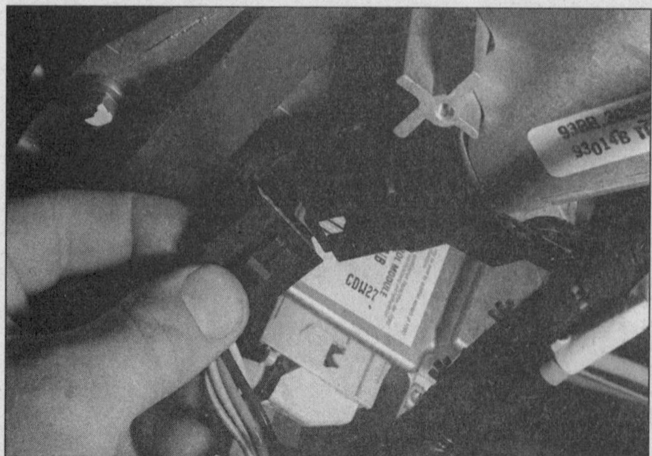
18.7a Disconnecting the multi-plug from the ignition switch

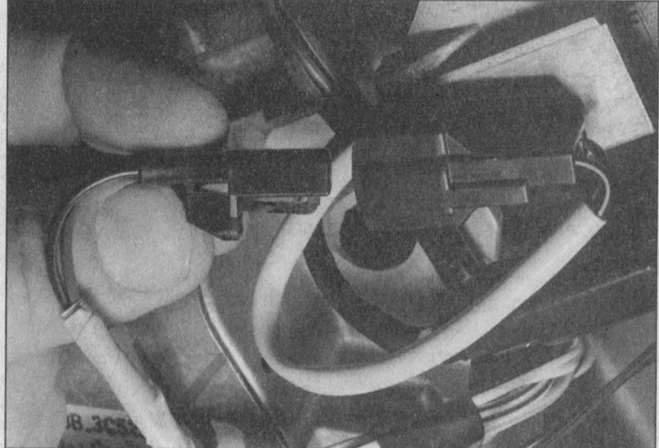
18.7b Disconnecting the small multi-plug . . .

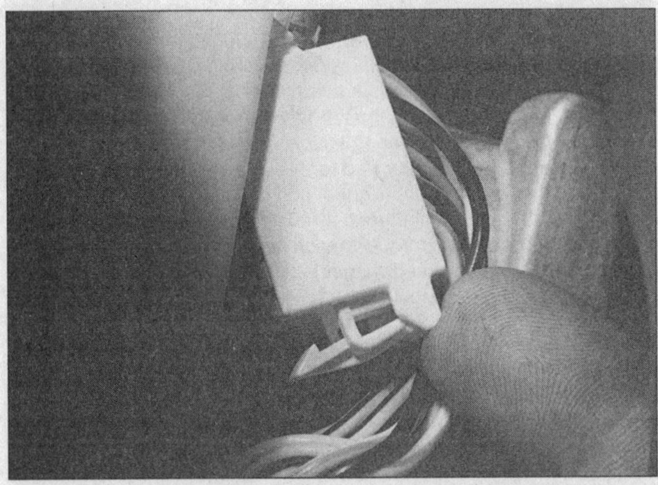

18.7c . . . and main multi-plug from the steering column

18.8 Removing the steering column

18.9 Steering column and universal fitting

10 Examine the height adjustment lever mechanism for wear and damage **(see illustration)**.

11 With the steering lock disengaged, turn the inner column, and check the upper and lower bearings for smooth operation. The bearings are obtainable separately, and should be replaced if necessary. Dismantling and reassembly of the column assembly is a relatively easy operation.

Installation

Refer to illustration 18.13

12 Locate the steering column on its bracket, making sure that the tab slides down into the groove correctly.

13 Insert the mounting bolts and tighten to the specified torque **(see illustration)**.

14 Reconnect the multi-plugs, and secure the wiring harness with the cable tie.

15 Locate the steering column shaft on the flexible coupling, swivel the clamp plate round, then insert the bolt and tighten to the specified torque.

16 Install the driver's side lower trim panel.

17 Install the steering column upper and lower shrouds.

18 Reconnect the battery negative lead.

19 Steering column flexible coupling - removal and installation

Removal

1 Disconnect the battery negative (ground) cable (refer to Chapter 5, Section 1).

2 Turn the steering wheel so that the front wheels are in the straight-ahead position. Remove the ignition key, then turn the steering wheel slightly as necessary until the steering lock engages.

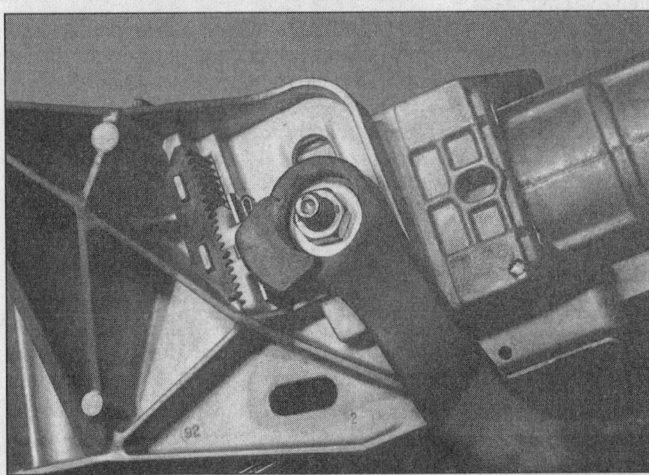

18.10 Height adjustment lever mechanism

18.13 Tightening the steering column mounting bolts

3 Unscrew the clamp plate bolt securing the steering column shaft to the flexible coupling. Swivel the clamp plate around, and disengage it from the flexible coupling stub.
4 Carefully pry the rubber boot from the firewall, and withdraw it into the passenger compartment. Take care not to damage the sealing lip of the boot.
5 Using an Allen key, unscrew the clamp bolt securing the flexible coupling to the pinion shaft on the steering gear, and withdraw the coupling from inside the vehicle.

Installation

6 Installation is a reversal of the removal procedure, but tighten the clamp bolts to the specified torque. Make sure that the rubber boot engages correctly in the firewall and on the flexible coupling.

20 Power steering gear - removal and installation

Removal

1 Disconnect the battery negative (ground) cable (refer to Chapter 5, Section 1).
2 Working inside the vehicle, unscrew the clamp plate bolt securing the steering column shaft to the flexible coupling. Swivel the clamp plate around, and disengage it from the flexible coupling stub.
3 Apply the parking brake, then jack up the front of the vehicle and support it on jackstands. Remove both wheels.
4 On manual transaxle models, disconnect the shift linkage and support rods from the transaxle, as described in Chapter 7, Part A.
5 Remove the exhaust downpipe complete, as described in Chapter 4.
6 Remove the cover from under the radiator by unscrewing the screws and releasing the clips.
7 Support the radiator in its raised position, by inserting cotter pins through the small holes in the radiator mounting extensions which protrude through the upper mountings.
8 Unbolt and remove the radiator lower mounting brackets.
9 Where applicable, unscrew the bolts securing the air conditioning accumulator to the subframe.
10 Working beneath the vehicle, unbolt the engine rear mounting from the transaxle and underbody.
11 Unscrew the front engine mounting-to-cylinder block bolts, and also the through-bolt.
12 Extract the cotter pins from the tie-rod end balljoint nuts, then unscrew the nuts, and detach the rods from the arms on the steering knuckles using a conventional balljoint removal tool. Take care not to damage the balljoint seals.
13 Working on each side in turn, unscrew the mounting nuts, and remove the stabilizer bar links from the front suspension struts. Note that, on models equipped with ABS, the ABS sensor wiring support brackets are located beneath the nuts.
14 Working on each side in turn, unscrew and remove the balljoint clamp bolt from the knuckle assembly. Lever the balljoint down from the knuckle - if it is tight, pry the joint open carefully using a large flat-bladed tool. Take care not to damage the balljoint seal during the separation procedure.
15 Support the weight of the front subframe assembly on two floor jacks.
16 Unscrew and remove the subframe mounting bolts, then lower the subframe sufficiently to gain access to the power steering fluid pipes on top of the steering gear. Note that the front subframe mounting bolts are gold in color - the rear ones are silver.
17 Position a suitable container beneath the steering gear, then unscrew the fitting nuts securing the power steering fluid supply, return, and cooler lines to the steering gear. Identify the lines for position, then unbolt the clamps, disconnect the lines, and allow the fluid to drain into the container. Cover the apertures in the steering gear and also the ends of the fluid pipes, to prevent the ingress of dust and dirt into the hydraulic circuit.
18 Lower the subframe, together with the power steering gear, to the ground.
19 Unscrew the mounting bolts and remove the power steering gear from the subframe.
20 Using a suitable Allen key, unscrew the clamp bolt securing the flexible coupling to the pinion shaft on the steering gear, and withdraw the coupling.
21 Refer to Section 23, Step 27 for details of replacing the Teflon rings.

Installation

22 Install the flexible coupling to the pinion shaft on the steering gear, then insert and tighten the clamp bolt using an Allen key.
23 Locate the power steering gear on the subframe, then insert the mounting bolts and tighten to the specified torque.
24 Raise the subframe until it is possible to install the fluid lines. Tighten the fitting nuts and clamps.
25 Raise the subframe, making sure that the alignment holes are in line with the holes in the underbody. At the same time, make sure that the flexible coupling locates correctly on the steering column. Technicians use a special tool to ensure that the subframe is correctly aligned - refer to Chapter 2C for more details of the alignment procedure. With the subframe aligned, insert and tighten the mounting bolts to the specified torque. Note that the front mounting bolts are gold in color - the rear bolts are silver.
26 Working on each side in turn, install the front suspension lower arm balljoint to the knuckle assembly, and insert the clamp bolt with its head facing forwards. Install the nut and tighten to the specified torque.
27 Working on each side in turn, install the stabilizer bar links and tighten the mounting nuts to the specified torque. On models equipped with ABS, don't forget to locate the wheel sensor wiring support brackets beneath the nuts.
28 Install the tie-rod end balljoints to the steering knuckles, and tighten the nuts to the specified torque. Check if the cotter pin holes are aligned, and if necessary turn the nuts to the nearest alignment, making sure that the torque wrench setting is still within the specified range. Insert new cotter pins, and bend them back to secure.
29 Install and tighten the engine front mounting bolts.
30 Install the engine rear mounting and tighten the bolts.
31 Where applicable, insert and tighten the air conditioning accumulator bolts.
32 Install the radiator lower mounting brackets and tighten the bolts.
33 Remove the cotter pins supporting the radiator in its raised position.
34 Install the cover under the radiator.
35 Install the exhaust downpipe as described in Chapter 4.
36 On manual transaxle models, reconnect the shift linkage and support rods.
37 Install the front wheels, and lower the vehicle to the ground.
38 Working inside the vehicle, reconnect the steering column clamp plate, then insert the bolt and tighten to the specified torque.
39 Reconnect the battery negative (ground) cable.
40 Bleed the power steering hydraulic system as described in Section 22.
41 Have the front wheel alignment checked, and if necessary adjusted, at the earliest opportunity (refer to Section 25).

21 Power steering gear boots - replacement

1 Remove the tie-rod end and its locknut from the tie-rod, as described in Section 24. Make sure that a note is made of the exact position of the tie-rod end on the tie-rod, in order to retain the front wheel alignment setting on installation.
2 Release the outer retaining clamp and inner plastic clamp band, and disconnect the boot from the steering gear housing.
3 Disconnect the breather from the boot, then slide the boot off the tie-rod.
4 Scrape off all grease from the old boot, and apply to the tie-rod inner joint. Wipe clean the seating areas on the steering gear housing and tie-rod.
5 Slide the new boot onto the tie-rod and steering gear housing, and reconnect the breather.
6 Install a new inner plastic clamp band and outer retaining clamp.
7 Install the tie-rod end as described in Section 24.
8 Have the front wheel alignment checked, and if necessary adjusted, at the earliest opportunity (refer to Section 25).

23.23 Remove the clamp securing the power steering pressure line to the right-hand engine support bracket

23.25 Before removing the drivebelt, loosen the power steering pump pulley bolts

22 Power steering hydraulic system - bleeding

1 Following any operation in which the power steering fluid lines have been disconnected, the power steering system must be bled, to remove any trapped air.

2 With the front wheels in the straight-ahead position, check the power steering fluid level in the reservoir and, if low, add fresh fluid until it reaches the "MAX" or "MAX COLD" mark. Pour the fluid slowly, to prevent air bubbles forming, and use only the specified fluid (refer to Chapter 1 Specifications).

3 Start the engine, and allow it to run at a fast idle. Check the hoses and connections for leaks.

4 Stop the engine, and recheck the fluid level. Add more if necessary, up to the "MAX" or "MAX COLD" mark.

5 Start the engine again, allow it to idle, then bleed the system by slowly turning the steering wheel from side to side several times. This should purge the system of all internal air. However, if air remains in the system (indicated by the steering operation being very noisy), leave the vehicle overnight, and repeat the procedure again the next day.

6 If air still remains in the system, it may be necessary to use a hand-held vacuum pump and an adapter that fits in place of the cap on the fluid reservoir. Turn the steering to the right until it is near the stop, then install the vacuum pump to the fluid reservoir, and apply vacuum. Maintain the vacuum for a minimum of 5 minutes, then repeat the procedure with the steering turned to the left.

7 Keep the fluid level topped-up throughout the bleeding procedure; note that, as the fluid temperature increases, the level will rise.

8 On completion, switch off the engine, and return the front wheels to the straight-ahead position.

23 Power steering pump - removal and installation

Four-cylinder models

Removal

1 Disconnect the cable from the negative battery terminal (refer to Chapter 5, Section 1).

2 Unscrew and remove the bolt securing the hydraulic fluid line support to the engine lifting bracket on the right-hand side of the engine.

3 Unscrew and remove the bolt securing the hydraulic fluid line support to the pump mounting bracket.

4 Position a suitable container beneath the power steering pump, to catch spilled fluid.

5 Loosen the clamp, and disconnect the fluid supply hose from the pump inlet. Plug the hose, to prevent the ingress of dust and dirt.

6 Unscrew the union nut, and disconnect the high-pressure line from the pump. Allow the fluid to drain into the container.

7 Apply the parking brake, then jack up the front of the vehicle and support it on jackstands. Remove the right front wheel.

8 Disconnect and remove the lower drivebelt cover.

9 Using a wrench, rotate the drivebelt tensioner in a clockwise direction to release the belt tension, then slip the drivebelt off the pulleys and remove from the vehicle. Refer to Chapter 1 if necessary.

10 Unscrew and remove the four mounting bolts, and withdraw the power steering pump from its bracket. Access to the bolts on the right-hand side of the engine is gained by turning the pump pulley until a hole lines up with the bolt.

Installation

11 Locate the power steering pump on the mounting bracket, and secure with the four bolts. Tighten the bolts to the specified torque.

12 Slip the drivebelt over the pulleys, then rotate the drivebelt tensioner in a clockwise direction, and locate the drivebelt on it. Release the tensioner to tension the drivebelt.

13 Install the lower belt cover.

14 Install the right-hand front wheel, and lower the vehicle to the ground.

15 If necessary, the sealing ring on the high-pressure outlet should be replaced, using the same procedure as described in Step 27.

16 Reconnect the high-pressure line to the pump, and tighten the union nut.

17 Reconnect the fluid supply hose to the pump inlet, and tighten the clamp.

18 Install the hydraulic fluid line support to the pump mounting bracket, and tighten the bolt.

19 Install the hydraulic fluid line support to the engine lifting bracket on the right-hand side of the engine, and tighten the bolt.

20 Reconnect the battery negative lead.

21 Bleed the power steering hydraulic system as described in Section 22.

V6 models

Removal

Refer to illustrations 23.23, 23.25 and 23.26

22 Disconnect the cable from the negative battery terminal (see Chapter 5, Section 1).

23 Remove the bolt or nut securing the power steering pressure line to the right-hand engine support bracket **(see illustration)**.

24 Disconnect the power steering pressure line from the pump and allow the fluid to drain into a suitable container. Disconnect the power steering low-pressure hose from the pump.

25 Loosen the power steering pump pulley mounting screws, then remove the drivebelt **(see illustration)**. Rotate the belt tensioner clockwise to relieve the tension on the belt and remove it.

23.26 Remove the six nuts and five bolts that secure the power steering pump and bracket to the engine, then remove the pump and bracket

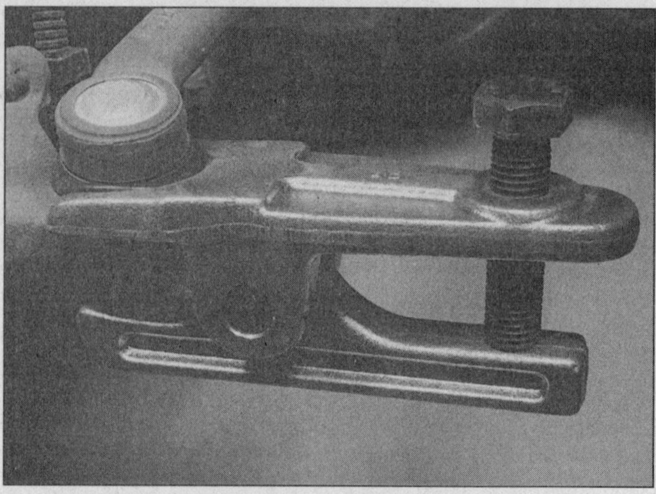

24.4 Using a balljoint separator tool to release the tie-rod end balljoint

26 Remove the pulley from the pump. Remove the six nuts and five bolts from the power steering pump bracket and remove the pump and bracket. **(see illustration)**. If necessary, separate the pump from the pump bracket.

Installation

27 If necessary, the sealing ring on the high-pressure fitting should be replaced. To do this the rings must be expanded individually onto a fitting adapter then located in the grooves of the fitting nuts.
28 Reconnect the high-pressure line to the pump, and tighten the fitting nut.
29 Reconnect the fluid supply hose to the pump inlet.
30 Install the hydraulic fluid line support to the pump mounting bracket, and tighten the bolt.
31 Install the pressure line clamp to the engine support bracket.
32 Reconnect the negative battery cable.
33 Fill the power steering reservoir and bleed the power steering hydraulic system as described in Section 22.

24 Tie-rod end - replacement

Refer to illustration 24.4

1 Apply the parking brake, then jack up the front of the vehicle and support it on axle stands. Remove the appropriate front wheel.
2 Using a suitable wrench, loosen the locknut on the tie-rod by a quarter-turn. Hold the tie-rod end stationary with another wrench engaged with the special flats while loosening the locknut.
3 Extract the cotter pin, then unscrew and remove the tie-rod end balljoint retaining nut.
4 To release the tapered shank of the balljoint from the steering knuckle arm, use a balljoint separator tool (if the balljoint is to be re-used, take care not to damage the dust cover when using the separator tool) **(see illustration)**.
5 Count the number of exposed threads visible on the inner section of the tie-rod, and record this figure.
6 Unscrew the tie-rod end from the tie-rod, counting the number of turns necessary to remove it. If necessary, hold the tie-rod stationary with grips.
7 Screw the tie-rod end onto the tie-rod by the number of turns noted during removal, until it just contacts the locknut.
8 Engage the shank of the balljoint with the steering knuckle arm, and install the nut. Tighten the nut to the specified torque. If the balljoint shank turns while the nut is being tightened, press down on the balljoint. The tapered part of the shank will lock it, and prevent rotation as the nut is tightened.
9 Check that the cotter pin holes in the nut and balljoint shank are aligned. If necessary turn the nut to the nearest alignment, making sure that the torque wrench setting is still within the specified range. Insert a new cotter pin, and bend it back to secure.
10 Now tighten the locknut, while holding the tie-rod end as before.
11 Install the wheel, and lower the vehicle to the ground. Tighten the lug nuts to the torque listed in the Chapter 1 Specifications.
12 Have the front wheel alignment checked, and if necessary adjusted, at the earliest opportunity (see Section 25).

25 Wheel alignment and steering angles - general information

Refer to illustration 25.2

1 Accurate front wheel alignment is essential to provide positive steering, and to prevent excessive tire wear. Before considering the steering/suspension geometry, check that the tires are correctly inflated, that the front wheels are not buckled, and that the steering linkage and suspension joints are in good order, without slackness or wear.
2 Wheel alignment consists of four factors **(see illustration)**:

Camber is the angle at which the front wheels are set from the vertical, when viewed from the front of the vehicle. "Positive camber" is the amount (in degrees) that the wheels are tilted outward at the top of the vertical.

Caster is the angle between the steering axis and a vertical line, when viewed from each side of the car. "Positive caster" is when the steering axis is inclined rearward at the top.

Steering axis inclination is the angle (when viewed from the front of the vehicle) between the vertical and an imaginary line drawn through the suspension strut upper mounting and the lower suspension arm balljoint.

Toe setting is the amount by which the distance between the front inside edges of the wheels (measured at hub height) differs from the diametrically opposite distance measured between the rear inside edges of the front wheels.

3 With the exception of the toe setting, all other steering angles are set during manufacture, and no adjustment is possible. It can be assumed, therefore, that unless the vehicle has suffered accident damage, all the preset steering angles will be correct. Should there be some doubt about their accuracy, it will be necessary to seek the help of a dealer or an alignment shop, as special gauges are needed to check the steering angles.
4 Two methods are available to the home mechanic for checking the toe setting. One method is to use a gauge to measure the distance between the front and rear inside edges of the wheels. The other method is to use a scuff plate, in which each front wheel is rolled across a movable plate which records any deviation, or scuff, of the tire from the straight-ahead position as it moves across the plate. Relatively inexpensive equipment of both types is available from accessory outlets.

5 If, after checking the toe setting using whichever method is preferable, it is found that adjustment is necessary, proceed as follows.

6 Turn the steering wheel onto full-left lock, and record the number of exposed threads on the right-hand tie-rod. Now turn the steering onto full-right lock, and record the number of threads on the left-hand tie-rod. If there are the same number of threads visible on both sides, then subsequent adjustment can be made equally on both sides. If there are more threads visible on one side than the other, it will be necessary to compensate for this during adjustment. *After adjustment, there must be the same number of threads visible on each tie-rod. This is most important.*

7 To alter the toe setting, loosen the locknut on the tie-rod, and turn the tie-rod using self-locking pliers to achieve the desired setting. When viewed from the side of the car, turning the rod clockwise will increase the toe-in, turning it counterclockwise will increase the toe-out. Only turn the tie-rods by a quarter of a turn each time, and then recheck the setting.

8 After adjustment, tighten the locknuts. Reposition the steering gear boots, to remove any twist caused by turning the tie-rods.

9 The rear wheel toe-setting may also be checked and adjusted, but as this additionally requires alignment with the front wheels, it should be left to a dealer service department or an alignment shop.

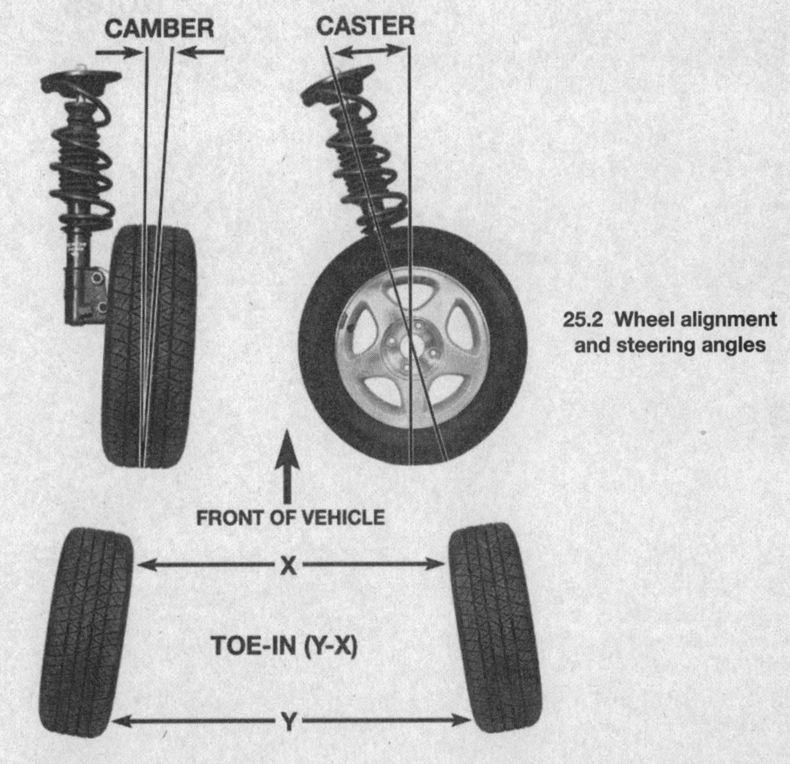

25.2 Wheel alignment and steering angles

Notes

Chapter 11 Body

Contents

Specifications

Torque specifications

	Ft-lbs (unless otherwise indicated)
Hood and tailgate hinges	18
Trunk lid	84 in-lbs
Front seat mounting bolts	28
Seat belt mounting nuts and bolts	28
Bumper mounting nuts	84 in-lbs

1 General information

The bodyshell and underframe on all models is of all-steel welded construction, incorporating progressive crumple zones at the front and rear, and a rigid center safety cell. The firewall behind the engine compartment incorporates crash grooves which determine its energy-absorption characteristics, and special beams to prevent the intrusion of the front wheels into the passenger compartment during a serious accident. All passenger doors incorporate side impact bars.

All sheet metal surfaces which are prone to corrosion are galvanized. The painting process includes a base color which closely matches the final topcoat, so that any stone damage is not noticeable.

Automatic seat belts are installed on all models, and the front seat belt stalks are mounted on automatic tensioners (also known as "grabbers"). In the event of a serious front impact, a spring mass sensor releases a coil spring which pulls the stalk buckle downwards and tensions the seat belt. It is not possible to reset the tensioner once fired, and it must therefore be replaced.

Central locking is optional on all models. Where double-locking is installed, the lock mechanism is disconnected (when the system is in use) from the interior door handles, making it impossible to open any of the doors or the tailgate/trunk lid from inside the vehicle. This means that, even if a thief should break a side window, he will not be able to open the door using the interior handle. Models with the double-locking system are installed with a control module located beneath the dash on the right-hand side. In the event of a serious accident, a crash sensor unlocks all doors if they were previously locked.

Many of the procedures in this Chapter require the battery to be disconnected. Refer to Chapter 5, Section 1 first.

2 Body - maintenance

The general condition of a vehicle's bodywork is the one thing that significantly affects its value. Maintenance is easy, but needs to be regular. Neglect, particularly after minor damage, can lead quickly to further deterioration and costly repair bills. It is important also to keep watch on those parts of the vehicle not immediately visible, for instance the underside, inside all the wheel arches, and the lower part of the engine compartment.

The basic maintenance routine for the bodywork is washing - preferably with a lot of water, from a hose. This will remove all the loose solids which may have stuck to the vehicle. It is important to flush these off in such a way as to prevent grit from scratching the finish. The wheel arches and underframe need washing in the same way, to remove any accumulated mud, which will retain moisture and tend to encourage rust. Paradoxically enough, the best time to clean the underframe and wheel arches is in wet weather, when the mud is thoroughly wet and soft. In very wet weather, the underframe is usually cleaned of large accumulations automatically, and this is a good time for inspection.

Periodically, except on vehicles with a wax-based underbody protective coating, it is a good idea to have the whole of the underframe of the vehicle steam-cleaned, engine compartment included, so that a thorough inspection can be carried out to see what minor repairs and renovations are necessary. Steam-cleaning is available at many garages, and is necessary for the removal of the accumulation of oily grime, which sometimes is allowed to become thick in certain areas. If steam-cleaning facilities are not available, there are some excellent grease solvents available which can be brush-applied; the dirt can then be simply hosed off. Note that these methods should not be used on vehicles with wax-based underbody protective coating, or the coating will be removed. Such vehicles should be inspected annually, preferably just prior to Winter, when the underbody should be washed down, and any damage to the wax coating repaired. Ideally, a completely fresh coat should be applied. It would also be worth considering the use of such wax-based protection for injection into door panels, sills, box sections, etc., as an additional safeguard against rust damage, where such protection is not provided by the vehicle manufacturer.

After washing paintwork, wipe off with a chamois leather to give an unspotted clear finish. A coat of clear protective wax polish will give added protection against chemical pollutants in the air. If the paintwork sheen has dulled or oxidized, use a cleaner/polisher combination to restore the brilliance of the shine. This requires a little effort, but such dulling is usually caused because regular washing has been neglected. Care needs to be taken with metallic paintwork, as special non-abrasive cleaner/polisher is required to avoid damage to the finish. Always check that the door and ventilator opening drain holes and pipes are completely clear, so that water can be drained out. Trim should be treated in the same way as paintwork. Windshields and windows can be kept clear of the smeary film which often appears, by the use of proprietary glass cleaner. Never use any form of wax or other body or chromium polish on glass.

3 Upholstery and carpets - maintenance

Mats and carpets should be brushed or vacuum-cleaned regularly, to keep them free of grit. If they are badly stained, remove them from the vehicle for scrubbing or sponging, and make quite sure they are dry before installation. Seats and interior trim panels can be kept clean by wiping with a damp cloth. If they do become stained (which can be more apparent on light-colored upholstery), use a little liquid detergent and a soft nail brush to scour the grime out of the grain of the material. Do not forget to keep the headlining clean in the same way as the upholstery. When using liquid cleaners inside the vehicle, do not over-wet the surfaces being cleaned. Excessive damp could get into the seams and padded interior, causing stains, offensive odors or even rot.

If the inside of the vehicle gets wet accidentally, it is worthwhile taking some trouble to dry it out properly, particularly where carpets are involved. *Do not leave oil or electric heaters inside the vehicle for this purpose.*

4 Minor body damage - repair

Repairs of minor scratches in bodywork

If the scratch is very superficial, and does not penetrate to the metal of the bodywork, repair is very simple. Lightly rub the area of the scratch with a paintwork renovator, or a very fine cutting paste, to remove loose paint from the scratch, and to clear the surrounding bodywork of wax polish. Rinse the area with clean water.

Apply touch-up paint to the scratch using a fine paint brush; continue to apply fine layers of paint until the surface of the paint in the scratch is level with the surrounding paintwork. Allow the new paint at least two weeks to harden, then blend it into the surrounding paintwork by rubbing the scratch area with a paintwork renovator or a very fine cutting paste. Finally, apply wax polish.

Where the scratch has penetrated right through to the metal of the bodywork, causing the metal to rust, a different repair technique is required. Remove any loose rust from the bottom of the scratch with a penknife, then apply rust-inhibiting paint to prevent the formation of rust in the future. Using a rubber or nylon applicator, fill the scratch with bodyfiller paste. If required, this paste can be mixed with cellulose thinners to provide a very thin paste which is ideal for filling narrow scratches. Before the stopper-paste in the scratch hardens, wrap a piece of smooth cotton rag around the top of a finger. Dip the finger in cellulose thinners, and quickly sweep it across the surface of the stopper-paste in the scratch; this will ensure that the surface of the stopper-paste is slightly hollowed. The scratch can now be painted over as described earlier in this Section.

Repairs of dents in bodywork

When deep denting of the vehicle's bodywork has taken place, the first task is to pull the dent out, until the affected bodywork almost attains its original shape. There is little point in trying to restore the original shape completely, as the metal in the damaged area will have stretched on impact, and cannot be reshaped fully to its original contour. It is better to bring the level of the dent up to a point which is about 3 mm below the level of the surrounding bodywork. In cases where the dent is very shallow anyway, it is not worth trying to pull it out at all. If the underside of the dent is accessible, it can be hammered out gently from behind, using a mallet with a wooden or plastic head. While doing this, hold a suitable block of wood firmly against the outside of the panel, to absorb the impact from the hammer blows and thus prevent a large area of the bodywork from being "belled-out".

Should the dent be in a section of the bodywork which has a double skin, or some other factor making it inaccessible from behind, a different technique is called for. Drill several small holes through the metal inside the area - particularly in the deeper section. Then screw long self-tapping screws into the holes, just sufficiently for them to gain a good purchase in the metal. Now the dent can be pulled out by pulling on the protruding heads of the screws with a pair of pliers.

The next stage of the repair is the removal of the paint from the damaged area, and from an inch or so of the surrounding "sound" bodywork. This is accomplished most easily by using a wire brush or abrasive pad on a power drill, although it can be done just as effectively by hand, using sheets of abrasive paper. To complete the preparation for filling, score the surface of the bare metal with a screwdriver or the tang of a file, or alternatively, drill small holes in the affected area. This will provide a really good "key" for the filler paste.

To complete the repair, see the Section on filling and re-spraying.

Repairs of rust holes or gashes in bodywork

Remove all paint from the affected area, and from an inch or so of the surrounding "sound" bodywork, using an abrasive pad or a wire brush on a power drill. If these are not available, a few sheets of abrasive paper will do the job most effectively. With the paint removed, you will be able to judge the severity of the corrosion, and therefore decide whether to replace the whole panel (if this is possible) or to repair the affected area. New body panels are not as expensive as most people think, and it is often quicker and more satisfactory to install a new panel than to attempt to repair large areas of corrosion.

Remove all attachments from the affected area, except those which will act as a guide to the original shape of the damaged bodywork (e.g. headlight shells etc.). Then, using tin snips or a hacksaw blade, remove all loose metal and any other metal badly affected by corrosion. Hammer the edges of the hole inwards, in order to create a slight vacuum for the filler paste.

Wire-brush the affected area to remove the powdery rust from the surface of the remaining metal. Paint the affected area with rust-inhibiting paint, if the back of the rusted area is accessible, treat this also.

These photos illustrate a method of repairing simple dents. They are intended to supplement *Body repair - minor damage* in this Chapter and should not be used as the sole instructions for body repair on these vehicles.

1 If you can't access the backside of the body panel to hammer out the dent, pull it out with a slide-hammer-type dent puller. In the deepest portion of the dent or along the crease line, drill or punch hole(s) at least one inch apart . . .

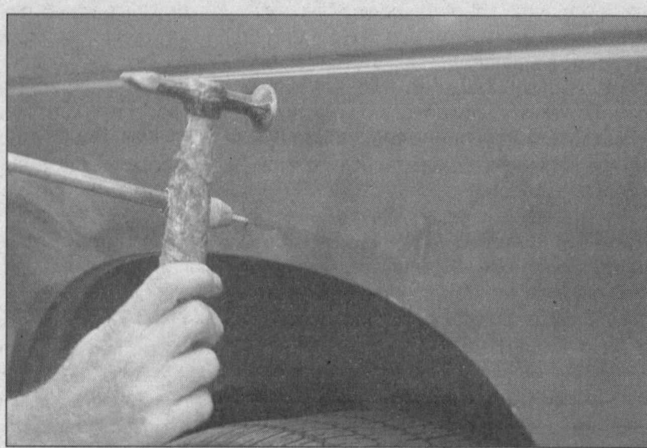

2 . . . then screw the slide-hammer into the hole and operate it. Tap with a hammer near the edge of the dent to help 'pop' the metal back to its original shape. When you're finished, the dent area should be close to its original contour and about 1/8-inch below the surface of the surrounding metal

3 Using coarse-grit sandpaper, remove the paint down to the bare metal. Hand sanding works fine, but the disc sander shown here makes the job faster. Use finer (about 320-grit) sandpaper to feather-edge the paint at least one inch around the dent area

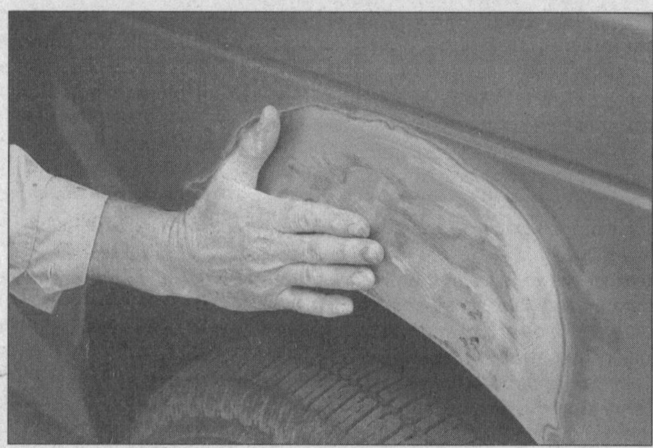

4 When the paint is removed, touch will probably be more helpful than sight for telling if the metal is straight. Hammer down the high spots or raise the low spots as necessary. Clean the repair area with wax/silicone remover

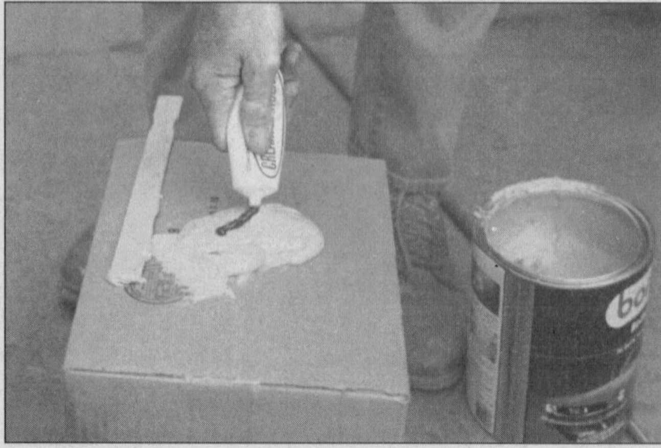

5 Following label instructions, mix up a batch of plastic filler and hardener. The ratio of filler to hardener is critical, and, if you mix it incorrectly, it will either not cure properly or cure too quickly (you won't have time to file and sand it into shape)

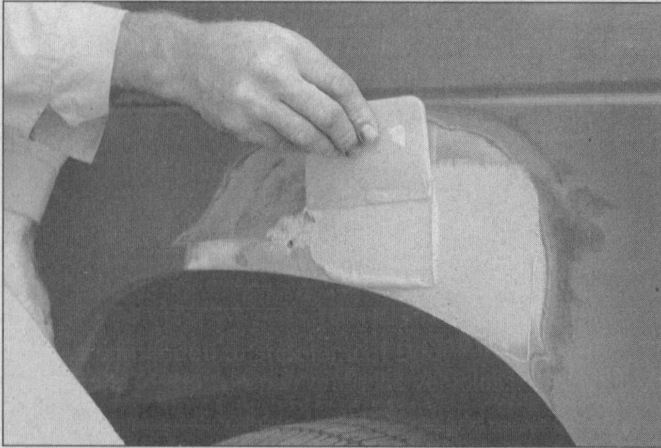

6 Working quickly so the filler doesn't harden, use a plastic applicator to press the body filler firmly into the metal, assuring it bonds completely. Work the filler until it matches the original contour and is slightly above the surrounding metal

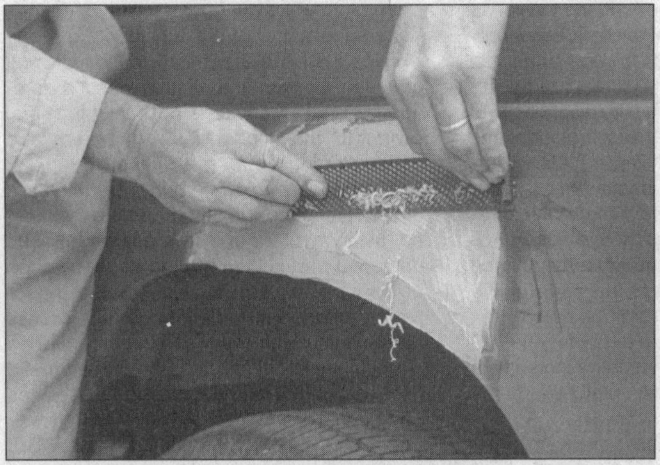

7 Let the filler harden until you can just dent it with your fingernail. Use a body file or Surform tool (shown here) to rough-shape the filler

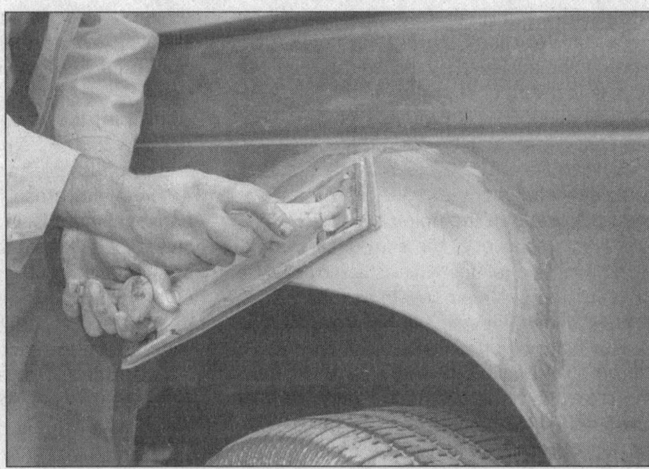

8 Use coarse-grit sandpaper and a sanding board or block to work the filler down until it's smooth and even. Work down to finer grits of sandpaper - always using a board or block - ending up with 360 or 400 grit

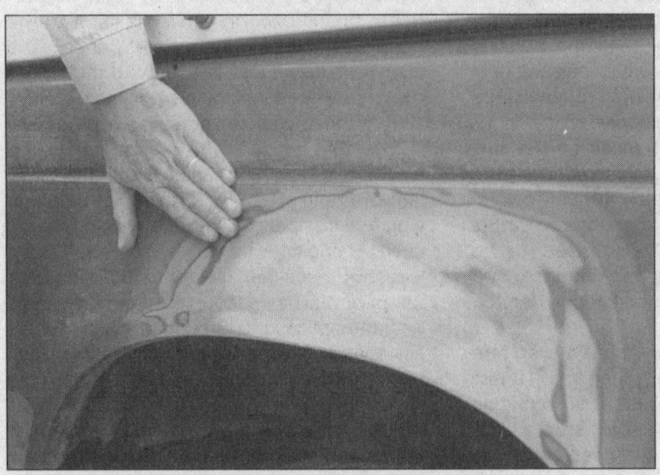

9 You shouldn't be able to feel any ridge at the transition from the filler to the bare metal or from the bare metal to the old paint. As soon as the repair is flat and uniform, remove the dust and mask off the adjacent panels or trim pieces

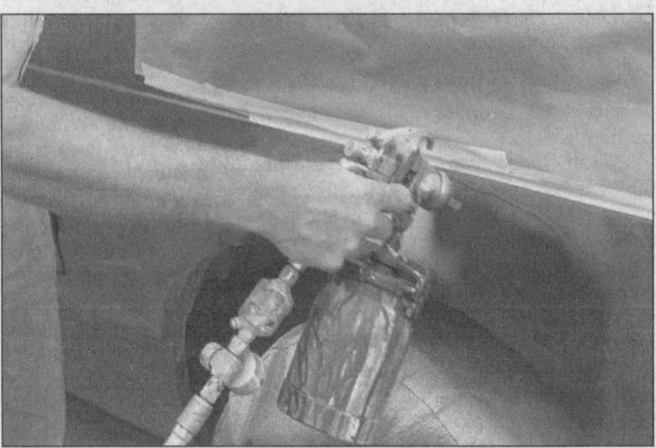

10 Apply several layers of primer to the area. Don't spray the primer on too heavy, so it sags or runs, and make sure each coat is dry before you spray on the next one. A professional-type spray gun is being used here, but aerosol spray primer is available inexpensively from auto parts stores

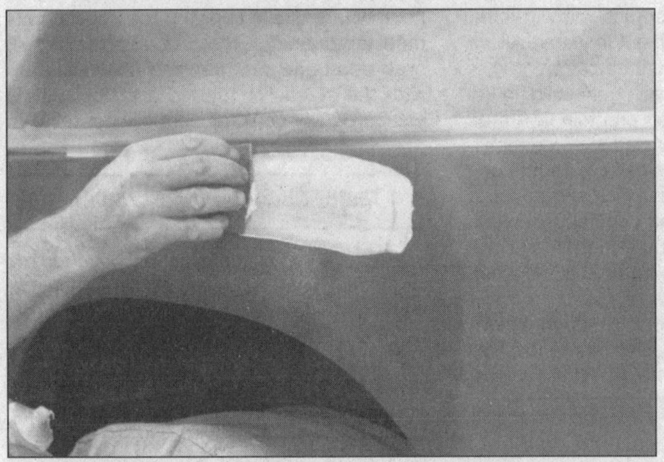

11 The primer will help reveal imperfections or scratches. Fill these with glazing compound. Follow the label instructions and sand it with 360 or 400-grit sandpaper until it's smooth. Repeat the glazing, sanding and respraying until the primer reveals a perfectly smooth surface

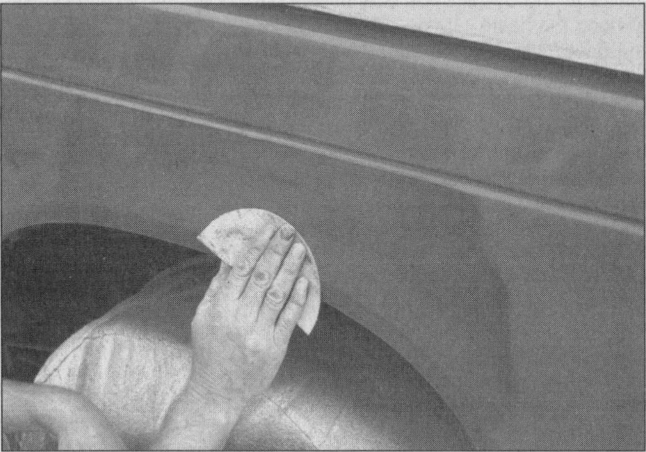

12 Finish sand the primer with very fine sandpaper (400 or 600-grit) to remove the primer overspray. Clean the area with water and allow it to dry. Use a tack rag to remove any dust, then apply the finish coat. Don't attempt to rub out or wax the repair area until the paint has dried completely (at least two weeks)

Before filling can take place, it will be necessary to block the hole in some way. This can be achieved by the use of aluminum or plastic mesh, or aluminum tape.

Aluminum or plastic mesh, or glass-fiber matting, is probably the best material to use for a large hole. Cut a piece to the approximate size and shape of the hole to be filled, then position it in the hole so that its edges are below the level of the surrounding bodywork. It can be retained in position by several blobs of filler paste around its periphery.

Aluminum tape should be used for small or very narrow holes. Pull a piece off the roll, trim it to the approximate size and shape required, then pull off the backing paper (if used) and stick the tape over the hole; it can be overlapped if the thickness of one piece is insufficient. Burnish down the edges of the tape with the handle of a screwdriver or similar, to ensure that the tape is securely attached to the metal underneath.

Bodywork repairs - filling and re-spraying

Before using this Section, see the Sections on dent, deep scratch, rust holes and gash repairs.

Many types of bodyfiller are available, but generally speaking, those proprietary kits which contain a tin of filler paste and a tube of resin hardener are best for this type of repair. A wide, flexible plastic or nylon applicator will be found invaluable for imparting a smooth and well-contoured finish to the surface of the filler.

Mix up a little filler on a clean piece of card or board - measure the hardener carefully (follow the maker's instructions on the pack), otherwise the filler will set too rapidly or too slowly. Using the applicator, apply the filler paste to the prepared area; draw the applicator across the surface of the filler to achieve the correct contour and to level the surface. As soon as a contour that approximates to the correct one is achieved, stop working the paste - if you carry on too long, the paste will become sticky and begin to "pick-up" on the applicator. Continue to add thin layers of filler paste at 20-minute intervals, until the level of the filler is just proud of the surrounding bodywork.

Once the filler has hardened, the excess can be removed using a metal plane or file. From then on, progressively-finer grades of abrasive paper should be used, starting with a 40-grade production paper, and finishing with a 400-grade wet-and-dry paper. Always wrap the abrasive paper around a flat rubber, cork, or wooden block - otherwise the surface of the filler will not be completely flat. During the smoothing of the filler surface, the wet-and-dry paper should be periodically rinsed in water. This will ensure that a very smooth finish is imparted to the filler at the final stage.

At this stage, the "dent" should be surrounded by a ring of bare metal, which in turn should be encircled by the finely "feathered" edge of the good paintwork. Rinse the repair area with clean water, until all of the dust produced by the rubbing-down operation has gone.

Spray the whole area with a light coat of primer - this will show up any imperfections in the surface of the filler. Repair these imperfections with fresh filler paste or bodyfiller, and once more smooth the surface with abrasive paper. Repeat this spray-and-repair procedure until you are satisfied that the surface of the filler, and the feathered edge of the paintwork, are perfect. Clean the repair area with clean water, and allow to dry fully.

If bodyfiller is used, it can be mixed with cellulose thinners, to form a really thin paste which is ideal for filling small holes.

The repair area is now ready for final spraying. Paint spraying must be carried out in a warm, dry, windless and dust-free atmosphere. This condition can be created artificially if you have access to a large indoor working area, but if you are forced to work in the open, you will have to pick your day very carefully. If you are working indoors, dousing the floor in the work area with water will help to settle the dust which would otherwise be in the atmosphere. If the repair area is confined to one body panel, mask off the surrounding panels; this will help to minimize the effects of a slight mismatch in paint colors. Bodywork attachments (e.g. chrome strips, door handles etc.) will also need to be masked off. Use genuine masking tape, and several thicknesses of newspaper, for the masking operations.

Before commencing to spray, agitate the aerosol can thoroughly, then spray a test area (an old tin, or similar) until the technique is mastered. Cover the repair area with a thick coat of primer; the thickness should be built up using several thin layers of paint, rather than one thick one. Using 400-grade wet-and-dry paper, rub down the surface of the primer until it is really smooth. While doing this, the work area should be thoroughly doused with water, and the wet-and-dry paper periodically rinsed in water. Allow to dry before spraying on more paint.

Spray on the top coat, again building up the thickness by using several thin layers of paint. Start spraying at one edge of the repair area, and then, using a side-to-side motion, work until the whole repair area and about 2 inches of the surrounding original paintwork is covered. Remove all masking material 10 to 15 minutes after spraying on the final coat of paint.

Allow the new paint at least two weeks to harden, then, using a paintwork renovator, or a very fine cutting paste, blend the edges of the paint into the existing paintwork. Finally, apply wax polish.

Plastic components

With the use of more and more plastic body components by the vehicle manufacturers (e.g. bumpers. spoilers, and in some cases major body panels), rectification of more serious damage to such items has become a matter of either entrusting repair work to a specialist in this field, or replacing complete components. Repair of such damage by the DIY owner is not really feasible, owing to the cost of the equipment and materials required for effecting such repairs. The basic technique involves making a groove along the line of the crack in the plastic, using a rotary burr in a power drill. The damaged part is then welded back together, using a hot-air gun to heat up and fuse a plastic filler rod into the groove. Any excess plastic is then removed, and the area rubbed down to a smooth finish. It is important that a filler rod of the correct plastic is used, as body components can be made of a variety of different types (e.g. polycarbonate, ABS, polypropylene).

Damage of a less serious nature (abrasions, minor cracks etc.) can be repaired by the DIY owner using a two-part epoxy filler repair material. Once mixed in equal proportions, this is used in similar fashion to the bodywork filler used on metal panels. The filler is usually cured in twenty to thirty minutes, ready for sanding and painting.

If the owner is replacing a complete component himself, or if he has repaired it with epoxy filler, he will be left with the problem of finding a suitable paint for finishing which is compatible with the type of plastic used. At one time, the use of a universal paint was not possible, owing to the complex range of plastics encountered in body component applications. Standard paints, generally speaking, will not bond to plastic or rubber satisfactorily. However, it is now possible to obtain a plastic body parts finishing kit which consists of a pre-primer treatment, a primer and colored top coat. Full instructions are normally supplied with a kit, but basically, the method of use is to first apply the pre-primer to the component concerned, and allow it to dry for up to 30 minutes. Then the primer is applied, and left to dry for about an hour before finally applying the special-colored top coat. The result is a correctly-colored component, where the paint will flex with the plastic or rubber, a property that standard paint does not normally possess.

5 Major body damage - repair

Where serious damage has occurred, or large areas need replacement due to neglect, it means that complete new panels will need welding-in; this is best left to professionals. If the damage is due to impact, it will also be necessary to check completely the alignment of the bodyshell; this can only be carried out accurately by a dealer, using special jigs. If the body is left misaligned, it is primarily dangerous, as the car will not handle properly, and secondly, uneven stresses will be imposed on the steering, suspension and possibly transaxle, causing abnormal wear or complete failure, particularly to items such as the tires.

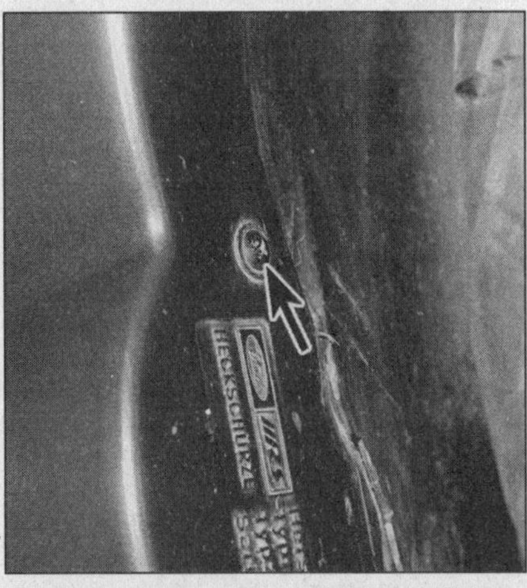
6.4 Screw securing the wheel arch liner to the front bumper

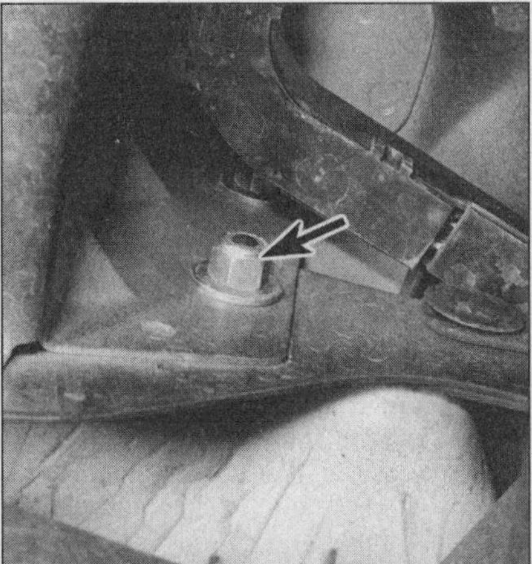
6.5a Front bumper mounting bolt

6.5b Disconnect the front bumper from the side guides

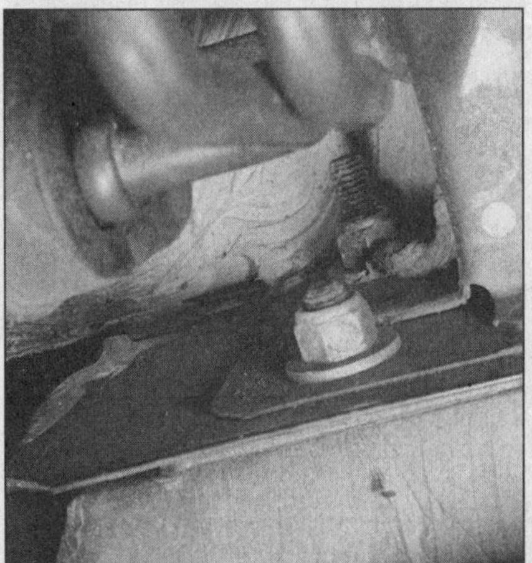
6.9 Rear bumper mounting nuts

7.2 Removing a radiator grille mounting screw

7.3 Unclip the radiator grille from the front panel

6 Bumpers - removal and installation

Removal

Front bumper - 1995 through 1998

Refer to illustrations 6.4, 6.5a and 6.5b

1 Apply the parking brake, jack up the front of the vehicle and support it on jackstands.

2 Where applicable, remove the foglights from the front bumper (Chapter 12).

3 Where applicable, disconnect the tubing from the headlight washer jets.

4 Unscrew the screws securing the wheel arch liners to the front bumper **(see illustration)**.

5 Unscrew the bumper mounting nuts, and withdraw the bumper forwards from the vehicle, at the same time disconnecting the guides from the side pins **(see illustrations)**.

Rear bumper

Refer to illustration 6.9

6 Chock the front wheels, jack up the rear of the vehicle and support it on jackstands.

7 Disconnect the rear exhaust mounting rubber, and support the exhaust system on a jackstand.

8 Remove the screws securing the wheel arch liners to the rear bumper. On later models, pull back the splash guard and remove the screw securing the bumper to the rear fenders.

9 Unscrew the bumper mounting nuts, and withdraw the bumper rearwards from the vehicle, at the same time disconnecting the guides from the side pins **(see illustration)**.

Front bumper - 1999 and later

10 Raise the vehicle and support it securely on jackstands. Remove the large splash guard from beneath the radiator.

11 Remove the grille. Remove two the upper bumper clips at the top of the bumper.

12 Disconnect the side support arms by removing the clips. Disconnect the center support brackets.

13 Remove the screws securing the bumper at the wheel arch.

14 Remove the bumper cover.

15 Remove the four bumper-to-frame mounting nuts. With the help of an assistant, lift the front bumper off.

Installation

Front and rear bumpers

16 Installation is a reversal of the removal procedure. Make sure that the guides locate correctly on the side pins.

7 Radiator grille - removal and installation

Removal

Refer to illustrations 7.2 and 7.3

1 Support the hood in the open position.

2 Using a Torx driver, unscrew the radiator grille mounting screws **(see illustration)**.

3 Unclip the radiator grille from the front panel **(see illustration)**.

Installation

4 Installation is a reversal of the removal procedure.

8 Hood - removal, installation and adjustment

Removal

Refer to illustrations 8.5, 8.7 and 8.8

1 Open the hood, and support it in the open position using the stay.

2 Disconnect the battery negative cable (Chapter 5, Section 1).

3 Pry out the clips from the insulator on the underside of the hood, for access to the windshield washer hoses and engine compartment light. It is not necessary to completely remove the insulator.

4 Disconnect the wiring from the engine compartment light, and unclip the wiring from the hood.

5 Unbolt the ground wire from the hood **(see illustration)**.

6 Disconnect the windshield washer hoses from the bottom of the jets, and unclip the hose from the hood.

7 To assist in correctly realigning the hood when installing it, mark the outline of the hinges with a soft pencil. Loosen the two hinge retaining bolts on each side **(see illustration)**.

8 With the help of an assistant, unscrew the four bolts, release the stay, and lift the hood from the vehicle **(see illustration)**.

Installation

Refer to illustration 8.9

9 Installation is a reversal of the removal procedure. Position the hood hinges within the outline marks made during removal, but if necessary alter its position to provide a uniform gap all round. Adjust the rear height of the hood by repositioning it on the hinges. Adjust the front height by repositioning the lock (see Section 10) and turning the rubber buffers on the engine compartment front cross panel up or down to support the hood **(see illustration)**.

9 Hood release cable and lever - removal and installation

Removal

Refer to illustration 9.3

1 With the hood open, disconnect the battery negative cable (Chapter 5, Section 1).

2 Working inside the vehicle, remove the trim from the "B" pillar, and pull off the door weatherstrips from the bottom of the door apertures.

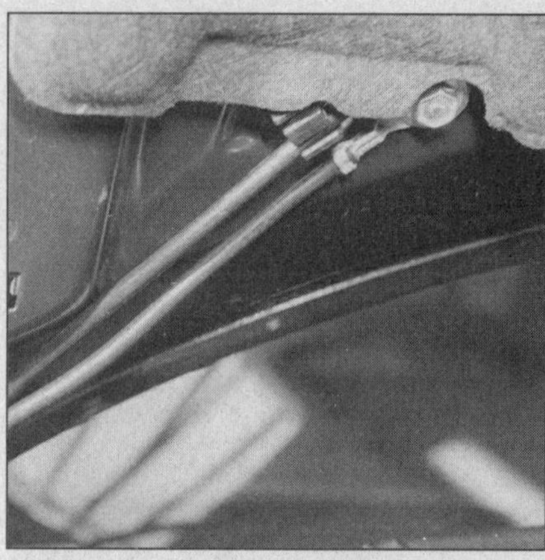

8.5 Ground wire and washer hoses on the underside of the hood

3 Remove the clips and screws, and withdraw the lower side trim, to give access to the hood release lever **(see illustration)**.

4 Release the outer cable from the lever bracket.

5 Unscrew and remove the lever mounting

8.7 Mark around the hood hinges with a soft pencil before removal

8.8 Removing the hood

8.9 Buffer for adjustment of the hood front height

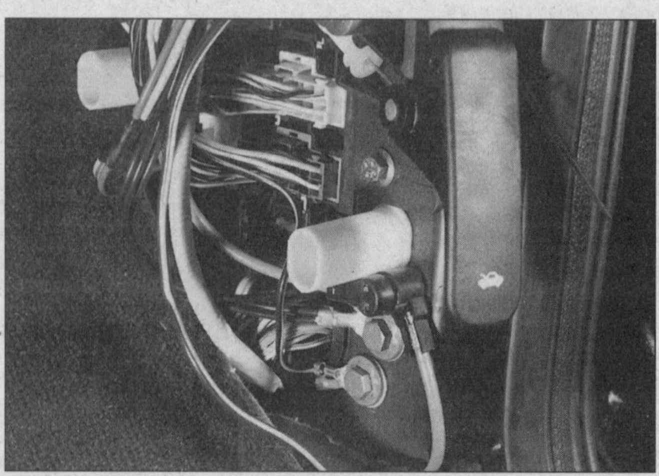

9.3 Hood release lever

11.2a Pry out the plastic cover . . .

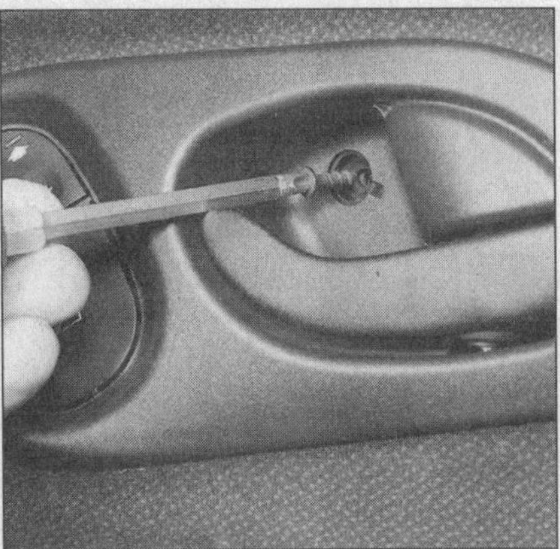
11.2b . . . remove the screw . . .

11.2c . . . and withdraw the bezel from the inner door handle

screws, and turn the lever clockwise through a quarter-turn to disconnect it from the cable.

6 Remove the radiator grille (Section 7). Also remove the backing panel from the engine compartment front crossmember.

7 Release the inner and outer cables from the lock.

8 Withdraw the cable from the engine compartment, feeding it through the front crossmember, and removing the grommet from the firewall.

Installation

9 Installation is a reversal of the removal procedure.

10 Hood lock - removal, installation and adjustment

Removal

1 Remove the radiator grille (Section 7).

2 Release the inner and outer cables from the hood lock.

3 Mark the position of the lock on the crossmember, then unscrew the mounting nuts and withdraw the lock.

Installation and adjustment

4 Installation is a reversal of the removal procedure, starting by positioning the lock as noted before removal.

5 If the front of the hood is not level with the front fenders, the lock may be moved up or down within the mounting holes. After making an adjustment, raise or lower the rubber buffers to support the hood correctly.

11 Door inner trim panel - removal and installation

Removal

Refer to illustrations 11.2a, 11.2b, 11.2c, 11.3a and 11.3b

1 Disconnect the battery negative cable (Chapter 5, Section 1).

2 Carefully pry out the plastic cover with a small screwdriver. Remove the screw, and ease the bezel off the inner door handle **(see illustrations)**.

3 Where applicable, remove the window operating switch and disconnect the multi-plug **(see illustrations)**.

Front door

Refer to illustrations 11.4a, 11.4b, 11.5a and 11.5b

4 Carefully pry out the cover, remove the screws and withdraw the door pull handle **(see illustrations)**.

5 Pry off the plastic cap, remove the screw, and withdraw the quarter bezel from the front of the window opening **(see illustrations)**.

11.3a Remove the window operating switch . . .

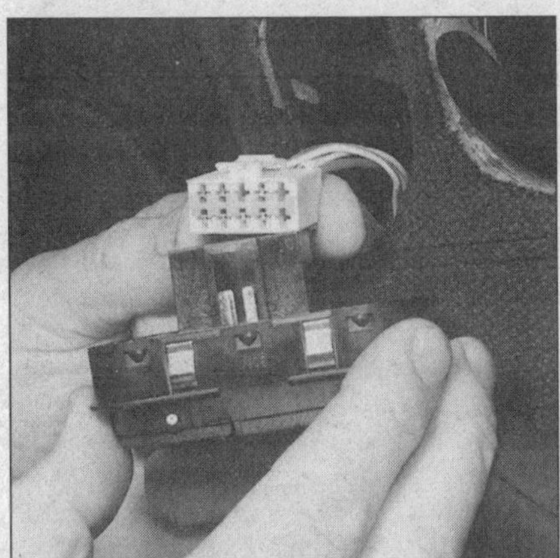
11.3b . . . and disconnect the multi-plug

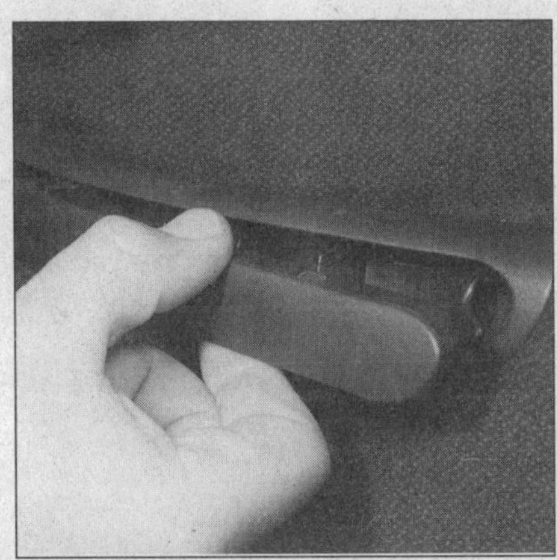
11.4a Remove the cover . . .

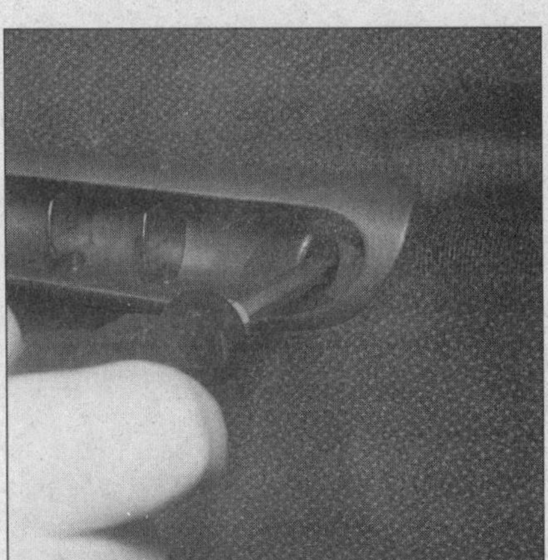
11.4b . . . then remove the screws and withdraw the door pull handle

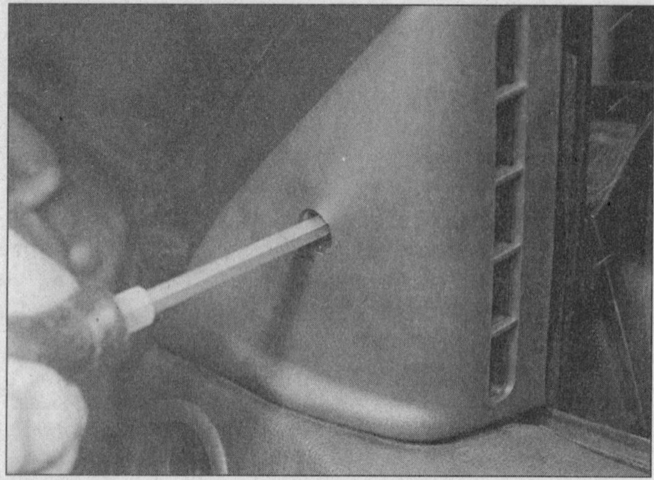

11.5a Remove the plastic cap and the screw . . .

11.5b . . . then withdraw the quarter bezel

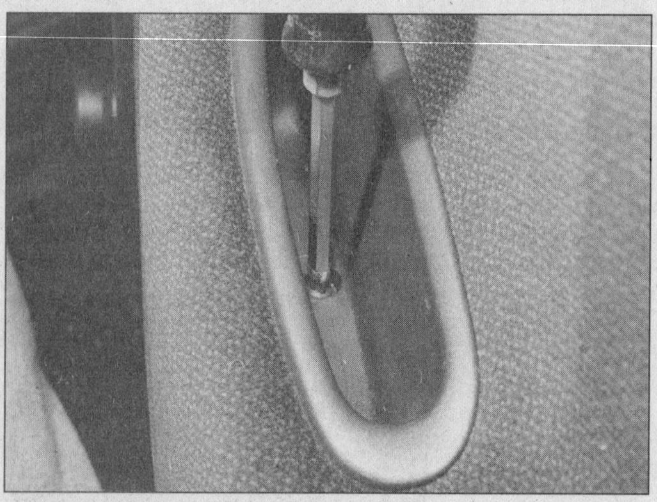

11.6a Remove the screw . . .

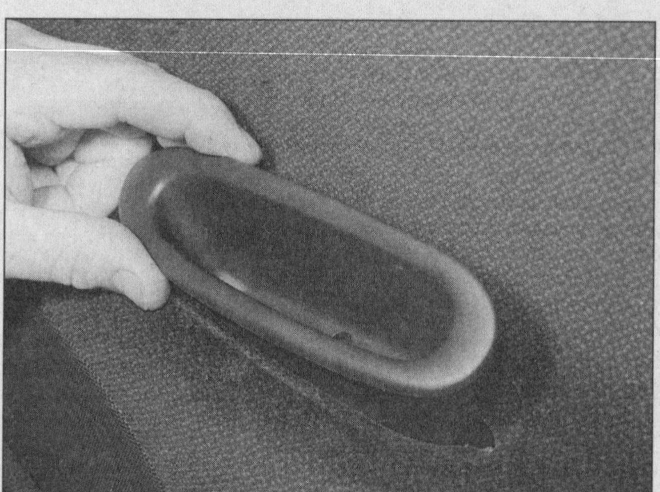

11.6b . . . and withdraw the rear door pull handle

Rear door

Refer to illustrations 11.6a and 11.6b

6 Pry off the cap, then remove the screw and withdraw the door pull handle **(see illustrations)**.

Front and rear doors

Refer to illustrations 11.7a, 11.7b, 11.7c, 11.8a, 11.8b, 11.8c, 11.8d, 11.10, 11.11 and 11.12

7 On models equipped with manual (i.e. non-electric) windows, fully shut the window, and note the position of the regulator handle. Release the spring clip by inserting a clean cloth between the handle and the door trim. Pull the cloth against the open ends of the

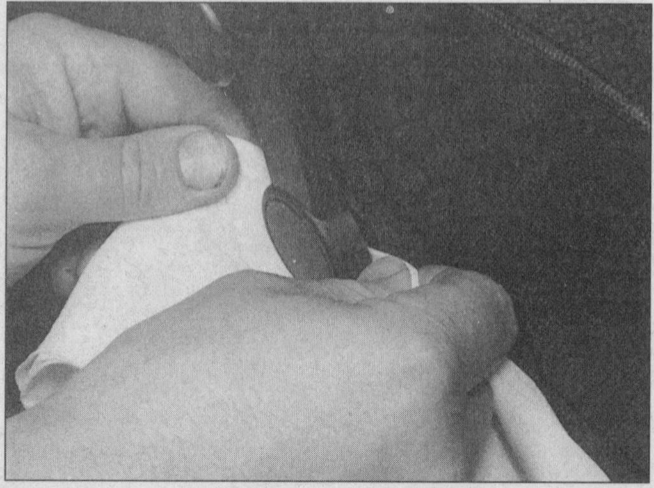

11.7a Using a clean cloth to release the spring clip from the window regulator handle

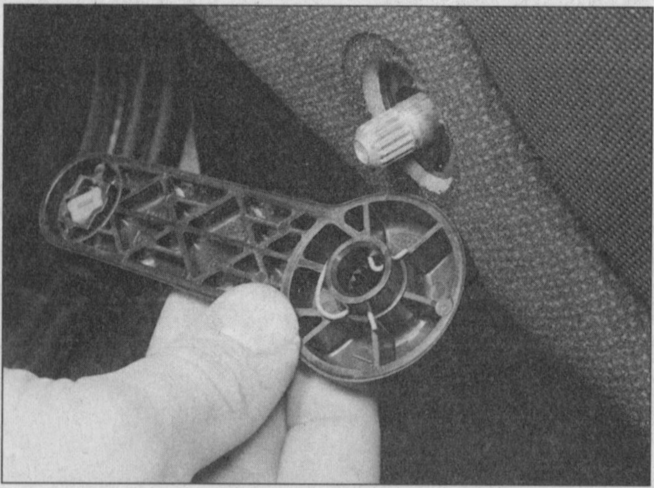

11.7b Withdrawing the window regulator handle

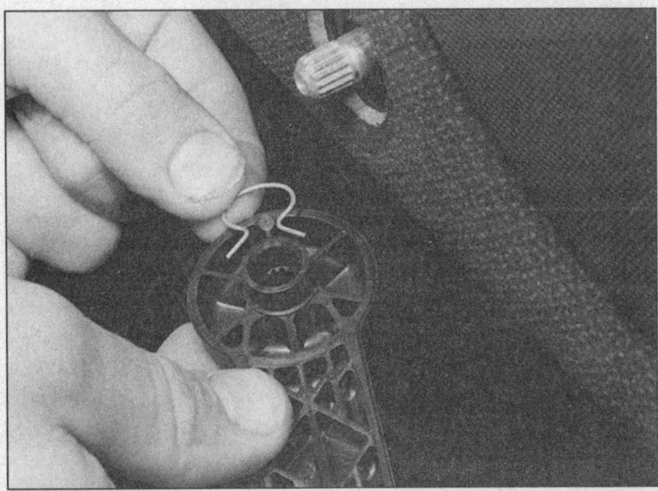
11.7c Recover the spring clip from the window regulator handle

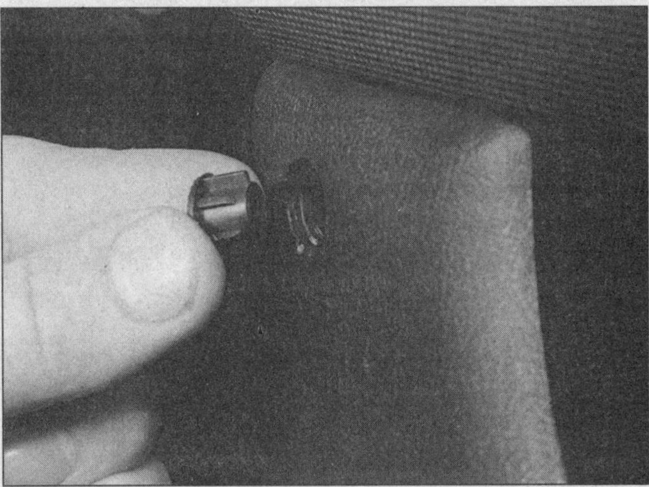
11.8a Pry out the caps . . .

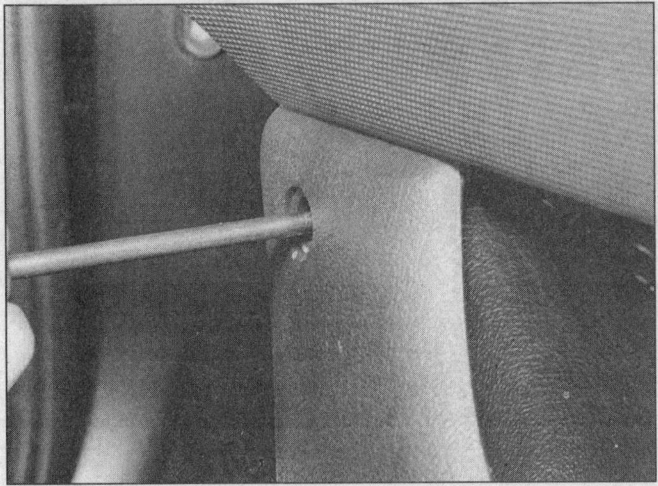
11.8b . . . remove the inner-facing screws . . .

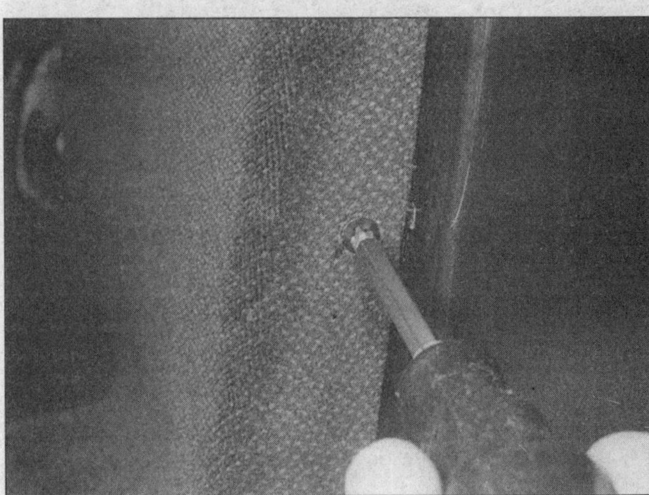
11.8c . . . and the side screws . . .

clip to release it, at the same time pulling the handle from the regulator shaft splines. Withdraw the handle (and if equipped, the spacer) and recover the clip **(see illustrations)**.

8 Pry the caps from the trim panel retaining screws, then remove the screws and lift off the panel. Where a speaker is attached to the trim panel, disconnect the multi-plug **(see illustrations)**.

9 If necessary, the foam insulation may be removed from the door. First remove the speaker as described in Chapter 12.

10 On models with manual windows, remove the foam spacer from the regulator spindle **(see illustration)**.

11 On the rear door, unscrew the screws and remove the door pull bracket **(see illustration)**.

11.8d . . . then lift off the trim panel

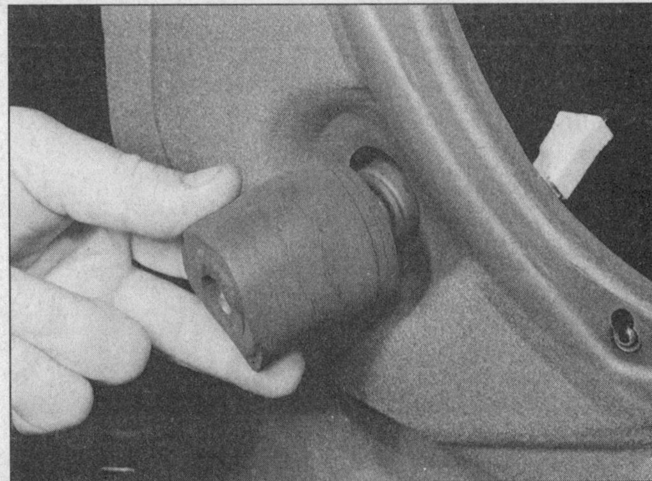
11.10 Removing the foam spacer

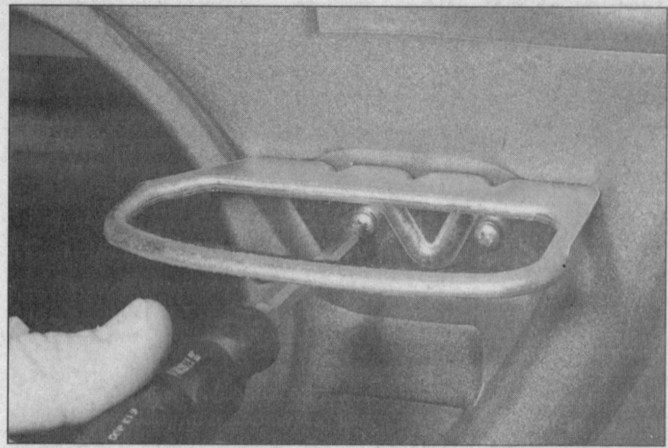

11.11 Removing the door pull bracket from a rear door

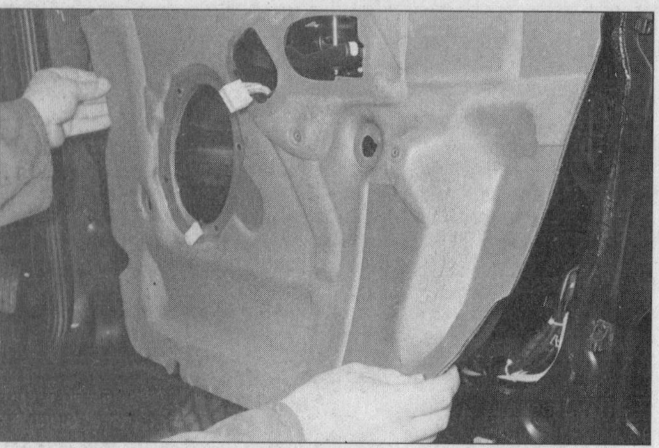

11.12 Removing the foam insulation

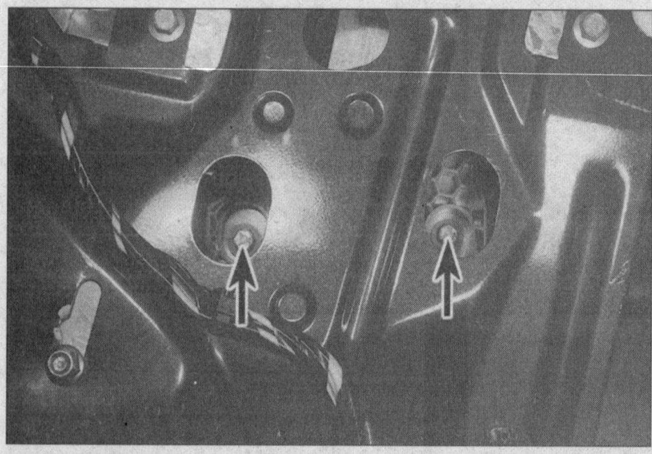

12.12 Window support bracket bolts viewed through the holes in the door inner panel

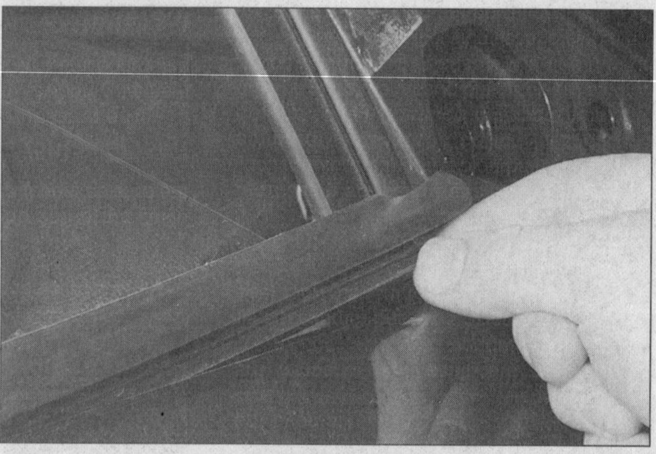

12.13 Removing the weatherstrip from the outside of the door

12 Carefully cut the adhesive with a knife, and remove the foam insulation **(see illustration)**.

Installation

13 Installation is a reversal of the removal procedure.

12 Door window glass - removal and installation

Removal

Front (manual/non-electric)

1 Disconnect the battery negative cable (Chapter 5, Section 1).

2 Remove the door inner trim panel (Section 11).

3 Remove the door exterior mirror (Section 16).

4 Temporarily install the regulator handle on its splines.

5 Lower the window until the glass support bracket is visible through the holes in the door inner panel. Remove the regulator handle.

6 Carefully pry off the weatherstrip from the outside of the door.

7 Support the glass, then unscrew the bolts from the support bracket.

8 Lift the glass from the door while tilting it at the rear, and withdraw it from the outside.

Front (electric)

Refer to illustrations 12.12, 12.13, and 12.15

9 Disconnect the battery negative cable (Chapter 5, Section 1).

10 Remove the door inner trim panel (Section 11).

11 Remove the door exterior mirror (Section 16).

12 Temporarily reconnect the battery and the window operating switch. Lower the window until the support bracket and bolts are visible through the holes in the door inner panel **(see illustration)**. Disconnect the battery lead and the operating switch again.

13 Carefully pry off the weatherstrip from the outside of the door **(see illustration)**.

14 Support the glass, then unscrew the bolts from the support bracket.

15 Lift the glass from the door while tilting it at the rear, and withdraw it from the outside **(see illustration)**.

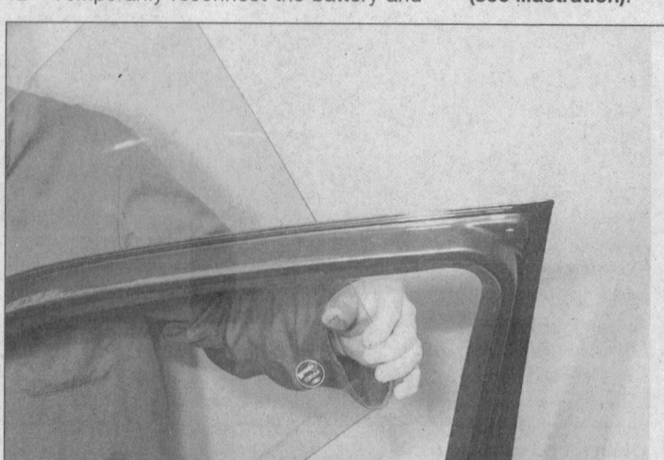

12.15 Lifting the glass from the front door

Rear (manual/non-electric)

Refer to illustrations 12.21a, 12.21b and 12.26

16 Disconnect the battery negative cable (Chapter 5, Section 1).

17 Remove the door inner trim panel (Section 11).

18 Temporarily install the regulator handle on its splines.

19 Lower the window until the glass support bracket and bolts are visible through the holes in the door inner panel. Remove the regulator handle.

20 Support the glass, then unscrew the bolts from the support bracket.

21 Unscrew the screws, and remove the air vent grilles from the rear of the rear door **(see illustrations)**.

22 Carefully pry off the weatherstrip from the outside of the door.

23 Have an assistant raise the glass from the outside, and hold it near its shut position.

24 Loosen (but do not remove) the three regulator mounting bolts, then slide the top bolts to the right, and push them out. Slide the bottom bolt upwards, and push it out. Lower the regulator assembly inside the door.

25 Working inside the door, lower the glass until it is below the regulator position, and move the glass to the outer side of its channels.

26 With the help of an assistant, lift the glass out of the door, and withdraw it from the outside **(see illustration)**.

12.21a Unscrew the screws . . .

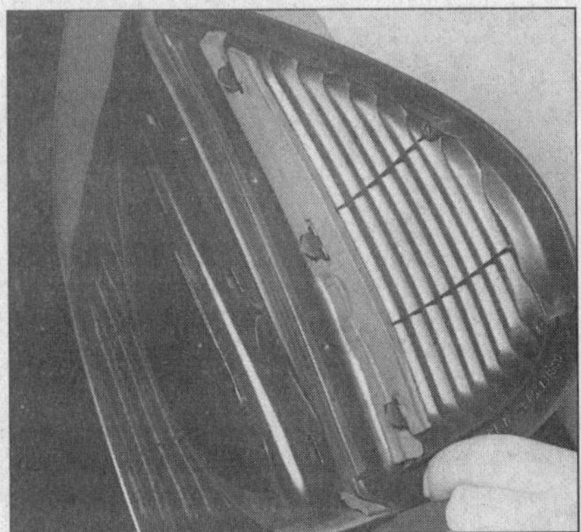

12.21b . . . and remove the air vent grilles from the rear door

Rear (electric)

27 The procedure is as just described for manual windows, making allowances for the difference in the regulator mechanism.

Installation

All doors

28 Installation is a reversal of the removal procedure, making sure that the glass is correctly located in the support bracket.

13 Door window regulator - removal and installation

Removal

Refer to illustrations 13.2a, 13.2b, 13.2c, 13.2d, 13.5, 13.6a, 13.6b, 13.6c and 13.6d

1 Remove the window glass (Section 12).

2 Loosen (but do not remove) the regulator and manual winder/electric motor mounting bolts **(see illustrations)**.

3 Twist the winder or motor (as applicable) in the bolt slots, and push it inwards.

12.26 Lifting the glass from the rear door

13.2a Window regulator upper mounting bolts (front door)

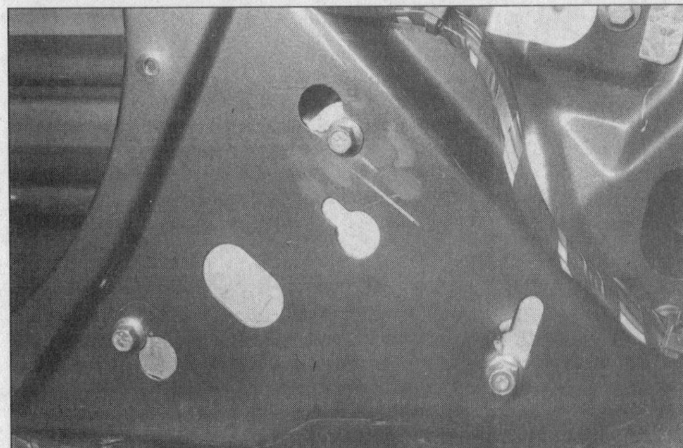

13.2b Electric window motor mounting bolts (front door)

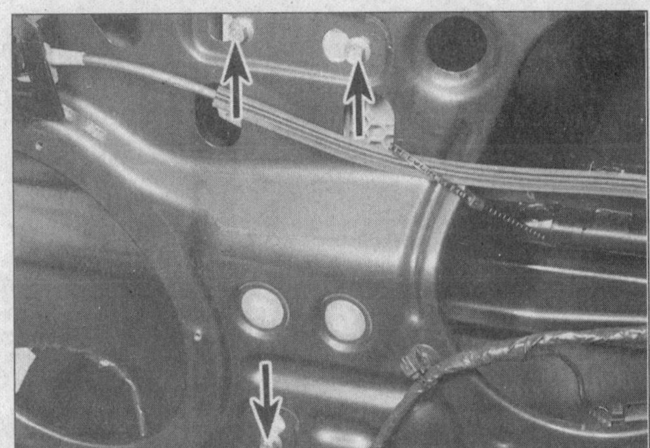

13.2c Window regulator mounting bolts - (rear door)

11

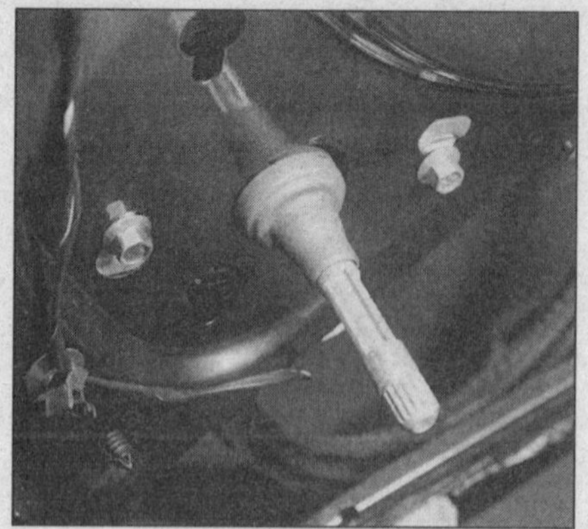
13.2d Manual winder mounting bolts (rear door)

13.5 Disconnecting the wiring multi-plug from an electrically-operated window

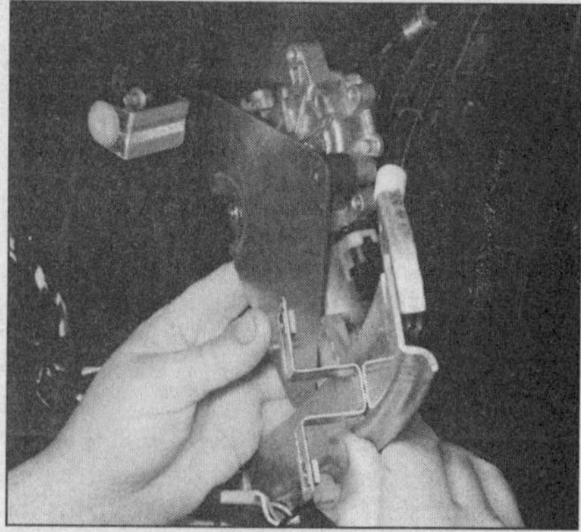
13.6a Removing the window regulator mechanism from the front door

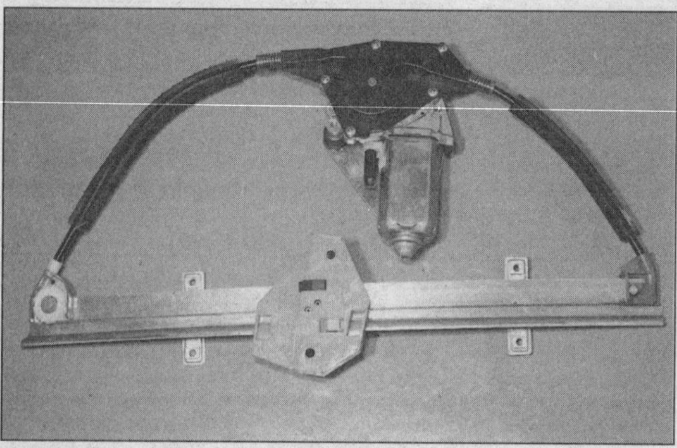
13.6b Front door window regulator removed from the vehicle

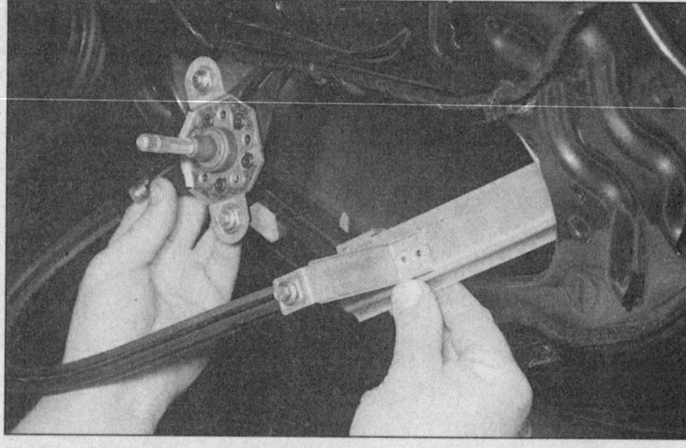
13.6c Removing the window regulator mechanism from the rear door

4 Slide the top bolts to the right, and push them out. Slide the bottom bolt upwards, and push it out.
5 On electric windows, disconnect the wiring multi-plug from the motor **(see illustration)**.
6 Withdraw the window regulator mechanism from inside the door, through the hole in the inner panel **(see illustrations)**.

Installation

7 Installation is a reversal of the removal procedure.

14 Door handle and lock components - removal and installation

Removal

Front door exterior handle

Refer to illustrations 14.3a, 14.3b, 14.4a, 14.4b, 14.4c, 14.5, 14.7a, 14.7b, 14.8a, 14.8b, 14.9, 14.10 and 14.11

1 Remove the door inner trim panel (Section 11).
2 Use a knife to cut through the adhesive strip, so that the foam insulator can be peeled back locally for access to the lock. *Do not* peel back the foam insulator without first cutting through the adhesive strip, otherwise the insulator will be damaged. To ensure a good seal when the insulator is pressed back, do not touch the adhesive strip.
3 Unscrew and remove the two bolts for the exterior handle outer bezel, and remove the bezel **(see illustrations)**.
4 Unscrew and remove the lock mounting bolts on the inner rear edge of the door, and

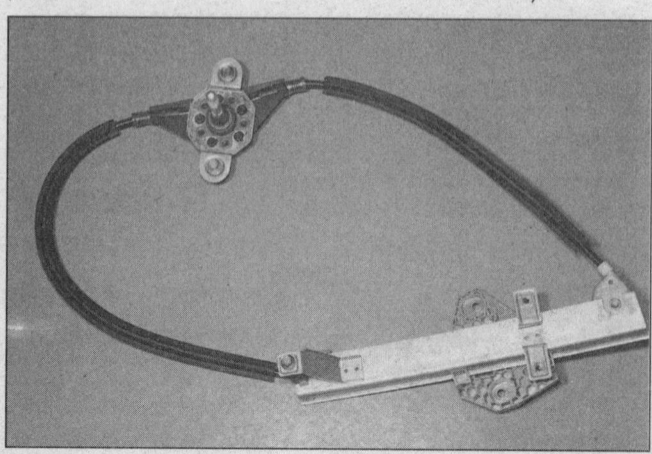
13.6d Rear door window regulator removed from the vehicle

14.3a Remove the two bolts . . .

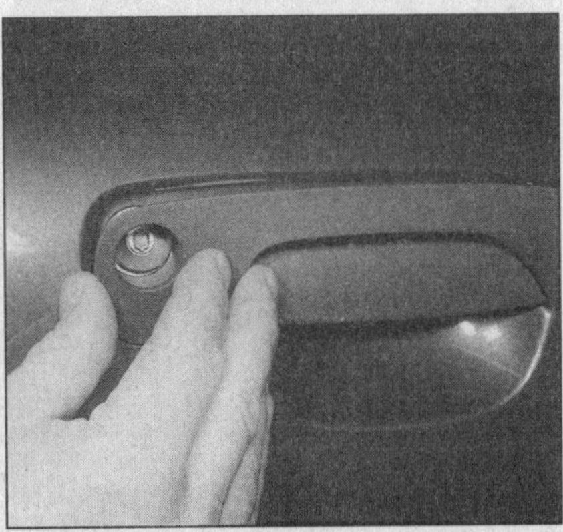

14.3b . . . followed by the exterior handle bezel

14.4a Unscrew the lock mounting bolts . . .

14.4b . . . and remove the plate

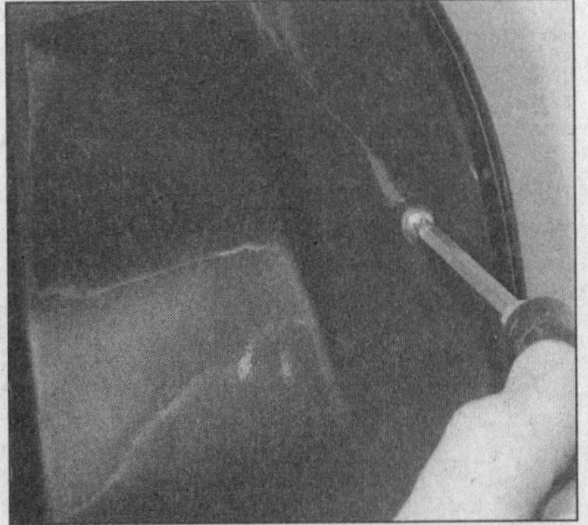

14.4c Removing the additional support screw

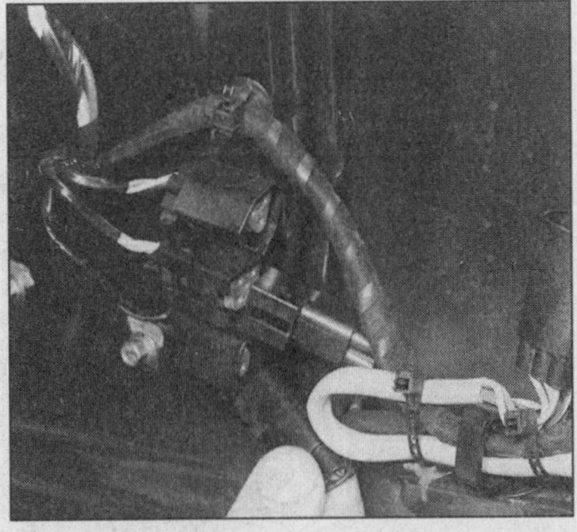

14.5 Disconnecting the central locking and alarm system wiring multi-plugs

14.7a Removing the inner handle

remove the plate. Also remove the additional support screw **(see illustrations)**.

5 Unclip and disconnect the wiring multi-plugs for the central locking and alarm systems **(see illustration)**.

6 Disconnect the wiring multi-plug from the door lock.

7 Disconnect the inner handle illumination light. Undo the screws and remove the inner handle. Disconnect the operating cable from the inner handle, as described later in this Section **(see illustrations)**.

8 Manipulate the lock and handle assembly as necessary, and disconnect the wiring multi-plugs for the alarm sensor and central locking. Withdraw the complete assembly from inside the door **(see illustrations)**.

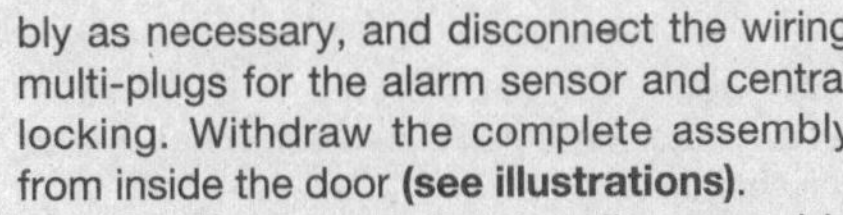

9 To disconnect the handle assembly from the lock bracket, slide the rubber posts inwards, and push out the assembly **(see illustration)**.

10 To remove the handle itself, twist the door handle through a quarter-turn, and pull out the connecting rods **(see illustration)**.

11 Remove the alarm sensor and the central locking "Set-reset" sensor **(see illustration)**.

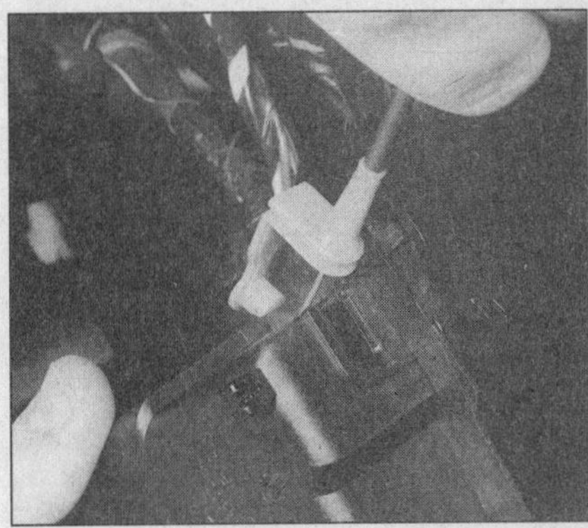

14.7b Disconnecting the operating cable from the inner handle

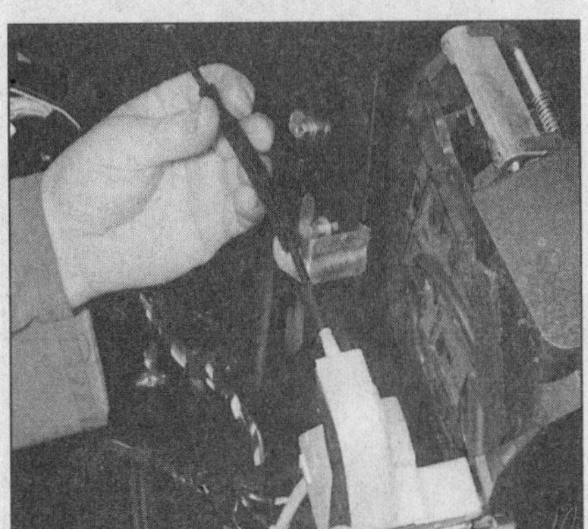

14.8a Removing the lock and exterior handle assembly from inside the door

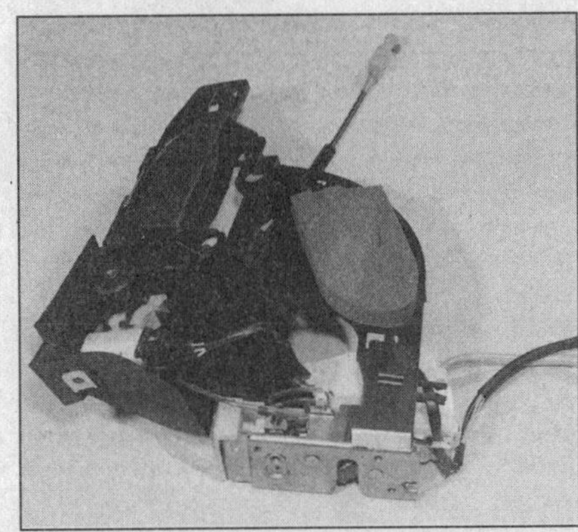

14.8b Front door lock and exterior handle assembly removed from the vehicle

14.9 Disconnecting the handle assembly from the lock bracket

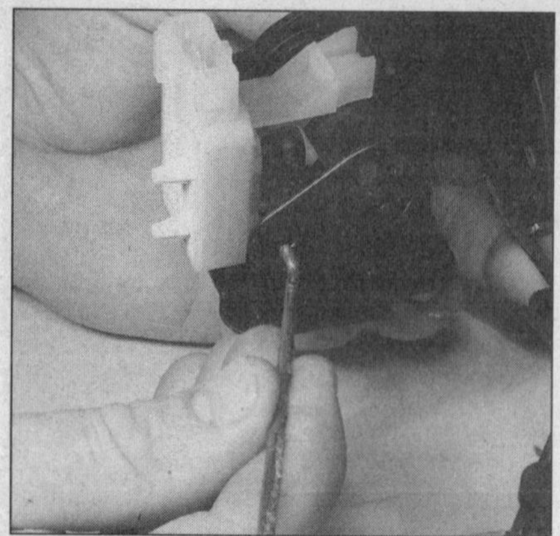

14.10 Pulling out the handle connecting rods

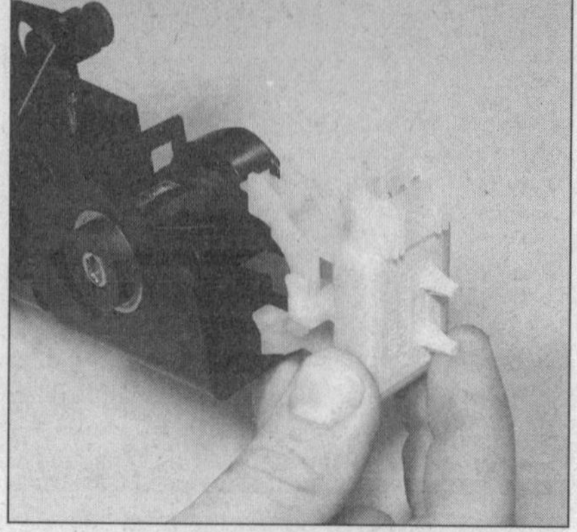

14.11 Removing the central locking "Set-reset" sensor

14.14a Pry out the plug . . .

Rear door exterior handle

Refer to illustrations 14.14a, 14.14b, 14.15 and 14.16

12 Remove the door inner trim panel (Section 11).

13 Use a knife to cut through the adhesive strip, so that the foam insulator can be peeled back for access to the lock. *Do not* peel back the foam insulator without first cutting through the adhesive strip. To ensure a good seal when the insulator is pressed back, do not touch the adhesive strip.

14 Pry out the plug from the rear edge of the door, then unscrew the handle mounting nuts **(see illustrations)**.

15 Pry up the clip, and disconnect the operating rod from the lock **(see illustration)**.

16 Withdraw the handle from the outside of the door **(see illustration)**.

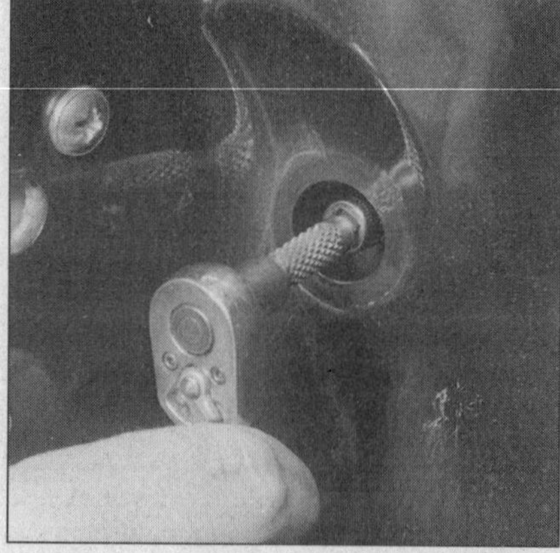

14.14b . . . and unscrew the handle mounting nuts

14.15 Disconnect the operating rod from the lock

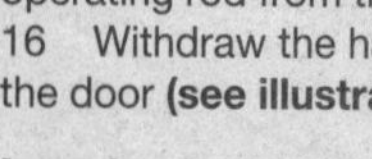

Interior handle

17 Remove the door inner trim panel (Section 11).

18 Use a knife to cut through the adhesive strip, so that the foam insulator can be peeled back for access to the lock. *Do not* peel back the foam insulator without first cutting through the adhesive strip. To ensure a good seal when the insulator is pressed back, do not touch the adhesive strip.

19 Disconnect the interior handle illumination light.

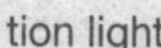

20 Undo the screws and remove the interior handle.

21 To remove the cable, first pull back the plastic outer cable end and blanking piece. Apply light inward pressure to the control lever, with the lever in the locked position, until the inner cable is aligned with the release slot in the bottom of the cable holder.

22 Push down on the cable ferrule, and disconnect the inner cable. Remove the handle assembly.

Lock cylinder

Refer to illustrations 14.24 and 14.25

23 Remove the exterior handle as described earlier in this Section.

24 Pry out the lock cylinder retaining tab from the handle body, using a small screwdriver **(see illustration)**.

25 Insert the key, turn it so that it engages the lock cylinder, then pull out the lock cylinder **(see illustration)**.

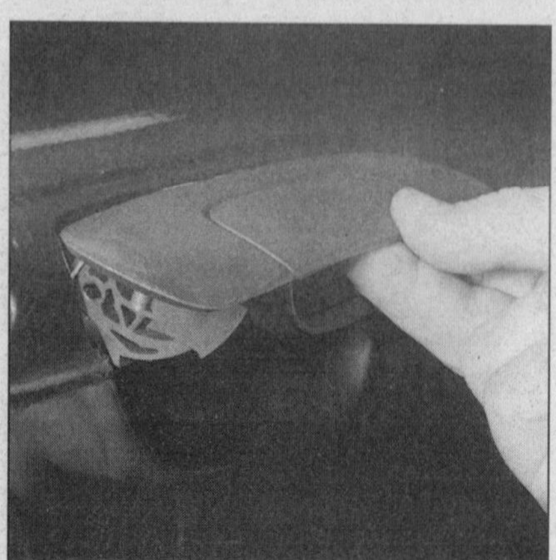

14.16 Removing the rear door exterior handle

14.24 Pry out the lock cylinder retaining tab . . .

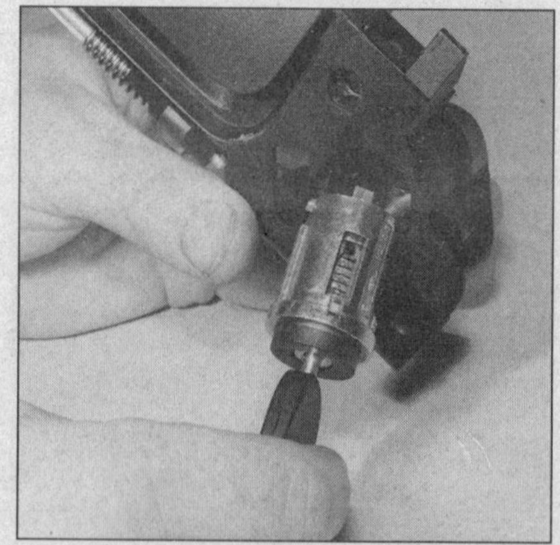

14.25 . . . and pull out the lock cylinder

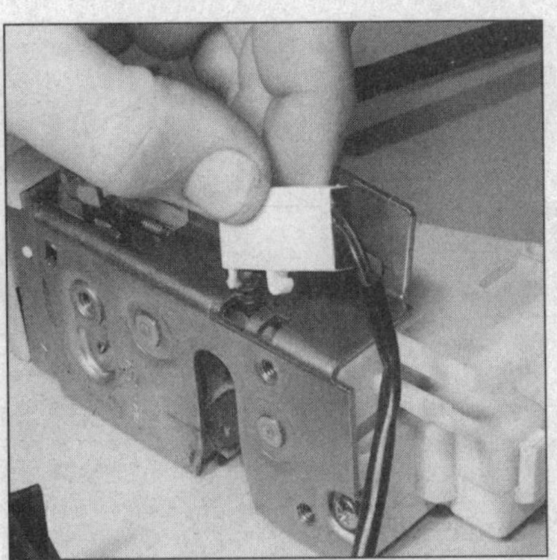

14.31 **Unclipping the door-ajar sensor**

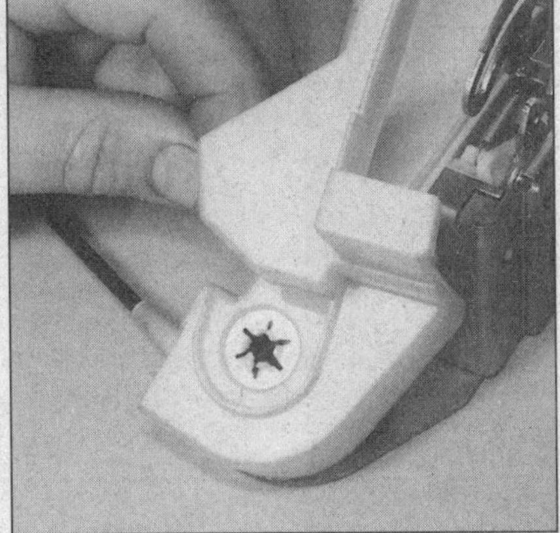

14.32 **Removing the plastic shield from the locating post**

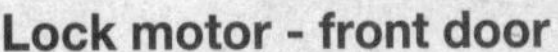

Lock motor - front door

Refer to illustrations 14.31, 14.32, 14.33 and 14.34

26 Remove the exterior handle as described earlier in this Section.

27 Extract the clip, and pull out the operating rod.

28 Remove the operating rod from the plastic bushing, by turning it through a quarter-turn.

29 Release the sensor wiring harness from the clip.

30 Detach the mounting plate from the lock.

31 Release the door-ajar sensor from the clip **(see illustration)**.

32 Pry the plastic shield from the locating post **(see illustration)**.

33 Slide the outer cable from the lock bracket **(see illustration)**, then turn the inner cable through a quarter-turn to remove it from the bell crank.

34 Unscrew the mounting screws and remove the lock motor **(see illustration)**.

Lock motor - rear door

35 Remove the exterior handle as described earlier in this Section.

36 Unscrew and remove the three lock mounting screws.

37 Release the sensor wiring harness from the clip on the door.

38 Disconnect the wiring multi-plug from the door lock.

39 Disconnect the interior handle illumination light.

40 Remove the screws, and remove the interior handle.

41 Remove the lock assembly.

42 Release the door-ajar sensor from the clip.

43 Pry the plastic shield from the locating post.

44 Slide the outer cable from the lock bracket, then turn the inner cable through a quarter-turn to remove it from the bell crank.

45 Unscrew the mounting screws and remove the lock motor.

Striker

46 Using a pencil, mark the position of the striker.

47 Undo the mounting screws using a Torx driver, and remove the striker.

Check strap

48 Disconnect the battery negative cable (Chapter 5, Section 1).

49 Using a Torx driver, unscrew and remove the check strap mounting screw(s). On the front door, there are two screws; on the rear door, there is only one.

50 Pry the rubber grommet from the door aperture, then unscrew the mounting nuts and withdraw the check strap from the door.

Installation

Handles (exterior and interior)

51 Installation is a reversal of the removal procedure.

Lock cylinder

52 Check that the retaining clip is installed correctly.

53 Align the grooves on the lock cylinder with the grooves on the body and operating lever, then carefully push the lock cylinder into the handle until it engages the clip.

54 The remaining installation procedure is a reversal of removal.

Lock motor

55 Installation is a reversal of the removal procedure.

Striker

56 Installation is a reversal of the removal procedure, but check that the door lock passes over the striker centrally. If necessary, re-position the striker before fully tightening the mounting screws.

Check strap

59 Installation is a reversal of the removal procedure.

15 Door - removal and installation

Removal

Refer to illustrations 15.2a, 15.2b, 15.3, 15.4, 15.5a and 15.5b

1 Disconnect the battery negative cable (Chapter 5, Section 1).

2 Using a Torx driver, unscrew and remove the check strap mounting screw(s). On the front door, there are two screws; on the rear door, there is only one **(see illustrations)**.

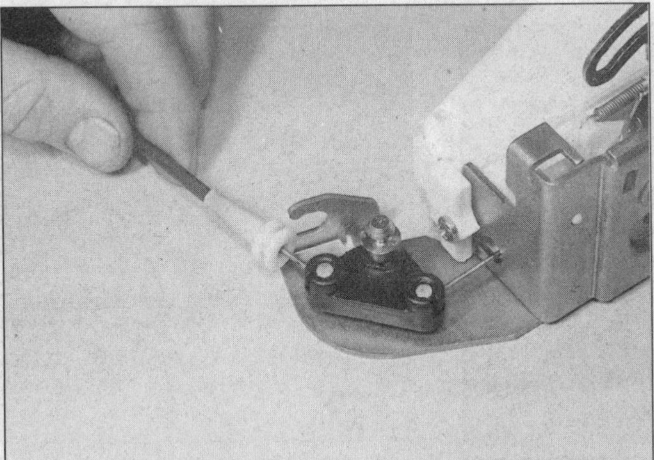

14.33 **Slide the outer cable from the lock bracket**

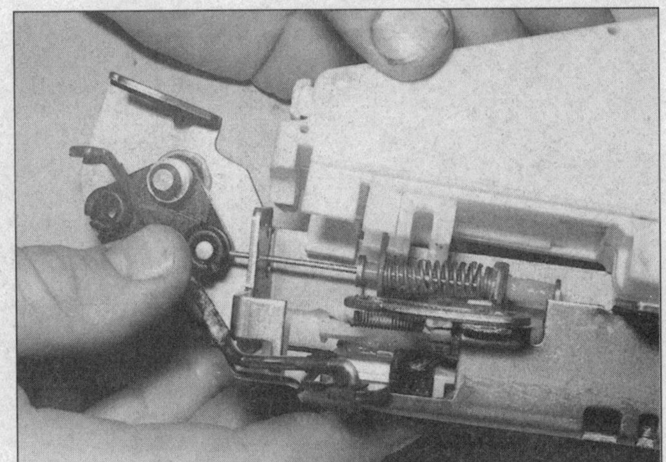

14.34 **Removing a lock motor**

15.2a Front door check strap mounting screw removal

15.2b Front door check strap removed

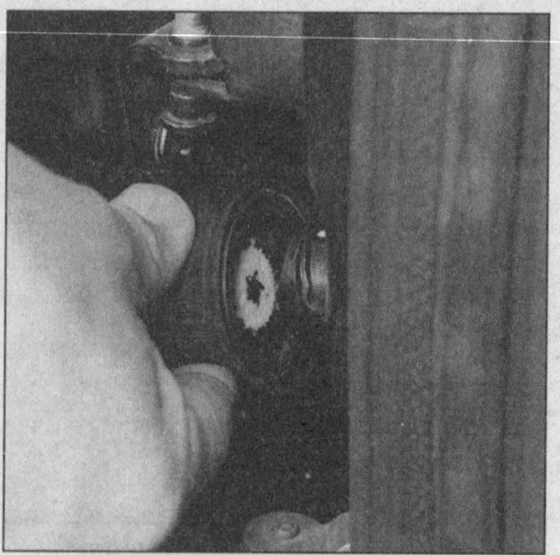

15.3 Disconnecting a door wiring connector

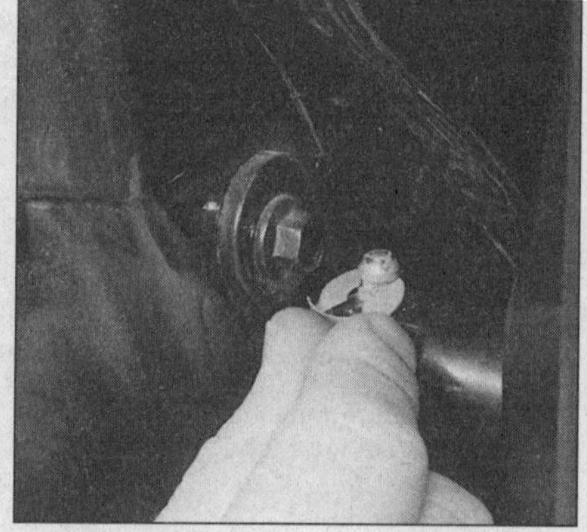

15.4 Extract the small circlips . . .

15.5a . . . then drive out the hinge pins . . .

3 Disconnect the wiring connector(s) by twisting them counterclockwise. On the front door, there are two connectors; on the rear door, there is only one **(see illustration)**.

4 Extract the small circlips from the top of the upper and lower hinge pins **(see illustration)**.

5 Have an assistant support the weight of the door, then drive the hinge pins down through the hinges using a small drift **(see illustrations)**.

6 Carefully withdraw the door from the hinges.

Installation

7 Installation is a reversal of the removal procedure, but check that the door lock passes over the striker centrally. If necessary, re-position the striker.

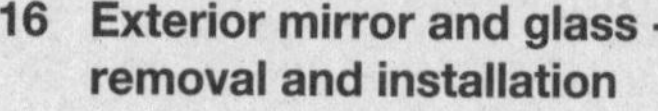

16 Exterior mirror and glass - removal and installation

Removal

Refer to illustrations 16.4, 16.5a and 16.5b

1 Where electric mirrors are installed, disconnect the battery negative (ground) lead (Chapter 5, Section 1).

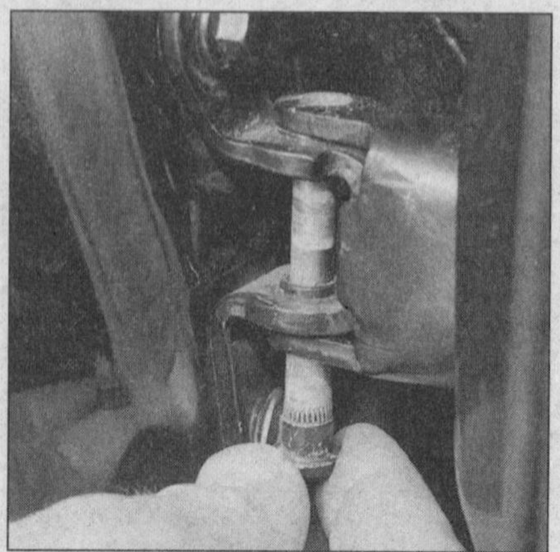

15.5b . . . and remove them

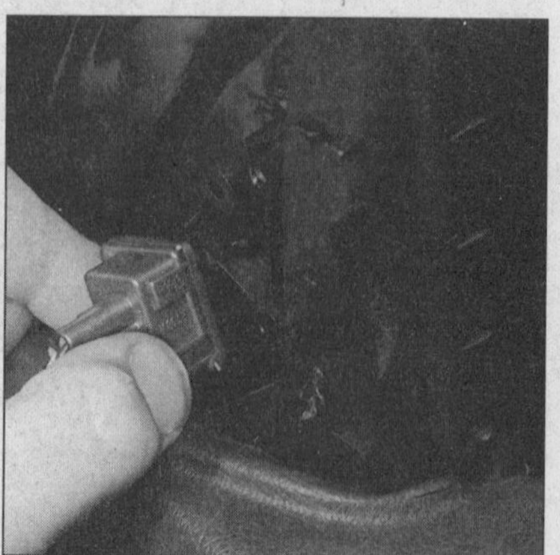

16.4 Disconnecting the wiring multi-plug from an electric exterior mirror

16.5a Unscrew the screws . . .

16.5b . . . and withdraw the mirror

2 Pry off the cap, unscrew the screw, and remove the quarter bezel from the front of the window opening.
3 On manual mirrors, detach the adjustment lever.
4 On electric mirrors, disconnect the wiring multi-plug **(see illustration)**.
5 On both types of mirror, use a Torx driver to unscrew the mirror mounting screws, then withdraw the mirror from the outside of the door **(see illustrations)**. Recover the gasket.

Installation

6 Installation is a reversal of the removal procedure.

17 Interior mirror - removal and installation

Removal

1 Using a length of strong thin cord or fishing line, break the adhesive bond between the base of the mirror and the glass. Have an assistant support and remove the mirror as it is released.
2 If the original mirror is to be reinstalled, thoroughly clean its base with rubbing alcohol and a lint-free cloth. Allow a period of one minute for the spirit to evaporate. Clean the windshield black patch in a similar manner.

Installation

3 During the installation of the mirror, it is important that the mirror base, windshield black patch and the adhesive patch are not touched or contaminated in any way, otherwise poor adhesion will result.
4 Prior to installing the mirror, the vehicle should have been at an ambient temperature of at least 68-degrees F.
5 With the contact surfaces thoroughly cleaned, remove the protective tape from one side of the adhesive patch, and press it firmly into contact with the mirror base.
6 If installing the mirror to a new windshield, the protective tape must also be removed from the windshield black patch.
7 Using a hairdryer or a hot air gun, warm the mirror base and the adhesive patch for about 30 seconds to a temperature of 120 to 160-degrees F. Peel back the protective tape from the other side of the adhesive patch on the mirror base. Align the mirror base and the windshield patch, and press the mirror firmly into position. Hold the base of the mirror firmly against the windshield for a minimum period of two minutes, to ensure full adhesion.
8 Wait at least thirty minutes before adjusting the mirror position.

18 Trunk lid - removal and installation

Removal

1 Disconnect the battery negative cable (Chapter 5, Section 1), and open the trunk lid.
2 Where applicable, pull off the trim covering, and release the wiring on the hinge arm.
3 If equipped, remove the trim from inside the trunk lid.
4 Disconnect the wiring at the connectors visible through the trunk lid inner skin aperture.
5 Attach a length of strong cord to the end of the wires in the aperture, to act as an aid to guiding the wiring through the lid when it is installed.
6 Release the cable guide rubber grommet, and withdraw the wiring harness through it. Untie the cord, and leave it in the trunk lid.
7 Mark the position of the hinge arms with a pencil.
8 Place rags beneath each corner of the trunk lid, to prevent damage to the paintwork.
9 With the help of an assistant, unscrew the mounting bolts and lift the trunk lid from the car.

Installation

10 Installation is a reversal of the removal procedure. Check that the trunk lid is correctly aligned with the surrounding bodywork, with an equal clearance around its edge. Adjustment is made by loosening the hinge bolts, and moving the trunk lid within the elongated mounting holes. Check that the lock enters the striker centrally when the trunk lid is closed.

19 Trunk lid lock components - removal and installation

Removal

Lock cylinder

1 Disconnect the battery negative cable (Chapter 5, Section 1).
2 With the trunk lid open, remove the luggage space trim from the right-hand rear corner.
3 Remove the screws, and pry out the rear light trim cover from the guides.
4 Release the door-ajar sensor from the clip near the lock.
5 Slide the outer cable from the lock bracket. Raise the inner cable until it is aligned with the slot in the lock cylinder lever, and disconnect it.
6 Pull out the lock locating spring clip.
7 Detach the cable mounting bracket from the lock cylinder, and remove the lock cylinder.

Lock

8 Disconnect the battery negative (ground) lead (Chapter 5, Section 1).
9 With the trunk lid open, pry out the clips and remove the trim from inside the trunk lid.
10 Release the door-ajar sensor from the clip near the lock.
11 Using a Torx driver, unscrew the lock mounting screws, and withdraw the lock for access to the cables.
12 Disconnect both the inner and outer cables from the lock bracket.
13 Pry open the plastic lip, and remove the central locking control rod.
14 Withdraw the lock assembly.

Installation

Lock cylinder and lock

15 Installation is a reversal of the removal procedure.

20 Central locking system components - testing, removal and installation

Testing

1 The central locking module incorporates a service-test mode, which is activated by operating one of the lock position switches 8 times within 10 seconds. A buzzer will sound, to indicate that the service-test mode is operating, and to indicate that no faults have been found in the system. If a fault has been found, the system should be checked by a dealer or electrical specialist. The central locking module also incorporates the alarm system module.

Removal

Central locking/alarm module

2 To remove the module, first remove the glovebox.
3 Disconnect the battery negative cable (Chapter 5, Section 1).
4 Unscrew the mounting bolts, and remove the module from the bracket beneath the dash.
5 Disconnect the wiring multi-plug, and withdraw the module from inside the vehicle.
6 Note that a different module is used for models without an anti-theft alarm.

24.2a Unscrew the Torx-headed screws . . .

24.2b . . . and remove the mounting trims for access to the front seat rear mounting bolts

Central locking set/reset switch

7 This procedure is covered in Section 14, under front door handle removal.

Central locking door-ajar switch

8 This procedure is covered in Section 14, under front door lock motor removal.

Installation

Central locking/alarm module

9 Installation is a reversal of the removal procedure.

Central locking set/reset switch

10 Installation is a reversal of the removal procedure.

Central locking door-ajar switch

11 Installation is a reversal of the removal procedure.

21 Windshield and fixed windows - removal and installation

1 The windshield and rear window on all models are bonded in place with special mastic. Special tools are required to cut free the old units and install replacements; special cleaning solutions and primer are also required. It is therefore recommended that this work is entrusted to a dealer or windshield replacement specialist.

2 Note that the windshield contributes towards the structural strength of the vehicle as a whole, so it is important that it is correctly installed.

22 Body side-trim moldings and adhesive emblems - removal and installation

Removal

1 Insert a length of strong cord (fishing line is ideal) behind the molding or emblem concerned. With a sawing action, break the adhesive bond between the molding or emblem and the panel.

2 Thoroughly clean all traces of adhesive from the panel using rubbing alcohol, and allow the location to dry.

Installation

3 Peel back the protective paper from the rear face of the new molding or emblem. Carefully place it into position on the panel concerned, but take care not to touch the adhesive. When in position, apply hand pressure to the molding/emblem for a short period, to ensure maximum adhesion to the panel.

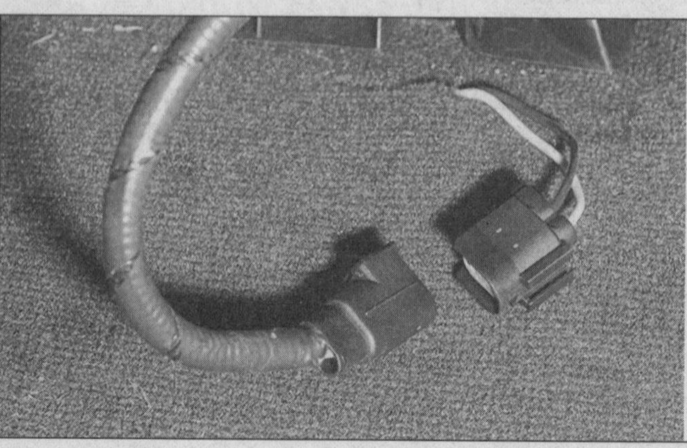
24.4 Disconnecting an electric seat multi-plug

23 Sunroof - general information and adjustment

1 The sunroof should operate freely, without sticking or binding, as it is opened and closed. When in the closed position, check that the panel is flush with the surrounding roof panel.

2 If adjustment is required, open the sun blind, but leave the glass panel shut. Unscrew and remove the three lower frame-to-glass panel retaining screws. Slide the lower frame back into the roof.

3 Loosen the central and front securing screws. Adjust the glass roof panel so that it is flush at its front edge with the roof panel, then retighten the securing screws.

4 Pull the lower frame forwards, and insert and tighten its retaining screws to complete.

24 Seats - removal and installation

Removal

Front seat

Refer to illustrations 24.2a, 24.2b, 24.4 and 24.5

1 Release the seat belt, and slide the seat fully forwards.

2 Using a Torx driver, undo the screws and remove the rear mounting trims, then unscrew the rear mounting bolts **(see illustrations)**.

3 Slide the seat fully rearwards.

4 Where electric seats are installed, disconnect the battery negative cable (Chapter 5, Section 1). Disconnect the seat wiring multi-plugs **(see illustration)**.

5 Unscrew the front mounting bolts, and remove the seat from the vehicle **(see illustration)**.

24.5 Front seat front mounting bolt

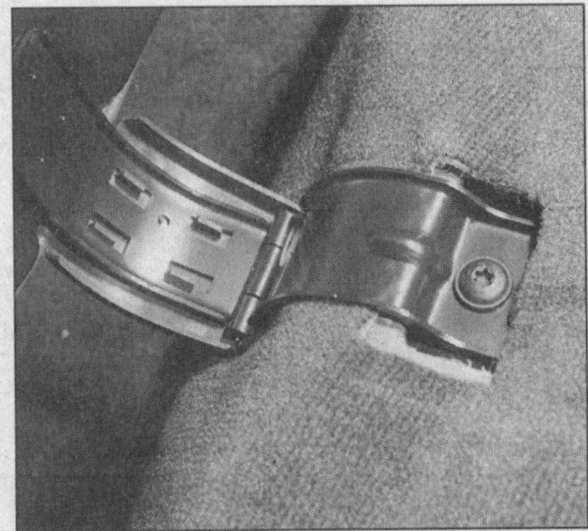

24.6 Rear seat cushion hinge bolt

24.10 Rear seat backrest mounting bolts

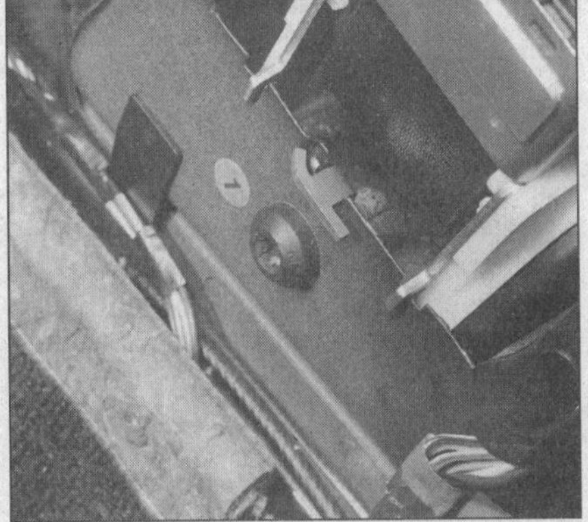

25.2 Front seat belt reel unit lower mounting bolt

25.3a Front seat belt guide and mounting bolt

25.3b Front seat belt shackle and mounting nut

Rear seat cushion

Refer to illustration 24.6

6 Fold the rear seat cushion forwards. (Note that, on some models, the seat cushion is held in place by screws which must be removed first.) Using a Torx driver, unscrew and remove the mounting bolts from the hinges on each side **(see illustration)**.

7 Withdraw the seat cushion from the vehicle.

Rear seat backrest

Refer to illustration 24.10

8 Fold the rear seat cushion and both backrests forwards.

9 Unclip the backrest rear trims, if equipped, and raise them.

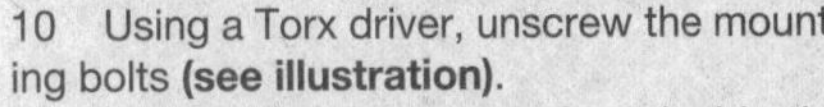

10 Using a Torx driver, unscrew the mounting bolts **(see illustration)**.

11 Withdraw the backrest from inside the vehicle.

Rear seat side bolster

12 Fold the rear seat backrest forwards.

13 On low-series models, remove the screw and pull the bolster forwards to disengage the clips. On high-series models, simply pull the bolster upwards to disengage the clips.

Installation

14 Installation is a reversal of the removal procedure, but tighten the mounting bolts to the specified torque.

25.4 Front seat stalk mounting nut

25 Seat belts - removal and installation

Warning: *Be careful when handling the seat belt tensioning device ("grabber"). It contains a powerful spring, which could cause injury if released in an uncontrolled fashion. Once fired, the grabber cannot be reset, and must be replaced. Note also that seat belts and associated components which have been subject to impact loads must be replaced.*

Removal

Front seat belt

Refer to illustrations 25.2, 25.3a, 25.3b, 25.4, 25.5a, 25.5b and 25.5c

1 Remove the trim from the "B" pillar and the sill plate.

2 Unscrew the mounting bolts and remove the seat belt reel unit **(see illustration)**.

3 Unscrew the bolt securing the seat belt guide to the "B" pillar, then unscrew the nut securing the seat belt shackle **(see illustrations)**.

4 Detach the stalk cable, then undo the mounting nut, and remove the stalk and grabber assembly from the front seat **(see illustrations)**. **Warning:** *There is a potential risk of the grabber firing during removal, so it should be handled carefully. As an extra precaution, a spacer may be installed on the*

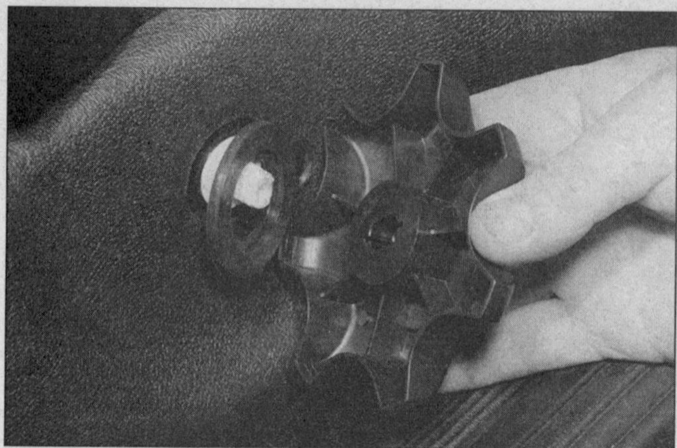
25.5a Remove the recline adjustment knob . . .

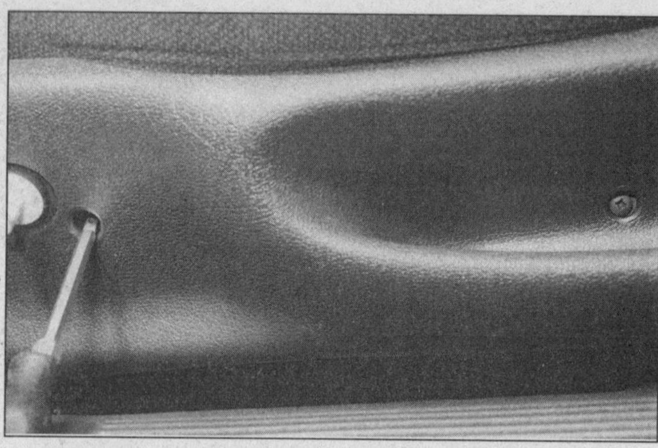
25.5b . . . unscrew the trim retaining screws . . .

cable before removal. Hold the adjustment lever in the "adjust" position while inserting the spacer.

5 Remove the recline adjustment knob and trim from the outer side of the front seat, then unscrew the bolt and remove the seat belt end from the seat **(see illustrations)**.

Rear side seat belt

Refer to illustrations 25.6a, 25.6b, 25.7a, 25.7b and 25.8

6 Unscrew the screws and remove the trim from the "C" pillar. It will be necessary to detach the rear seat release cable, and remove the plastic cover from the rear seat lock **(see illustrations)**.

7 Fold the rear seat cushions forward. Unscrew the mounting bolts from the seat belt shackle and reel **(see illustrations)**.

8 Unscrew the mounting bolt securing the seat belt stalk, and withdraw the stalk. Also unscrew the mounting bolt from the lower anchorage, where applicable **(see illustration)**.

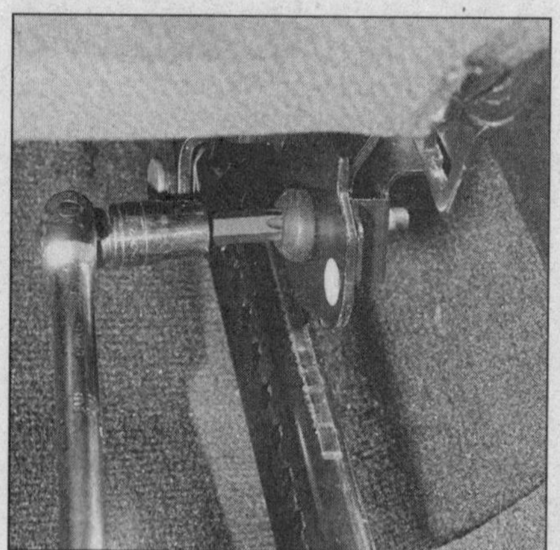
25.5c . . . and unscrew the seat belt end retaining bolt

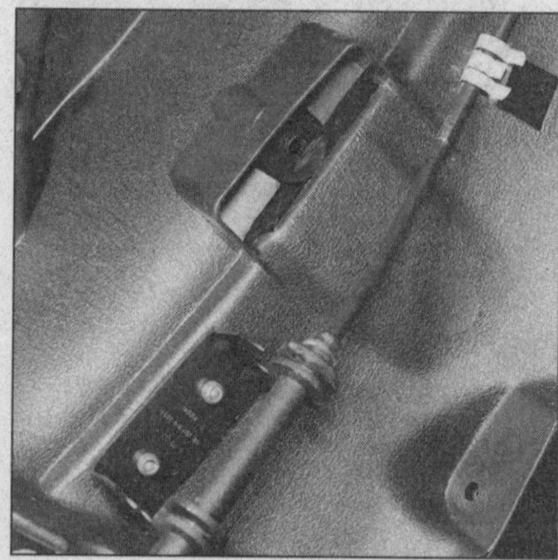
25.6a Detach the rear seat release cable

25.6b Removing the plastic cover from the rear seat lock

25.7a Rear seat belt shackle mounting bolt

25.7b Rear seat belt reel mounting bolt

25.8 Rear seat belt lower anchorage

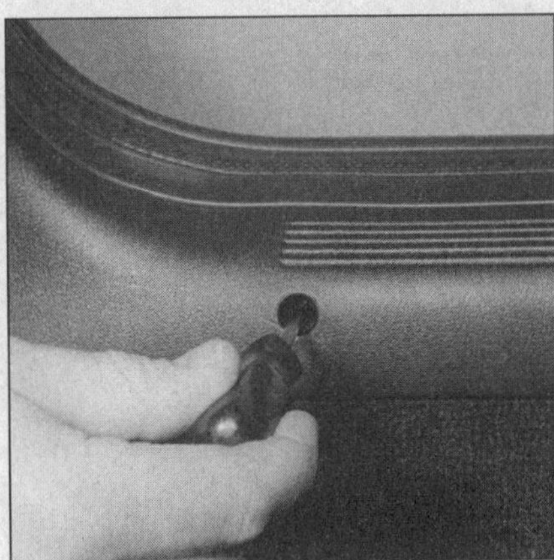

26.10a Removing a middle screw from the lower trim

Rear center seat belt

9 Unscrew the mounting bolts securing the seat belt and stalks to the floor. Note that the stalks are handed, and are marked Left or Right.

Installation

10 Installation is a reversal of the removal procedure. Tighten the mounting nuts and bolts to the specified torque.

26 Interior trim panels - removal and installation

Removal

Sun visor

1 Disconnect the wiring for the vanity mirror light, if equipped.

2 Unscrew the mounting screws and remove the visor.

3 Pry up the cover, unscrew the inner bracket mounting screws, and remove the bracket.

Passenger grab handle

4 Pry up the covers, then unscrew the mounting screws and remove the grab handle.

"A" pillar trim

5 Pull away the door weatherstrip in the area of the trim.

6 Release the alarm and aerial wiring from the upper and middle clips.

7 Carefully press the trim away from the upper and middle clips, and pull the trim upwards. Recover the lower sealing strip.

8 Remove the upper and middle clips from the pillar.

"B" pillar and cowl side trim

Refer to illustrations 26.10a, 26.10b and 26.11

9 Pull away the door weatherstrip in the area of the trim.

10 Undo the screws, release the fasteners and remove the lower trim **(see illustrations)**.

11 Carefully separate the lower trim from the upper trim, using a screwdriver if necessary **(see illustration)**.

12 Unscrew the seat belt mounting bolt from under the front seat, remove the remaining trim from the "B" pillar, and feed the belt through the trim.

"C" pillar trim

Refer to illustrations 26.15a and 26.15b

13 Pull away the door weatherstrip in the area of the trim.

14 Fold the rear seat cushion forwards.

15 Pull up the rear seat bolster, and release the upper hook. Note that, on low-series models, the bolster is retained with a screw **(see illustrations)**.

16 Undo the screw, release the clips, and detach the upper trim.

17 Remove the rear seat belt lower mounting bolt, then remove the trim, and pass the seat belt through it.

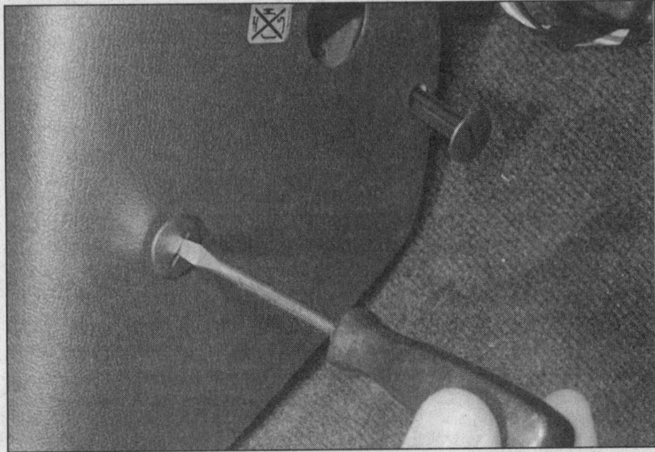

26.10b Releasing the fasteners from the cowl side trim

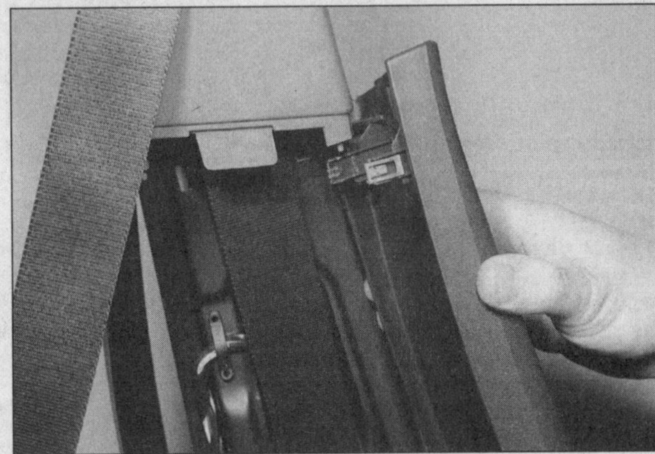

26.11 Separating the "B" pillar lower and upper trim

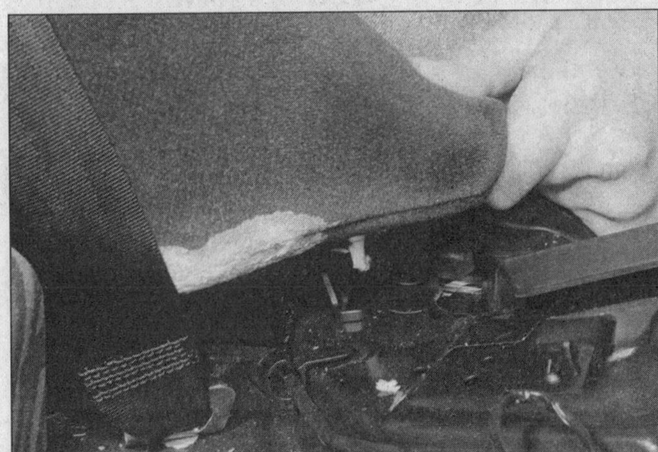

26.15a Pull up the rear seat bolster . . .

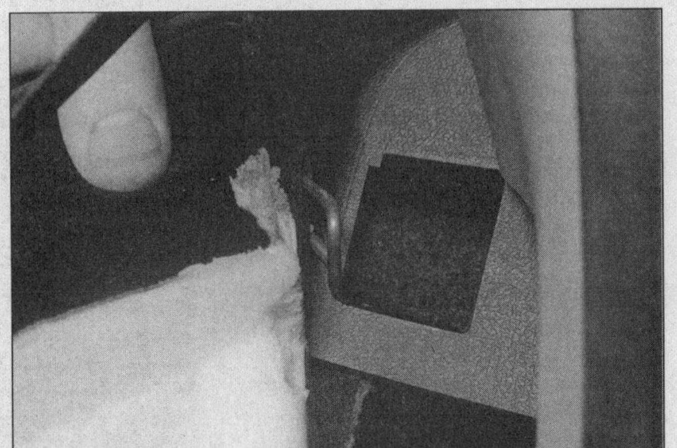

26.15b . . . and release the upper hook

26.19a Unscrew the mounting screws from the upper corners . . .

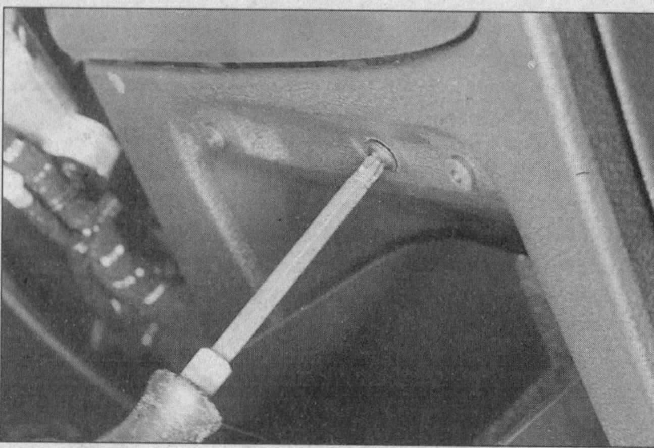
26.19b . . . and above the coin tray position . . .

26.19c . . . and withdraw the lower dash panel

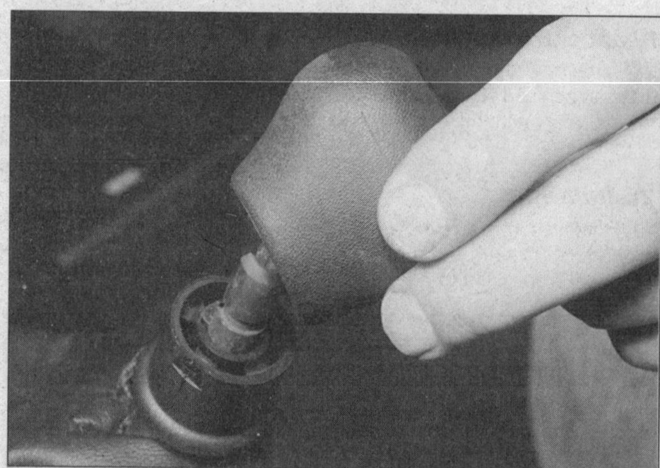
27.3 Shift lever knob removal

Lower dash panel

Refer to illustrations 26.19a, 26.19b and 26.19c

18 Remove the steering column top and bottom shrouds.

19 Unscrew the mounting screws from the upper corners and above the coin tray position, and withdraw the lower dash panel from the dash **(see illustrations)**.

Installation

20 Installation is a reversal of the removal procedure. Where seat belt fastenings have been disturbed, make sure that they are tightened to the specified torque.

27 Center console - removal and installation

Removal

Refer to illustrations 27.3, 27.4, 27.6a, 27.6b, 27.6c, 27.6d, 27.7a, 27.7b and 27.8

1 Disconnect the battery negative cable (Chapter 5, Section 1).

2 Pull the ashtray from the dash.

3 Pull off the shift lever (or selector lever) knob **(see illustration)**.

4 Using a screwdriver, carefully pry out the shift lever boot/switch panel or selector lever panel, as applicable. When necessary, disconnect the wiring multi-plugs **(see illustration)**.

5 Remove the adaptive damping switch, when equipped (Chapter 12).

6 Pry off the plastic caps, then unscrew the center console mounting screws. These are located on each side, on the front top, and inside the cassette storage box. The screws with the washers go on the side of the console; the front screws are smaller than the others, and black in color **(see illustrations)**.

7 Fully apply the parking brake lever. Withdraw the center console, at the same time passing the boot over the parking brake lever **(see illustrations)**.

8 Disconnect the cigar lighter wiring **(see illustration)**.

Installation

9 Installation is a reversal of the removal procedure.

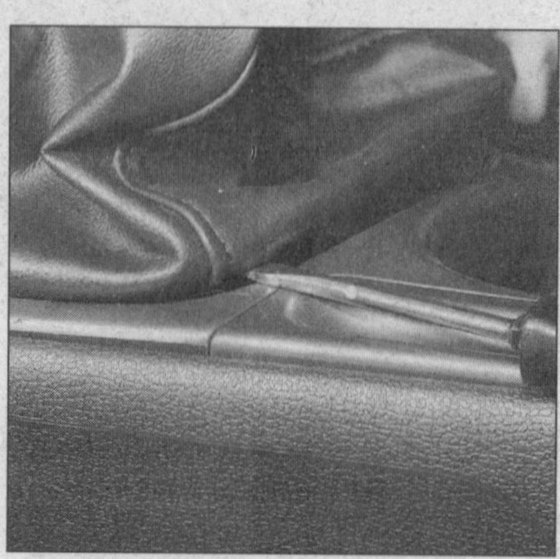
27.4 Prying out the shift lever boot

27.6a Pry off the plastic caps . . .

27.6b . . . and unscrew the mounting screws at the front top . . .

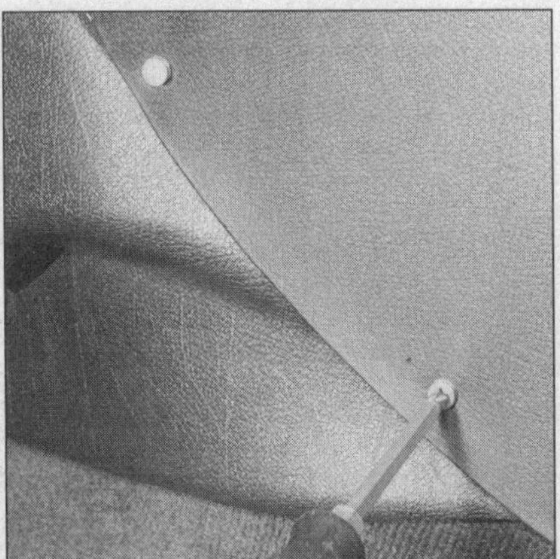

27.6c . . . at the sides . . .

27.6d . . . and inside the cassette storage box

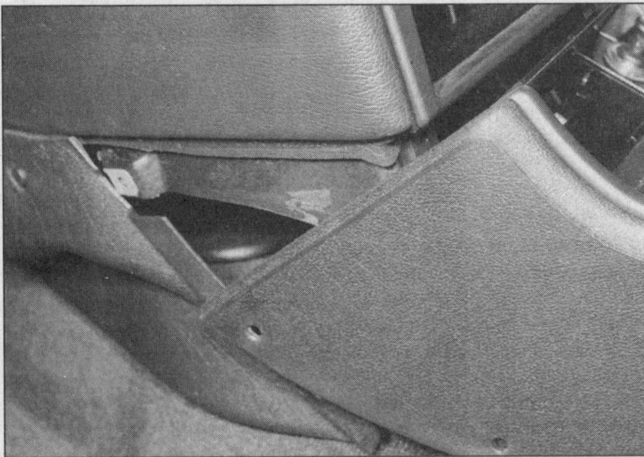

27.7a Withdrawing the front of the console from the dash

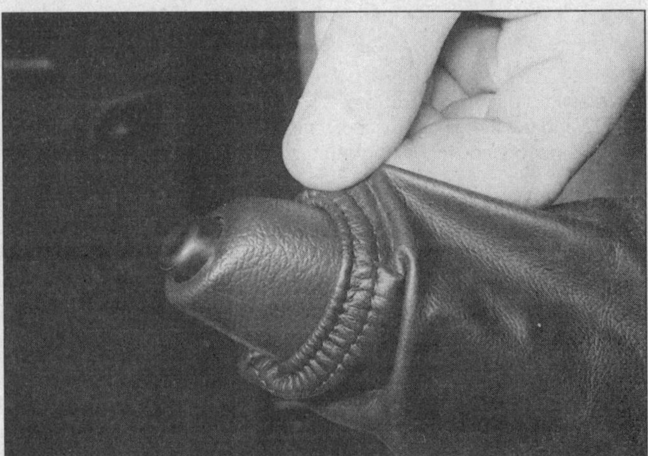

27.7b Passing the boot over the parking brake lever

28 Overhead console - removal and installation

Removal

Refer to illustration 28.3

1 Disconnect the battery negative cable (Chapter 5, Section 1).

2 When applicable, remove the sunroof switch (Chapter 12).

3 When applicable, remove the sunroof handle, after undoing the securing screw **(see illustration)**.

3 Push the console towards the windshield, to disengage it from the clips.

Installation

4 Installation is a reversal of the removal procedure.

29 Glovebox - removal and installation

Removal

Refer to illustration 29.1

1 Open the glovebox. Using a screwdriver, carefully press in one side of the glovebox near the hinge, to release it from

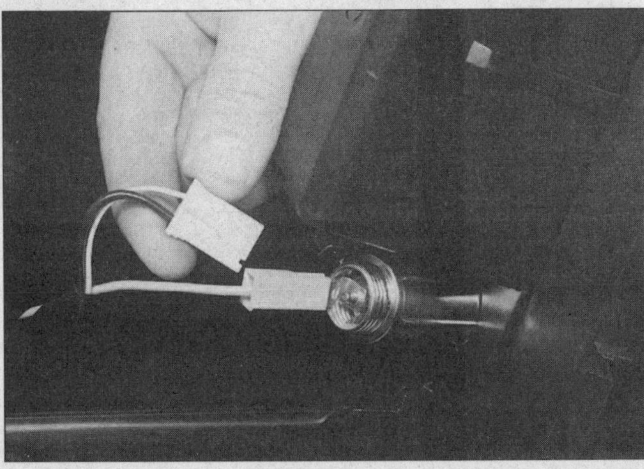

27.8 Disconnecting the cigar lighter wiring

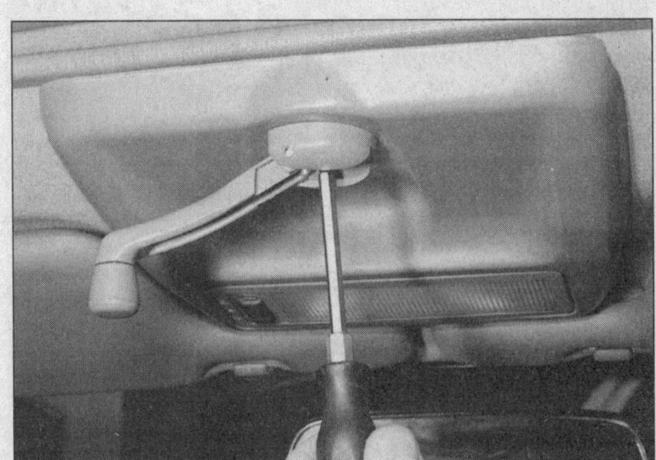

28.3 Removing the sunroof handle securing screw

29.1 Glovebox removal

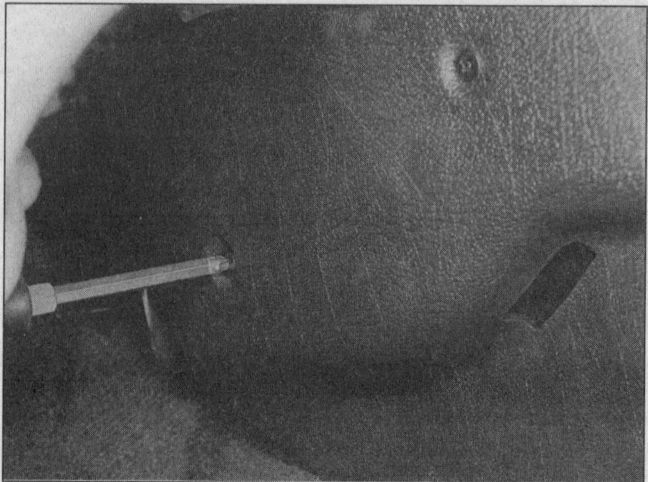

30.3a Unscrew the screws . . .

the plastic clip **(see illustration)**.

2 Withdraw the glovebox and, where necessary, disconnect the wiring multi-plug for the light.

3 If necessary, the lock may be removed by unscrewing the mounting screws and removing the lock plate and spring from the glove box door.

4 To remove the lock cylinder, depress the spring tabs.

Installation

5 Locate the cylinder in the lock plate, making sure that the clips are fully engaged.

6 Hold the latch pins together, and engage the right-hand pin of the lock plate.

7 Install the spring, and engage the left-hand pin of the lock plate.

8 Install the lock plate, and tighten the screws.

9 Reconnect the wiring multi-plug and install the glovebox, making sure that it is fully inserted in the plastic clips.

30 Dash - removal and installation

Removal

Refer to illustrations 30.3a, 30.3b, 30.18a, 30.18b, 30.20a, 30.20b, 30.20c and 30.22

1 Disconnect the battery negative cable (Chapter 5, Section 1).

2 Remove the windshield wiper arms (Chapter 12), then remove the cowl from just in front of the windshield. The cowl is in two sections, with retaining screws located along its front edge. With the cowl removed, disconnect the speedometer cable by pulling it from the intermediate inner cable extension.

3 Remove the center console (Section 30), then unscrew the screws and remove the heater side covers **(see illustrations)**.

4 Remove the steering column (Chapter 10).

5 Remove the instrument cluster (Chapter 12).

6 If equipped, unscrew the screws and remove the automatic warning system display.

7 Remove the radio and (if fitted) the CD player (Chapter 12).

8 Remove the heater control panel (Chapter 3).

9 Using a screwdriver, carefully pry out the headlight switch panel, and disconnect the wiring multi-plugs.

10 Remove the glovebox (Section 32).

11 Remove the small piece of carpet from under the passenger side of the dash.

12 Remove the side trim panels from the "A" and "B" pillars on each side of the vehicle (Section 29). The upper panels on the "B" pillars can be left in position.

13 At the base of the right-hand "A" pillar, disconnect the wiring multi-plugs, ground leads and aerial, noting their installed positions.

14 Identify the position of the wiring multi-plugs on the fuse box, then disconnect them.

15 Disconnect the wiring from the footwell lights, if equipped.

16 Pry out the speedometer cable rubber grommet at the firewall near the pedal bracket, then release the cable from the clips.

30.3b . . . and remove the heater side covers

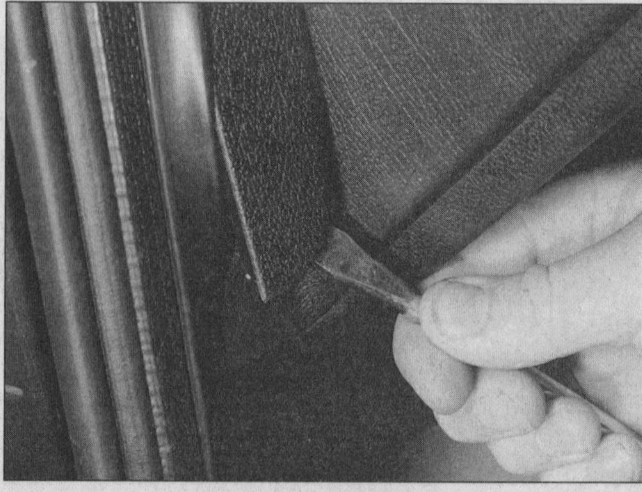

30.18a Pry off the covers . . .

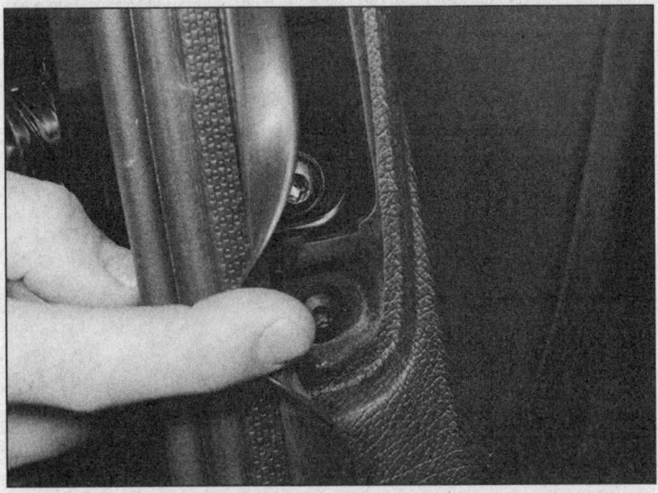
30.18b . . . and pull away the weatherstrip to reveal the dash mounting bolts

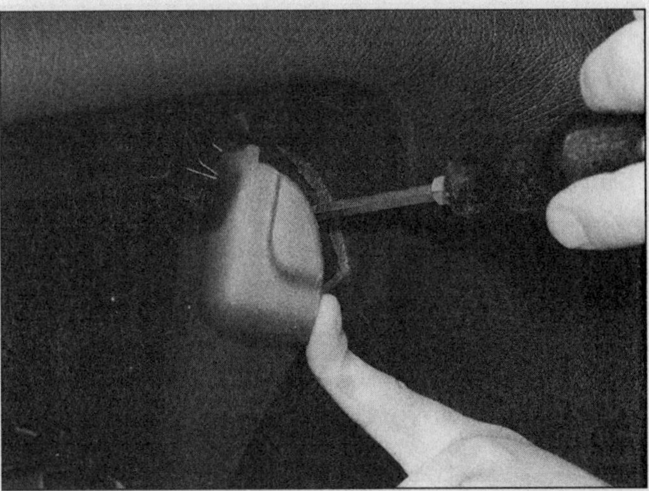
30.20a Dash mounting bolt next to the glovebox

30.20b Dash center mounting bolt next to the heater panel

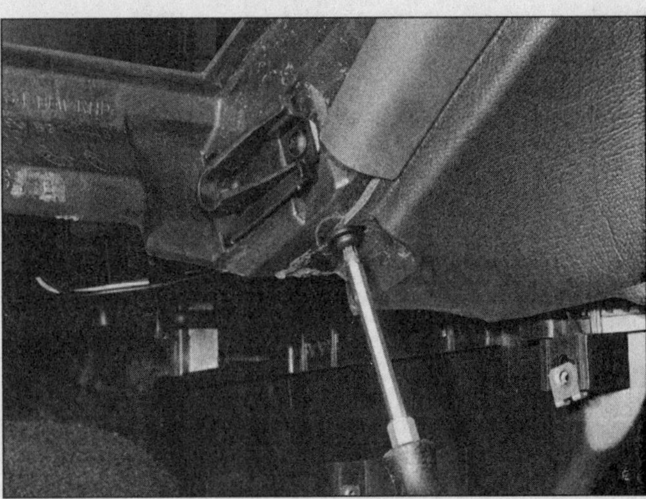
30.20c Dash mounting bolt near the heater

17 Remove the screws and withdraw the glovebox side trim, for access to the side dash mounting screw.

18 Open the front doors. Pry off the trim covers, then pull away the door weatherstrip by the side mounting bolt positions on each side **(see illustrations)**.

19 Unscrew the dash side mounting bolts.

20 Unscrew the dash center mounting bolts **(see illustrations)**.

21 Withdraw the dash from the firewall, far enough to be able to reach in behind it.

30.22 Disconnecting the fresh air hoses

22 Disconnect the remaining multi-plugs and connections, noting their locations on the various components for correct installation. It will also be necessary to release some wiring harness holders, clips and plastic ties, and the fresh air vent hoses **(see illustration)**.

23 Withdraw the dash from one side of the vehicle.

Installation

24 Installation is a reversal of the removal procedure. On completion, check the operation of all electrical components.

31 Wheel arch liner - removal and installation

Removal

Front

Refer to illustrations 31.3 and 31.4

1 Apply the parking brake, jack up the front of the vehicle and support it on jack-

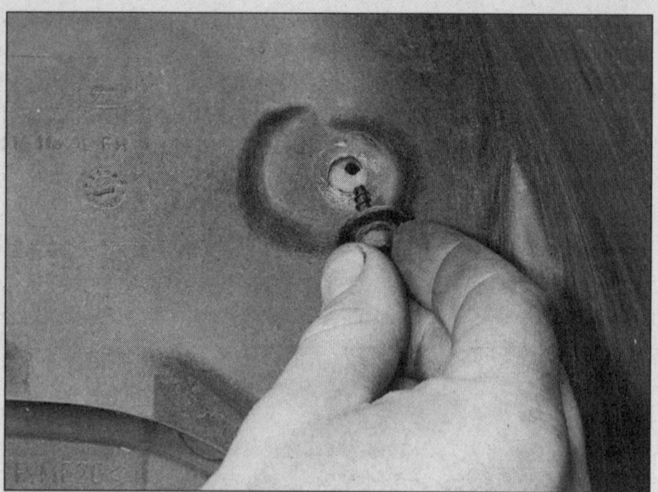

31.3 Removing a wheel arch liner retaining screw

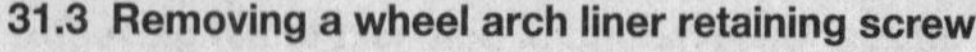

31.4 Removing a front wheel arch liner

stands. If wished, remove the wheel to improve access.

2 Pry out the stud clip on the front lower edge of the liner.

3 Using a Torx driver, unscrew the screws securing the liner to the inner wheel arch panel **(see illustration)**.

4 Remove the screws and clips securing the liner to the outer edge of the wheel arch and bumper. Withdraw the liner from under the vehicle **(see illustration)**.

Rear

5 Chock the front wheels, jack up the rear of the vehicle and support it on jackstands. If wished, remove the wheel to improve access.

6 Unscrew and remove the nuts, located on either side of the coil spring, securing the central section of the liner.

7 Using a Torx driver, unscrew the screws securing the liner to the center of the inner wheel arch panel.

8 Remove the clips securing the liner to the outer edge of the wheel arch, and withdraw the liner from under the vehicle.

Installation

9 Installation is a reversal of the removal procedure. If the wheels were removed, tighten the wheel nuts to the specified torque.

Chapter 12
Body electrical system

Contents

Specifications

Fuses (auxiliary fuse box in engine compartment)

Note: *Fuse ratings and circuits are liable to change from year to year. Consult the owner's manual supplied with the vehicle, or consult a dealer, for specific information.*

Fuse No	Rating	Color	Circuit(s) protected
1	80	Black	Power supply to main fuse box
2	60	Yellow	Radiator electric cooling fans
3	60	Yellow	ABS braking system
4	20	Yellow	Daytime running lights
5	30	Light green	Fog lamp
6	30	Light green	Not used
7	30	Light green	ABS braking system
8	30	Light green	Air pump
9	20	Light blue	PCM module
10	20	Light blue	Ignition switch
11	3	Violet	PCM memory
12	15	Light blue	Horn and hazard flasher warning system
13	15	Light blue	Oxygen sensor
14	15	Light blue	Fuel pump

Fuses (main fuse box in passenger compartment)

Note: *Fuse ratings and circuits change from year to year. Consult the vehicle owners manual or a dealer for specific information.*

Fuse	Rating	Color	Circuit(s) protected
15	10	Red	Right-hand low beam headlight
16	10	Red	Left-hand low beam headlight
17	10	Red	Right-hand high beam
18	10	Red	Left-hand high beam
19	7.5	Brown	Heated door mirrors
20	10	Black	Windshield wipers (circuit breaker)
21	30	Light green	Electric windows
22	7.5	Brown	ABS module
23	15	Light blue	Backup lights
24	15	Light blue	Stop-lights
25	20	Yellow	Door locks
26	20	Yellow	Main light
27	15	Light blue	Cigar lighter
28	30	Light green	Power seats
29	30	Light green	Heated rear window
30	7.5	Brown	Engine management system
31	7.5	Brown	Instrument panel illumination
32	7.5	Brown	Radio
33	7.5	Brown	Front and rear sidelights (left-hand side)
34	7.5	Brown	Interior lighting and digital clock
35	7.5	Brown	Front and rear sidelights (right-hand side)
36	30	Light green	Air bag
37	30	Light green	Heater blower
38			Not used

Relays (auxiliary fuse box in engine compartment)

Relay	Color	Circuit(s) protected
R1	Green	Daytime running lights (Canada)
R2	Black	Radiator electric cooling fan (high speed)
R3	Blue	Air conditioning cut-out
R4	Brown	Air conditioning clutch relay
R5	Dark green	Radiator electric cooling fan (low speed)
R6	Yellow	Starter solenoid
R7	Brown	Horns
R8	Brown	Fuel pump
R9	White	Low beam headlights
R10	White	High beam headlights
R11	Brown	PCM power supply

Relays (main fuse box in passenger compartment)

Relay	Color	Circuit(s) protected
R12	White	Interior and courtesy lights
R13	Yellow	Heated rear window
R14	Yellow	Heater blower
R15	Green	Windshield wiper motor
R16	Black	Ignition

Auxiliary relays (not in the fuse boxes)

Relay	Color	Circuit(s) protected	Location
R17		Not used	
R18	Black	Express down windows	Driver's door
R19	Blue	Speed control cut-off	Central fuse box bracket below the instrument panel
R20		Not used	
R21		Not used	
R22	White	Foglights	Interface module bracket
R23	Black	Turn signals	Steering column
R24	White	Left-hand flasher	Door lock module bracket
R25	White	Right-hand flasher	Door lock module bracket
R26		Not used	

Bulbs	Wattage	Type
Headlight main beam	55	Halogen
Headlight low beam	55	Halogen
Fog lamps	55	Halogen
Sidelights	5	Wedge
Turn signal lights	21	Bayonet
Side repeater lights	5	Wedge
Stop-lights	21	Bayonet
Backup lights	21	Bayonet
Rear fog/tail lights	21/4	Bayonet
Rear tail light	5	Bayonet
License plate lights	5	Festoon
Engine compartment	10	Wedge
Interior lights	10	Festoon
Map light	5	Wedge

Torque specifications	Ft-lbs
Windshield wiper motor bolts	
Into old motor (see text)	6
Into new motor (see text)	9

1 General information

Warning: *Before carrying out any work on the electrical system, read through the precautions given in* Safety first! *at the beginning of this manual.*

The electrical system is of 12-volt negative ground type. Power for the lights and all electrical accessories is supplied by a lead/acid battery which is charged by the alternator.

This Chapter covers repair and service procedures for the various electrical components not associated with the engine. Information on the battery, ignition system, alternator, and starter motor can be found in Chapter 5.

All models are equipped with a driver's air bag, which is designed to prevent serious chest and head injuries to the driver during an accident. A similar bag for the front seat passenger is also available The sensor and electronic unit for the air bag is located next to the steering column inside the vehicle, and contains a back-up capacitor, crash sensor, decelerometer, safety sensor, integrated circuit and microprocessor. The air bag is inflated by a gas generator, which forces the bag out of the module cover in the center of the steering wheel. A "clock spring" ensures that a good electrical connection is maintained with the air bag at all times - as the steering wheel is turned in each direction, the spring winds and unwinds.

Some models are equipped with an alarm system incorporating a movement sensor and ignition immobilize. The alarm system horn is located on the left-hand side of the luggage.

Some models are equipped with a headlight leveling system, which is controlled by a knob on the dash. On position "0", the headlights are in their base position, and on position "5", the headlights are in their maximum inclined angle.

It should be noted that, when portions of the electrical system are serviced, the cable should be disconnected from the battery negative terminal, to prevent electrical shorts and fires. **Caution:** *When disconnecting the battery for work described in the following Sections, refer to Chapter 5, Section 1.*

2 Electrical fault finding - general information

Note: *Refer to the precautions given in "Safety first!" and in Section 1 of this Chapter before starting work. The following tests relate to testing of the main electrical circuits, and should not be used to test delicate electronic circuits (such as engine management systems, anti-lock braking systems, etc.), particularly where an electronic control module is used. Also refer to the precautions given in Chapter 5, Section 1.*

General

1 A typical electrical circuit consists of an electrical component, any switches, relays, motors, fuses, fusible links or circuit breakers related to that component, and the wiring and connectors which link the component to both the battery and the chassis. To help to pinpoint a problem in an electrical circuit, wiring diagrams are included at the end of this manual.

2 Before attempting to diagnose an electrical fault, first study the appropriate wiring diagram, to obtain a complete understanding of the components included in the particular circuit concerned. The possible sources of a fault can be narrowed down by noting if other components related to the circuit are operating properly. If several components or circuits fail at one time, the problem is likely to be related to a shared fuse or ground connection.

3 Electrical problems usually stem from simple causes, such as loose or corroded connections, a faulty ground connection, a blown fuse, a melted fusible link, or a faulty relay (refer to Section 3 for details of testing relays). Visually inspect the condition of all fuses, wires and connections in a problem circuit before testing the components. Use the wiring diagrams to determine which terminal connections will need to be checked in order to pinpoint the trouble-spot.

4 The basic tools required for electrical fault-finding include a circuit tester or voltmeter (a 12-volt bulb with a set of test leads can also be used for certain tests); an ohmmeter (to measure resistance and check for continuity); a battery and set of test leads; and a jumper wire, preferably with a circuit breaker or fuse incorporated, which can be used to bypass suspect wires or electrical components. Before attempting to locate a problem with test instruments, use the wiring diagram to determine where to make the connections.

5 To find the source of an intermittent wiring fault (usually due to a poor or dirty connection, or damaged wiring insulation), a "wiggle" test can be performed on the wiring. This involves wiggling the wiring by hand to see if the fault occurs as the wiring is moved. It should be possible to narrow down the source of the fault to a particular section of wiring. This method of testing can be used in conjunction with any of the tests described in the following sub-Sections.

6 Apart from problems due to poor connections, two basic types of fault can occur in an electrical circuit - open-circuit, or short-circuit.

7 Open-circuit faults are caused by a break somewhere in the circuit, which prevents current from flowing. An open-circuit fault will prevent a component from working.

8 Short-circuit faults are caused by a "short" somewhere in the circuit, which allows the current flowing in the circuit to "escape" along an alternative route, usually to ground. Short-circuit faults are normally caused by a breakdown in wiring insulation, which allows a feed wire to touch either another wire, or an grounded component such as the bodyshell. A short-circuit fault will normally cause the relevant circuit fuse to blow.

Finding an open-circuit

9 To check for an open-circuit, connect one lead of a circuit tester or the negative lead of a voltmeter either to the battery negative terminal or to a known good ground.

10 Connect the other lead to a connector in the circuit being tested, preferably nearest to the battery or fuse. At this point, battery voltage should be present, unless the lead from the battery or the fuse itself is faulty (bearing in mind that some circuits are live only when the ignition switch is moved to a particular position).

11 Switch on the circuit, then connect the tester lead to the connector nearest the circuit switch on the component side.

12 If voltage is present (indicated either by the tester bulb lighting or a voltmeter reading, as applicable), this means that the section of the circuit between the relevant connector and the switch is problem-free.

13 Continue to check the remainder of the circuit in the same fashion.

14 When a point is reached at which no voltage is present, the problem must lie between that point and the previous test point with voltage. Most problems can be traced to a broken, corroded or loose connection.

Finding a short-circuit

15 To check for a short-circuit, first disconnect the load(s) from the circuit (loads are the components which draw current from a circuit, such as bulbs, motors, heating elements, etc.).

16 Remove the relevant fuse from the circuit, and connect a circuit tester or voltmeter to the fuse connections.

17 Switch on the circuit, bearing in mind that some circuits are live only when the ignition switch is moved to a particular position.

18 If voltage is present (indicated either by the tester bulb lighting or a voltmeter reading, as applicable), this means that there is a short-circuit.

19 If no voltage is present during this test, but the fuse still blows with the load(s) reconnected, this indicates an internal fault in the load(s).

Finding an ground fault

20 The battery negative terminal is connected to "ground" - the metal of the engine/transaxle unit and the vehicle body - and many systems are wired so that they only receive a positive feed, the current returning via the metal of the car body. This means that the component mounting and the body form part of that circuit. Loose or corroded mountings can therefore cause a range of electrical faults, ranging from total failure of a circuit, to

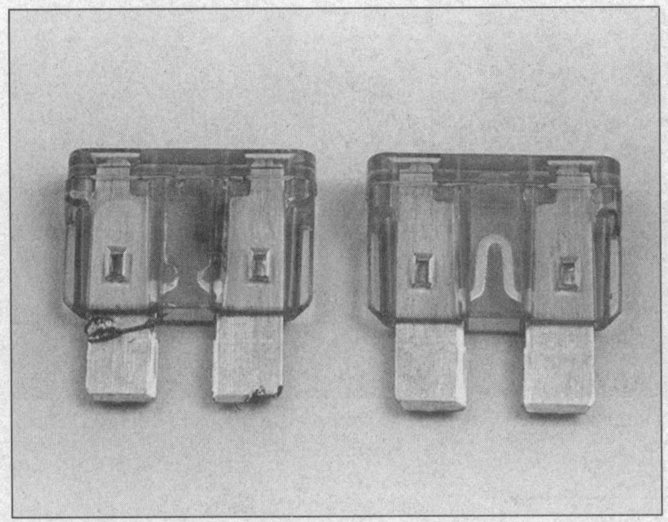

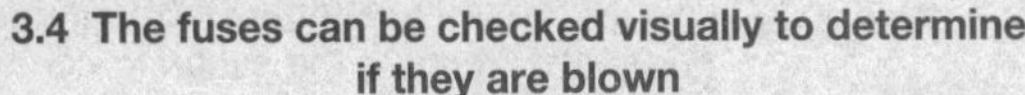
3.4 The fuses can be checked visually to determine if they are blown

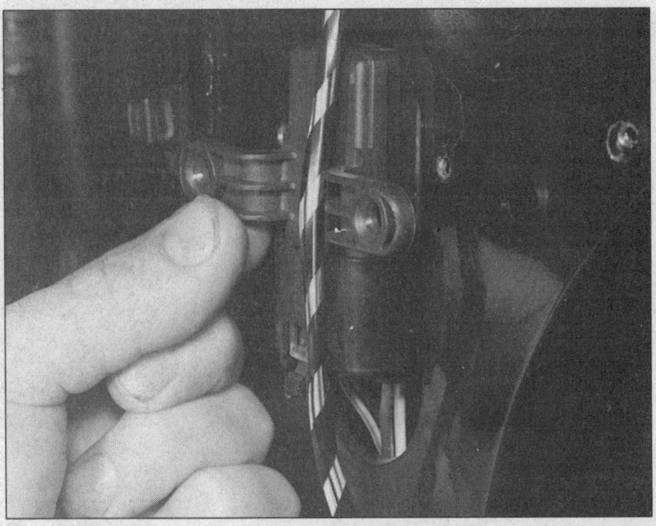

3.7 "One-touch down" window relay in the driver's door

a puzzling partial failure. In particular, lights may shine dimly (especially when another circuit sharing the same ground point is in operation), motors (e.g. wiper motors or the radiator cooling fan motor) may run slowly, and the operation of one circuit may have an apparently-unrelated effect on another. Note that on many vehicles, ground straps are used between certain components, such as the engine/transaxle and the body, usually where there is no metal-to-metal contact between components, due to flexible rubber mountings, etc.

21 To check whether a component is properly grounded, disconnect the battery (refer to Chapter 5, Section 1) and connect one lead of an ohmmeter to a known good ground point. Connect the other lead to the wire or ground connection being tested. The resistance reading should be zero; if not, check the connection as follows.

22 If an ground connection is thought to be faulty, disassemble the connection, and clean both the bodyshell and the wire terminal (or the component ground connection mating surface) back to bare metal. Be careful to remove all traces of dirt and corrosion, then use a knife to trim away any paint, so that a clean metal-to-metal fitting is made. On reassembly, tighten the fitting fasteners securely; if a wire terminal is being installed, use serrated washers between the terminal and the bodyshell, to ensure a clean and secure connection. When the connection is remade, prevent the onset of corrosion in the future by applying a coat of petroleum jelly or silicone-based grease, or by spraying on (at regular intervals) a proprietary ignition sealer such as Holts Damp Start, or a water-dispersant lubricant such as Holts Wet Start.

3 Fuses, relays and timer module - testing and replacement

Refer to illustrations 3.4 and 3.7

Note: *It is important to note that the ignition switch and the appropriate electrical circuit must always be switched off before any of the fuses (or relays) are removed and replaced. In the event of the fuse/relay unit having to be removed, the battery ground lead must be disconnected. When reconnecting the battery, reference should be made to Chapter 5.*

1 Fuses are designed to break a circuit when a predetermined current is reached, in order to protect components and wiring which could be damaged by excessive current flow. Any excessive current flow will be due to a fault in the circuit, usually a short-circuit (see Section 2). The main fuse box, which also carries some relays, is located inside the vehicle below the dash panel on the passenger's side, and is accessed by a lever behind the glovebox.

2 A central timer module is located on the bottom of the main fuse box. This module contains the time control elements for the heated rear window, interior lights and intermittent wiper operation. The module also activates a warning buzzer/chime when the vehicle is left with the lights switched on, or if a vehicle equipped with automatic transaxle is not parked in position "P".

3 The auxiliary fuse box is located on the front left-hand side of the engine compartment, and is accessed by unclipping and removing the cover. The auxiliary fuse box also contains some relays. Each circuit is identified by numbers on the main fuse box and on the inside of the auxiliary fuse box cover. Reference to the fuse chart in the Specifications at the start of this Chapter will indicate the circuits protected by each fuse. Plastic tweezers are attached to the main fuse box and to the inside face of the auxiliary fuse and block cover, to remove and install the fuses and relays.

4 To remove a fuse, use the tweezers provided to pull it out of the holder. Slide the fuse sideways from the tweezers. The wire within the fuse is clearly visible, and it will be broken if the fuse is blown **(see illustration)**.

5 Always replace a fuse with one of an identical rating. Never substitute a fuse of a higher rating, or make temporary repairs using wire or metal foil; more serious damage, or even fire, could result. The fuse rating is stamped on top of the fuse. Never replace a fuse more than once without tracing the source of the trouble.

6 Spare fuses of various current ratings are provided in the cover of the auxiliary fuse box. Note that if the vehicle is to be laid up for a long period, fuse 34 in the main fuse box should be removed, to prevent the ancillary electrical components from discharging the battery.

7 Relays are electrically-operated switches, which are used in certain circuits. The various relays can be removed from their respective locations by carefully pulling them from the sockets. Each relay in the fuse boxes has a plastic bar on its upper surface to enable the use of the tweezers. The locations and functions of the various relays are given in the Specifications **(see illustration)**.

8 If a component controlled by a relay becomes inoperative and the relay is suspect, listen to the relay as the circuit is oper-

WRONG it's underneath dash on drivers side left
release retaining clip (push button)
See page from "Chiltons" Ref.

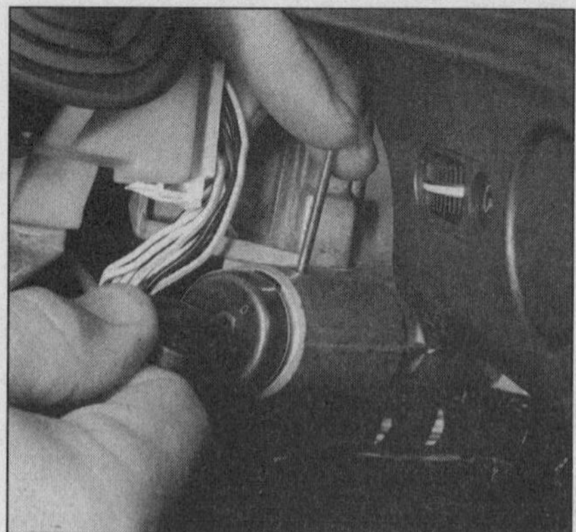
4.3a Depress the locking plunger . . .

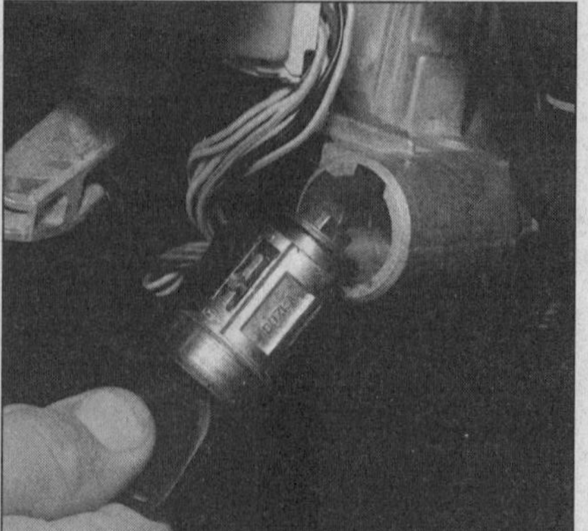
4.3b . . . and withdraw the ignition lock cylinder

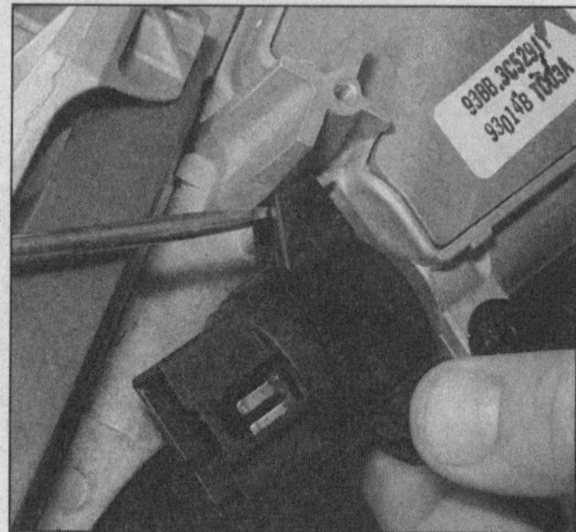
4.4a Release the retaining tab . . .

ated. If the relay is functioning, it should be possible to hear it click as it is energized. If the relay proves satisfactory, the fault lies with the components or wiring of the system. If the relay is not being energized, then either the relay is not receiving a switching voltage, or the relay itself is faulty. (Do not overlook the relay socket terminals when tracing faults.) Testing is by the substitution of a known good unit, but be careful; while some relays are identical in appearance and in operation, others look similar, but perform different functions.

9 The central timer module located on the bottom of the main fuse box incorporates its own self-diagnosis function. Note that diagnosis cannot take place if the heated rear window is defective.

10 To activate the system, press the heated rear window button while the ignition is being switched on, then release the button. Operate the light switch, washer pump switch and all of the door switches one after the other, and check that the buzzer confirms that the input signals are correct.

11 Now move the wiper lever to the intermittent wipe position, and check the output signals by operating the same switches.

12 The self-diagnosis function is turned off by switching the ignition off and on again.

4 Switches - removal and installation

Removal

Ignition switch and lock cylinder

Refer to illustrations 4.3a, 4.3b, 4.4a and 4.4b

1 Disconnect the battery negative cable (refer to Chapter 5, Section 1).

2 Remove the rubber boots and locking rings, then remove the securing screws and take off the steering column upper and lower shrouds.

3 Insert the ignition key, and turn it to the accessory position. Using a small screwdriver or twist drill through the hole in the side of the lock housing, depress the locking plunger and withdraw the lock cylinder **(see illustrations)**.

4 The switch may be removed from the steering column assembly by disconnecting the multi-plug, then using a screwdriver to release the switch retaining tab **(see illustrations)**.

Windshield wiper multi-function switch

Refer to illustrations 4.7, 4.8a and 4.8b

5 Disconnect the battery negative cable (refer to Chapter 5, Section 1).

6 Remove the rubber boots and locking rings, then remove the securing screws and take off the steering column upper shroud.

7 Disconnect the multi-plug **(see illustration)**.

8 Depress the plastic tab with a screwdriver, and lift the switch assembly from the steering column **(see illustrations)**.

Main light, auxiliary foglight and rear foglight combination switch

Refer to illustrations 4.10 and 4.11

9 Disconnect the battery negative cable (refer to Chapter 5, Section 1).

10 Carefully pry the switch panel from the dash, using a screwdriver against a cloth pad to prevent damage to the dash **(see illustration)**.

11 Disconnect the multi-plugs and withdraw the switch panel **(see illustration)**.

12 Unscrew the four mounting screws, and remove the switch from the panel.

13 Pull off the switch control knob, and remove the blanking plug and retainer.

14 Depress the plastic tabs, and remove the front cover and switch.

Instrument light rheostat

15 Disconnect the battery negative cable

4.4b . . . and remove the ignition switch

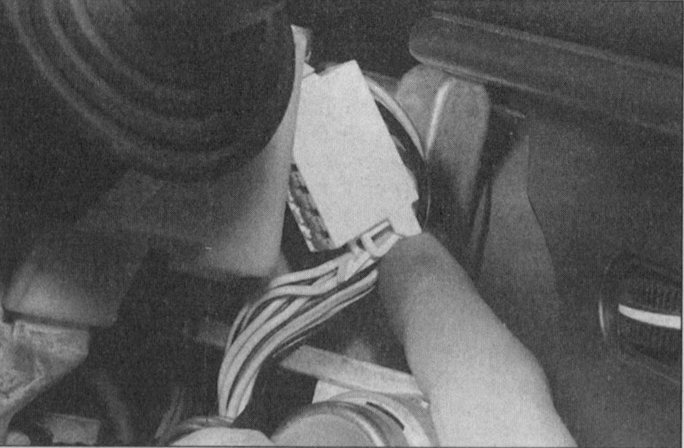
4.7 Disconnecting the multi-plug from the windshield wiper multi-function switch

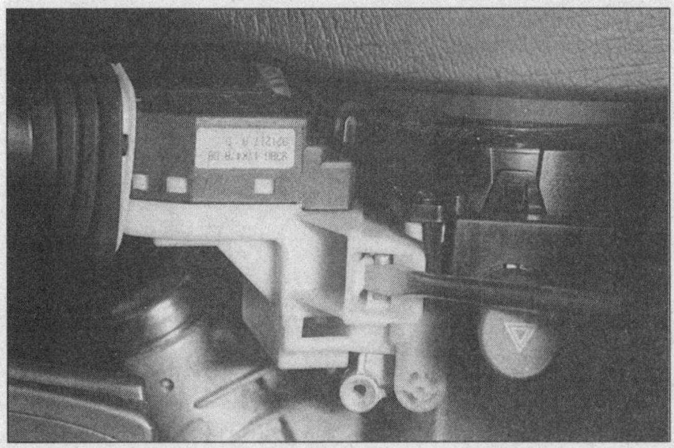

4.8a Depress the plastic tab with a screwdriver . . .

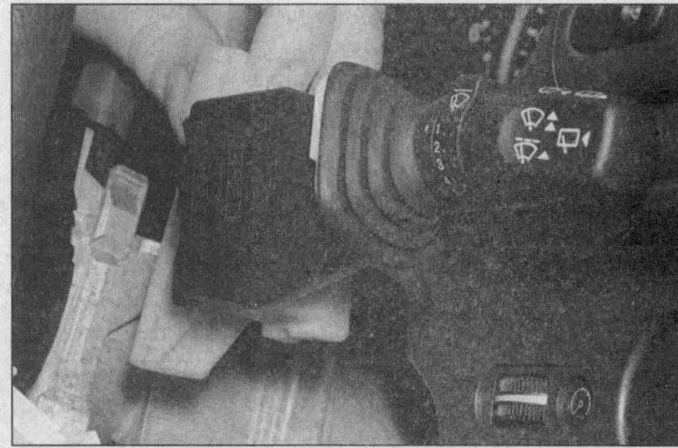

4.8b . . . and remove the windshield wiper multi-function switch

(refer to Chapter 5, Section 1).

16 Carefully pry the light switch panel from the dash, using a screwdriver against a cloth pad to prevent damage to the dash.

17 Disconnect the multi-plugs from the rear of the switch, then remove the screws and withdraw the instrument light rheostat from the panel.

Door mirror control switch

18 Disconnect the battery negative cable (refer to Chapter 5, Section 1).

19 Carefully pry the switch from the dash, using a screwdriver against a cloth pad to prevent damage to the dash.

20 Disconnect the multi-plug and withdraw the switch.

Direction indicator, headlight dimmer and hazard flasher multi-function switch

Refer to illustration 4.23

21 Disconnect the battery negative (ground) lead (refer to Chapter 5, Section 1).

22 Remove the rubber boots and locking rings, then remove the screws and take off the steering column upper shroud.

23 Depress the retaining lug and withdraw the switch assembly, then disconnect the multi-plug **(see illustration)**.

24 With the switch assembly removed, pull out the direction indicator relay if required.

Horn switch (steering wheel without air bag)

Note: *When an air bag is installed, the horn switch is removed with the air bag unit. Refer to Section 28.*

25 Disconnect the battery negative cable (refer to Chapter 5, Section 1).

26 Carefully pull off the padded center of the steering wheel which incorporates the horn switch.

27 Disconnect the wiring and remove the switch assembly.

Luggage compartment switch

28 Disconnect the battery negative cable (refer to Chapter 5, Section 1).

29 With the tailgate/trunk lid open, pull the weatherstrip from the center of the rear cross panel.

30 Carefully pry out the trim fasteners from the bottom corners of the rear trim, then unscrew the retaining screws and remove the trim panel.

31 Disconnect the wiring multi-plug, and pull out the switch.

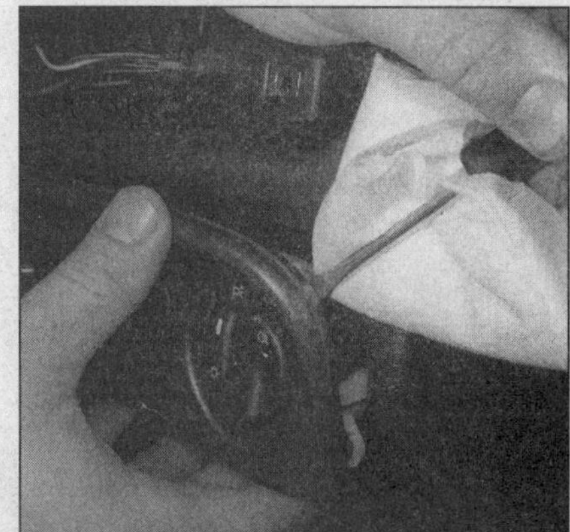

4.10 Prying out the light switch

Electrically-operated window switch (single)

32 Disconnect the battery negative cable (refer to Chapter 5, Section 1).

33 Carefully pry out the switch from the door inner trim panel, using a cloth pad to prevent damage to the trim.

34 Disconnect the multi-plug and remove the switch.

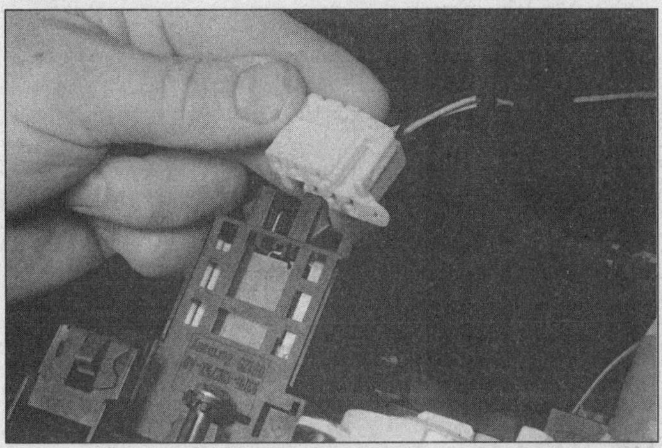

4.11 Disconnecting the multi-plugs from the light switch and rheostat

4.23 Removing the direction indicator, headlight dimmer hazard flasher multi-function switch. Direction indicator relay (flasher unit) is attached

Electrically-operated window switch (multiple) and isolator

35 Disconnect the battery negative cable (refer to Chapter 5, Section 1).

36 Pry the blanking cap from inside the inner door handle cavity, and remove the screw.

37 Hold the inner door handle in its open position, then remove the bezel and withdraw it over the handle.

38 Depress the retaining lug and remove the switch assembly, then disconnect the multi-plug.

Electrically-operated sunroof switch and traction control switch

39 Disconnect the battery negative cable (refer to Chapter 5, Section 1).

40 Carefully pry out the switch with a screwdriver, using a cloth pad to prevent damage to the trim.

41 Disconnect the multi-plug and remove the switch.

Parking brake-on warning switch

Refer to illustration 4.44

42 Disconnect the battery negative cable (refer to Chapter 5, Section 1).

43 Remove the center console as described in Chapter 11.

44 Disconnect the multi-plug, then remove the screw and withdraw the switch from the parking brake lever mounting bracket **(see illustration)**.

"Economy/Sport" mode switch (automatic transaxle models)

45 Disconnect the battery negative cable (refer to Chapter 5, Section 1).

46 Select Neutral, then pry out the selector indicator panel, using a cloth pad to prevent damage to the surrounding trim.

47 Push the switch out of the panel, and disconnect the multi-plug.

Heated windshield switch and heated rear window switch

Refer to illustrations 4.49 and 4.50

48 Disconnect the battery negative cable (refer to Chapter 5, Section 1).

49 Carefully pry out the switch, using a cloth pad to prevent damage to the trim **(see illustration)**.

50 Disconnect the multi-plug and remove the switch **(see illustration)**.

Electrically-operated seat switch and heated seat switch

51 Disconnect the battery negative cable (refer to Chapter 5, Section 1).

52 Carefully pry out the switch, using a cloth pad to prevent damage to the trim.

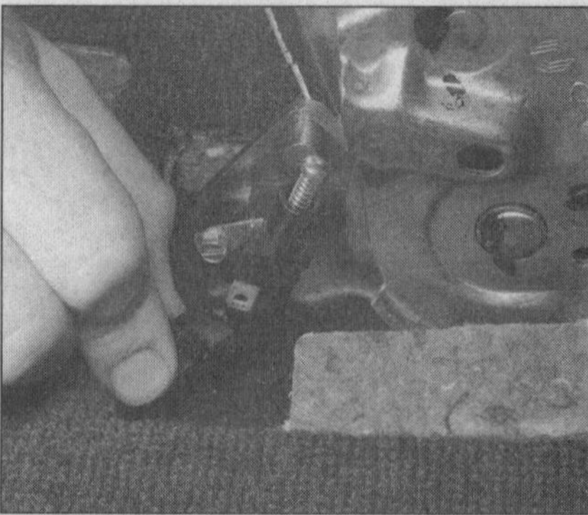

4.44 Disconnecting the multi-plug from the parking brake lever

53 Disconnect the multi-plug and remove the switch.

Adaptive damping switch

54 Disconnect the battery negative (ground) lead (refer to Chapter 5, Section 1).

55 Carefully pry out the switch, using a cloth pad to prevent damage to the trim.

56 Disconnect the multi-plug and remove the switch.

Courtesy light door switch

Refer to illustrations 4.57a and 4.57b

57 Open the door, then unscrew the cross-

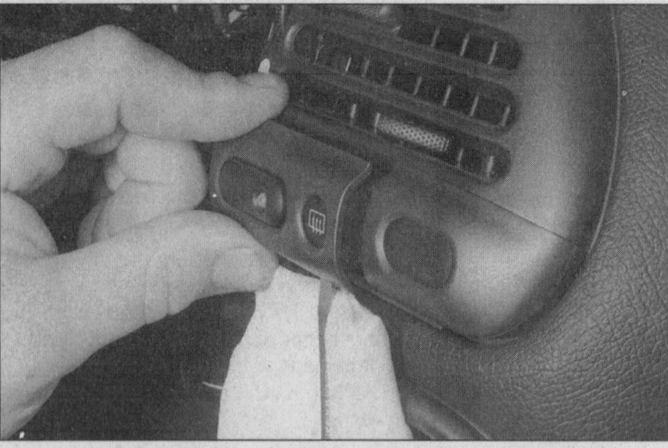

4.49 Prying out the heated rear window switch

4.50 Disconnecting the multi-plug from the heated rear window switch

4.57a Unscrew the cross-head screw . . .

4.57b . . . and pull out the courtesy light switch

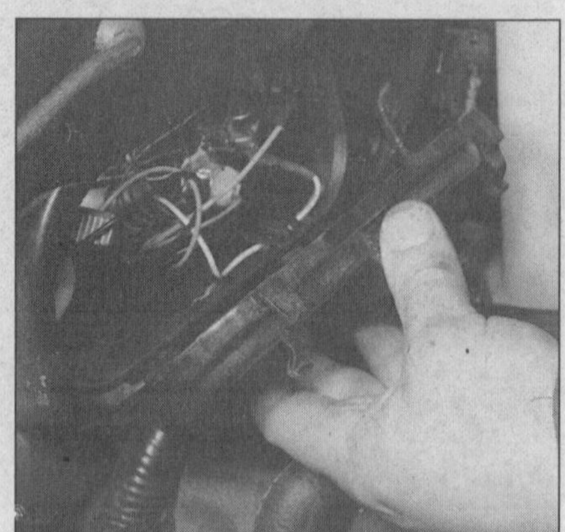

5.1 Removing the cover from the rear of the headlight

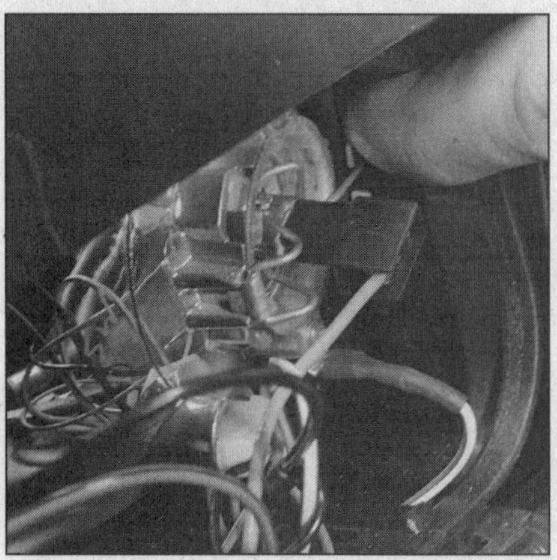
5.2a Release the spring clip . . .

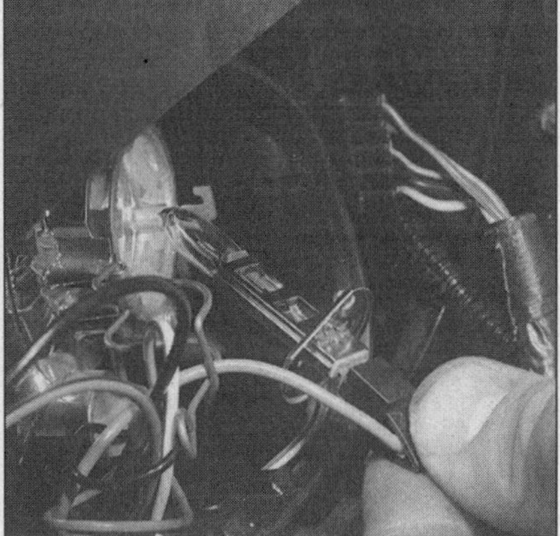
5.2b . . . and withdraw the headlight bulb

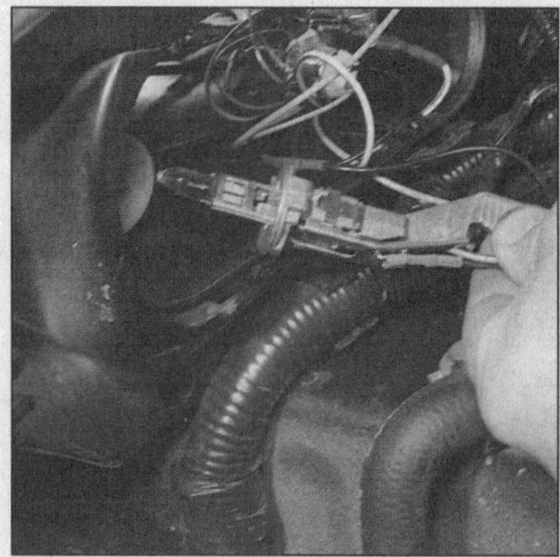
5.5 Removing the headlight (main beam) bulbholder

head screw and carefully pull the switch from the pillar **(see illustrations)**. Take care not to force the wire from the switch terminal, otherwise it will be difficult to retrieve it from the pillar.

58 Disconnect the wire, and tie it in a loose knot to prevent it dropping back into the pillar.

Installation

59 Installation of all switches is a reversal of the removal procedure.

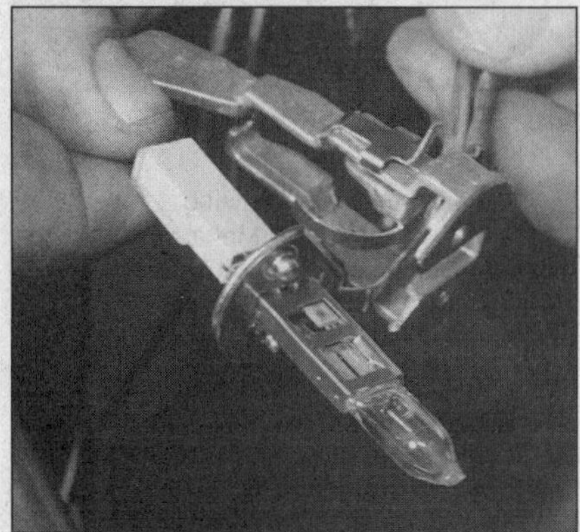
5.6 Removing the headlight (main beam) bulb from the bulbholder

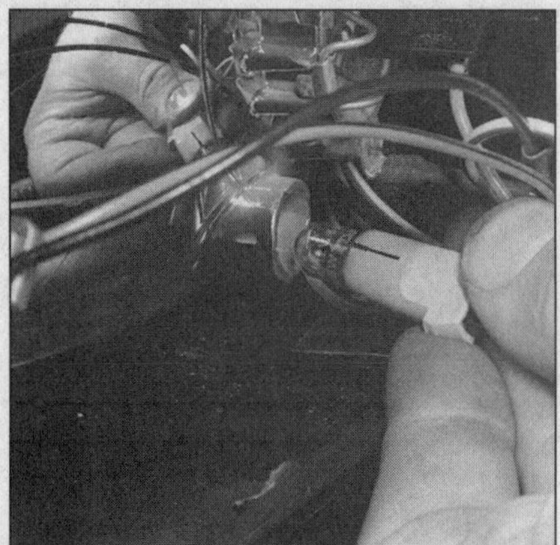
5.9 Removing the front sidelight bulbholder from the rear of the headlight unit

5 Bulbs (exterior lights) - replacement

Note: *Ensure that all exterior lights are switched off before disconnecting the wiring connectors from any exterior light bulbs. Do not touch the glass of halogen-type bulbs (headlights, front foglights) with the fingers; if the glass is accidentally touched, clean it with rubbing alcohol.*

Headlight (dipped beam)

Refer to illustrations 5.1, 5.2a and 5.2b

1 Working under the hood, depress the plastic clips and remove the cover from the rear of the headlight unit **(see illustration)**.

2 Release the spring clip and withdraw the bulb, then disconnect the wiring lead **(see illustrations)**.

3 Install the new bulb using a reversal of the removal procedure. Have the headlight beam alignment checked as described later in this Chapter.

Headlight (main beam)

Refer to illustrations 5.5 and 5.6

4 Working under the hood, depress the plastic clips and remove the cover from the rear of the headlight unit.

5 Turn the bulbholder counterclockwise, and remove it from the rear of the headlight unit **(see illustration)**.

6 Pull out the bulb and disconnect the wiring lead **(see illustration)**.

7 Install the new bulb using a reversal of the removal procedure, making sure that the bulbholder is correctly located in the headlight unit. Have the headlight beam alignment checked as described later in this Chapter.

Front sidelight

Refer to illustrations 5.9 and 5.10

8 Working under the hood, depress the plastic clips and remove the cover from the rear of the headlight unit.

9 Pull the bulbholder from the rear of the headlight unit **(see illustration)**.

10 Pull the bulb from the bulbholder **(see illustration)**.

11 Install the new bulb using a reversal of the removal procedure.

Front direction indicator

Refer to illustration 5.15

12 Open the hood. Loosen (but do not remove) the screw located above the front direction indicator **(see illustration 7.10)**.

13 Withdraw the front direction indicator light unit.

14 Rotate the bulbholder counterclockwise, and withdraw it from the light unit.

15 Twist the bulb counterclockwise, and remove it from the bulbholder **(see illustration)**.

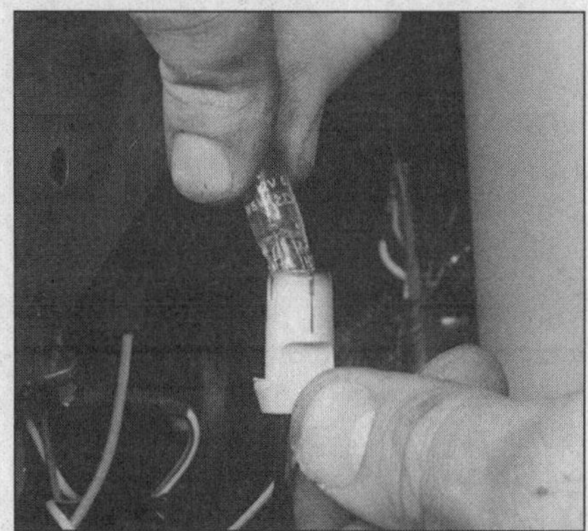
5.10 Pulling the bulb from the bulbholder

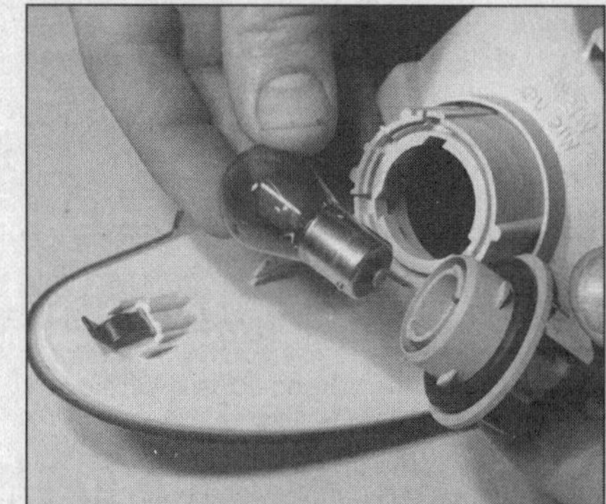
5.15 Removing the front direction indicator bulb

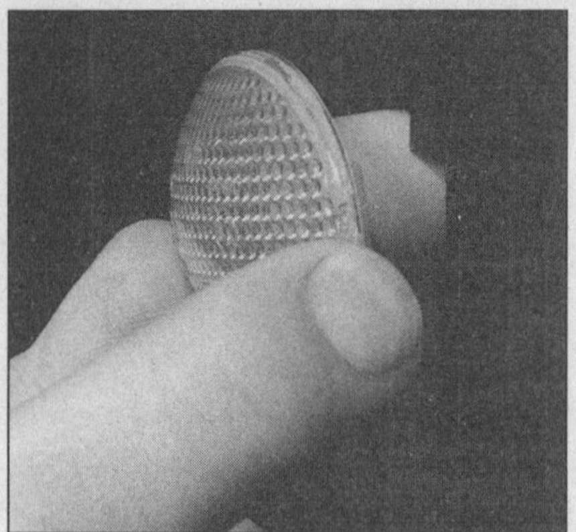

5.18 Removing the side repeater from the front fender

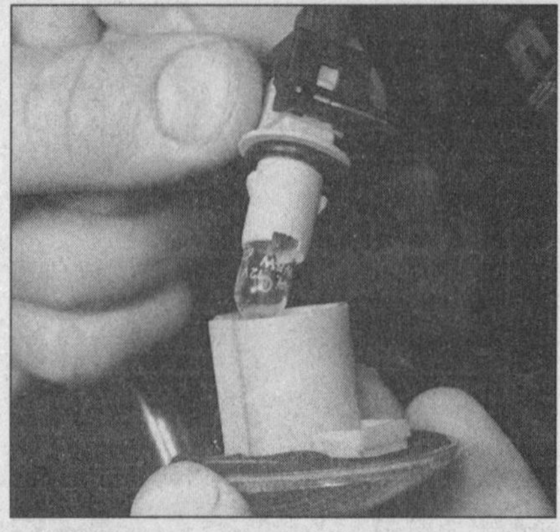

5.19 Removing the bulbholder from the side repeater lens/bulbholder

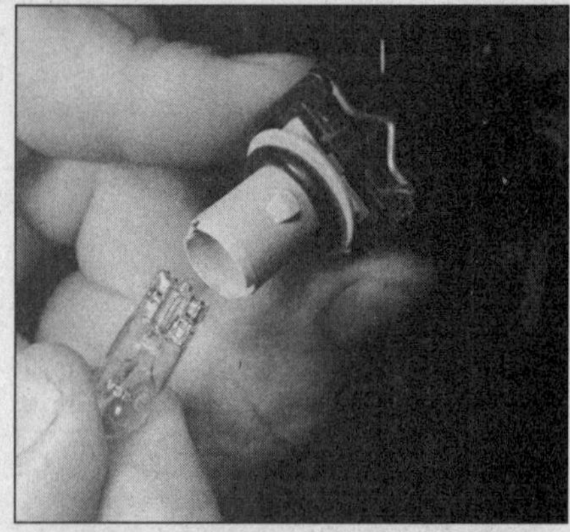

5.20 Removing the bulb from the side repeater bulbholder

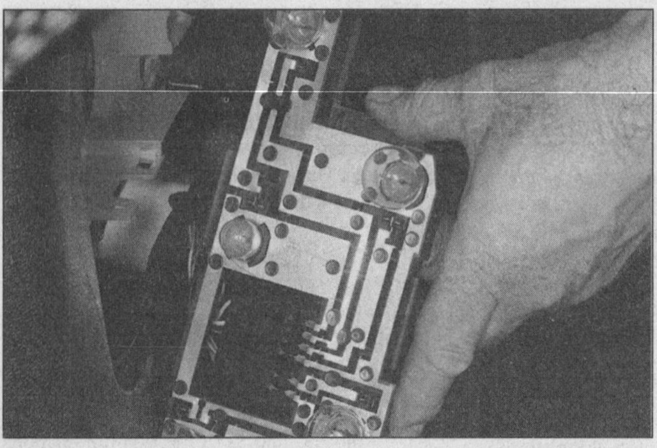

5.27 Removing the rear light cluster

5.28 Removing a bulb from the rear light cluster bulbholder

16 Install the new bulb using a reversal of the removal procedure, but before installation the light unit, first insert the holding spring in its bore.

Side repeaters

Refer to illustrations 5.18, 5.19 and 5.20

17 The side repeater light is held in position by spring pressure.

18 Depending on how the light unit was previously installed, press it either forwards or rearwards, and remove it from the front fender **(see illustration)**.

19 Turn the bulbholder counterclockwise, and disconnect it from the housing **(see illustration)**.

20 Pull the bulb from the holder **(see illustration)**.

21 Install the new bulb using a reversal of the removal procedure.

Front foglight

22 Unscrew the cross-head screws securing the front foglight unit to the valance, and withdraw the light unit.

23 Pry open the plastic clips and remove the rear cover from the light unit.

24 Release the spring clips and withdraw the bulb, then pull off the wiring connector.

25 Install the new bulb using a reversal of the removal procedure.

Rear light cluster

Refer to illustrations 5.27 and 5.28

26 With the trunk lid open, flip open the trim cover to reveal the bulbholder in the rear corner of the luggage compartment.

27 Press the two plastic locking tabs together, and withdraw the complete rear light cluster **(see illustration)**.

28 Depress and twist the appropriate bulb to remove it from the bulbholder **(see illustration)**.

29 Install the new bulb using a reversal of the removal procedure. Make sure that the rear light cluster is fully inserted.

License plate light

Refer to illustrations 5.30 and 5.31

30 Remove the cross-head screws from the license plate light, and remove the light unit **(see illustration)**.

5.30 Remove the cross-head screws . . .

5.31 . . . for access to the bulb

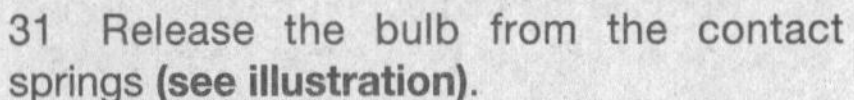

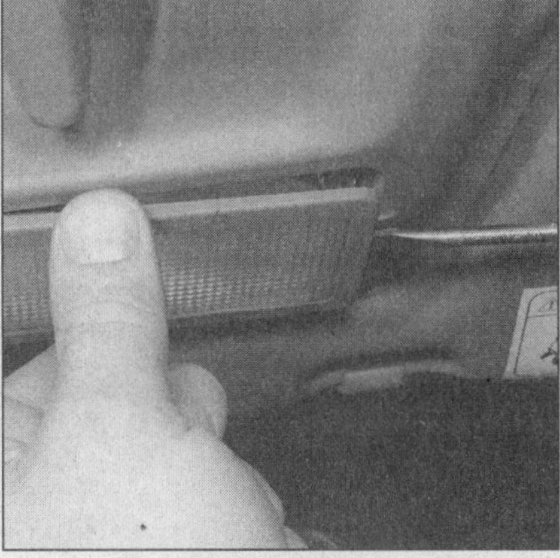

6.4 Pry out the interior light with a screwdriver

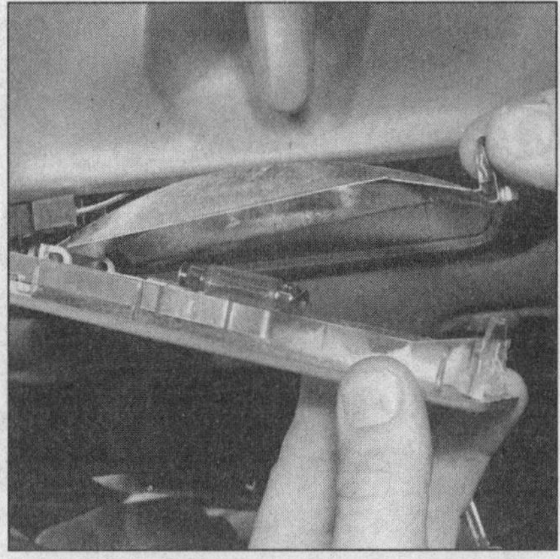

6.5 Lifting the reflector from the interior light

31 Release the bulb from the contact springs **(see illustration)**.

32 Install the new bulb using a reversal of the removal procedure. Make sure that the tension of the contact springs is sufficient to hold the bulb firmly.

6 Bulbs (interior lights) - replacement

Engine compartment light

1 With the hood open, pull the bulb from the bulbholder.

2 Install the new bulb using a reversal of the removal procedure.

Interior lights

Refer to illustrations 6.4 and 6.5

3 Switch off the interior light by locating the switch in its middle position.

4 Using a small screwdriver, carefully pry out the light or bulb cover, as applicable **(see illustration)**.

5 Lift up the reflector, then release the bulb from the contact springs **(see illustration)**.

6 Install the new bulb using a reversal of the removal procedure. Make sure that the tension of the contact springs is sufficient to hold the bulb firmly.

Reading light

7 With the reading light switched off, pry out the light using a small screwdriver.

8 Hinge back the contact plate, and release the bulb from the contact springs.

9 Install the new bulb using a reversal of the removal procedure. Make sure that the tension of the contact springs is sufficient to hold the bulb firmly.

Instrument panel illumination and warning lights

Refer to illustration 6.11

10 Remove the instrument panel as described in Section 10.

11 Twist the bulbholder counterclockwise to remove it **(see illustration)**.

12 Install the new bulbholder using a reversal of the removal procedure.

Foglight warning indicator

13 Using a screwdriver, pry out the indicator from the dash, and disconnect the multi-plug.

14 Twist the bulbholder counterclockwise with the screwdriver, and remove it.

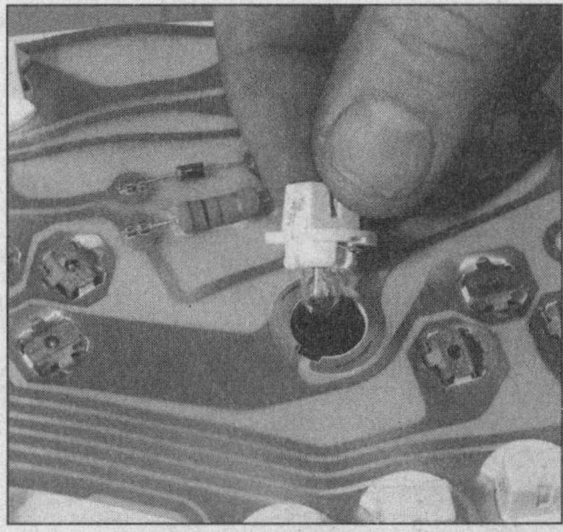

6.11 Removing a bulb from the rear of the instrument panel

15 Install the new bulb using a reversal of the removal procedure.

Hazard warning light

Refer to illustrations 6.16a and 6.16b

16 Pull the cover directly up from the switch, then remove the bulb **(see illustrations)**.

17 Install the new bulb using a reversal of the removal procedure.

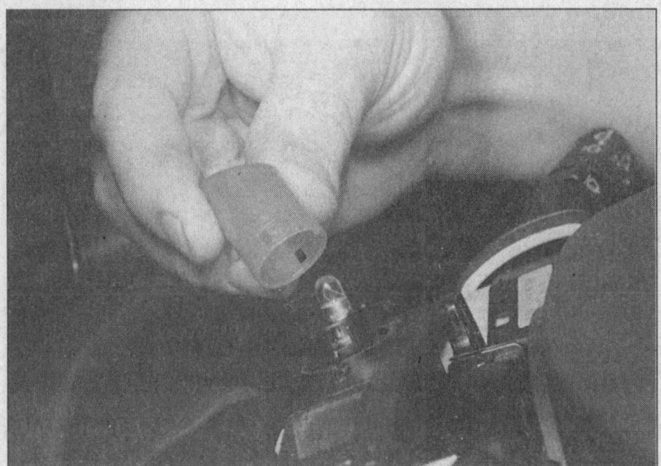

6.16a Pull off the hazard warning light cover . . .

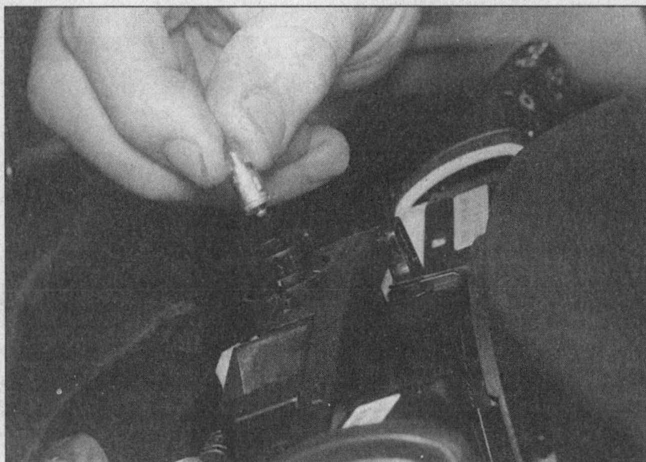

6.16b . . . and remove the bulb

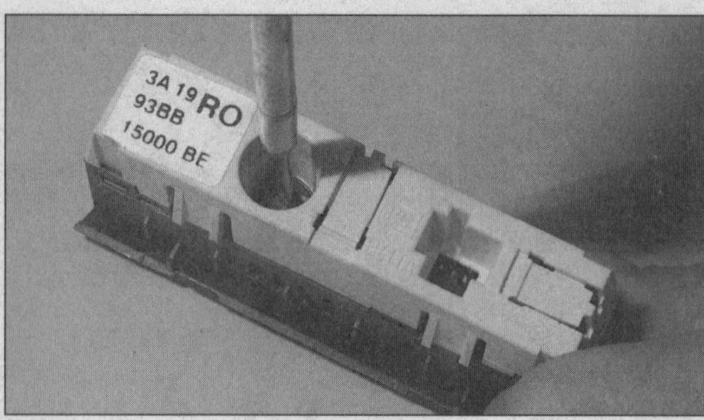

6.32a Twist the bulbholder counterclockwise . . .

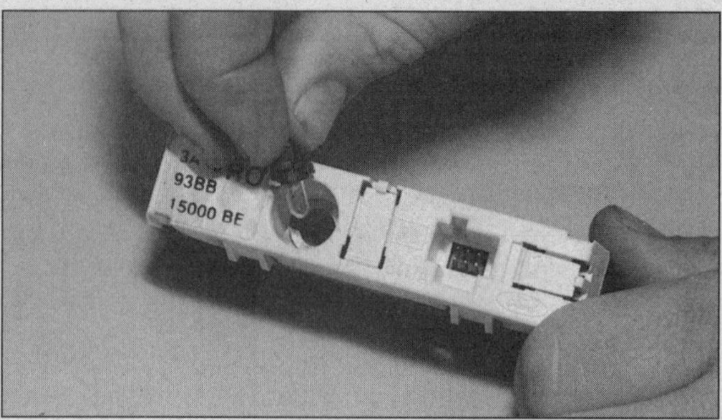
6.32b . . . and remove it from the rear of the clock

Glovebox light

18 Open the glovebox, then pull out the bulb from the light located under the upper edge.

Heater fan switch illumination

19 Pull off the switch knob, then depress and twist the bulb to remove it.

Automatic transaxle selector panel illumination

20 Disconnect the battery negative cable (refer to Chapter 5, Section 1).

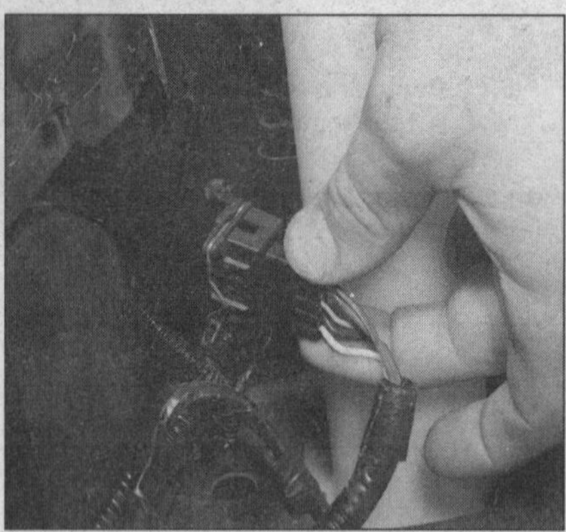
7.4 Disconnecting the headlight unit wiring multi-plug

21 Remove the ashtray.
22 Select Neutral, then pry out the panel from the center console.
23 Disconnect the multi-plug from the overdrive control switch.
24 Disconnect the bulbholder and pull out the bulb.
25 Install the new bulb using a reversal of the removal procedure.

Interior door handle illumination

26 Disconnect the battery negative cable (refer to Chapter 5, Section 1).
27 Remove the door interior trim panel as described in Chapter 11.
28 Using a knife, cut free the foam watershield for access to the rear of the interior door handle.
29 Pull out the bulbholder and remove the bulb.

Clock illumination

Refer to illustrations 6.32a and 6.32b

30 Disconnect the battery negative cable (refer to Chapter 5, Section 1).
31 Remove the clock as described in Section 13.
32 Twist the bulbholder counterclockwise using a screwdriver, then remove the bulbholder from the rear of the clock **(see illustrations)**.

Heater control illumination

33 Remove the heater control panel (Chapter 3), then twist the bulbholder counterclockwise and remove the bulb from the rear of the panel.

7 Exterior light units - removal and installation

Removal

1 Disconnect the battery negative cable (refer to Chapter 5, Section 1).

Headlight unit

Refer to illustrations 7.4, 7.8a, 7.8b, 7.8c, 7.9a and 7.9b

2 With the hood supported in its open position, loosen (but do not remove) the screw located above the front direction indicator.
3 Withdraw the front direction indicator unit forwards, and disconnect the wiring multi-plug. Place the unit to one side.
4 Disconnect the wiring multi-plug for the headlight unit **(see illustration)**.
5 Remove the radiator grille as described in Chapter 11.
6 Remove the front bumper as described in Chapter 11.
7 The headlights installed from new are a single unit, joined by a plastic back-piece

7.8a Unscrew the outer mounting screws . . .

7.8b . . . and inner mounting screws . . .

7.8c . . . and withdraw the headlight unit assembly

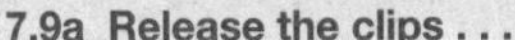

7.9a Release the clips . . .

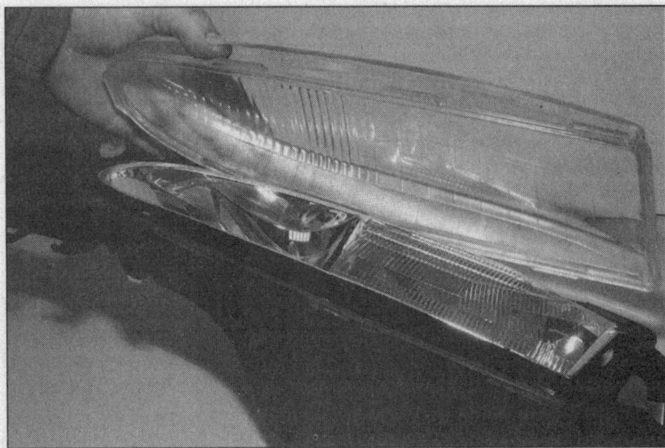

7.9b . . . and remove the headlight lens

running across the front of the vehicle. However, if it is required to replace a headlight unit on one side only, the back-piece must first be removed complete.

8 Unscrew the mounting bolts from each side of the headlight unit, and withdraw the unit from the front of the vehicle **(see illustrations)**. Reach behind the headlight unit, remove the clips retaining the headlight housing to the unit and remove the headlight housing.

9 If necessary, the lens may be removed separately by releasing the clips **(see illustrations)**. To remove the diffuser, release the clips, then remove the rubber seal.

7.10 Loosen the front direction indicator retaining screw

Front direction indicator

Refer to illustration 7.10 and 7.12

10 With the hood supported in its open position, loosen (but do not remove) the screw located above the front direction indicator **(see illustration)**.

11 Withdraw the front direction indicator light unit.

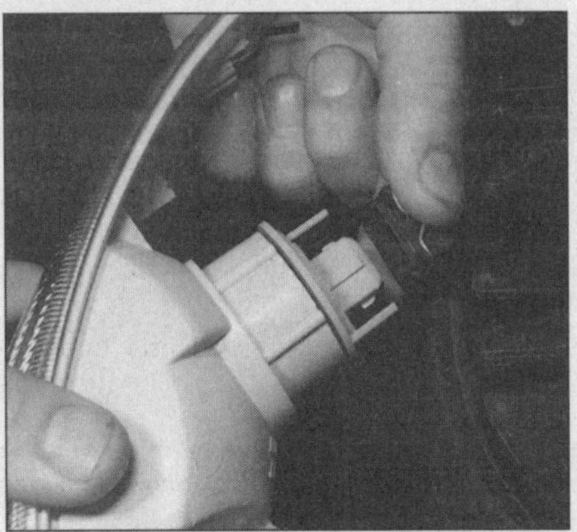

7.12 Disconnecting the wiring plug from the indicator bulbholder

12 Rotate the bulbholder counterclockwise, and withdraw it from the light unit. Alternatively, the wiring plug can be disconnected from the bulbholder, leaving the bulb in position **(see illustration)**. Remove the light unit.

Foglight (front)

13 Unscrew the cross-head screws securing the front foglight unit to the valance, and withdraw the light unit from the valance.

14 Pry open the plastic clips, and remove the rear cover from the light unit.

15 Release the spring clips and withdraw the bulb, then pull off the wiring connector. Remove the foglight unit.

Rear light cluster

Refer to illustrations 7.20a and 7.20b

16 With the trunk lid open, unhook the parcel net (if equipped) from the rear of the luggage compartment.

17 Remove the screws, release the clips, and remove the trim panel from the rear cross panel.

18 Remove the screws, and press the rear light trim cover from the guides (where applicable).

19 Disconnect the wiring multi-plug.

20 Unscrew the four mounting nuts, and withdraw the light unit from the outside of the vehicle **(see illustrations)**.

7.20a Rear light cluster mounting nuts

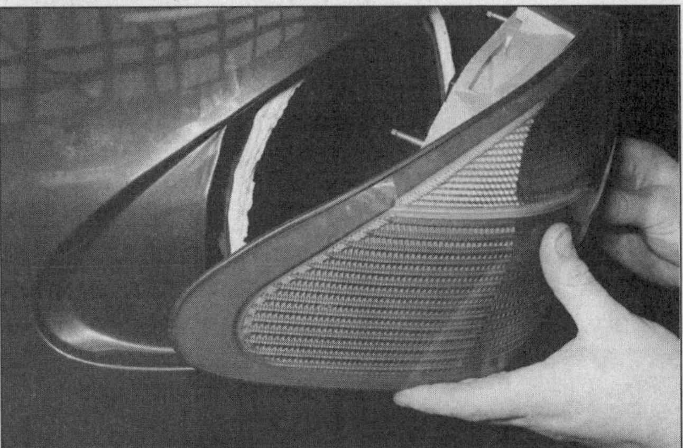

7.20b Removing the rear light cluster unit

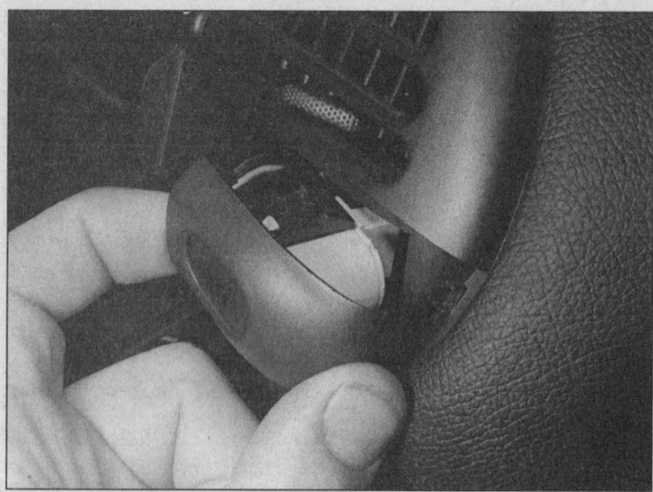

10.6 Removing the foglight warning indicator

10.7 Removing a switch blanking cover

Rear license plate light assembly

21 Remove both license plate lights as described in Section 5.

22 With the trunk lid open, remove the screws and withdraw the inner trim panel.

23 Unscrew the nuts, and remove the outer cover and license plate base.

24 Disconnect the multi-plug and remove the light assembly.

Installation

25 Installation of all the external light units is a reversal of the removal procedure, noting the following points:

a) *When installation the rubber seal on the headlight unit, note that it has a tapered seat.*

b) *If one or both headlights have been disturbed, have the beam alignment checked as described in the next Section.*

c) *When installation the rear light cluster, check the condition of the sealer on the body panel, and if necessary replace it.*

8 Headlight beam alignment - checking and adjustment

1 Accurate adjustment of the headlight beam is only possible using optical beam-setting equipment. This work should therefore be carried out by a dealer, or other service station with the necessary facilities.

2 Temporary adjustment can be made after replacement of a headlight bulb or unit, or as an emergency measure if the alignment is incorrect following accident damage. Turn the adjustment screws on the top of the headlight unit to make the adjustment.

3 Before making any adjustments to the settings, it is important that the tire pressures are correct, and that the vehicle is standing on level ground. Bounce the front of the vehicle a few times to settle the suspension. Ideally, somebody of average size should sit in the driver's seat during the adjustment, and the vehicle should have a full tank of fuel. Where a vehicle is installed with an electrical beam leveling system, set the switch to the "O" position before making any adjustments.

4 Whenever temporary adjustments are made, the settings must be checked and if necessary reset by a dealer or other qualified person as soon as possible.

9 Headlight leveling motor - removal and installation

Removal

1 Remove the headlight unit as described in Section 7, then remove the cover.

2 Disconnect the wiring multi-plug from the motor.

3 Rotate the motor upwards approximately 60-degrees, then pull it forwards slightly.

4 Disconnect the adjustment spindle by pressing the ball coupling to one side, away from the socket on the reflector.

5 Withdraw the motor from the headlight unit.

Installation

6 Installation is a reversal of the removal procedure, but make sure that the motor is turned down until it engages the stop.

10 Instrument cluster - removal and installation

Removal

Refer to illustrations 10.6, 10.7, 10.8a, 10.8b, 10.8c, 10.9 and 10.10

1 Disconnect the battery negative cable (refer to Chapter 5, Section 1).

2 If equipped, remove the clock as described in Section 13.

3 If equipped, remove the trip computer module as described in Section 18.

4 Remove the heated rear window switch as described in Section 4.

5 If equipped, remove the heated windshield switch.

6 If equipped, remove the display assembly warning indicator for the foglights **(see illustration)**.

7 Remove any blanking covers from the unused switch positions **(see illustration)**.

8 Pry out the blanking covers, then unscrew the retaining screws and remove the instrument cluster surround **(see illustrations)**.

9 Unscrew the mounting screws, and withdraw the instrument cluster a little way from the dash **(see illustration)**.

10 Disconnect the two multi-plugs from the rear of the instrument cluster **(see illustration)**.

11 Withdraw the instrument cluster from the dash, at the same time releasing the speedometer intermediate cable.

Installation

12 Installation is a reversal of the removal procedure.

10.8a With the blanking covers removed, unscrew the concealed screws . . .

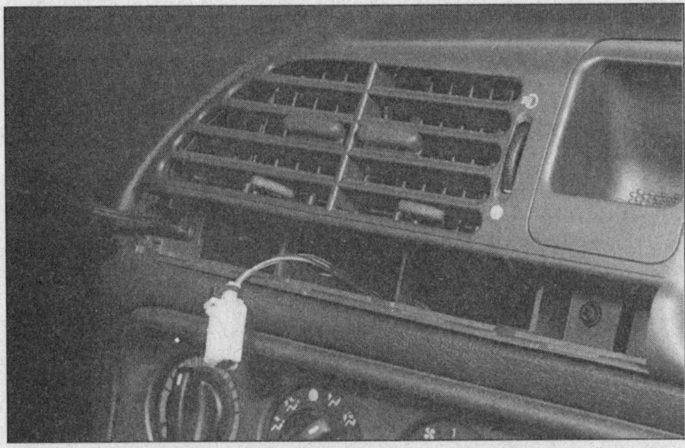
10.8b . . . and the remaining screws . . .

10.8c . . . and lift out the instrument cluster surround

10.9 Three of the instrument cluster mounting screws

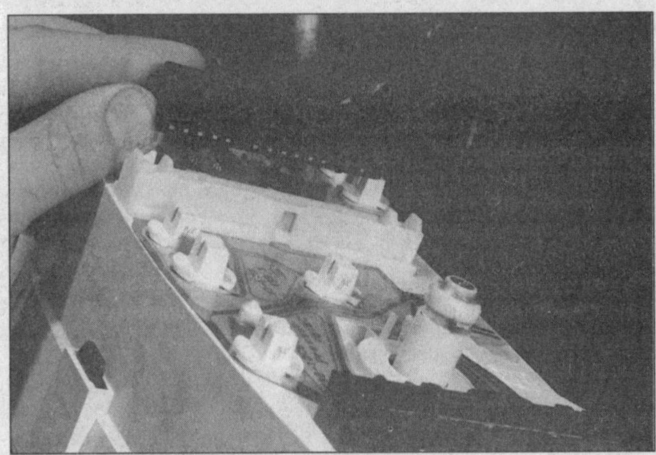
10.10 Disconnecting the multi-plugs from the rear of the instrument cluster

11 Instrument cluster components - removal and installation

Removal

Refer to illustrations 11.1 and 11.2

1 Remove the warning light and illumination bulbs by twisting them counterclockwise **(see illustration)**.

2 Carefully pry off the glass and bezel from the front of the instrument cluster, noting the positions of the retaining lugs **(see illustration)**.

3 Note the positions of the five diffusers, then remove them from the instrument cluster.

4 To remove the speedometer head, unscrew the three mounting screws and withdraw the head from the housing.

5 To remove the tachometer, unscrew the single screw and withdraw it from the housing.

6 Similarly remove the fuel gauge and temperature gauge by unscrewing the single screws.

7 Remove all the pin contacts.

8 Using a small punch, push in the multi-plug securing pins, and remove the multi-plugs.

9 Carefully lift the printed circuit from the location dowels on the housing, taking care not to damage it.

Installation

10 Installation is a reversal of the removal procedure.

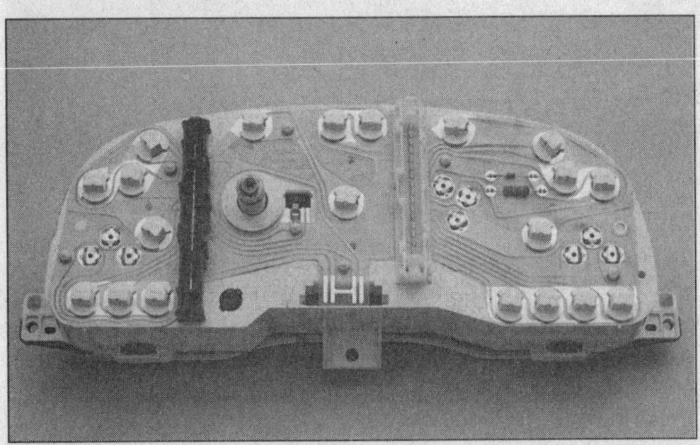
11.1 Rear view of the instrument cluster, showing bulbholders

11.2 Bezel retaining lug on the instrument cluster

12.7a Squeeze the collar . . .

12.7b . . . and disconnect the speedometer main cable from the intermediate cable

12.9a Unscrew the cable nut . . .

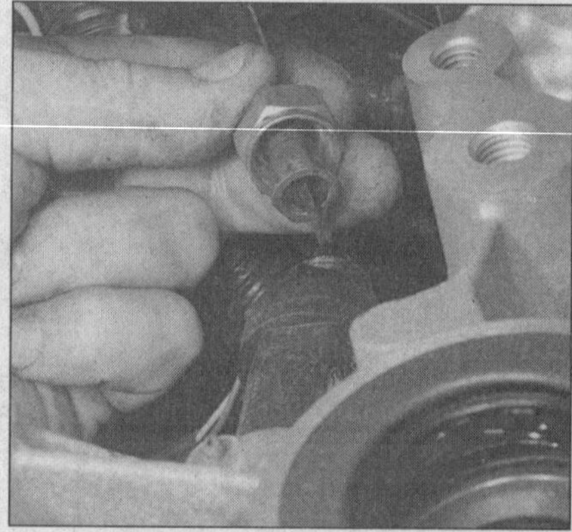

12.9b . . . and disconnect the speedometer cable from the vehicle speed sensor

12 Speedometer drive cable - removal and installation

Removal

Refer to illustrations 12.7a, 12.7b, 12.9a and 12.9b

1 Remove the windshield wiper arms as described in Section 15.

2 With the hood closed, release the grille panel upper edge from just in front of the windshield, by prying off the caps and unscrewing the upper retaining screws.

3 Open the hood, and support with the stay.

4 Pull off the sealing strip from the cross panel at the rear of the engine compartment.

5 Unscrew the lower screws, and remove the grille panel halves from in front of the windshield, withdrawing first one side and then the other.

6 Disconnect the battery negative cable (refer to Chapter 5, Section 1).

7 Reach in behind the firewall. Squeeze the collar on the upper end of the speedometer cable, where it is attached to the intermediate cable from the rear of the speedometer head. Disconnect the cable, and withdraw it from the firewall inner panel, together with the rubber grommet **(see illustrations)**.

8 Apply the parking brake, jack up the front of the vehicle and support it on jackstands.

9 Unscrew the nut and disconnect the speedometer cable from the vehicle speed sensor on the transaxle, then withdraw the cable from within the engine compartment. Use two spanners to loosen the nut - one to counterhold the sensor, and the other to unscrew the cable nut **(see illustrations)**.

Installation

10 Installation is a reversal of the removal procedure.

13 Clock - removal and installation

Removal

Refer to illustrations 13.2 and 13.3

1 Disconnect the battery negative cable (refer to Chapter 5, Section 1).

Contour models

2 Using a small screwdriver, pry the clock out of the dash **(see illustration)**. To prevent damage to the dash, place a cloth pad beneath the screwdriver.

Mystique models

3 Remove the three instrument cluster bezel screw covers and retaining screws. Remove the instrument cluster bezel.

4 Disconnect the multi-plug from the rear of the clock, and withdraw the clock **(see illustration)**.

Installation

5 Installation is a reversal of the removal procedure. Reset the clock on completion.

13.2 Prying the clock out of the dash (Contour)

13.4 Disconnecting the multi-plug from the rear of the clock

14.4 Horn and mounting bracket

15.3 Loosening the wiper arm retaining nut

15.5 Removing the wiper arm from the spindle

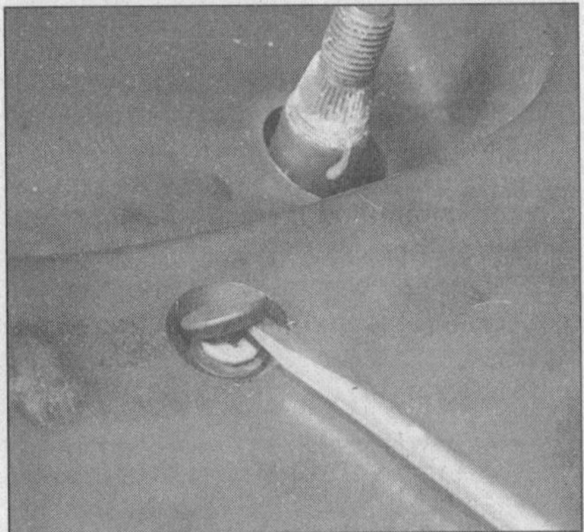
16.3a Pry off the cap . . .

14 Horn - removal and installation

Removal

Refer to illustration 14.4

1 Apply the parking brake, jack up the front of the vehicle and support it on jackstands.

2 Unscrew the bolts, and release the clips securing the radiator lower cover to the front of the vehicle.

3 Disconnect the wiring from the horn terminal.

4 Unscrew the mounting bolt and withdraw the horn with its mounting bracket from under the vehicle **(see illustration)**.

Installation

5 Installation is a reversal of the removal procedure.

15 Wiper arms - removal and installation

Removal

Refer to illustration 15.3 and 15.5

1 Disconnect the battery negative cable (refer to Chapter 5, Section 1). If the windshield wiper arms are to be removed, close the hood.

2 With the wiper(s) "parked" (i.e. in the normal at-rest position), mark the positions of the blade(s) on the screen using a wax crayon or strips of masking tape.

3 Lift up the plastic cap from the bottom of the wiper arm, and loosen the nut one or two turns **(see illustration)**.

4 Lift the wiper arm and release it from the taper on the spindle by moving it to one side.

5 Completely remove the nut, and withdraw the wiper arm from the spindle **(see illustration)**.

Installation

6 Installation is a reversal of the removal procedure. Make sure that the arm is installed in the previously-noted position.

16 Windshield wiper motor and linkage - removal and installation

Removal

Refer to illustrations 16.3a, 16.3b, 16.5, 16.6a, 16.6b, 16.7, 16.9 and 16.10

1 Disconnect the battery negative cable (refer to Chapter 5, Section 1).

2 Remove the wiper arms as described in Section 15.

3 With the hood closed, release the grille panel upper edge from just in front of the windshield by prying off the caps and unscrewing the upper retaining screws **(see illustrations)**.

4 Open the hood and support it with the stay.

5 Pull off the hood sealing strip from the cross panel at the rear of the engine compartment **(see illustration)**.

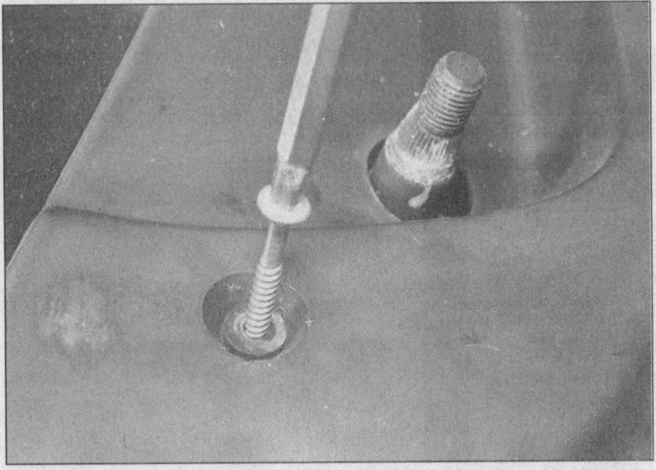
16.3b . . . and remove the upper retaining screws

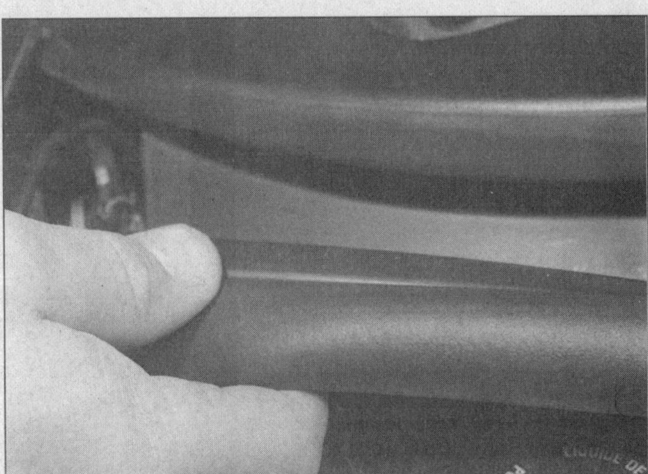
16.5 Removing the hood sealing strip

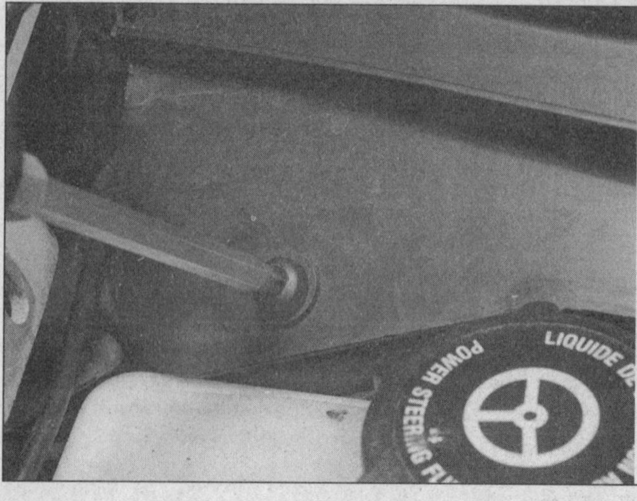

16.6a Unscrew the lower screws . . .

6 Unscrew the lower screws, and remove the grille panel halves from in front of the windshield, withdrawing one side then the other side **(see illustrations)**.
7 Unscrew the mounting bolts securing the wiper motor and linkage to the firewall **(see illustration)**.
8 Disconnect the wiper motor multi-plug.
9 Withdraw the wiper motor, complete with the linkage, from the firewall **(see illustration)**.
10 Mark the position of the motor arm on the mounting plate, then unscrew the center nut **(see illustration)**.
11 Unscrew the motor mounting bolts and separate the motor from the linkage assembly.

Installation

12 Installation is a reversal of the removal procedure. There are two tightening torques for the motor mounting bolts - the lower one for bolts that are being re-inserted into an old motor and the higher ones for bolts that are being inserted into a new motor. Make sure that the wiper motor is in its "parked" position before installing the motor arm, and check that the wiper linkage is in line with the motor arm.

17 Trip computer module - removal and installation

Removal

1 Disconnect the battery negative cable (refer to Chapter 5, Section 1).
2 Using a small screwdriver, pry the trip computer module out of the dash. To prevent damage to the dash, place a cloth pad beneath the screwdriver.
3 Disconnect the multi-plug from the rear of the trip computer module and withdraw the unit.

16.6b . . . and remove the grille panel from in front of the windshield

16.7 Wiper motor mounting bolt locations

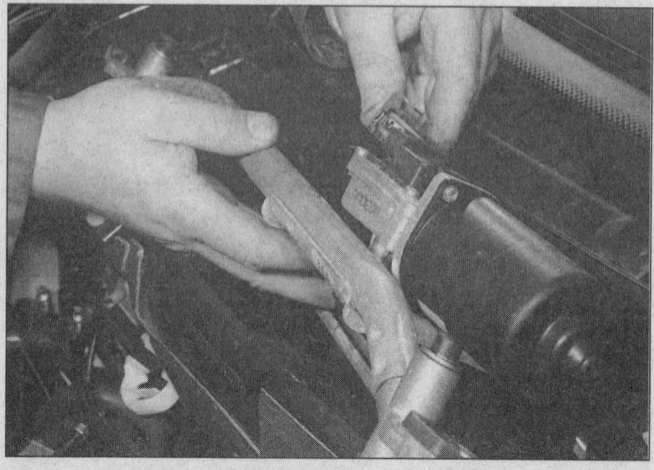
16.9 Removing the wiper motor and linkage

16.10 Wiper motor arm and mounting plate located on the motor

19.3a Disconnecting a movement sensor multi-plug

19.3b Removing a movement sensor

4 If necessary, the bulb can be removed by twisting it counterclockwise.

Installation

5 Installation is a reversal of the removal procedure.

18 Auxiliary warning system - general information and component replacement

1 Some models are equipped with an auxiliary warning system, which monitors brake lights, sidelights, headlight dimmer and tail lights, external temperature, and door/tailgate/trunk lid opening. An engine oil level warning light on the instrument cluster is also part of the system.

2 The auxiliary warning system module and graphic warning display are combined into one unit.

Component replacement

3 The following paragraphs describe brief removal procedures for the auxiliary warning system components. Disconnect the battery cable lead before commencing work (refer to Chapter 5, Section 1). Installation procedures are a reversal of removal.

Display warning bulb

4 Remove the control assembly.

5 Pry off the cover, and pull out the relevant bulb and bulbholder.

Low air temperature warning sender unit

6 Remove the front bumper.

7 Unclip the sender unit and disconnect the multi-plug.

Engine oil level sensor

8 Apply the parking brake, jack up the front of the vehicle and support it on jackstands.

9 Place a container beneath the oil level sensor, to catch any spilled oil.

10 Unscrew the screws and remove the cover from the sensor.

11 Disconnect the multi-plug.

12 Unscrew and remove the sensor, and remove the seal.

Door ajar sensor

13 Remove the door lock as described in Chapter 11, Section 14.

14 Unclip the sensor and disconnect the multi-plug.

Low coolant warning switch

15 Refer to Chapter 3, Section 6.

Low washer fluid switch

16 Disconnect the multi-plug from the washer fluid reservoir.

17 Drain or siphon out the fluid from the reservoir.

18 Using a screwdriver, lever out the switch from the reservoir.

Service indicator reset switch

19 Remove the glove compartment lid as described in Chapter 11, Section 32.

20 Carefully lever out the switch using a small screwdriver.

21 Remove the rear cover and disconnect the wiring.

Control assembly

22 Remove the instrument cluster surround, referring to Section 10.

23 Unscrew the mounting screws, disconnect the multi-plugs and remove the assembly.

Bulb failure module

24 Remove the lower dash panel from under the steering wheel.

25 Unclip the bulb failure module and disconnect the multi-plug.

19 Anti-theft alarm system - general information

Refer to illustrations 19.3a, 19.3b and 19.7

1 Some models are equipped with an anti-theft alarm system, incorporating movement sensors and an ignition immobilize. The system is activated when the vehicle is locked.

2 The system includes a start inhibitor circuit, which makes it impossible to start the engine with the system armed.

3 The movement sensors consist of two ultrasonic units, located in the "B" pillars, incorporating transmitters and receivers **(see illustrations)**. The receivers check that the echo frequency matches the original frequency. If there is any significant difference, the system triggers the alarm.

4 The system module is located on a bracket beneath the right-hand side of the dash. The set and reset switches are located in a housing by the lock cylinder holder in the doors or trunk lid.

5 To allow temporary opening of the trunk lid, an inhibit switch is attached to the lock cylinder. This suppresses the alarm system until the trunk lid is closed again.

6 Where remote central locking is installed, an infra-red receiver is located on the exterior door handle. Note that excessive heat can destroy this receiver; therefore, it should be covered with aluminum tape if (for instance) a paint-drying heat process is to be used.

7 The alarm system is installed with its own horn. It is located on the left-hand side of the luggage compartment **(see illustration)**.

8 The alarm system incorporates a self-test function, which can be activated by operating the hood switch or one of the lock position switches eight times within 10 seconds. During the check, the horn or buzzer issues acoustic signals which should occur every time a door, hood or trunk lid is opened. If the doors are double-locked, the signal will occur when something is moved

within the passenger compartment. A more comprehensive test can be made using the manufacturers diagnostic tester.
9 The door lock switches associated with the alarm system are located behind the door trim panels.

20 Cruise control system - general information

1 Cruise control is available as an option on some models.
2 The cruise control system is active at road speeds between 25 mph and 125 mph.
3 The system comprises an electronic speed control unit with integral actuator and switches mounted in the engine compartment with a control cable connected to the throttle valve actuator, driver-operated switches, brake and clutch pedal switches, an indicator light, and a road speed sensor.
4 The driver-operated switches are mounted on the steering wheel, and allow the driver to control the various functions.
5 The vehicle speed sensor uses the speedometer cable drive pinion to generate pulses which are fed to the speed control unit.
6 The brake light switch, brake pedal switch and (when applicable) clutch pedal switch are used to disable the cruise control system. The brake light switch is activated when the brake pedal is applied gently, and the brake pedal switch is activated when the brake pedal is applied forcibly.
7 An indicator light on the instrument panel is illuminated when the system is in operation.
8 The following paragraphs describe brief removal procedures for the cruise control system components. The battery negative cable should be disconnected before commencing work (refer to Chapter 5, Section 1). Installation is a reversal of removal.

Speed control switch

9 Remove the steering column upper and lower shrouds, with reference to Chapter 10.
10 Remove the air bag module as described in Section 29.
11 Disconnect the multi-plugs, then unscrew the screws and remove the switch.

Disable switches

12 Remove the lower dash panel from under the steering column.
13 Disconnect the multi-plugs from the clutch switch, brake pedal switch and brake light switch.
14 To remove the clutch and brake pedal switches, twist them counterclockwise. To remove the brake light switch, twist it clockwise.
15 Installation is the reverse of removal. To ensure correct operation of the brake pedal switches, reset the switch by fully extending its plunger. Depress the pedal until the distance between it and the mounting bracket is approximately one-inch. Hold the pedal in this position, clip the switch securely into position and gently raise the pedal to the at-rest position. This will automatically set the position of the switch.

19.7 Alarm system horn location on Hatchback and Saloon models

Speed control actuator

16 Remove the air cleaner as described in Chapter 4.
17 Disconnect the actuator cable from the throttle linkage on the throttle body, by releasing the inner cable end attachment from the segment and unclipping the outer cable from the bracket.
18 Unscrew the actuator mounting bolt, then slide the actuator out of the mounting pin holes.
19 Disconnect the multi-plug and remove the assembly.
20 Depress the actuating cable cap locking arm, and remove the cap by turning it counterclockwise.
21 Gently raise the cable retaining lug by a maximum of 0.5 mm, and push the cable end out of the slot in the pulley.
22 When installation, make sure that the cable end locks into the slot in the pulley.
23 To locate the cable cap onto the actuator pulley, keep the cable taut and in the pulley groove, and pull the throttle linkage end of the cable to draw the cable cap onto the pulley.
24 To install the cable cap, keep the cable taut and the pulley still, then install the cable cap tabs into the actuator slots; turn the cap clockwise until the locking arm locates on the locking stop. **Note:** *Incorrect assembly of the cable onto the pulley may result in a high idle speed. Check that the throttle lever is in its idle position after installation the actuator.*

21 Windshield washer system components - removal and installation

Removal

Washer reservoir and pump

Refer to illustrations 21.2, 21.3 and 21.6

1 Unscrew the bolts, and release the clips to remove the radiator lower cover.
2 Unscrew the mounting bolts, and pull the reservoir forwards slightly **(see illustration)**. For better access, it may be necessary to remove the front bumper.
3 Disconnect the multi-plugs for the windshield washer pump and fluid level sensor **(see illustration)**.
4 Disconnect the hoses from the windshield washer pump and (where applicable) from the headlight washer pump. Anticipate some loss of fluid by placing a container beneath the reservoir.
5 Withdraw the reservoir from the vehicle.
6 Pull the level sensor, the windshield washer pump, and (where applicable) the headlight washer pump, from the reservoir **(see illustration)**.
7 Remove the rubber seals.

Washer nozzle

8 With the hood supported in its open position, carefully disconnect the washer tube from the bottom of the nozzle.
9 Using a screwdriver and working from under the hood, carefully pry out the nozzle. Where necessary, disconnect the wiring for the nozzle heater.

Installation

10 Installation is a reversal of the removal procedure. In the case of the washer nozzles, press them in until they are fully engaged. The rear window washer nozzle must rest against the rubber seal.

22 Radio/cassette player - coding, removal and installation

Note: *Special tools are required to remove the radio.*

Coding

1 If a factory "Keycode" unit is installed, and the unit and/or the battery is disconnected, the unit will not function again on reconnection until the correct security code is entered. Details of this procedure are given in the "Audio Systems Operating Guide" supplied with the vehicle when new, with the

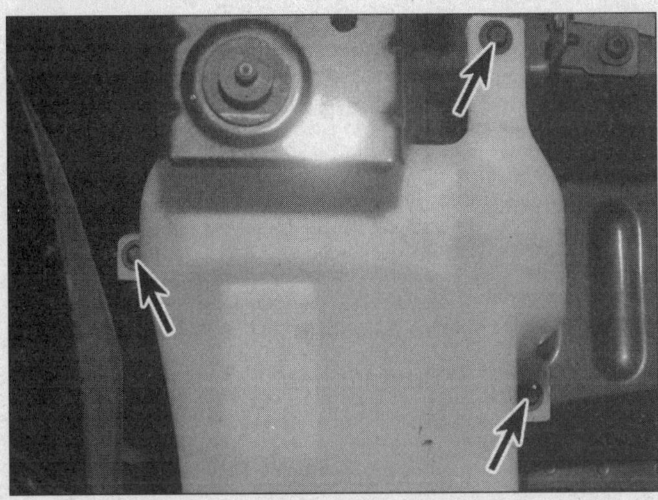

21.2 Washer reservoir mounting bolts

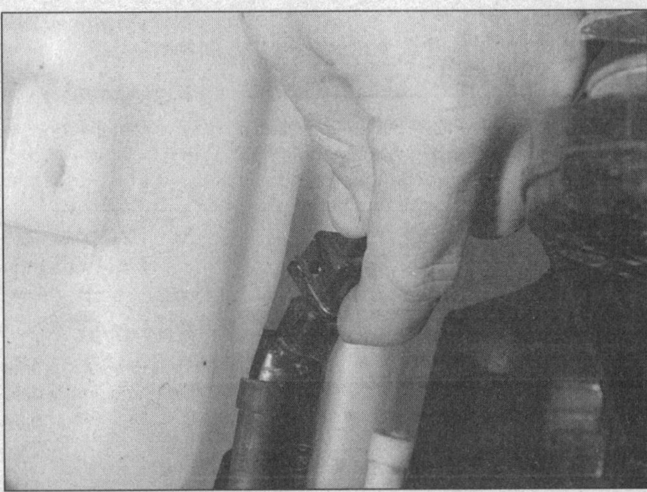

21.3 Disconnecting the washer pump and level sensor multi-plugs

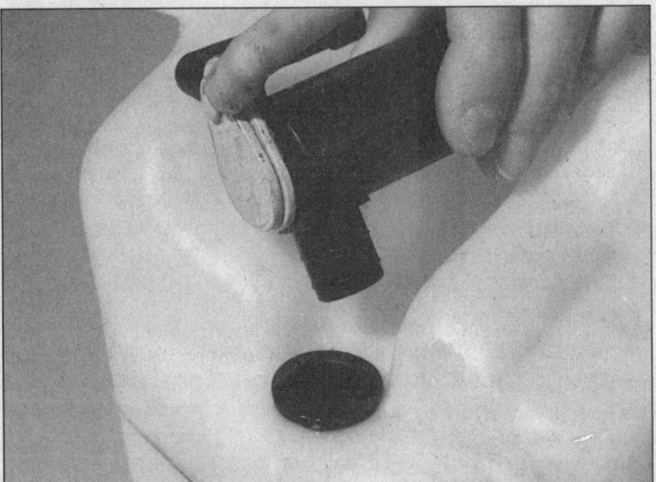

21.6 Pulling the windshield washer pump from the reservoir

22.6 Using the special U-shaped rods to remove the radio

code itself being given in a "Radio Passport" and/or a "Keycode Label" at the same time.

2 For obvious security reasons, the re-coding procedure is not given in this manual - if you do not have the code or details of the correct procedure, but can supply proof of ownership and a legitimate reason for wanting this information, the vehicle's selling dealer may be able to help.

3 Note that these units will allow only ten attempts at entering the code - any further attempts will render the unit permanently inoperative until it has been reprogrammed by the dealer themselves. At first, three consecutive attempts are allowed; if all three are incorrect, a 30-minute delay is required before another attempt can be made. Each of any subsequent attempts (up to the maximum of ten) can be made only after a similar delay.

Removal

Refer to illustration 22.6

4 Disconnect the battery negative cable.

5 If equipped, pry the cover/surround from the front of the radio/cassette player. Note that the cover is not installed in all models.

6 In order to release the radio retaining clips, two U-shaped rods must be inserted into the special holes on each side of the radio **(see illustration)**. If possible, it is preferable to obtain purpose-made rods from an audio specialist, as these have cut-outs which snap firmly into the clips so that the radio can be pulled out. Pull the unit squarely from its aperture, or it may jam. If the unit proves difficult to withdraw, remove the cassette tray (or where applicable, the CD player) from beneath the unit, then reach through the aperture and ease it out from behind.

7 With the radio partly withdrawn, disconnect the feed, ground, aerial and speaker leads. Where applicable, also detach and remove the plastic support bracket from the rear of the unit.

Installation

8 Installation is a reversal of removal. With the leads reconnected to the rear of the unit, press it into position until the retaining clips are felt to engage. Reactivate the unit by entering the correct code in accordance with the maker's instructions.

23 Radio/cassette player power amplifier - removal and installation

Removal

1 Disconnect the battery negative cable. See Chapter 5, Section 1.

2 Unscrew the screws and remove the lower dash panel.

3 The radio/cassette player power amplifier is located beneath the dash.

4 Unscrew the cross-head screws, disconnect the wiring and remove the amplifier.

Installation

5 Installation is a reversal of the removal procedure.

24 Compact disc player - removal and installation

1 A compact disc (CD) player is available as an optional extra on most models. On some models, an autochanger version is available, which can hold a number of discs at a time.

Removal

2 The battery negative cable should be disconnected before commencing work.

CD player or autochanger control unit

3 The procedure is identical to that for the radio/cassette player described in Section 22.

CD player autochanger

4 The CD player autochanger unit is mounted on the right-hand side of the luggage compartment **(see illustration)**. The wiring harness passes up the "C" pillar, across to the left-hand side "A" pillar, then to the center console area.
5 Remove the trim cover from the autochanger unit.
6 Unscrew the mounting screws, and remove the autochanger unit from its mounting bracket.
7 Disconnect the multi-plug and remove the unit from inside the vehicle.

Installation

8 Installation is a reversal of the removal procedure.

25 Speakers - removal and installation

Removal

1 Remove the door trim panel as described in Chapter 11.
2 Unscrew the cross-head screws, and withdraw the speaker from the door inner panel.
3 Disconnect the wiring and remove the speaker.

Installation

4 Installation is a reversal of the removal procedure.

26 Radio aerial - removal and installation

Removal

1 Pry out the trim cover from the headlining immediately below the base of the aerial.
2 Unscrew the cross-head screw from the base of the aerial, and remove the aerial mast.

Installation

3 Installation is a reversal of the removal procedure.

27 Air bag unit (driver's side) - removal and installation

Warning: *Handle the air bag unit with extreme care, as a precaution against personal injury, and always hold it with the cover facing away from the body. If in doubt concerning any proposed work involving the air bag unit or its control circuitry, consult a dealer or other qualified specialist.*

Removal

Refer to illustrations 27.3 and 27.4

1 Disconnect the battery negative cable (refer to Chapter 5, Section 1). **Warning:** *Before proceeding, wait a minimum of 15 minutes, as a precaution against accidental firing of the air bag unit. This period ensures that any stored energy in the back-up capacitor is dissipated.*
2 Rotate the steering wheel so that one of the mounting bolt holes is visible above the steering column upper shroud.
3 Unscrew and remove the first mounting bolt, then turn the steering wheel as necessary and remove the remaining mounting bolts **(see illustration)**.
4 Carefully withdraw the air bag unit from the steering wheel far enough to disconnect the wiring multi-plug, then remove it from inside the vehicle **(see illustration)**. **Warning:** *Stand the unit with the cover pointed up and do not expose it to heat sources in excess of 212-degrees F. Do not attempt to open or repair the air bag unit, or apply any electrical current to it. Do not use any air bag unit which is visibly damaged or which has been tampered with.*

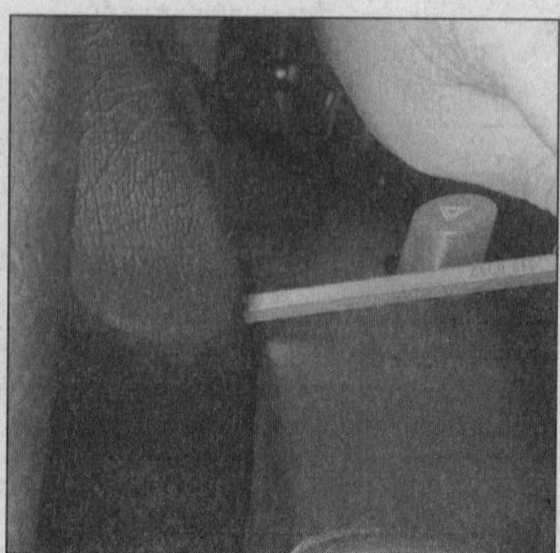

27.3 Unscrewing an air bag mounting bolt

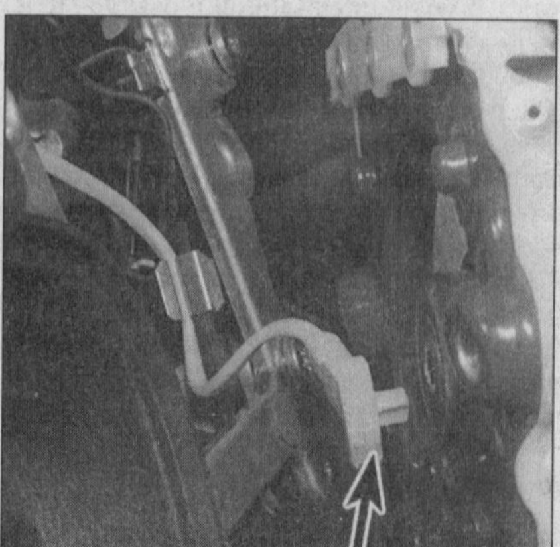

27.4 Disconnecting the air bag wiring multi-plug

Installation

5 Installation is a reversal of the removal procedure.

28 Air bag control module - removal and installation

Removal

1 Disconnect the battery negative cable (refer to Chapter 5, Section 1). **Warning:** *Before proceeding, wait a minimum of 15 minutes, as a precaution against accidental firing of the air bag unit. This period ensures that any stored energy in the back-up capacitor is dissipated.*
2 Remove the dash panel as described in Chapter 11.
3 Disconnect the multi-plug from the module, by pressing the locking tab upwards and swiveling the retaining strap.
4 Unscrew the mounting bolts and remove the module from the vehicle.

Installation

5 Installation is a reversal of the removal procedure.

29 Air bag clock spring - removal and installation

Removal

1 Remove the air bag unit as described in Section 28.
2 Disconnect the horn switch multi-plug.
3 If installed, disconnect the multi-plugs for the cruise control.
4 Remove the steering wheel and shrouds.
5 Using a small screwdriver, release the retaining tabs, then remove the clock spring from the steering column.

Installation

6 Installation is a reversal of the removal procedure, but make sure that the steering wheel is centralized. The clock spring must be installed in its central position, with the special alignment marks aligned and the TOP mark uppermost. To check for this position, turn the clock spring housing counterclockwise until it is tight, then turn in the opposite direction by two-and-three-quarter turns.

KEY TO SYMBOLS

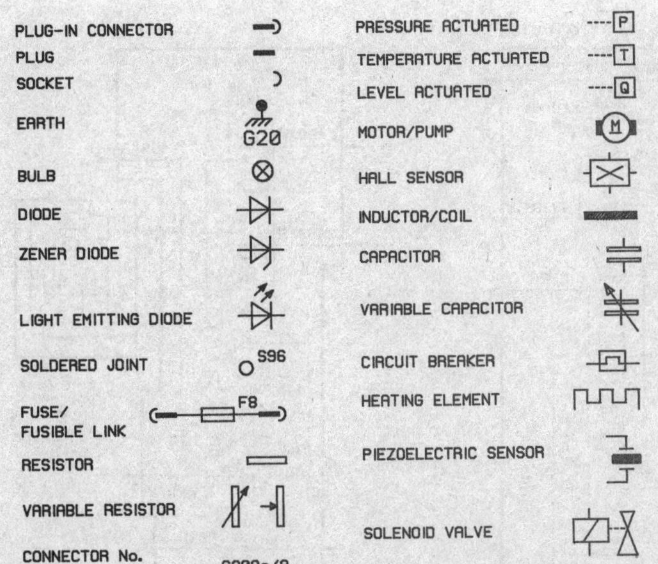

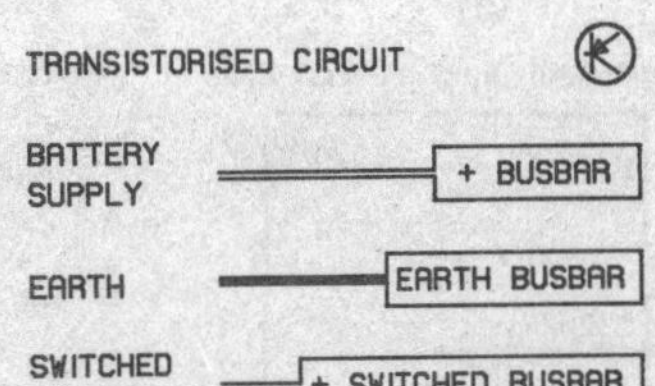

NOTES:

1. All diagrams are divided into numbered circuits depending on function e.g. Diagram 11 : Exterior lighting.
2. Items are arranged in relation to a plan view of the vehicle.
3. Wires may interconnect between diagrams and are located by using a grid reference e.g. 2/A1 denotes a position on diagram 2 grid location A1.
4. Complex items appear on the diagrams in sections and are shown in full on the internal connections page (see below).
5. Brackets show how the circuit may be connected in more than one way.
6. Items with a broken border have other connections shown elsewhere.
7. Not all items are fitted to all models.

INTERNAL CONNECTION DETAILS

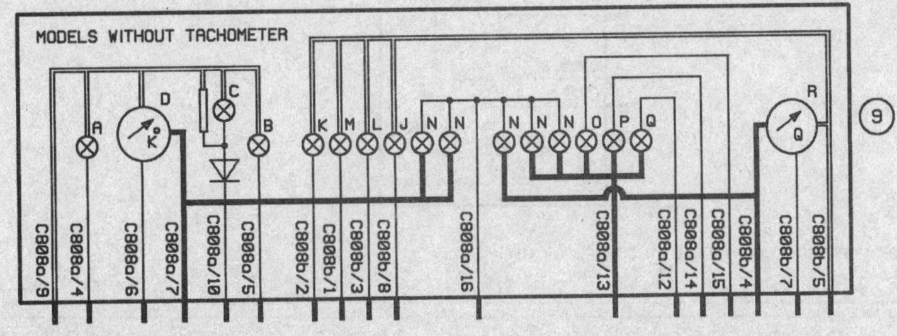

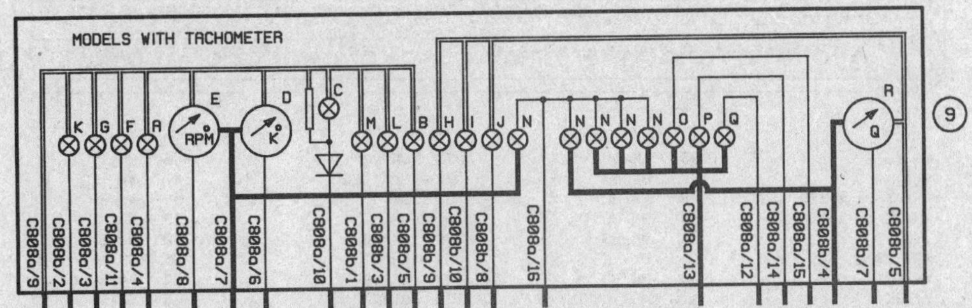

KEY TO INSTRUMENT CLUSTER (ITEM 9)

A = Traction Control Warning Light
B = Airbag Warning Light
C = No Charge Warning Light
D = Temperature Gauge
E = Tachometer
F = Cruse Control Warning Light
G = Low Oil Level Warning Light
H = Overdrive Off Warning Light
I = Sport Warning Light
J = Adaptive Damping Warning Light
K = Anti-lock Braking Warning Light
L = Low Brake Fluid Level/ Handbrake-on Warning Light
M = Low Oil Pressure Warning Light
N = Instrument Illumination
O = Direction Indicator Warning Light LH
P = Direction Indicator Warning Light RH
Q = High Beam Warning Light
R = Fuel Gauge

H24540
T.M.MARKE

Notes, internal connection details and key to symbols

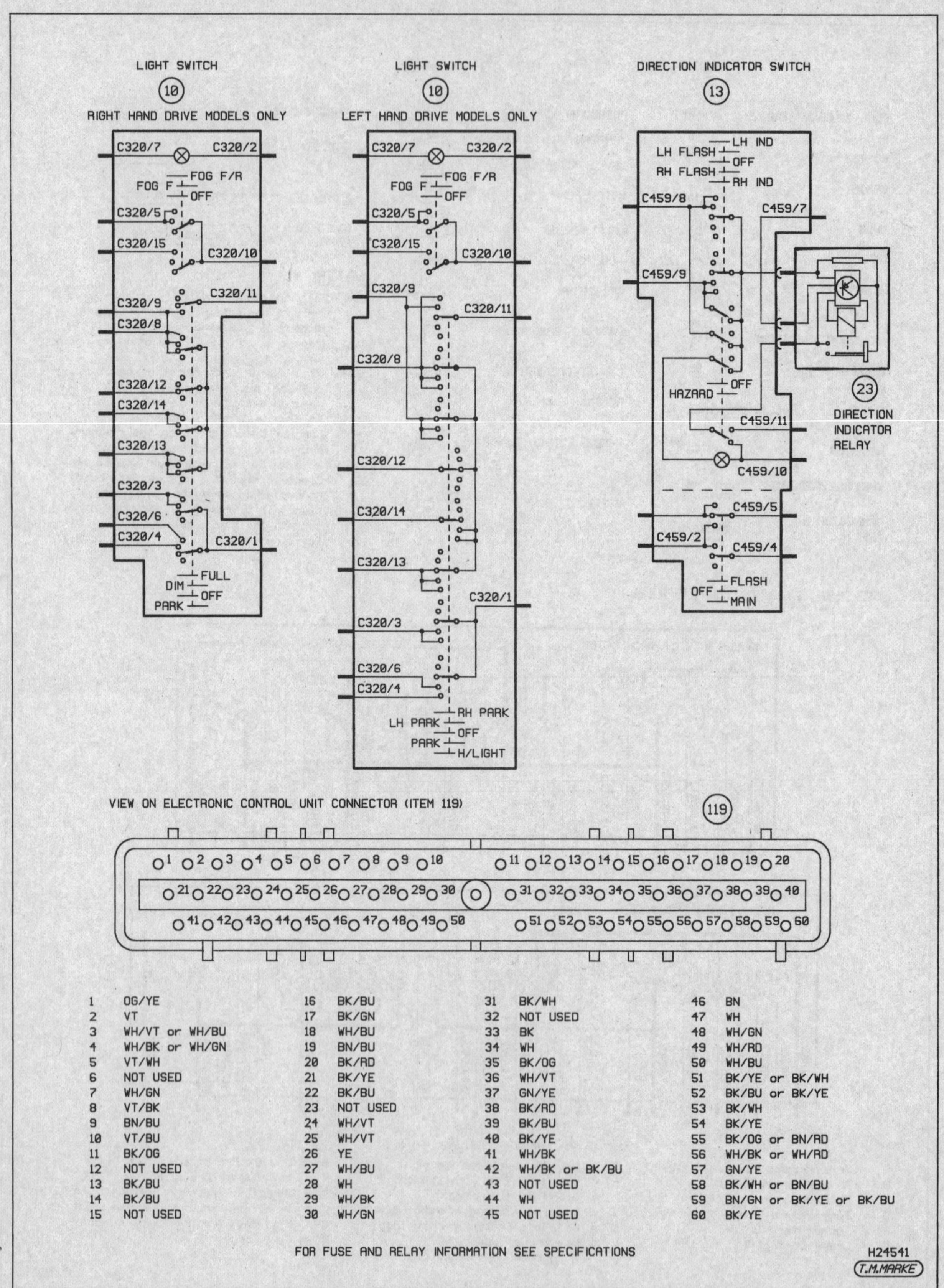

Pin	Colour	Pin	Colour	Pin	Colour	Pin	Colour
1	OG/YE	16	BK/BU	31	BK/WH	46	BN
2	VT	17	BK/GN	32	NOT USED	47	WH
3	WH/VT or WH/BU	18	WH/BU	33	BK	48	WH/GN
4	WH/BK or WH/GN	19	BN/BU	34	WH	49	WH/RD
5	VT/WH	20	BK/RD	35	BK/OG	50	WH/BU
6	NOT USED	21	BK/YE	36	WH/VT	51	BK/YE or BK/WH
7	WH/GN	22	BK/BU	37	GN/YE	52	BK/BU or BK/YE
8	VT/BK	23	NOT USED	38	BK/RD	53	BK/WH
9	BN/BU	24	WH/VT	39	BK/BU	54	BK/YE
10	VT/BU	25	WH/VT	40	BK/YE	55	BK/OG or BN/RD
11	BK/OG	26	YE	41	WH/BK	56	WH/BK or WH/RD
12	NOT USED	27	WH/BU	42	WH/BK or BK/BU	57	GN/YE
13	BK/BU	28	WH	43	NOT USED	58	BK/WH or BN/BU
14	BK/BU	29	WH/BK	44	WH	59	BN/GN or BK/YE or BK/BU
15	NOT USED	30	WH/GN	45	NOT USED	60	BK/YE

Internal connection details continued

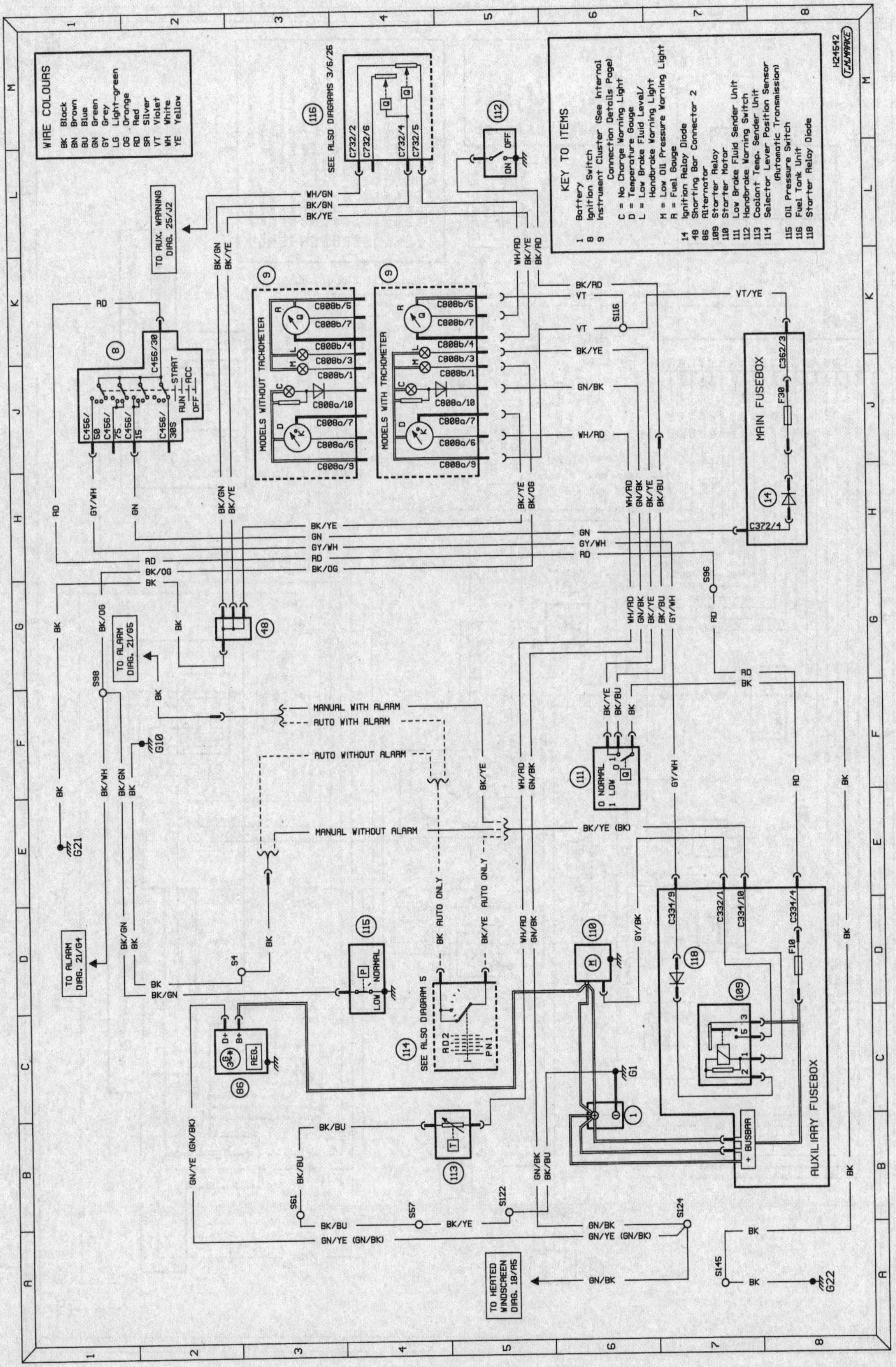

WIRE COLOURS

BK	Black
BN	Brown
BU	Blue
GN	Green
GY	Grey
LG	Light-green
OG	Orange
RD	Red
SR	Silver
VT	Violet
WH	White
YE	Yellow

KEY TO ITEMS

1 Battery
8 Ignition Switch
9 Instrument Cluster (See Internal Connection Details Page)
C = No Charge Warning Light
D = Temperature Gauge
L = Low Brake Fluid Level/ Handbrake Warning Light
M = Low Oil Pressure Warning Light
R = Fuel Gauge
14 Ignition Relay Diode
48 Shorting Bar Connector 2
86 Alternator
109 Starter Relay
110 Starter Motor
111 Low Brake Fluid Sender Unit
112 Handbrake Warning Switch
113 Coolant Temp. Sender Unit
114 Selector Lever Position Sensor (Automatic Transmission)
115 Oil Pressure Switch
116 Fuel Tank Unit
118 Starter Relay Diode

H24542

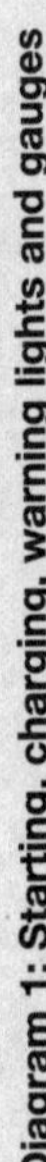
Diagram 1: Starting, charging, warning lights and gauges

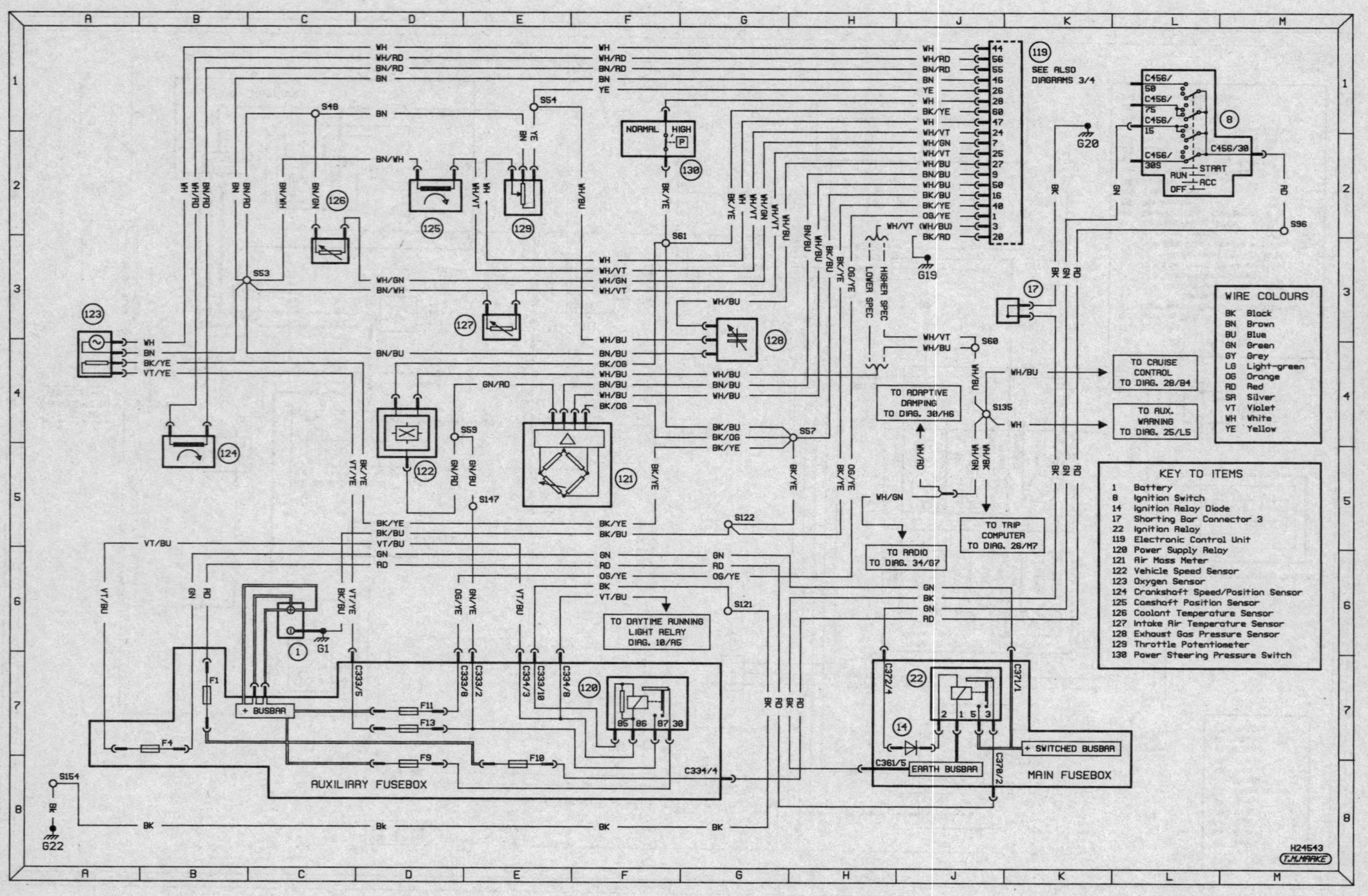

Diagram 2: Engine management – sensor inputs (manual transmission models)

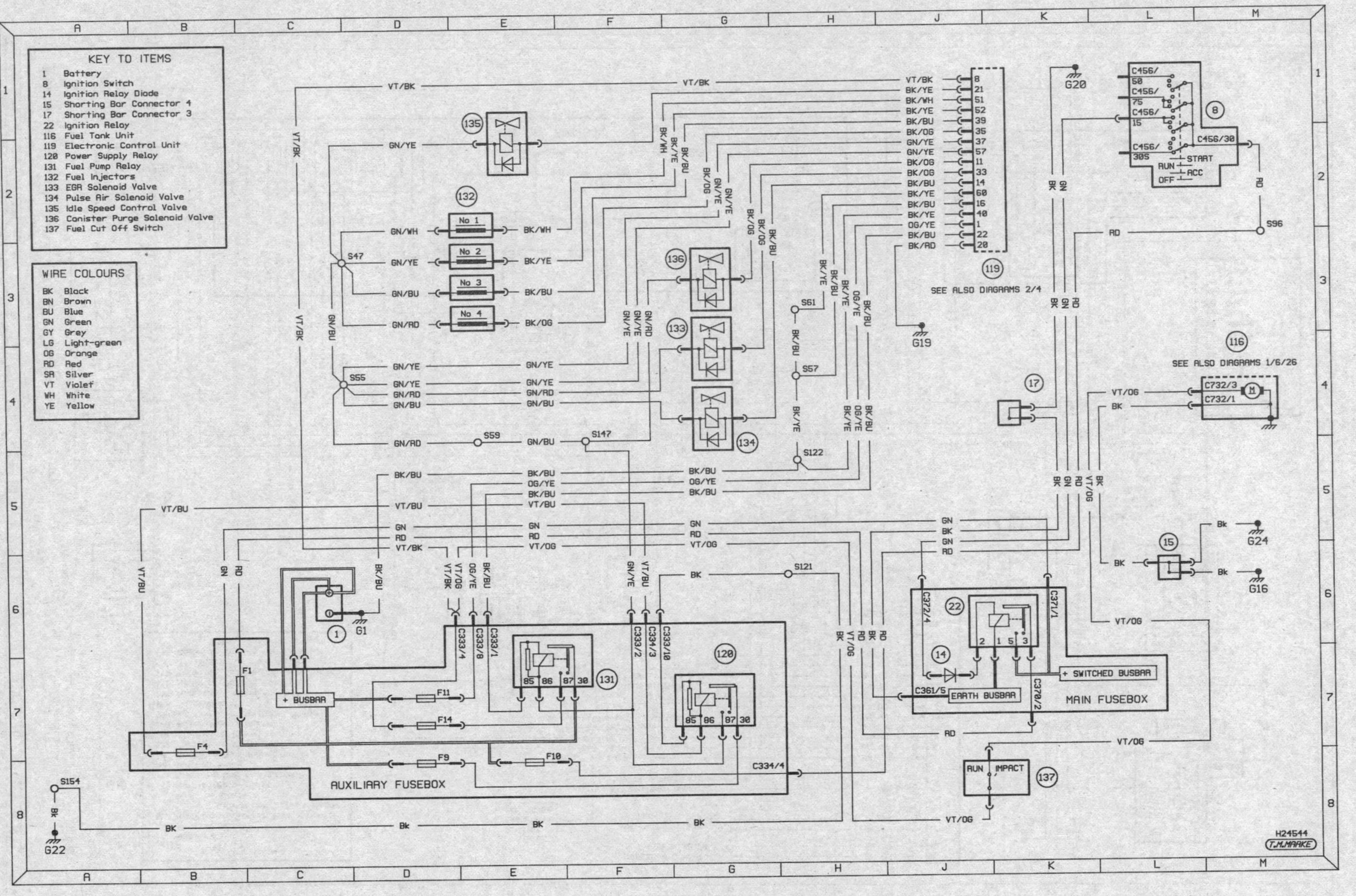

Diagram 3: Engine management – solenoid outputs and fuel pump (manual transmission models)

KEY TO ITEMS
1 Battery
8 Ignition Switch
9 Instrument Cluster (See Internal Connection Details Page)
E = Tachometer
14 Ignition Relay Diode
17 Shorting Bar Connector 3
22 Ignition Relay
48 Shorting Bar Connector 2
108 Dual Pressure Switch
119 Electronic Control Unit
120 Power Supply Relay
138 Ignition Coil And Spark Plugs
139 Suppressor
140 Radiator Cooling Fan Motor
141 Radiator Cooling Fan Relay
142 Radiator Cooling Fan High Speed Relay (Air Conditioning Only)
143 Radiator Cooling Fan Resistor (Air Conditioning Only)
WIRE COLOURS
BK Black
BN Brown
BU Blue
GN Green
GY Grey
LG Light-green
OG Orange
RD Red
SR Silver
VT Violet
WH White
YE Yellow
NOTE
DASHED LINES DENOTE WIRING VARIATION FOR MODELS WITH AIR CONDITIONING
H24545
MAIN FUSEBOX
AUXILIARY FUSEBOX
DIAGNOSIS CONNECTOR (FOR FDS2000)
SELF-TEST CONNECTOR (FOR STAR TESTER)
SERVICE CONNECTOR (FOR OCTANE ADJUST)
MODELS WITH TACHOMETER
TO IGNITION MODULE DIAG. 6/L3
TO AIR CONDITIONING DIAG. 19/C8
TO TRIP COMPUTER DIAG. 26/L6
TO ADAPTIVE DAMPING DIAG. 30/H7
SEE ALSO DIAGRAMS 2/3
SEE ALSO DIAGRAMS 7/19
SUPPRESSOR
WITH AIR COND.
WITHOUT AIR COND.
HIGH SPEC
LOW SPEC

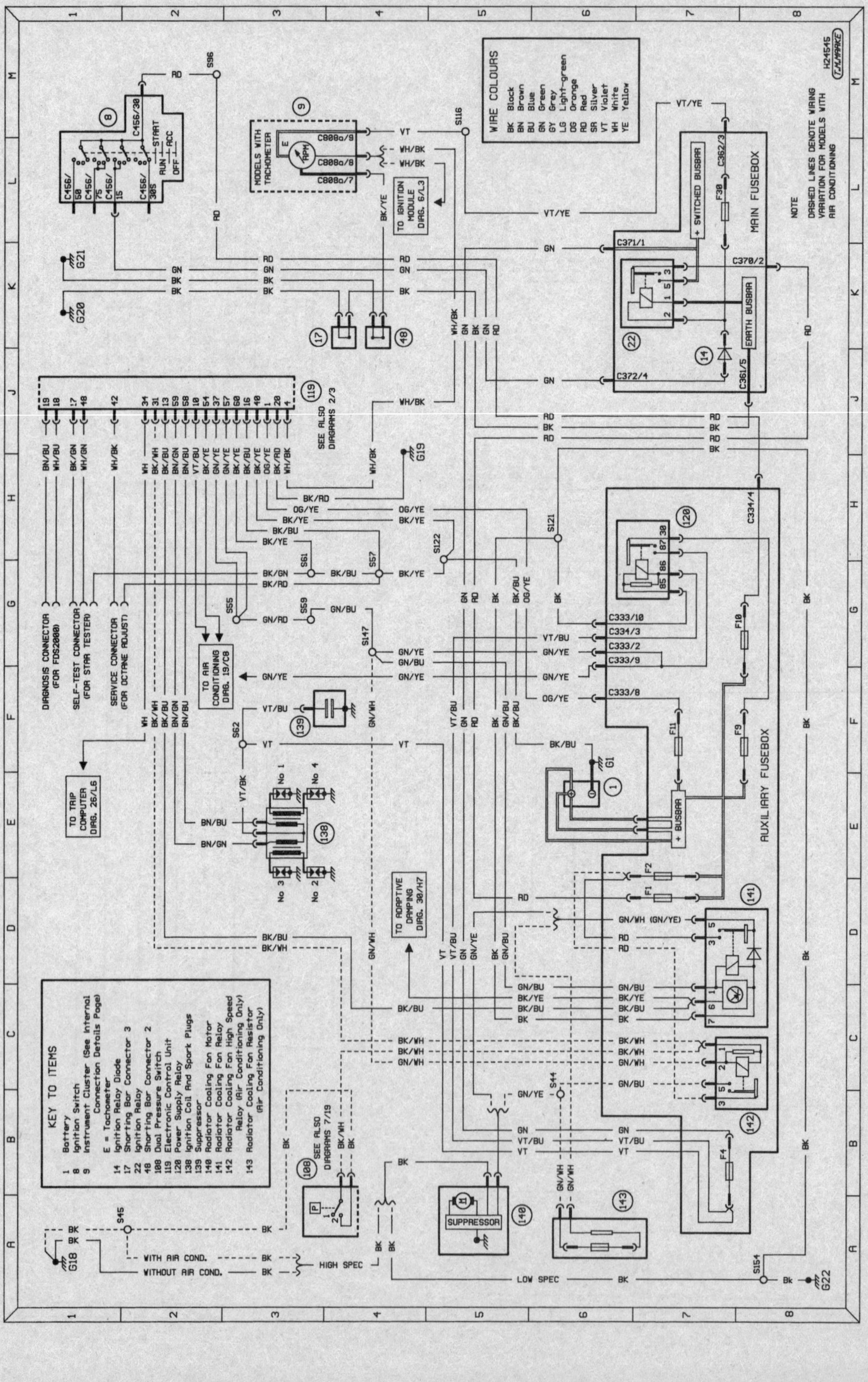

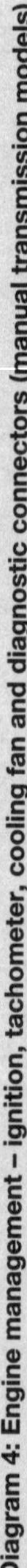

Diagram 4: Engine management – ignition, tachometer, cooling fan and diagnostic connectors (manual transmission models)

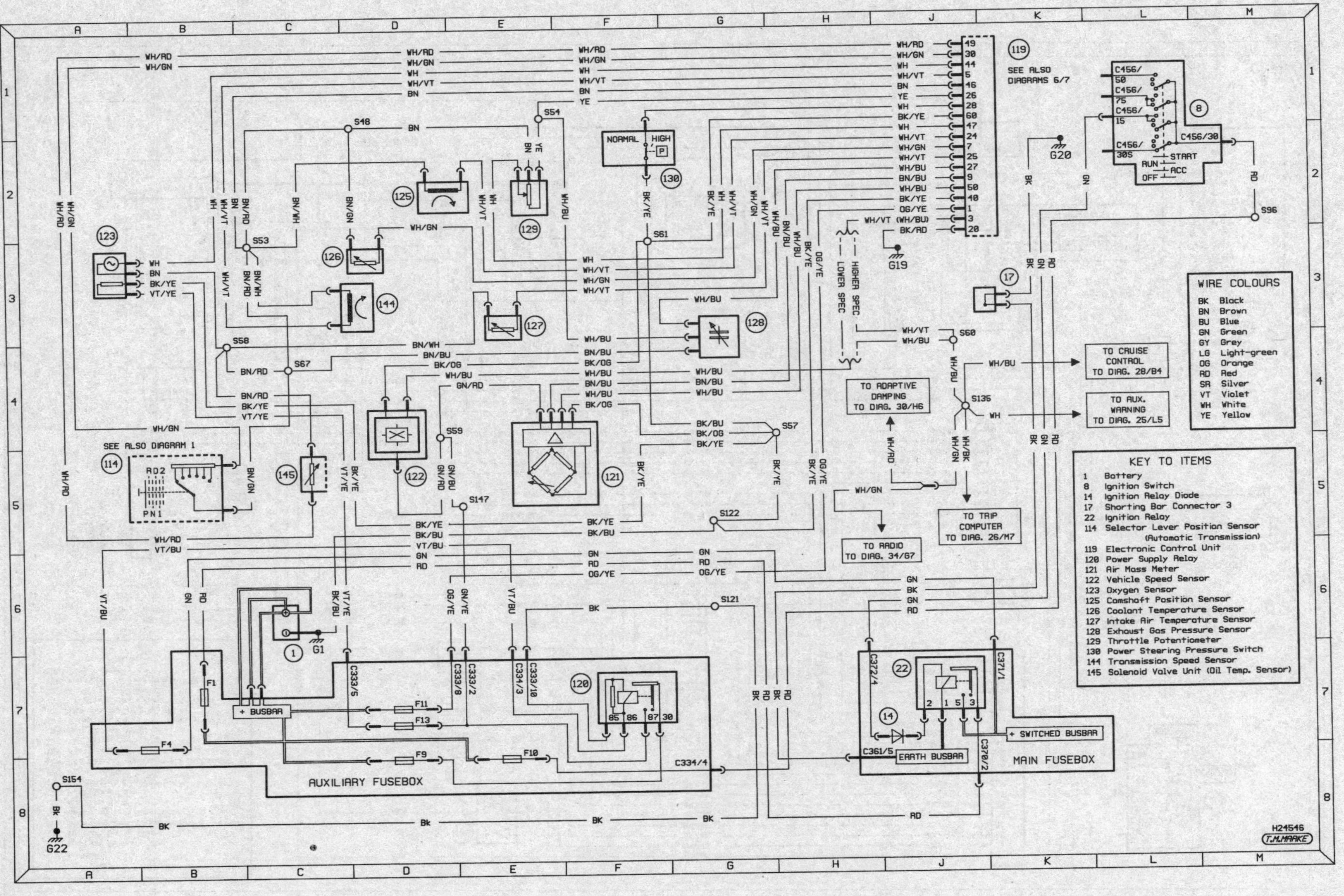

Diagram 5: Engine management – sensor inputs (automatic transmission models)

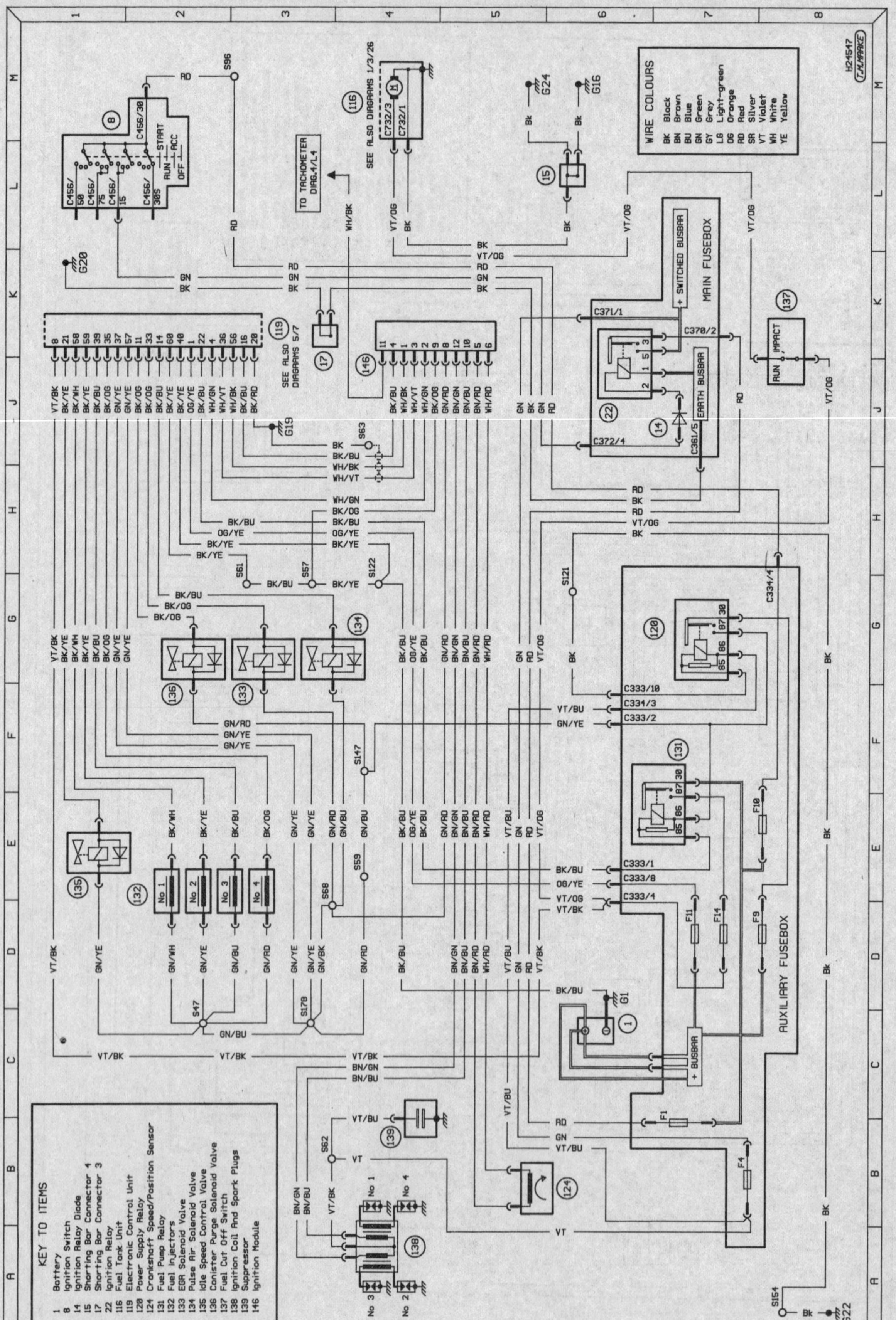

KEY TO ITEMS

1 Battery
8 Ignition Switch
14 Ignition Relay Diode
15 Shorting Bar Connector 4
17 Shorting Bar Connector 3
22 Ignition Relay
116 Fuel Tank Unit
119 Electronic Control Unit
120 Power Supply Relay
124 Crankshaft Speed/Position Sensor
131 Fuel Pump Relay
132 Fuel Injectors
133 EGR Solenoid Valve
134 Pulse Air Solenoid Valve
135 Idle Speed Control Valve
136 Canister Purge Solenoid Valve
137 Fuel Cut Off Switch
138 Ignition Coil And Spark Plugs
139 Suppressor
146 Ignition Module

WIRE COLOURS

BK Black
BN Brown
BU Blue
GN Green
GY Grey
LG Light-green
OG Orange
RD Red
SR Silver
VT Violet
WH White
YE Yellow

H24547

Diagram 6: Engine management – solenoid outputs, ignition and fuel pump (automatic transmission models)

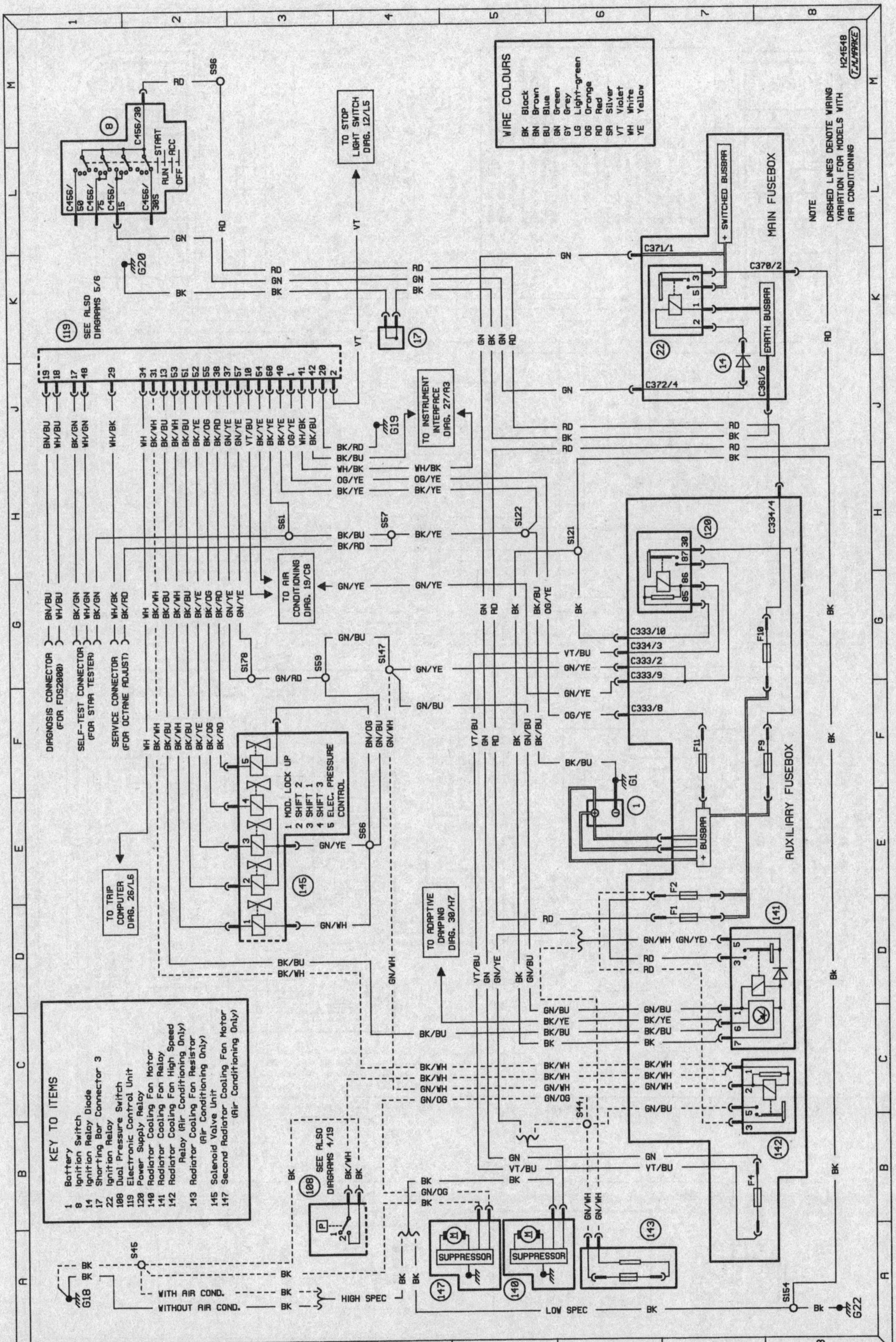

KEY TO ITEMS

1	Battery
8	Ignition Switch
14	Ignition Relay Diode
17	Shorting Bar Connector 3
22	Ignition Relay
108	Dual Pressure Switch
119	Electronic Control Unit
120	Power Supply Relay
140	Radiator Cooling Fan Motor
141	Radiator Cooling Fan Relay
142	Radiator Cooling Fan High Speed Relay (Air Conditioning Only)
143	Radiator Cooling Fan Resistor (Air Conditioning Only)
145	Solenoid Valve Unit
147	Second Radiator Cooling Fan Motor (Air Conditioning Only)

WIRE COLOURS

BK	Black
BN	Brown
BU	Blue
GN	Green
GY	Grey
LG	Light-green
OG	Orange
RD	Red
SR	Silver
VT	Violet
WH	White
YE	Yellow

NOTE
DASHED LINES DENOTE WIRING VARIATION FOR MODELS WITH AIR CONDITIONING

H24548

Diagram 7: Engine management – cooling fan, solenoid valve unit and diagnostic connectors (automatic transmission models)

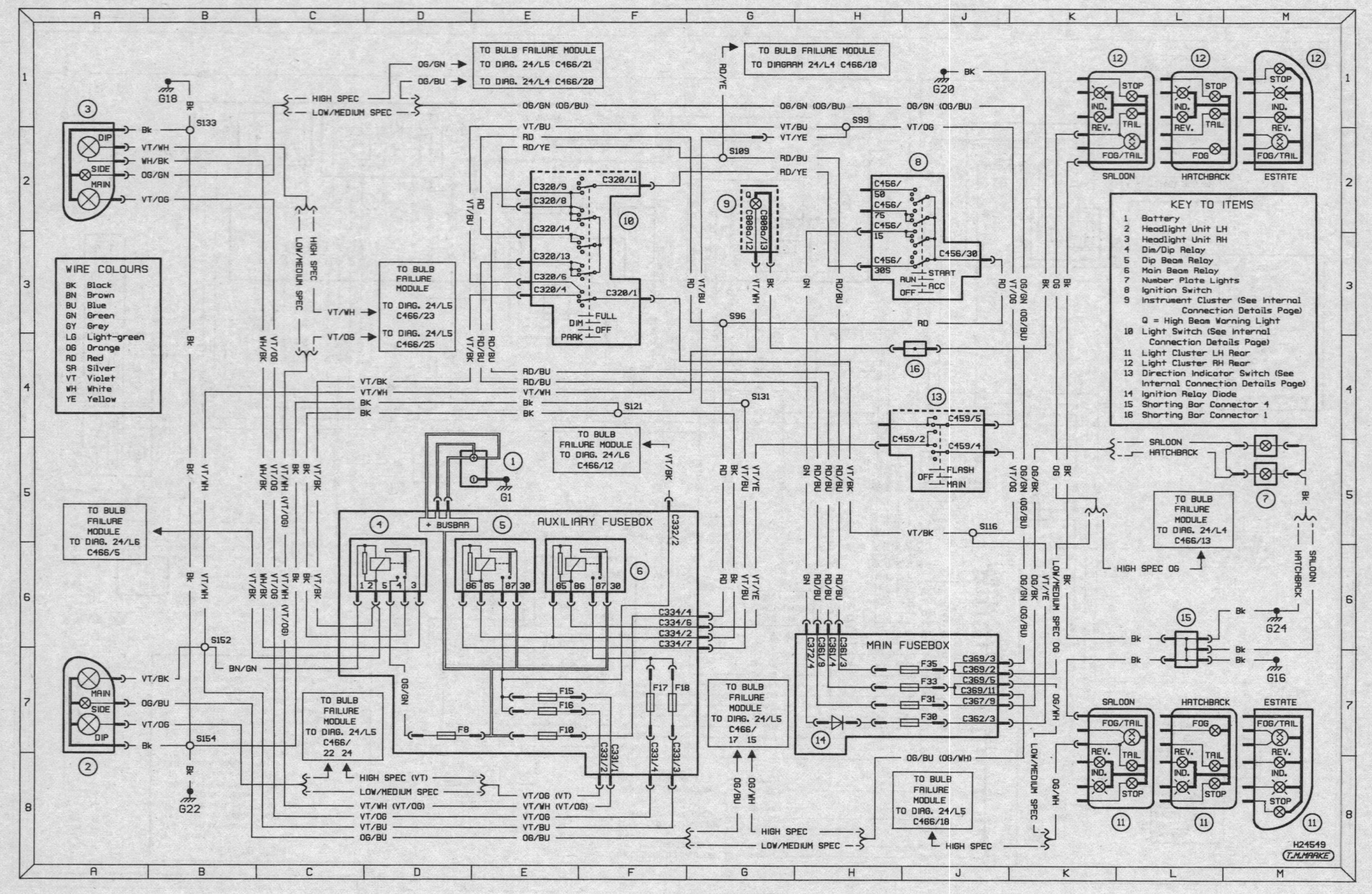

Diagram 8: Exterior lighting – side and headlights (dim-dip)

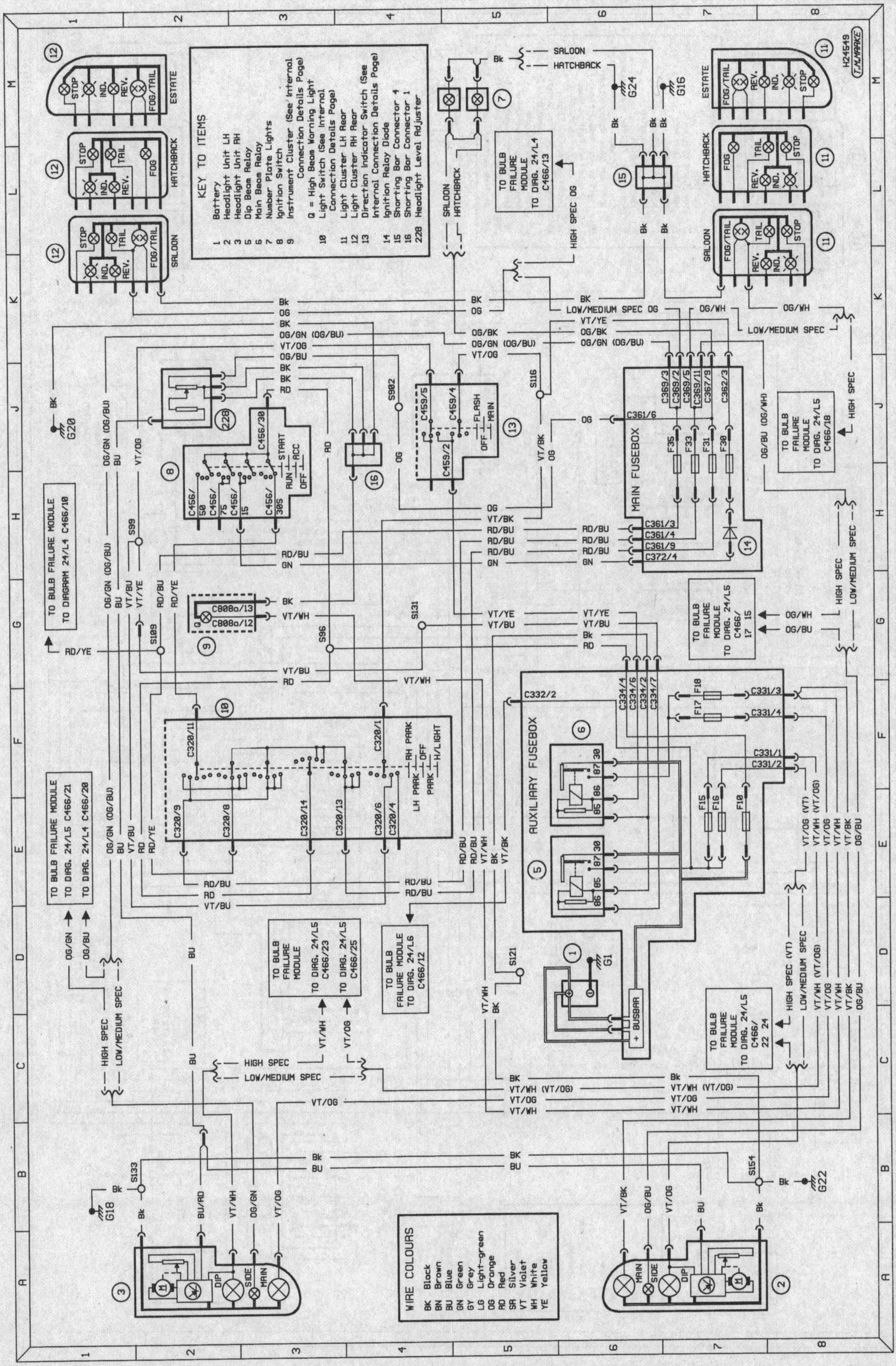

KEY TO ITEMS

1 Battery
2 Headlight Unit LH
3 Headlight Unit RH
5 Dip Beam Relay
6 Main Beam Relay
7 Number Plate Lights
8 Ignition Switch
9 Instrument Cluster (See Internal Connection Details Page)
Q = High Beam Warning Light
10 Light Switch (See Internal Connection Details Page)
11 Light Cluster LH Rear
12 Light Cluster RH Rear
13 Direction Indicator Switch (See Internal Connection Details Page)
14 Ignition Relay Diode
15 Shorting Bar Connector 4
16 Shorting Bar Connector 1
228 Headlight Level Adjuster

WIRE COLOURS

BK	Black
BN	Brown
BU	Blue
GN	Green
GY	Grey
LG	Light-green
OG	Orange
RD	Red
SR	Silver
VT	Violet
WH	White
YE	Yellow

Diagram 9: Exterior lighting – side and headlights (non dim-dip)

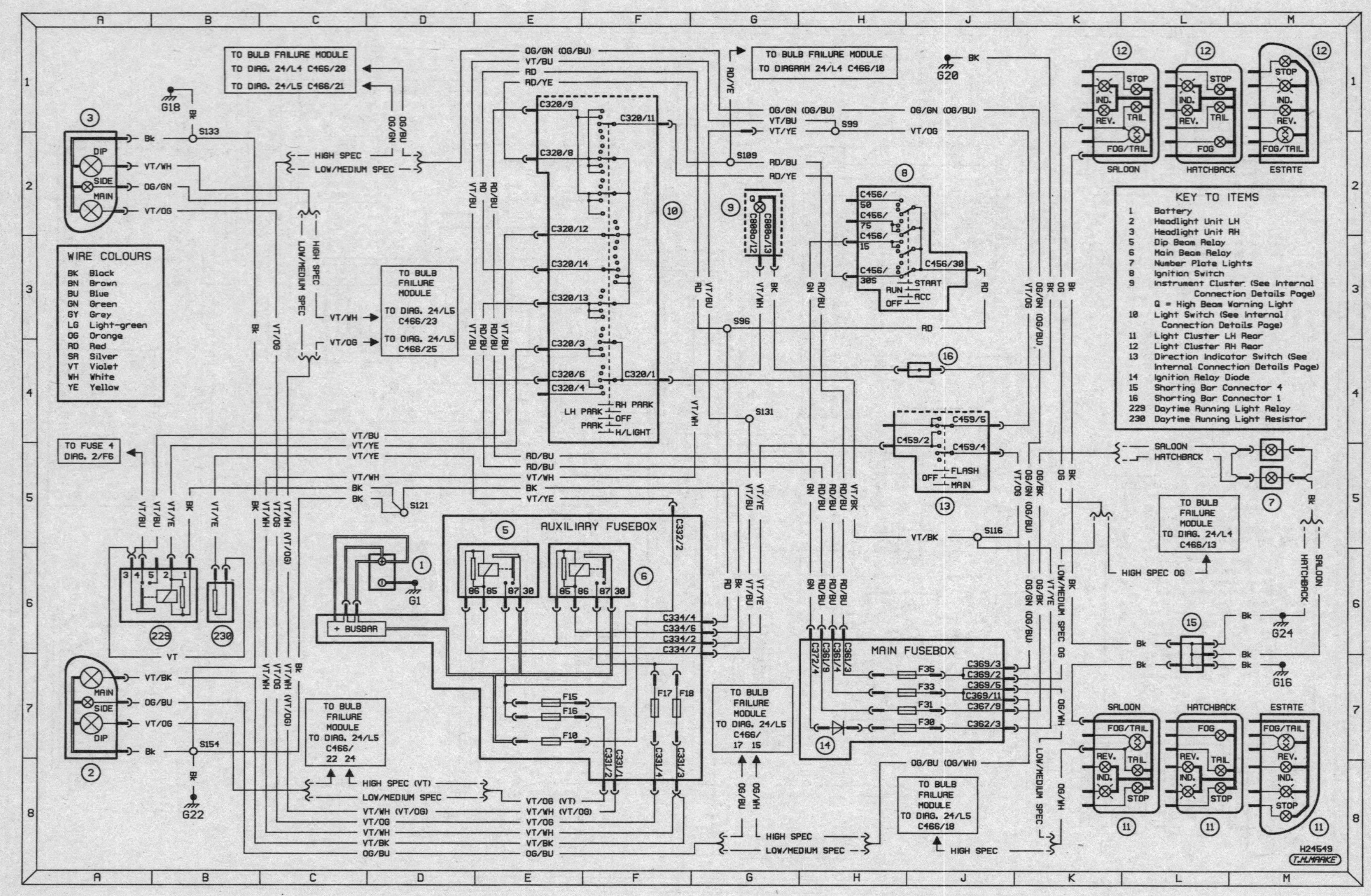

Diagram 10: Exterior lighting – side and headlights (daytime running lights)

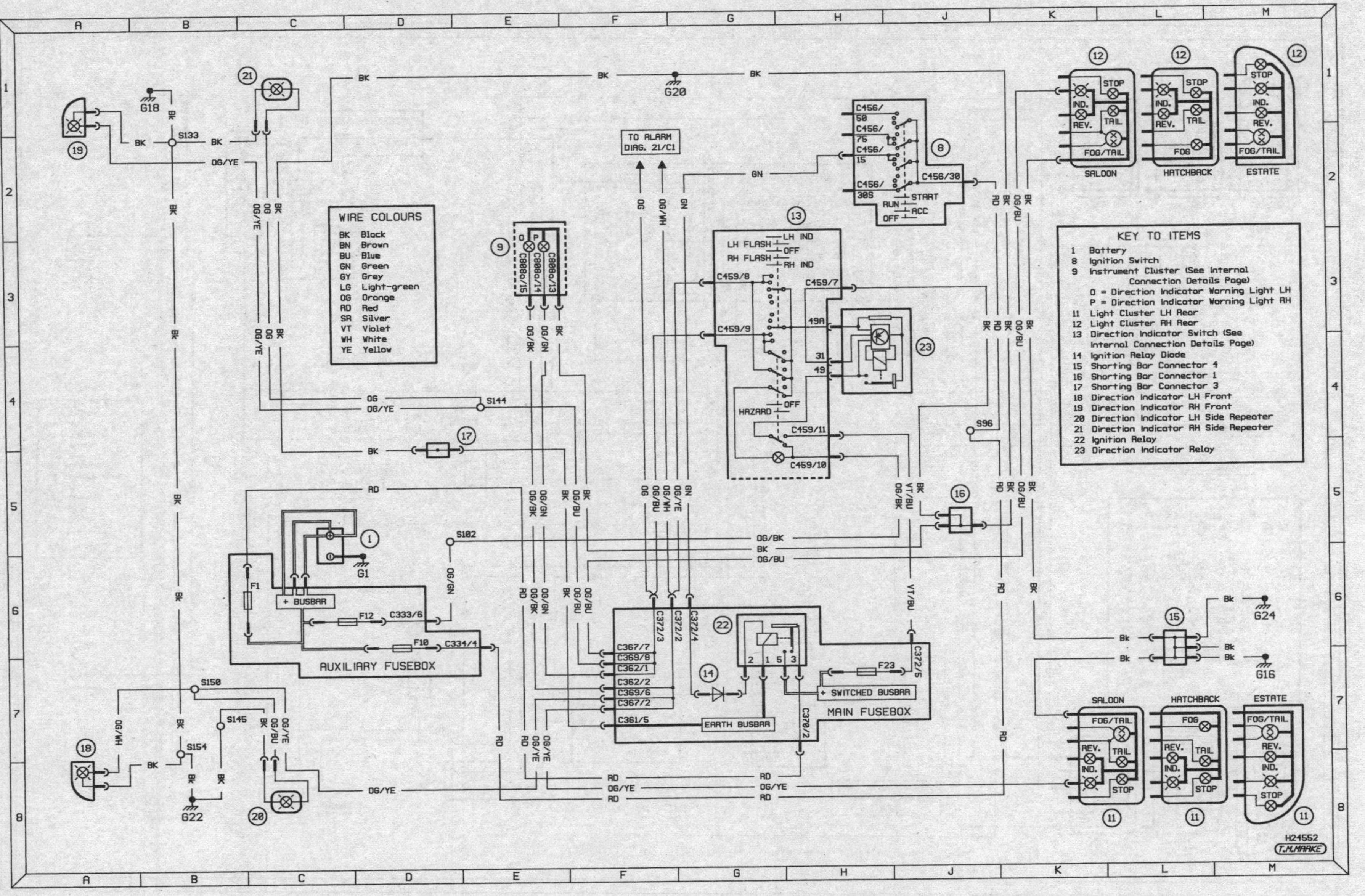

Diagram 11: Exterior lighting – hazard flasher and direction indicators

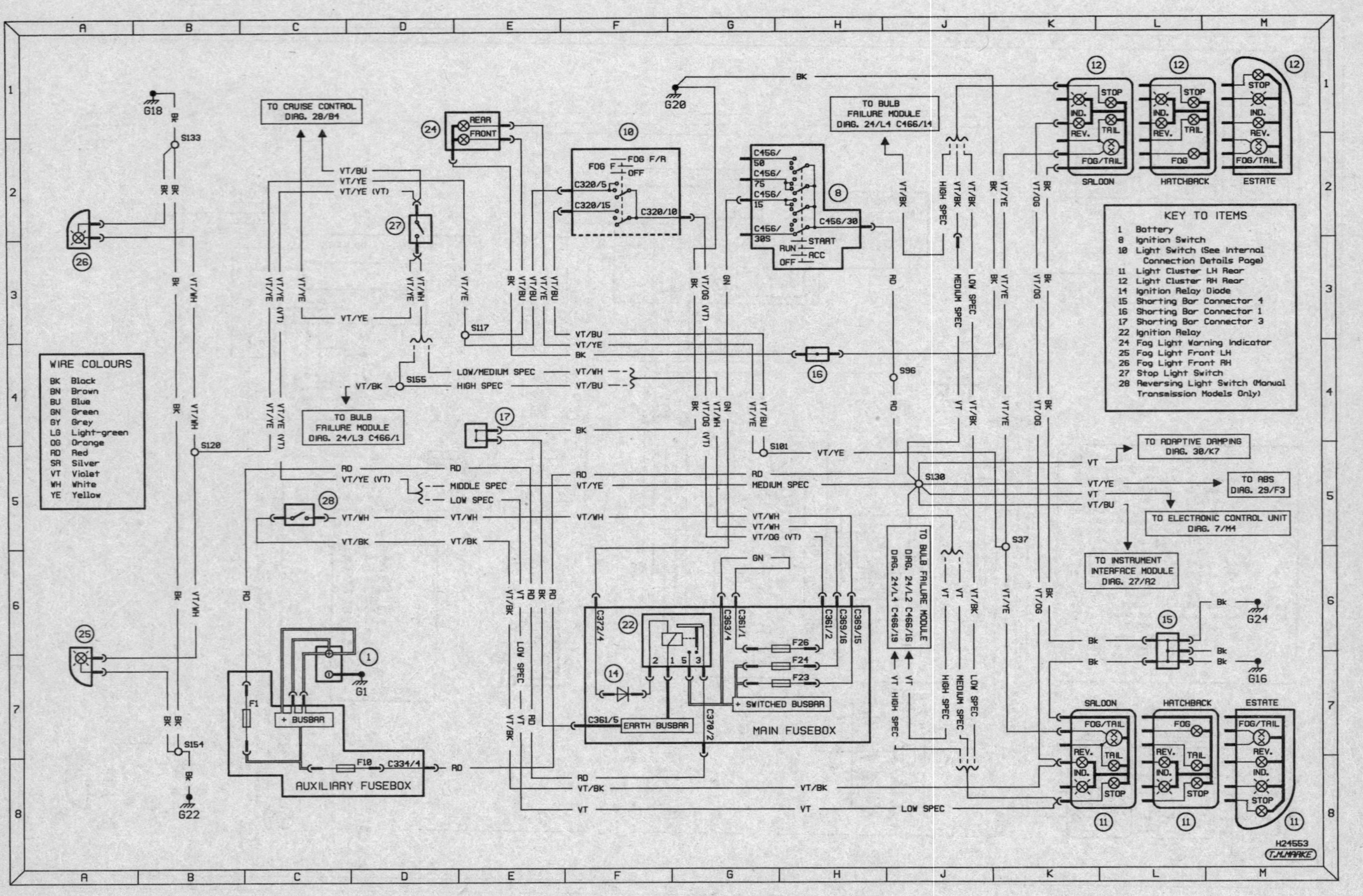

Diagram 12: Exterior lighting – foglights, stop-lights and reversing lights

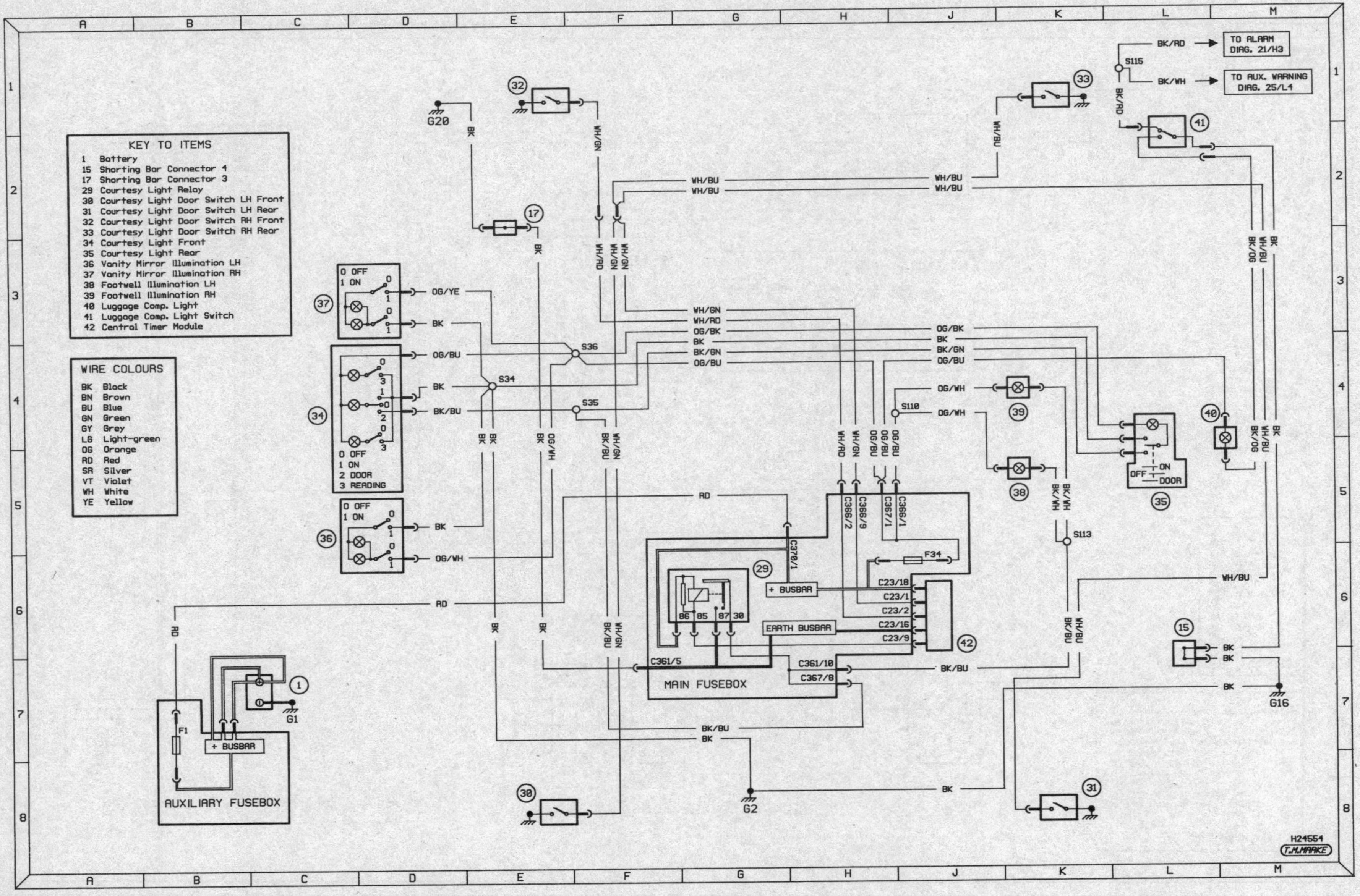

KEY TO ITEMS
1 Battery
15 Shorting Bar Connector 4
17 Shorting Bar Connector 3
29 Courtesy Light Relay
30 Courtesy Light Door Switch LH Front
31 Courtesy Light Door Switch LH Rear
32 Courtesy Light Door Switch RH Front
33 Courtesy Light Door Switch RH Rear
34 Courtesy Light Front
35 Courtesy Light Rear
36 Vanity Mirror Illumination LH
37 Vanity Mirror Illumination RH
38 Footwell Illumination LH
39 Footwell Illumination RH
40 Luggage Comp. Light
41 Luggage Comp. Light Switch
42 Central Timer Module
WIRE COLOURS
BK Black
BN Brown
BU Blue
GN Green
GY Grey
LG Light-green
OG Orange
RD Red
SR Silver
VT Violet
WH White
YE Yellow
TO ALARM DIAG. 21/H3
TO AUX. WARNING DIAG. 25/L4
MAIN FUSEBOX
AUXILIARY FUSEBOX
+ BUSBAR
EARTH BUSBAR
0 OFF
1 ON
2 DOOR
3 READING
H24554

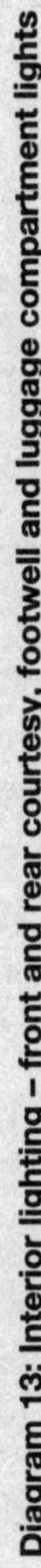

Diagram 13: Interior lighting – front and rear courtesy, footwell and luggage compartment lights

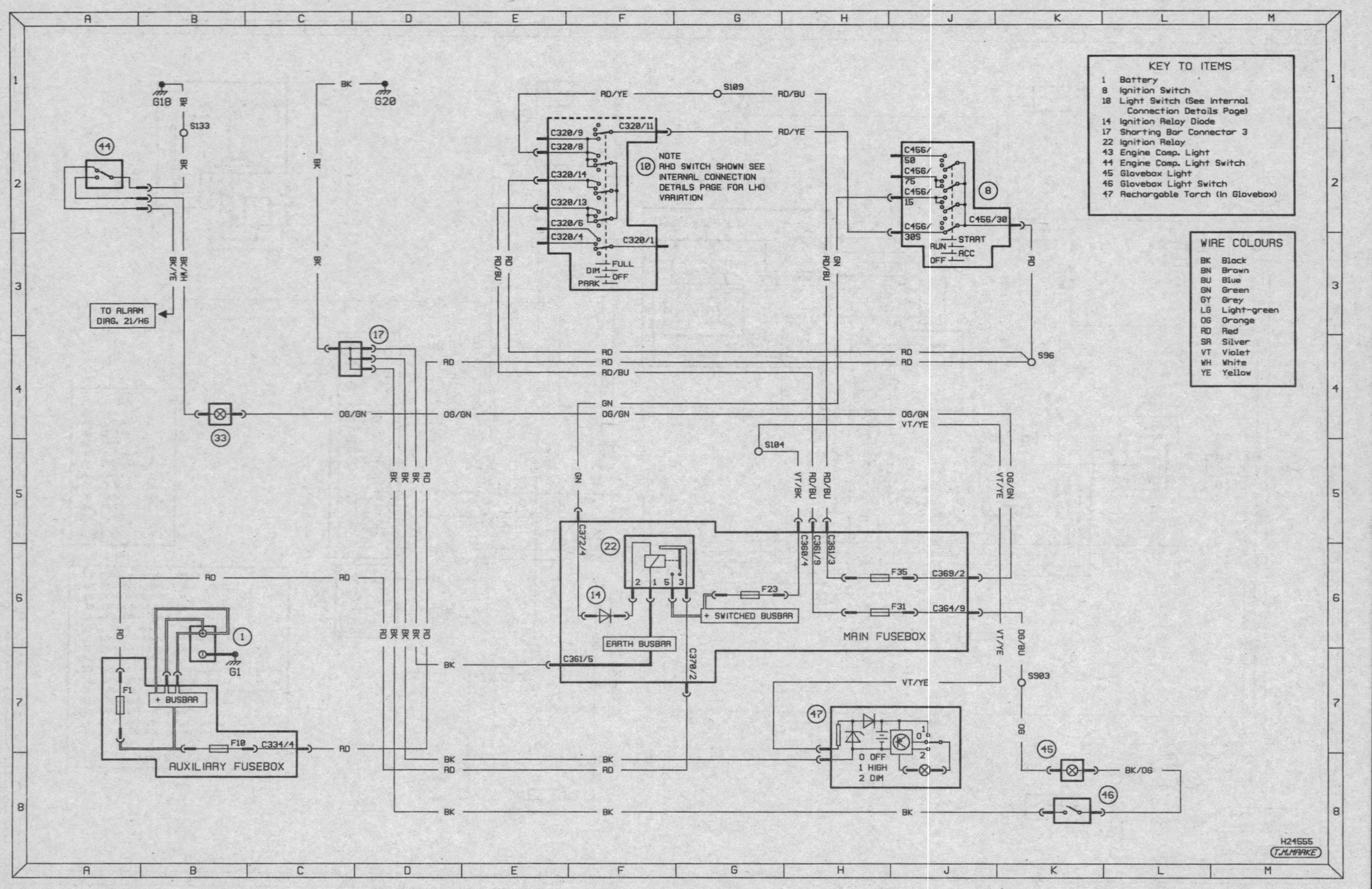

Diagram 14: Interior lighting – glovebox and engine compartment lights

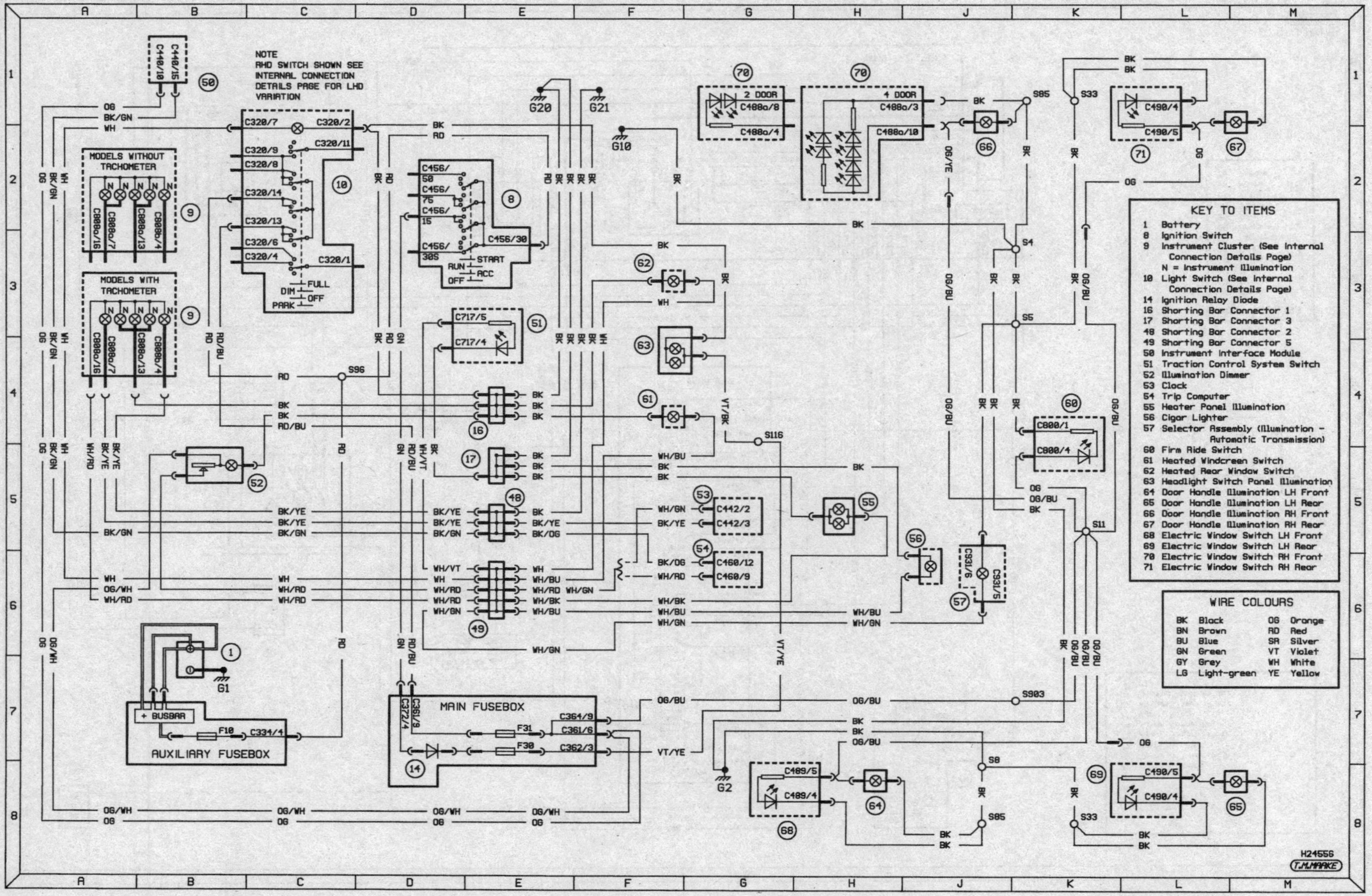

NOTE
RHD SWITCH SHOWN SEE
INTERNAL CONNECTION
DETAILS PAGE FOR LHD
VARIATION
KEY TO ITEMS
1 Battery
8 Ignition Switch
9 Instrument Cluster (See Internal Connection Details Page)
N = Instrument Illumination
10 Light Switch (See Internal Connection Details Page)
14 Ignition Relay Diode
16 Shorting Bar Connector 1
17 Shorting Bar Connector 3
48 Shorting Bar Connector 2
49 Shorting Bar Connector 5
50 Instrument Interface Module
51 Traction Control System Switch
52 Illumination Dimmer
53 Clock
54 Trip Computer
55 Heater Panel Illumination
56 Cigar Lighter
57 Selector Assembly (Illumination - Automatic Transmission)
60 Firm Ride Switch
61 Heated Windscreen Switch
62 Heated Rear Window Switch
63 Headlight Switch Panel Illumination
64 Door Handle Illumination LH Front
65 Door Handle Illumination LH Rear
66 Door Handle Illumination RH Front
67 Door Handle Illumination RH Rear
68 Electric Window Switch LH Front
69 Electric Window Switch LH Rear
70 Electric Window Switch RH Front
71 Electric Window Switch RH Rear
WIRE COLOURS
BK Black
BN Brown
BU Blue
GN Green
GY Grey
LG Light-green
OG Orange
RD Red
SR Silver
VT Violet
WH White
YE Yellow
MAIN FUSEBOX
AUXILIARY FUSEBOX
MODELS WITHOUT TACHOMETER
MODELS WITH TACHOMETER
2 DOOR
4 DOOR
H24556
T.M.MARKE

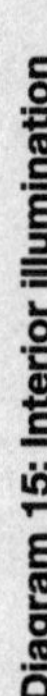

Diagram 15: Interior illumination

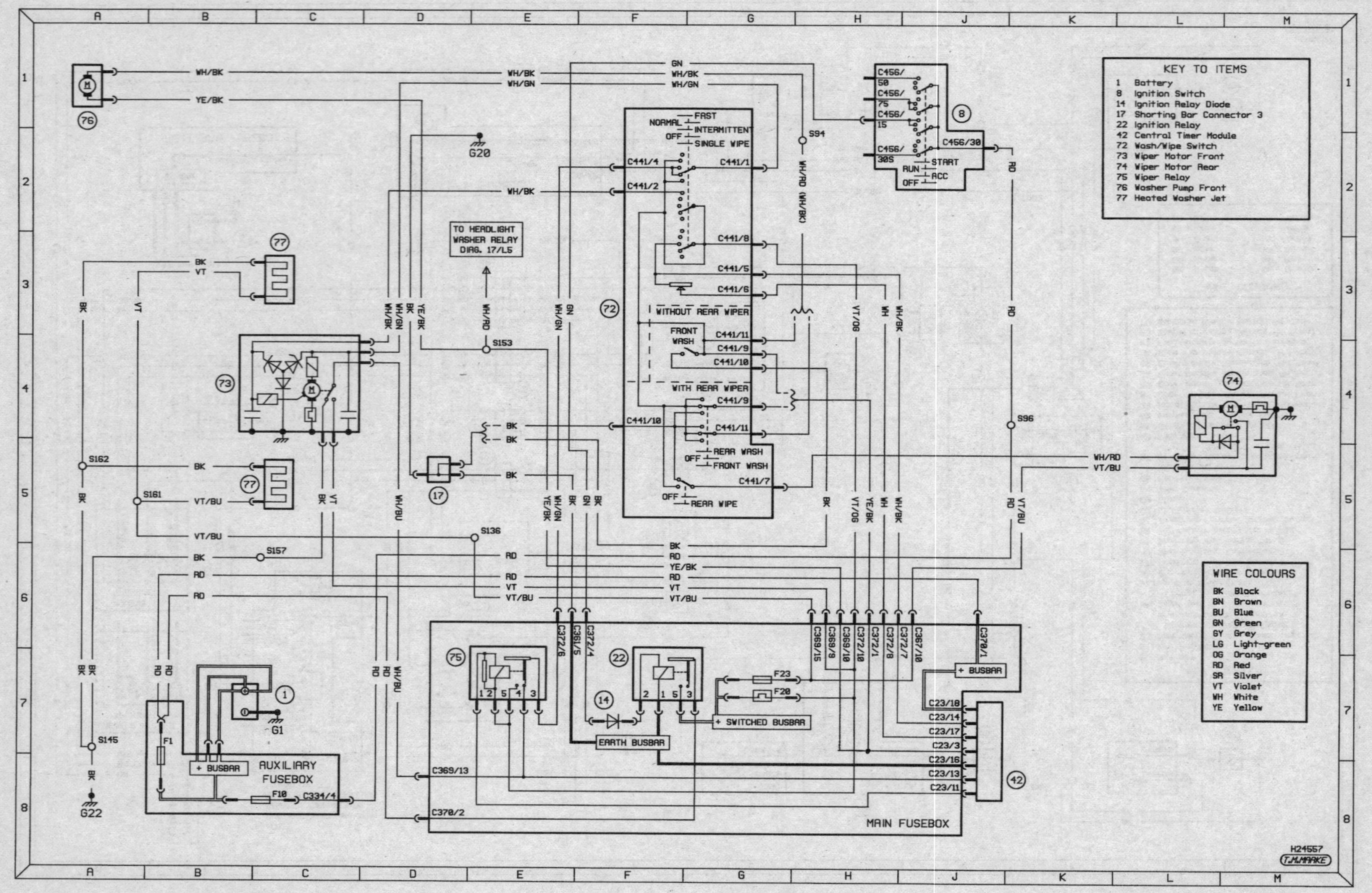

Diagram 16: Wash/wipe and heated washer jets

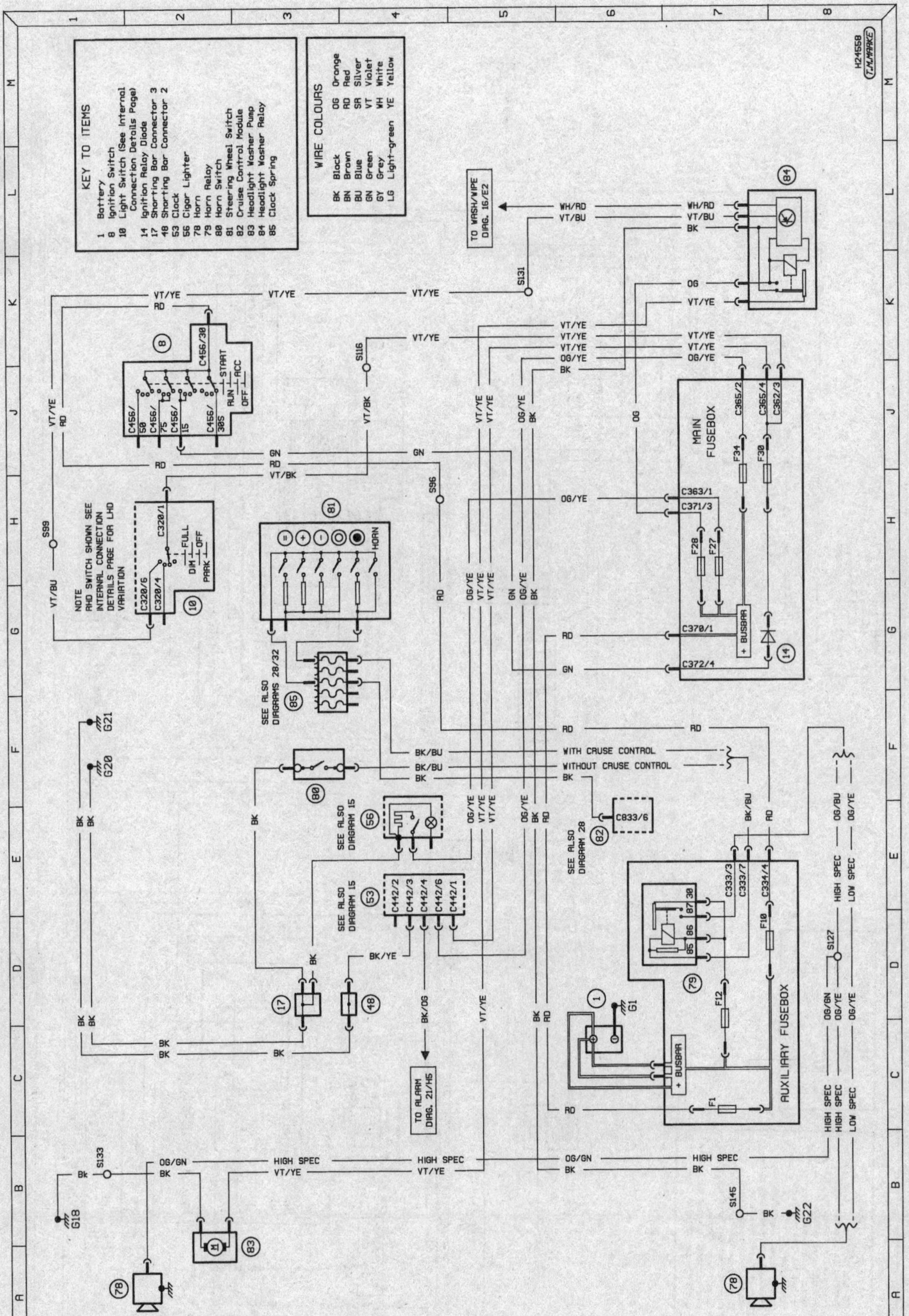

KEY TO ITEMS

1 Battery
8 Ignition Switch
10 Light Switch (See Internal Connection Details Page)
14 Ignition Relay Diode
17 Shorting Bar Connector 3
48 Shorting Bar Connector 2
53 Clock
56 Cigar Lighter
78 Horn
79 Horn Relay
80 Horn Switch
81 Steering Wheel Switch
82 Cruise Control Module
83 Headlight Washer Pump
84 Headlight Washer Relay
85 Clock Spring

WIRE COLOURS

BK	Black	OG	Orange
BN	Brown	RD	Red
BU	Blue	SR	Silver
GN	Green	VT	Violet
GY	Grey	WH	White
LG	Light-green	YE	Yellow

Diagram 17: Headlight washer, horn, clock and cigar lighter

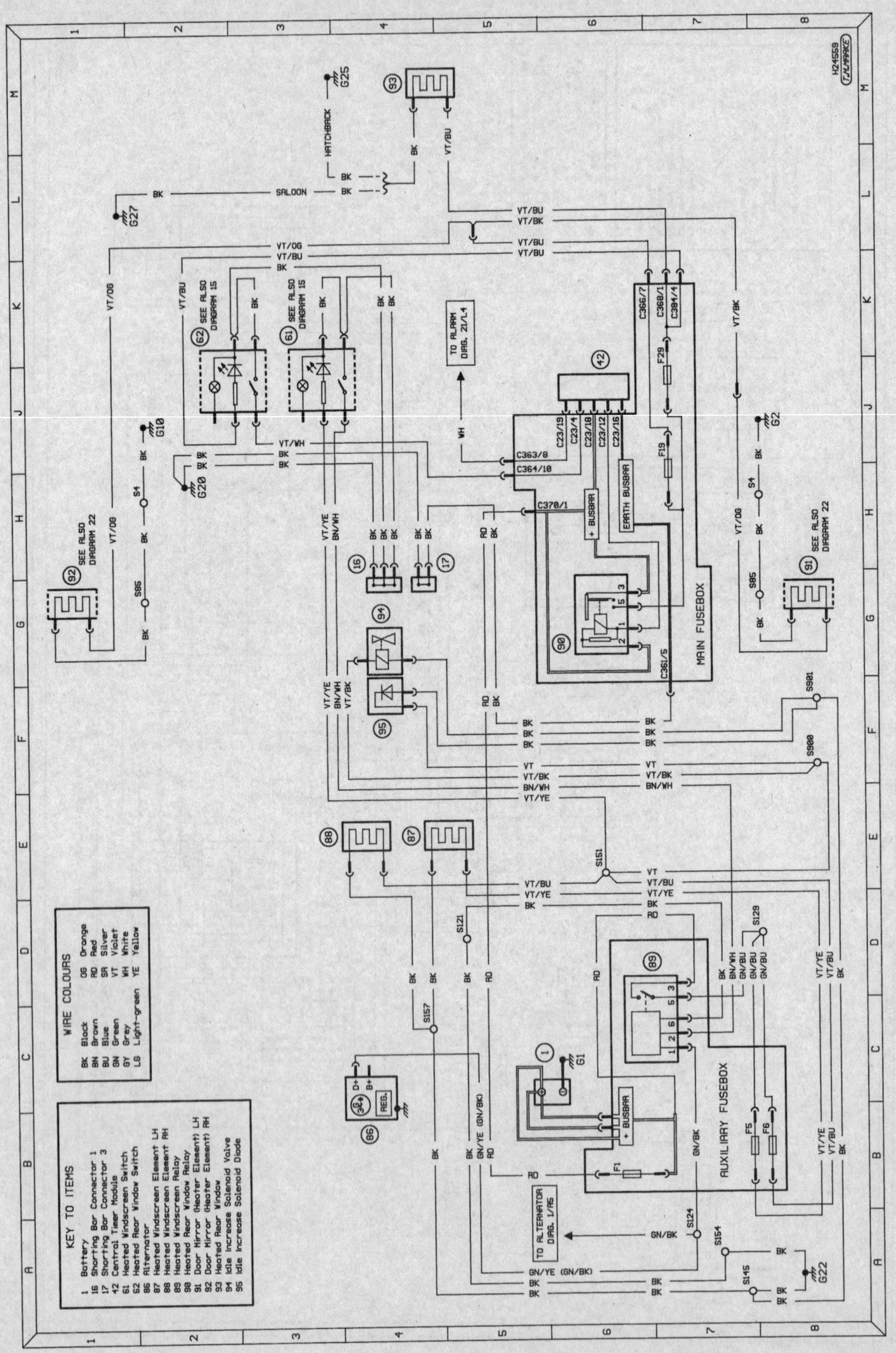

Diagram 18: Heated mirrors and heated front/rear windshield

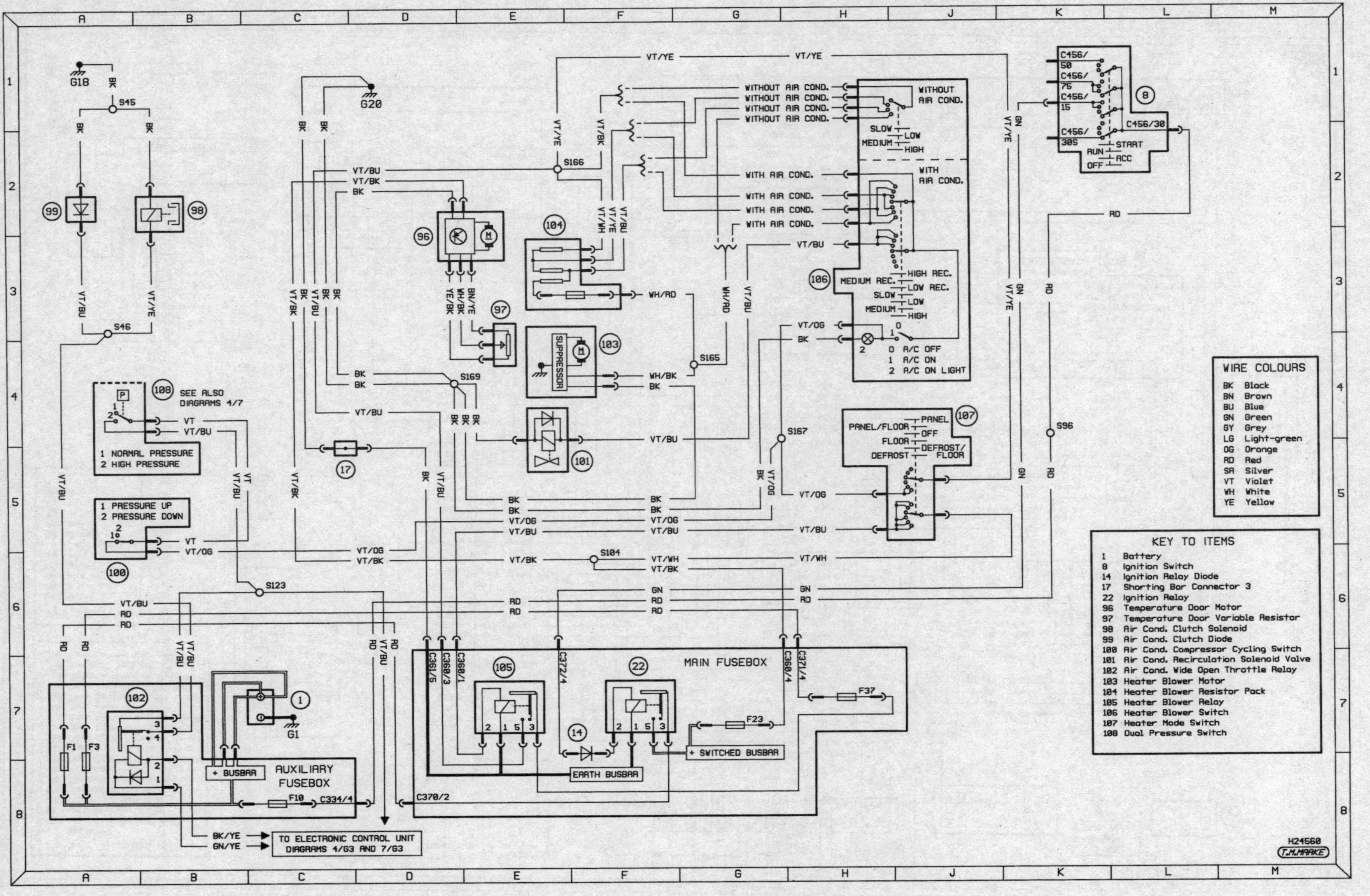

Diagram 19: Air conditioning and heater blower

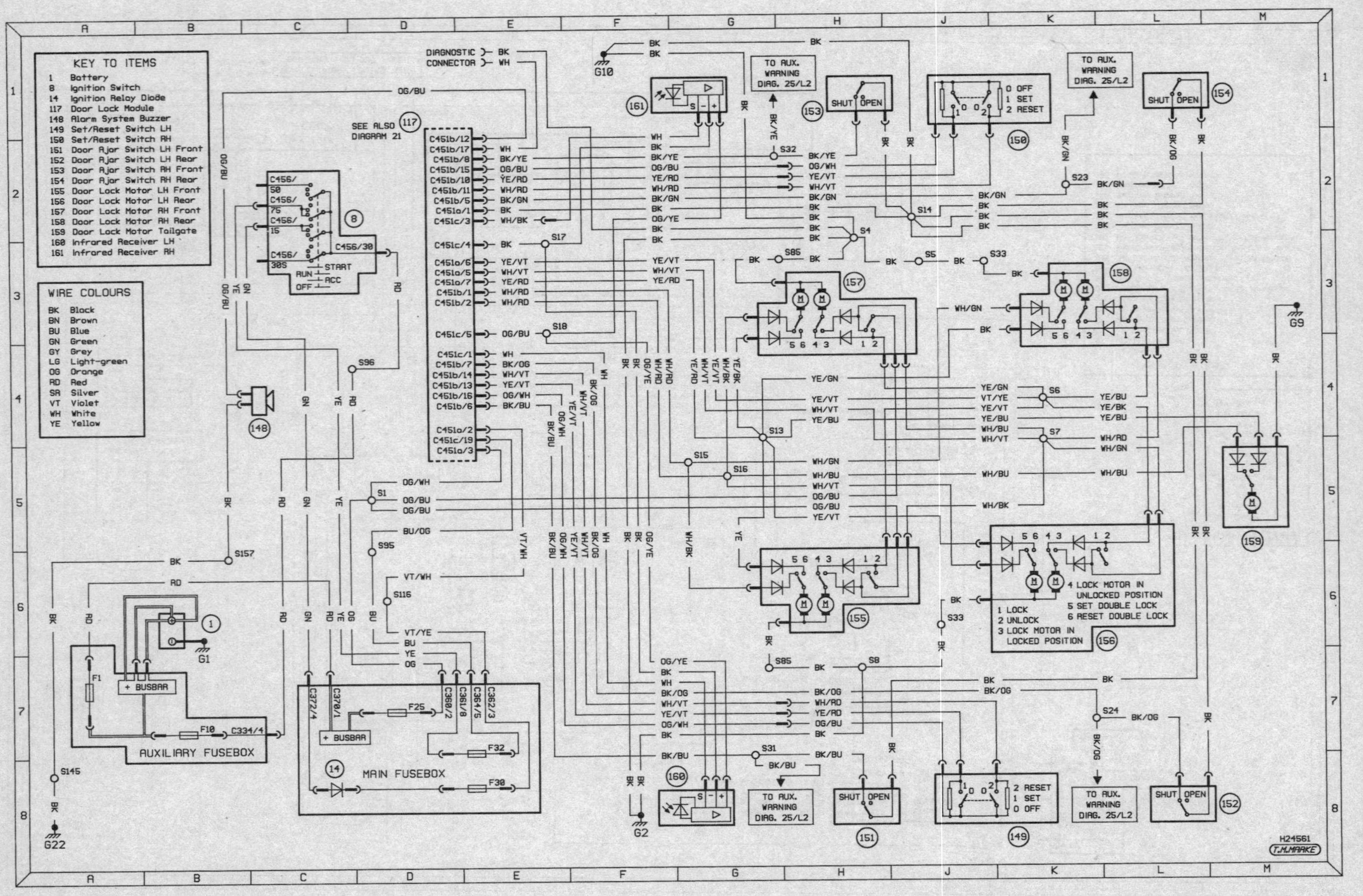

Diagram 20: Central door locking (with double locking)

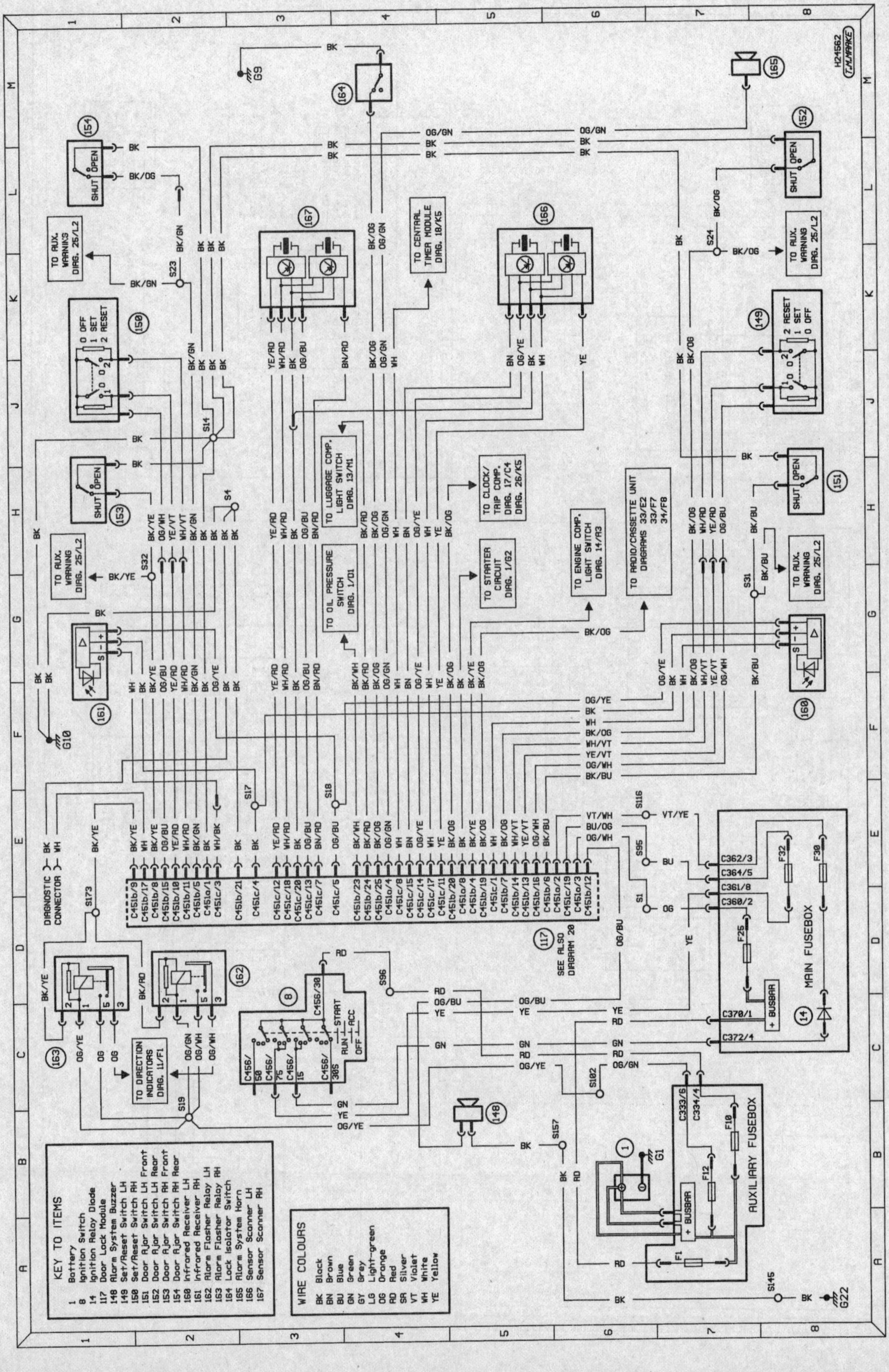

KEY TO ITEMS
1 Battery
8 Ignition Switch
14 Ignition Relay Diode
117 Door Lock Module
148 Alarm System Buzzer
149 Set/Reset Switch LH
150 Set/Reset Switch RH
151 Door Ajar Switch LH Front
152 Door Ajar Switch LH Rear
153 Door Ajar Switch RH Front
154 Door Ajar Switch RH Rear
160 Infrared Receiver LH
161 Infrared Receiver RH
162 Alarm Flasher Relay LH
163 Alarm Flasher Relay RH
164 Lock Isolator Switch
165 Alarm System Horn
166 Sensor Scanner LH
167 Sensor Scanner RH
WIRE COLOURS
BK Black
BN Brown
BU Blue
GN Green
GY Grey
LG Light-green
OG Orange
RD Red
SR Silver
VT Violet
WH White
YE Yellow
MAIN FUSEBOX
AUXILIARY FUSEBOX
DIAGNOSTIC CONNECTOR
H24562

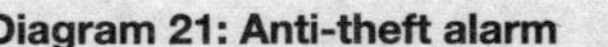

Diagram 21: Anti-theft alarm

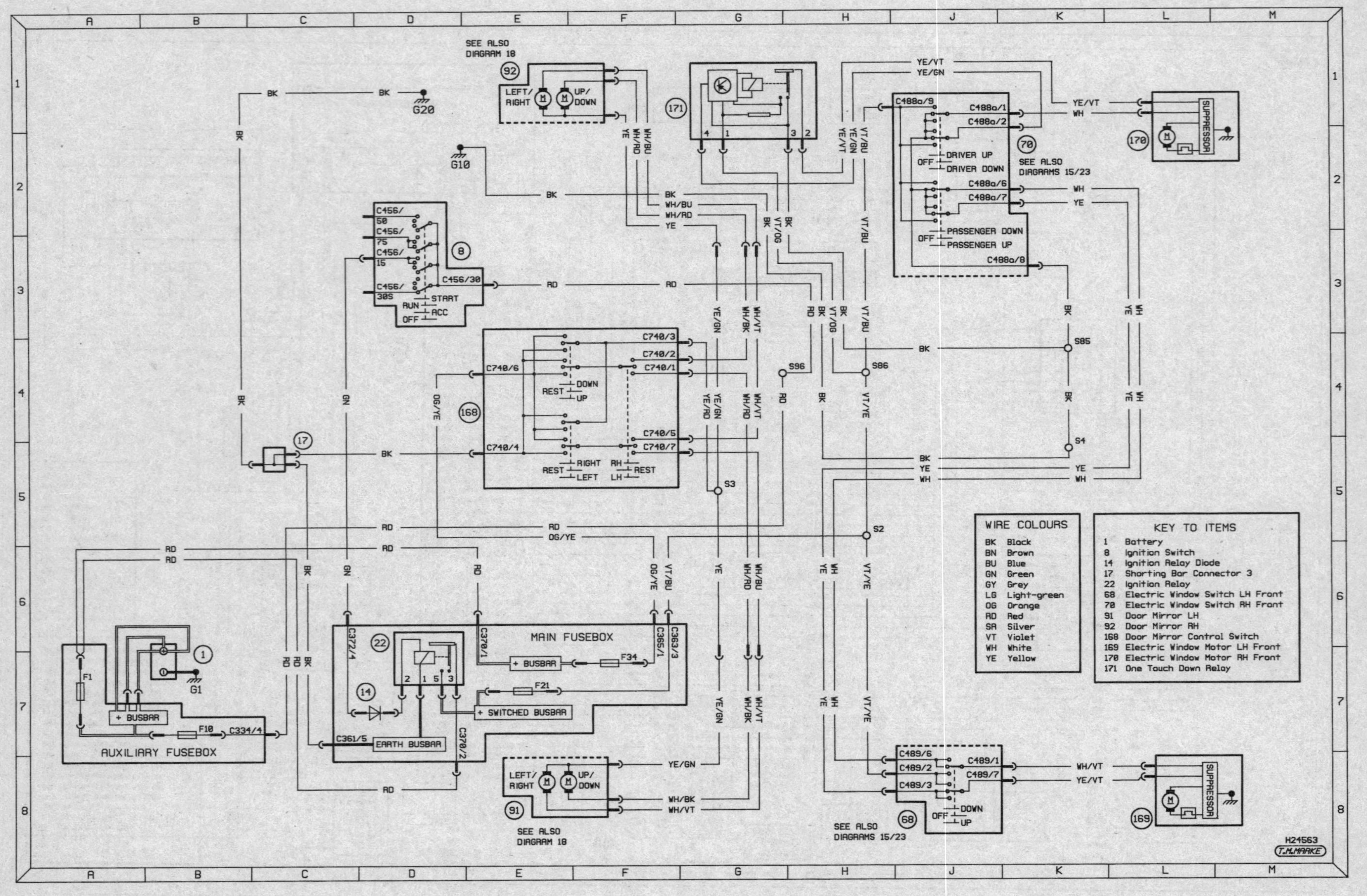

Diagram 22: Electric mirrors and (front) electric window

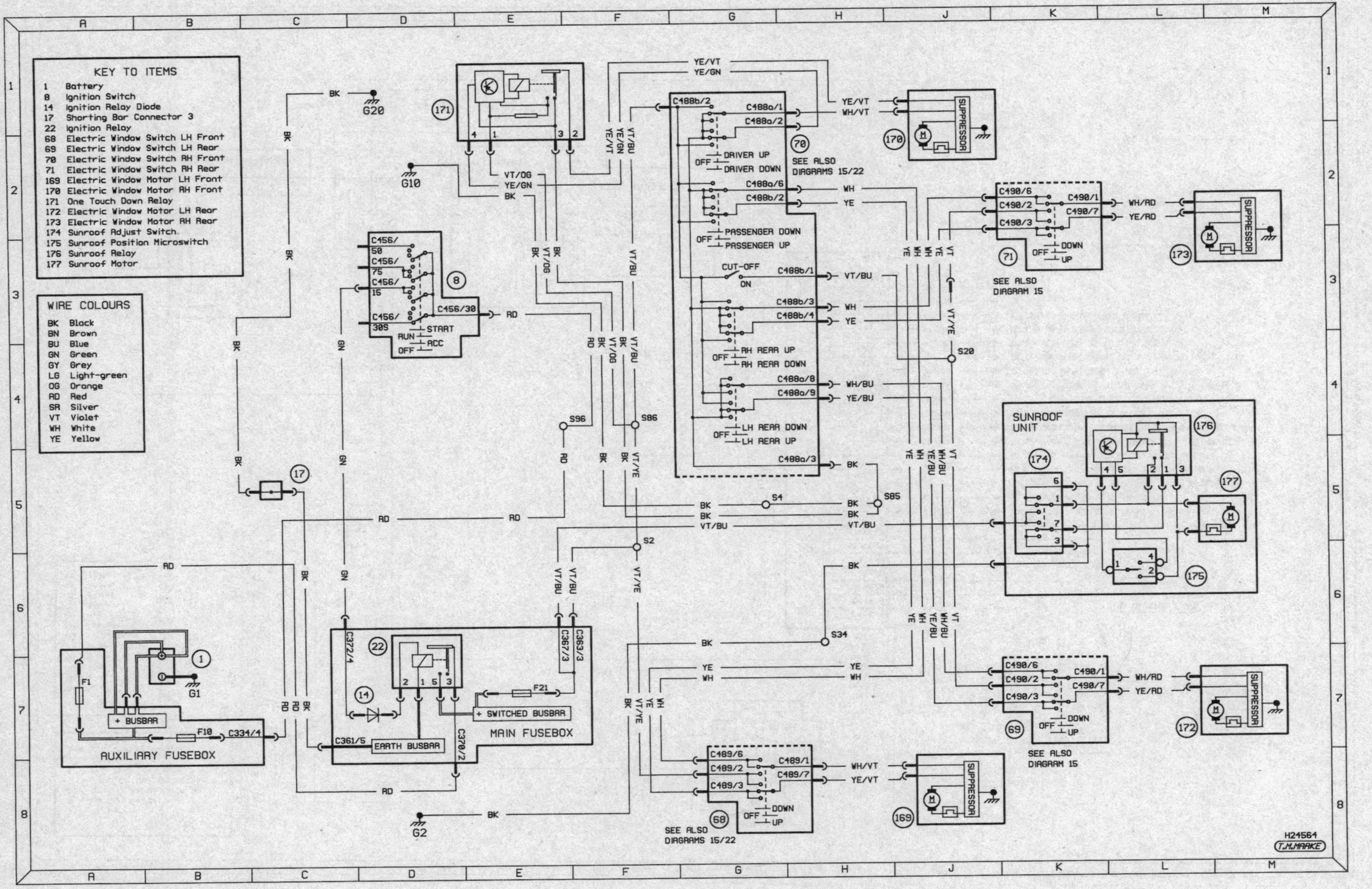

Diagram 23: Electric sunroof and (front and rear) electric windows

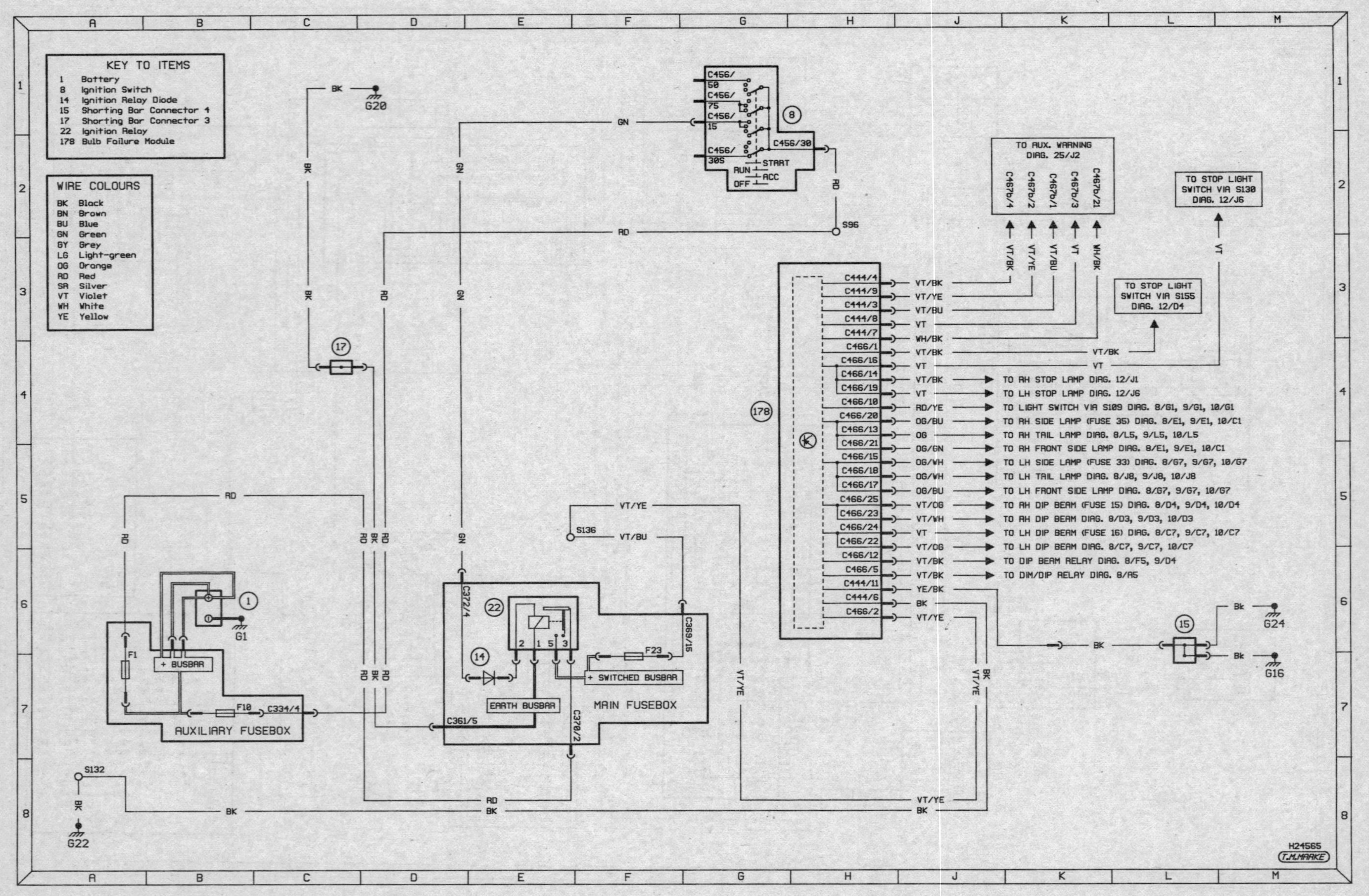

Diagram 24: Bulb failure warning system

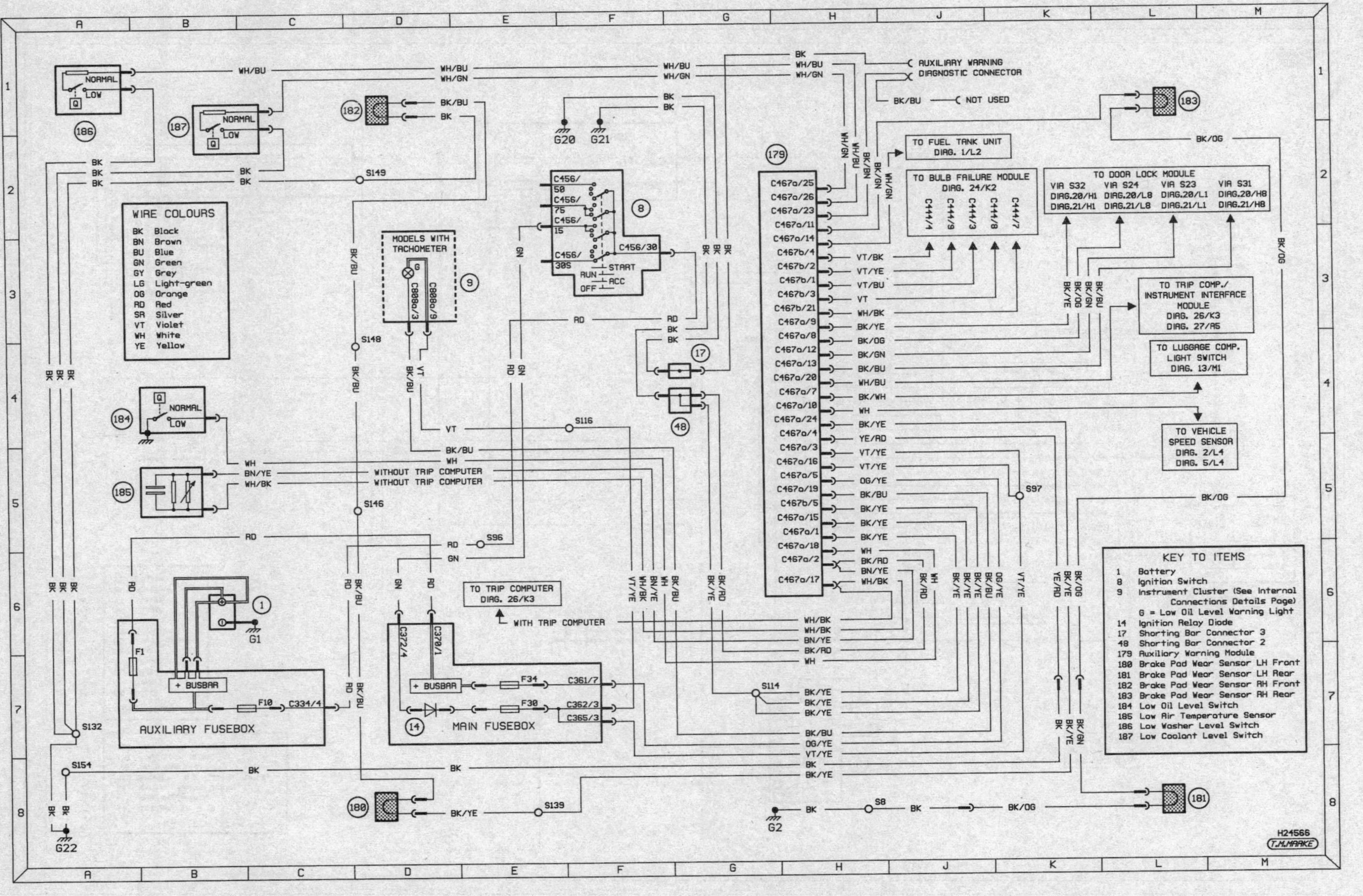

Diagram 25: Auxiliary warning system

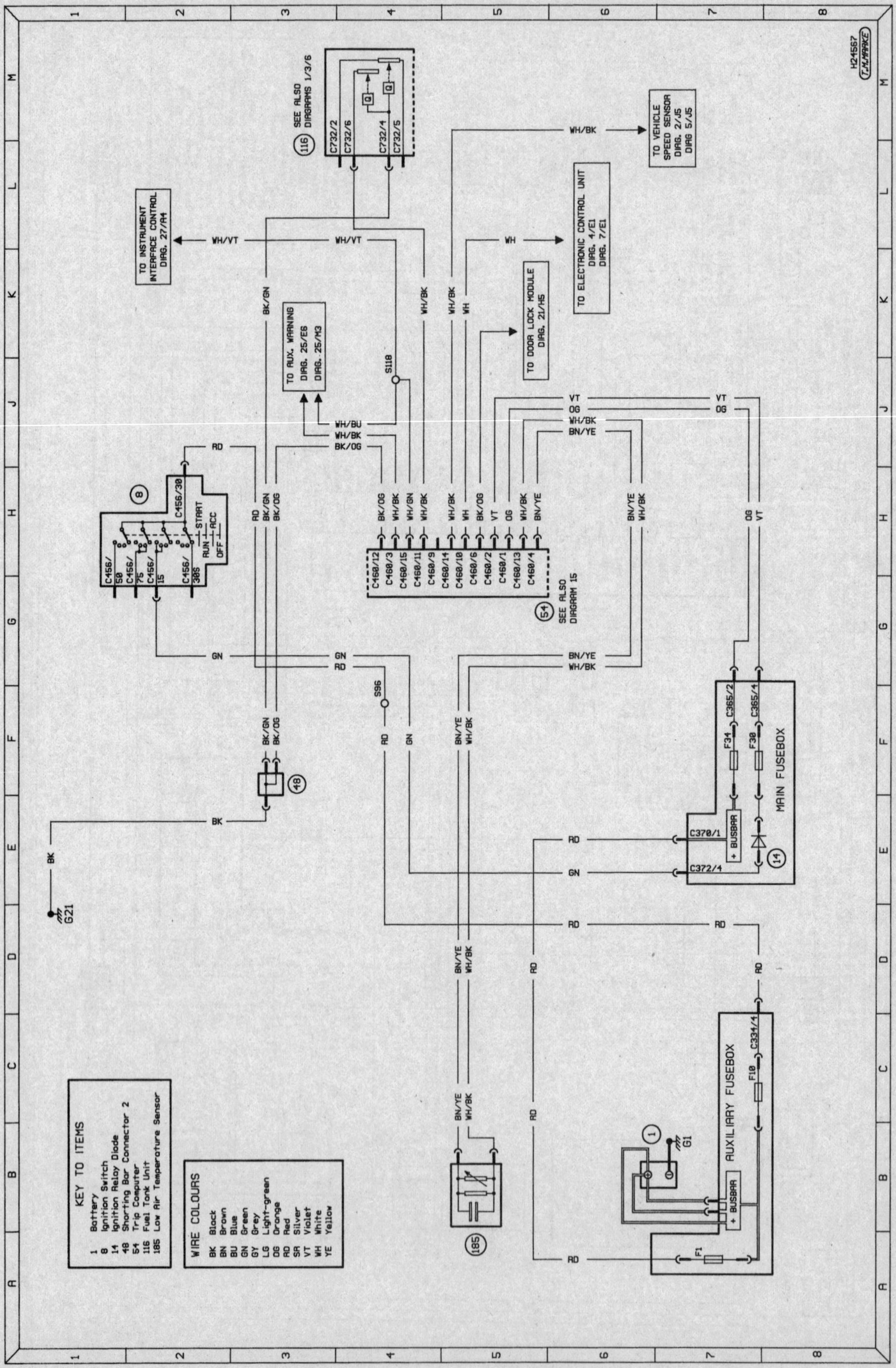

KEY TO ITEMS
1 Battery
8 Ignition Switch
14 Ignition Relay Diode
48 Shorting Bar Connector 2
54 Trip Computer
116 Fuel Tank Unit
185 Low Air Temperature Sensor
WIRE COLOURS
BK Black
BN Brown
BU Blue
GN Green
GY Grey
LG Light-green
OG Orange
RD Red
SR Silver
VT Violet
WH White
YE Yellow
MAIN FUSEBOX
AUXILIARY FUSEBOX
TO INSTRUMENT INTERFACE CONTROL DIAG. 27/A4
TO AUX. WARNING DIAG. 25/E6 DIAG. 25/M3
TO DOOR LOCK MODULE DIAG. 21/H5
TO ELECTRONIC CONTROL UNIT DIAG. 4/E1 DIAG. 7/E1
TO VEHICLE SPEED SENSOR DIAG. 2/J5 DIAG 5/J5
SEE ALSO DIAGRAMS 1/3/6
SEE ALSO DIAGRAM 15
H24567

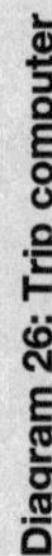

Diagram 26: Trip computer

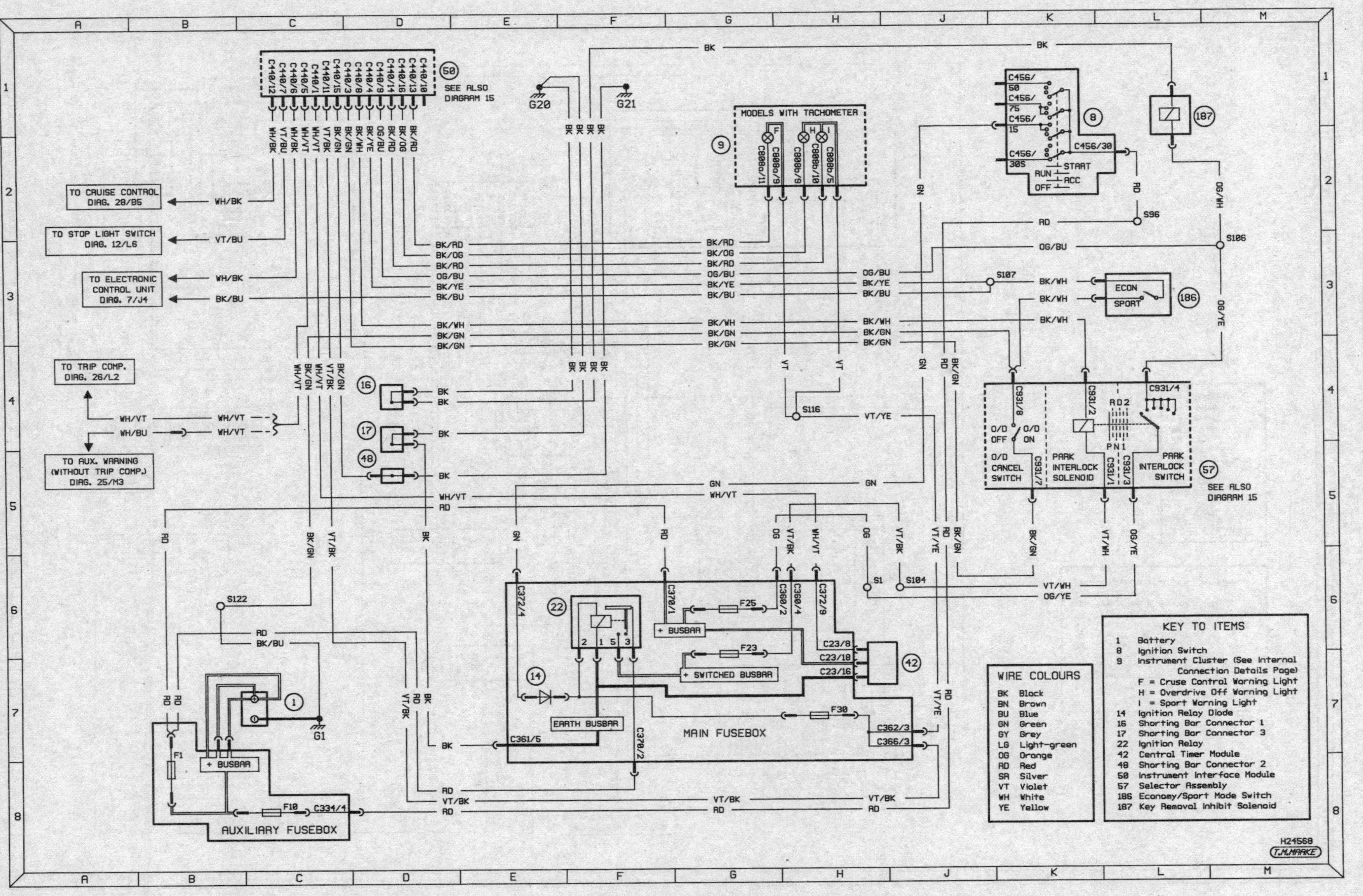

Diagram 27: Instrument interface control

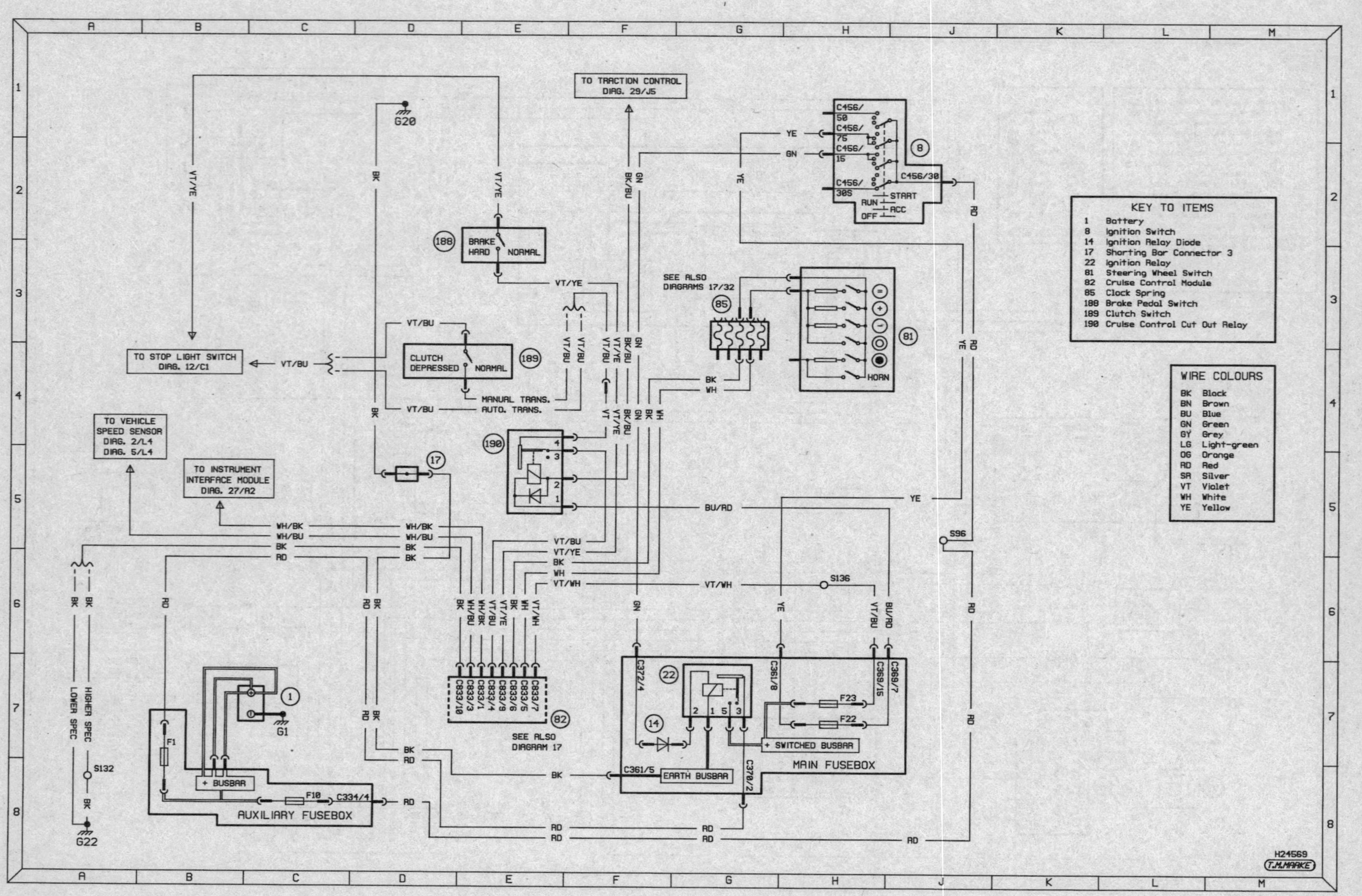

Diagram 28: Cruise control

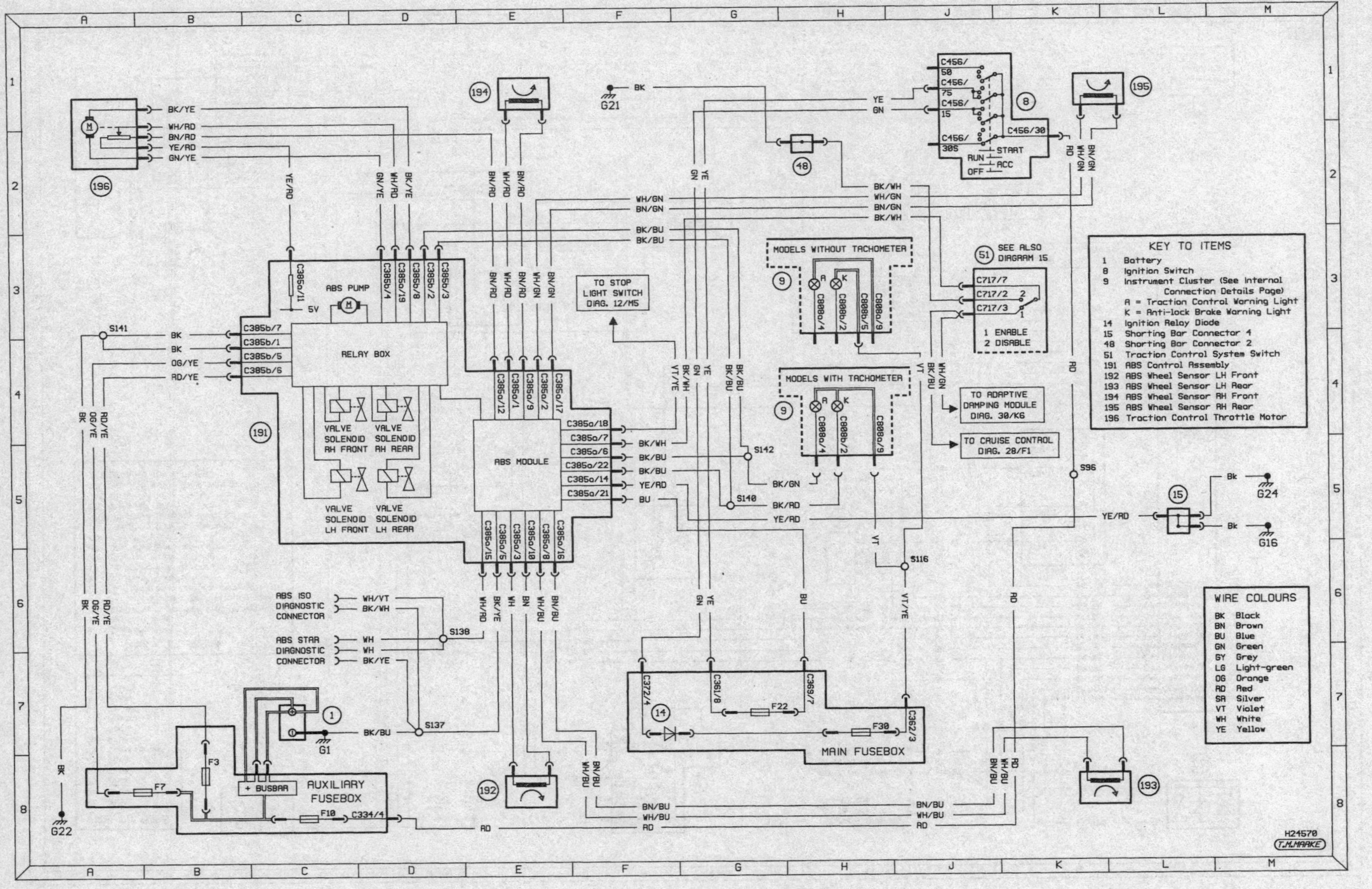

Diagram 29: ABS with traction control

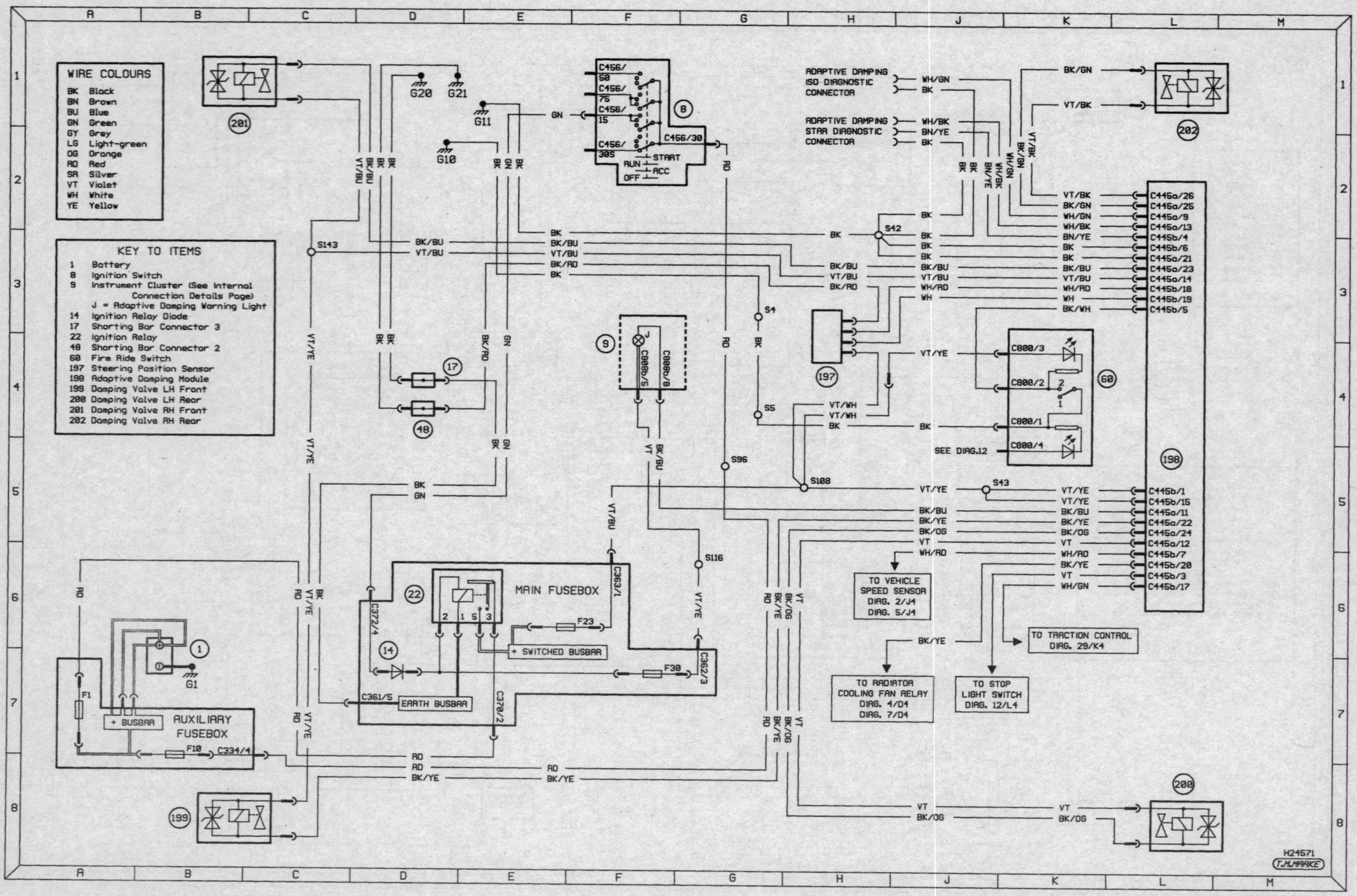
WIRE COLOURS
BK Black
BN Brown
BU Blue
GN Green
GY Grey
LG Light-green
OG Orange
RD Red
SR Silver
VT Violet
WH White
YE Yellow
KEY TO ITEMS
1 Battery
8 Ignition Switch
9 Instrument Cluster (See Internal Connection Details Page)
J = Adaptive Damping Warning Light
14 Ignition Relay Diode
17 Shorting Bar Connector 3
22 Ignition Relay
48 Shorting Bar Connector 2
60 Firm Ride Switch
197 Steering Position Sensor
198 Adaptive Damping Module
199 Damping Valve LH Front
200 Damping Valve LH Rear
201 Damping Valve RH Front
202 Damping Valve RH Rear
ADAPTIVE DAMPING ISO DIAGNOSTIC CONNECTOR
ADAPTIVE DAMPING STAR DIAGNOSTIC CONNECTOR
MAIN FUSEBOX
AUXILIARY FUSEBOX
SWITCHED BUSBAR
EARTH BUSBAR
TO VEHICLE SPEED SENSOR DIAG. 2/J4 DIAG. 5/J4
TO RADIATOR COOLING FAN RELAY DIAG. 4/D4 DIAG. 7/D4
TO STOP LIGHT SWITCH DIAG. 12/L4
TO TRACTION CONTROL DIAG. 29/K4
SEE DIAG.12
H24571
T.M.MARKE

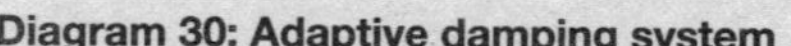

Diagram 30: Adaptive damping system

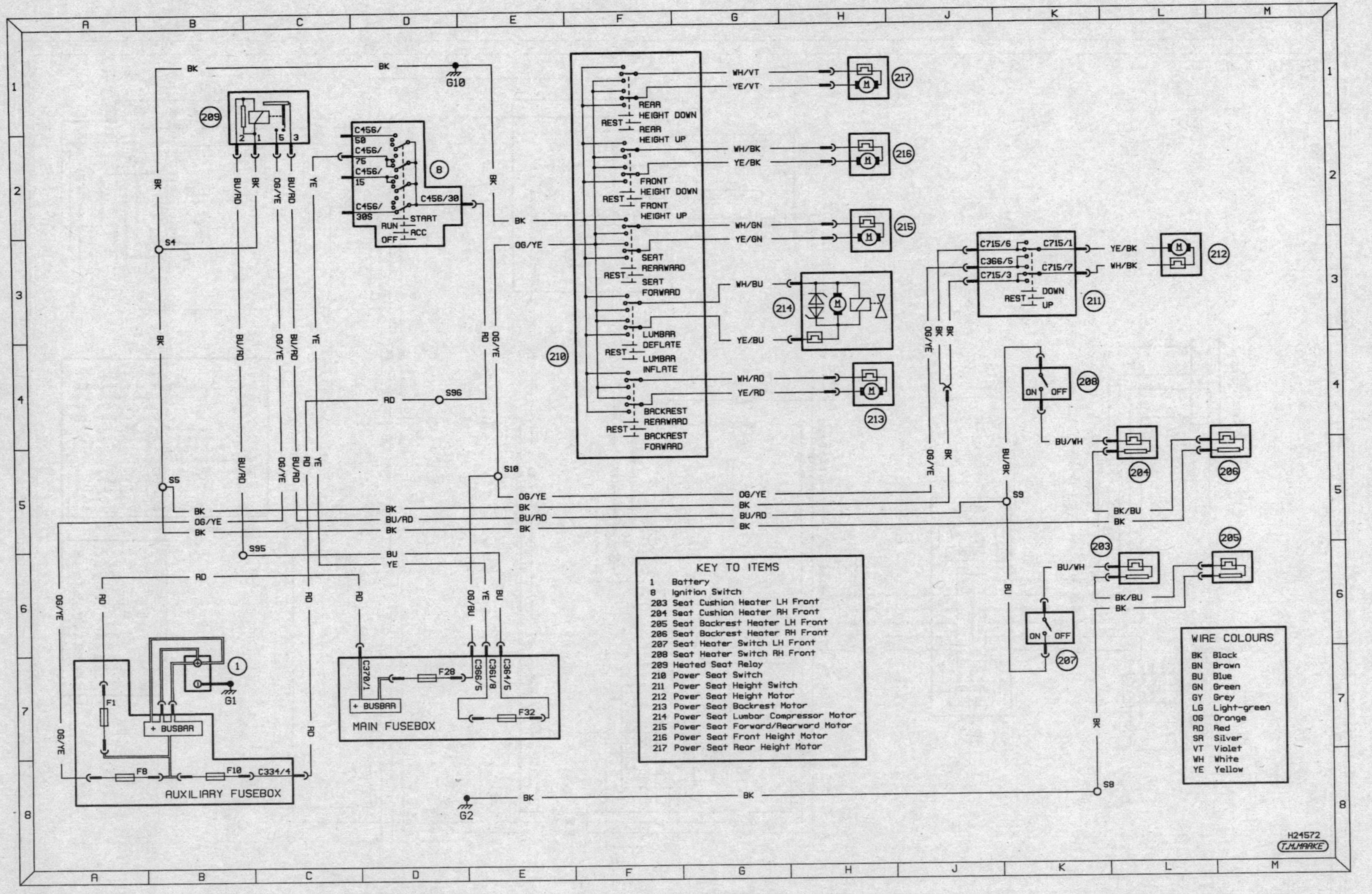

Diagram 31: Heated seats and driver's seat electric adjustment

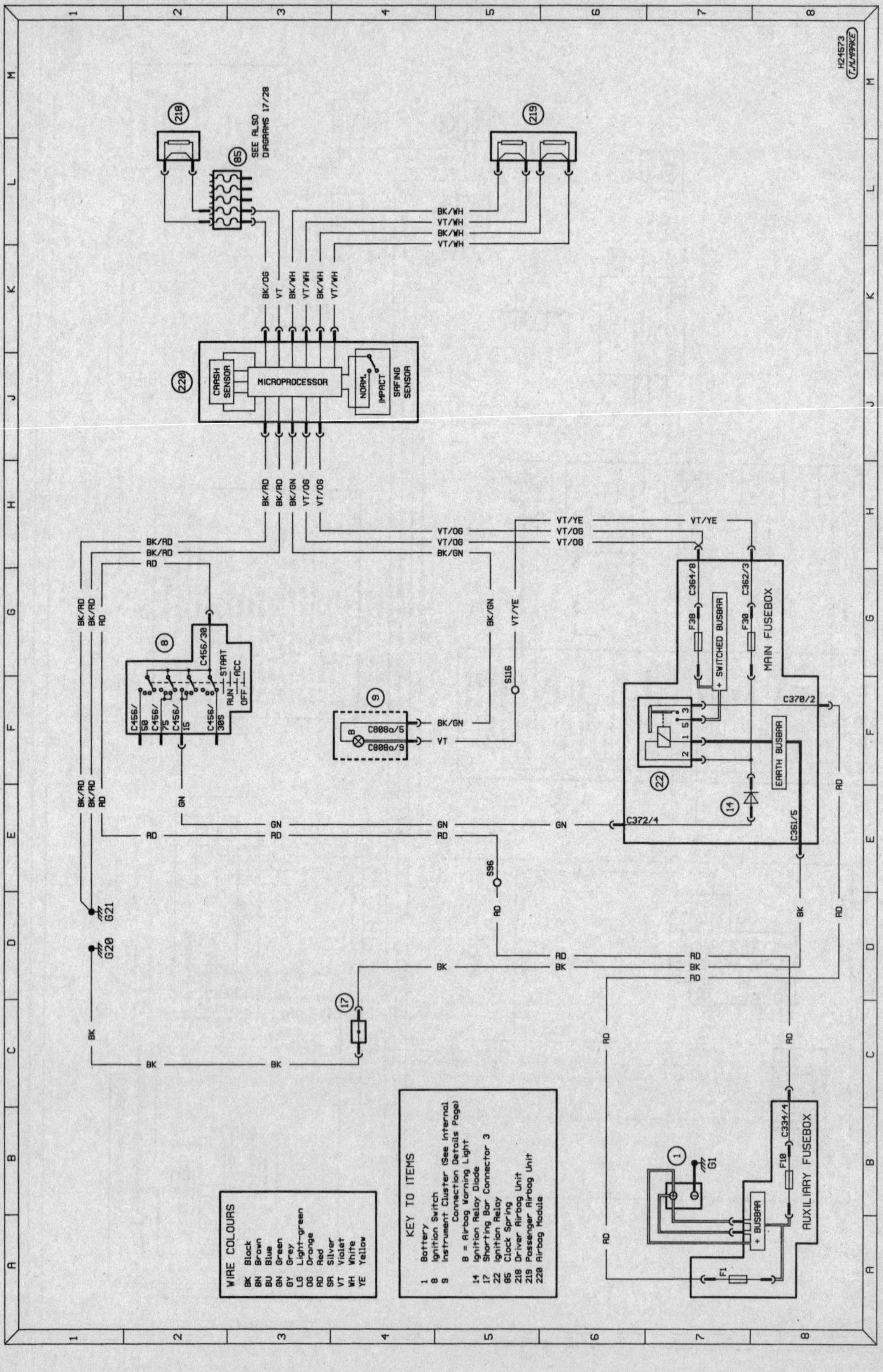

H24573
WIRE COLOURS
BK Black
BN Brown
BU Blue
GN Green
GY Grey
LG Light-green
OG Orange
RD Red
SR Silver
VT Violet
WH White
YE Yellow
KEY TO ITEMS
1 Battery
8 Ignition Switch
9 Instrument Cluster (See Internal Connection Details Page)
B = Airbag Warning Light
14 Ignition Relay Diode
17 Shorting Bar Connector 3
22 Ignition Relay
85 Clock Spring
218 Driver Airbag Unit
219 Passenger Airbag Unit
220 Airbag Module
SEE ALSO DIAGRAMS 17/28
CRASH SENSOR
MICROPROCESSOR
SAFING SENSOR
NORM.
IMPACT
MAIN FUSEBOX
SWITCHED BUSBAR
EARTH BUSBAR
AUXILIARY FUSEBOX
BUSBAR
START
RUN
ACC
OFF

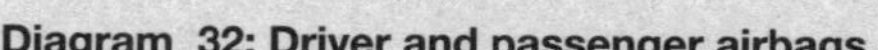

Diagram 32: Driver and passenger airbags

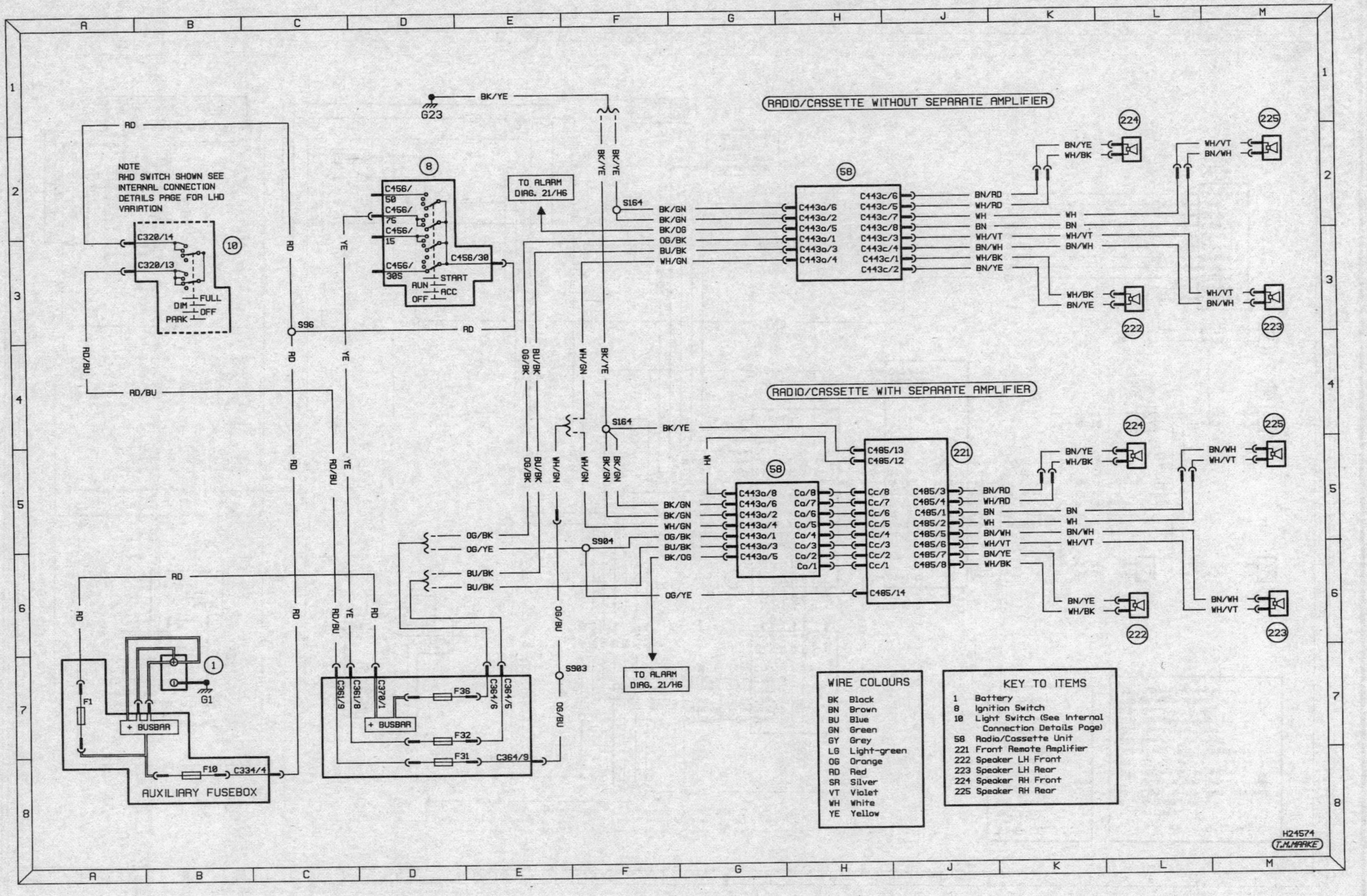

Diagram 33: Radio/cassette (with amplifier)

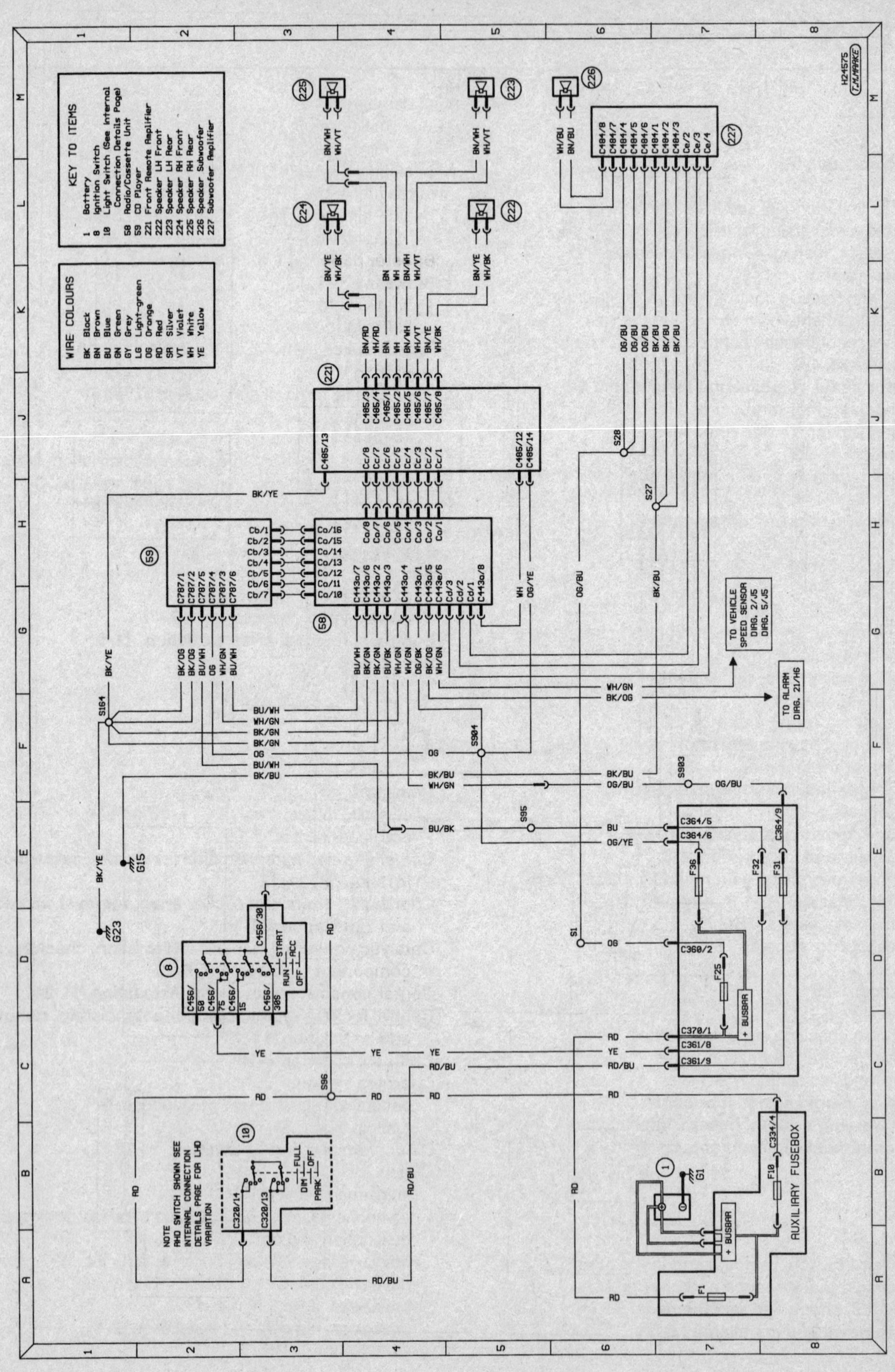

Diagram 34: Radio/cassette and CD player (with subwoofer)

Index

A

B

C

D

E

J

M

O

P

R

S

T

U

V

W

Haynes Automotive Manuals

NOTE: New manuals are added to this list on a periodic basis. If you do not see a listing for your vehicle, consult your local Haynes dealer for the latest product information.

ACURA
12020 **Integra** '86 thru '89 & **Legend** '86 thru '90
12021 **Integra** '90 thru '93 & **Legend** '91 thru '95

AMC
Jeep CJ - *see JEEP (50020)*
14020 Concord/Hornet/Gremlin/Spirit '70 thru '83
14025 **(Renault) Alliance & Encore** '83 thru '87

AUDI
15020 **4000** all models '80 thru '87
15025 **5000** all models '77 thru '83
15026 **5000** all models '84 thru '88

AUSTIN
Healey Sprite - *see MG Midget (66015)*

BMW
*18020 **3/5 Series** '82 thru '92
18021 **3 Series** including Z3 models '92 thru '98
18025 **320i** all 4 cyl models '75 thru '83
18050 **1500 thru 2002** except Turbo '59 thru '77

BUICK
*19010 **Buick Century** '97 thru '02
Century (FWD) - *see GM (38005)*
*19020 **Buick, Oldsmobile & Pontiac Full-size (Front wheel drive)** '85 thru '02
19025 **Buick Oldsmobile & Pontiac Full-size (Rear wheel drive)** '70 thru '90
19030 **Mid-size Regal & Century** '74 thru '87
Regal - *see GENERAL MOTORS (38010)*
Skyhawk - *see GM (38030)*
Skylark - *see GM (38020, 38025)*
Somerset - *see GENERAL MOTORS (38025)*

CADILLAC
21030 **Cadillac Rear Wheel Drive** '70 thru '93
Cimarron, Eldorado & Seville - *see GM (38015, 38030, 38031)*

CHEVROLET
10305 **Chevrolet Engine Overhaul Manual**
*24010 **Astro & GMC Safari Mini-vans** '85 thru '02
24015 **Camaro V8** all models '70 thru '81
24016 **Camaro** all models '82 thru '92
Cavalier - *see GM (38015)*
Celebrity - *see GM (38005)*
24017 **Camaro & Firebird** '93 thru '00
24020 **Chevelle, Malibu, El Camino** '69 thru '87
24024 **Chevette & Pontiac T1000** '76 thru '87
Citation - *see GENERAL MOTORS (38020)*
24032 **Corsica/Beretta** all models '87 thru '96
24040 **Corvette** all V8 models '68 thru '82
24041 **Corvette** all models '84 thru '96
24045 **Full-size Sedans** Caprice, Impala, Biscayne, Bel Air & Wagons '69 thru '90
24046 **Impala SS & Caprice and Buick Roadmaster** '91 thru '96
Lumina '90 thru '94 - *see GM (38010)*
*24048 **Lumina & Monte Carlo** '95 thru '01
Lumina APV - *see GM (38035)*
24050 **Luv Pick-up** all 2WD & 4WD '72 thru '82
Malibu - *see GM (38026)*
24055 **Monte Carlo** all models '70 thru '88
Monte Carlo '95 thru '01 - *see LUMINA*
24059 **Nova** all V8 models '69 thru '79
24060 **Nova/Geo Prizm** '85 thru '92
24064 **Pick-ups '67 thru '87** - Chevrolet & GMC, all V8 & in-line 6 cyl, 2WD & 4WD '67 thru '87; Suburbans, Blazers & Jimmys '67 thru '91
24065 **Pick-ups '88 thru '98** - Chevrolet & GMC, all full-size models '88 thru '98; C/K Classic '99 & '00; Blazer & Jimmy '92 thru '94; Suburban '92 thru '99; Tahoe & Yukon '95 thru '99
*24066 **Pick-ups '99 thru '02** - Chevrolet Silverado & GMC Sierra '99 thru '02; Suburban/Tahoe/Yukon/Yukon XL '00 thru '02
24070 **S-10 & GMC S-15 Pick-ups** '82 thru '93
*24071 S-10, Gmc S-15 & Jimmy '94 thru '01
*24072 **Chevrolet TrailBlazer & TrailBlazer EXT, GMC Envoy & Envoy XL, Oldsmobile Bravada** '02 and '03
24075 **Sprint** '85 thru '88, **Geo Metro** '89 thru '01
24080 **Vans - Chevrolet & GMC** '68 thru '96

CHRYSLER
10310 **Chrysler Engine Overhaul Manual**
25015 **Chrysler Cirrus, Dodge Stratus, Plymouth Breeze**, '95 thru '98
25020 **Full-size Front-Wheel Drive** '88 thru '93
K-Cars - *see DODGE Aries (30008)*
Laser - *see DODGE Daytona (30030)*
25025 **Chrysler LHS, Concorde & New Yorker, Dodge** Intrepid, **Eagle** Vision, '93 thru '97
*25026 **Chrysler LHS, Concorde, 300M, Dodge** Intrepid '98 thru '03
25030 **Chrysler/Plym. Mid-size** '82 thru '95
Rear-wheel Drive - *see DODGE (30050)*
*25035 **PT Cruiser** all models '01 thru '03
*25040 **Chrysler Sebring/Dodge Avenger** '95 thru '02

DATSUN
28005 **200SX** all models '80 thru '83
28007 **B-210** all models '73 thru '78
28009 **210** all models '78 thru '82
28012 **240Z, 260Z & 280Z** Coupe '70 thru '78
28014 **280ZX** Coupe & 2+2 '79 thru '83
300ZX - *see NISSAN (72010)*
28016 **310** all models '78 thru '82
28018 **510 & PL521 Pick-up** '68 thru '73
28020 **510** all models '78 thru '81
28022 **620 Series Pick-up** all models '73 thru '79
720 Series Pick-up - *NISSAN (72030)*
28025 **810/Maxima** all gas models, '77 thru '84

DODGE
400 & 600 - *see CHRYSLER (25030)*
30008 **Aries & Plymouth Reliant** '81 thru '89
30010 **Caravan & Ply. Voyager** '84 thru '95
*30011 **Caravan & Ply. Voyager** '96 thru '02
30012 **Challenger/Plymouth Saporro** '78 thru '83
Challenger '67-'76 - *see DART (30025)*
30016 **Colt/Plymouth Champ** '78 thru '87
30020 **Dakota Pick-ups** all models '87 thru '96
*30021 **Durango** '98 & '99, **Dakota** '97 thru '99
30025 **Dart, Challenger/Plymouth Barracuda & Valiant** 6 cyl models '67 thru '76
30030 **Daytona & Chrysler Laser** '84 thru '89
Intrepid - *see Chrysler (25025, 25026)*
*30034 **Dodge & Plymouth Neon** '95 thru '99
*30035 **Omni & Plymouth Horizon** '78 thru '90
30040 **Pick-ups** all full-size models '74 thru '93
*30041 **Pick-ups** all full-size models '94 thru '01
*30045 **Ram 50/D50 Pick-ups & Raider and Plymouth Arrow Pick-ups** '79 thru '93
30050 **Dodge/Ply./Chrysler RWD** '71 thru '89
30055 **Shadow/Plymouth Sundance** '87 thru '94
30060 **Spirit & Plymouth Acclaim** '89 thru '95
*30065 **Vans - Dodge & Plymouth** '71 thru '03

EAGLE
Talon - *see MITSUBISHI (68030, 68031)*
Vision - *see CHRYSLER (25025)*

FIAT
34010 **124 Sport Coupe & Spider** '68 thru '78
34025 **X1/9** all models '74 thru '80

FORD
10355 **Ford Automatic Transmission Overhaul**
10320 **Ford Engine Overhaul Manual**
36004 **Aerostar Mini-vans** '86 thru '97
Aspire - *see FORD Festiva (36030)*
36006 **Contour/Mercury Mystique** '95 thru '00
36008 **Courier Pick-up** all models '72 thru '82
*36012 **Crown Victoria & Mercury Grand Marquis** '88 thru '00
36016 **Escort/Mercury Lynx** '81 thru '90
36020 **Escort/Mercury Tracer** '91 thru '00
Expedition - *see FORD Pick-up (36059)*
36022 **Ford Escape & Mazda Tribute** '01 thru '03
*36024 **Explorer & Mazda Navajo** '91 thru '01
36025 **Ford Explorer & Mercury Mountaineer** '02 and '03
36028 **Fairmont & Mercury Zephyr** '78 thru '83
36030 **Festiva & Aspire** '88 thru '97
36032 **Fiesta** all models '77 thru '80
*36034 **Focus** all models '00 and '01
36036 **Ford & Mercury Full-size** '75 thru '87
36044 **Ford & Mercury Mid-size** '75 thru '86
36048 **Mustang V8** all models '64-1/2 thru '73
36049 **Mustang II** 4 cyl, V6 & V8 '74 thru '78
36050 **Mustang & Mercury Capri** '79 thru '86
*36051 **Mustang** all models '94 thru '03
36054 **Pick-ups and Bronco** '73 thru '79
36058 **Pick-ups and Bronco** '80 thru '96
*36059 **Pick-ups, Expedition & Lincoln Navigator** '97 thru '02
*36060 **Super Duty Pick-up, Excursion** '97 thru '02
36062 **Pinto & Mercury Bobcat** '75 thru '80
36066 **Probe** all models '89 thru '92
36070 **Ranger/Bronco II** gas models '83 thru '92
*36071 **Ford Ranger** '93 thru '00 & **Mazda Pick-ups** '94 thru '00
36074 **Taurus & Mercury Sable** '86 thru '95
*36075 **Taurus & Mercury Sable** '96 thru '01
36078 **Tempo & Mercury Topaz** '84 thru '94
36082 **Thunderbird/Mercury Cougar** '83 thru '88
36086 **Thunderbird/Mercury Cougar** '89 thru '97
36090 **Vans** all V8 Econoline models '69 thru '91
*36094 **Vans** full size '92 thru '01
*36097 **Windstar Mini-van** '95 thru '03

GENERAL MOTORS
10360 **GM Automatic Transmission Overhaul**
38005 **Buick Century, Chevrolet Celebrity, Olds Cutlass Ciera & Pontiac 6000** '82 thru '96
*38010 **Buick Regal, Chevrolet Lumina, Oldsmobile Cutlass Supreme & Pontiac Grand Prix** front wheel drive '88 thru '02
38015 **Buick Skyhawk, Cadillac Cimarron, Chevrolet Cavalier, Oldsmobile Firenza Pontiac J-2000 & Sunbird** '82 thru '94
*38016 **Chevrolet Cavalier/Pontiac Sunfire** '95 thru '01
38020 **Buick Skylark, Chevrolet Citation, Olds Omega, Pontiac Phoenix** '80 thru '85
38025 **Buick Skylark & Somerset, Olds Achieva, Calais & Pontiac Grand Am** '85 thru '98
*38026 **Chevrolet Malibu, Olds Alero & Cutlass, Pontiac Grand Am** '97 thru '00
38030 **Cadillac Eldorado & Oldsmobile Toronado** '71 thru '85, Seville '80 thru '85, **Buick Riviera** '79 thru '85
*38031 **Cadillac Eldorado & Seville** '86 thru '91, **DeVille & Buick Riviera** '86 thru '93, **Fleetwood & Olds Toronado** '86 thru '92
38032 **DeVille** '94 thru '02, **Seville** '92 thru '02
38035 **Chevrolet Lumina APV, Oldsmobile Silhouette & Pontiac Trans Sport** '90 thru '96
*38036 **Chevrolet Venture, Olds Silhouette, Pontiac Trans Sport & Montana** '97 thru '01
General Motors Full-size Rear-wheel Drive - *see BUICK (19025)*

GEO
Metro - *see CHEVROLET Sprint (24075)*
Prizm - *see CHEVROLET (24060) or TOYOTA (92036)*
40030 **Storm** all models '90 thru '93
Tracker - *see SUZUKI Samurai (90010)*

GMC
Vans & Pick-ups - *see CHEVROLET*

HONDA
42010 **Accord CVCC** all models '76 thru '83
42011 **Accord** all models '84 thru '89
42012 **Accord** all models '90 thru '93
42013 **Accord** all models '94 thru '97
*42014 **Accord** all models '98 and '99
42020 **Civic 1200** all models '73 thru '79
42021 **Civic 1300 & 1500 CVCC** '80 thru '83
42022 **Civic 1500 CVCC** all models '75 thru '79
42023 **Civic** all models '84 thru '91
42024 **Civic** & del Sol '92 thru '95
*42025 **Civic** '96 thru '00, **CR-V** '97 thru '00, **Acura Integra** '94 thru '00
Passport - *see ISUZU Rodeo (47017)*
*42040 **Prelude CVCC** all models '79 thru '89

HYUNDAI
*43010 Elantra all models '96 thru '01
43015 Excel & Accent all models '86 thru '98

ISUZU
Hombre - *see CHEVROLET S-10 (24071)*
*47017 **Rodeo** '91 thru '02, **Amigo** '89 thru '02, **Honda Passport** '95 thru '02
47020 **Trooper** '84 thru '91, **Pick-up** '81 thru '93

JAGUAR
49010 **XJ6** all 6 cyl models '68 thru '86
49011 **XJ6** all models '88 thru '94
49015 **XJ12 & XJS** all 12 cyl models '72 thru '85

JEEP
50010 **Cherokee, Comanche & Wagoneer Limited** all models '84 thru '00
50020 **CJ** all models '49 thru '86
*50025 **Grand Cherokee** all models '93 thru '00
50029 **Grand Wagoneer & Pick-up** '72 thru '91
*50030 **Wrangler** all models '87 thru '00

LEXUS
ES 300 - *see TOYOTA Camry (92007)*

LINCOLN
Navigator - *see FORD Pick-up (36059)*
*59010 **Rear Wheel Drive** all models '70 thru '01

MAZDA
61010 **GLC (rear wheel drive)** '77 thru '83
61011 **GLC (front wheel drive)** '81 thru '85
61015 **323 & Protegé** '90 thru '00
*61016 **MX-5 Miata** '90 thru '97
61020 **MPV** all models '89 thru '94
Navajo - *see FORD Explorer (36024)*
61030 **Pick-ups** '72 thru '93
Pick-ups '94 on - *see Ford (36071)*
61035 **RX-7** all models '79 thru '85
61036 **RX-7** all models '86 thru '91
61040 **626** (rear wheel drive) '79 thru '82
61041 **626 & MX-6 (front wheel drive)** '83 thru '91
61042 **626** '93 thru '01, & **MX-6/Ford Probe** '93 thru '97

MERCEDES-BENZ
63012 **123 Series Diesel** '76 thru '85
63015 **190 Series** 4-cyl gas models, '84 thru '88
63020 **230, 250 & 280** 6 cyl sohc '68 thru '72
63025 **280 123 Series** gas models '77 thru '81
63030 **350 & 450** all models '71 thru '80

MERCURY
64200 **Villager & Nissan Quest** '93 thru '01
All other titles, see FORD listing.

MG
66010 **MGB** Roadster & GT Coupe '62 thru '80
66015 **MG Midget & Austin Healey Sprite Roadster** '58 thru '80

MITSUBISHI
68020 **Cordia, Tredia, Galant, Precis & Mirage** '83 thru '93
68030 **Eclipse, Eagle Talon & Plymouth Laser** '90 thru '94
*68031 **Eclipse** '95 thru '01, **Eagle Talon** '95 thru '98
68035 **Mitsubishi Galant** '94 thru '03
68040 **Pick-up** '83 thru '96, **Montero** '83 thru '93

NISSAN
72010 **300ZX** all models incl. Turbo '84 thru '89
72015 **Altima** all models '93 thru '01
72020 **Maxima** all models '85 thru '92
*72021 **Maxima** all models '93 thru '01
72030 **Pick-ups** '80 thru '97, **Pathfinder** '87 thru '95
*72031 **Frontier Pick-up** '98 thru '01, Xterra '00 & '01, Pathfinder '96 thru '01
72040 **Pulsar** all models '83 thru '86
72050 **Sentra** all models '82 thru '94
72051 **Sentra & 200SX** all models '95 thru '99
72060 **Stanza** all models '82 thru '90

OLDSMOBILE
*73015 **Cutlass** '74 thru '88
For other OLDSMOBILE titles, see BUICK, CHEVROLET or GM listings.

PLYMOUTH
For PLYMOUTH titles, see DODGE.

PONTIAC
79008 **Fiero** all models '84 thru '88
79018 **Firebird** V8 models except Turbo '70 thru '81
79019 **Firebird** all models '82 thru '92
79040 **Mid-size Rear-wheel Drive** '70 thru '87
For other PONTIAC titles, see BUICK, CHEVROLET or GM listings.

PORSCHE
80020 **911** Coupe & Targa models '65 thru '89
80025 **914** all 4 cyl models '69 thru '76
80030 **924** all models incl. Turbo '76 thru '82
80035 **944** all models incl. Turbo '83 thru '89

RENAULT
Alliance, Encore - *see AMC (14020)*

SAAB
*84010 **900** including Turbo '79 thru '88

SATURN
*87010 **Saturn** all models '91 thru '02
87020 **Saturn** all L-series models '00 thru '04

SUBARU
89002 **1100, 1300, 1400 & 1600** '71 thru '79
89003 **1600 & 1800** 2WD & 4WD '80 thru '94

SUZUKI
90010 **Samurai/Sidekick/Geo Tracker** '86 thru '01

TOYOTA
92005 **Camry** all models '83 thru '91
92006 **Camry** all models '92 thru '96
*92007 **Camry/Avalon/Solara/Lexus ES 300** '97 thru '01
92015 **Celica Rear Wheel Drive** '71 thru '85
92020 **Celica Front Wheel Drive** '86 thru '99
92025 **Celica Supra** all models '79 thru '92
92030 **Corolla** all models '75 thru '79
92032 **Corolla** rear wheel drive models '80 thru '87
92035 **Corolla** front wheel drive models '84 thru '92
92036 **Corolla & Geo Prizm** '93 thru '02
92040 **Corolla Tercel** all models '80 thru '82
92045 **Corona** all models '74 thru '82
92050 **Cressida** all models '78 thru '82
92055 **Land Cruiser** FJ40/43/45/55 '68 thru '82
92056 **Land Cruiser** FJ60/62/80/FZJ80 '80 thru '96
92065 **MR2** all models '85 thru '87
92070 **Pick-up** all models '69 thru '78
92075 **Pick-up** all models '79 thru '95
*92076 **Tacoma** '95 thru '00, **4Runner** '96 thru '00, **T100** '93 thru '98
*92078 **Tundra** '00 thru '02, **Sequoia** '01 thru '02
92080 **Previa** all models '91 thru '95
*92082 **RAV4** all models '96 thru '02
92085 **Tercel** all models '87 thru '94

TRIUMPH
94007 **Spitfire** all models '62 thru '81
94010 **TR7** all models '75 thru '81

VW
96008 **Beetle & Karmann Ghia** '54 thru '79
*96009 **New Beetle** '98 thru '00
96016 **Rabbit, Jetta, Scirocco, & Pick-up** gas models '74 thru '91 & Convertible '80 thru '92
96017 **Golf, GTI & Jetta** '93 thru '98, **Cabrio** '95 thru '98
*96018 **Golf, GTI, Jetta & Cabrio** '98 thru '02
96020 **Rabbit, Jetta, Pick-up** diesel '77 thru '84
96023 **Passat** '98 thru '01, **Audi A4** '96 thru '01
96030 **Transporter 1600** all models '68 thru '79
96035 **Transporter 1700, 1800, 2000** '72 thru '79
96040 **Type 3 1500 & 1600** '63 thru '73
96045 **Vanagon** air-cooled models '80 thru '83

VOLVO
97010 **120, 130 Series & 1800 Sports** '61 thru '73
97015 **140 Series** all models '66 thru '74
97020 **240 Series** all models '76 thru '93
97025 **260 Series** all models '75 thru '82
97040 **740 & 760 Series** all models '82 thru '88

TECHBOOK MANUALS
10205 **Automotive Computer Codes**
10210 **Automotive Emissions Control Manual**
10215 **Fuel Injection Manual, 1978 thru 1985**
10220 **Fuel Injection Manual, 1986 thru 1999**
10225 **Holley Carburetor Manual**
10230 **Rochester Carburetor Manual**
10240 **Weber/Zenith/Stromberg/SU Carburetor**
10305 **Chevrolet Engine Overhaul Manual**
10310 **Chrysler Engine Overhaul Manual**
10320 **Ford Engine Overhaul Manual**
10330 **GM and Ford Diesel Engine Repair**
10340 **Small Engine Repair Manual**
10345 **Suspension, Steering & Driveline**
10355 **Ford Automatic Transmission Overhaul**
10360 **GM Automatic Transmission Overhaul**
10405 **Automotive Body Repair & Painting**
10410 **Automotive Brake Manual**
10415 **Automotive Detailing Manual**
10420 **Automotive Eelectrical Manual**
10425 **Automotive Heating & Air Conditioning**
10430 **Automotive Reference Dictionary**
10435 **Automotive Tools Manual**
10440 **Used Car Buying Guide**
10445 **Welding Manual**
10450 **ATV Basics**

SPANISH MANUALS
98903 **Reparación de Carrocería & Pintura**
98905 **Códigos Automotrices de la Computadora**
98910 **Frenos Automotriz**
98915 **Inyección de Combustible 1986 al 1999**
99040 **Chevrolet & GMC Camionetas** '67 al '87
99041 **Chevrolet & GMC Camionetas** '88 al '98
99042 **Chevrolet Camionetas Cerradas** '68 al '95
99055 **Dodge Caravan/Ply. Voyager** '84 al '95
99075 **Ford Camionetas y Bronco** '80 al '94
99077 **Ford Camionetas Cerradas** '69 al '91
99088 **Ford Modelos de Tamaño Mediano** '75 al '86
99091 **Ford Taurus & Mercury Sable** '86 al '95
99095 **GM Modelos de Tamaño Grande** '70 al '90
99100 **GM Modelos de Tamaño Mediano** '70 al '88
99110 **Nissan Camionetas** '80 al '96, Pathfinder '87 al '95
99118 **Nissan Sentra** '82 al '94
99125 **Toyota Camionetas y 4-Runner** '79 al '95

** Listings shown with an asterisk (*) indicate model coverage as of this printing. These titles will be periodically updated to include later model years - consult your Haynes dealer for more information.*

Nearly 100 Haynes motorcycle manuals also available

9-04

Haynes North America, Inc., 861 Lawrence Drive, Newbury Park, CA 91320 • (805) 498-6703